General
Architectural
Drafting

Mr. and Mrs. Jack Schoonover

General
ARCHITECTURAL DRAFTING

WILLIAM E. WYATT

Practical Arts Division Head
J. Sterling Morton High School
Cicero, Illinois

CHAS. A. BENNETT CO., INC.
Peoria, Illinois 61614

● ACKNOWLEDGMENTS

The author wishes to express his thanks to the many persons, firms, and associations that have been of assistance during preparation of this book. When drawings or photographs supplied by others are presented, a credit line accompanies each illustration. Many illustrations are based upon information supplied by others and their contribution is acknowledged herewith.

Alan Clemons
Albert Benda
American Plywood Association
American Standard Products
Anaconda American Brass Co.
Artcrest Products Co., Inc.
California Redwood Association
Carpet Institute Inc.
Charles Bruning Co.
Charles Voight
Cicero, Illinois
Commonwealth Edison Co.
Erwyn H. James
Eugene Dietzgen Co.
Federal Housing Administration
First Federal Savings & Loan
    Berwyn, Illinois
Formica Corporation
Forest Studios
Fred Reuten Inc.
Frederick Post Co.
General Electric Co.
Honeywell Corporation
Jack Williams
John Deere Corporation
Joseph T. Ryerson and Son, Inc.
Kitchen Maid Corporation
Kueffel and Esser Co.
Knape and Vogt Mfg. Co.

Kroehler Mfg. Co.
Life Newspapers
Long Bell Division,
    International Paper Co.
Meadow Steel Products Co.
Morgan Sash and Door Co.
Mosaic Tile Co.
Mueller Climatrol,
    Worthington Industries
National Assn. of Home Builders
National Homes
National Lumber Mfg. Assn.
National Woodwork Mfg. Assn.
Paratone Inc.
Paul Roise
P. M. Bolton and Associates
Pittsburgh Plate Glass Co.
Plumbing-Heating-Cooling
    Information Bureau
Portland Cement Association
Robert Borlik
Rohm and Haas Co.
Scholz Homes Inc.
Simpson Logging Co.
Steel City Electric Co.
Steel Joist Institute
Symons Mfg. Co.
The Ceco Corporation
Unit Structures Inc.
United States Plywood Co.
West Coast Lumberman's Assn.
Western Wood Products Assn.
Weyerhaeuser Company
Wire Reinforcement Institute

SPECIAL CREDIT:
The author wishes to express his special thanks to Mr. Raymond Hagood, Mr. Patrick McFall, and Mr. George Voyta for their drafting assistance on illustrations for this book.

● INTRODUCTION

This book is in three parts:
- PART I describes building materials and explains construction principles.
- PART II presents information necessary for building planning and design.
- PART III presents information necessary for drawing building plans.

It is the author's belief that a person must be familiar with building materials, construction principles, and their terminology before it is possible to draw technical plans requiring such information. Most discussions and illustrations are related to homes or other light construction because these are less complex than buildings of heavy construction. Drawing principles for heavy construction are the same as for light construction except that many more details must be mastered. Many explanations in this book are lengthy, but no discussion presents all there is to know about a given subject! Rather, the book gives a broad overview of many different areas.

Examination of the book reveals that some drawings are in a single color while others are in multi-color. When a drawing is printed entirely in blue, it is drawn as a working plan. Pictorial drawings and working plans *illustrating specific points* are often multi-color and are not intended for use on building plans exactly as shown. Naturally, any applicable information can be used on your plan, but it will generally require modification.

Illustrative working drawings in the book are usually drawn to the smallest scale recommended for a given item. For example, all symbols shown in Chapter 38 are drawn to a scale of $\frac{1}{4}'' = 1'\text{-}0''$ because this is the size most often used on floor plan and elevation drawings. Individual drawings for the building plans in Chapter 49 are drawn to their *smallest* allowable size for working drawings. They are only half the size *normally* used, so they fit on book pages.

Questions following chapters are designed to cover each major topic presented, and are an invaluable study guide.

Spelling words and terms are listed at the end of chapters. A good draftsman must be able to spell properly, as well as understand his terms.

Table of Contents

PART ONE
STRUCTURE—AN ARCHITECTURAL
OBLIGATION

PART TWO
FUNCTION AND BEAUTY—ESSENTIALS OF PLANNING

Color Illustrations

12

Part One

STRUCTURE—
AN ARCHITECTURAL
OBLIGATION

Laying Out and Excavating

Selection of Building Location on the Lot

In choosing a building location, you must know the exact property boundaries of the building site. It is not enough to take the word of the person from whom the property is being purchased. He may be entirely honest in his *beliefs* when he describes the boundaries of the property. But the only way to be absolutely sure is to have a survey of the property made, following the legal description as given in the abstract. An *abstract* gives the exact legal description of property, stating boundaries as measured from latitudes, longitudes, and meridians. Much of the country is divided by government survey into *sections* of one square mile each. Sections are divided into subsections of halves and quarters. These are divided into further halves and quarters. A legal description of property and its use might read as follows:

> The property known and described as Lots nineteen (19) and twenty (20) in Block two (2) in J. C. McCartney and Co. Subdivision of the South half of the Southeast quarter of the

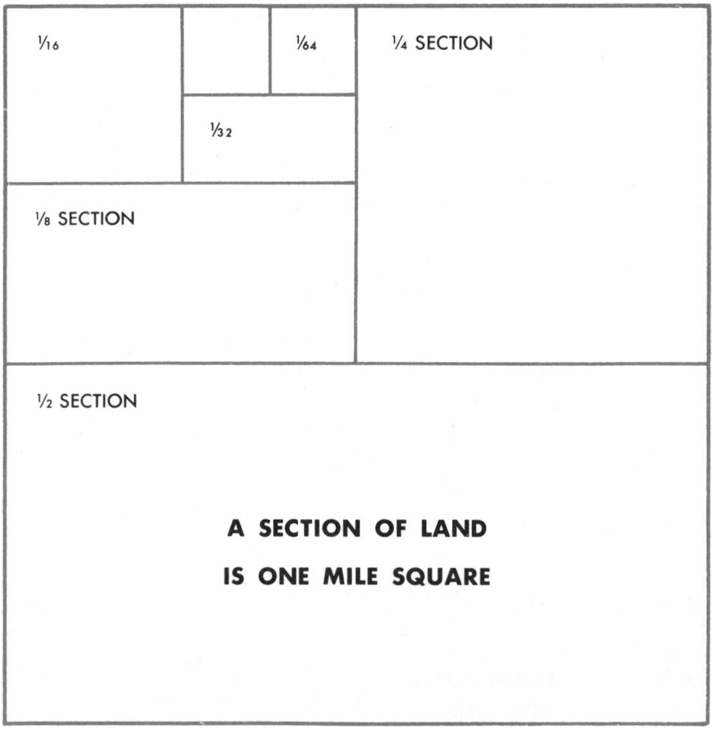

¹⁄₁₆		¹⁄₆₄	¼ SECTION
	¹⁄₃₂		
⅛ SECTION			
½ SECTION			

A SECTION OF LAND IS ONE MILE SQUARE

The indicated divisions are described as follows:

½ = South half of section.
¼ = Northeast quarter of section.
⅛ = South half of northwest quarter of section.
¹⁄₁₆ = Northwest quarter of the northwest quarter of section.
¹⁄₃₂ = South half of the northeast quarter of the northwest quarter of section.
¹⁄₆₄ = Northeast quarter of the northeast quarter of the northwest quarter of section.

Divisions of one section of land (1 sq. mi.)

Northwest quarter and the East half of the Northeast quarter of the Southwest quarter of the Northeast quarter, Section 20, Township 39 North, Resubdivision of Blocks one (1) to five (5), is to be zoned as a Second Commercial District.

An abstract also shows previous owners of the property, and dates acquired and transferred to new owners. Amounts of money or other considerations of the transaction are usually stated. Money borrowed against the property and a record of the repayments may be recorded.

Deed Restrictions

An owner may add any restriction he desires regulating future use. Future owners are bound to them. For example, an owner may require all future buildings to be of masonry construction. The cost and quality of future buildings may be predetermined. Uses of the property may be specified.

hearings, the rezoning will either be approved or denied.

Besides zoning ordinances, regulations usually define the methods of construction to be used. It is also common practice for a local ordinance to state the amount of ground area the building can occupy in relation to the total area of the property, and the distance one must allow from the edges of the building to the property lines. In many instances the height of buildings is determined by local ordinance. All ordinances governing construction requirements are usually assembled and published in booklet form called the building code.

Local Ordinances and Zoning Laws

Before construction can begin, check the local ordinances and zoning laws. Most communities have regulations stating where certain types of structures may be located. For example, it would not be possible to build an industrial plant in a new residential neighborhood. Zones are usually classified as (1) first residential—single family, (2) second residential—multi-family, (3) apartments, (4) first commercial, (5) second commercial, (6) light industrial, (7) heavy industrial. These names and ratings may vary from one locality to another. Many areas were built up before adequate zoning ordinances were established. In these areas one may find a variety of buildings, constructed for many different purposes. Other areas have been zoned after construction of at least a part of the buildings. In these older areas it may be difficult to tell exactly into which zoning category property should be placed.

If the property is zoned and a builder wishes to introduce another kind of structure, he may apply to the governing body to have the property rezoned into a different class. The case will be reviewed and public hearings will be held to give all property owners in the area an opportunity to express their wishes. After the

Determining Building Location

Other homes in the area help determine the location of a new house on the property. If all other structures are built in a row, a given distance from the front of the lot, the new structure should be in line with them.

NOTICE

A public hearing will be held by the Town of Cicero's Zoning Board of Appeals at 7:30 P.M., on Monday, July —, 196—, in the Cicero Town Hall, located at 4937 West 25th Street, Cicero, Illinois, at which time the following proposal will be considered:

That property known and described as Lot 36 and the East ½ of Lot 35 in Block 3 in Householder's Addition to Morton Park in the East ½ of Section 28, Township 39 North, Range 13, East of the Third Principal Meridian in Cook County, Illinois, commonly known as 4808 West 24th Place, Cicero, Illinois, be rezoned from First Residential to First Commercial.

Notice is hereby given that a copy of the proposed amendment to the Zoning Ordinance will be available for inspection by any interested person at the meeting effecting such classification.

Zoning Board of Appeals
of the Town of Cicero
WILLIAM MAGUIRE
Secretary

Public newspaper notice of rezoning request

Laws usually prohibit new construction that extends over this line. On the other hand, a setback behind other structures will tend to obstruct the view from the new building.

When planning the location of a structure it is well to take into consideration trees and other growth. Many times the location of the building can be adjusted to allow existing natural features to remain. This not only is a saving in cost but can add to the value of the property because it gives it an established look. Many large developers move into an area and proceed to remove all trees, shrubs, hills, and even existing lawns. When they are finished the area looks like a barren wasteland. If this happens it may take years before the area will again have the harmonious, enriched look of belonging, unless large sums are spent on sodding, transplanting, or terracing. The natural terrain may offer the best basic landscape possible. Some examples of construction in which the natural landscape has been preserved are shown on these two pages.

16   The beauty of this home is enhanced by nature's landscaping.

Western Wood Products Association

Anderson Corporation, Bayport, Minnesota

Preserving existing trees around a building site adds beauty to the structure.

17

This modern plywood home blends well with its natural setting.

American Plywood Association

Plot Plan

The working drawings should show a plot plan giving the outline and shape of the property. This plan is dimensioned, showing locations of all streets, sidewalks, alleys, and easements for utilities. Generally the property owner can use easement space for yards and gardens, but the utility company still reserves the right of access for placement and repair of utility services.

The location and outline of buildings to be placed on the property should be drawn on the plot plan. Dimensions from each of the property boundaries are given. The plan also includes all driveways, sidewalks, patios, terraces, and other items to be constructed. These are dimensioned when it is necessary to determine their location. Trees, shrubs, and other obstructions should be shown when their presence has a bearing upon the construction. *Contour lines* showing the elevations above sea level of the property are included on some plot plans.

Additional methods of showing working plot plans are included in Chapter 41.

Establishing the Grade

The grade or relationship of the building to ground is very important. The *grade line* is the point at which the earth touches the foundation of the building. One usually selects the highest point on the perimeter of the building when starting to lay out the building's location. All dimensions applying to the grade line are taken from this reference point—or bench mark, as it is sometimes called.

Recent preference in building has tended to keep the floor line close to the grade. The omission of the basement in many new homes has been one of the primary reasons. Yet one must be careful not to place the building too close to the ground because of the danger of dampness and rot. Most communities have regulations governing the distance floors or wood parts of a building must be above grade. The FHA— Federal Housing Adminstration —places a minimum of 8 inches as the distance wood parts must be above grade. There are exceptions to this rule, if adequate pro-

vision is made to prevent moisture, rot and termite damage.

If one places the building high above grade, it is likely to look as though it were built on stilts. However, if families live in basement apartments, the structure may be built high enough so the basement windows will be above ground. The less underground depth a basement has, the less waterproofing is required. Some codes determine the maximum depth if the basement rooms are to be used for living purposes. Yet development of new building materials has, for all practical purposes, made this code obsolete. Recent developments have enabled buildings to be placed entirely below grade.

When the grade is being established, adjoining terrain must be given consideration. The ground should slope away in all directions. Otherwise, water from adjoining property may drain across and cause erosion, or it may back up against foundation and basement walls and cause moisture problems inside. One must also consider what surface water from a new site is going to do to adjoining property.

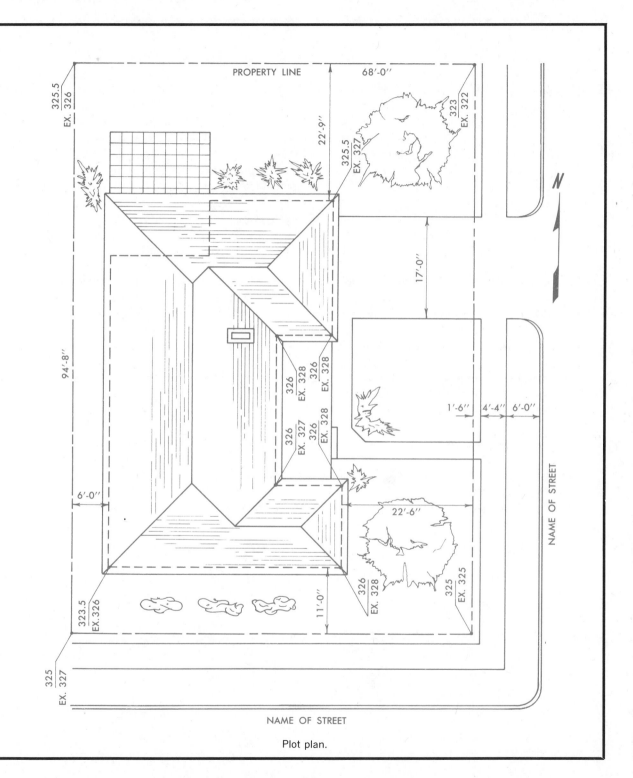

Plot plan.

Staking Out

When staking out a building, the distance of setback from the front property line is usually determined first. A line is stretched across to represent the front edge of the building. Then drive a small stake in the ground at the exact front corner of each end of the building. A small tack or nail can then be driven into the stake to mark the exact location. The stakes should be driven almost flush with the ground. A batter board, such as the one shown, should then be constructed at the two front corners, using 2x4 stakes of a suitable length, tapered at one end with a hatchet or power saw. The batter boards should be placed no closer than 4 feet from the outside edge of the footing line. Then 1x6 boards are used to connect the stakes. The top edges of the 1x6's should be straight—level and equi-distant above the grade line.

Next an approximate layout of the footing is measured off and batter boards set up for the remainder of the building. Single batter boards, as shown, may be used for marking offsets or indentations. The corners must be exactly square; using a transit level, or employing the 6-8-10 method of establishing a right triangle. This is an application of the Pythagorean theorem, which states: In any right triangle the square of the hypotenuse is equal to the sum of the squares of the other two sides. See illustration.

Taut, or tightly stretched, lines of "staging," or carpenter's twine, are fastened over the batter boards to outline sections of the footing. These lines are usually fastened by cutting notches in the batter boards to line with the edges of the footing, by looping string around the boards, and tying. The strings can also be fastened around nails driven in the boards.

The diagonal method is good for checking the square. See illustration. If the tape measure reads the same when the area is checked diagonally in both directions, the building is square. After the outlines of the building have been established, they can be marked on the ground with marking lime. The line or staging is removed for excavation.

Very simple rectangular structures, as in the illustration, may be *staked out* as a single section, or all at the same time. However, most structures must be staked out in sections, or different parts at a time, because of the irregularity of the outlines of the building. Additional offsets, as for bay windows, recessed entries, areaways, and porches, require special laying out and forming.

The shape of a building should be kept as simple as possible because irregular shapes require more material and labor to construct. This is not only true for excavation and forming and pouring footings and foundations, but also for all other parts of the building. The layout of a building with irregular outlines, and sections, is shown.

"L" shaped batter boards.

Straight batter board.

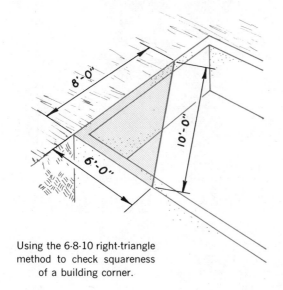

Using the 6-8-10 right-triangle method to check squareness of a building corner.

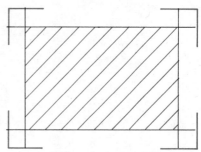

Batter boards and string layout for a rectangular building.

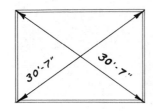

Checking for squareness, using the diagonal method.

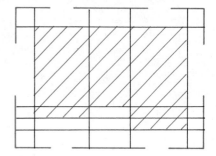

Batter boards and string layout for an irregular shaped building.

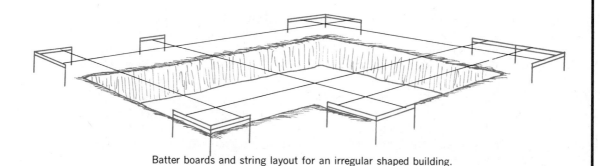

Batter boards and string layout for an irregular shaped building.

Excavating at a construction site.

Excavating

The excavated earth is transported far enough from the immediate vicinity of the building site to prevent interference with construction work and so as not to interfere with deliveries and stockpiling of materials.

Top soil is a very scarce commodity in most regions and sells for a premium price. For this reason the top soil and the subsoil should be piled in two separate locations. It is not always easy to get the contractor to do this because of the time involved; therefore it should be stated clearly in the plans and specifications.

While the earth is being moved and while construction is in progress, care should be taken to keep the excavated material free of debris and rubble. At least a portion of the earth will be used as backfill and should be as clean as possible. Backfill with trash in it can be a haven for termites and may cause both water pockets and settling around the foundation wall.

The terrain and the condition of the soil should be checked carefully before actual selection of a site is made. Firm clay makes an ideal base for a building of lightweight construction, whereas a

Earthmoving equipment performs many operations during construction

building of heavy construction would need piles or footings to extend to bedrock. Rock formations near the surface might require blasting and heavy equipment for removal, which would add considerably to the cost.

If loose sand were encountered, added width would be required for the footings. Excavation might be much more difficult because sand from surrounding areas would tend to fill in. This would require excavating an area considerably larger than the size of the building.

Excavating can be done in many different ways. The old way is to use a shovel and other hand tools. However, much of the hand labor has been eliminated and replaced with power tools such as trenchers, crane and dragline, backhoes, and bulldozers. See illustrations.

The method of excavation is dependent to a large extent upon the conditions of the soil to be removed. If the soil is quite firm, it is not uncommon to use the sides of the excavation as the outside form for pouring concrete. This is more typical for light construction. In heavy construction, the earth is removed from a larger area than the building will occupy, and forms are constructed to retain the concrete for footings and foundations.

Leveling the construction site with a landscape rake.

Questions to Reinforce Knowledge

1. What is the purpose of having a survey of the property before construction begins?

2. What is an abstract?

3. What is meant by a section of land?

4. What is meant by deed restrictions?

5. What is a zoning ordinance?

6. How is it possible to have a zoning ordinance changed?

7. What is a building code?

8. How do other buildings in an area help determine the location of a building that is to be constructed?

9. How can existing trees affect building construction?

10. What extra expenses may be incurred if a developer completely clears an area before construction is started?

11. What is the value of a plot plan?

12. What is meant by the term "legal description"?

13. What is meant by "grade"?

14. What is a bench mark?

15. Why are floors usually built closer to the ground than formerly?

16. What is meant by the term "terrain"?

17. What is meant by the term "staking out"?

18. What is a batter board?

19. What is staging?

20. How does the Pythagorean theorem apply to laying out a building?

21. What is meant by the term "diagonal method"?

22. Why should rubble and debris be kept from backfill material?

Excavating a trench with a backhoe-loader.

Terms To Spell and Know

property	neighborhood	terrace	adjoining
boundaries	apartment	easement	erosion
purchased	commercial	utilities	basement
abstract	locality	obstructions	staking
surveyor	height	bearing	batter
regulations	barren	contour	transit
community	terrain	elevation	Pythagorean
structure	approaches	legal	hypotenuse
industrial	site	foundation	staging
residential	driveway	perimeter	

2

Concrete

Ingredients of Concrete

The chief ingredients of concrete are cement—a mixture of lime and powdered clay—sand, crushed stone or gravel, and water.

Proportions of Mix

The proportions of the ingredients will vary with the job the concrete is to perform. Generally speaking, the more cement in the mixture, the stronger it will be. Cement is relatively expensive; therefore only enough is used to assure that the concrete will perform its job. For ordinary concrete, such as in basement floors, drives, and sidewalks, the mix usually consists of one 94 pound bag of cement to every 2½ cu. ft. of clean sand and 3 cu. ft. of crushed stone or ¾″ screened, washed gravel. The FHA minimum requirement is *one part* cement, *three parts* sand, and *five parts* gravel or crushed stone. Washed gravel should not be confused with ordinary road gravel, which is not only unwashed but also may contain a large quantity of sand and other foreign matter such as twigs and clay.

The amount of water will vary somewhat, depending upon the desired plasticity of the concrete mix. The more water one adds to the mixture the more plastic or pliable the material becomes. However, additional water weakens the finished concrete. Use only enough to allow the mixture to reach corners and recesses of the form. *Six gallons* of water *per bag* of cement is the quantity usually recommended. NOTE: Any water in the mixture *includes the free water* in the sand and gravel. Damp materials, of course, would require the addition of less water than would dry materials.

Lightweight Aggregates

Concrete may not be required to support loads. Concrete usually weighs about 145 pounds per cubic foot. In order to reduce the weight per cubic foot, lightweight aggregates are sometimes used in the place of the crushed stone or gravel. The more common are *lava slag, cinders,* and *blast furnace slag.*

Effects of Temperature and Moisture

Besides water, the temperature at which concrete is poured and cured has a tremendous effect upon the strength of the finished product. NOTE: Under no circumstances should the concrete be allowed to *freeze* during the setting period. If the temperature is near freezing, yet concrete work must be done, the mix may be heated before it is poured. Also chemicals are available that, when added to the mixture, generate heat which helps prevent freezing; and temporary shelters may be built around, or covers placed over, the concrete, and heat supplied from portable heaters.

The setting time is much faster in warm weather than in cold. However, extreme warmth can cause a problem because the concrete may become solid before the desired finish is achieved. It is necessary to add more water in very hot weather and, for added protection, to cover it with a material such as canvas or sisalkraft paper. This will help to retain the moisture for proper curing. It is also a good idea to dampen the concrete daily for about five days during curing.

If the temperature is *either* too cold or too hot during the curing process, damage and flaking of the surface may result.

Forms

Being a semi-liquid, concrete mix must have a "container" while it is taking shape. Such containers are called forms. Forms are made of lumber, plywood, hardboards, or metal. They may either be built on the construction site or ready-made forms can be set in place on the job. Most larger jobs require the use of both. For large straight foundation walls the manufactured forms are convenient. For posts, columns, footings, and special shapes, job-built ones are usually more satisfactory. NOTE: If round posts are to be poured, the forms are usually made from *cardboard* tubes.

After the concrete is thoroughly set, the forms are then removed or "stripped." If walls are being poured, the forms are held to the correct shape by wire or strap ties. After the forms are removed, these wires remain in the concrete and are sometimes objectionable to the appearance of the finished work. Most ties can be broken back beneath the finished surface by turning them. The cavity where the tie is removed should be filled or "painted"

Reinforcing

The strength of the concrete and a resistance to cracking and shifting position can be improved by the addition of metal reinforcement.

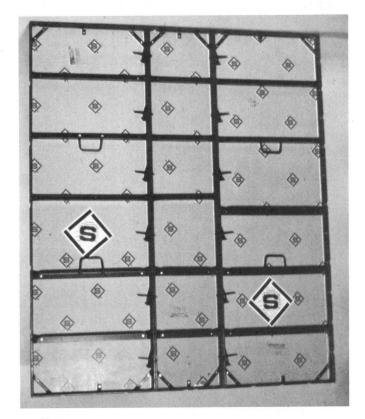

Manufactured concrete forms.

Concrete forms being raised in place with a crane.

Symons Manufacturing Co.

27

This reinforcement is either deformed—not smooth—metal *rod,* the diameter of which is dependent upon the amount of strength required, or *wire* which has been welded into square or rectangular mesh. Examples are illustrated and summarized in Chapter 5, Structural Metal. Reinforcing in slab concrete should be kept near the bottom. While the pouring is in progress, the workman should use a hoe or similar device to lift the mesh slightly so it will be embedded firmly in the concrete. Reinforcing rods must also be held up from the *bottom* of the excavation if they are to be of any value.

Ryerson Steel

Deformed reinforcing bar.

American Stair Corporation

Steel stair forms being prepared
for installation.

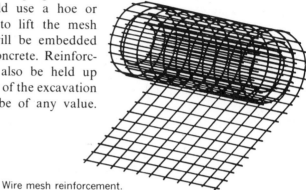

Wire mesh reinforcement.

Complex forms for a foundation wall.

Symons Manufacturing Co.

Mixing and Pouring Concrete

This was originally a hand operation. The cement was delivered in bags; the sand and gravel were dumped near the site where the concrete was to be mixed. On some very small jobs it is still handled in this manner. The workman shovels the dry ingredients into a wooden or metal mixing box; the water is added from a bucket; and the entire contents is mixed thoroughly with a hoe or shovel. The concrete is then shoveled into a wheelbarrow and transported to the point where it is to be used. This method is laborious and time consuming on larger jobs.

A concrete mixer, usually equipped with a gasoline engine, helped make the mixing of concrete less of a chore. The mixer of today is usually mounted on the back of a truck. The ingredients are measured into it from large hoppers located at a central supply point. The concrete is mixed while the truck is on the road to the construction site. When the order is placed, the customer can specify what mix he desires. If the concrete arrives at the construction site with a low pouring consistency, water from a tank on the truck is added as required. The mixer has a short trough attached for dumping the concrete to the job. Several extensions for the trough are kept on the truck to enable the operator to reach work points. If the construction job is large enough to warrant, large hoppers and mixers may be *set up* at the site.

It is not always possible to reach the point where the concrete is to be used. On smaller jobs it will probably be transported in a wheelbarrow. On larger jobs it may be placed on a *conveyor*, or pumped through large flexible *hoses* that can be moved as the work progresses. For high work, *cranes* or *lifts* are employed.

Concrete being poured from a ready-mix truck is shown.

Symons Mfg. Co.

Concrete is often transported to upper levels by conveyor.

Symons Mfg. Co.

A multistory building formed for pouring.

Forms being set for the foundation of a large house.

Symons Mfg. Co.

Vibrating

When concrete is being poured, either the stiffness of the mixture or air trapped in the form may prevent the mix from completely filling the space. Voids or pockets may weaken the structure or allow water to pass through a wall. Vibrating the fresh concrete with poles helps settle the mix. These poles have motors or compressed air hoses attached to vibrate them. Vibrating helps form a more dense material.

When concrete is being poured for a floor, walk, or other large, flat surface, it is sometimes tamped with a "jitterbug" to settle the coarse aggregate below the surface. Remaining aggregate, cement, and sand will be smooth when the concrete is troweled. NOTE: Excessive tamping will cause the aggregate to settle to the bottom of the slab, reducing the strength of the concrete.

Screeding

After the concrete has been poured on a flat surface, the mix must be leveled to the desired height. The straightedge used is called a screed. The screed is moved back and forth across the surface, dragging the concrete to the desired level. Motor driven screeds are sometimes used on large jobs.

Topping

During the leveling process, aggregate may work to the surface, exposing gravel or crushed stone. A smooth surface is usually desired. Topping the concrete with a mixture of cement, sand, and

Wood float used for a textured finish.

water is one method of achieving a smooth finish, but much faulty construction has resulted from such attempts. A good product has a monolithic or one-piece finish. If the topping is added after the base coat of concrete has set, the finish coat will not adhere properly to the base coat. The topping is likely to break away, leaving the rough aggregate exposed. The topping must be placed over the base coat while the mix is still *plastic* or pliable. However, if the base coat is relatively smooth, a rich mixture of dry cement and sand may be sprinkled directly on and troweled to the desired finish. The surface must be troweled until moisture from the mix is worked to the surface to insure a monolithic slab.

Troweling

Smaller surfaces are smoothed with a hand trowel, moved in a circular motion, on partly hardened concrete. On large jobs this is too time-consuming. Troweling machines accomplish the job in a much shorter time, with less manual effort.

Textured surfaces are sometimes desired. A wood float, as shown in the illustration, can be used to achieve this. The float replaces the trowel during the finishing operation. If a striated—

straight, shallow, grooved—face is desired, the troweled surface is swept with a coarse broom, the brush strokes going in the direction the striations are to run.

Exposed Aggregate

For decorative purposes on some concrete work, it is desirable to leave the aggregate protruding above the surface. This is called "exposed aggregate" concrete. The rough surface, as shown, is achieved by leveling the concrete in the customary manner, except that it is *not troweled*. A chemical retarder is placed on the concrete after the screeding is completed. The sub-surface of the concrete hardens in the usual manner but the retarder prevents the surface from hardening. After the sub-surface has set, the surface is washed with a hose, which removes the top mix but allows the aggregate to remain firmly attached in the hardened concrete below.

Retarders can also be added to ordinary concrete to slow the setting time.

Expansion Joints

Large, uninterrupted areas of concrete are likely to crack because of expansion and contraction due to changes in temperature. Therefore lines are usually scored in the surface to allow the concrete to "move" in unobjectionable places. If the surface is quite large, expansion joints are used to allow for expansion and contraction. These joints are filled with tar or a fibrous material which has been impregnated with tar. The joints are placed so as

Portland Cement Association

Exposed aggregate concrete is used for this patio floor.

not to present an objectionable appearance.

Purchased by the Cubic Yard

Concrete is purchased by the cubic yard. Imagine a piece of concrete 3'x3'x3'. This represents one cubic yard. Concrete will not usually pour out full measure. Loss of the water by evaporation and absorption into adjacent ma-

terials is the cause. When figuring concrete, consider 25 cubic feet as one cubic yard instead of the customary 27 cubic feet. One desires to figure a job as close as is possible, but it is better to have too much concrete than not enough. Serious delays and faulty construction can result from ordering too little concrete for a continuous pour.

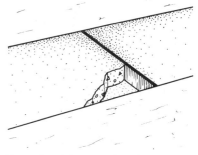

Expansion joints control cracking of concrete surfaces.

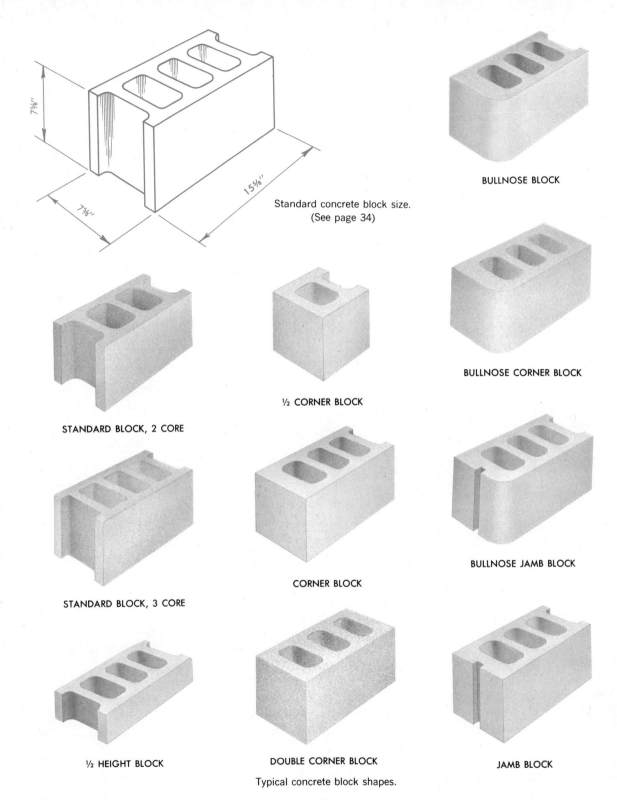

7⅝″

7⅜″

15⅝″

Standard concrete block size.
(See page 34)

BULLNOSE BLOCK

½ CORNER BLOCK

BULLNOSE CORNER BLOCK

STANDARD BLOCK, 2 CORE

CORNER BLOCK

BULLNOSE JAMB BLOCK

STANDARD BLOCK, 3 CORE

½ HEIGHT BLOCK

DOUBLE CORNER BLOCK

JAMB BLOCK

Typical concrete block shapes.

OFFSET BLOCK

SOFFIT BLOCK

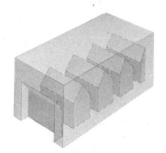

CAP BLOCK

OFFSET BLOCK

SILL BLOCK

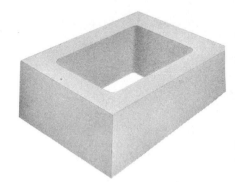

FLUE BLOCK

OFFSET BLOCK

LINTEL BLOCK

PILASTER BLOCK

HEADER BLOCK

LINTEL JAMB BLOCK

PARTITION OR SOLID BLOCK

Typical concrete block shapes.

Concrete Blocks

Exposed aggregate panels are frequently used for vertical installations.

Concrete can also be purchased in the form of ready-made blocks. These are composed of cement, sand, and a fine aggregate. Small gravel is the usual aggregate, but blocks are also made with other materials. Cinder and haydite are added to make a lightweight block. These are not designed to be load bearing, or supporting. They will support only their own weight. Beams support the floors and walls. The block are used to wall off areas in a building and to form outer walls. Concrete blocks can be purchased which have *decorative* aggregates such as marble or granite chips.

The standard size of concrete blocks is 8″x8″x16″. This is called the *nominal* size. The *actual* size is ⅜″ less on all measurements. The reason is to allow for the mortar joint and still lay up the block at the given size. The reasons for the 16″ measurement will be discussed later.

There are many sizes and shapes of concrete blocks. *Patterns* for laying of concrete blocks are limited only by the imagination of the designer. Samples of frequently used patterns for laying concrete blocks are shown in Chapter 8.

Concrete blocks are purchased by the hundred or, on smaller jobs, by the individual unit.

Extensive use of concrete adds to the beauty of this home.

Questions to Reinforce Knowledge

1. From what materials is ordinary concrete usually made?

2. Why does one sometimes vary the proportions of the ingredients of concrete?

3. What is the difference between road gravel and washed gravel?

4. When concrete is not required to be load bearing, what aggregates are sometimes used?

5. What two things are likely to happen if concrete is poured in freezing conditions?

6. How are the ingredients of concrete warmed and kept warm for use?

7. What is the name of the item that holds the concrete in place while it is curing?

8. What material is sometimes used as a form when pouring round posts?

9. What are some of the materials used in form construction?

10. What is the process of removing the forms from the concrete called?

11. What is reinforcing rod?

12. What is reinforcing mesh?

13. Why is reinforcing rod held away from the bottom of the excavation?

14. Describe a ready-mix truck.

15. How can the consistency of concrete be varied?

16. What difficulties can result from having voids in the concrete?

17. What is meant by the term vibrating the concrete?

18. What is meant by the term tamping the concrete?

19. What is the process of leveling the concrete called?

20. What tool is used for leveling concrete?

21. What is meant by the term topping?

22. What is meant by the term monolithic concrete?

23. What is meant by the term machine troweling?

24. What is a broom finish, and how is it achieved?

25. What is exposed aggregate concrete?

26. What is a retarder, and why is it used?

27. From what materials are ordinary concrete blocks made?

28. What are lightweight concrete blocks? When are they used?

29. How is concrete purchased?

30. What are decorative concrete blocks?

31. What is the standard size of a concrete block?

Portland Cement Association

Concrete privacy screen.

Terms To Spell and Know

concrete	columns	flaking	expansion
ingredients	reinforcement	hardboard	fibrous
plastic	deformed	texture	impregnated
aggregates	wheelbarrow	striated	evaporation
sisalkraft	hopper	retarder	absorption
curing	consistency	screeding	trough

Extra strength forms are frequently necessary for heavy construction.

Symons Mfg. Co.

3

Footings and Foundations

Footing and Foundation Size

Two factors which influence the size of a footing and foundation are:

- Load-bearing ability of the soil.
- Weight of the structure as distributed.

For large construction projects the load-bearing ability of the soil should be determined by an engineer. For most light construction the accompanying table will be adequate.

When determining the weight which one lineal foot must support, the weight of all materials in the same foot of building must be considered.

Minimum Requirements for Footings and Foundations

For most light construction it is not necessary to make mathematical calculations to determine the sizes to be used. The Federal Housing Administration minimum requirements for firm soil

LOAD BEARING ABILITY OF SOILS	
SOIL TYPES	**TONS SQ. FT.**
Hard Pan	10
Rocks or Gravel	6
Coarse Sand—Compact	4
Stiff Clay	4
Fine Sand—Dry	3
Fine Sand—Damp	2
Medium Clay	2
Soft Clay	1

Definition of a Footing

A footing is the concrete or other solid, enlarged base which supports the foundation, a column, pier, or other weight. The footing helps distribute the load.

Definition of a Foundation

A foundation is that portion of the walls of a building which is below the floor joist. Usually most of the foundation is beneath the finished grade.

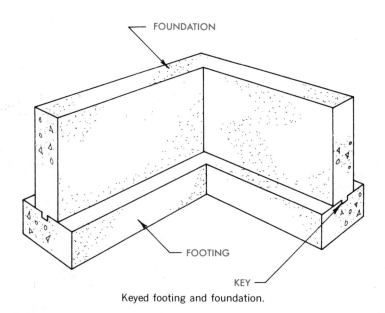

Keyed footing and foundation.

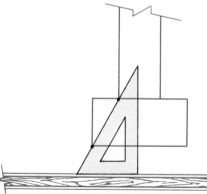

When footing thickness and foundation width are the same, the footing width may be determined by the 30°-60° method.

state that the foundation must be at least as wide as the materials to be supported. The footing must be at least twice as wide as the foundation wall. The minimum thickness of a bearing foundation of poured concrete is 6″. However, local codes frequently require the use of a greater thickness. For frame buildings an 8″ thickness is often used. Masonry veneer and solid masonry buildings may require 10″ or 12″ foundation thickness. The width of a concrete block foundation wall should be 8″ minimum. The thickness or height of the footing should be the same as the width of the foundation.

The 30°-60° method of determining the footing width and the thickness or height is also sometimes used. An example of this method is shown.

Individual building codes differ widely as to required sizes. Before a plan is drawn the building code for the locality should be consulted.

Footing Shapes

For lightweight, thin-walled buildings such as garages and storage sheds, the load may not require the use of a footing other than the foundation. If slightly more weight must be supported, and the earth is firm, it is permissible to use a flared footing. The foundation is dug to the desired depth and the base is widened with a shovel to give a slightly larger base.

The typical foundation is rectangular. The footing and foundation are usually poured at separate times. This forms a joint where the sections meet. The joint can cause two problems: Water may enter the area between the two parts or settling may cause the footing and foundation to separate. A *key* may be placed in the footing to help remedy these problems.

If a stronger support is desired, a monolithic footing and foundation may be poured. Because of the irregular shape, the form construction and pour is difficult. It is used only in cases of necessity.

When the floor of a building is to be of concrete, the floor, foundation, and footing are sometimes poured as a single-unit floating slab. This type construction is used more often in moderate climates where it is not necessary to add a great amount of insulation. The insulation is placed on the exterior perimeter of the foundation wall and must extend to the top of the floor. (NOTE: It is exposed and does not present a desirable appearance.) The insulation is then faced with asbestos board or other inorganic material.

(See next two pages.)

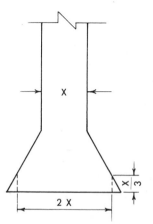

On a flared footing the effective bearing width should be at least twice the foundation width.

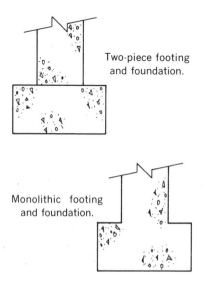

Two-piece footing and foundation.

Monolithic footing and foundation.

FOOTING SHAPES

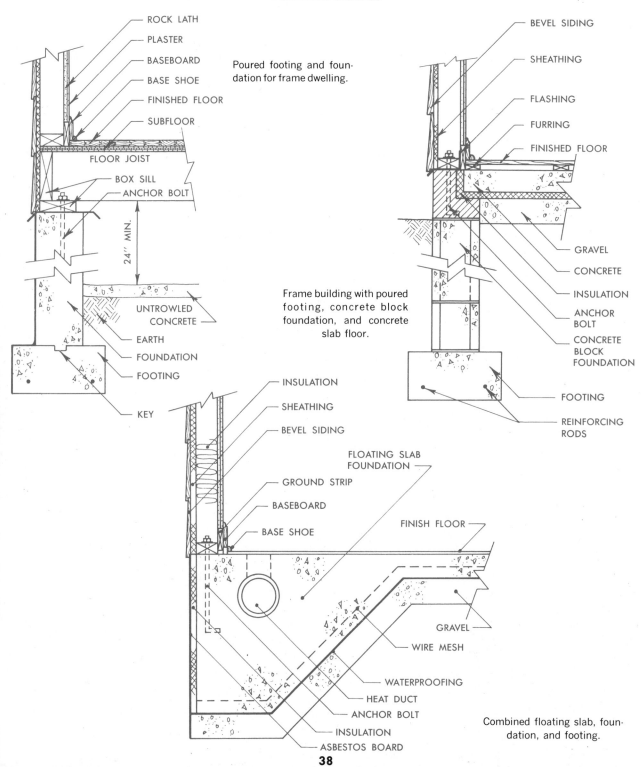

ROCK LATH
PLASTER
BASEBOARD
BASE SHOE
FINISHED FLOOR
SUBFLOOR
FLOOR JOIST
BOX SILL
ANCHOR BOLT
24" MIN.
UNTROWLED CONCRETE
EARTH
FOUNDATION
FOOTING
KEY

Poured footing and foundation for frame dwelling.

BEVEL SIDING
SHEATHING
FLASHING
FURRING
FINISHED FLOOR
GRAVEL
CONCRETE
INSULATION
ANCHOR BOLT
CONCRETE BLOCK FOUNDATION
FOOTING
REINFORCING RODS

Frame building with poured footing, concrete block foundation, and concrete slab floor.

INSULATION
SHEATHING
BEVEL SIDING
GROUND STRIP
BASEBOARD
BASE SHOE
FLOATING SLAB FOUNDATION
FINISH FLOOR
GRAVEL
WIRE MESH
WATERPROOFING
HEAT DUCT
ANCHOR BOLT
INSULATION
ASBESTOS BOARD

Combined floating slab, foundation, and footing.

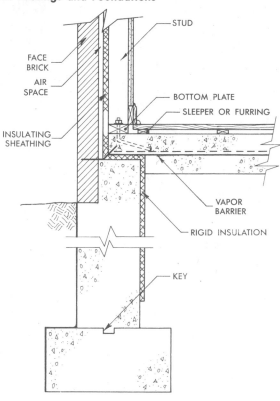

STUD

FACE BRICK

AIR SPACE

INSULATING SHEATHING

BOTTOM PLATE

SLEEPER OR FURRING

VAPOR BARRIER

RIGID INSULATION

KEY

Poured footing and foundation for frame
veneer house with a slab floor.

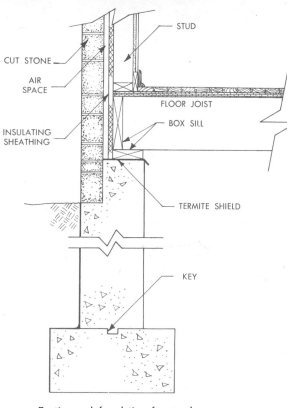

STUD

CUT STONE

AIR SPACE

INSULATING SHEATHING

FLOOR JOIST

BOX SILL

TERMITE SHIELD

KEY

Footing and foundation for wood
joists and masonry veneer wall.

Footing and foundation for a solid
masonry building.

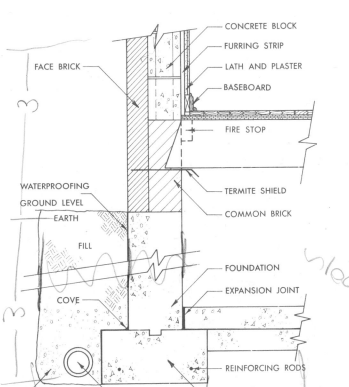

CONCRETE BLOCK

FURRING STRIP

LATH AND PLASTER

BASEBOARD

FACE BRICK

FIRE STOP

WATERPROOFING

GROUND LEVEL

EARTH

FILL

COVE

TERMITE SHIELD

COMMON BRICK

FOUNDATION

EXPANSION JOINT

REINFORCING RODS

GRAVEL FILL

DRAIN TILE

FOOTING

39

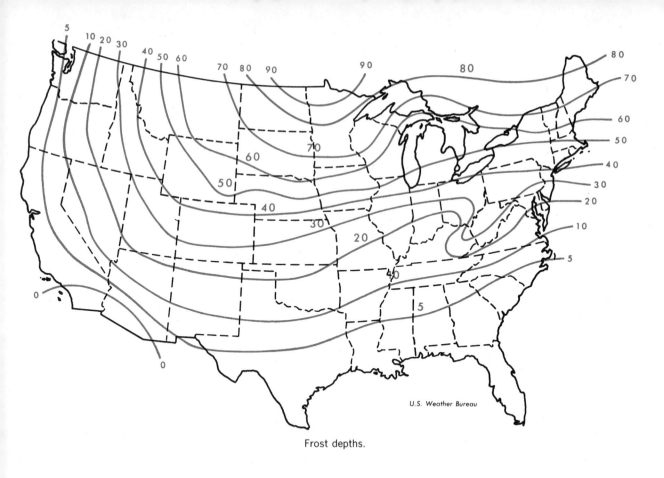

Frost depths.

Frost Line

The depth of the footing is determined by the depth to which the ground is likely to freeze. Freezing and thawing cause the ground to expand and contract. If the ground freezes below the footing it will force the wall to move, which will cause cracking. The accompanying map shows minimum footing depths for different sections of the United States, based upon the maximum depth frost is likely to occur. However, this cannot be used as an absolute guide. Many local codes specify depths that vary from recommended government standards. Local codes must be consulted before plans are drawn.

The FHA places the minimum height of basement ceilings at 6'-10". If the basement is to be finished as habitable rooms, 7'-6" or 8'-0" is more desirable.

Unexcavated Areas

The minimum distance between the bottom of wood floor joists and the ground is 24". (The earth should be scraped free of all organic material.) This space will allow adequate air circulation and workmen can move about without difficulty. If dampness is likely to occur, provision for draining the area should be made. Many builders place a 3" slab of concrete over the excavated area. NOTE: A screed is used to level the concrete but it is not troweled to a smooth finish.

Space between the earth and

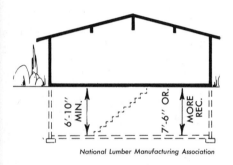

National Lumber Manufacturing Association

Basement ceiling heights.

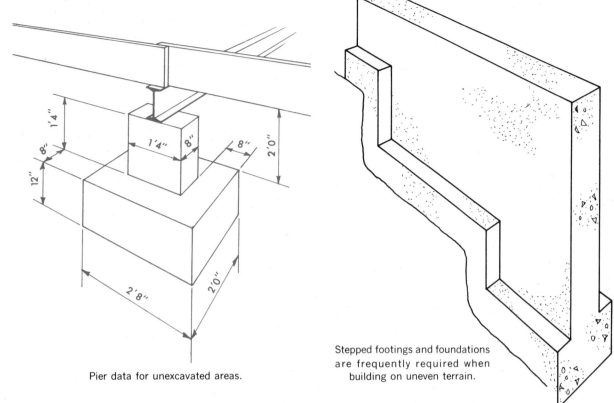

Pier data for unexcavated areas.

Stepped footings and foundations are frequently required when building on uneven terrain.

floor joist must not be confused with height above grade.

Steps in Footing

If the terrain is uneven, it is not always possible to make a level base for the footing and foundation. Then the footing must conform to the shape of the ground, although the *base* is always kept level. To vary the height, place *steps* in the footing. The step heights should not exceed 2'-0". The horizontal distance between steps should be no less than 2'-0". The horizontal portion should be the same thickness or height as other footing. The vertical member should be at least 4" thick, and the same width as the footing.

Footing and Foundation Reinforcement

Most construction requires the addition of reinforcing rod to the footing to minimize cracking and shifting of the concrete. Two ½" rods are usually adequate. They should not be placed above the center of the footing.

Rod may also be placed in the foundation walls to increase their strength.

Breaks in the Pour

If all the concrete cannot be poured at one time and breaks or splices must be made in the footing, they should not occur close to a step or pilaster. The breaks should be kept clean and should be thoroughly dampened

before the next pour is made. This allows the concrete to bond together.

Pilaster

A pilaster is a post built into the wall. It may occur in the foundation wall or the supporting walls above the foundation. To be effective, a pilaster is placed on the inside of the building, when additional weight must be supported. For example, if a large beam is to span a basement, a pilaster might be used to support the end of the beam.

Foundation Wall Materials

Although poured concrete is used commonly for foundation walls, it is relatively expensive.

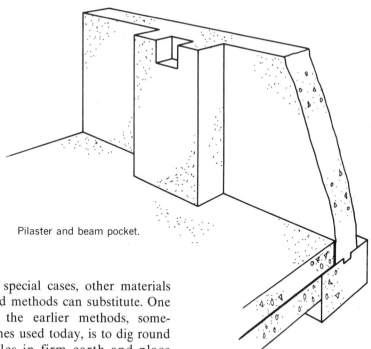

Pilaster and beam pocket.

In special cases, other materials and methods can substitute. One of the earlier methods, sometimes used today, is to dig round holes in firm earth and place *wooden posts* in the holes. The tops of the posts are made level, so the building can be constructed upon them. In pole construction, these posts also act as the vertical framework for the walls. Cypress, cedar, and redwood are materials well suited for this method of construction. Other kinds of wood may be used but they require the addition of a pressure-treated preservative, such as creosote, to retard decay.

Wood piles can be expected to last about thirty years. The part of the pile subjected to the weather deteriorates much more rapidly than that below grade or submerged in water. A shallow foundation wall can be used to cap the tops of the poles to prolong their life. This wall also acts as a level base for the sills. *Concrete posts* are sometimes used for

a lightweight foundation of this type. The installation is the same as for wood posts.

Hard varieties of *stone* and *brick* are also used as foundation materials. Both materials are likely to disintegrate from excessive moisture if soft and porous. A tile drain around foundations of these types is necessary. A stone foundation or retaining wall can be *battered* or sloped, as shown, to gain added strength.

Concrete Block

Concrete block is used quite extensively as a foundation material. The joints must be completely filled with mortar. Metal reinforcing, as shown in the illustration, is recommended between alternate courses of block to help minimize cracking. Hollow block walls are less waterproof than solid concrete, so more

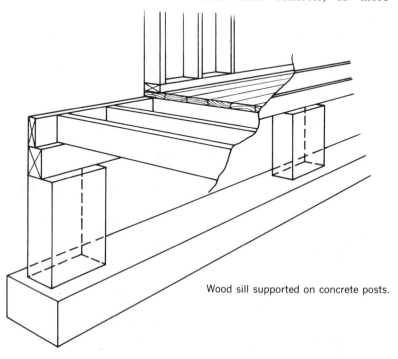

Wood sill supported on concrete posts.

waterproofing is required to keep the moisture from penetrating.

Drain Tile

When the foundation serves as a basement wall, or if water might not drain properly otherwise, a 4″ inside-diameter drain tile should be placed around the perimeter of the building. The tile is placed at the same level as the footing, and about 6″ outside of it. The tile should be laid in a bed of gravel or crushed stone. The joints between the tile should be left open about ⅜″. These are covered with strips of building paper or roll roofing to prevent gravel above the tile from entering it. The material for the tile may be field clay, concrete, or bituminous fiber. The drain tile should be connected to the sanitary sewer (unless a code prohibits it), a storm sewer, or a dry well. The joints between the tile leading to the sewer or other drain should be cemented.

Battered stone foundation.

Concrete block reinforcement.

When a basement floor extends to a footing, the drain tile is positioned adjacent to the footing.

When a basement floor does not extend to the footing, the drain tile is placed near the same level as the floor.

Waterproofing Foundation Walls

As was stated earlier, concrete can be made more dense by adding adulterants of other materials to the mix. This may make the wall more waterproof, but it should not be the only measure taken. Also, some building codes prohibit the use of adulterants. Coatings of waterproof materials are placed on the outside of the foundation wall. One of the best known methods is to mop a layer, or layers, of *tar* on the outside of the foundation wall. The use of *plastic film* between the layers is an excellent newer method. A 1″ coating of *cement mortar* is specified by some codes. Others require cement in addition to tar.

At the juncture of the wall and footing, extra care should be taken. The tar or mortar should be rounded in the corner to form a cove which will flow water away from the joint. See illustration, page 43.

Many products are available that are advertised to waterproof a wall from the *inside*. Some of these may work to a degree. However, such waterproofing is not usually very satisfactory. If water penetrates the masonry wall, pressure exerted against the protective coat will probably cause the wall to scale and blister. Outside waterproofing may be built up in layers and has the wall to help resist pressure.

Areaways or Window Wells

The purpose of an areaway is to keep the earth away from an opening, such as a window, in

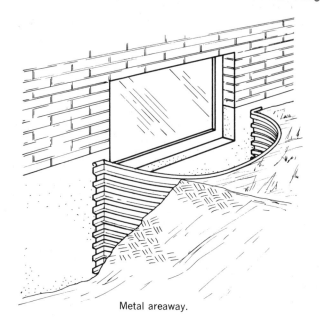

Metal areaway.

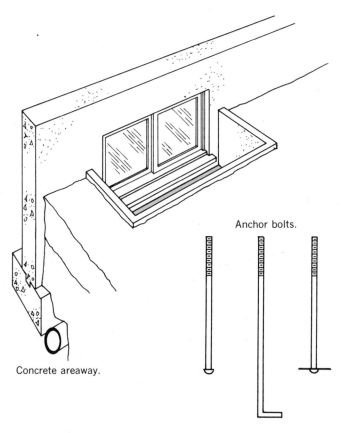

Concrete areaway.

Anchor bolts.

the foundation wall. The areaway may be made of metal or concrete. Its inside width should be about 1' more than the wall opening. The top of a window in a foundation wall must be above the grade line; the distance the areaway extends from the building should be the same as the depth of the window below grade. The minimum distance from the edge of the building is 1'-0"; the areaway should extend below the window sill at least 6". The bottom of the areaway should be covered with gravel or crushed stone. Provisions should be made for draining surface water from the well. If the bottom of the well is more than 2' deep, a guard rail should be provided.

Height Above Grade

Unless special provisions have been made for protection against rot and termites, the top of the foundation should be a minimum of 8" above the finished grade. No *wood parts* should be closer than 8" to the ground. Offsets may be placed in the top of the foundation to allow masonry to end even with the grade. An example is shown on the footing and foundation detail on page 39.

Anchor Bolts

Anchor bolts help tie the framework of the building to the foundation. They should be at least ½" in diameter. They should extend into a poured concrete wall at least 6" and into a masonry wall at least 15". When anchor bolts are placed in piers, a hole slightly larger than the diameter of the bolt should be drilled in a

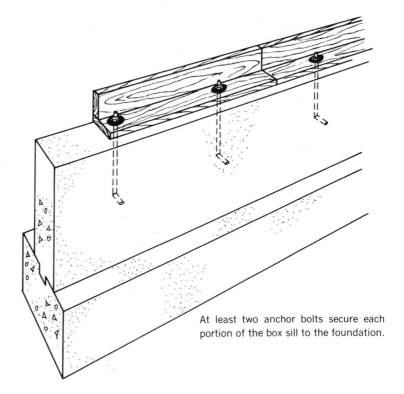

At least two anchor bolts secure each portion of the box sill to the foundation.

⅛"x3"x3" steel plate. Place the bolt through the plate so the head of the bolt is in contact with the steel plate. Bolts are placed in the foundation walls no more than 8'-0" apart (on center). Every board to be anchored must have at least two bolts.

Foundation Vents

The crawl space or unexcavated area beneath a building must have ventilation to remove moisture and circulate the air. If the area is not ventilated, mold and rot will result.

Vents for foundation walls are usually 8"x16", and cast of iron or aluminum. When the wall is of brick it is possible to omit mortar from some of the vertical joints, or place a series of bricks in a vertical position with open spaces between each brick. Vents should be provied with a screen of not less than eight squares per lineal inch. The minimum amount of ventilation for crawl spaces is 1 square foot for each 150 square feet of ground area. Vents should be placed near the corners of the building in such a manner as to provide adequate cross ventilation.

It is not necessary to place foundation vents in the wall if the building's crawl space opens directly into a basement and one half the space between the floor joist and crawl space floor is open.

8"x16" foundation vents.

Questions to Reinforce Knowledge

1. What is a footing?
2. What is a foundation?
3. What is the most common material for a footing? Others?
4. What are two kinds of concrete forms frequently used for foundation walls?
5. What two factors determine the size of a footing?
6. What is the FHA minimum requirement for foundation thickness?
7. To meet minimum standards, on normal-weight construction, what is the difference between the width of the foundation wall and the width of the footing?
8. To meet minimum standards, what is the relationship between the width of the foundation wall and the thickness or height of the footing?
9. What is meant by the term 30°-60° method of determining footing size?
10. What is meant when one says a key is placed between the footing and foundation?
11. What is a flared footing? When is it used? What are its advantages?
12. What is meant by the term monolithic footing and foundation?
13. What is the frost line?
14. Why must one be concerned with this line?
15. What is meant by stepped footing? Why is it used?
16. What is the maximum height of the steps?
17. What is the minimum horizontal distance between steps?
18. What is the minimum thickness of the concrete connecting the steps?
19. What is a pilaster?
20. Why is cypress frequently used as a pile?
21. How can the life of wood posts be extended?
22. If soft brick is used for a foundation wall what is likely to happen?
23. Waterproofing is applied on which side of a foundation wall? Why?
24. Explain the function of the drain tile placed around the exterior of the building.
25. What is the minimum distance, on a wood building, the foundation should extend above grade? Why?
26. How does one determine the number of anchor bolts needed?
27. What is a foundation vent?

Terms to Spell and Know

lineal	preservative	termite
flared	creosote	anchor
thawing	submerged	ventilation
pilaster	juncture	pier
cypress	penetrate	ceiling
cedar	bituminous	horizontal
redwood	areaway	vertical

Poured Concrete Slabs

Prepared Earth as a Base

If concrete is to be used on the outside of a building, or if moisture does not have to be considered on the inside, the concrete may be poured directly on smooth, firm earth. If the earth has been disturbed from its natural state, is should be well tamped or compacted to eliminate

Definition of Concrete Slab

A concrete slab is any thin, broad, flat shape, such as a floor, driveway, walk, porch, or any other broad, flat surface.

For most applications the minimum thickness of a concrete slab is 4″ nominal size. NOTE: A nominal size is only approximate. The actual size would conform to the dimensions of the lumber being used as a form. Dimension lumber is usually smaller than the stated size. For example, a 2x4 is only 1⅝″x3⅝″ the other ⅜″ is wasted in planing and smoothing down before you purchase it.

settling. Concrete should never be poured over lose fill. As the fill settles, the concrete will crack. It is then necessary to drill holes in the concrete and pump a mixture of cement, earth, and water under it to make it level again. This is very costly.

When plans are being drawn for a building the preparation of the earth is clearly stated. For example, if earth beneath a floor is to be filled, leveled, and compacted this should be noted on the working plans.

Under-Floor Fill

When a concrete slab serves as a floor on the inside of a building, some material is usually placed between the earth and concrete. Recommended is clean sand, gravel, or crushed stone. Cinders are sometimes used but they tend to deteriorate, leaving voids beneath the concrete. The right materials help level the surface. They also absorb surface water and help drain it away from the floor.

The minimum thickness of the under-floor fill is 4″, preferably 6″, if load bearing.

Vapor Barriers

Concrete is porous. Water in contact with the under side of the floor will cause the top side to become damp. Concrete floors in habitable structures require a vapor or moisture barrier between the fill and the concrete. At the present time the most widely used material is sheet plastic film. This may be obtained in rolls up to 40′ in width, thus minimizing the number of splices needed. NOTE: An adhesive should be applied to joint splices to insure waterproofing.

The vapor barrier also makes pouring and finishing of the concrete less difficult. If concrete is poured directly onto the fill, the porous material tends to absorb water, thus making it harder to achieve the desired finish.

Reinforcement

Most building codes require the addition of wire fabric to concrete slabs. If the concrete cracks, the wire fabric will prevent separation, thus holding the crack to a minimum. Electrically welded fabric with 6″x6″ spacing is frequently used.

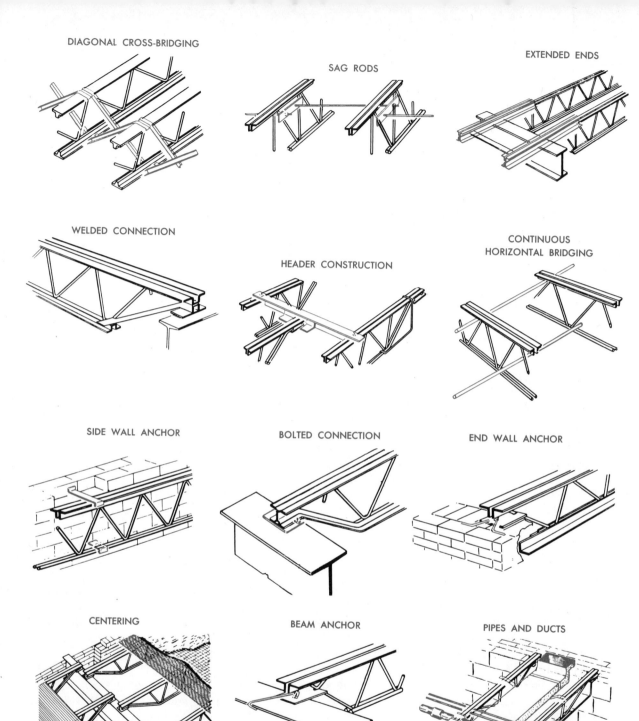

DIAGONAL CROSS-BRIDGING

SAG RODS

EXTENDED ENDS

WELDED CONNECTION

HEADER CONSTRUCTION

CONTINUOUS
HORIZONTAL BRIDGING

SIDE WALL ANCHOR

BOLTED CONNECTION

END WALL ANCHOR

CENTERING

BEAM ANCHOR

PIPES AND DUCTS

Steel Joist Institute

Steel joist assemblies.

Suspended Concrete Floors

Concrete floors, in addition to being fireproof, give a structure a rigidity found with no other method of construction.

Many times it is desired to lay floors of concrete in locations other than on or below grade. When used above grade, a method of supporting the concrete is necessary. Open web bar joists as shown in the illustration are sometimes used to span the area where the floor is desired. The size and spacing of the joist is determined by the span and the load to be supported. Corrugated or ribbed metal is attached across the joist as a base for the concrete. Manufactured materials for floor and roof decks, as shown, are also available.

For most light construction, bar joist spacing on 24″ centers makes maximum use of other building materials. For example,

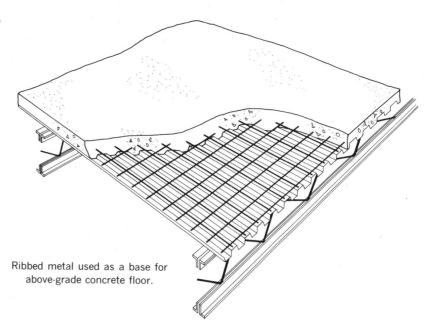

Ribbed metal used as a base for above-grade concrete floor.

the metal for the deck might be 8′-0″ long, plus 2′ increments over this basic length. The length of manufactured sheet materials are fabricated in even foot measures. By utilizing these full lengths, we keep waste to a minimum.

Other materials also serve as a base for the concrete. Lumber, plywood, or fiber board is frequently used. The exterior grain of plywood should be placed across the joist. Fiber boards work best for roof decks where no great live load is to be supported.

Pan type forms can add to both structure and beauty. Beams and floor are poured as one unit with steel forms.

The Ceco Corporation, M. Scilingo Photo

Two kinds of *loads* must be supported by the floor and roof decks: (1) A dead load is the actual weight of the materials in the floor, or bearing upon it. (2) A live load is weight in addition to the materials. For example, people, furniture, and automobiles are live loads.

Precast Joist

Precast joists are manufactured in a plant away from the job site. Reinforcing rod under tension (prestressed) is placed in a form, and the concrete is poured around the rod. Examples of precast joists are shown.

Monolithic Beam and Floor

When a one-piece floor system is desired, it is possible to build a single form for the floors and beams. Necessary reinforcing is wired in place and the concrete is poured as for an ordinary slab. However, the mix must be vibrated and worked into place so the exposed under side will be smooth and have a finished appearance.

A floor or roof of this type is usually quite expensive. In addition to the time and materials needed for the forms, some arrangement must be made for supporting them in their proper place. Wood or metal posts with cross T's at the top are placed beneath the form to hold it while the concrete is being poured and cured. These posts are called *shoring*.

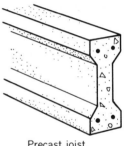

Precast joist.

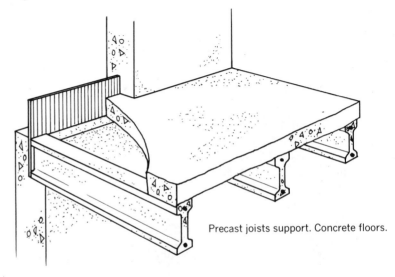

Precast joists support. Concrete floors.

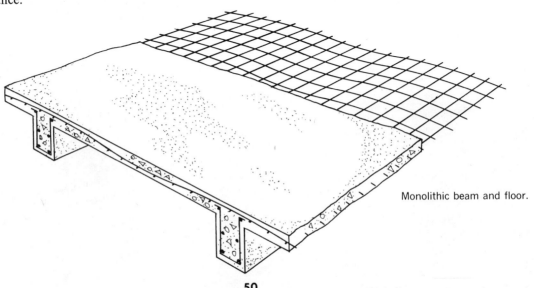

Monolithic beam and floor.

Steel dome pans form a monolithic concrete floor system that can also serve as a finished ceiling of rooms below.

The Ceco Corporation, M. Scilingo Photo

Crawl Spaces for Pipes

When a concrete floor is used, place major plumbing and wiring beneath it in such a manner that it is readily accessible for repair and service, using a pipe trench or crawl space as shown. A 3″ concrete floor for the trench will greatly improve working conditions and help eliminate moisture under the floor.

Lightweight Aggregates for Floor and Roof Construction

Insulation from sound and temperature can be improved with the addition of a layer of lightweight aggregate as shown. It is not usually load supporting. Added thickness would be required if the floor or roof must support a live load.

Ordinary roof systems use lightweight aggregates exclusively.

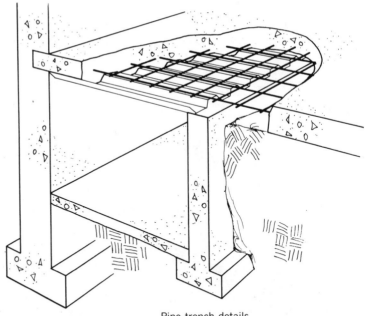

Pipe trench details.

Questions to Reinforce Knowledge

1. What is a concrete slab?

2. What is the thickness recommended for a live load-supporting concrete slab?

3. Why is a 2x4 not actually 2″x4″?

4. When may concrete be poured directly on undistorted or firm earth?

5. Why is concrete not poured over loose fill?

6. What is under-floor fill? What materials are commonly used?

7. Why are cinders a poor choice for fill?

8. What is the minimum thickness of under-floor fill?

9. What is a vapor barrier?

10. What is a good material to use as a vapor barrier?

11. What are two advantages of having a barrier between the floor and fill?

12. What is meant by the term suspended concrete floor?

13. What is an open web bar joist?

14. What determines the size bar joist to use?

15. Name four materials that might be used over the joist to support the concrete floor.

16. Why is 24″ on center a good choice for bar joist spacing? What other spacings might also be satisfactory?

17. What is meant by the term dead load?

18. What is meant by the term live load?

19. What is a precast joist?

20. What is meant by the term prestressed joist?

21. What is a pipe trench?

22. Why is a floor advisable for a pipe trench?

23. Why may lightweight aggregate be used in ordinary roof systems?

Terms to Spell and Know

applications	expanded
planing	corrugated
settling	increments
cinders	plywood
vapor	fiber board
barrier	precast
adhesive	prestressed
electrically	monolithic
rigidity	shoring
	wiring

5

Structural Metal

Scope

Structural metal is any metal part that adds strength to the building. It usually supports or distributes weight other than its own. Because of the technical nature of the topic it is impossible to do more than acquaint you with the problems involved. Most cities and codes do not permit the draftsman to make actual strength calculations. When he does, they must be checked and approved by a registered architect or engineer, who then assumes responsibility for the calculations. The tables and charts shown in the chapter are satisfactory for preliminary calculations, but engineering data is to be verified before construction proceeds.

Factors That Influence

One does not design *all* structural parts, using complete mathematical calculations. This would result in much unnecessary duplication of work. Many requirements have been previously determined from similar construction and the results have been incorporated into tables and charts.

It is very important to check local codes before establishing strength requirements and structural shapes and sizes, to meet the desired standards. Each local code will have its own strength and size requirements. If no code is available, one may consult government recommendations or published industry standards.

Assumptions

As previously stated, *all* building parts must support at least their own weight or the *dead load*. In addition, some structural parts must support the weight of superimposed or *live loads*.

Before one can determine the size of any structural part he must know its weight and the weight of the load to be supported. This is difficult to know at the beginning stages of planning. For example, if one is designing a beam to support floor joists, he must first know all of the materials that will bear upon the joists, and the weight of these materials. He must also determine the size, number, and weight of all joists to bear upon the beam. The weight of the beam itself must be taken into consideration. When determining beam size, one must also know what proportion of the weight is distributed to foundations and columns, and whether the load is quiescent (no movement) or is subject to movement.

It is readily apparent that many assumptions must be made and/or considered before actual structural parts can be planned.

To find the weight of materials, one cannot weigh samples of building materials! Therefore manufacturers supply pertinent data concerning their products and this information is incorporated into tables and charts to be used for planning purposes, before construction starts.

Welded Wire Fabric

Welded wire fabric is a prefabricated steel reinforcing material. It is manufactured of cold-drawn steel. It is a rigid material, due to its electrically welded connections at all wire intersections, yet it is ductile and has the ability to lie flat in both light and heavy styles. Its main advantages are speed of installation and ease of handling on the job. It is especially suitable as a reinforcement.

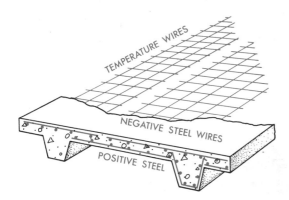

One-way monolithic concrete slab floor.

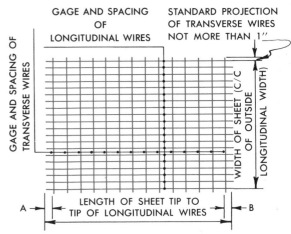

Welded wire fabric detailing sheet.

Concrete floors, roofs, walls, and other concrete structural elements usually require wire reinforcement.

Heavy mats with wires in excess of ½″ eliminate the necessity of using individual reinforcing rods which must be wired together at all rod intersections; this increases possible uses of welded wire fabric. Built-in spacing of wires is a time saver, assuring perfect alignment of members.

When a slab is on grade, location of welded wire fabric will depend on the slab thickness. In slabs 6″ or more in thickness, the fabric should be placed at a minimum depth of 2″ below the surface and a maximum depth equal to ⅓ the slab thickness. For slabs less than 6″, the fabric may be placed in the middle. Experience indicates that the minimum sizes of welded wire fabric should be No. 10 gage for basement floors and sidewalks; No. 6 gage for driveways and filling stations; and No. 4 gage for heavy duty industrial floors.

A good rule for wire spacing, regardless of wire size or pattern formed by cross wires is that wire spacing should not exceed twice the thickness of the slab and maximum spacing is 12″. It is customary to limit spacing of both longitudinal and transverse wires to a maximum of 6″ in slabs less than 6″ thick. Reinforcing fabric should not be carried through construction or expansion joints. It should extend to within 2 to 4 inches of the joints and edges of the slab.

Suspended concrete—or one-way floors and roofs used in combination with structural steel frame, steel joists, precast or poured-in place beams, joist and pan or other construction—involves an entirely different engineering concept. Therefore additional engineering data should be consulted prior to their design.[1]

---

[1] *Adapted from Building Design Handbook, Wire Reinforcement Institute.*

Reinforcement Sizes

Wire gage sizes as used in welded wire fabric are not to be confused with reinforcing rod sizes. Both materials have *number* sizes, so confusion could possibly result. A comparison of sizes is shown in the table below.

WIRE SIZE	
Gage No.	Diameter
½″	.5000
0000000	.4900
000000	.4615
00000	.4305
0000	.3938
000	.3625
00	.3310
0	.3065
1	.2830
2	.2625
¼	.2500
3	.2437
4	.2253
5	.2070
6	.1920
7	.1770
8	.1620
9	.1483
10	.1350
11	.1250
12	.1055

Kinds and Use of I Beams

To Support Floors

For planning purposes, assume you are designing a wood frame building, dimensions of which are 30'x48'. This building is to have two stories as shown in the illustration. The floor joists are placed across the short dimension. This 30' span is too great for continuous wood floor joists, therefore they must be spliced. The splice is ordinarily made above a wood girder or steel beam, and beneath the bearing walls of the area above. Excessive *deflection* or sagging of the floor joists will occur if the bearing wall is not placed above the beam.

Two kinds of steel beams are commonly used. These are: American Standard I beams and Wide Flange I beams. The main difference between the two is that the latter has a much wider horizontal width or *flange*. Wide flange beams will support much greater weights and will withstand greater *lateral* or sidewise pressure.

Weight Beam Is to Support

When load-supporting walls are located beneath the spliced joists or wall of the area above, no beam is necessary. When a wall beneath the joists is not designed to be load supporting, a beam is required. The beam is placed at right angles to the joists. If placed as shown in the foundation illustration, the span is 48'. (See page 59.)

Local codes usually specify minimum amounts of weight that floors and other building parts must support. To simplify the calculations, all weights have been based on the tables shown in this text.

Using the section through the building shown in the illustration, the weights are as follows:

First floor
Live load	40	pounds per square foot
Dead load	10	" " " "
Net load	50	" " " "

Second floor
Live load	40	" " " "
Dead load	10	" " " "
Net load	50	" " " "

Ceiling
Live load	20	" " " "
Dead load	10	" " " "
Net load	30	" " " "

Roof   0 bearing upon joists or interior wall for transmission to beam

Walls
Live load	0
Dead load	10 pounds per square foot

REINFORCING BARS		
ar No.	Bar Size	Diameter
2	* ¼ rd.	.250
3	* ⅜ rd.	.375
4	½ rd.	.500
5	⅝ rd.	.625
6	¾ rd.	.750
7	⅞ rd.	.875
8	1 rd.	1.000
9	** 1 sq.	1.128
10	** 1⅛ sq.	1.270
11	** 1¼ sq.	1.410
14	** 1½ sq.	1.693
18	** 2 sq.	2.257

¼" bars are plain round; ⅜" bars, plain round or deformed.

All bars are round. These sizes are equivalent in cross section area to the standard square new billet reinforcing bar sizes indicated.

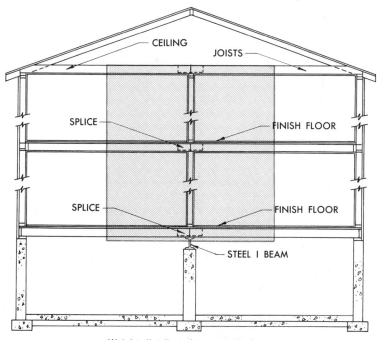

Weight distributed to a center beam.

Fiber Stress—20,000 # per square inch

I Beams — American Standard
Allowable Uniform Loads in Kips for Beams Laterally Supported

SPAN IN FEET

SIZE	WEIGHT	4	6	8	10	12	14	16	18	20	22	24	26	28	30	32	34	36	38	40	42	44	46	48	50
4 x 2¾	7.7	10.0	6.7	5.0																					
	9.5	11.0	7.3	5.5																					
5 x 3	10.0	16.0	10.7	8.0	6.4																				
		20.0	13.3	10.0	8.0																				
6 x 3⅜	12.5	24.0	16.2	12.2	9.7	8.1																			
	17.25	29.0	19.3	14.5	11.6	9.7																			
7 x 3⅝	15.3	35.0	23.0	17.3	13.9	11.6	9.9																		
	20.0	40.0	27.0	20.0	16.0	15.2	13.3																		
8 x 4	18.4	47.0	32.0	24.0	18.9	15.8	13.5	11.8																	
	23.0	53.0	36.0	27.0	21.0	17.8	15.2	13.3																	
10 x 4¾	25.4	80.0	54.0	41.0	33.0	27.0	23.0	20.0	18.1	16.3															
	35.0	97.0	65.0	49.0	39.0	32.0	28.0	24.0	22.0	19.5															
12 x 5	31.8	110.0	80.0	60.0	48.0	40.0	34.0	30.0	27.0	24.0	22.0	20.0													
	35.0	126.0	84.0	63.0	50.0	42.0	36.0	32.0	28.0	25.0	23.0	21.0													
12 x 5¼	40.8	144.0	100.0	75.0	60.0	50.0	43.0	37.0	33.0	30.0	27.0	25.0													
	50.0	168.0	112.0	84.0	67.0	56.0	48.0	42.0	37.0	34.0	31.0	28.0													
15 x 5½	42.9	160.0	131.0	98.0	79.0	65.0	56.0	49.0	44.0	39.0	36.0	33.0	30.0	28.0	26.0	25.0									
	50.0	214.0	143.0	107.0	86.0	71.0	61.0	54.0	48.0	43.0	39.0	36.0	33.0	31.0	29.0	27.0									
18 x 6	54.7	332.0	196.0	147.0	118.0	98.0	84.0	74.0	66.0	59.0	54.0	49.0	45.0	42.0	39.0	37.0	35.0	33.0	31.0						
	70.0		226.0	170.0	136.0	113.0	97.0	85.0	76.0	68.0	62.0	57.0	52.0	49.0	45.0	43.0	40.0	38.0	36.0						
20 x 6¼	65.4		260.0	195.0	156.0	130.0	111.0	97.0	87.0	78.0	71.0	65.0	60.0	56.0	52.0	49.0	46.0	43.0	41.0	39.0	37.0				
	75.0		281.0	211.0	169.0	140.0	120.0	105.0	94.0	84.0	77.0	70.0	65.0	60.0	56.0	53.0	50.0	47.0	44.0	42.0	40.0				
20 x 7	85.0		334.0	250.0	200.0	167.0	143.0	125.0	111.0	100.0	91.0	84.0	77.0	72.0	67.0	63.0	59.0	56.0	53.0	50.0	48.0				
	95.0		356.0	267.0	213.0	178.0	152.0	133.0	118.0	107.0	97.0	89.0	82.0	76.0	71.0	67.0	63.0	59.0	56.0	53.0	51.0				
24 x 7	79.9		390.0	290.0	232.0	193.0	166.0	145.0	129.0	116.0	105.0	97.0	89.0	83.0	77.0	73.0	68.0	64.0	61.0	58.0	55.0	53.0	50.0	48.0	46.0
	90.0			310.0	248.0	206.0	177.0	155.0	138.0	124.0	113.0	103.0	95.0	89.0	83.0	77.0	73.0	69.0	65.0	62.0	59.0	56.0	54.0	52.0	50.0
	100.0		439.0	329.0	264.0	220.0	188.0	165.0	146.0	132.0	126.0	110.0	101.0	94.0	88.0	82.0	78.0	73.0	69.0	66.0	63.0	60.0	57.0	55.0	53.0
24 x 7⅞	105.0		498.0	390.0	312.0	260.0	223.0	195.0	174.0	156.0	142.0	130.0	120.0	112.0	104.0	98.0	92.0	87.0	82.0	78.0	74.0	71.0	68.0	65.0	63.0
	120.0			418.0	335.0	279.0	239.0	209.0	186.0	167.0	152.0	139.0	129.0	126.0	112.0	105.0	98.0	93.0	88.0	84.0	80.0	76.0	73.0	70.0	67.0

Fiber Stress — 20,000 # per square inch
I Beams — Wide Flange
Allowable Uniform Loads in Kips for Beams Laterally Supported

SPAN IN FEET

SIZE	WEIGHT	4	6	8	10	12	14	16	18	20	22	24	26	28	30	32	34	36	38	40	42	44	46	48	50
8 x 5¼	17	47.0	31.0	24.0	18.8	15.7	13.4	11.7																	
8 x 6½	24		46.0	35.0	28.0	23.0	19.8	17.3																	
8 x 8	31		60.0	46.0	37.0	30.0	26.0	23.0	20.0	18.0	16.0														
10 x 5¼	21	62.0	48.0	36.0	29.0	24.0	21.0	17.9	15.9	14.3															
10 x 8	33		74.0	58.0	47.0	39.0	33.0	29.0	26.0	23.0															
10 x 10	49			88.0	73.0	61.0	52.0	46.0	40.0	36.0	33.0	30.0	28.0	26.0											
12 x 6½	27		74.0	57.0	45.0	38.0	32.0	28.0	25.0	23.0	21.0	19.0													
12 x 8	40		87.0	69.0	58.0	49.0	43.0	38.0	35.0	32.0	29.0														
12 x 10	53			108.0	94.0	79.0	67.0	59.0	52.0	47.0	43.0	39.0													
12 x 12	65				117.0	98.0	84.0	73.0	65.0	59.0	53.0	49.0	45.0	42.0	39.0										
14 x 6¾	30		93.0	70.0	56.0	46.0	40.0	35.0	31.0	28.0	25.0	23.0	21.0	19.9	18.6										
14 x 8	43			105.0	84.0	70.0	60.0	52.0	46.0	42.0	38.0	35.0	32.0	30.0	28.0										
14 x 10	61				123.0	102.0	88.0	77.0	68.0	62.0	56.0	51.0	47.0	44.0	41.0										
14 x 12	78				156.0	135.0	115.0	101.0	90.0	81.0	73.0	67.0	62.0	58.0	54.0										
14 x 14½	87					152.0	132.0	115.0	102.0	92.0	84.0	77.0	71.0	66.0	61.0	57.0	54.0	51.0							
16 x 7	36		124.0	94.0	75.0	63.0	54.0	47.0	42.0	38.0	34.0	31.0	29.0	27.0	25.0	24.0	22.0								
16 x 8½	58			157.0	126.0	105.0	90.0	78.0	70.0	63.0	57.0	52.0	48.0	45.0	42.0	39.0	37.0								
16 x 11½	88				202.0	168.0	144.0	126.0	112.0	101.0	92.0	84.0	78.0	72.0	67.0	63.0	59.0								
18 x 7½	50			148.0	119.0	99.0	85.0	74.0	66.0	59.0	54.0	49.0	46.0	42.0	40.0	37.0	35.0	33.0	31.0						
18 x 8¾	64			188.0	156.0	130.0	111.0	98.0	87.0	78.0	71.0	65.0	60.0	56.0	52.0	49.0	46.0	43.0	41.0						
18 x 11¾	96				224.0	189.0	176.0	154.0	137.0	123.0	112.0	103.0	95.0	88.0	82.0	77.0	72.0	68.0	65.0						
21 x 8¼	62			211.0	169.0	141.0	120.0	105.0	94.0	84.0	77.0	70.0	65.0	60.0	56.0	53.0	50.0	47.0	44.0	42.0	40.0	38.0			
21 x 9	82			270.0	224.0	187.0	160.0	140.0	124.0	112.0	102.0	93.0	86.0	80.0	75.0	70.0	66.0	62.0	59.0	56.0	53.0	51.0			
21 x 13	112					277.0	238.0	208.0	185.0	166.0	151.0	139.0	128.0	119.0	111.0	104.0	98.0	93.0	88.0	83.0	79.0	76.0			
24 x 9	74				234.0	195.0	167.0	146.0	130.0	117.0	106.0	98.0	90.0	84.0	78.0	73.0	69.0	65.0	61.0	58.0	56.0	53.0	51.0	49.0	47.0
24 x 12	100			274.0		277.0	237.0	207.0	184.0	166.0	151.0	138.0	128.0	119.0	111.0	104.0	98.0	92.0	87.0	83.0	79.0	75.0	72.0	69.0	66.0
24 x 14	130					356.0	315.0	276.0	245.0	221.0	200.0	184.0	170.0	158.0	147.0	138.0	130.0	123.0	116.0	110.0	105.0	100.0	96.0	92.0	88.0
27 x 14	145					420.0	384.0	336.0	298.0	269.0	244.0	224.0	207.0	192.0	179.0	168.0	158.0	149.0	141.0	134.0	128.0	122.0	117.0	112.0	108.0
33 x 11½	130				498.0	449.0	385.0	337.0	300.0	269.0	245.0	225.0	207.0	193.0	179.0	168.0	159.0	150.0	142.0	135.0	128.0	122.0	117.0	112.0	108.0

Width x length = Area

30' x 48' = 1,440 square feet of floor
area for each floor

8' x 48' = 384 square feet of wall
area for each wall

Weight per square foot x number of square feet =
total weight

Weight of first floor	=	72,000 pounds
Weight of second floor	=	72,000 pounds
Weight of ceiling	=	43,000 pounds
Roof bearing to beam	=	00,000 pounds
		187,000 pounds

One half weight bears on center beam	=	93,500 pounds
Weight of first wall	=	3,840 pounds
Weight of second wall	=	3,840 pounds
Weight bearing upon beam	=	101,180 pounds

This weight appears quite large, but one
must remember that two stories are involved in the calculations.

The tables on pages 56 and 57 give the greatest safe load (uniformly distributed over the entire beam length) which the steel I beams will carry. The building on page 55 has a uniformly distributed load.

The safe loads are given in kips. One kip equals 1,000 pounds.

The loads shown in the tables include the weight of the beam, which must be deducted to obtain the net load.

The loads shown are based on a *fiber stress,* or pressure they will withstand, of 20,000 pounds per square inch. This stress is entirely reliable for ordinary conditions where the loads are *quiescent* (subject to no movement) as in most buildings. It is a good idea to check strength requirements of local codes, because some require materials of greater or less strength. However, proportions or ratios can be determined and the tables still be used, as follows:

$$\frac{\text{Local code 16 Kips}}{\text{Tables} \quad 20 \text{ Kips}} - \frac{x \text{ feet}}{30 \text{ feet}} = 24' \text{ span}$$

or

$$\frac{16}{20} - \frac{30 \text{ Kips}}{x \text{ Kips}} = 16x = 600 \text{ or } x = 37.5 \text{ Kips}$$

For fluctuating loads causing vibration, especially if the beams are long as compared to depth (vertical thickness), the loads shown in the tables should be reduced one-fifth; for rapidly moving loads, or where loads are suddenly applied with slight impact, the loads shown should be reduced one-third.

The illustration of *structural metal shapes,* below, gives the names of structural metal shapes

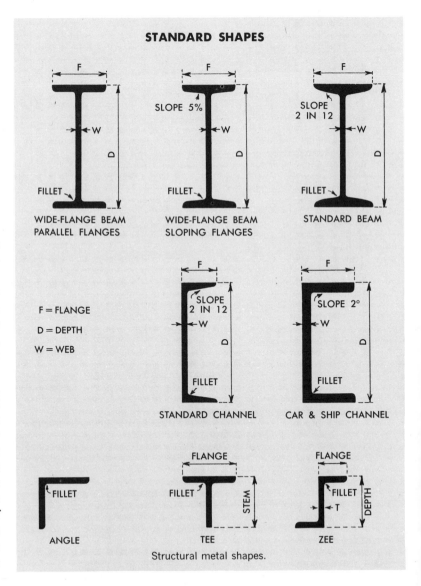

STANDARD SHAPES

F = FLANGE
D = DEPTH
W = WEB

WIDE-FLANGE BEAM PARALLEL FLANGES

WIDE-FLANGE BEAM SLOPING FLANGES — SLOPE 5%

STANDARD BEAM — SLOPE 2 IN 12

STANDARD CHANNEL — SLOPE 2 IN 12

CAR & SHIP CHANNEL — SLOPE 2°

ANGLE

TEE

ZEE

Structural metal shapes.

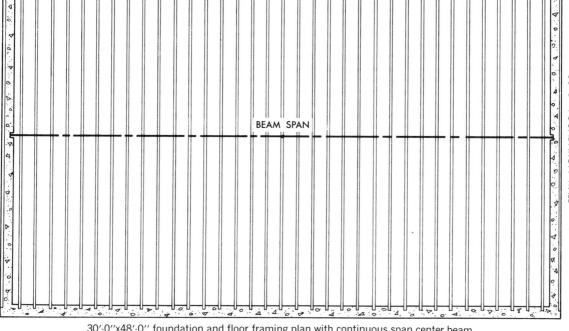

48'-0'' FOUNDATION WALL

30'-0'' FOUNDATION WALL

BEAM SPAN

30'-0''x48'-0'' foundation and floor framing plan with continuous span center beam.

and parts. It is assumed that the beams are stiffened sideways to prevent buckling in the compression flange; otherwise, loads must be reduced as shown in the following table, observing that the *laterally* or sideways unsupported length of beams shall not exceed 40 times the width of the compression flange.

The allowable deflection or sagging for plastered ceilings is $1/360$ of the span. This limit is not reached on the span lengths shown in the tables. The deflection will be reduced in the same ratio as the load on the beam.

Distribution of Loads

The following illustrations on page 60 show different load distributions and the percentage of weight they will support as compared to the allowable loads shown in the preceding tables. (See pages 56 and 57.)

Calculating Beam Strength and Size

The illustration on this page shows a foundation plan 30'x48'; the beam is placed the 48' direc-tion. (If no posts support the beam, the span is 48'.) Actual span is the distance from one inside edge of the foundation to the opposite inside edge. To simplify the calculations, how-ever, the span has been shown as the entire building length. Note that after the procedure is mastered, only the true beam span should be used for making the calculations.

Unbraced Length of Beam	Proportion to be used	Unbraced Length of Beam	Proportion to be used
15 × flange width	100% tab. load	30 × flange width	77% tab. load
20 × flange width	92% tab. load	35 × flange width	69% tab. load
25 × flange width	85% tab. load	40 × flange width	62% tab. load

Percentages of calculated loads when beam lengths are laterally unbraced.

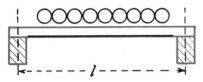

Safe load = that given in tables. Maximum bending moment at

$$\text{center} = \frac{Wl}{8}.$$

Deflection as in tables.

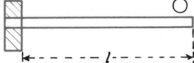

Safe load = ½ that given in tables.

$$M = \frac{Wl}{4}.$$

Deflection = 8/10 that given in tables.

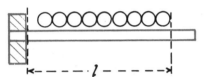

Safe load = ¼ that given in tables.

$$M = \frac{Wl}{2}.$$

Deflections = 2.4 that given in tables.

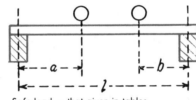

Safe load = ⅛ that given in tables.

M at point of support = W.

Deflections = 3.2 that given in tables

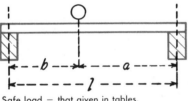

Safe load = that given in tables.

$$\times \frac{l2}{8ab}.$$

Maximum bending moment, $M = \dfrac{Wab}{l}.$

Safe load = that given in tables.

$$\times \frac{l}{4a}.$$

Maximum bending moment between loads = ½ Wa.

Load distribution.

From previous calculations, the weight bearing upon the beam was figured to be 101,180 pounds. This is represented by the colored area on page 55.

Since the weight as calculated is in pounds and the safe load tables are in kips, convert the weight into kips. Using the tables for American Standard I Beams, find the column at the top of the chart that represents 48 feet span.

Follow down the chart until 102 kips is shown. When one does this, 70 kips is the largest number shown. This is not adequate for the span. Add piers or columns under the beam to divide the length into the required short spans. The number of posts is determined by the amount of open span desired. (The longer the span the greater the beam weight.) Steel is purchased by

the pound, so it is advisable to use the smallest size that will do the job.

If the building has no basement and piers are used, it is advisable to place them on approximate 8' centers. Many local codes specify minimum distance between piers. A large number of piers is not objectionable because the space between the floor joist and earth is used only as crawl space for maintenance. Posts in a basement *may* be objectionable. If so, a large beam size is justified.

Using the same 30'x48' building described earlier but adding three posts as shown in the accompanying illustration reduces the beam span to 12'. This is represented by the shaded area on the plan. When the total bearing weight on the beam is divided by 4, this is found to be 25,295 pounds or 25.3 kips. At the top of the chart locate the 12 foot span and follow down the column until 25.3 kips is reached. This exact size is not shown on the chart, so one must locate the next larger weight. This is shown as 27 kips. Then, as previously stated, the weight of the beam must be added to the net weight or load because the beam must support its own weight in addition to the building weight. From the 27 kips on the chart, follow the column to the left to the vertical column showing weight per foot. This column gives a weight of 25.4 pounds per lineal foot. When multiplied by the span of 12' a beam weight of 304.8 pounds is shown. Add this .305 kips to previous load of 25.3 kips. This gives a total load

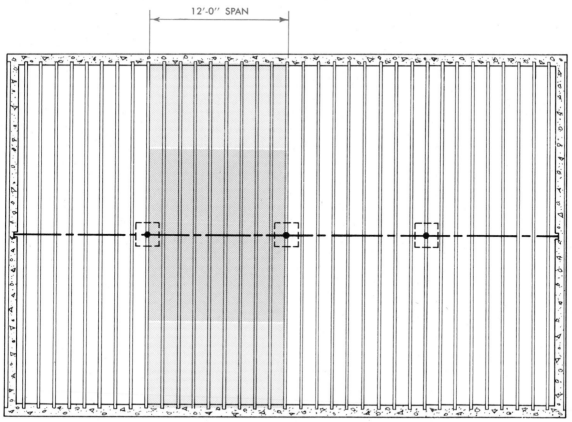

12'-0'' SPAN

30'-0''x48'-0'' foundation and floor framing plan with center beam supported by 3 equally spaced posts to reduce beam span to 12'-0'' o.c. Light shaded area is supported by foundation walls. Dark shaded area is supported by the center beam and supporting posts.

of 25.6 kips. This size is still adequate to support the described load, so it is not necessary to move to the next larger beam size. One should repeat the strength calculations to be absolutely sure the beam size is satisfactory. (Refer to the charts on pages 56 and 57.)

The beam selected is 10''x4¾'' and weighs 25.4 pounds per lineal foot. Since all building spans shown are the same and since the weight is uniformly distributed, all beams will be the same size. If the spans between posts are *not* the same or if the weight is not uniformly distributed, it is necessary to make separate calculations for each beam span.

Steel Posts or Columns
To Support Beams

Posts, columns, or piers transmit the load imposed on the beam or girder to the footing and on to the ground. The building shown in the shaded illustration has beam spans of 12'-0'', and the total load for each span is 25,295 pounds. This was previously determined when making strength and weight calculations. The beam carrying this load is supported by two posts or columns, one at each end. Thus half of the load is supported by each post. The load transmitted to *each post* is called the *beam reaction.* Therefore, the beam reaction is 12,647.5 pounds. Since two beams terminate over the same post, the total reactions of the two beams must be considered. The beams and the loads are the same; therefore, the total weight to be supported ıs 25,295 pounds.

STANDARD STEEL PIPE COLUMNS

Safe Loads in Thousands of Pounds

Nominal Size, Inches	External Diam., Inches	Internal Diam., Inches	Weight per Ft., Lbs.	Unbraced Length in Feet									Metal Area, Inches	Radius of Gyration, Inches	Moment of Inertia, Inches
				6	8	10	12	14	16	18	20	22			
3	3.500	3.068	7.58	33	30	26	21	18	16	13			2.228	1.16	3.017
3½	4.000	3.548	9.11	42	38	35	30	25	22	19	17	15	2.680	1.34	4.788
4	4.500	4.026	10.79	50	47	44	40	34	30	26	23	21	3.174	1.51	7.233
5	5.563	5.047	14.62	70	68	64	61	56	51	45	41	37	4.300	1.88	15.16
6	6.625	6.065	18.97	92	90	86	82	79	74	69	63	56	5.581	2.25	28.14
8	8.625	8.071	24.70	121	120	118	115	112	109	105	100	95	7.265	2.95	63.35
	8.625	7.981	28.55	140	138	136	133	129	125	121	115	109	8.399	2.94	72.49
10	10.750	10.192	31.20	154	153	151	149	147	144	141	137	133	9.178	3.70	125.9
	10.750	10.136	34.24	169	168	166	164	161	158	154	151	146	10.07	3.69	137.4
	10.750	10.020	40.48	200	199	196	194	190	187	182	178	172	11.91	3.67	160.7
12	12.750	12.090	43.77	217	216	214	212	210	207	204	200	196	12.88	4.39	248.5
	12.750	12.000	49.56	246	244	243	240	237	234	231	227	222	14.58	4.38	279.3

Standard steel pipe columns.

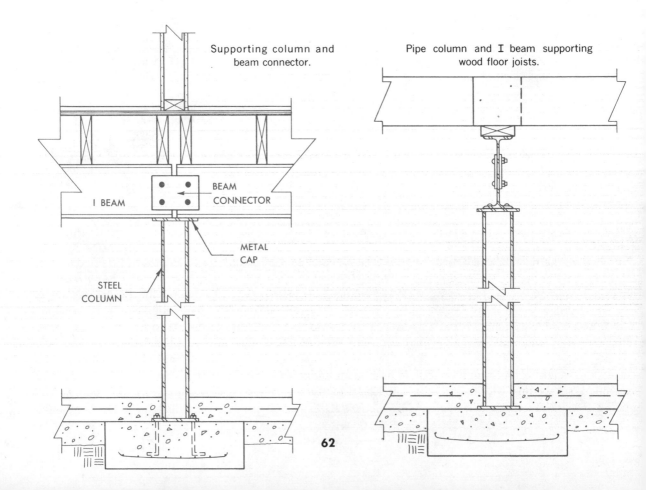

Supporting column and beam connector.

Pipe column and I beam supporting wood floor joists.

BEAM CONNECTOR

I BEAM

METAL CAP

STEEL COLUMN

WEIGHTS, DIMENSIONS AND DATA
STANDARD STEEL I BEAMS

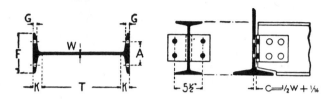

Depth of Beam, Inches	Wt. Per Ft., Lbs.	Dimensions, in Inches							Maximum Rivet or Bolt, Inch
		F	W	T	K	G	A	C	
24	120	8	13/16	20 1/8	1 15/16	1 1/8	4	1/2	1
	105.9	7 7/8	5/8	20 1/4	1 15/16	1 1/8	4	3/8	1
	100	7 1/4	3/4	20 3/4	1 5/8	7/8	4	7/16	1
	90	7 1/8	5/8	20 3/4	1 5/8	7/8	4	3/8	1
	79.9	7	1/2	20 3/4	1 5/8	7/8	4	5/16	1
20	95	7 1/4	13/16	16 1/2	1 3/4	15/16	4	1/2	1
	85	7	11/16	16 1/2	1 3/4	15/16	4	7/16	1
	75	6 3/8	5/8	17	1 9/16	13/16	3 1/2	7/16	7/8
	65.4	6 1/4	1/2	17	1 9/16	13/16	3 1/2	5/16	7/8
18	70	6 1/4	3/4	15 1/4	1 3/8	11/16	3 1/2	7/16	7/8
	54.7	6	1/2	15 1/4	1 3/8	11/16	3 1/2	5/16	7/8
15	50	5 5/8	9/16	12 1/2	1 1/4	5/8	3 1/2	3/8	3/4
	42.9	5 1/2	7/16	12 1/2	1 1/4	5/8	3 1/2	1/4	3/4
12	50	5 1/2	11/16	9 3/8	1 5/16	11/16	3	7/16	3/4
	40.8	5 1/4	1/2	9 3/8	1 5/16	11/16	3	5/16	3/4
	35	5 1/8	7/16	9 3/4	1 1/8	9/16	3	5/16	3/4
	31.8	5	3/8	9 3/4	1 1/8	9/16	3	1/4	3/4
10	35	5	5/8	8	1	1/2	2 3/4	3/8	3/4
	25.4	4 5/8	5/16	8	1	1/2	2 3/4	1/4	3/4
8	23	4 1/8	7/16	6 1/4	13/16	7/16	2 1/4	5/16	3/4
	18.4	4	5/16	6 1/4	13/16	7/16	2 1/4	3/16	3/4
7	20	3 7/8	7/16	5 3/8	7/8	3/8	2 1/4	5/16	5/8
	15.3	3 5/8	1/4	5 3/8	7/8	3/8	2 1/4	3/16	5/8
6	17.25	3 5/8	1/2	4 1/2	3/4	3/8	2	5/16	5/8
	12.5	3 3/8	1/4	4 1/2	3/4	3/8	2	3/16	5/8
5	14.75	3 1/4	1/2	3 5/8	11/16	5/16	1 3/4	5/16	1/2
	10	3	1/4	3 5/8	11/16	5/16	1 3/4	3/16	1/2
4	9.5	2 3/4	5/16	2 3/4	5/8	5/16	1 1/2	1/4	1/2
	7.7	2 5/8	3/16	2 3/4	5/8	5/16	1 1/2	3/16	1/2
3	5.7	2 1/2	3/8	1 7/8	9/16	1/4	1 1/2	1/4	3/8
	5.7	2 3/8	3/16	1 7/8	9/16	1/4	1 1/2	3/16	3/8

Weights, dimensions, and data of standard steel I beams.

(If the two beams are of different sizes and the loads are not the same, the reactions will not be equal.) NOTE: Since the end of only one beam is supported by the foundation, the beam reaction *at this location* is 12,647.5 pounds, or one-half the total weight transmitted to the posts.

Kinds of Steel Posts Used

Several kinds of steel posts are used. Some of the more common are: ordinary steel pipe, heavy duty steel pipe, steel pipe filled with concrete, Standard and Wide Flange I beams and H columns.

Since standard steel posts or columns are frequently used for light construction, their sizes and safe loads are shown in the table.

Joining Structural Steel Members

When beams are end joined they must be fastened to each other as well as to a column or columns supporting them. Standard connectors using bolts or rivets are recommended. Tables of safe loads in this text are calculated based on standard "B" series connectors. Holes in the connectors and beams, as illustrated by the black circles, should be spaced on approximate 5½" centers.

Column Caps

Pipe columns have steel plates welded to each end to increase their surface area and permit fastening of parts. The cap is secured to concrete footings by pre-positioning anchor bolts in the concrete so the bolts correspond with the holes in the plate.

Column cap bolted to I beam.

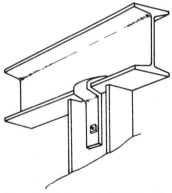

Column and I beam fastened together with metal strap.

Suitable methods of connecting structural metal parts are shown in the accompanying illustrations.

Steel Lintels

Steel lintels are constructed of angle iron. These may be purchased as equal angles, with both legs of equal size, or as unequal angles with legs of different sizes. The accompanying table shows pertinent information concerning angles.

Lintel Spans

The actual window, door, or other opening width is the true span. This opening size is used for determining the size lintel required. (See page 67.)

ELEMENTS OF EQUAL ANGLES

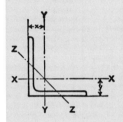

Size in Inches	Wt. Per Ft., Lbs.	Area of Section, Inches	Axis X-X and X-Y				Axis Z-Z
			I Inches	S Inches	r Inches	x or y Inches	r Inches
1 x1 x ⅛	0.80	0.23	0.02	0.03	0.31	0.30	0.19
1 x1 x 3/16	1.16	0.34	0.03	0.04	0.30	0.32	0.19
1 x1 x ¼	1.49	0.44	0.04	0.06	0.29	0.34	0.19
1¼x1¼x ⅛	1.01	0.30	0.04	0.05	0.38	0.35	0.25
1¼x1¼x 3/16	1.48	0.43	0.06	0.07	0.38	0.38	0.24
1¼x1¼x ¼	1.92	0.56	0.08	0.09	0.37	0.40	0.24
1½x1½x ⅛	1.23	0.36	0.08	0.07	0.46	0.42	0.30
1½x1½x 3/16	1.80	0.53	0.11	0.10	0.46	0.44	0.29
1½x1½x ¼	2.34	0.69	0.14	0.13	0.45	0.47	0.29
1¾x1¾x ⅛	1.44	0.42	0.13	0.10	0.55	0.48	0.35
1¾x1¾x 3/16	2.12	0.62	0.18	0.14	0.54	0.51	0.34
1¾x1¾x ¼	2.77	0.81	0.23	0.19	0.53	0.53	0.34
2 x2 x ⅛	1.65	0.48	0.19	0.13	0.63	0.55	0.40
2 x2 x 3/16	2.44	0.71	0.28	0.19	0.62	0.57	0.40
2 x2 x ¼	3.19	0.94	0.35	0.25	0.61	0.59	0.39
2 x2 x 5/16	3.92	1.15	0.42	0.30	0.60	0.61	0.39
2 x2 x ⅜	4.70	1.36	0.48	0.35	0.59	0.64	0.39
2½x2½x 3/16	3.07	0.90	0.55	0.30	0.78	0.69	0.49
2½x2½x ¼	4.10	1.19	0.70	0.39	0.77	0.72	0.49
2½x2½x 5/16	5.00	1.47	0.85	0.48	0.76	0.74	0.49
2½x2½x ⅜	5.90	1.73	0.98	0.57	0.75	0.76	0.48
3 x3 x ¼	4.9	1.44	1.2	0.58	0.93	0.84	0.59
3 x3 x 5/16	6.1	1.78	1.5	0.71	0.92	0.87	0.59
3 x3 x ⅜	7.2	2.11	1.8	0.83	0.91	0.89	0.58
3 x3 x 7/16	8.3	2.43	2.0	0.95	0.91	0.91	0.58
3 x3 x ½	9.4	2.75	2.2	1.1	0.90	0.93	0.58
3½x3½x ¼	5.8	1.69	2.0	0.79	1.09	0.97	0.69
3½x3½x 5/16	7.2	2.09	2.5	0.98	1.08	0.99	0.69
3½x3½x ⅜	8.5	2.48	2.9	1.2	1.07	1.01	0.69
3½x3½x 7/16	9.8	2.87	3.3	1.3	1.07	1.04	0.68
3½x3½x ½	11.1	3.25	3.6	1.5	1.06	1.06	0.68
4 x4 x ¼	6.6	1.94	3.0	1.0	1.25	1.09	0.79
4 x4 x 5/16	8.2	2.40	3.7	1.3	1.24	1.12	0.79
4 x4 x ⅜	9.8	2.86	4.4	1.5	1.23	1.14	0.79
4 x4 x 7/16	11.3	3.31	5.0	1.8	1.23	1.16	0.78
4 x4 x ½	12.8	3.75	5.6	2.0	1.22	1.18	0.78
4 x4 x ⅝	15.7	4.61	6.7	2.4	1.20	1.23	0.77
4 x4 x ¾	18.5	5.44	7.7	2.8	1.19	1.27	0.77
5 x5 x ⅜	12.3	3.61	8.7	2.4	1.56	1.39	0.99
5 x5 x ½	16.2	4.75	11.3	3.2	1.54	1.43	0.98
5 x5 x ⅝	20.0	5.86	13.6	3.9	1.52	1.48	0.97
6 x6 x ⅜	14.9	4.36	15.4	3.5	1.88	1.64	1.19
6 x6 x 7/16	17.2	5.06	17.7	4.1	1.87	1.66	1.19
6 x6 x ½	19.6	5.75	19.9	4.6	1.86	1.68	1.18
6 x6 x 9/16	21.9	6.43	22.1	5.1	1.85	1.71	1.18
6 x6 x ⅝	24.2	7.11	24.2	5.7	1.84	1.73	1.18
6 x6 x ¾	28.7	8.44	28.2	6.7	1.83	1.78	1.17
6 x6 x ⅞	33.1	9.73	31.9	7.6	1.81	1.82	1.17
8 x8 x ½	26.4	7.75	48.6	8.4	2.51	2.19	1.58
8 x8 x ⅝	32.7	9.61	59.4	10.3	2.49	2.23	1.58
8 x8 x ¾	38.9	11.44	69.7	12.2	2.47	2.28	1.57
8 x8 x ⅞	45.0	13.23	79.6	14.0	2.45	2.32	1.56
8 x8 x1	51.0	15.00	89.0	15.8	2.44	2.37	1.56
8 x8 x1⅛	56.9	16.73	98.0	17.5	2.42	2.41	1.55

ELEMENTS OF UNEQUAL ANGLES

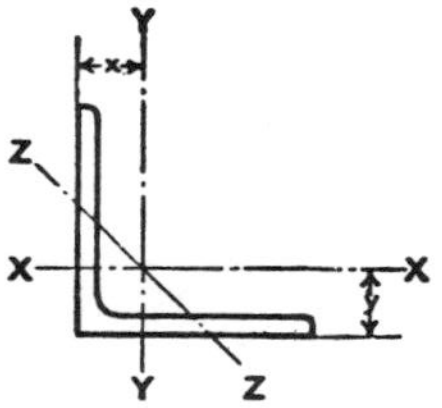

Size in Inches	Wt. Per Ft., Lbs.	Area of Section Inches	Axis Y-Y I In.	S In.	r In.	X In.	Axis X-X I In.	S In.	r In.	Y In.	Axis Z-Z r In.
2 x1½x ⅛	1.44	0.42	0.17	0.13	0.64	0.62	0.09	0.08	0.45	0.37	0.33
2 x1½x 3/16	2.12	0.62	0.25	0.18	0.63	0.64	0.12	0.11	0.44	0.39	0.32
2 x1½x ¼	2.77	0.81	0.32	0.24	0.62	0.66	0.15	0.14	0.43	0.41	0.32
2½x2 x3/16	2.75	0.81	0.51	0.29	0.79	0.76	0.20	0.20	0.60	0.51	0.43
2½x2 x¼	3.62	1.06	0.65	0.38	0.78	0.79	0.37	0.25	0.59	0.54	0.42
2½x2 x5/16	4.5	1.31	0.79	0.47	0.78	0.81	0.45	0.31	0.58	0.56	0.42
2½x2 x⅜	5.3	1.55	0.91	0.55	0.77	0.83	0.51	0.36	0.58	0.58	0.42
3 x2 x¼	4.1	1.19	1.1	0.54	0.95	0.99	0.39	0.26	0.57	0.49	0.43
3 x2 x5/16	5.0	1.47	1.3	0.66	0.95	1.02	0.47	0.32	0.57	0.52	0.43
3 x2 x⅜	5.9	1.73	1.5	0.78	0.94	1.04	0.54	0.37	0.56	0.54	0.43
3 x2½x¼	4.5	1.31	1.2	0.56	0.95	0.91	0.74	0.40	0.75	0.66	0.53
3 x2½x5/16	5.6	1.62	1.4	0.69	0.94	0.93	0.90	0.49	0.74	0.68	0.53
3 x2½x⅜	6.6	1.92	1.7	0.81	0.93	0.96	1.00	0.58	0.74	0.71	0.52
3½x2½x¼	4.9	1.44	1.8	0.75	1.12	1.11	0.78	0.41	0.74	0.61	0.54
3½x2½x5/16	6.1	1.78	2.2	0.93	1.11	1.14	0.94	0.50	0.73	0.64	0.54
3½x2½x⅜	7.2	2.11	2.6	1.1	1.10	1.16	1.1	0.59	0.72	0.66	0.54
3½x2½x7/16	8.3	2.43	2.9	1.3	1.09	1.18	1.2	0.68	0.71	0.68	0.54
3½x2½x½	9.4	2.75	3.2	1.4	1.09	1.20	1.4	0.76	0.70	0.70	0.53
3½x3 x¼	5.4	1.56	1.9	0.78	1.11	1.04	1.3	0.59	0.91	0.79	0.63
3½x3 x5/16	6.6	1.93	2.3	0.95	1.10	1.06	1.6	0.72	0.90	0.81	0.63
3½x3 x⅜	7.9	2.30	2.7	1.1	1.09	1.08	1.9	0.85	0.90	0.83	0.62
3½x3 x½	10.2	3.00	3.5	1.5	1.07	1.13	2.3	1.1	0.88	0.88	0.62
4 x3 x¼	5.8	1.69	2.8	1.0	1.28	1.24	1.4	0.60	0.90	0.74	0.65
4 x3 x5/16	7.2	2.09	3.4	1.2	1.27	1.26	1.7	0.73	0.89	0.76	0.65
4 x3 x⅜	8.5	2.48	4.0	1.5	1.26	1.28	1.9	0.87	0.88	0.78	0.64
4 x3 x7/16	9.8	2.87	4.5	1.7	1.25	1.30	2.2	1.0	0.87	0.80	0.64
4 x3 x½	11.1	3.25	5.1	1.9	1.25	1.33	2.4	1.1	0.86	0.83	0.64
4 x3 x⅝	13.6	3.98	6.0	2.3	1.23	1.37	2.9	1.4	0.85	0.87	0.64
4 x3½x ⅜	9.1	2.67	4.2	1.5	1.25	1.21	3.0	1.2	1.06	0.96	0.73
4 x3½x ½	11.9	3.50	5.3	1.9	1.23	1.25	3.8	1.5	1.04	1.00	0.72
4 x3½x ⅝	14.7	4.30	6.4	2.4	1.22	1.29	4.5	1.8	1.03	1.04	0.72
5 x3 x 5/16	8.2	2.40	6.3	1.9	1.61	1.68	1.8	0.75	0.85	0.68	0.66
5 x3 x ⅜	9.8	2.86	7.4	2.2	1.61	1.70	2.0	0.89	0.84	0.70	0.65
5 x3 x 7/16	11.3	3.31	8.4	2.6	1.60	1.73	2.3	1.0	0.84	0.73	0.65
5 x3 x ½	12.8	3.75	9.5	2.9	1.59	1.75	2.6	1.1	0.83	0.75	0.65
5 x3½x 5/16	8.7	2.56	6.6	1.9	1.61	1.59	2.7	1.0	1.03	0.84	0.76
5 x3½x ⅜	10.4	3.05	7.8	2.3	1.60	1.61	3.2	1.2	1.02	0.86	0.76
5 x3½x 7/16	12.0	3.53	8.9	2.6	1.59	1.63	3.6	1.4	1.01	0.88	0.76
5 x3½x ½	13.6	4.00	10.0	3.0	1.58	1.66	4.1	1.6	1.01	0.91	0.75
5 x3½x ⅝	16.8	4.92	12.0	3.7	1.56	1.70	4.8	1.9	0.99	0.95	0.75
6 x3½x ⅜	11.7	3.42	12.9	3.2	1.94	2.04	3.3	1.2	0.99	0.79	0.77
6 x3½x 7/16	13.5	3.97	14.8	3.7	1.93	2.06	3.8	1.4	0.98	0.81	0.76
6 x3½x ½	15.3	4.50	16.6	4.2	1.92	2.08	4.3	1.6	0.97	0.83	0.76
6 x3½x ⅝	18.9	5.55	20.1	5.2	1.90	2.13	5.1	1.9	0.96	0.88	0.75
6 x4 x⅜	12.3	3.61	13.5	3.3	1.93	1.94	4.9	1.6	1.17	0.94	0.88
6 x4 x7/16	14.3	4.18	15.5	3.8	1.92	1.96	5.6	1.9	1.16	0.96	0.87
6 x4 x½	16.2	4.75	17.4	4.3	1.91	1.99	6.3	2.1	1.15	0.99	0.87
6 x4 x9/16	18.1	5.31	19.3	4.8	1.90	2.01	6.9	2.3	1.14	1.01	0.87
6 x4 x⅝	20.0	5.86	21.1	5.3	1.90	2.03	7.5	2.5	1.13	1.03	0.86
6 x4 x¾	23.6	6.94	24.5	6.2	1.88	2.08	8.7	3.0	1.12	1.08	0.86
8 x4 x ½	19.6	5.75	38.5	7.5	2.59	2.86	6.7	2.2	1.08	0.86	0.86
8 x4 x ⅝	24.2	7.11	46.9	9.2	2.57	2.91	8.1	2.6	1.07	0.91	0.86
8 x4 x ¾	28.7	8.44	54.9	10.9	2.55	2.95	9.4	3.1	1.05	0.95	0.85
8 x4 x ⅞	33.1	9.73	62.5	12.5	2.53	3.00	10.5	3.5	1.04	1.00	0.85
8 x4 x1	37.4	11.00	69.6	14.1	2.52	3.05	11.6	3.9	1.03	1.05	0.85
8 x6 x ½	23.0	6.75	44.3	8.0	2.56	2.47	21.7	4.8	1.79	1.47	1.30
8 x6 x ¾	33.8	9.94	63.4	11.7	2.53	2.56	30.7	6.9	1.76	1.56	1.29
8 x6 x ⅞	39.1	11.48	72.3	13.4	2.51	2.61	34.9	7.9	1.74	1.61	1.28
8 x6 x1	44.2	13.00	80.8	15.1	2.49	2.65	38.8	8.9	1.73	1.65	1.28

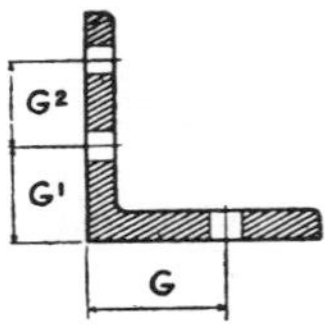

Standard Steel Angles

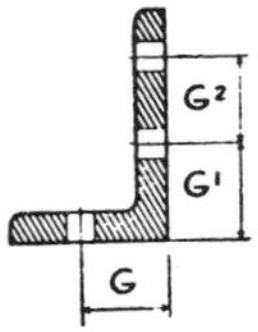

WEIGHTS, DIMENSIONS AND DATA

EQUAL LEG ANGLES—STRUCTURAL SIZES

Size of Angle, Inches	THICKNESS IN INCHES													USUAL GAUGES			Max. Rivet or Bolt
	1⅛	1	⅞	¾	⅝	9/16	½	7/16	⅜	5/16	¼	3/16	⅛	G	G1	G2	
8 x8	56.9	51.0	45.0	38.9	32.7	29.6	26.4							4½	3	3	1
6 x6		37.4	33.1	28.7	24.2	21.9	19.6	17.2	14.9	12.6				3½	2¼	2½	⅞
5 x5			27.2	23.6	20.0		16.2	14.3	12.3	10.3				3	2	1¾	⅞
4 x4				18.5	15.7		12.8	11.3	9.8	8.2	6.6			2½			⅞
3½x3½							11.1	9.8	8.5	7.2	5.8			2			⅞
3 x3							9.4	8.3	7.2	6.1	4.9	*3.71		1¾			¾

UNEQUAL LEG ANGLES—STRUCTURAL SIZES

Size of Angle, Inches	THICKNESS IN INCHES												USUAL GAUGES			Max. Rivet or Bolt
	1	⅞	¾	⅝	9/16	½	7/16	⅜	5/16	¼	3/16	⅛	G	G1	G2	
8 x6	44.2	39.1	33.8	28.5	25.7	23.0	20.2						3½	3	3	⅞
8 x4	37.4	33.1	28.7	24.2	21.9	19.6	17.2									
7 x4		30.2	26.2	22.1	20.0	17.9	15.8	13.6					2½	2½	3	⅞
6 x4		27.2	23.6	20.0	18.1	16.2	14.3	12.3	10.3				2½	2¼	2½	⅞
6 x3½						15.3		11.7	9.8	7.9			2	2¼	2½	⅞
5 x3½			19.8	16.8		13.6	12.0	10.4	8.7	7.0			2	2	1¾	⅞
5 x3						12.8	11.3	9.8	8.2	6.6			1¾	2	1¾	¾
4 x3½				14.7		11.9	10.6	9.1	7.7	6.2			2	2½		⅞
4 x3				13.6		11.1	9.8	8.5	7.2	5.8			1¾	2½		¾
3½x3				12.5		10.2	9.1	7.9	6.6	5.4			1¾	2		¾
3½x2½				11.5		9.4	8.3	7.2	6.1	4.9			1⅜	2		¾
3 x2½						8.5	7.6	6.6	5.6	4.5			1⅜	1¾		¾
3 x2						7.7	6.8	5.9	5.0	4.1	*3.07		1⅛	1¾		⅝

*Bar Mill Sizes.

Weights, dimensions, and data of standard steel angles.

Channels—American Standard
Allowable Uniform Loads in Kips
For Channels Laterally Supported

For channels laterally unsupported, allowable loads must be reduced.

Span in Feet	18x4			Deflection Inches	15x3½			Deflection Inches
	51.9	**45.8**	**42.7**		**50**	**40**	**33.9**	
2					280			
3	280	234	210		238	202	156	.01
4	230	212	203	.02	178	154	139	.02
5	184	170	163	.03	143	123	111	.03
6	154	142	136	.04	119	103	93	.05
7	132	121	116	.06	102	88	79	.07
8	115	106	102	.07	89	77	70	.09
9	102	94	90	.09	79	68	62	.11
10	92	85	81	.12	71	62	56	.14
11	84	77	74	.14	65	56	51	.17
12	77	71	68	.17	59	51	46	.20
13	71	65	63	.19	55	47	43	.23
14	66	61	58	.23	51	44	40	.27
15	61	57	54	.26	48	41	37	.31
16	58	53	51	.29	45	39	35	.35
17	54	50	48	.33	42	36	33	.40
18	51	47	45	.37	40	34	31	.45
19	49	45	43	.42	38	32	29	.50
20	46	43	41	.46	36	31	28	.55
21	44	40	39	.51	34	29	27	.61
22	42	39	37	.56	32	28	25	.67
23	40	37	35	.61	31	27	24	.73
24	38	35	34	.66	30	26	23	.79
25	37	34	33	.72	29	25	22	.86
26	35	33	31	.78	27	24	21	.93
27	34	32	30	.84	26	23	21	1.01
28	33	30	29	.90	26	22	19.9	1.08
29	32	29	28	.97	25	21	19.2	1.16
30	31	28	27	1.03	24	21	18.5	1.24
31	30	27	26	1.11	23	19.9	17.9	1.33
32	29	27	25	1.18	22	19.3	17.4	1.41
33	28	26	25	1.25	22	18.7	16.8	1.50
34	27	25	24	1.33	21	18.1	16.4	1.60
35	26	24	23	1.41	20	17.6	15.9	1.69

PROPERTIES AND REACTION VALUES

S in.³	69.1	63.7	61.0		53.6	46.2	41.7
V kips	140	117	105		140	101	78
R kips	69	58	52		83	60	46
G kips	14.4	12.0	10.8		17.2	12.5	9.6
N in.	8.4	8.4	8.4		6.8	6.8	6.8

The total length of the lintel should be 8″ greater than the opening. The 8″ allowance is made so the lintel will have 4″ of bearing surface on each side of the opening.

To determine lintel size, *weight* of all materials and desired *live load,* if any, are calculated the same as for weight of walls and other structural parts, previously described in this chapter. The accompanying tables give the total safe load that may be supported by each lintel size.

For preliminary calculations only, it is not always desirable to figure exact size requirements, which takes unnecessary time and effort. The following table may be used:

STEEL ANGLE IRONS TO SUPPORT FOUR-INCH MASONRY WALLS

SPAN	SIZE OF LINTELS
0 to 5 feet	3″ x 3″ x ¼″
5⁺ feet to 9 feet	3½″ x 3½″ x 5⁄16″
9⁺ feet to 10 feet	4″ x 4″ x 5⁄16″
10⁺ feet to 11 feet	4″ x 4″ x 3⁄8″
11⁺ feet to 15 feet	6″ x 4″ x 3⁄8″
15⁺ feet to 16 feet	6″ x 4″ x ½″

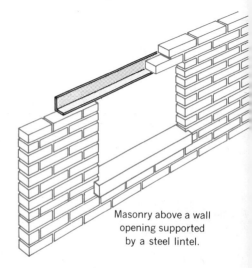

Masonry above a wall opening supported by a steel lintel.

Open Web Steel Joists
"J" SERIES

Total Safe Loads in Lbs. per Lineal Ft. (For nominal joist depths 8″ to 14″ incl.)

Span in Feet	8J2	10J2	10J3	10J4	12J2	12J3	12J4	12J5	12J6	14J3	14J4	14J5	14J6	14J7
8	475													
9	422													
10	373	400	440	480										
11	309	364	400	436										
12	259	324	367	400	367	383	417	450	500					
13	221	276	338	369	335	354	385	415	462					
14	190	238	303	343	289	329	357	386	429	343	400	443	486	529
15	166	207	264	320	252	307	333	360	400	320	373	413	453	493
16	146	182	232	289	221	281	313	338	375	300	350	388	425	463
17		161	205	256	196	249	294	318	353	282	329	365	400	435
18		144	183	228	175	222	278	300	333	261	311	344	378	411
19		129	164	205	157	199	249	284	316	235	294	326	358	389
20			117	148	185	142	180	225	268	300	212	265	310	340	370
21					128	163	204	243	286	192	240	287	324	352
22					117	149	186	222	270	175	219	262	309	336
23					107	136	170	203	247	160	200	239	290	322
24					98	125	156	186	227	147	184	220	266	308
25										135	170	203	245	294
26										125	157	187	227	272
27										116	145	174	210	252
28										108	135	162	196	235

Total Safe Loads in Lbs. per Lineal Ft. (For nominal joist depths 16″ to 24″ incl.)

Span in Feet	16J4	16J5	16J6	16J7	16J8	18J5	18J6	18J7	18J8	20J5	20J6	20J7	20J8	22J6	22J7	22J8	24J6	24J7	24J8
16	375	413	450	500	538														
18	333	367	400	444	478	389	433	467	500										
20	288	330	360	400	430	350	390	420	450	380	410	430	460						
22	238	298	327	364	391	318	355	382	409	345	373	391	418	382	409	436			
24	200	250	299	333	358	281	325	350	375	307	342	358	383	350	375	400	367	392	417
26	171	213	254	306	331	240	289	323	346	261	312	331	354	323	346	369	338	362	385
28	147	184	219	264	305	207	249	299	321	225	269	307	329	285	321	343	312	336	357
30	128	160	191	230	266	180	217	261	300	196	234	283	307	248	300	320	272	313	333
32	113	141	168	202	234	158	191	229	264	173	206	249	288	218	273	300	239	294	313
34						140	169	203	234	153	182	220	262	193	242	282	212	265	294
36						125	151	181	209	136	163	197	234	172	216	254	189	237	278
38										122	146	176	210	155	194	228	169	212	249
40										110	132	159	190	140	175	205	153	192	225
42														127	159	186	139	174	204
44														115	145	170	126	158	186
46																	116	145	170
48																	106	133	156

Steel Joist Institute, Standard Specifications and Load Tables Open Web Steel Joists.

Bar Joists

Bar joists, as illustrated and discussed briefly in Chapter 4, may be used as structural floor and roof framing. Because of the large number of sizes and weights available, it is not possible to include descriptions and tables for all joists. The two most common are the "J" or junior joists and the "H" or long span joists.

Limit the clear span of J-series joists to 24 times depth.

The ends of steel joists shall extend a distance of not less than 4 inches over *masonry* or poured concrete supports. The ends shall extend not less than 2½ inches over *steel* supports except where opposite joists butt over a narrow steel support and attachment is made by welding or bolting.

Bridging-spacing

In no case shall the spacing of bridging or sag rods be greater than given in the following table:

Clear Span	Number of Lines of Bridging
Up to 14 feet	One row near center.
14 to 21 feet	Two rows placed at approximately ⅓ points of span.
21 to 32 feet	Three rows placed at approximately ¼ points of span
32 to 40 feet	Four rows placed at approximately 1/5 points of span
40 to 48 feet	Five rows placed at approximately 1/6 points of span.

Joist Spacing

Joists shall be so spaced that the loading on each does not exceed the allowable load given for the particular designation and span in load table. For floors, it is recommended that maximum spacing be not greater than 24".[1]

[1]*Structural Steel Data, J. T. Ryerson & Son, Inc.*

Structural steel for a movable dome.

Rohm & Haas Photograph

Completed dome showing swimming pool through roof that can be opened.

Rohm & Haas Photograph

Questions to Reinforce Knowledge

1. What is structural metal?

2. Who may make official structural calculations? Why?

3. How are weights of materials determined?

4. Are all structural parts always calculated by using mathematical data? Explain.

5. How do individual local codes influence strength requirements and calculations?

6. If no code is required in a specific area, where can one obtain pertinent information concerning required strengths and sizes of structural parts?

7. What is a dead load?

8. What is a live load?

9. What is meant when one says, "The load is quiescent"?

10. What is welded wire fabric?

11. Where is welded wire fabric used?

12. How is its size determined?

13. Can you think of reasons why welded wire fabric should not be carried through construction or expansion joints?

14. What is the difference between wire gage sizes and reinforcing rod sizes?

15. From the wire fabric illustrations, can you describe the difference between positive and negative steel?

16. What is the apparent value of a detail sheet for welded wire fabric?

17. What do we mean when we say a reinforcing rod is *deformed*?

18. Are all reinforcing rods deformed?

19. What is the difference between a Standard and a Wide Flange I beam?

20. What is deflection? Is it important, or a problem?

21. When used in a building, do steel beams support all floors? Explain.

22. What is the recommended live load which floors in dwellings should carry?

23. What is a kip?

24. What is meant when one says the load is uniformly distributed?

25. What is "fiber stress"?

26. If a safe load table is based on a fiber stress of 20,000 pounds per square inch, and the local code specifies 16,000 pounds per square inch, how can the table be used to make the required calculations?

27. What is a compression flange?

28. When one says lateral support, what is meant?

29. What is the allowable deflection for plastered ceilings?

30. How does one determine beam size from the load tables shown in the text?

31. What is meant by the term "beam span"?

32. What is a pipe column?

33. Why are steel plates placed on the top and bottom of steel columns?

34. How is column spacing determined?

35. How is column size determined?

36. What is "beam reaction"?

37. Can one have two beam reactions on the same column? Explain.

38. How are posts or columns joined to beams?

39. How are steel columns secured to concrete footings or floors?

40. What are steel lintels?

41. How is their size determined?

42. What is a bar joist?

43. Is there more than one kind?

44. How much bearing surface on masonry must a bar joist have?

45. Do you know why bridging is used on steel joists?

Terms to Spell and Know

structural	welded	spliced
distribute	connectors	flange
technical	intersections	lateral
verified	ductile	kip
calculations	install	impact
duplication	alignment	buckling
incorporated	gage	deflection
recommendation	longitudinal	allowable
assumptions	transverse	represented
superimposed	suspended	transmit
proportion	data	reaction
quiescent	equivalent	terminate
pertinent	billet	

Sill and Floor Construction

Sills

The sill is a wood beam that rests on the foundation. The sill is pressed carefully into the mortar to insure a good seal. Washers are placed over the anchor bolts, and nuts are tightened to hold the sill in place. The anchor bolts prevent the sill from slipping on the foundation and also secure the frame to the foundation during high winds.

Methods of Floor Framing

Two methods of floor framing are illustrated. *Western* or *platform* framing is most widely used. This method allows workmen to complete the base or platform in a minimum amount of time, thus giving them a firm, clean walking and storage surface for the remainder of construction. Another advantage is that the solid subfloor over the box sill helps eliminate drafts, which can be a fire hazard.

The box sill is composed of two parts. The horizontal member is the bed plate. The vertical member is a header.

The chief disadvantage is

shrinkage of lumber across the grain. This is undesirable when the exterior of the building is to be faced with masonry veneer or stucco. Expansion and contraction of framing will cause cracking of the exterior surface, or separation of masonry from the wood frame.

The major advantage of *balloon framing* is its dimensional stability. Studding extending to the sill prevents any change of shape on the outside of the building. When used with masonry veneer, this allows the materials to be attached without danger of shifting or separating.

One disadvantage is the time necessary for "letting in" or notching the studs to receive the ribbon. (See page 512.) The ribbon is *usually* made of 1″ material. A notch for thicker materials would weaken the studs. Another disadvantage is that the studs must be *raised* or put in place at the same time as the floor joists. Working over an excavation or basement is difficult.

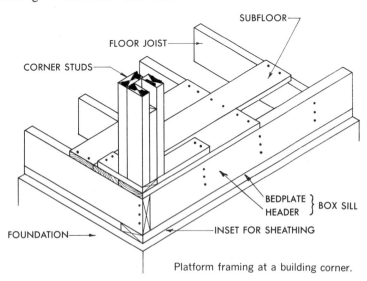

Platform framing at a building corner.

Pressure Treated or Applied Preservatives

Floor framing near moisture or earth is susceptible to decay and termites. Preservatives should be added to the framing to prolong its life. The best protection is gained by applying the preservative under pressure. Deep penetration is insured. Bulk preservatives may be purchased and job-applied; however, this is time consuming and the results are not permanent.

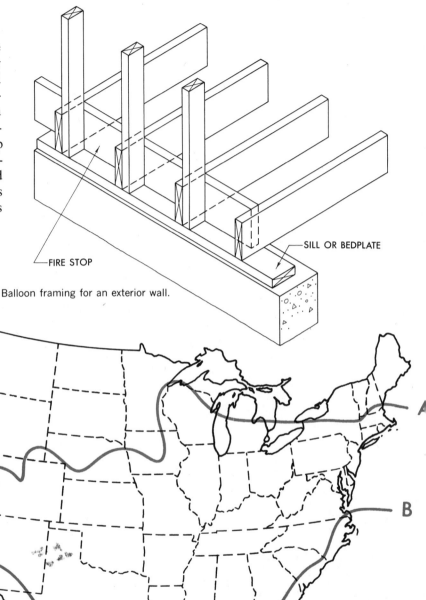

SILL OR BEDPLATE

FIRE STOP

Balloon framing for an exterior wall.

U.S. Department of Agriculture

Map showing (line AA) the northern limit of damage by subterranean termites in the United States; BB, the northern limit of damage by dry-wood or nonsubterranean termites.

Termite Shield

A termite shield is placed over the foundation and piers. It should extend past the edges of the foundation two inches and be bent down to a 45° angle. The purpose of the bend is to help prevent termites from bypassing. A termite is a boring insect. It builds tunnels in wood material. It cannot tunnel through the shield.

Holes must be cut in the shield for anchor bolts. Tar or some other plastic material should be used to seal around the bolts. When pieces of termite shield must be end joined, or when joints are made at the corners, this seam should also be sealed. The joint is best *closed* by soldering.

Materials used for termite shields are: copper, copper coated kraft paper, or aluminum. Roll roofing is sometimes used and meets minimum requirements of some codes, but this is not recommended. The material is soft and is likely to decay. The edges do not stay at the proper angle.

Grout or Mortar with Shield

A thin layer of grout or mortar, about ⅜″, is placed over the shield. This acts as a base for wood parts. The grout helps level the top of the foundation and acts as a weather seal.

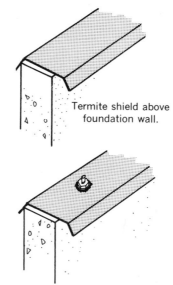

Termite shield above foundation wall.

Openings in termite shields as those for anchor bolts must be completely sealed.

Floor Joist

Many woods are suitable for floor joists. Because of their abundance, workability, and strength, softwoods are most frequently used. The light weight of this group makes them easy to cut and handle. Southern, long leaf yellow pine is the strongest of the native softwoods. Douglas fir, hemlock, and spruce have slightly less strength but are suitable.

Spacing for floor joists may be 12″, 16″, 20″, or 24″ o.c. (on center). Spacing of 16″ o.c. is most frequently used. When laying out for floor joists, measurements are begun at the outside edge of the first or header joist. It is 16″ from the outside of the edge joist (header) to the center of the second joist, and then 16″ o.c. for remaining joists—except the last

one, which will end with uneven spacing. The spacing of the last joist would be 16″ if modular construction were used. A discussion of this topic begins on page 135.

In wood frame construction, the first joist or header of the box sill is frequently placed ¾″ from the outside edge of the foundation wall.

Size of floor joists is determined by the total load to be supported and the distance they must span. Charts showing the comparative strength of different woods and the maximum allowable span for dimension lumber are shown. See page 75.

Nominal 2″ lumber is most frequently used for *conventional* framing. The term nominal means "not actual." Finished size is smaller than 2″. When greater thickness is desired, the cost is usually considerably greater. When several joist sizes are required, it is not unusual to select the largest size needed, and use this size for the entire structure. This is especially true when the under sides of the joists form a base for a finish ceiling.

When joists must be end joined over a beam or girder, some provision must be made for tying them together. They should be lapped a minimum of 4″ and be nailed firmly to secure, or a scab of lumber should be nailed across the joint as shown in the second illustration on page 74.

Posts, beams, and girders which might be considered a part of floor framing are discussed in Chapter 11.

When framing floor openings, all the joists should be doubled.

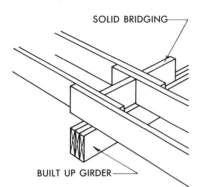

Floor joists lapped over a built-up girder.

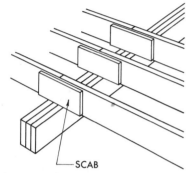

Joists spliced above a built-up girder.

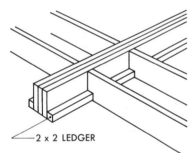

A ledger provides bearing surface at joist and girder intersections.

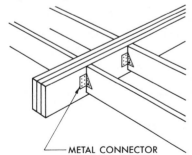

Joists may be secured to a girder with metal connectors.

Framing

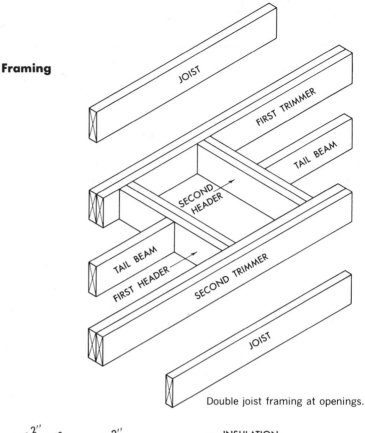

Double joist framing at openings.

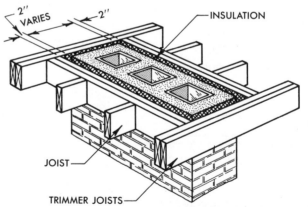

Joist framing for flues or fireplaces.

The illustration shows the method of framing openings and names of the parts involved. When framing openings for fireplaces and flues, the area between the wood and masonry should be filled with a fireproof insulation. Wood framing should be spaced a minimum of 2″ from the masonry. Note also that ends of joists may not terminate in a chimney or fireplace and that all framing beneath load bearing walls should be doubled.

Floor Joists

DOUGLAS FIR—COAST REGION

Nominal sizes (inches)	Spacing (inches o. c.)	Association Lumber Grades									
		Select Structural	Dense Construction	Construction	Standard	Utility	Select Structural	Dense Construction	Construction	Standard	Utility
		1950 f	1700 f	1450 f	1200 f	(1)	1950 f	1700 f	1450 f	1200 f	(1)
		30 LB. LIVE LOAD					40 LB. LIVE LOAD				
		Ft. In.	Ft. In.	Ft. In.	Ft. In.	Ft. In.	Ft. In.	Ft. In.	Ft. In.	Ft. In.	Ft. In.
2 x 6	12	11 4	11 4	11 4	11 4	8 4	10 6	10 6	10 6	10 6	7 4
	16	10 4	10 4	10 4	10 4	7 2	9 8	9 8	9 8	9 8	6 4
	24	9 0	9 0	9 0	9 0	5 10	8 4	8 4	8 4	8 2	5 2
2 x 8	12	15 4	15 4	15 4	15 4	12 4	14 4	14 4	14 4	14 4	11 0
	16	14 0	14 0	14 0	14 0	10 8	13 0	13 0	13 0	13 0	9 6
	24	12 4	12 4	12 4	12 4	8 8	11 6	11 6	11 6	11 0	7 10
2 x 10	12	18 4	18 4	18 4	18 4	16 10	17 4	17 4	17 4	17 4	15 2
	16	17 0	17 0	17 0	17 0	14 8	16 2	16 2	16 2	16 2	13 0
	24	15 6	15 6	15 6	15 6	12 0	14 6	14 6	14 6	14 0	10 8
2 x 12	12	21 2	21 2	21 2	21 2	19 8	20 0	20 0	20 0	20 0	17 8
	16	19 8	19 8	19 8	19 8	17 0	18 8	18 8	18 8	18 8	15 4
	24	17 10	17 10	17 10	17 10	14 0	16 10	16 10	16 10	16 10	12 6

1. Denotes Grade is not a stress grade

SOUTHERN YELLOW PINE—MEDIUM GRAIN

Nominal size (inches)	Spacing (inches o. c.)	Association Lumber Grades							
		No. 1 Dense K. D. 2″ Dimension	No. 2 Dense K. D. 2″ Dimension	No. 1 Dense 2″ Dimension	No. 2 Dense 2″ Dimension	No. 1 Dense K. D. 2″ Dimension	No. 2 Dense K. D. 2″ Dimension	No. 1 Dense 2″ Dimension	No. 2 Dense 2″ Dimension
		1700 f	1500 f	1450 f	1200 f	1700 f	1200 f	1450 f	1200 f
		30 LB. LIVE LOAD				40 LB. LIVE LOAD			
		Ft. In.	Ft. In.	Ft. In.	Ft. In.	Ft. In.	Ft. In.	Ft. In.	Ft. In.
2 x 6[1]	12	11 4	11 4	11 4	11 4	10 6	10 6	10 6	10 6
	16	10 4	10 4	10 4	10 4	9 8	9 8	9 8	9 8
	24	9 0	9 0	9 0	9 0	8 4	8 4	8 4	8 2
2 x 8	12	15 4	15 4	15 4	15 4	14 4	14 4	14 4	14 4
	16	14 0	14 0	14 0	14 0	13 0	13 0	13 0	13 0
	24	12 4	12 4	12 4	12 4	11 6	11 6	11 6	11 0
2 x 10	12	18 4	18 4	18 4	18 4	17 4	17 4	17 4	17 4
	16	17 0	17 0	17 0	17 0	16 2	16 2	16 2	16 2
	24	15 6	15 6	15 6	15 6	14 6	14 6	14 6	14 0
2 x 12	12	21 2	21 2	21 2	21 2	20 0	20 0	20 0	20 0
	16	19 8	19 8	19 8	19 8	18 8	18 8	18 8	18 8
	24	17 10	17 10	17 10	17 10	16 10	16 10	16 10	16 10

[1] Spans for 2″x6″ lumber having actual dressed size of 1⅝″x5⅝″ may be increased 2½ percent.

Notes: (a) Spans may be increased 5 percent from those shown for rough lumber or lumber surfaced two edges (S2E).

(b) Spans shall be decreased 5 percent from those shown for lumber more than 2 percent but not more than 5 percent scant from American Lumber Standards sizes measured at a moisture content of 19 percent or less. Lumber scant more than 5 percent not acceptable.

Table of floor joist sizes and their spans.

Bridging

Bridging is used between joists to stiffen the floor and spread the concentrated load over a greater area. Cross bridging is the type most commonly used. Bridging as shown in the framing diagram is usually constructed of 1"x3" lumber. The ends are cut at an angle to allow them to fit against the joist. Bridging may also be made of metal.

The top of the bridging is nailed before the subfloor is nailed in place. The lower ends remain loose. After the finished floor is in place, the lower ends are pulled flush with the bottom of the joists and nailed. If the joists are warped, the crowns are placed near the top. When the lower ends are nailed, it tends to level the floor. Actual strength gained from the addition of bridging is questionable, but most codes require their use. Most minimum requirements space the bridging not less than 8'-0" apart. This means most typical rooms will have one row in the center. If the span is more than 16' 0", two rows would be required.

Subfloor

Three materials are commonly used for wood subfloors. Plywood now is most popular.

(1) Until recently, the most common was tongue and groove lumber. Minimum thickness is $^{25}/_{32}$" and maximum width is 8". Excessive warpage can result from using wider lumber.

(2) Lumber surfaced four sides (S4S), is also sometimes used. The size required is the same as for tongue and groove lumber. The

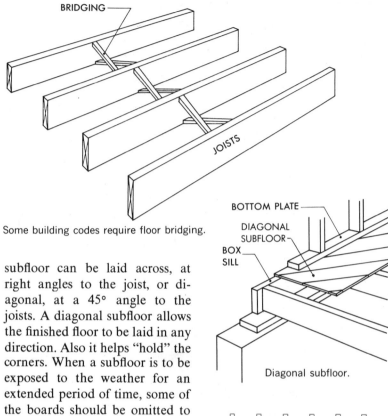

Some building codes require floor bridging.

subfloor can be laid across, at right angles to the joist, or diagonal, at a 45° angle to the joists. A diagonal subfloor allows the finished floor to be laid in any direction. Also it helps "hold" the corners. When a subfloor is to be exposed to the weather for an extended period of time, some of the boards should be omitted to allow for drainage of water.

End joining of boards for the subfloor should be done over floor joist. In some cases, when end matched tongue and groove lumber is used, the joints can be made between joists. However, the lumber should bear, or rest upon, at least two joists and no joints in succeeding boards should be made over or between the same joists.

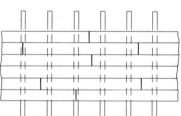

Diagonal subfloor.

Tongue and groove subflooring is sometimes spliced between joists.

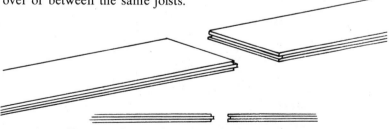

Tongue and groove lumber provides strength at joints.

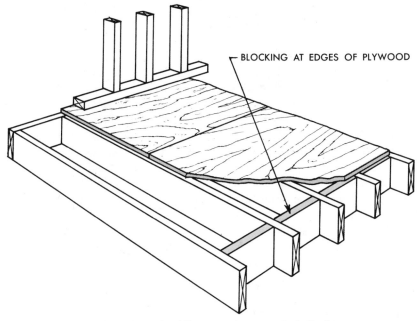

BLOCKING AT EDGES OF PLYWOOD

Most plywood subfloors require support at all edges.

(3) Plywood has become widely used as a material for subfloors. The large size of the sheets, and the speed with which they can be nailed, offsets the slightly higher cost of material. Greater care must be taken when spacing the joists. Any discrepancy in spacing will prevent the ends of panels from resting on the joists; excessive waste of material and time will result from poor spacing. When using 16″ spacing for floor joists, ½″ plywood is adequate. The outer grain of the plywood should be placed across the joist. End joints should be staggered so successive panels do not break, or end over the same joist. Unless tongue and groove plywood is used, blocking is required to support edges. A low-grade sheathing of unsanded plywood is usually used.

Joist Framing for Solid Masonry

When solid masonry is used for exterior walls, no box sill is required. The joist ends are imbedded in, or placed on a ledge of the wall. Two methods of setting joists are shown in the illustration. Joist ends should have 3″ minimum bearing on solid masonry.

Pockets for beam ends should be provided in foundation walls.

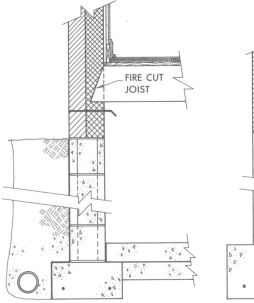

FIRE CUT JOIST

Foundation and wall with fire cut joist.

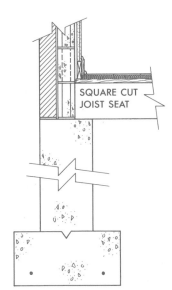

SQUARE CUT JOIST SEAT

Section through a wall showing square cut joist seat.

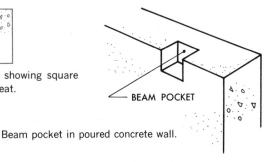

BEAM POCKET

Beam pocket in poured concrete wall.

Minimum bearing surface for beam ends is 4″. When wood beams are used, ½″ clearance should be provided at the sides and ends of the beam. This allows for expansion and contraction and permits air to circulate around the beam. Minor adjustments of alignment can also be made.

Questions to Reinforce Knowledge

1. What is a termite shield?

2. What is the purpose of bending the termite shield?

3. Why are the joints soldered or otherwise closed in the shield?

4. Why is mortar placed over the termite shield?

5. What part of a wood structure is placed upon this mortar?

6. What are two methods of wood wall framing? Explain each.

7. What is meant by the term "letting in" when referring to a ribbon?

8. What advantage do pressure-applied preservatives for termite protection have over brush-applied ones?

9. What is a floor joist?

10. What is the strongest of the native softwoods?

11. What is the most frequently used spacing for wood floor joists?

12. Why is the box sill sometimes placed ¾″ inside the edge of the foundation?

13. Why are joists sometimes lapped over a beam?

14. What are some other methods of end-joining joists?

15. When added strength is required at floor openings, what is done to the joists?

16. Why is framing not placed against chimneys and fireplaces?

17. What is the minimum distance between framing and a chimney?

18. What material is placed in this space?

19. What is bridging? When is it used?

20. Why is the bottom of bridging not nailed until after the subfloor is laid?

21. What are three materials frequently used for subfloors? Which is becoming most popular? Why?

22. Why are joints not broken over the same joists when laying subfloors?

Terms to Spell and Know

seam	spruce
soldering	nominal
aluminum	ceiling
grout	scab
shrinkage	bridging
ribbon	subfloor
softwoods	discrepancy
hemlock	

7

Frame Wall Construction

Wall Section

During this discussion the frame wall of a building is considered as a single unit, even though it is composed of many individual parts. Framing a wood wall was originally done one piece at a time, on the construction site. This is no longer true. Only on very small jobs would the framing be done in this manner. Wall sections are usually completed and then raised in place. On some light construc-tion the wall section might be assembled on the subfloor and then erected.

In volume production, the parts are cut and assembled in a shop or factory. Volume pro-duction can increase quality and reduce the number of man hours of labor per unit, as well as im-proving working conditions be-cause of the efficiency. Parts for a structure being cut and assembled in this manner do not necessarily indicate a trend toward total prefabrication as the ultimate in progress of con-struction methods. The merits of total prefabrication and the use of components in building will not be discussed at this time. Custom built, or one-of-a-kind building, can also be framed very efficiently in this manner. Quality of materials and workmanship usually exceeds that of a build-ing totally assembled on the site.

Sole Plate

The sole plate is a 2x4, with its wide dimension contacting the subfloor. It is placed beneath all stud walls.

When used on exterior walls it is customary to align the edge of the bed plate flush with the edge of the foundation, as shown to the left. Another arrangement is sometimes substituted as shown in the illustration at the right.

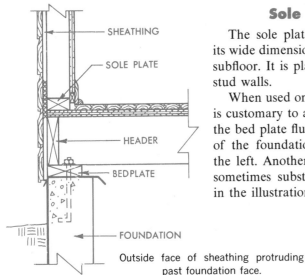

SHEATHING

SOLE PLATE

HEADER

BEDPLATE

FOUNDATION

Outside face of sheathing protruding past foundation face.

SHEATHING

SOLE PLATE

HEADER

BEDPLATE

Outside face of sheathing flush with foundation face.

The sole plate acts as an anchor for the studs and helps hold their proper spacing. It also serves as a means of attaching the wall to the subfloor. It is sometimes placed around the entire perimeter of the wall, including door openings. This helps make the wall more rigid while it is being erected. After the wall is nailed in place the plate is removed from the openings. When bearing walls are parallel to floor joists, and in line with them, the joists should be doubled. When the wall is between joists, blocking as shown in the illustration is used to prevent the floor from sagging between joists.

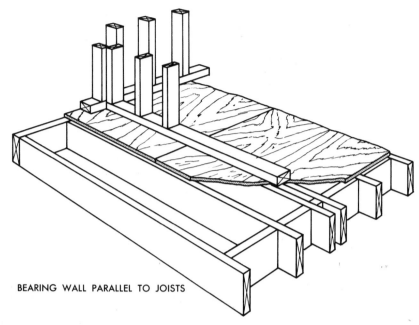

BEARING WALL PARALLEL TO JOISTS

Joists are doubled beneath bearing walls. Double joists may be joined together, or separated by spacers to accommodate wires or pipes.

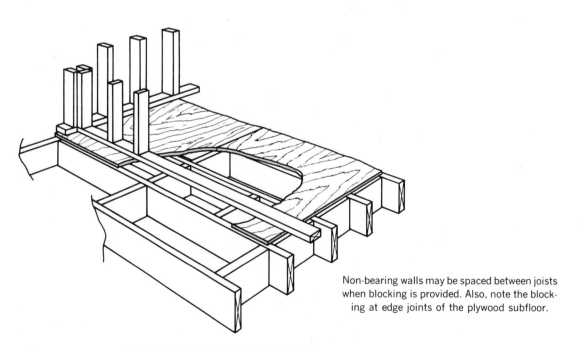

Non-bearing walls may be spaced between joists when blocking is provided. Also, note the blocking at edge joints of the plywood subfloor.

NON-BEARING WALL PARALLEL TO JOISTS

Top Plate

Plates are placed over the top of all studs. They serve as spacers and tie the top of the studs in place. All plates on outside walls should be doubled because the weight of ceiling joists and rafters bears upon them. It is sometimes permissible to use single top plates for interior walls if no load is to be supported. However, the extra time involved to cut and handle different length studs usually offsets the amount of material saved.

When top plates must be end joined, the splice should be made over a stud. When splices must be made in both top plates, the splices should not be made over the same stud.

When the top plate is joined at a corner, the plate should be lapped so the corner can be tied together as in the illustration.

When panels of modular construction are used for walls, the top plates are sometimes stood on edge as shown to the right, and serve as a header around the perimeter of outside walls.

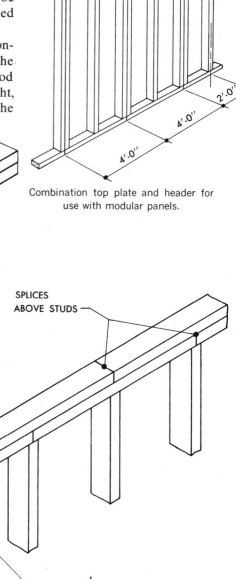

Combination top plate and header for use with modular panels.

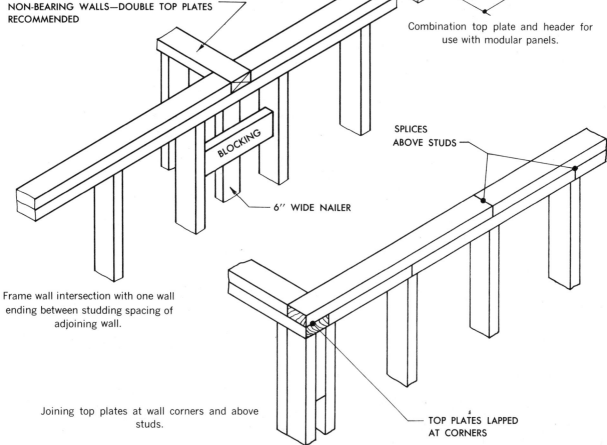

SINGLE TOP PLATE PERMITTED FOR INTERIOR NON-BEARING WALLS—DOUBLE TOP PLATES RECOMMENDED

BLOCKING

6" WIDE NAILER

Frame wall intersection with one wall ending between studding spacing of adjoining wall.

SPLICES ABOVE STUDS

Joining top plates at wall corners and above studs.

TOP PLATES LAPPED AT CORNERS

81

Studding

Studs are the slender wood uprights that form the vertical framework of the walls of a structure. Studs are usually made of 2x4's actual size of which is 1½"x3½". One notable exception to the standard thickness of frame walls is the area which must accommodate the larger soil stack or vent pipe for the bathroom plumbing fixtures. This wall is usually constructed of 2x6's.

The studding should be of uniform length, which is determined by the ceiling height desired. For conventional, flat ceilings of homes, 8'0" is the most common ceiling height. NOTE: This measurement is not the stud length, it is only used in *determining* length. Studs are usually spaced 16" on centers. The stud is turned so the wide dimension forms the thickness of the wall. In rare cases where no load must be supported, as in a closet wall, the stud may be turned so the short dimension represents the thickness of the wall. This is done only if space is at a premium. The 16" spacing works well in "hanging a curtain" of most wall materials.

In some very light construction it is permissible to use 24" spacing. For example, studs for a garage or shed might be so spaced.

The uniform spacing is usually continued over window and door openings.

It is impossible to start measuring stud spacing at the outside corner of a building and keep the studs on 16" centers on the inside of the building at the same

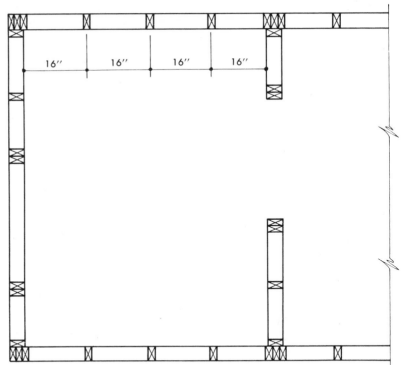

Studs spaced 16" o.c. from inside building.

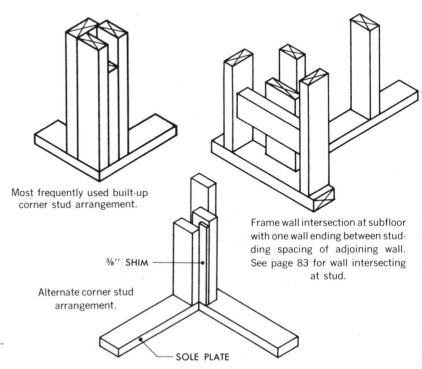

Most frequently used built-up corner stud arrangement.

Frame wall intersection at subfloor with one wall ending between studding spacing of adjoining wall. See page 83 for wall intersecting at stud.

⅜" SHIM

Alternate corner stud arrangement.

SOLE PLATE

time. One of the spacings (inside or outside) must necessarily be off the 16″ module. It is customary to start the spacing from the inside as shown in the stud layout diagram. Then studs can be more easily located when nailing through plaster is required.

It is desirable—but impossible—to purchase lumber that is perfectly straight, with no warp or wind (twist). Yet only the straightest lumber should be selected for studs. If studs are noticeably warped, the crowns, or high points, should be alternated, placing one toward the outside and the next toward the inside. When sheathing or wall covering is applied, this helps pull the wall into a straight position. If an occasional stud is extremely warped, but must be used, it can be partially cut and pulled into a straight position. A scab or extra piece is then nailed over the cut to hold the stud firm.

Corner Studs

When two exterior corners meet, studs must be joined to form a corner post. Two methods are shown. The first illustration shows the method most frequently used. The short wood sections between the studs are blocking used to help form the post. Short scrap boards are used, thus eliminating one extra full stud.

Studs To Fill Between an Inside Wall and an Outside Wall

Inside and outside walls may be joined as shown. The arrangement to use will be determined by the position of the inside wall

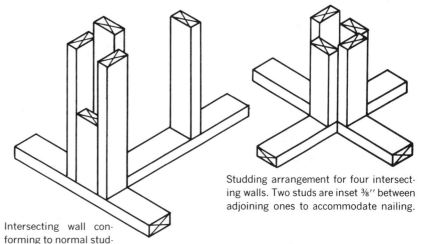

Intersecting wall conforming to normal studding spacing.

Studding arrangement for four intersecting walls. Two studs are inset ⅜″ between adjoining ones to accommodate nailing.

surface, in relation to the stud arrangement. If an inside wall ends between studs, the first arrangement (page 82) is used. If it ends on wall studs, the second (page 83) would be used.

Stud Intersections

At wall intersections on the interior of the building, the studs are arranged as shown.

Studs at Wall Openings

Double studs are placed at all door, window, and other openings. The outside stud extends from the bottom to the top plate. The inside stud is cut to receive the headers over the opening. If no weight is to be supported for a second floor, the portion of studding above the header is sometimes omitted. The studs are used in addition to the ones on the 16″ spacing. However, when possible, window and door placement are arranged to conform with the stud spacing. The stud next to the opening is used for normal spacing.

OMITTED WHEN NO SECOND STORY.

Framing for a window opening.

Framing for a door opening. This method is not as frequently used as the other method shown on page 84.

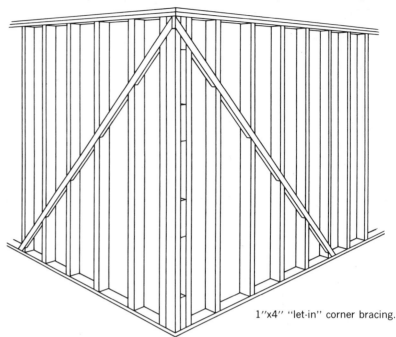

1"x4" "let-in" corner bracing.

Base Blocks

Short scraps of lumber the same thickness and width as studding are placed against the studs opposite the opening to provide for nailing the ends of baseboard and casing.

Corner Bracing

Temporary corner braces may be used at studded wall openings and room corners to insure a square corner. They are applied at a 45° angle to the studs. If rigid sheathing is not to be applied to the exterior, it is necessary to place *permanent* braces on the outside of the studs. These are made from 1"x4" lumber and are *"let in"* to the studs. As said, if plywood or rigid insulating sheathing is used, no additional bracing is required.

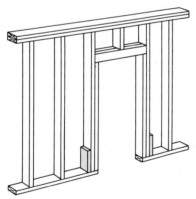

Frequently used method of framing a door opening. Small blocks of 2"x4" called base blocks afford additional nailing surface for securing casing and baseboard. A crippled stud is added above the header.

Firestop and Nailers

Balloon framing leaves an open space along the studs. This space acts as a flue if fire occurs. Western framing is not as open, but both walls should have lumber placed between the studs to serve as a firestop. Two methods of installation are shown. When vertical coverings, such as plywood or hardboard paneling, are applied directly to the studs, these boards also act as backing. This makes the wall firm and provides additional nailing surface. See page 85.

Headers

Joists, rafters, and additional floors above, must be supported over doors, windows, and other openings. Headers of lumber on edge or plywood laminated beams, as shown in the illustrations, are used.

The accompanying chart shows the header size required for various spans. See page 86.

Two methods of installing the header are shown. The older method requires short studs over the header. Newer construction methods use a large header to fill the entire space above the opening. The additional material required would not be as great as the labor for laying out, cutting, and installing crippled studs. Additional material can be saved when applying sheathing or inside wall coverings because the parts need not be spaced on the 16" module.

Plywood box beams are very desirable as headers when long spans are needed. They have an exceptionally good weight-to-strength ratio. Such beams are also used with post and beam structural systems.

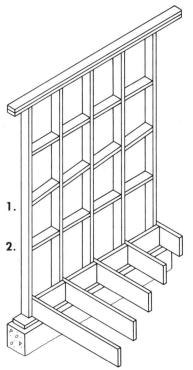

Two methods of installing firestop between studs.

⅜" THICK SHIM

Dimension lumber nailed together to form a header.

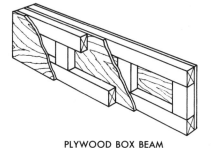

PLYWOOD BOX BEAM

For wide openings plywood box beams make excellent headers.

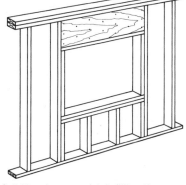

Solid headers completely filling the space above an opening give added strength, require uniform width lumber, and speed construction.

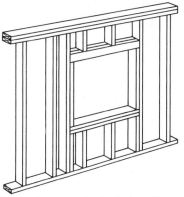

Conventional method of installing a header above an opening.

Framing Diagrams

When construction was entirely a one-part-at-a-time operation, it was necessary to draw complete framing diagrams to show the workmen how to assemble the structure. At the present this is not always done. However, any information not placed on the working drawings leaves the final decision of framing location to the builder.

Any person planning a structure should be able to show the location of the framing members. If the parts are assembled away from the site, the planning must be exact, to assure a proper fit when the building is assembled.

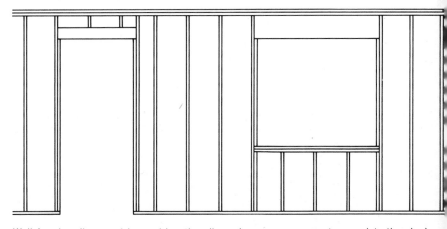

Wall framing diagram (size and location dimensions are necessary to complete the plan).

Headers—Exterior Openings

Width of structure	Header size (on edge)	Roof construction		
		Roof joist with bearing partition, slope 3 in 12 or less / Braced rafters with bearing partition — Slope over 3 in 12	Rafters with bearing partition — Slope over 3 in 12 / Trussed rafters — Slope 3 in 12 or less	Trussed rafters slope over 3 in 12 / Rafters with bearing partition — Habitable space
		1 story		
Up to 26 feet wide.	2—2 x 4s...	3′ 6″	3′ 0″	2′ 6″
	2—2 x 6s...	6′ 6″	5′ 0″	4′ 6″
	2—2 x 8s...	8′ 6″	7′ 0″	6′ 0″
	2—2 x 10s...	11′ 0″	8′ 6″	[1] 8′ 0″
	2—2 x 12s..	13′ 6″	[1] 10′ 6″	[1] 9′ 6″
		1½ or 2 story		
	2—2 x 4s...	2′ 6″	. . . . .	. . . . .
	2—2 x 6s...	4′ 6″	4′ 0″	3′ 6″
	2—2 x 8s...	6′ 0″	5′ 6″	5′ 0″
	2—2 x 10s..	7′ 6″	[1] 6′ 6″	[1] 6′ 0″
	2—2 x 12s..	9′ 0″	[1] 8′ 0″	[1] 7′ 6″
		1 story		
26 to 32 feet wide.	2—2 x 4s...	3′ 0″	2′ 6″	. . . . .
	2—2 x 6s...	6′ 0″	4′ 6″	4′ 0″
	2—2 x 8s...	8′ 0″	6′ 0″	5′ 6″
	2—2 x 10s..	[1] 10′ 0″	[1] 8′ 0″	[1] 7′ 0″
	2—2 x 12s..	[1] 12′ 0″	[1] 9′ 6″	[1] 8′ 6″
		1½ or 2 story		
	2—2 x 4s...	. . . . .	. . . . .	. . . . .
	2—2 x 6s...	4′ 0″	3′ 6″	3′ 6″
	2—2 x 8s...	5′ 6″	5′ 0″	4′ 6″
	2—2 x 10s..	[1] 7′ 0″	[1] 6′ 0″	[1] 5′ 6″
	2—2 x 12s..	[1] 8′ 6″	[1] 7′ 6″	[1] 7′ 0″

Note: The above spans are based on allowable fiber stresses in bending as follows: For 2 x 4s, 800 psi; for 2 x 6s and larger, 1,200 psi. These allowable stresses are average values taking into consideration upgrading for doubling of members. Where 2 x 4s having allowable fiber stress exceeding 800 are used, the spans for 2 x 4s may be increased by 20 percent. Where conditions vary from these assumptions, design headers in accordance with standard engineering practice.

[1] *Triple studs at jamb opening; headers to bear on 2-2 x 4s.*

A sample wall framing diagram for a small structure is shown. See drawing, bottom of page 85.

A typical schedule of header sizes for a building is shown in the illustration. This is very convenient for workmen, as it eliminates the need to locate and figure the length for each header.

HEADER SCHEDULE

KEY	QUAN.	HEADER WIDTH	HEADER HEIGHT	CLEAR SPAN	HEADER LENGTH
1	4	4″	4″	3'-0″	3'-3¼″
2	2	4″	6″	5'-0″	5'-3¼″
3	2	4″	8″	7'-0″	7'-3¼″
4	1	4″	12″	10'-5″	10'-9¾″

Questions to Reinforce Knowledge

1. What is meant by the term "raising the wall"?

2. What is the purpose of a soleplate?

3. What is a top plate? Why is it made from two pieces of lumber?

4. Why are the plates lapped at corners and where inside walls join outside walls?

5. What is a stud, or studding?

6. What size material is usually used for studs?

7. What is their normal spacing?

8. When may they be placed so the small dimension represents the thickness of the frame wall?

9. When referring to lumber, what is warp? What is wind?

10. What is a scab?

11. Why is blocking sometimes used when forming a corner post?

12. What are two methods of joining an inside wall to an outside wall?

13. How are interior wall intersections framed?

14. How are the studs arranged at openings for doors and windows?

15. What is a base block?

16. What is corner bracing? How is it applied?

17. What is a firestop? What material is normally used?

18. What is a header? Explain its construction.

19. What is a framing diagram?

20. How is the size of headers determined?

21. Why is a schedule for headers sometimes included on working drawings?

Terms To Spell and Know

prefabricated	perimeter
component	modular
workmanship	sheathing
sole plate	scab
studding	blocking
studs	firestop
header	

An architect and a builder discussing the framing plans during construction of the building.

Western Wood Products Assn.

8

Masonry Wall Construction

Masonry Materials

Stone, brick, concrete block, clay tile, terra-cotta, or specially processed forms of each are classified as masonry.

Masonry Construction

Any wall constructed entirely of the above materials is considered a masonry wall. However, other materials may be used as the interior finish and the provision for attaching the finish to the masonry. When more than one wythe (thickness) of masonry is used, they must be bonded or fastened securely together.

Solid Masonry

As said, a solid masonry wall is constructed without a framework of studding or space between wythes. All wythes are bonded with mortar and reinforcement. This bond is not sufficient to prevent the wythes from separating. Therefore individual bricks or stones are placed crosswise of the wythes so they tie the two together. Or, instead of placing individual units across both wythes, *header courses,* as shown in the illustration, are used. The

Many masonry materials were used to construct this luxury home.

P.M. Bolton and Assoc.

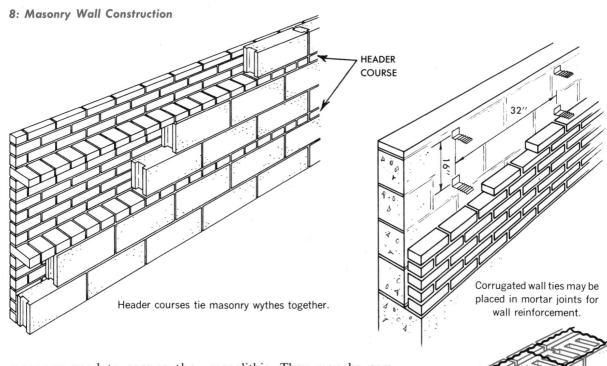

Header courses tie masonry wythes together.

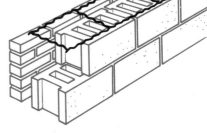

Corrugated wall ties may be placed in mortar joints for wall reinforcement.

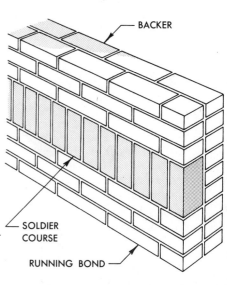

Welded wire reinforcement adds strength and holds wythes in position.

Soldier course in running bond brick.

masonry used to secure the wythes should equal at least 4% of the outer wall surface, and should extend at least 4″ into the interior wythe. The interior wythe is called a backing. When concrete block is the backing and it is faced with brick, every seventh course of brick is placed as a header course. This allows the header course to tie across each second course of block backing.

When face brick is used as a decorative exterior covering, one sometimes desires not to disrupt the facing pattern with header courses. Then the practice is to tie the wythes with corrugated wall ties or other metal reinforcement. Minimum spacing of such ties is 16″ on center vertically and 32″ horizontally.

Masonry Cavity Walls

All masonry walls are not monolithic. They may be composed of separated wythes spaced apart to represent a specified wall thickness. To be classed as a cavity wall, the minimum cavity width is 2″ and the maximum is 4″.

Since masonry transmits heat, cold, and moisture, the cavity between wythes *may* be filled with insulation. Sprayed foam insulations are especially good. They are inert and are not subject to rot and mold.

The space between masonry units must be bridged with reinforcement.

Hollow Masonry

Any wall constructed of masonry units or blocks which have interior voids—the area of which exceeds 25% of the total cross-sectional area—is classed as hollow masonry.

89

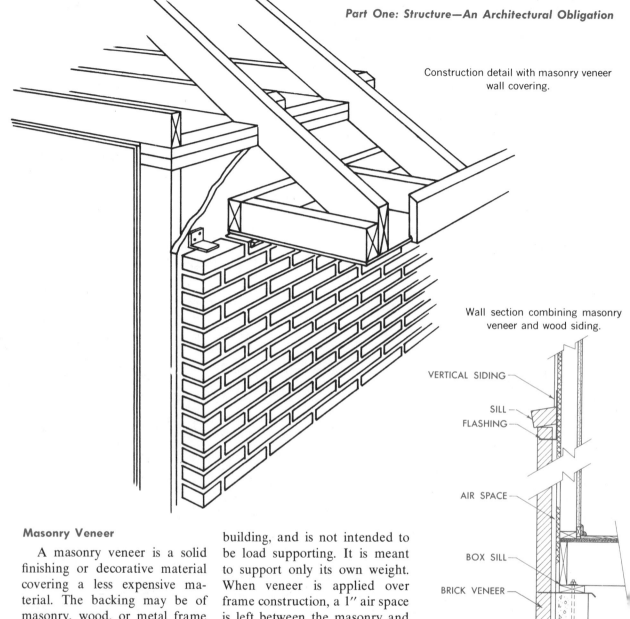

Construction detail with masonry veneer wall covering.

Wall section combining masonry veneer and wood siding.

VERTICAL SIDING

SILL

FLASHING

AIR SPACE

BOX SILL

BRICK VENEER

Masonry Veneer

A masonry veneer is a solid finishing or decorative material covering a less expensive material. The backing may be of masonry, wood, or metal frame construction. However, the term veneer is usually intended to mean that masonry is applied as a covering over a material other than masonry. When veneer is applied over other masonry, it is usually referred to as *facing*.

Veneer placed over wood frame is not a true structural part of the building, and is not intended to be load supporting. It is meant to support only its own weight. When veneer is applied over frame construction, a 1″ air space is left between the masonry and wall sheathing. The veneer is attached to the *frame* with metal wall ties. Normal spacing for the ties is 16″ vertically and 32″ horizontally. The air space allows for variations in the thickness of the masonry, and resists transmission of heat, cold, and penetrating moisture.

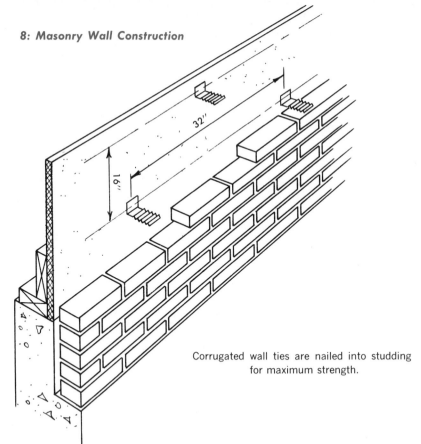

Corrugated wall ties are nailed into studding
for maximum strength.

peak or gable may be of 6″ masonry. NOTE: This is accepted primarily in low-cost buildings. Most codes would not permit it. Generally, walls less than 35′ high may be of 8″ solid masonry. Walls more than 35′ must be 12″ solid masonry. Most codes will permit first story walls to be 12″ and second story walls 8″.

The minimum thickness of *veneer* for two-story structures is 4″.

Parging

Parging is a layer of rough (not smooth finished) plaster made from sand and portland cement. It is used as a waterproofing on exterior foundation walls, between solid masonry walls and interior coverings and between masonry wythes. This prevents the masonry backing from discoloring exposed decorative masonry.

Weep Holes for Cavity and Veneer Walls

Temperature differences between interior and exterior walls lead to moisture condensation. This must be ventilated. Special vents may be used, or vertical mortar joints may be omitted every 4′ in the bottom course.

Masonry Wall Thickness and Height

Wall thickness and height for materials used in masonry will vary with local codes. These must be checked before wall planning can be completed. The FHA gives the following minimum standards: Solid or hollow cavity walls less than 9′ high at the top wall plate line and 15′ or less at

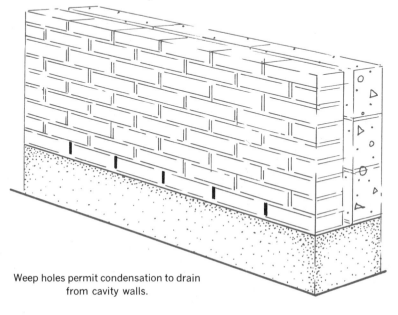

Weep holes permit condensation to drain
from cavity walls.

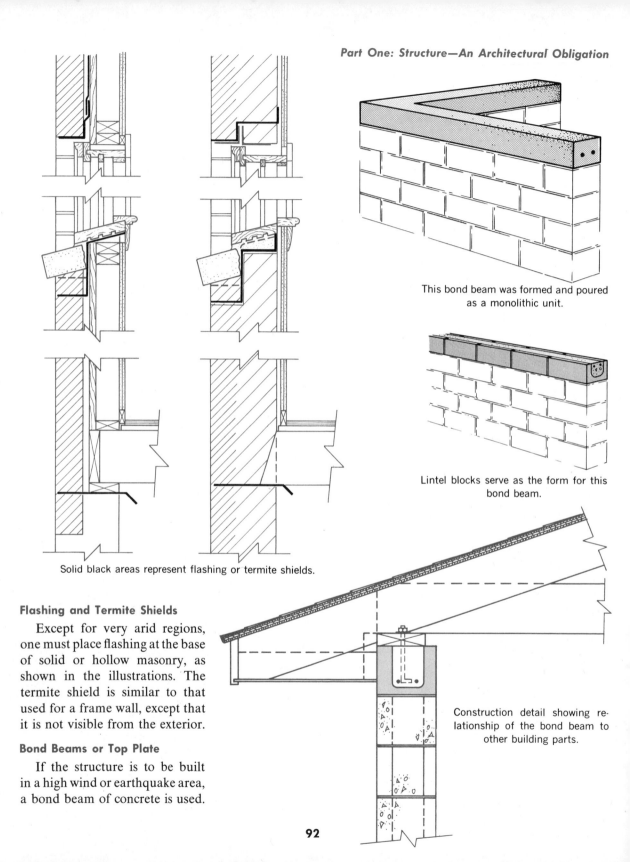

This bond beam was formed and poured as a monolithic unit.

Lintel blocks serve as the form for this bond beam.

Solid black areas represent flashing or termite shields.

Construction detail showing relationship of the bond beam to other building parts.

Flashing and Termite Shields

Except for very arid regions, one must place flashing at the base of solid or hollow masonry, as shown in the illustrations. The termite shield is similar to that used for a frame wall, except that it is not visible from the exterior.

Bond Beams or Top Plate

If the structure is to be built in a high wind or earthquake area, a bond beam of concrete is used.

With solid masonry, this is a reinforced concrete band, extending around the perimeter of the building. For 8″ and 12″ walls, two No. 4 reinforcing rods are required. If the building is constructed of *hollow* concrete block units, the bond beam is formed with lintel blocks as shown and two No. 4 reinforcement rods added; then the units of the reinforced band are filled with concrete.

If in neither a high wind nor earthquake area, a single top plate may be placed over *both* wythes for masonry and firmly secured with anchor bolts. These should be placed as for foundations. When hollow units are used, the voids in the top course are filled with concrete.

Lintels

When openings in masonry are required, as for windows or doors, masonry above the openings must be supported. When wall recesses are required, as for flush radiators, pipe chases, and other equipment, these openings must also be supported by lintels. A lintel is a horizontal construction member over the opening.

Lintels may be constructed of poured concrete, pre-cast concrete, or concrete lintel blocks. These are held to their proper position with wood temporary vertical supports called shoring; reinforcement is added and the voids filled with concrete. Arches of masonry may also serve as lintels. When concealed lintels are desired, structural metal may be used. Ends of the lintel extend a minimum of 4″ into the masonry wall.

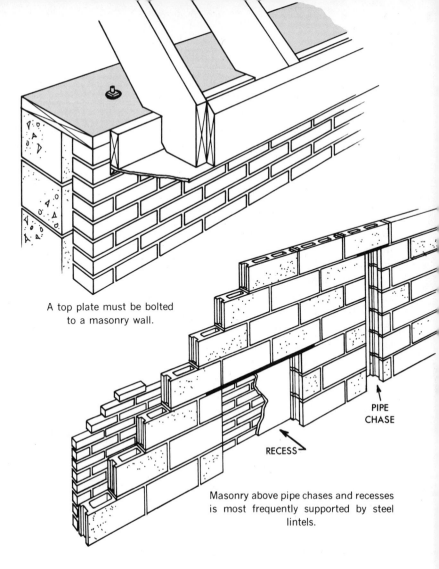

A top plate must be bolted to a masonry wall.

PIPE CHASE

RECESS

Masonry above pipe chases and recesses is most frequently supported by steel lintels.

A masonry arch gives its own support, so no steel lintel is required.

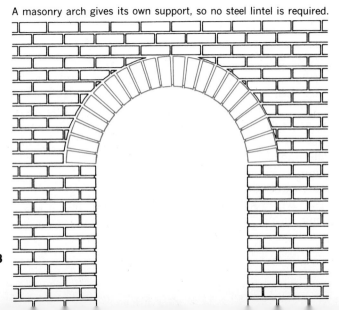

93

A table of steel lintel sizes is shown in Chapter 5, Structural Metal. Lintels must be clearly indicated on the working drawing; a schedule of lintel sizes, coded to specific openings is most desirable.

Damp-proofing

Since capillary action draws moisture from a damp exterior surface toward the interior, something must be done to stop this flow.

Silicone spray on exterior masonry surfaces will help. Parging, or rough plastering the wall on the inside with a coating of Portland cement mortar and then coating this surface with bituminous damp-proofing will retard the flow of moisture. When a cavity wall is used, the damp-proofing may be placed between the wythes. Since a cavity wall is not

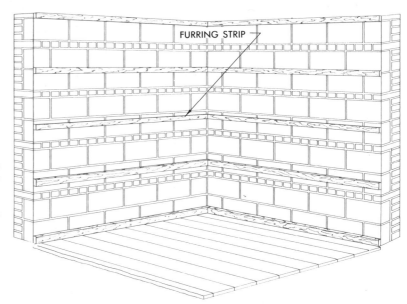

FURRING STRIP

Furring strips block moisture transfer and serve as nailers for wall coverings.

in direct contact with the exterior, this is sufficient.

Interior finishes may be applied directly to the masonry cavity wall. However, when solid masonry is used, additional precautions must be taken. Furring strips, at least ¾″ in thickness must be placed over the damp-proofing.

Brick

Brick is a baked clay product. The finished color is determined by the natural color of the clay, or earth colors may be added during manufacture. Red and buff are the most common. However, brick is manfactured in almost every color imaginable. Bricks may be purchased in quantities of a single color, or they may vary within specified limits, as determined from manufacturers' samples. Variant colors and textures are obtained by using glazed brick, which has a coating of ceramic on the face.

Bricks used as an exposed decorative material are called *face bricks*. They are uniform in size (usually within 1/16″ limits), have neat, square corners and close quality control during manufacture. Common bricks are not uniform in size or color. They are used primarily as backing material, or sometimes on the sides and back of a building, if partially obscured by other structures. These are porous, and absorb dirt readily. They eventually present an unsightly appearance. The expense of a quality

product is the only excuse for using this material on prominent exteriors. It is the author's opinion that common brick on exterior walls suggests more of a run-down appearance than any other single factor of construction.

Names and Sizes of Brick

The names of brick shapes are well standardized; however, the exact sizes are not. A chart showing names and approximate sizes is given on page 96. Individual manufacturers may vary ⅛″ from the sizes shown.

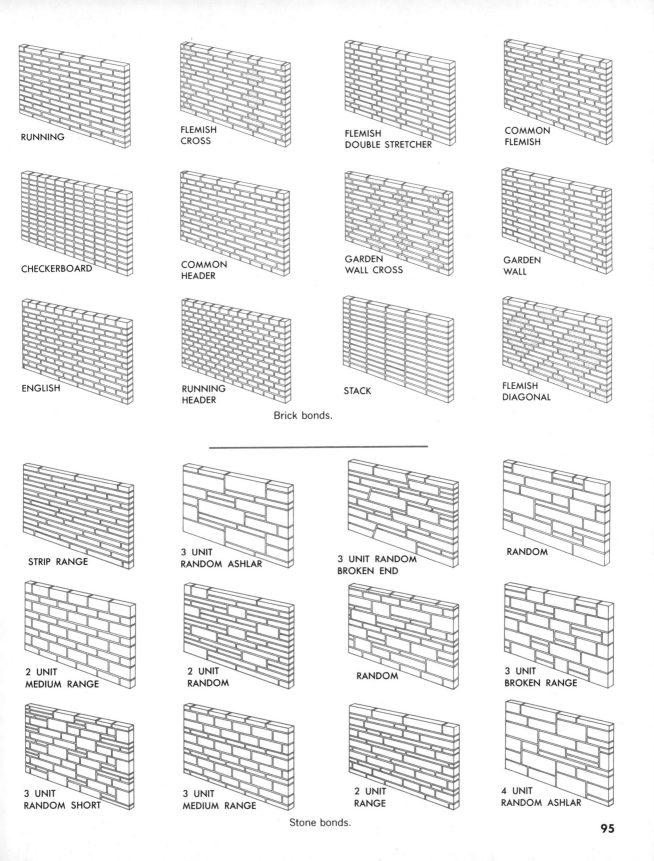

RUNNING

FLEMISH
CROSS

FLEMISH
DOUBLE STRETCHER

COMMON
FLEMISH

CHECKERBOARD

COMMON
HEADER

GARDEN
WALL CROSS

GARDEN
WALL

ENGLISH

RUNNING
HEADER

STACK

FLEMISH
DIAGONAL

Brick bonds.

STRIP RANGE

3 UNIT
RANDOM ASHLAR

3 UNIT RANDOM
BROKEN END

RANDOM

2 UNIT
MEDIUM RANGE

2 UNIT
RANDOM

RANDOM

3 UNIT
BROKEN RANGE

3 UNIT
RANDOM SHORT

3 UNIT
MEDIUM RANGE

2 UNIT
RANGE

4 UNIT
RANDOM ASHLAR

Stone bonds.

Standard	. . .	2¼″x3¾″x8″
Modular	. . . .	2¼″x3⅝″x7⅝″
Jumbo	. . . . .	2¾″x3¾″x8″
Norman	. . . .	2¼″x3⅝″x11⅝″
S.C.R.*	. . .	2⅛″x5½″x11½″
Roman	. . . . .	1⅝″x3⅝″x11⅝″
Baby Roman	.	1⅝″x3⅝″x7⅝″
Fire Brick	. . .	2½″x3⅝″x9″
Oversize	. . . .	Size may vary with manufacturer

*Registered trade-mark. This brick is intended as a single thickness, low cost, one-story masonry wall.

Brick Bonds

Differing feelings for architectural beauty, and different ways of solving construction problems, have resulted in identification of certain styles and methods with the people who developed them. Some of the more common brick bonds, and their application to wall areas, are shown in the illustrations on page 95.

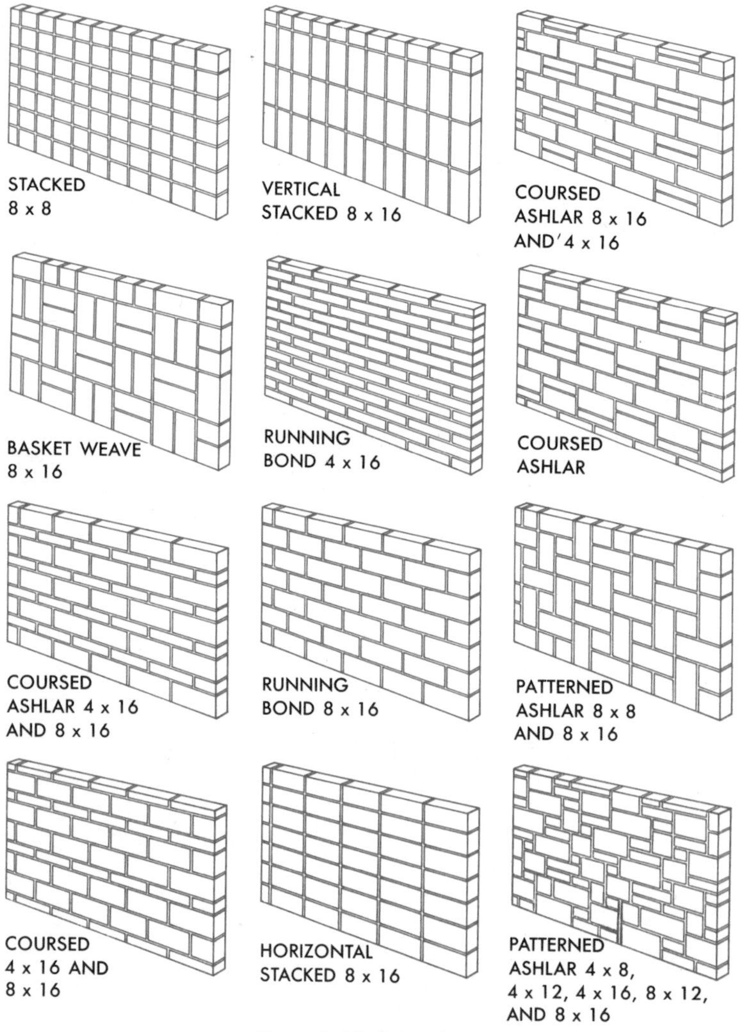

STACKED
8 x 8

VERTICAL
STACKED 8 x 16

COURSED
ASHLAR 8 x 16
AND 4 x 16

BASKET WEAVE
8 x 16

RUNNING
BOND 4 x 16

COURSED
ASHLAR

COURSED
ASHLAR 4 x 16
AND 8 x 16

RUNNING
BOND 8 x 16

PATTERNED
ASHLAR 8 x 8
AND 8 x 16

COURSED
4 x 16 AND
8 x 16

HORIZONTAL
STACKED 8 x 16

PATTERNED
ASHLAR 4 x 8,
4 x 12, 4 x 16, 8 x 12,
AND 8 x 16

Concrete block bonds.

Building Stone

Stones most commonly used in building are: sandstone, limestone, granite, and marble. Lava, quartz and other stone sometimes are used in decorative details. Manufactured stone is made from aggregates of natural stone bonded into a monolithic unit, with mortar or synthetics as the bonding agent. This stone may have a rough textured or smooth polished face, depending upon aggregates used and effect desired. This material should not be confused with "soft" imitations, which try to simulate or copy the appearance of true materials.

Shapes of Building Stone

Rubble is stone as found in nature. When used in building construction no processing is done to produce a more regular shape, although large natural stones may be broken to make them more suitable for building purposes. Two kinds of rubble are:

(1) Fieldstone, or stone as one might find it in a field. It usually has a rather smooth, rounded surface of irregular shape. The stones are fitted at random to form a wall. The backs may be cut for a more uniform thickness.

(2) Stratified stone, which is found in thin broken layers may be broken into pieces suitable for building. It may be laid with the strata in a vertical or horizontal position. When laid vertically, the stones present many irregular faces to the viewer. When laid horizontally they may be coursed or uncoursed (random).

Random stone adds to the beauty of this home.

Stratified stone as used on the front wall of this home gives a rugged effect.

Purchase of Stone

Stone is purchased by the ton. The quoted price is usually based on pick-up at the quarry. Transportation costs must be added to this.

When 3½" stone is used, a ton will lay approximately 50 square feet.

Ashlar. Imagine a piece of stone 10'x10'x20' being taken from a quarry. From this one large stone, many small rectangular building stones are to be cut. These manufactured rectangular shapes are called ashlar. The stone is cut into pieces about 3½" thick, with heights of 2¼", 5", 7¾" and 10½". When mortar is added between horizontal joints, the courses will work well with other modular materials. For example, if 2¼" and 5" stones are placed on top of each other, and a ⅜" mortar joint is used between, the total height is 7⅝". This is the same height as one 8" nominal concrete block or 3 bricks with mortar between. Lengths may be specified, but ashlar stone is usually purchased in random lengths. Ends are irregular, or if specified at additional cost, they can be cut to predetermined lengths. When buying stone one must specify the quantity proportion of each height desired; stated as a percentage.

The face of ashlar is either sawed or split. The sawed patterns may have many textures, depending upon the type saw used. When a split face is used, shallow saw cuts are made the length of the stone along the top and bottom edge. The stone is then broken along this weakened line. When selecting stone, one should consult the manufacturer's or supplier's literature concerning the product.

Facing Stone

As stated earlier, facing is usually applied over other masonry. When it is placed over concrete, the wall must be parged to keep the concrete from staining the stone. Facing may be either in the form of large square or rectangular stones of a uniform thickness or it may be specially shaped with decoration cut into the face. When planning the building, the architect specifies individual stone shapes. Each shape is located by number on the plan and the stone is then cut to the desired shape. Each stone would not have an individual shape, but rather a series of shapes would be repeated in the allover plan. All like stones, of course, would have the same number. When the stones are delivered to the building site, they are stacked according to number as marked on by the manufacturer. Each stone has this identifying number to correspond with the working drawings.

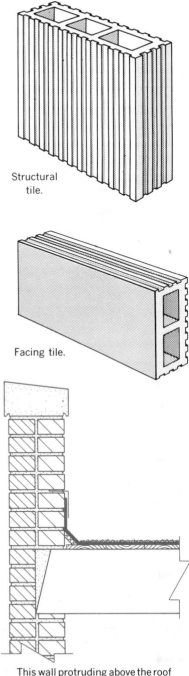

Structural tile.

Facing tile.

This wall protruding above the roof is called a parapet. The stone covering is called a coping. Also note the built-up roof and flashing detail plus the 45° cant strip.

98

Structural and Facing Tile

Tile is a baked clay product similar to brick. The main difference is the cavities built into the tile. These lighten its weight. Structural tile is made as a backing material or with one finished face or more. When used in a single unit wall, both faces are finished. The exterior may be finished as a brick face, or a ceramic glaze may be applied. When a ceramic glaze is added, the material is called facing tile.

Sills

Masonry buildings usually have a stone sill beneath all openings. Some manufacturers may have standard sizes more popular than any others; however, there is no degree of uniformity as to the size and shape of sills. One cannot give as a standard answer that sills generally have a certain size. They may range from 2½″ to 5″ in thickness. Modern buildings tend to use the thinner sill. Modern design trends will be discussed later.

Parapet, Coping

A parapet is a low enclosing wall, usually extending above a roof. Exposed masonry must be capped to prevent moisture from entering between wythes and mortar joints. This cap or covering, usually of stone, or terra-cotta, is called a *coping*.

Mortar Joints

Two kinds of mortar are used: (1) cement or (2) hydrated lime— or combinations of both, with sand as the aggregate.

The desired finished appear-

Weyerhaeuser Company

Glazed facing tile is easy to maintain and withstands much abuse while retaining its beauty.

ance determines the size mortar joint to use. For ashlar a ½″ mortar joint is typical, but by no means the only size that may be used. Rustic type buildings may have mortar joints in excess of 1″. On rubble walls it is not uncommon to use 3″ of mortar between irregular spaces.

Questions to Reinforce Knowledge

1. What is masonry?
2. What is a solid masonry wall?
3. What is a masonry cavity wall?
4. What is a masonry veneer wall?
5. What is meant by the term header course?
6. What is a wall tie?
7. What is a wythe?
8. What is a hollow masonry unit?
9. How are two or more wythes of a cavity wall joined?
10. What is meant by the term facing?
11. What is a weep hole; where is it located?
12. How does one determine required thickness of a masonry wall?
13. What is the purpose of flashing; from the illustrations, what are two places where it is used?
14. What is a bond beam; why is it used?
15. How is a top plate secured to a masonry wall?

16. How many reinforcing rods are placed in a bond beam; where are they located?

17. What is parging, and what is its function?

18. When may plaster be applied directly to a masonry wall?

19. Think of two reasons for using furring strips on masonry walls.

20. Brick is available in how many standard colors?

21. What is face brick; where is it used?

22. What is common brick; where is it used?

23. Name five different kinds of brick and their sizes.

24. Name as many patterns of face brick as you can.

25. What is rubble? Is there more than one kind? Explain.

26. What is ashlar?

27. What is a coursed pattern for a masonry wall?

28. What are the common heights of ashlar? Thickness?

29. What is meant by the term split face?

30. How does one show and specify special stone shapes?

31. What is the standard thickness or height of stone sills?

32. How is stone purchased, in terms of weight and price?

Terms to Spell and Know

veneer	matt	shoring
terra cotta	velour	rubble
attaching	architectural	coursed
wythe	sandstone	ashlar
flashing	limestone	quarry
lintel block	granite	mortar
damp-proofing	marble	chat sawed
arches	lava	hydrated
capillary	quartz	rustic
silicone	strata	coping
parging	stratified	parapet
glazed	fieldstone	textures

9

Ceiling Joists and Roof Construction

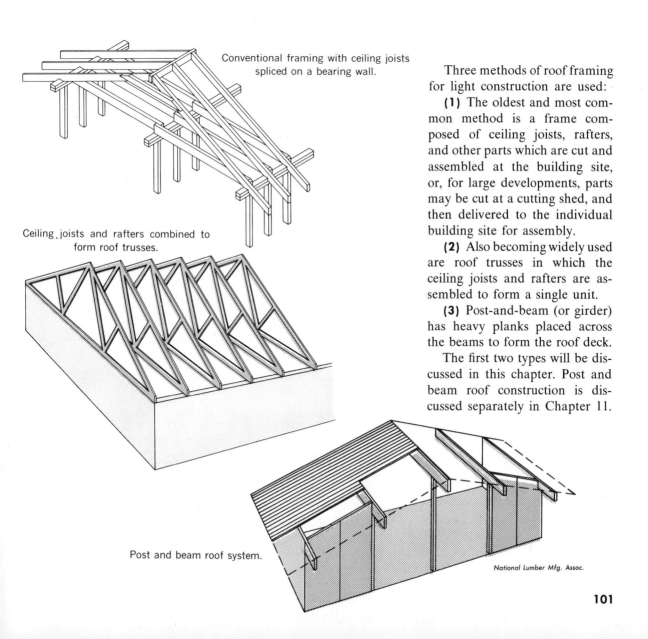

Conventional framing with ceiling joists spliced on a bearing wall.

Ceiling joists and rafters combined to form roof trusses.

Post and beam roof system.

National Lumber Mfg. Assoc.

Three methods of roof framing for light construction are used:

(1) The oldest and most common method is a frame composed of ceiling joists, rafters, and other parts which are cut and assembled at the building site, or, for large developments, parts may be cut at a cutting shed, and then delivered to the individual building site for assembly.

(2) Also becoming widely used are roof trusses in which the ceiling joists and rafters are assembled to form a single unit.

(3) Post-and-beam (or girder) has heavy planks placed across the beams to form the roof deck.

The first two types will be discussed in this chapter. Post and beam roof construction is discussed separately in Chapter 11.

Ceiling joists and rafters are in very close proximity and serve to counteract thrust forces of each other. Many times they are constructed as a single unit, as in roof trusses, or one of them may be omitted and the remaining member will be required to serve as both. For these reasons the discussion of ceiling joists and roof construction will be given in the same unit.

The discussion is primarily about light wood frame construction. However, other materials can serve equally well. For example, steel and aluminum manufacturers are supplying structural parts for light construction.

Ceiling Joists

Ceiling joists are structural members that support the finished ceiling and also floors of occupied space above. In addition, they act as tension members to resist the outward thrust of the rafters. The rafters exert constant outward pressure on the outside walls. The ceiling joists tie the building and prevent the tops of outside walls from spreading apart because of this pressure.

Splices in Ceiling Joists

If continuous ceiling joists do not extend across the building, they are spliced *over* an interior wall. When a wall supports the ceiling joists in this manner, we say the wall is *load bearing*. When joists are spliced they must be secured together and also secured to the wall supporting them. The joists may be lapped and *spiked* together, or a scab may be nailed

to the sides as shown in the illustration.

Determining Joist Size

Joist size is determined by the strength of the wood species to be used, by the joist span, and by the *net load* the ceiling is to support.

Since it is difficult to determine the exact weight of all structural parts, and since research and past experience indicate sizes that can be expected to support the structure, exact engineering data will not usually be compiled for light construction. It is common practice to use established minimum sizes from existing tables and charts.

The tables for ceiling joists and rafters used in this text show minimum standards established by the FHA. As mentioned earlier, one must check local codes to be certain these tables satisfy legal requirements.

Minimum Loads for Ceiling Joists

If the space above the ceiling joists is not to be used for occupancy, the rafter slope is greater than 3″ in 12″, and attic storage is desired, a *net load* of 30 pounds per square foot (psf) is adequate. This allows 20 psf. for live load and 10 psf. for dead load. If the slope of the roof is 3″ in 12″ or less and no attic storage is desired, the total net load may be 15 psf. The accompanying tables are based upon these strengths.

When ceiling joists serve as floor joists for occupancy above, strength requirements should be the same as for floor joists.

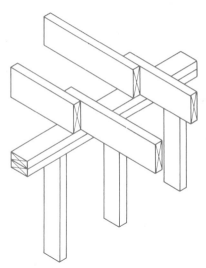

Ceiling joists may be lapped above a bearing wall.

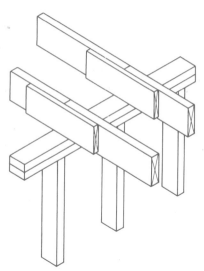

When ceiling joists are end joined above a bearing wall, scabs should be ¼″ above the lower edge of the joists.

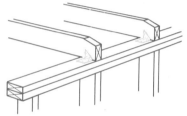

Ceiling joists may be secured to wall plates with metal connectors.

Ceiling Joists

DOUGLAS FIR, COAST REGION—ASSOCIATION LUMBER GRADES

Nominal size (inches)	Spacing (inches o.c.)	Select Structural 1950 f	Dense Construction 1700 f	Construction 1450 f	Standard 1200 f	Utility (¹)	Select Structural 1950 f	Dense Construction 1700 f	Construction 1450 f	Standard 1200 f	Utility (¹)
		NO ATTIC STORAGE					**LIMITED ATTIC STORAGE**				
2 x 4²	12	11 10	. . .	11 8	8 10	. . .	9 6	. . .	8 2	6 4	. . .
	16	10 10	. . .	10 0	7 8	. . .	8 6	. . .	7 2	5 6	. . .
	24	9 6	. . .	8 2	6 4	. . .	7 6	. . .	5 10	4 6	. . .
2 x 6	12	17 2	17 2	17 2	17 2	13 6	14 4	14 4	14 4	14 4	9 6
	16	16 0	16 0	16 0	16 0	11 8	13 0	13 0	13 0	12 10	8 4
	24	14 4	14 4	14 4	14 4	9 6	11 4	11 4	11 4	10 6	6 8
2 x 8	12	21 8	21 8	21 8	21 8	20 2	18 4	18 4	18 4	18 4	14 4
	16	20 2	20 2	20 2	20 2	17 6	17 0	17 0	17 0	17 0	12 4
	24	18 4	18 4	18 4	18 4	14 4	15 4	15 4	15 4	14 4	10 0
2 x 10	12	24 0	24 0	24 0	24 0	24 0	21 10	21 10	21 10	21 10	19 6
	16	24 0	24 0	24 0	24 0	22 6	20 4	20 4	20 4	20 4	16 10
	24	21 10	21 10	21 10	21 10	19 6	18 4	18 4	18 4	18 0	13 10

¹ Denotes grade is not a stress grade.
² Denotes light framing grade. (Not Industrial Light Framing)
Notes:
(a) Spans may be increased 5 percent from those shown for rough lumber or lumber surfaced two edges (S2E).

(b) Spans shall be decreased 5 percent from those shown for lumber more than 2 percent but not more than 5 percent scant from American Lumber Standards sizes measured at a moisture content of 19 percent or less. Lumber scant more than 5 percent will not be acceptable.

SOUTHERN YELLOW PINE—(MEDIUM GRAIN)—ASSOCIATION LUMBER GRADES

Nominal size (inches)	Spacing (inches o.c.)	No. 1 K.D. 2" Dimension 1700 f	No. 2 K.D. 2" Dimension 1500 f	No. 1 2" Dimension 1450 f	No. 2 2" Dimension 1200 f	No. 1 K.D. 2" Dimension 1700 f	No. 2 K.D. 2" Dimension 1500 f	No. 1 2" Dimension 1450 f	No. 2 2" Dimension 1200 f
		NO ATTIC STORAGE				**LIMITED ATTIC STORAGE**			
2 x 4	12	11 10	11 10	11 10	11 10	9 6	9 6	9 6	9 6
	16	10 10	10 10	10 10	10 10	8 6	8 6	8 6	8 6
	24	9 6	9 6	9 6	9 6	7 6	7 6	7 6	6 10
2 x 6¹	12	17 2	17 2	17 2	17 2	14 4	14 4	14 4	14 4
	16	16 0	16 0	16 0	16 0	13 0	13 0	13 0	12 10
	24	14 4	14 4	14 4	14 4	11 4	11 4	11 4	10 6
2 x 8	12	21 8	21 8	21 8	21 8	18 4	18 4	18 4	18 4
	16	20 2	20 2	20 2	20 2	17 0	17 0	17 0	17 0
	24	18 4	18 4	18 4	18 4	15 4	15 4	15 4	14 4
2 x 10	12	24 0	24 0	24 0	24 0	21 10	21 10	21 10	21 10
	16	24 0	24 0	24 0	24 0	20 4	20 4	20 4	20 4
	24	21 10	21 10	21 10	21 10	18 4	18 4	18 4	18 0

¹ Spans for 2" x 6" lumber having actual dressed size of 1⅝" x 5⅝" may be increased 2½ percent.
Notes:
(a) Spans may be increased 5 percent from those shown for rough lumber or lumber surfaced two edges (S2E).

(b) Spans shall be decreased 5 percent from those shown for lumber more than 2 percent but not more than 5 percent scant from American Lumber Standards sizes measured at a moisture content of 19 percent or less. Lumber scant more than 5 percent will not be acceptable.

Ceiling joist sizes and spacings.

Ceiling Joist Spacing

Ceiling joists are normally spaced on 16″ or 24″ centers, with the 16″ spacing usually preferred because this gives more support to the finished ceiling. When the 24″ spacing is specified and the ceiling is to be installed using prefinished materials, furring strips are sometimes placed at right angles to the joists on spacings that conform to the size of the material. When large sheet materials are used, as 4′x8′ panels, 16″ spacing is normally specified.

Framing for Attic Opening

Framing for openings should conform to good practice as described in Chapter 6, page 74. Attic access is usually provided in an inconspicuous place. Access to an attic with no storage space is frequently placed in a closet, while access to attic storage is frequently placed in the utility room or a hall. A disappearing stairway is convenient for gaining access to frequently used attic storage space.

Rafters

Rafters are the sloping structural members designed to support roof loads. Rafter size is determined by the strength of the wood species, by the sloping or rafter span, and by the net load the roof is to support.

From general observation you may have noticed roofs that were practically flat and ones that were very steep or any angle of slope in between. Climate is one of the determining factors of roof slope. In colder climates it is customary to build the slope quite steep to shed snow and ice, while in warmer climates this is not necessary, so roof slopes are generally quite low. A low slope represents a considerable saving in materials. However, low slope roofs must have greater strength to support additional live loads, such as an unusual snowfall. Current design tends to favor low slopes when at all permissible.

Securing Ceiling Joists to Wall

When ceiling joists and walls of the rooms *below* the joists are parallel to each other but the joists do not bear upon the wall, some provision must be made for securing the two together. Two methods of joining walls and ceilings are shown in the illustrations.

Beam or Girder to Support Joists Above Openings

If ceiling joists are at a right angle to an opening between rooms, as when a living and dining room have no wall between (open plan), a beam or girder must support the opening. If the beam protrudes below the finished ceiling, the joists may be lapped or spliced over the beam. However, if a smooth ceiling is desired between the two rooms, a ledger may be added to the beam as shown and the joists supported on the ledger. The ledger should equal ⅓ the total beam depth.

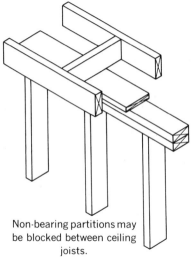

Non-bearing partitions may be blocked between ceiling joists.

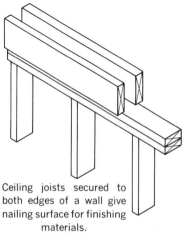

Ceiling joists secured to both edges of a wall give nailing surface for finishing materials.

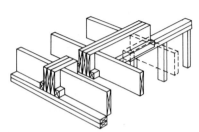

Built-up girders with ledgers permit level ceilings between rooms.

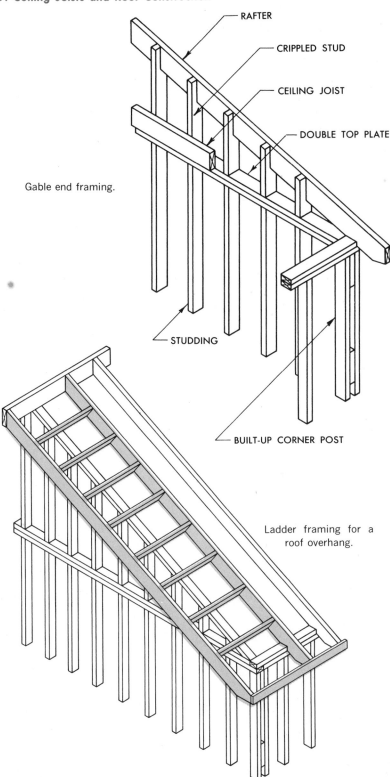

RAFTER

CRIPPLED STUD

CEILING JOIST

DOUBLE TOP PLATE

Gable end framing.

STUDDING

BUILT-UP CORNER POST

Ladder framing for a roof overhang.

Roof Types

Traditional design has developed standard roof types. The more common are shown in the illustrations on page 106.

These are not the only solutions to placing a roof on a structure. Modern design and experimentation have offered many unusual shapes. Some of the new shapes, based on an expanding technology, will certainly become standard forms of construction. Others are merely an attempt to find something new and different and have no structural advantage over existing types. Some of the more promising new shapes are illustrated.

To design a good roof requires a basic knowledge of the parts and how these parts are assembled into a finished structure. When complicated design is involved, it is necessary for the designer to supply framing plans describing the parts and their locations in relation to the other structural members.

Gable Roof

The gable roof is the most frequently used type. When more complicated types are used, the gable usually forms the basic part of the shape.

Building Span

Ceiling joists and rafters are usually placed across the shortest building dimension. The distance from one outer corner of the top plate to the opposite outer corner is the building span.

Frequently used roof shapes.

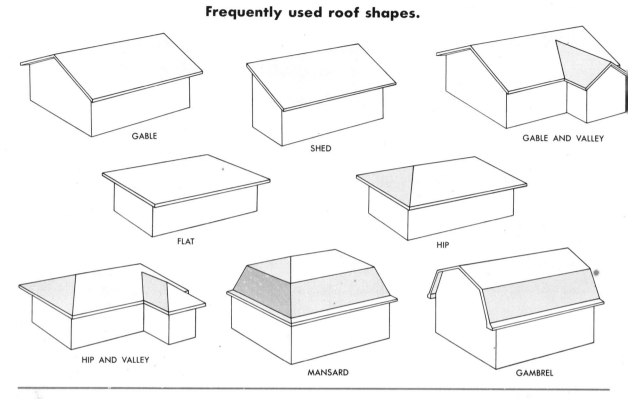

GABLE

SHED

GABLE AND VALLEY

FLAT

HIP

HIP AND VALLEY

MANSARD

GAMBREL

Roof shapes frequently used on contemporary buildings.

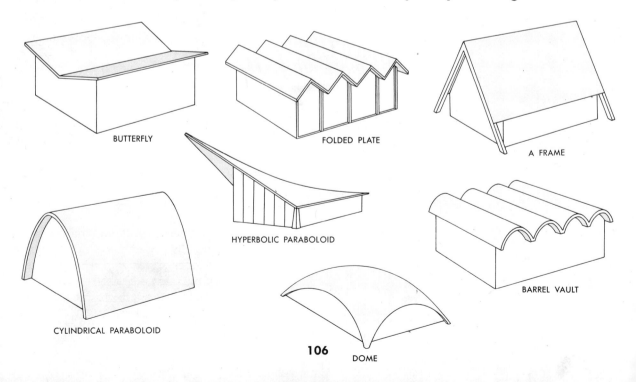

BUTTERFLY

FOLDED PLATE

A FRAME

HYPERBOLIC PARABOLOID

BARREL VAULT

CYLINDRICAL PARABOLOID

DOME

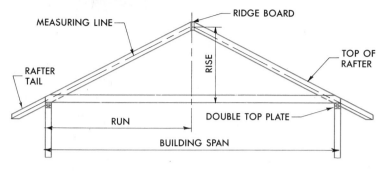

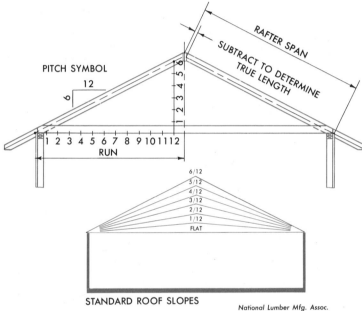

Roof construction data.

National Lumber Mfg. Assoc.

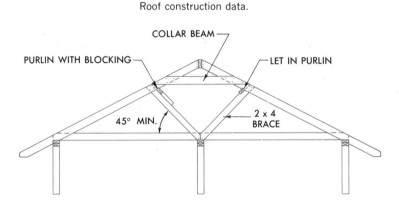

Collar beams and braces strengthen roof construction.

Rafter Run

The rafter run is the horizontal distance from one end of the rafter to the opposite end. When a ridge board is placed at the upper end of the rafters, the center of this board is considered as the point where each run terminates.

Rafter Notch at Top Plate

A flat bearing surface is necessary where rafters bear upon the top plate. A notch ("bird's mouth") is cut on the lower edge of the rafter so the notch is equal in width to the 2x4 top plate. When solid masonry walls are used and a wide top plate is placed covering both wythes, the notch is still made only 4″ wide. This is slightly variable.

Measuring Line of Rafter

The measuring line is an imaginary line running parallel to the edge of the rafter so that it passes through the inside 90° corner formed by the notch and extends the entire length of the rafter.

Rafter Tail

The rafter tail is the amount of rafter extending past the side of the building to form the overhang. The tail is not considered a part of the actual rafter length.

Rafter Span

The rafter span is the inclined or actual rafter length, measured from the 90° corner of the notch and following the measuring line to the center of the ridge board. NOTE: It is very easy to confuse rafter span with building span. Be sure you understand it. Also see illustrations on page 108.

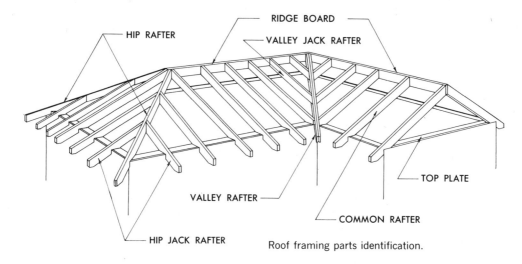

Roof framing parts identification.

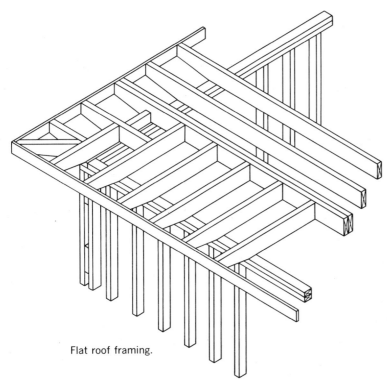

Flat roof framing.

(1) It is stated as a fraction, as full pitch, ½ pitch, ⅓, ¼, etc. On a full-pitch roof the rise is equal to twice the rafter run. This is also equal to the building span. On a ½ pitch roof the rise is equal to the rafter run. (2) The pitch is also stated as the amount of rise in inches in proportion to each 12 inches of run. Examples are 4/12, 5/12, 6/12, 10/12, or 12/12. This might also be stated as "6 inches to the foot," "10 inches to the foot," etc.

Rafter Angle

As stated earlier the rafter is designed in a ratio of rise to run. The rafter tables on the carpenter's framing square are also based on this ratio. The tables are tabulated in even inches of rise in proportion to 12″ or 1′ of run. It is not wise to design a roof with an uneven pitch such as 4½/12 because this prevents the workmen from using the tables on the framing square, greatly increasing labor costs because of the extra time involved.

Rise

Rise is the vertical distance from the lower edge of the ceiling joists to the rafter measuring line, when measured at the end of the rafter run.

Pitch

Pitch is the amount of slope or slant of the roof. It is described as the proportion or ratio of rise in relation to each foot of rafter run. Pitch is stated in two ways:

LOW SLOPE ROOF JOISTS OR RAFTERS

(Roof slope 3 in 12 or less)

DOUGLAS FIR, COAST REGION—ASSOCIATION LUMBER GRADES

Nominal size (inches)	Spacing (inches o. c.)	Select Structural 1950 f		Dense Construction 1700 f		Construction 1450 f		Standard 1200 f		Utility (1)		Select Structural 1950 f		Dense Construction 1700 f		Construction 1450 f		Standard 1200 f		Utility (1)	
		Light Roofing										Light Roofing									
		NOT SUPPORTING FINISHED CEILING										SUPPORTING FINISHED CEILING									
		FT.	In.	Ft.	In.	Ft.	In.	Ft.	In.	Ft.	In.	Ft.	In.	Ft.	In.	Ft.	In.	Ft.	In.	Ft.	In.
2 x 6	12	14	4	14	4	14	4	14	4	9	6	13	8	13	8	13	8	13	8	8	10
	16	13	0	13	0	13	0	12	10	8	4	12	4	12	4	12	4	11	10	7	8
	24	11	4	11	4	11	4	10	6	6	8	10	10	10	10	10	8	9	8	6	2
2 x 8	12	18	4	18	4	18	4	18	4	14	4	17	8	17	8	17	8	17	8	13	2
	16	17	0	17	0	17	0	17	0	12	4	16	4	16	4	16	4	16	2	11	6
	24	15	4	15	4	15	4	14	4	10	0	14	8	14	8	14	6	13	2	9	4
2 x 10	12	21	10	21	10	21	10	21	10	19	6	21	0	21	0	21	0	21	0	18	0
	16	20	4	20	4	20	4	20	4	16	10	19	6	19	6	19	6	19	6	15	8
	24	18	4	18	4	18	4	18	0	13	10	17	8	17	8	17	8	16	8	12	10
2 x 12	12	24	0	24	0	24	0	24	0	22	8	24	0	24	0	24	0	24	0	21	0
	16	23	6	23	6	23	6	23	6	19	8	22	6	22	6	22	6	22	6	18	2
	24	21	2	21	2	21	2	21	2	16	2	20	4	20	4	20	4	20	2	14	10

(Roof slope 3 in 12 or less)

SOUTHERN YELLOW PINE (Medium Grain)—ASSOCIATION LUMBER GRADES

Nominal size (inches)	Spacing (inches o. c.)	No. 1 K. D. 2″ Dimension 1700 f		No. 2 K. D. 2″ Dimension 1500 f		No. 1 2″ Dimension 1450 f		No. 2 2″ Dimension 1200 f		No. 1 K. D. 2″ Dimension 1700 f		No. 2 K. D. 2″ Dimension 1500 f		No. 1 2″ Dimension 1450 f		No. 2 2″ Dimension 1200 f	
		Light Roofing								Light Roofing							
		NOT SUPPORTING FINISHED CEILING								SUPPORTING FINISHED CEILING							
		Ft.	In.	Ft.	In.	Ft.	In.	Ft.	In.	Ft.	In.	Ft.	In.	Ft.	In.	Ft.	In.
2 x 6[1]	12	14	4	14	4	14	4	14	4	13	8	13	8	13	8	13	8
	16	13	0	13	0	13	0	12	10	12	4	12	4	12	4	11	10
	24	11	4	11	4	11	4	10	6	10	10	10	10	10	8	9	8
2 x 8	12	18	4	18	4	18	4	18	4	17	8	17	8	17	8	17	8
	16	17	0	17	0	17	0	17	0	16	4	16	4	16	4	16	2
	24	15	4	15	4	15	4	14	4	14	8	14	8	14	6	13	2
2 x 10	12	21	10	21	10	21	10	21	10	21	0	21	0	21	0	21	0
	16	20	4	20	4	20	4	20	4	19	6	19	6	19	6	19	6
	24	18	4	18	4	18	4	18	0	17	8	17	8	17	8	16	8
2 x 12	12	24	0	24	0	24	0	24	0	24	0	24	0	24	0	24	0
	16	23	6	23	6	23	6	23	6	22	6	22	6	22	6	22	6
	24	21	2	21	2	21	2	21	2	20	4	20	4	20	4	20	2

[1] Spans for 2″x6″ lumber having actual dressed size of 1⅝″x5⅝″ may be increased by 2½ percent.

Notes: (a) Spans may be increased 5 percent from those shown for rough lumber or lumber surfaced two edges (S2E).

(b) Spans shall be decreased 5 percent from those shown for lumber more than 2 percent but not more than 5 percent scant from American Lumber Standards sizes measured at a moisture content of 19 percent or less. Lumber scant more than 5 percent will not be acceptable.

Low slope rafter sizes and spacings.

RAFTERS

(Roof Slope over 3 in 12)

DOUGLAS FIR—COAST REGION—ASSOCIATION LUMBER GRADES

Nominal size (inches)	Spacing (inches o.c.)	LIGHT ROOFING Select Structural 1950 f	Dense Construction 1700 f	Construction 1405 f	Standard 1200 f	Utility (1)	HEAVY ROOFING Select Structural 1950 f	Dense Construction 1700 f	Construction 1450 f	Standard 1200 f	Utility (1)
2 x 4²	12	11 6	. . . .	9 6	7 4	. . . .	10 4	. . . .	8 2	6 4	. . . .
	16	10 6	. . . .	8 4	6 4	. . . .	9 6	. . . .	7 2	5 6	. . . .
	24	9 2	. . . .	6 10	5 2	. . . .	8 4	. . . .	5 10	4 6	. . . .
2 x 6	12	16 10	16 10	16 10	16 10	11 2	15 6	15 6	15 6	14 10	9 6
	16	15 8	15 8	15 8	15 0	9 8	14 4	14 4	14 0	12 10	8 4
	24	13 10	13 10	13 6	12 2	7 10	12 6	12 6	11 6	10 6	6 8
2 x 8	12	21 2	21 2	21 2	21 2	16 8	19 8	19 8	19 8	19 8	14 4
	16	19 10	19 10	19 10	19 10	14 4	18 4	18 4	18 4	17 6	12 4
	24	17 10	17 10	17 10	16 8	11 10	16 6	16 6	15 8	14 4	10 0
2 x 10	12	24 0	24 0	24 0	24 0	22 10	23 6	23 6	23 6	23 6	19 6
	16	23 8	23 8	23 8	23 8	19 8	21 10	21 10	21 10	21 10	16 10
	24	21 4	21 4	21 4	21 0	16 2	19 8	19 8	19 8	18 0	13 10

[1] Denotes grade is not a stress grade.

[2] Denotes light framing grade. (Not Industrial Light Framing)

Notes:

(a) Spans may be increased 5 percent from those shown for rough lumber or lumber surfaced two edges (S2E).

(b) Spans shall be decreased 5 percent from those shown for lumber more than 2 percent but not more than 5 percent scant from American Lumber Standards sizes measured at a moisture content of 19 percent or less. Lumber scant more than 5 percent will not be acceptable.

(Roof slope over 3 in 12)

SOUTHERN YELLOW PINE—MEDIUM GRAIN—ASSOCIATION LUMBER GRADES

Nominal size (inches)	Spacing (inches o.c.)	LIGHT ROOFING No. 1 K. D. 2" Dimension 1700 f	No. 2 K. D. 2" Dimension 1500 f	No. 1 2" Dimension 1450 f	No. 2 2" Dimension 1200 f	HEAVY ROOFING No. 1 K. D. 2" Dimension 1700 f	No. 2 K. D. 2" Dimension 1500 f	No. 1 2" Dimension 1450 f	No. 2 2" Dimension 1200 f
2 x 4	12	11 6	11 6	11 6	11 4	10 4	10 4	10 4	9 8
	16	10 6	10 6	10 6	9 10	9 6	9 6	9 4	8 6
	24	9 2	9 0	8 10	8 0	8 2	7 8	7 6	6 10
2 x 6¹	12	16 10	16 10	16 10	16 10	15 6	15 6	15 6	14 10
	16	15 8	15 8	15 8	15 0	14 4	14 4	14 0	12 10
	24	13 10	13 8	13 4	12 2	12 6	11 8	11 6	10 6
2 x 8	12	21 2	21 2	21 2	21 2	19 8	19 8	19 8	19 8
	16	19 10	19 10	19 10	19 10	18 4	18 4	18 4	17 6
	24	17 10	17 10	17 10	16 8	16 6	16 0	15 8	14 4
2 x 10	12	24 0	24 0	24 0	24 0	23 6	23 6	23 6	23 6
	16	23 8	23 8	23 8	23 8	21 10	21 10	21 10	21 10
	24	21 4	21 4	21 4	21 0	19 8	19 8	19 8	18 0

[1] Spans for 2"x6" lumber having actual dressed size of 1⅝"x5⅝" may be increased 2½ percent.

Notes: (a) Spans may be increased 5 percent from those shown for rough lumber or lumber surfaced two edges (S2E).

(b) Spans shall be decreased 5 percent from those shown for lumber more than 2 percent but not more than 5 percent scant from American Lumber Standards sizes measured at a moisture content of 19 percent or less. Lumber scant more than 5 percent will not be acceptable.

Rafter sizes and spacings.

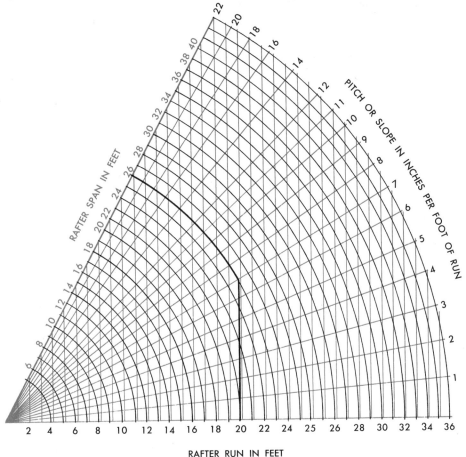

RAFTER RUN IN FEET

Rafter span conversion diagram.

Knowing the names of roof parts is very important if one is to convey their descriptions to other persons. Therefore study carefully the illustrations naming the parts. Proper methods of joining the parts can also be determined by studying the illustrations.

Rafter Tables Used in Text

Rafters for low slope roofs may also serve as a base for the finished ceiling on their lower side. In this case the same members serve as rafters and ceiling joists.

There are two sets of rafter tables in the text: one for *low slope* rafters and/or roof joists and one for *normal* rafters with a slope greater than 3″ in 12″ pitch. Each table is divided into two sections. The low slope tables are divided so the unfinished ceiling is to the left and the chart for finished ceilings is to the right. Rafters with a low slope are designed to accommodate lightweight roofing, which weighs less than four pounds per square foot. Any roofing that weights more than four

pounds per square foot is classed as a heavyweight roofing.

The low slope tables covering support of finished ceilings are based on a total design load for both stress and deflection of 35 pounds per square foot. The dead load has been calculated at 15 psf and the live load at 20 psf. Deflection is not to exceed $1/240$ of the clear span up to 15 feet. If the joists are longer than 15 feet the total deflection must not exceed ·¾″. See tables on pages 109 and 110.

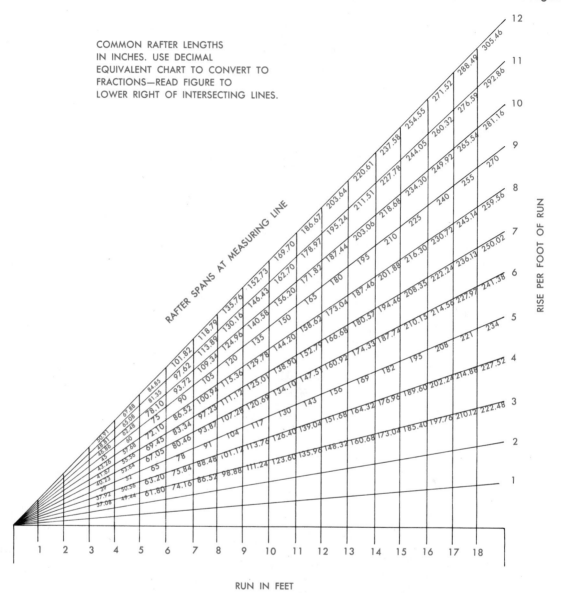

COMMON RAFTER LENGTHS
IN INCHES. USE DECIMAL
EQUIVALENT CHART TO CONVERT TO
FRACTIONS—READ FIGURE TO
LOWER RIGHT OF INTERSECTING LINES.

RAFTER SPANS AT MEASURING LINE

RISE PER FOOT OF RUN

RUN IN FEET

Low slope tables used in figuring supports for finished ceilings are based on a total design load for both stress and deflection of 30 psf. The dead load has been calculated at 10 psf and the live load at 20 psf. The allowable deflection is the same as for low slope roofs with finished ceilings. Study and compare rafter tables.

Rafters with a slope greater than 3″ in 12″ and designed for lightweight roofing are based on a total design load of 22 psf. The dead load has been calculated at 7 psf and the live load at 15 psf. Rafters designed for heavyweight roofing are based on a total load of 30 psf. The dead load has been calculated at 15 psf and the live load at 15 psf. Deflection is not to exceed $1/180$ of the clear span up to 15′. Over 15′ the deflection is not to exceed 1″.

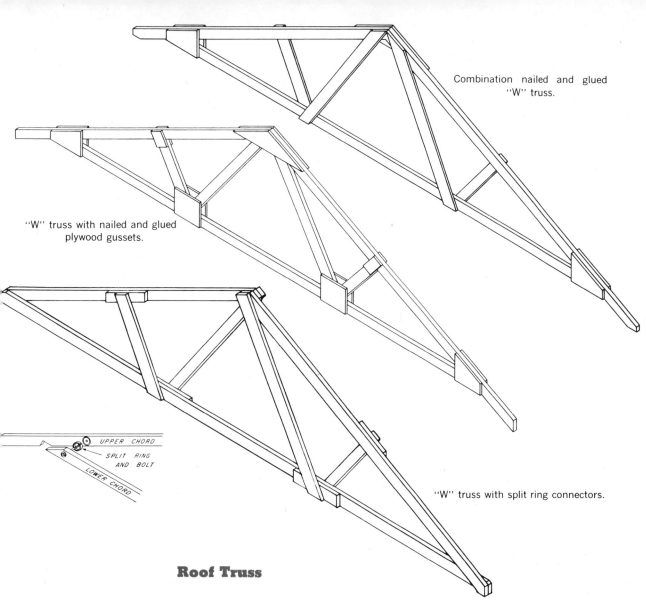

Combination nailed and glued "W" truss.

"W" truss with nailed and glued plywood gussets.

UPPER CHORD

SPLIT RING AND BOLT

LOWER CHORD

"W" truss with split ring connectors.

Roof Truss

Ceiling joists and rafters may be cut and assembled as a single unit, with structural support between the members. The triangular unit thus formed is called a roof truss. The truss has many advantages over conventional framing methods. (1) The structural members can be smaller than conventional framing and still furnish the same strength. (2) They may be purchased, thus reducing construction time and labor costs. (3) A truss bears only upon the outside walls, thus permitting a clear span the entire width of the building. This eliminates the need for bearing walls and permits the building to be framed as one large room. The building can be *closed in* after a minimum of time and the area used for working during the remainder of construction. Since no bearing walls are required, interior walls can be placed in any desired location.

Methods of Assembling Roof Truss

There are two common methods of assembling roof trusses. One method makes use of metal connectors and the other is by gluing and/or nailing. When a nailed, glued truss is used, plywood gussets, are used at joints.

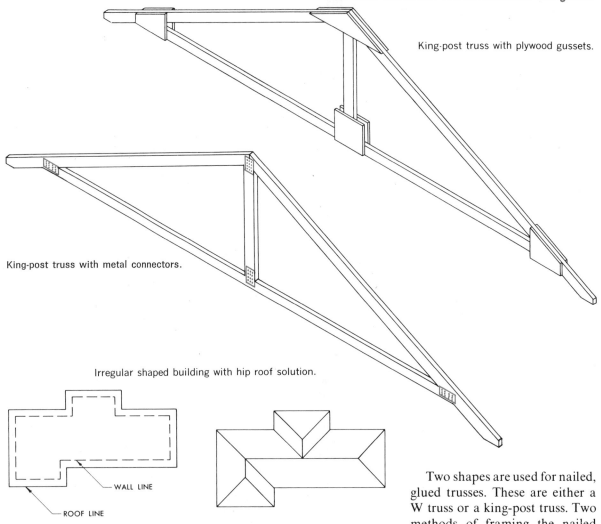

King-post truss with plywood gussets.

King-post truss with metal connectors.

Irregular shaped building with hip roof solution.

WALL LINE

ROOF LINE

Preliminary Design for Nailed Glued Trusses

Pitch 2/12 to 4/12	Span	Chords
W - Truss	20'-8" to 28'-8"	2 x 4
W - Truss	28'-9" to 40'-0"	2 x 6
Kingpost	18'-0" to 24'-0"	2 x 4
Kingpost	25'-0" to 32'-0"	2 x 6

Table of truss cords.

Two shapes are used for nailed, glued trusses. These are either a W truss or a king-post truss. Two methods of framing the nailed and glued W truss are shown, with the latter preferred.

All trusses should be designed conforming to standard engineering practice. Note that it is more practical to purchase them as manufactured units than to construct them at the building site.

Truss Spacing

The most common spacing for wood roof trusses is 2'-0" on center (o.c.). However, this is not the only spacing that may be used.

Questions to Reinforce Knowledge

1. What are three common methods of roof framing?

2. What are ceiling joists?

3. Where are splices in ceiling joists made?

4. What is a load bearing wall?

5. What is meant by a scab being nailed onto a joist?

6. What three factors determine ceiling joist size?

7. When do ceiling joists also serve as floor joists?

8. What is the preferred ceiling joist spacing?

9. What determines spacing of furring strips placed at right angles to the ceiling joists?

10. What are two methods of securing ceiling joists to walls parallel to the joists? Use sketches, if necessary.

11. If there is no wall between two adjoining rooms (open plan), how are the ceiling joists supported?

12. What special provision should be made when there is an opening through ceiling joists?

13. What is a rafter?

14. What factors determine roof slope?

15. Why are low slope roofs quite popular at the present time?

16. Name and describe as many roof types as you can.

17. What is the most frequently used roof type? Why?

18. What is meant by the term *building span*?

19. What is meant by the term *rafter run*?

20. Why is a rafter notched where it joins the top plate?

21. What is another name for the rafter notch?

22. Where is the rafter measuring line located? What kind of line is this?

23. What is a rafter tail?

24. What is rafter span?

25. What is rise?

26. What is pitch?

27. How are rise and run related to pitch?

28. What is a dormer?

29. What is a crippled stud?

30. From your own reasoning, why are rafters doubled at openings?

31. What special provision must be made when framing a gable to accommodate masonry veneer?

32. What is a ridge board, and what is its purpose? Do all buildings with a sloping roof have one?

33. What is a low slope roof?

34. What is lightweight roofing? Heavyweight?

35. What is a roof truss?

36. What are the advantages of a truss roof over conventional framing methods?

37. What are two methods of assembling roof trusses?

38. What is a W truss?

39. What is a king post truss?

40. Which is the stronger?

41. For typical light construction, what is the truss spacing most frequently used?

Terms to Spell and Know

counteract	prefinished
framing	furring
joists	traditional
rafters	gable
assembly	mansard
truss	gambrel
girder	butterfly
planks	parabola
roof deck	hyperparabola
tension	barrel
thrust	overhang
spiked	lightweight
nailed	heavyweight
species	W truss
slope	king post truss

10

Roofings

Definition of Roof Sheathing

Roof sheathing is the solid base material placed over the rafters or roof framing members to support the roof covering.

Concrete or Gypsum Base Sheathing

If a structure is of masonry and has steel or concrete roof framing members, the roof deck may be of concrete or gypsum. Sometimes this deck is made of concrete planks or it can be formed and poured. When gypsum is used as a roof deck it is not intended to support live loads other than water or snow. Gypsum is prepared with water in a mixer and sprayed onto the roof through a hose. It is leveled in much the same manner as concrete. When gypsum is used as a base for roofing it coats a form of fiberboard or corrugated metal. This form material is not removed; it acts as a sub-base for the roof. Two advantages of gypsum over concrete are its light weight and the short setting time for the material.

Concrete or gypsum roofs are covered with built-up roofing.

This type roof may be flat. Roofs of these materials are usually reserved for buildings of heavy construction. However, the concrete plank systems are used quite extensively in small masonry apartments and light commercial buildings. Two advantages are the speed of erection and its fire rating, which is Class A, as determined by Underwriters Laboratories. The planks are also very low in noise transmission, which makes them satisfactory as a flooring system.

Wood Roof Sheathing

Wood frame roofs using either

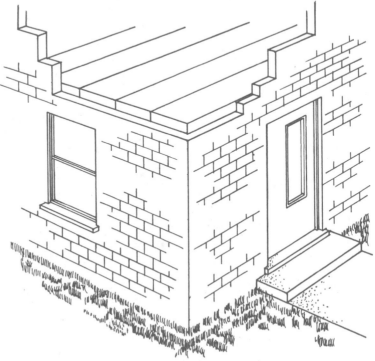

Concrete planks may be installed for floor or roof systems.

116

rafters or roof trusses are usually covered with a wood sheathing.

When wood shingles are to be used as a roof covering, 1"x3" strips are often placed across the rafters with vacant spaces between. This meets minimum requirements where wood shingles are permitted but makes additional work later if the shingles are replaced with other types of roofing, which requires that these spaces be filled in.

Solid Sheathing

Surfaced-four-sides (S4S) lumber is frequently used as roof sheathing. However, tongue-and-groove or shiplap lumber is more satisfactory because the edges are held securely together across the space between rafters.

Sheathing Lumber Sizes

When either S4S boards or edge-and-end matched lumber is used, and when minimum rafter spacing is 24" o.c. or less, nominal 1" (actually $25/32$") lumber is used. When greater rafter spacing is desired, additional sheathing thickness is also required. Tables of lumber thickness and spans are shown in Chapter 11, Post and Beam Construction. Tables of plywood thickness and spans are shown on page 118 of this chapter.

Breaking Joints in Sheathing

When S4S lumber is used, succeeding boards should not be spliced over the same rafter. The joints should be staggered or alternated. If end-matched lumber is used, a joint may be made between rafters but the board must rest upon at least two rafters.

Western Wood Products Assoc.

Wood strips are frequently used to replace solid sheathing when wood shingles are to form the finished roof.

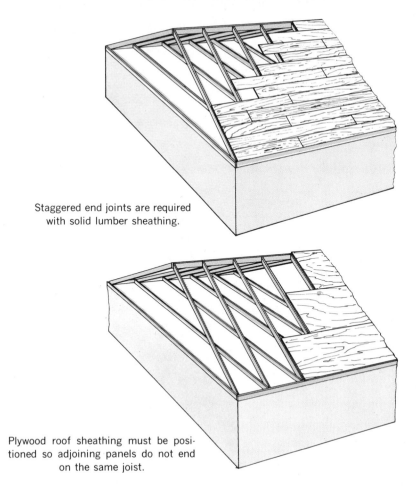

Staggered end joints are required with solid lumber sheathing.

Plywood roof sheathing must be positioned so adjoining panels do not end on the same joist.

ROOFS—Minimum Thicknesses, Spans and Nailing Schedules

(Grain of Face Plys. Across Supports; Stagger All Panel End Joints)

FHA requirements

When the minimum property standards of the FHA are met for each use, this agency allows the use of plywood in all parts of the home. This table sets out the basic FHA requirements.

SPECIES	PLY-WOOD THICK-NESS	MAXIMUM SUPPORT SPACING (Center to Center)					NAIL SIZE Common Nails (c)	NAIL SPACING	
		Asphalt or Wood Shingles or Shakes		(a) Built-up Roofing		Slate, Clay Tile or Asbestos-Cem. or Shingles Unblkd		Panel Edges	Inter-mediate
		Blkd (b)	Unblkd	Blkd (b)	Unblkd				
Douglas Fir, Western larch and Group 1 (C-C and C-D sheathing grades only) of Western softwood plywoods	5/16″	16″	16″	16″			6d	6″	12″
	3/8″	24″	20″	24″	16″		6d	6″	12″
	1/2″	32″	24″	32″	20″	16″	8d	6″	12″
	5/8″	42″	28″	42″	24″	24″	8d	6″	12″
	3/4″	48″	32″	48″	28″	32″	8d	6″	12″
Groups 2 and 3 of Western softwood plywood (d)	3/8″	16″	16″	16″			6d	6″	12″
	1/2″	24″	20″	24″	16″	16″	8d	6″	12″
	5/8″	32″	24″	32″	20″	20″	8d	6″	12″
	3/4″	42″	28″	42″	24″	28″	8d	6″	12″

(a) Flat roofs used for walking traffic such as sun decks shall use same construction as subflooring.

(b) Blocking of edges shall be by accurately cut wood blocking or by special metal clips designed for this purpose.

(c) Or 5d threaded nails for 5/16″ and 3/8″ plywood and 7d threaded nails for other thicknesses.

(d) This applies also to all grades identified as Group 1, excepting the sheathing grades (C-C and C-D) which if identified as Group 1 may take the same spans as Douglas fir.

American Plywood Assoc.

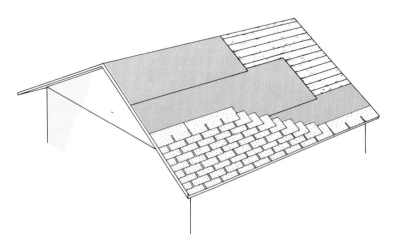

Building paper is fastened between roof sheathing and the exterior roof covering.

Width of Sheathing Boards

As stated in Chapter 6, wide boards warp more than narrow ones. When roof sheathing—also sometimes called decking or roof boards—warps, it presents an unsightly, irregular roof. It can also affect the quality because shingles may not lie flat, thus permitting wind to lift them from the roof. Boards no wider than 6″ are recommended.

Plywood Sheathing

Sheathing grade plywood (exterior unsanded) makes very fine roof sheathing. The advantages are the same as for sub-floors, discussed in Chapter 6. Tables for plywood roof sheathing are shown. Even though 5/16" and 3/8" thicknesses meet minimum requirements up to 30 pounds total live and dead loads for 24" rafter spacing, the deflection between rafters is sometimes visible to the observer. For this reason the author prefers a 1/2" minimum thickness, with 5/8" thickness more desirable if cost will permit.

When plywood sheathing is used, the face grain is placed across the joists. Examine carefully the notes at the bottom of the plywood sheathing tables to be sure all requirements are fulfilled.

Building Paper

After roof sheathing is in place, it is covered with felt building paper. Manufacturers recommend 15 pound paper for most applications. This protects the sheathing from the weather. It also serves as a partial vapor barrier. If the roofing is to be laid immediately, the building paper may be tacked in place with roofing nails or staples. However, with only nails holding the edges it is easily torn. Therefore it is usually held in place by tacking wood lath along the edges. This protects the paper from being torn by either the wind or workers' movements.

Roof Coverings

Built-up Roofing

Built-up roofing is used on flat or low slope roofs. It consists of alternate layers of asphalt and building felt. The final coat of asphalt is covered with gravel, slag, or stone chips (chat). The color and texture depend upon the material used. This type of roofing may be applied to almost any roof deck, since no nails or other mechanical fasteners are required. It is especially suitable for concrete and gypsum but may be used with wood, plywood, or fiberboard if adequate strength is provided at joints in the roof decking.

Most satisfactory results are obtained when the material is applied by a professional. Roof costs are based on the amount of time it can be expected to last. This depends upon the number of layers of asphalt and felt that are applied. It may be purchased with a 10, 15, or 20 year warranty.

Built-up roofing has several ad-vantages over other types. It has a Class A fire rating. It is easy to repair or replace and is very wind resistant.

The crushed stone placed in the outer layer serves chiefly as a decorative covering but also helps reflect the sun's rays.

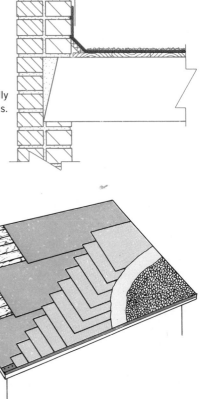

A built-up roof is long lasting and ideally suited to flat installations.

Low slope built-up roofs are widely used on contemporary homes.

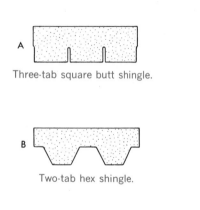

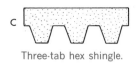

A — Three-tab square butt shingle.

B — Two-tab hex shingle.

C — Three-tab hex shingle.

D — Individual shingle.

E — Giant individual American shingle.

F — Dutch lap shingle.

Asphalt shingle patterns.

Asphalt Roll Roofing

Asphalt roll roofing is felt building paper impregnated with asphalt. It is purchased in rolls of 36″ width. It may be either smooth surfaced, with the asphalt exposed, or it may have stone granules imbedded in the outer surface. The granules may be distributed over the entire surface or they may be on only the lower half of the roll if double coverage (two layers) is not desired. Roll roofing may also be purchased with a patterned exposed edge.

This is a very inexpensive roof covering used on small utility farm structures or storage units where appearance is not a factor. This prohibits its use on most homes. Roll roofing is suitable for roof pitches of from 1/12 to 5/12. When it is used on low slope roofs, it is recommended that the lower edge be cemented and nailed to prevent water from running under the joint.

Asphalt Shingles

Asphalt shingles are of asphalt impregnated felt paper which is coated on the face with fine stone granules. They may be purchased in a wide variety of solid and variegated colors and in many different patterns. The more common are illustrated. Perhaps the most familiar is the 3-tab square butt shingle. The dimensions of strip shingles are 12″x36″. The amount of *tab* exposure to the weather (amount of shingle visible) is dependent upon the roof pitch and grade of shingle used. Five inches to the weather is a typical exposure. Low slope roofs or high wind areas may require cement under each tab to seal it to the roof, or the newer self-sealing shingles may be used.

For roof pitches of more than 2/12 the underlay paper should be head lapped 2″. For slopes less than 2/12 the underlay should be doubled. Asphalt shingles are purchased by the square, or 100 square feet. The standard weight is 215 pounds per square. However, some codes require up to a 275-pound weight.

Asphalt shingles are favored by many. They are easy to apply, have a good appearance, are fire resistant, and are reasonable in cost. They are usually applied over wood sheathing. When applying nails or staples to secure the roofing, care must be taken to avoid joints in the sheathing. If nails are not properly held they will work around in or through the outer surface, causing leaks.

Shingles are lapped over the gable rake and fascia from ¼″ to ⅜″ to prevent capillary action from drawing water under them. Metal edging or starter strip is recommended. When one observes asphalt strip shingles, the slits forming the tabs are seen. If the first course of shingles is placed on the roof in the regular manner, the felt underlay is exposed between the slits. One must use a strip of roll roofing or reversed shingles beneath this first course.

Asbestos Cement Shingles

Asbestos cement shingles are manufactured of asbestos fibers bonded in portland cement. They are usually striated or textured to resemble wood shingles. They are very durable except they are quite brittle and will shatter if struck a sharp blow. They are available in a great range of colors. There are no uniform standard sizes. Most companies manufacture individual shingles and wider widths resembling several shingles. These shingles are recommended for roofs with a pitch of 5/12 or greater but may be used on low slope roofs if special sealing precautions are taken. Asbestos cement shingles are fairly expensive and are therefore used primarily on institutional buildings and finer homes.

Corrugated asbestos cement sheets are used primarily for utility structures.

Clay Tile

Clay tile is manufactured of shale and clay in the form of baked masonry. There are many shapes of clay tile. If they are to be included in your plan secure detailed information from manufacturers literature. It is a very durable material and comes in a wide range of colors. It has several disadvantages. It is quite expensive, very heavy, and must be installed by an expert. It is used primarily for institutional buildings and expensive homes. It should be laid on a solid deck with 30 pound felt beneath the tile.

Wood Shingles

These shingles are used when a rustic appearance is desired. The thick butt (bottom end) provides a wide shadow line at the base. Wood shingles are manufactured of cedar, redwood, or cypress, with cedar being most frequently used. Wood shingles can actually be divided into two groups:

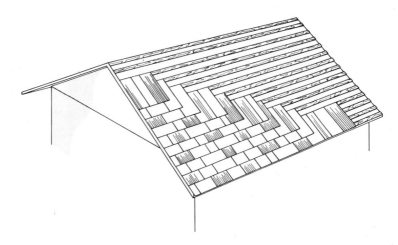

Random width wood shingles or shakes may be laid either on wood strips or solid roof sheathing covered with felt building paper.

(1) Wood shingles which are sawed to their shape and

(2) Wood shakes, split, either by machine or by hand.

The hand split is the more costly of the two. On less expensive split shakes the shingle is split on the face and then sawed (called resawing) to form a taper. In this way two shingles are formed from one piece of wood.

Many codes prohibit the use of wood shingles or shakes because of their fire hazard. However, when this is not a problem, they do present a pleasing appearance. They cost approximately three times the amount of a good quality asphalt shingle. As stated earlier, wood shingles are not usually laid on a solid roof deck. Strips are nailed across the rafters to conform to the amount of headlap desired.

Slate

Slate is a stone formed naturally into thin layers by earth forces. The shingle is the thickness of a layer but is cut into rectangles of the desired size. The surface may be smooth or rough, depending upon the effect desired. Slate makes a permanent roof but its high cost limits use. It is also easily broken if struck a sharp blow. It is installed in much the same manner as flat clay tile. Weight and cost are about the same.

Terne

Terne is sheet iron or steel coated with an alloy of tin and lead. It is purchased in rolls and may be applied on very low slope roofs. It may have either standing or flat locked seams. This roof should be painted or have a bituminous coating applied. It is installed over a solid roof deck. Terne is a good roof; if kept properly coated, under normal use, it will last indefinitely.

Properly designed standing seam metal roofs can contribute to overall architectural beauty.

It has very good fire and wind resistance. The cost is about three times as great as asphalt shingles.

Copper

Copper is purchased in rolls and applied in the same manner as terne. It is also a very durable material and makes a beautiful roof after the copper oxidizes to a warm green patina. The chief disadvantage of copper is its high initial cost, which prohibits its use on inexpensive structures.

Corrugated or Ribbed Galvanized Roofing

This comes in steel sheets formed with corrugations or ribs to add rigidity. The sheet is dipped into a hot zinc alloy to form a rust protective coating. The roofing is not intended for low slope roofs. It may be placed over a solid deck or may be placed vertically over purlins or furring without a roof deck. It is used primarily on utility structures as a finished roofing. However, it is sometimes used as a base for concrete, as previouly discussed. Because of the rust-resistant zinc coating, it may be left unfinished but painting assures better appearance and longer life. The sheets are 26″ wide and 6′ to 12′ long.

Corrugated or ribbed aluminum is similar in appearance and service to galvanized roofing. However, since aluminum does not rust, it need not be painted. The cost is slightly more than for galvanized but it is still primarily used for utility structures.

Corrugated and ribbed roofings also are often treated with fiber and bituminous coatings to prolong their life, improve appearance, and reduce noise.

Aluminum Shingles

Aluminum is also formed into individual and strip shingles, used for the same applications as asphalt shingles. The colors tend

Corrugated roofing is widely used on utility structures.

to be bright and have a glossy appearance. They are a very durable shingle. However, their noise transmission is great. They are lightweight and easy to apply. They are used on roofs with over a 4/12 pitch. Their cost is slightly more than for asphalt shingles.

Translucent Panels

These panels are manufactured in flat and corrugated styles. They are a relatively new product. Generally the panels are of either fiber glass or translucent acrylic plastic. Their uses are as varied as the imagination. They are especially suitable as inserts in roofs on industrial and utility structures, as they admit light but filter the sun's rays. Many buildings are being built using these panels as replacement for windows, or they are very satisfactory for carport and patio roofs. They work best on slopes over 4/12 but may be used on low slopes if the joints are calked or sealed. Panels are easy to cut and install using woodworking tools. The cost is greater than for metal roofing but is still satisfactory for low-priced structures.

Flashing

Where a vertical surface joins a roof the joint must be sealed. When two roof surfaces are joined they must also be sealed. Metal, plastic, or bituminous materials are placed in the joint to lead the water away. When planning a building the flashings must be described and specified. Examples of flashing at important locations are shown in the illustrations. These should be studied carefully.

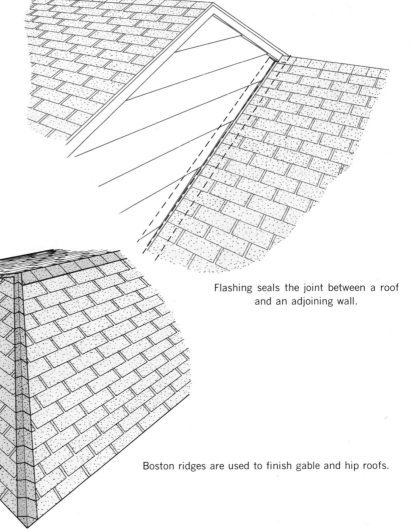

Flashing seals the joint between a roof and an adjoining wall.

Boston ridges are used to finish gable and hip roofs.

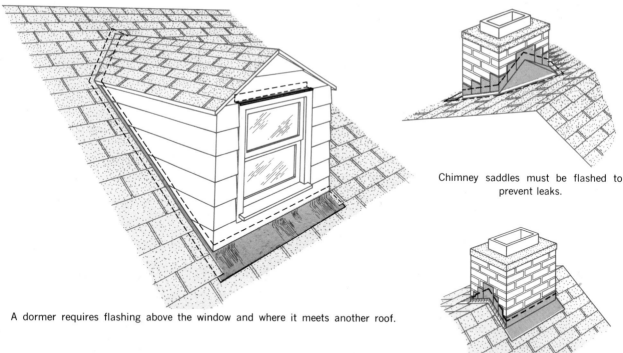

A dormer requires flashing above the window and where it meets another roof.

Chimney saddles must be flashed to prevent leaks.

Chimneys extending through a roof ridge should be flashed on all sides.

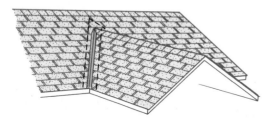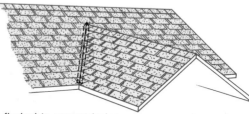

Both open and closed valleys should be flashed to prevent leaks.

Questions to Reinforce Knowledge

1. What is roof sheathing? What are two other names by which it is called?

2. When may concrete be used as a roof deck?

3. What are some of the advantages of a concrete roof deck?

4. When and why is gypsum used as a roof deck?

5. Are the forms removed when a gypsum roof deck is used? Explain.

6. What are some of the advantages of a gypsum roof deck? What is one disadvantage?

7. What are concrete planks, and why are they used?

8. Why is edge and end matched lumber better for roof sheathing than S4S lumber?

9. How thick is nominal 1″ lumber?

10. May boards ever be spliced between rafters? When?

11. Why are wide boards less satisfactory than narrow ones for roof sheathing?

12. What is likely to happen if wide boards are used?

13. What is sheathing grade plywood?

14. How does one determine what thickness of plywood to use?

15. What relationship does the face grain of the plywood have to the rafters?

16. What is building paper?

17. Why is building paper used beneath roofing?

18. How is it purchased?

19. What is built-up roofing?

20. Where is this most frequently used?

21. Is this a good material for flat roofs? Explain.

22. Why is crushed stone applied to the surface of built-up roofing?

23. What is asphalt roll roofing and where is it used?

24. How wide is asphalt roll roofing?

25. What are two surface treatments for asphalt roll roofing?

26. Can roll roofing be used on low slope roofs? Explain answer.

27. What are asphalt shingles? Is there more than one kind? Describe.

28. What is meant when one says 3-tab shingle?

29. When one says "to the weather," what is meant?

30. Are asphalt shingles widely used? Why or why not?

31. What special precaution must be taken when asphalt shingles are used on a low slope roof?

32. Why do shingles extend past the edge of a roof?

33. Why is the first course of asphalt shingles doubled?

34. What is an asbestos cement shingle? Is it a good shingle? Where is it most frequently used?

35. Is there more than one shape of clay tile? Explain.

36. What are the advantages of clay roofing tile?

37. Explain difference between wood shingle and a split shake.

38. Why do codes sometimes prohibit the use of wood shingles?

39. What is head lap on a shingle?

40. What is terne and how is it purchased?

41. Is terne a good roofing material?

42. Is terne suitable for flat roofs?

43. What is the life expectancy of terne?

44. Why does copper turn green?

45. What is corrugated roofing? Name the kinds and describe.

46. What are translucent corrugated panels and where are they used?

47. What is flashing? Is it a very important item on a building? Why?

Terms to Spell and Know

roofing	resistant	rustic
shingles	decorative	terne
matched	granules	bituminous
staggered	imbedded	oxidize
alternate	variegated	patina
decking	butt	ribbed
exterior	rake	zinc
staples	fascia	alloy
lath	tabs	fiber glass
asphalt	asbestos	acrylic
warranty	institution	translucent
	flashing	

11

Post, Plank and Beam Construction

Wood post and beam construction consists of a series of posts with heavy beams across them. The posts transmit the building load to the footing. The wall area between the posts does not add to the structural strength. The wall acts as a curtain to enclose the building. It may be a series of lightweight panels or may have conventional wall construction. A structure may be built in its entirety of post and beam or one section (such as a wall or roof) may be built using this method and the remainder may be built another way.

Post and beam is a very old method of construction. It was used extensively in early Ameri-

can building. It is also common in farm and utility structures. Even though modern building techniques and methods of joinery have improved, the basic principle is much the same as in earlier times. It is favored in heavy *mill construction* but not in homes.

New Uses

Because of post and beam application to modern structures, especially since the development of glued laminated beams, plywood box beams, and other laminated structural components, freedom of design has become virtually unlimited. Even so, the use of post and beam construction has not spread to all areas. Neverthe-

less, since the method is applied in modern structures, it is important.

Scope of Discussion

This unit is designed to familiarize you with the basic problems involved. It will also be an aid in preliminary design work. For final design purposes, engineering data and analysis should be studied.

Post and beam is a relatively simple system with many similarities to structural steel framing. However, because of the larger structural sizes, the need for framing connectors, and methods of joinery, the system presents new problems for one familiar with conventional framing.

Framing Systems

There are two general methods of beam placement. The first is called the *transverse* system. In this system, the roof beams follow the roof slope. The plank decking is at right angles to the beam, which permits roof decking to be placed in its customary position. The second method is called the *longitudinal* system. The beams

are at right angles to the roof slope. When decking is placed at right angles to the beams, it slopes from the highest to lowest point on the roof. See two drawings, top of next page.

Roof Slope

Post and beam construction is suitable for flat as well as all roof

slopes, which, as said, allows unlimited design possibilities.

Wood Posts

When floors are to be supported, 6"x6" wood posts are required. Posts for walls and to support ceiling beams should be 4"x4". Consult the codes, some require different calculations.

126

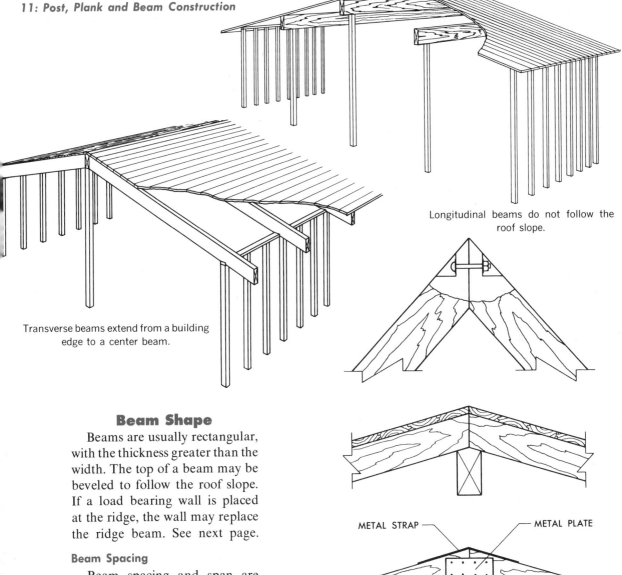

Longitudinal beams do not follow the roof slope.

Transverse beams extend from a building edge to a center beam.

Beam Shape

Beams are usually rectangular, with the thickness greater than the width. The top of a beam may be beveled to follow the roof slope. If a load bearing wall is placed at the ridge, the wall may replace the ridge beam. See next page.

Beam Spacing

Beam spacing and span are determined by the size and species of material used and by the total load to be supported.

When 2″ thick tongue-and-groove subfloor or roof deck is used the beam spacing is not to exceed 7′-0″. If greater beam spacing is desired, thicker planks must span the beams.

Three tables of beam sizes are given. See pages 129 and 130.

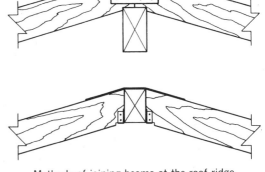

METAL STRAP — — METAL PLATE

Methods of joining beams at the roof ridge.

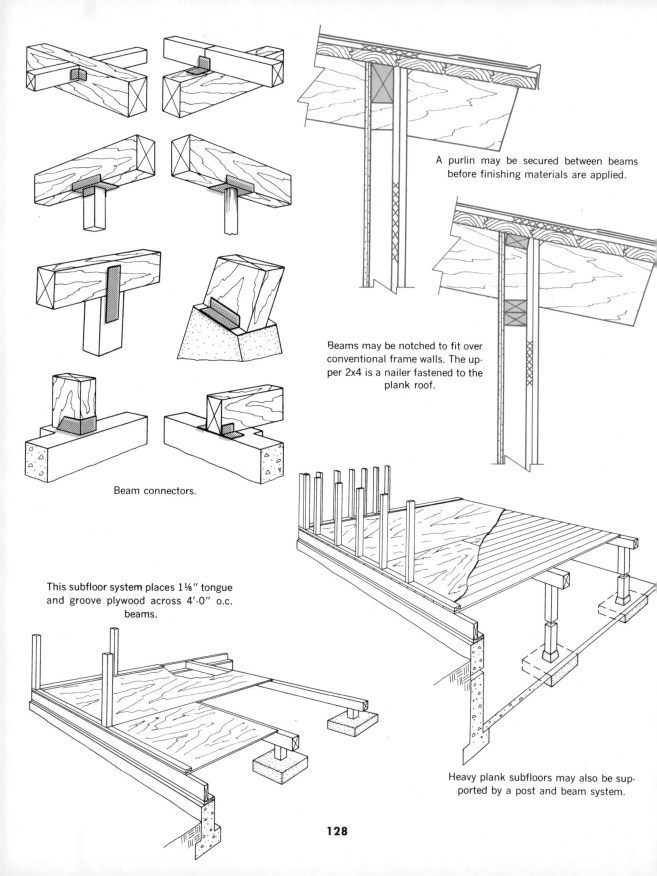

A purlin may be secured between beams before finishing materials are applied.

Beams may be notched to fit over conventional frame walls. The upper 2x4 is a nailer fastened to the plank roof.

Beam connectors.

This subfloor system places 1⅛″ tongue and groove plywood across 4′-0″ o.c. beams.

Heavy plank subfloors may also be supported by a post and beam system.

Maximum spans for floor beams using 2″ plank subfloor

Nominal Size	Spacing in feet	Douglas Fir S.Y. Pine	Redwood	Nominal Size	Spacing in feet	Douglas Fir S.Y. Pine	Redwood
1—3x10″	4'-0″	12'-8″	10'-4″	2—2x12″	4'-0″	16'-11″	13'-10″
	4'-6″	11'-11″	9'-9″		4'-6″	16'-0″	13'-1″
	5'-0″	11'-4″	9'-4″		5'-0″	15'-3″	12'-5″
	5'-6″	10'-10″	8'-11″		5'-6″	14'-6″	11'-10″
	6'-0″	10'-5″	8'-6″		6'-0″	13'-11″	11'-4″
	6'-6″	10'-0″	8'-2″		6'-6″	13'-5″	10'-11″
	7'-0″	9'-8″	7'-11″		7'-0″	12'-11″	10'-7″
2—2x10″	4'-0″	14'-0″	11'-6″	1—4x12″	4'-0″	17'-10″	14'-6″
	4'-6″	13'-3″	10'-9″		4'-6″	16'-10″	13'-9″
	5'-0″	12'-7″	10'-3″		5'-0″	16'-0″	13'-1″
	5'-6″	12'-0″	9'-10″		5'-6″	15'-3″	12'-6″
	6'-0″	11'-6″	9'-5″		6'-0″	14'-8″	12'-0″
	6'-6″	11'-1″	9'-1″		6'-6″	14'-1″	11'-6″
	7'-0″	10'-8″	8'-9″		7'-0″	13'-8″	11'-1″
1—4x10″	4'-0″	14'-9″	12'-1″	1—6x10″	4'-0″	17'-11″	14'-9″
	4'-6″	13'-11″	11'-5″		4'-6″	17'-0″	13'-11″
	5'-0″	13'-4″	10'-10″		5'-0″	16'-3″	13'-3″
	5'-6″	12'-9″	10'-4″		5'-6″	15'-6″	12'-8″
	6'-0″	12'-2″	9'-11″		6'-0″	14'-10″	12'-2″
	6'-6″	11'-9″	9'-7″		6'-6″	14'-3″	11'-8″
	7'-0″	11'-4″	9'-3″		7'-0″	13'-10″	11'-3″

Maximum spans for floor beams using 2″ plank subfloor. FHA

Maximum spans for roof beams using 2″ plank decking

Nominal size	Spacing in feet	Douglas Fir S.Y. Pine	Redwood	Nominal Size	Spacing in feet	Douglas Fir S.Y. Pine	Redwood
2—2x6″ or 1—4x6″	4'-0″	10'-1″	8'-3″	1—3x10″	4'-0″	15'-2″	12'-5″
	4'-6″	9'-7″	7'-10″		4'-6″	14'-4″	11'-9″
	5'-0″	9'-1″	7'-4″		5'-0″	13'-8″	11'-2″
	5'-6″	8'-8″	7'-0″		5'-6″	13'-0″	10'-8″
	6'-0″	8'-4″	6'-9″		6'-0″	12'-6″	10'-2″
	6'-6″	8'-0″	6'-6″		6'-6″	12'-0″	9'-10″
	7'-0″	7'-8″	6'-3″		7'-0″	11'-7″	9'-6″
2—2x8″ or 1—4x8″	4'-0″	13'-4″	10'-11″	2—2x10″ or 1—4x10″	4'-0″	16'-9″	13'-8″
	4'-6″	12'-8″	10'-4″		4'-6″	15'-10″	12'-11″
	5'-0″	12'-0″	9'-10″		5'-0″	15'-1″	12'-4″
	5'-6″	11'-6″	9'-4″		5'-6″	14'-5″	11'-10″
	6'-0″	11'-0″	9'-0″		6'-0″	13'-10″	11'-4″
	6'-6″	10'-7″	8'-8″		6'-6″	13'-4″	10'-10″
	7'-0″	10'-3″	8'-4″		7'-0″	12'-10″	10'-6″

Maximum spans for roof beams using 2″ plank decking. FHA

Typical Glued Laminated Beam and Purlin Sizes*

TOTAL LOAD (LIVE AND DEAD)

SPAN	SPCG.	30 P.S.F.	35 P.S.F.	40 P.S.F.	45 P.S.F.	50 P.S.F.	55 P.S.F.
12'	6'	3⅜" x 6½"	3⅜" x 6½"	3⅜" x 6½"	3⅜" x 8⅛"	3⅜" x 8⅛"	3⅜" x 8⅛"
	8'	3⅜" x 8⅛"	3⅜" x 8⅛"	3⅜" x 8⅛"	3⅜" x 8⅛"	3⅜" x 8⅛"	3⅜" x 9¾"
	12'	3⅜" x 8⅛"	3⅜" x 8⅛"	3⅜" x 9¾"	3⅜" x 9¾"	3⅜" x 11⅜"	3⅜" x 11⅜"
	16'	3⅜" x 9¾"	3⅜" x 9¾"	3⅜" x 11⅜"	3⅜" x 13"	3⅜" x 14⅝"	3⅜" x 14⅝"
16'	6'	3⅜" x 8⅛"	3⅜" x 9¾"	3⅜" x 9¾"	3⅜" x 9¾"	3⅜" x 9¾"	3⅜" x 9¾"
	8'	3⅜" x 9¾"	3⅜" x 9¾"	3⅜" x 9¾"	3⅜" x 11⅜"	3⅜" x 11⅜"	3⅜" x 11⅜"
	12'	3⅜" x 11⅜"	3⅜" x 11⅜"	3⅜" x 13"	3⅜" x 13"	3⅜" x 14⅝"	5¼" x 11⅜"
	16'	3⅜" x 13"	3⅜" x 13"	5¼" x 11⅜"	5¼" x 11⅜"	5¼" x 13"	5¼" x 13"
20'	8'	3⅜" x 11⅜"	3⅜" x 11⅜"	5¼" x 11⅜"	5¼" x 11⅜"	5¼" x 11⅜"	5¼" x 11⅜"
	12'	3⅜" x 13"	3⅜" x 14⅝"	5¼" x 13"	5¼" x 13"	5¼" x 13"	5¼" x 14⅝"
	16'	3⅜" x 14⅝"	5¼" x 13"	5¼" x 14⅝"	5¼" x 14⅝"	5¼" x 16¼"	5¼" x 16¼"
	18'	5¼" x 13"	5¼" x 14⅝"	5¼" x 14⅝"	5¼" x 16¼"	5¼" x 16¼"	5¼" x 17⅞"
24'	8'	3⅜" x 14⅝"	3⅜" x 14⅝"	3⅜" x 14⅝"	5¼" x 13"	5¼" x 14⅝"	5¼" x 14⅝"
	12'	3⅜" x 16¼"	5¼" x 13"	5¼" x 14⅝"	5¼" x 14⅝"	5¼" x 16¼"	5¼" x 16¼"
	16'	5¼" x 14⅝"	5¼" x 16¼"	5¼" x 16¼"	5¼" x 17⅞"	5¼" x 17⅞"	5¼" x 19½"
	18'	5¼" x 16¼"	5¼" x 16¼"	5¼" x 17⅞"	5¼" x 19½"	5¼" x 19½"	5¼" x 21⅛"
28'	8'	3⅜" x 16¼"	3⅜" x 16¼"	5¼" x 14⅝"	5¼" x 16¼"	5¼" x 16¼"	5¼" x 16¼"
	12'	5¼" x 16¼"	5¼" x 16¼"	5¼" x 17⅞"	5¼" x 17⅞"	5¼" x 17⅞"	5¼" x 19½"
	16'	5¼" x 17⅞"	5¼" x 17⅞"	5¼" x 19½"	5¼" x 21⅛"	5¼" x 21⅛"	5¼" x 22¾"
	18'	5¼" x 17⅞"	5¼" x 19½"	5¼" x 21⅛"	5¼" x 19½"	5¼" x 22¾"	5¼" x 24⅜"
32'	8'	5¼" x 16¼"	5¼" x 16¼"	5¼" x 17⅞"	5¼" x 17⅞"	5¼" x 17⅞"	5¼" x 19½"
	12'	5¼" x 17⅞"	5¼" x 19½"	5¼" x 19½"	5¼" x 19½"	5¼" x 21⅛"	5¼" x 22¾"
	16'	5¼" x 19½"	5¼" x 21⅛"	5¼" x 22¾"	5¼" x 22¾"	5¼" x 24⅜"	5¼" x 26"
	18'	5¼" x 19½"	5¼" x 21⅛"	5¼" x 22¾"	5¼" x 24⅜"	7" x 22¾"	7" x 24⅜"
40'	8'	5¼" x 19½"	5¼" x 21⅛"	5¼" x 21⅛"	5¼" x 22¾"	5¼" x 22¾"	5¼" x 24⅜"
	12'	5¼" x 22¾"	5¼" x 22¾"	5¼" x 24⅜"	5¼" x 24⅜"	5¼" x 26"	7" x 24⅜"
	16'	5¼" x 24⅜"	5¼" x 26"	7" x 24⅜"	7" x 24⅜"	7" x 26"	7" x 27⅝"
	18'	5¼" x 24⅜"	7" x 24⅜"	7" x 24⅜"	7" x 26"	7" x 27⅝"	7" x 29¼"
50'	12'	7" x 24⅜"	7" x 26"	7" x 27⅝"	7" x 27⅝"	7" x 29¼"	7" x 30⅞"
	16'	7" x 27⅝"	7" x 29¼"	7" x 30⅞"	7" x 30⅞"	7" x 32½"	9" x 30⅞"
	18'	7" x 29¼"	7" x 29¼"	7" x 30⅞"	7" x 32½"	9" x 30⅞"	9" x 32½"
	20'	7" x 29¼"	7" x 30⅞"	7" x 32½"	9" x 30⅞"	9" x 32½"	9" x 34⅛"
60'	12'	7" x 29¼"	7" x 30⅞"	9" x 30⅞"	9" x 30⅞"	9" x 32½"	9" x 34⅛"
	16'	9" x 30⅞"	9" x 32½"	9" x 32½"	9" x 34⅛"	9" x 35¾"	9" x 37⅜"
	18'	9" x 29⅞"	9" x 32½"	9" x 34⅛"	9" x 35¾"	9" x 37⅜"	9" x 39"
	20'	9" x 32½"	9" x 34⅛"	9" x 35¾"	9" x 37⅜"	9" x 39"	9" x 40⅝"

*This table of typical sizes is based on the following criteria.
1. The loading shown is total load of which 15 p.s.f. is assumed to be dead load.
2. Maximum bending stress is 2200 p.s.i. + 15% increase for short time loading.
3. Deflection limit is 1/240 of span for live load only or 1/180 of span for total load, whichever governs. This meets the A.I.T.C. deflection criteria for "Commercial and Institutiona l— Without Plaster Ceiling" use.

Weyerhaeuser Company

Glued laminated beam and purlin sizes.

The first table, page 129, is for floor beams using 2″ plank subfloor. The second table, same page, is for ceiling beams using 2″ wood plank decking. The third table is to be used if wider floor or ceiling beam spacing is desired. This table is calculated for glued laminated lumber. When solid beams are desired their strength is approximately the same. This table is suitable for coast region Douglas fir and medium-grain southern yellow pine. When other species are desired, consult other tables.

Roof Decking

There are three methods of laying roof planks: (1) They may form simple spans placed from one beam to the next beam; (2) they may be continuous over two beams or, (3) they may be placed at random. When placed at random, succeeding planks should not both end between the same beams. Illustrations showing the three methods of installation and tables of maximum spans are shown. Spans for roof planks for Douglas fir are also suitable for southern yellow pine. NOTE: Yellow pine has slightly greater strength.

Fiberboard roof decks are also used but their span is usually limited to 8′-0″.

Decking should be face and edge nailed according to the manufacturer's directions.

Insulation for Plank Roof

For most regions the roof decking will be sufficient insulation.

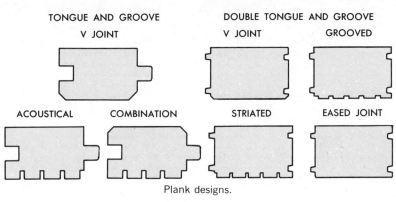

Plank designs.

Roof Decking

SIMPLE SPAN

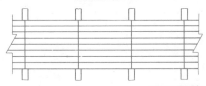

Douglas Fir

NOM. THICK.	GRADE AND PARA.	LIVE LOAD (Lbs. per Sq. Ft.) 20	30	40	50
3″	Select Dex—127-b	15′3″	13′3″	12′0″	11′3″
3″	Comm. Dex—127-c	15′3″	13′3″	12′0″	11′3″
4″	Select Dex—127-b	20′3″	17′9″	16′0″	15′0″
4″	Comm. Dex—127-c	20′3″	17′9″	16′0″	15′0″

Western Red Cedar

NOM. THICK.	GRADE AND PARA.	20	30	40	50
3″	Select Dex—427-b	13′0″	11′3″	10′3″	9′6″
3″	Comm. Dex—427-c	13′0″	11′3″	10′3″	9′6″
4″	Select Dex—427-b	17′3″	15′3″	13′9″	12′9″
4″	Comm. Dex—427-c	17′3″	15′3″	13′9″	12′9″

COMB. SIMPLE + 2-SPAN CONTINUOUS

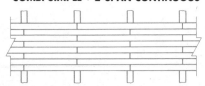

Douglas Fir

NOM. THICK.	GRADE AND PARA.	LIVE LOAD (Lbs. per Sq. Ft.) 20	30	40	50
3″	Select Dex—127-b	17′3″	15′0″	13′6″	12′6″
3″	Comm. Dex—127-c	17′3″	15′0″	13′6″	12′6″
4″	Select Dex—127-b	22′9″	20′0″	18′3″	16′9″
4″	Comm. Dex—127-c	22′9″	20′0″	18′3″	16′9″

Western Red Cedar

NOM. THICK.	GRADE AND PARA.	20	30	40	50
3″	Select Dex—427-b	14′9″	12′9″	11′9″	10′9″
3″	Comm. Dex—427-c	13′6″	12′0″	10′9″	10′0″
4″	Select Dex—427-b	19′6″	17′0″	15′6″	14′3″
4″	Comm. Dex—427-c	18′0″	16′0″	14′3″	13′3″

(Table continued on next page.)

Roof Decking
RANDOM LENGTH

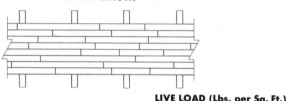

Douglas Fir					
NOM. THICK.	GRADE AND PARA.	20	30	40	50
3″	Select Dex—127-b	16′9″	14′6″	13′3″	12′3″
3″	Comm. Dex—127-c	16′9″	14′6″	13′3″	12′3″
4″	Select Dex—127-b	22′0″	19′3″	17′6″	16′3″
4″	Comm. Dex—127-c	22′0″	19′3″	17′6″	16′3″
Western Red Cedar					
3″	Select Dex—427-b	14′3″	12′3″	11′3″	10′6″
3″	Comm. Dex—427-c	13′6″	12′0″	10′9″	10′0″
4″	Select Dex—427-b	19′0″	16′3″	15′0″	14′0″
4″	Comm. Dex—427-c	18′0″	16′0″	14′9″	13′3″

LIVE LOAD (Lbs. per Sq. Ft.)

West Coast Lumberman's Association

When additional insulation is required, it may be placed above or below the decking. The planks are usually left exposed on the underneath side and rigid insulation is placed above the decking.

Purlins

When beam spacing is too great for plank spans, intermediate members may be placed across the top of—or hung between—the beams, and secured with metal connectors. These intermediate members are called purlins. When beams are to be left exposed but the plank decking is not (as when acoustic tile is the finished ceiling), purlins are usually used.

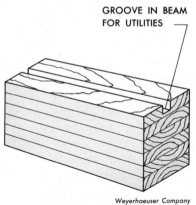

GROOVE IN BEAM FOR UTILITIES

Weyerhaeuser Company

Groove in beam for utilities.

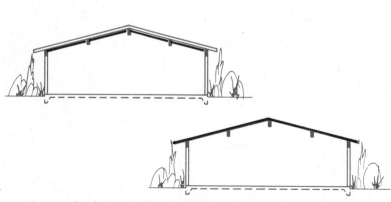

Insulation may be placed either above or below roof decking.

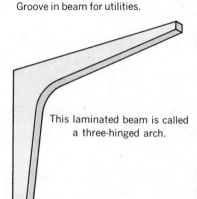

This laminated beam is called a three-hinged arch.

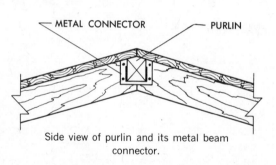

METAL CONNECTOR — PURLIN

Side view of purlin and its metal beam connector.

Provision for Utilities

One big disadvantage of this method is that there is no "attic" or space between framing for concealed wiring and other utilities. It is sometimes possible to rout grooves in the top of beams or to leave channels in built-up members to accommodate these utilities. However, when lighting fixtures are spaced between beams (on the planks) it is virtually impossible to conceal them. They are usually surface mounted.

Quite frequently the post and beam is constructed as a single unit, as in the three-hinged arch shown. Examples of buildings using plank and beam construction are illustrated on this page.

This gymnasium roof is supported by laminated beams and purlins.

133

Laminated beams are widely used in today's building. The arch is an example.

Questions to Reinforce Knowledge

1. What is wood post and beam (plank and beam) construction?

2. Is it a new method of construction?

3. Is it used in homes today?

4. Is it the most widely used method of construction?

5. What is the main difference in the ways it is now used as compared with the past?

6. What are glued laminated components?

7. Are posts and beams ever built as one unit? Explain.

8. What are the two beam placement systems? Discuss each.

9. What roof slope must one use with this type construction?

10. When wood posts support finished floors, what is their minimum size?

11. Posts for walls and to support ceiling beams are what minimum size?

12. Which of the two beam dimensions, vertical or horizontal, is largest?

13. If 2″ thick plank is used for subfloor or roof deck, what is the maximum beam spacing?

14. Are glued laminated and solid beams of the same species and other characteristics approximately the same strength?

15. What are three methods of placing planks across roof beams?

16. Which is the stronger, southern yellow pine or Douglas fir?

17. Why is insulation sometimes placed above the decking?

18. What is another name for decking?

19. What are purlins?

20. What are metal connectors? Do you know another name for them?

21. Why are electrical work and utilities sometimes difficult to place with this method of construction?

Terms to Spell and Know

joinery	planks
laminated	insulation
components	purlins
transverse	acoustic
longitudinal	rout
beveled	channels

12

Modular Construction

As stated in the first paragraph of Chapter 7, building construction has traditionally been done one piece at a time. There are many reasons why buildings can no longer be built entirely in this manner. No doubt you have heard the old saying, "Time is money." A builder must do everything within his power to complete a structure in the most efficient and economical manner possible. If he does not have a highly organized and efficient operation, he cannot survive in today's competitive market. Use of preassembled components, prefabrication, and modular coordination help him meet today's competition. These methods permit uniform sizes of parts, close quality control, and rapid erection.

Components

Components are large pre-assembled building parts such as roof trusses, window units, or framed panels for floors, walls, or roofs. The latter may be constructed using a variety of materials and different panel systems. Large sheet materials (plywood, drywall, fiberboard, hardboard, or others) are glued and nailed to a skeleton framework, forming main structural panels. These may be assembled at the job site to form a building shell or they may be purchased or constructed to varying stages of completion. For example, the panels might be studding covered with sheathing, or they might be completed wall sections ready for interior finish. There is no one standard panel system, many organizations have developed systems.

Large construction panels are not confined to any one material. Wood is most frequently used for light construction but metal and plastics work equally well. Plastics are usually used as coverings or decorative units. Curtain walls, exposed aggregate panels, and other masonry units all lend themselves to this modular system of construction.

Prefabrication

Prefabrication is the manufacture of all building parts in a factory. These parts are usually assembled into large panels before shipment to the building site. Prefabrication is not new. Earliest uses date to the latter part of the nineteenth century. However, the totally prefabricated structure with mass-production volume did not have a significant impact upon building construction until immediately following World War II.

Early attempts at production-line building left the manufacturers with a poor reputation. Insufficient research, poor design, and a "seller's market" made a victim of the consumer. Consequently, after supply and demand became reversed and the consumer could bargain better, prefabricated structures had lost favor. Prejudice from these early attempts still affects opinion of many people. Yet the prefabricated structure of today bears little resemblance to early attempts. For example, homes in the $100,000.00 class are now partially or substantially prefabricated before delivery.

The objection that all prefabricated structures were similar in appearance has been remedied. Stock models are supplied in a wide variety of designs and variations of architectural details. Many large manufacturers maintain their own architects and permit extensive design freedom to the buyer.

Building components of this prefabricated home are sized according to modular increments.   *Scholz Homes Inc.*

Designs are completed and the building is fabricated to order. Prefabrication has become widely used for every type of structure, including homes, commercial and industrial buildings. Structural parts may be of wood, metal, or more recently of masonry.

For those who do not desire a totally prefabricated building, one may purchase ready-cut parts and then have the individual parts assembled at the building site. The design is chosen from one of a series of stock plans which may be altered to meet any requirement, or some manufacturers will cut a complete building from the owner's plan. Each part is numbered as to its location in the finished structure. Ready-cut buildings may be purchased in any stage of completion to suit the wishes of the purchaser. These buildings are quite popular with amateur builders.

Need for Standardization

In order to make maximum use of building materials and construction labor, standardization of sizes and methods of construction are necessary. If each manufacturer were to decide all the dimensions of his products and manufacture them to any size he desired, complete chaos would result. Lumber thickness from one company would not match the thickness from another. There might not be a relationship between the size of concrete blocks and brick. Plywood or fiberboard sheathing sizes might differ from rock lath or plasterboard sizes, which would complicate studding placement. There might be no standard door thickness, which would require door jambs to be custom built. The list of possible size variations would be infinite. Standardization is necessary if volume and quality production is to be achieved.

Manufacturers, suppliers, architects, building contractors, and tradesmen agree that standardization of materials sizes, components, and construction methods is the key to a better structure at minimum cost.

It is very easy to say that standardization is necessary but very difficult to accomplish. Each of the groups of people mentioned above has little influence on the thinking of the others!

Size of Building Modules

The novice soon becomes familiar with the 16″ and 24″ spacing of framing members. Which is a step toward use of modular sizes. Since dimensions between framing members have already been accepted as standards, reason says they should be a part of basic modular sizes. Also, since most large sheet materials are already manufactured in 4'-0" widths, this size is considered the starting point for all standard sizes of material.

Imagine a group of building blocks (toys) that can be arranged into an unlimited number of complicated designs. Building modules are like these toys except they are larger. One module may be compared to a 4" block or cube. This is called a *module*. Imagine a 4'-0" cube constructed of 4" modules; this is called a *major module*. A 16" or 24" cube is called a *minor module*. Two 16" minor modules are sometimes combined to form a third minor module of 32".

Modular Coordination

The attempt to acquaint *all* people in every phase of the building industry with these three basic modules, and to persuade them to incorporate them into their products, designs, or construction is called *modular coordination*.

Efforts promoting the modular concept of building are directed toward the following:

• Acquainting individuals with the concept, terms, sizes, and uses of modules.

• Urging building material manufacturers to use modular sizes, and to coordinate sizes with other manufacturers.

• Urging builders of conventional frame structures to follow modular sizes.

• Development and prefabrication of modular components.

• Promoting modular drafting and design.

Most construction makes some use of modular materials and methods. Frequently this is without the builder's being aware of it, or possibly without his even knowing about modular construction! His efforts to make maximum use of building materials naturally leads to an attempt to find full sizes that fit plans.

Every good builder knows that framing members are spaced on 16" and 24" centers, in light wood frame construction. So he chooses materials that fit the spacing. When using small boards for subfloors and wall, or roof sheathing, framing members may vary from standard spacing without any serious consequences. But when large sheet materials are used, uneven spacing results in the sheets not ending on the framing. It is readily apparent that framing spacing is very important for maximum use of materials. The big difference between this and using all-modular construction methods is that, in the latter, one constantly maintains an awareness of standard sizes and pre-plans the work to make use of as many full-sized materials as possible.

Building Material Sizes

Much work is being done by building material manfacturers to change product sizes so they conform or will fit into the modular plan. Even though great strides have been made, at the present time the change-over is not complete. Materials used alone —as wall paneling, acoustic tile, and sheathing materials—are the full modular size. Other materials such as concrete block, brick, facing tile, and batt insulation are made smaller than the module so they will fit into the finished product. Even though smaller they adjust to the modular layout because they fit into the completed modular product without being cut or re-formed.

Building materials based on the 4" module will usually be one of the following sizes:

4"x8"	16"x96"
8"x16"	48"x48"
16"x16"	48"x96"
16"x32"	48"x120"
16"x48"	48"x144"

The 48"x96" size is most frequently used.

Some modular materials are based on a 3" module instead of the standard 4". Kitchen cabinets, appliances, and floor coverings are examples. These use 3" modules because their manufacturers standardized product sizes before the 4" module was adopted. These have not changed. Problems involved can be solved. These are not structural items; they are installed after other modular construction is complete.

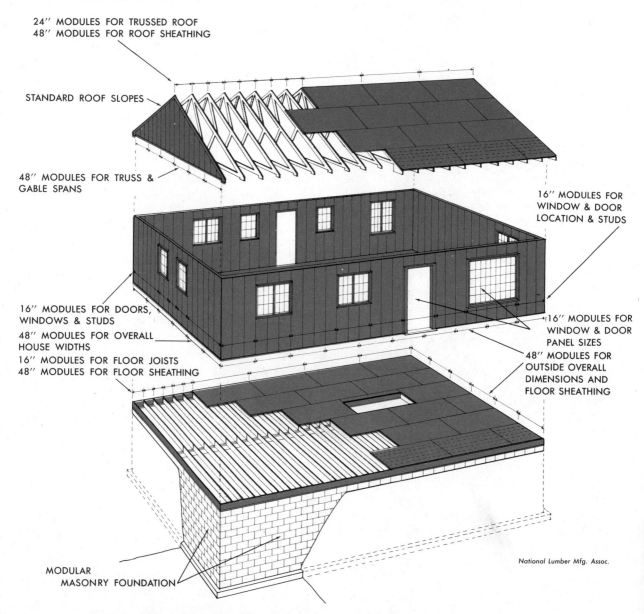

24" MODULES FOR TRUSSED ROOF
48" MODULES FOR ROOF SHEATHING

STANDARD ROOF SLOPES

48" MODULES FOR TRUSS & GABLE SPANS

16" MODULES FOR WINDOW & DOOR LOCATION & STUDS

16" MODULES FOR DOORS, WINDOWS & STUDS
48" MODULES FOR OVERALL HOUSE WIDTHS
16" MODULES FOR FLOOR JOISTS
48" MODULES FOR FLOOR SHEATHING

16" MODULES FOR WINDOW & DOOR PANEL SIZES
48" MODULES FOR OUTSIDE OVERALL DIMENSIONS AND FLOOR SHEATHING

MODULAR MASONRY FOUNDATION

National Lumber Mfg. Assoc.

MODULAR COORDINATION OF HOUSE ELEMENTS

All structural and aesthetic elements of a house are related. Coordinated modular increments of the structural elements, in an example house on the 48-inch module, are shown in the diagrammatic drawings. Standard sizes of various existing materials will easily fit the modular increments of the example shown.

Modular coordination of house elements. Also see column 1, page 139.

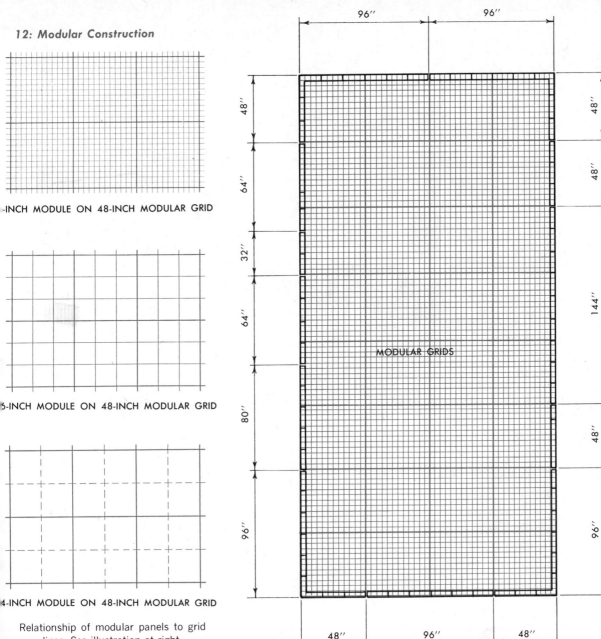

-INCH MODULE ON 48-INCH MODULAR GRID

6-INCH MODULE ON 48-INCH MODULAR GRID

4-INCH MODULE ON 48-INCH MODULAR GRID

Relationship of modular panels to grid lines. See illustration at right.

In any modular system (conventional framing or component parts) sizes conform to the *module* or vary only to accommodate other materials. Study the series of illustrations showing how building materials and components are used in modular construction.

Observation of the sample floor plan shows panel widths most frequently used. Framing members of components may be designed to conform to 16″ or 24″ spacing. (The panel spacing illustrated is placed on 16″ centers.) Component panel widths of most systems are 32″, 48″, 64″, 80″, 96″, and 144″, with 48″ being the basic major modular width. Half panels 24″ wide may be purchased, or "filler" panels can be made to order, to accommodate non-modular designs. Wall components are 8′-1½″ tall.

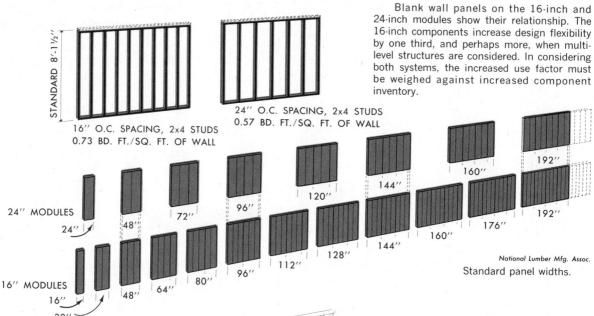

Blank wall panels on the 16-inch and 24-inch modules show their relationship. The 16-inch components increase design flexibility by one third, and perhaps more, when multi-level structures are considered. In considering both systems, the increased use factor must be weighed against increased component inventory.

STANDARD 8'-1½"

16" O.C. SPACING, 2x4 STUDS
0.73 BD. FT./SQ. FT. OF WALL

24" O.C. SPACING, 2x4 STUDS
0.57 BD. FT./SQ. FT. OF WALL

24" MODULES

24" 48" 72" 96" 120" 144" 160" 192"

16" MODULES

16" 32" 48" 64" 80" 96" 112" 128" 144" 160" 176" 192"

National Lumber Mfg. Assoc.
Standard panel widths.

The interior ceiling height will be 8'-0". Floor, roof, and truss components have modular lengths, usually even numbered, as 24'-0" or 26'-0".

Window and door components are designed to fit into the modular system. NOTE: When panels are used and placed edge to edge, double studs result at the edges. When such a panel is used with others, it fulfills the requirement of building codes that specify double studs at sides of door and window openings. Notice also that the studdings are continuous from bottom to top.

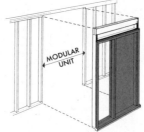

The 64-inch modular door and side-light panel is integrally designed to become a part of the 16-inch modular system for wall, door and window components. The pre-assembled unit with built-in header fits the 64-inch wall opening.

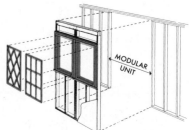

Two standard 32-inch casement window units are shown mullioned to become a 64-inch window unit to fit a 64-inch wall opening. The structural jambs of the window panel combine with adjacent blank wall studs to provide required double framing at openings.

Window panel construction details. *National Lumber Mfg. Assoc.*

Square-top high-wall and low-wall offsets, parallel to the standard height, 8-foot 1½-inch wall, extend the use of the modular system. Porch offsets, for sloping ceiling houses, often require high-wall units. Continuous roof slopes, on garages, may require low-wall offset storage areas.

National Lumber Mfg. Assoc.

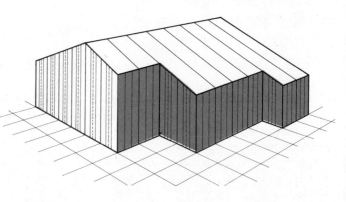

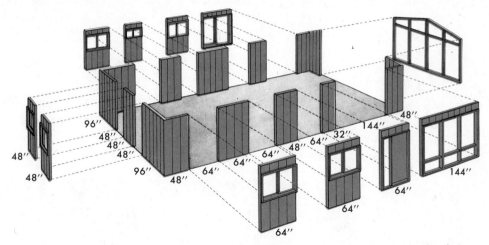

National Lumber Mfg. Assoc.

A series of blank wall areas and open areas form the walls of the house. The proportion of blank walls and "holes" is an important factor in the design of house exteriors and interiors. The materials used on the blank areas and the window and door design in the "holes" completes the exterior and interior wall composition. The illustration graphically shows the need for modular coordination in these components.

Large components are not confined to any one material. Wood is most frequently used for light construction but other materials work equally well. Metal, glass, and plastic, or curtain walls lend themselves to this system of construction. Masonry units—such as concrete panels, exposed aggregate panels, and others—are also used. When individual materials, as brick or stone, are laid to follow modular design, door and window openings conform to the module in both vertical and horizontal directions. The masonry bond (pattern) must also conform to modular increments.

Laminated beams and building panels contribute to the design of this modern clinic.

Weyerhaeuser Company

Modular building materials permit new design concepts for home building.

142

Curtain walls of this school are designed according to modular sizes.

Modular Design and Drafting

The architect or designer is responsible for achieving maximum use of modular materials and methods of construction, regardless of whether his planning is on conventional construction or components. He may promote modular coordination in the following ways:

• Select building materials that are modular in size.
• Specify *exactly* what materials are to be used.
• Design all major parts in modular increments, using materials selected.
• Have complete plans.
• Use modular grid lines on all plans.
• Show complete dimensioning, notes, and details.
• Use modular dimensioning to show modular and non-modular sizes.

No doubt you are familiar with ruled graph paper. Some drawing and tracing paper (descriptions in Chapter 32) use grid lines. Most of these have the lines spaced at ⅛″ or 1/10″. Grid lines for modular construction are similar except *module* grids are spaced at 4″ intervals (at whatever scale is being used). Large scale details include *module* and *major module* grid lines, while small scale drawings omit the *module* grid lines.

Because all building materials do not fit into modular sizes in every dimension, this complicates the job somewhat. Some edges of parts will not always be on the grid line. For example, one edge

Artcrest Products Company, Inc.
Modular sized building materials are used in this office interior.

of outside walls, partitions, windows, doors, masonry units will conform to one grid line, but the opposite edge will not, if the material size is non-modular. This must be shown on the plans. See modular dimensioning in Chapter 39.

Questions to Reinforce Knowledge

1. What are some of the factors which have brought about the need for modular construction?

2. What is a building component?

3. In what forms are building components manufactured?

4. What material is most frequently used for modular components?

5. What is prefabrication? Partial, total?

6. Is this a new development? Explain.

7. Is it true that only inexpensive buildings are prefabricated? Explain.

8. Are prefabricated structures confined to wood framing systems? What else?

9. What is a ready-cut building?

10. Why is standardization of building materials sizes necessary?

11. What is a *module*?

12. What is the underlying idea of the building module?

13. What is a *major module*?

14. What is a *minor module*?

15. What is the smallest *standard* building module?

16. What is the main difference between making the best use of modular materials in standard construction and actual modular construction?

17. What is being done by building materials manufacturers to further modular construction?

18. Why are some modular materials not based upon the 4″ module?

19. Are all building materials modular in size? Explain.

20. Framing of wood building components usually have what spacings of framing members?

21. What is the most frequently used panel size of modular building sheet materials?

22. What are the standard modular component widths?

23. How are windows and doors used with modular components or conventional modular framing?

24. What materials are used for modular components?

25. What measures may be taken by the architect to insure adequate use of modular construction?

26. Why is modular corrugated roofing 26″ wide instead of being on a module of 24″?

27. What is the difference between modular coordination and modular construction?

Terms to Spell and Know

component	building shell	major module
prefabrication	stock plans	minor module
modular coordination	plasterboard	facing tile
modular construction	module	

13

DOORS are used to protect an opening from the elements, to separate rooms, areas or compartments, to prevent or admit entrance or exit, and to add decorative architectural detail. In addition, a door may admit light and ventilation or expand vision.

Doors and Door Frames

Classification of Doors

Doors fall into two general design categories:

- Panel doors
- Flush doors

Panel doors. This door consists of a heavy framework around the outside and has a relatively thin panel placed within this framework to enclose the space. Frame size will vary slightly with different manufacturers. Different size doors will also have different width frames.

The inside edges of the frame and the panels are usually molded (shaped) into a decorative pattern. Panels may be of wood, glass, metal or other material. Panel doors are usually of wood but other materials are gaining in popularity.

Flush doors. Flush (sometimes called slab) doors are smooth on both faces. Wood is the material most frequently used. There are two types of flush doors, with many construction variations within each type. *Solid core* flush doors are solid throughout (no inner cavities). They are usually made of narrow strips of edge

grain lumber glued into a large sheet and covered on each face with ⅛″ plywood, or the core may be of particle board, which is reconstructed wood flakes and resins bound into solid sheets. See two illustrations, page 146.

Solid core flush construction is used primarily for front entrance doors and for institutions. They are sturdy and will take much abuse. Cost limits their use in small homes.

Hollow core flush doors look the same as solid ones. Their only difference is the interior construction. They have a light wood frame around the perimeter, but the interior is hollow. Without additional stiffening, ⅛″ plywood covering does not make the door rigid. Additional stiffeners are placed in the void. These may be cross bands of wood, expanded paper (thin strips, on edge, glued into a honeycomb shape), cardboard rings, circles of wood shavings, or plastic foam. Two methods of constructing hollow core doors are shown. These doors are inexpensive, present a fine appearance, and serve for most interior uses.

Both solid and hollow styles may have openings cut for glass or panels when desired. Moldings and panels may be applied to the surfaces for added decoration. These may be factory or job applied.

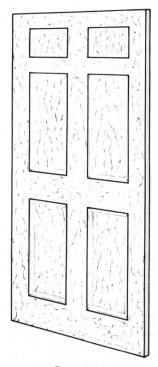

Panel door.

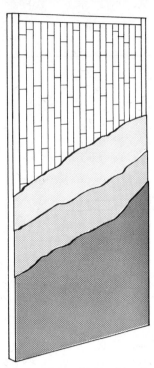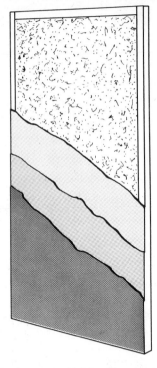

Solid core doors: (left) with edge grain lumber core; (right) with particle board core.

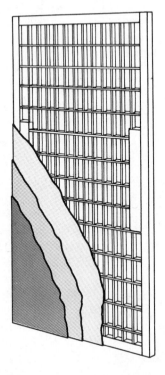

Hollow core doors.

Because of the great variety, complete lists of door sizes are not possible. Consult manufacturers' literature when making door selections.

The two most widely used door heights are 6'-8" and 7'-0". Both sizes are considered standard. Personal preference dictates the choice.

For homes and other small structures most codes specify the following minimum sizes:

Front entrance doors
$1\frac{3}{4}$"x3'-0"x6'-8"

Service entrance doors
$1\frac{3}{4}$"x2'-8"x6'-8"

Interior doors to rooms
$1\frac{3}{8}$"x2'-6"x6'-8"

Bathroom doors
$1\frac{3}{8}$"x2'-0"x6'-8"

Preferred bathroom doors
$1\frac{3}{8}$"x2'-4"x6'-8"

Single closet doors
$1\frac{3}{8}$"x2'-0"x6'-8"

Recommended minimum door sizes.

Although sizes of parts on a panel door vary with style and manufacturer, they approximate those shown below:

Stiles	$4\frac{3}{4}$"
Top rail	$4\frac{3}{4}$"
Cross rail	$4\frac{5}{8}$"
Lock rail	$5\frac{3}{8}$"
Mullion	$4\frac{5}{8}$"
Bottom rail	$9\frac{5}{8}$"
Bars (muntins)	$1\frac{3}{8}$"
Sticking	$\frac{7}{16}$"
Raised panels	$\frac{3}{4}$"

Approximate sizes of door parts.

Multiple Application of Same Door Type

There is minor confusion regarding designation of door types. Tradesmen and others sometimes refer to the following as door types:

- Hinged doors
- Bypass sliding
- Pocket doors
- Bi-fold or folding door units
- Double action hinged

These are *not* truly door types. They are simply standard doors using hardware designed for a specific purpose.

Hinged doors. Hinged doors are the most common. They must be located so the door swing does not interfere with passage or furniture arrangement. The door usually folds against an adjoining wall. On small structures such as homes doors open toward the rooms. On larger public buildings the doors open out. This is done so they cannot be forced closed if the building must be evacuated rapidly.

The face of a door is set flush with the edge of the jamb on the opening side. *Interior doors* in a home have two hinges. The top of the upper hinge is from 5″ to 7″ from the top of the door. The bottom of the lower hinge is 9″ to 11″ from the bottom of the door. *Exterior doors* and others subject to heavy use require three hinges. The third hinge is mounted midway between the top and bottom hinges. Height of door knobs and other controls is optional. Residential construction usually places their height at 36″. However, pre-hung doors sometimes have the knob at 40″ (½ door height) so they may be reversed up and down. Commercial and institutional doors are mounted with the knob at 42″ from the floor.

Determining door swing. On a closed door, with edges of hinges exposed, if the knob is to your right, this is a right-hand door. If the hinges are exposed and the knob is to the left, it is a left-hand door.

Bypass sliding doors *for interior use.* Bypass sliding doors are occasionally used at openings between rooms. However, they are much used with wide closets and storage areas. Any door type or style may be used. Frames, doors, and hardware may be purchased separately, or all necessary parts may be purchased in a *knocked-down* package, or the unit may be completely preassembled. Consult manufacturers' literature to become acquainted with the wide

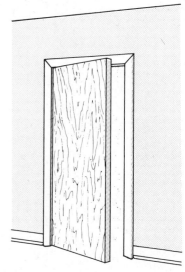

Hinged flush door.

variety of materials used, styles, and surface treatments.

Since these doors are hung so they will slide past each other, one edge of one door must be exposed. A clearance space (approximately ¼″) between doors is also visible. This space and door edge should not be visible as one enters, or stands in the center of the room.

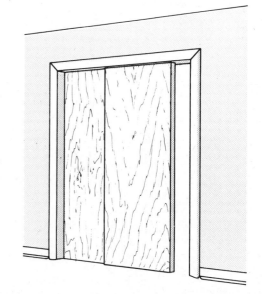

Bypass sliding doors.

When two doors are installed as a unit, the finished opening width is 1″ less than the total door widths. When there are three doors in the unit, the finished opening is 2″ less than the total door widths. For example, two 2′-0″ doors require a finished opening of 3′-11″. Three 2′-0″ doors require a finished opening of 5′-10″.

Bypass sliding doors for exterior use feature large glass areas with narrow stiles and rails. This permits a feeling of uninterrupted space. Both wood and aluminum units are popular. These units are usually purchased preassembled. They may be used in any climate. In cold climates insulating glass is required.

The units may be purchased with many combinations of fixed and sliding sections. On the illustrations notice the small "O" and "X" in the center of each section.

The "O" represents a fixed unit and the "X" a sliding unit.

Pocket door units are used when space is at a premium or when door swing is undesirable. However, they are more difficult to operate than hinged doors and are not convenient when they must be opened and closed frequently. They are especially useful as a means of closing off dining rooms from kitchens, studies from living rooms, or in compartmented bathrooms. They are not suitable as exterior doors. The door and pocket assembly is usually of wood with metal stiffeners in the jambs as shown. The units may be job built or prefabricated. The prefabricated type usually gives better service because of the close quality control during manufacture.

Double-action hinged doors. There are two general types of double-hinged doors. *Light-duty*

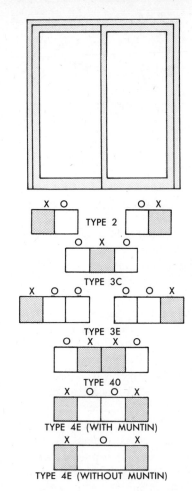

Combinations of fixed and sliding doors.

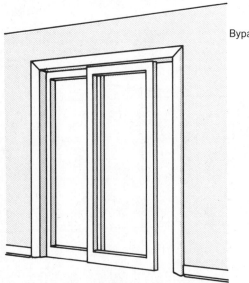

Bypass sliding glass doors for exterior use.

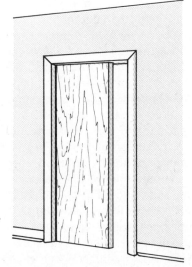

Pocket door.

148

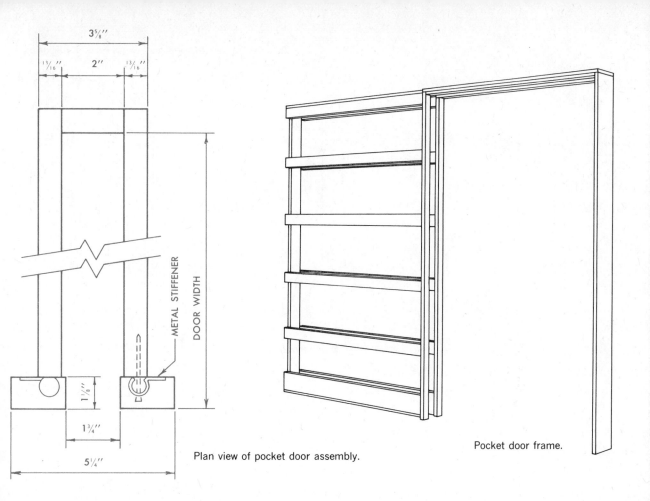

3⅝″

1³/₁₆″ 2″ 1³/₁₆″

METAL STIFFENER

DOOR WIDTH

1⅛″

1¾″

5¼″

Plan view of pocket door assembly.

Pocket door frame.

doors such as for cafes, as shown in the illustration, have spring hinges that will operate in either direction. They are mounted at the intersection of the door and side jamb. *Heavy-duty* doors have a pivot hinge at the top and bottom of the door. They also have a spring or hydraulic arrangement either in the bottom of the door or recessed in the floor to bring the door back to a closed position.

A door mounted in this manner may be placed in the center of the door frame or so one face is flush with the edge of the jamb.

Most frequent use is between the kitchen and other rooms.

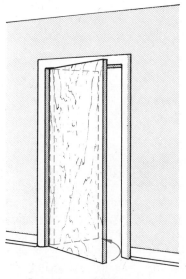

Double-action hinged door.

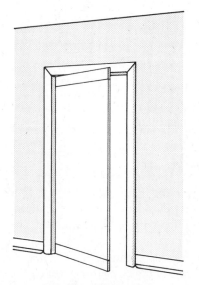

Pivot hinged glass door.

Wood folding door.

Plastic folding or accordion door.

Bi-fold door.

French doors.

Café doors (double action).

Folding doors are composed of narrow strips (about 3″) of wood, rigid plastic, or other material. Each strip is hinged to adjoining ones. Folding doors may also have a metal skeleton which is covered with cloth or pliable plastic. These units are sometimes called accor-dion doors because they fold in an accordion or bellows fashion. Small sizes are made to fit standard or special openings. Large sizes may be custom fabricated for individual jobs. Large installations may be equipped with motorized controls.

Bi-fold doors. Bi means "two parts". A typical unit consists of four doors, two of which are mounted on each side jamb. However, additional sections may be mounted in a similar manner. In practice, any door of any material or style may be mounted as a bi-

Dutch door.

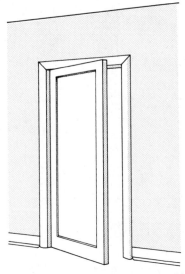

Wood or metal frame with panel of wood, plastic, or glass.

fold door. The frame and hardware may be purchased as a unit and the doors purchased separately, or the entire unit may be purchased completely prefabricated and ready-hung.

These doors are very popular for wide closets and are sometimes used as doors between rooms or as room dividers.

Individual door widths are usually between 1'-0" and 2'-0".

Using special folding hardware, any standard doors may be mounted so they "fold" to enclose any amount of space. When mounted in this manner, all doors in the group will be the same size. When open, all doors are *stacked* at right angles to the wall with their faces against each other.

Definition of Door Frame

A door frame is the finishing materials surrounding a door to conceal or beautify structural building parts.

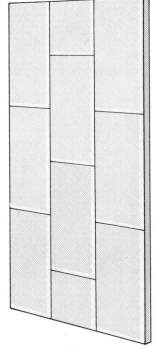

Metal clad fire door.

Door Jambs

A door jamb (buck) is the part of the frame which fits inside the masonry opening or rough frame opening. Jambs may be of wood or metal. Wood has been the traditional material but steel and aluminum have gained much popularity, especially in heavy-duty installations. They are not uncommon in homes.

A jamb consists of three parts. There are two *side jambs* and a *head jamb* across the top. There may be an additional head jamb if a transom—which is a glass or solid panel opening above a door —is required. Transoms have lost popularity in the immediate past but are now enjoying a new flair. Recent adaptations place the transom so it extends to the ceiling, thus eliminating framing and finishing over the door. This is especially suitable f o r non-bearing walls.

Metal jambs are made in a wide variety of shapes and sizes, some of which are illustrated on page 152. NOTE: The *stop*—which is the protrusion the face of the door closes against—is an integral part of the frame. Exterior wood door jambs also have the stop as a part of the jamb.

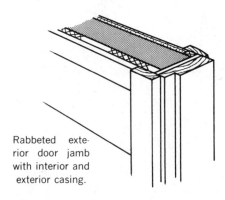

Rabbeted exterior door jamb with interior and exterior casing.

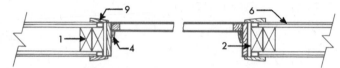

A

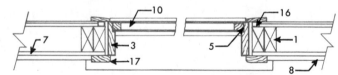

Plan view of interior door and its framing.

B

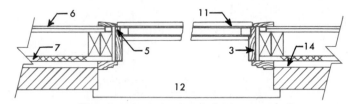

Plan view of exterior door in frame wall.

C

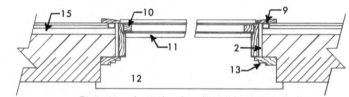

Plan view of exterior door in brick veneer wall.

D

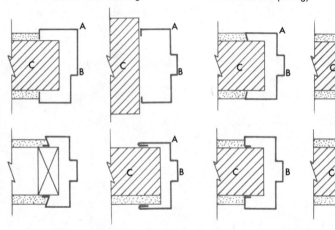

Plan view of exterior door in solid masonry wall.

Parts identification

1. Wall studs
2. Space for leveling door jamb
3. Side jamb
4. Door stop
5. Rabbeted stop
6. Plaster or other interior wall finish
7. Sheathing
8. Exterior wall covering
9. Interior casing
10. Door (hollow core shown)
11. Threshold
12. Sill
13. Brick mold
14. Air space
15. Furring strips
16. Plaster grounds
17. Exterior trim (casing)

Thickness of exterior wood jambs is 1⅛″, with a ½″ rabbet serving as a stop. On interior door jambs the thickness is approximately ¾″ (using nominal 1″ material) and the stop is applied to the face of the jamb.

Wood jambs are manufactured in two standard widths. Jambs for lath and plaster are 5¼″ wide, while those for drywall are 4⅝″ wide. Jambs may easily be cut to fit walls of less thickness. If walls are slightly thicker than the jambs, strips of wood are nailed on to form an extension. Also, jambs may be custom made to any desired size for a slight additional cost. Jambs may be purchased knocked down (not assembled), assembled with just exterior casing or brick mold applied, or assembled with the door pre-hung in the opening.

Pre-hung door units are also available with split jambs to permit rapid installation and to allow for any variation in wall thickness.

Metal door jamb shapes

A. Jamb profile
B. Integral stop
C. Masonry wall

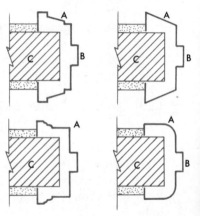

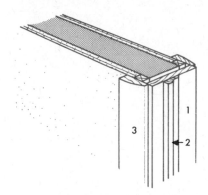

Interior door jamb (1) with stop (2) and casings (3) installed.

Modern use sometimes eliminates wood casings around door and window openings. Metal corners, as shown, protect wall finish materials.

Exterior Trim

On exterior wood jambs the trim (brick mold or casing) is purchased as a part of the jamb. When used in a wood frame wall, a *drip cap* may be placed over the top of the trim. When masonry is to be placed over the opening, it must be supported on lintels. Jambs in masonry do not require a drip cap. On one-story buildings, it is common practice to design a building so no masonry is required above openings. This space is filled with paneling or molding.

Door Sills

A sill extends across the bottom of an outside door and connects the two side jambs. Interior doors do not usually have a sill. A sill helps hold the lower part of the side jambs in their proper location. The top of the sill is sloped to provide a *wash* to drain water away from the door. If the door unit is to be installed in a wood frame wall, a wood sill is used. A masonry building requires a masonry sill.

A sill has considerable thickness and extends below the top edge of floor joists. The joists must be notched or special framing may be required to accommodate the sill. Examples of framing when the sill is at right angles to the joists, and when it is parallel, are shown on page 154.

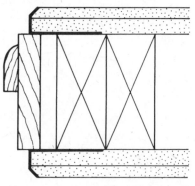

Metal corners frequently replace wood casing.

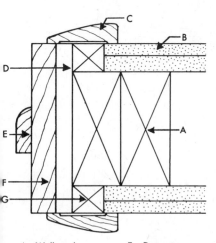

A. Wall studs
B. Plaster on rock lath
C. Casing
D. Space for leveling door jamb
E. Door stop
F. Door jamb
G. Plaster grounds

Plan view of door frame detail in plastered frame wall.

Interior Trim

Interior trim is not a part of the door jamb, so it is purchased separately. NOTE: All parts may sometimes be included in the same package, but this is an exception rather than standard practice. Illustrations of a variety of casing and other wood trim shapes are shown.

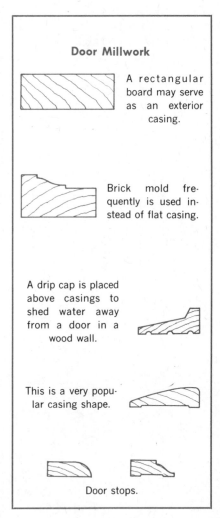

Door Millwork

A rectangular board may serve as an exterior casing.

Brick mold frequently is used instead of flat casing.

A drip cap is placed above casings to shed water away from a door in a wood wall.

This is a very popular casing shape.

Door stops.

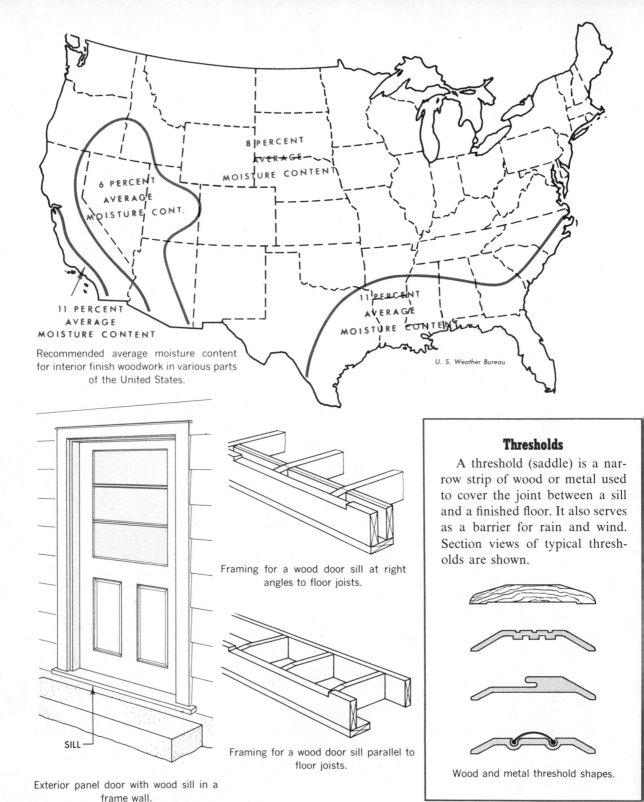

Recommended average moisture content for interior finish woodwork in various parts of the United States.

6 PERCENT AVERAGE MOISTURE CONT.

8 PERCENT AVERAGE MOISTURE CONTENT

11 PERCENT AVERAGE MOISTURE CONTENT

11 PERCENT AVERAGE MOISTURE CONTENT

U. S. Weather Bureau

SILL

Exterior panel door with wood sill in a frame wall.

Framing for a wood door sill at right angles to floor joists.

Framing for a wood door sill parallel to floor joists.

Thresholds

A threshold (saddle) is a narrow strip of wood or metal used to cover the joint between a sill and a finished floor. It also serves as a barrier for rain and wind. Section views of typical thresholds are shown.

Wood and metal threshold shapes.

Carpet pile weather-stripping.

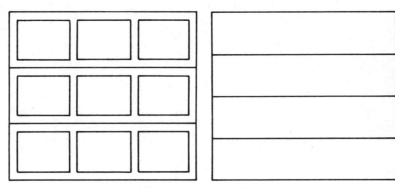

Two frequently used garage door styles.

Weatherproofing

Flexible metal, pile (fiber, as on a carpet), or felt may be fastened around exterior doors to make a permanent seal in maintaining inside temperature.

Entrance Door Details

Entrance doors are given special architectural emphasis to enhance their beauty and serve as a focal point. They may be job built or purchased as prefabricated units. When space permits, double entry doors are frequently used.

Garage Doors

Garage doors are usually the overhead type. They may be spring operated. Some doors have radio or "electric-eye" operators. The latter units add slightly to the building cost but give a feeling of quality construction to the building. Because of the wide variety of materials used, differing construction of doors, and sizes available, consult manufacturers literature before door selection is made.

The most common residential garage door sizes are shown above. These are actual sizes; framing around them is not shown.

| Single garage doors | | Double garage doors | |
Height	Width	Height	Width
6'-6'' x 8'-0''		6'-6'' x 15'-0''	
7'-0'' x 8'-0''		7'-0'' x 15'-0''	
6'-6'' x 9'-0''		6'-6'' x 16'-0''	
7'-0'' x 9'-0''		7'-0'' x 16'-0''	

Questions to Reinforce Knowledge

1. Explain the construction of a wood panel door.

2. What are the two kinds of flush wood doors?

3. Are all panel doors constructed of wood? Explain.

4. Describe the two types of folding doors.

5. How is the term "folding door" sometimes misused?

6. What is meant when one says doors fold in a stacking arrangement?

7. What is the largest size folding door?

8. What are the two standard door heights?

9. How does one determine which height to use?

10. What is the thickness of most exterior doors?

11. What is the thickness of most interior doors?

12. What is the minimum face size of front entrance doors?

13. What is a service entrance door? What is its minimum size?

14. What is the minimum size of interior residential doors?

15. What is the minimum size of bathroom doors?

16. What is a better size for bathroom doors?

17. From the panel door illustration, explain, in your own words, the following terms.

- stile
- top rail
- cross rail
- lock rail
- mullion
- muntin or bar
- bottom rail
- sticking
- raised panel

18. What is a hinged door?

19. When are two hinges required?

20. When are three hinges required?

21. Why are doors in public buildings hinged so they swing toward the outside?

22. What is the relationship of the face of a door and the edge of a jamb?

23. What is the normal height of the knob on a residential door?

24. What is the normal height of the knob or panic bar on public buildings?

25. What is meant by the "hand" of a door? Explain how it is determined.

26. What are bypass sliding closet doors? Is this actually a kind of door? Explain.

27. How may units for these be purchased?

28. What kinds of doors may be used for bypass sliding doors?

29. Explain the finished opening widths required for these units.

30. How does one determine which door to place toward the front of the unit? (Closest to the observer.)

31. How are bypass sliding doors used at exterior openings?

32. What does the "X" and "O" on a sliding door elevation represent?

33. What is a pocket door unit? Describe the construction of the pocket.

34. When is a pocket door unit more satisfactory than a hinged door?

35. What is their biggest disadvantage?

36. What is a bi-fold door unit?

37. What is a double action hinge? Describe two kinds.

38. What is a door jamb?

39. What is a transom? In what types of building might you find them?

40. What is a door stop?

41. What generally is the thickness of an interior wood jamb?

42. What generally is the thickness of an exterior wood jamb?

43. What generally is the width of a wood jamb to be used with lath and plaster?

44. What generally is the width of a wood jamb to be used with drywall?

45. Explain two methods of altering these widths.

46. What is meant when one says a door jamb is purchased "knocked down"?

47. What is a split jamb, and why is it used?

48. What is a brick mold? What is the difference between this and an exterior casing?

49. Describe the shape and function of a drip cap.

50. Is interior trim normally purchased as a part of the door jamb? What construction might call for this?

51. What is a door sill and why is it used?

52. What is a threshold? Describe four kinds.

53. Why is an entrance door given special design emphasis?

Terms to Spell and Know

door frame	cross rail	buck
panel door	bar	transom
flush door	sticking	drywall
folding door	hinge	lath
molding	bypass sliding door	plaster
slab	pocket door	knocked-down
solid core	bi-fold door	brick mold
particle board	double action hinge	sill
hollow core	side jamb	threshold
stacking	head jamb	

14

Windows and Glass

Each window manufacturing association (wood, steel, and aluminum) and each individual manufacturer make claims that their material is best for windows. Each material has advantages and disadvantages. A material may be more suitable for one installation, but under different conditions another material may be more practical. No attempt will be made here to evaluate the merits of each window material.

Wood Windows

Wood windows are usually manufactured of white pine. This wood is favored because of its abundance and the fact that it is soft but still machines and sands to a fine finish. The grain structure is close, which permits a wide variety of possible finishes. Hardwood windows are available, but their high cost limits their use.

Steel Windows

Steel windows may be purchased with a prime coat of paint or they may be purchased completely finished in many decorative colors. Industrial, commercial, and institutional construction make widespread use of steel windows, but they are not used extensively in residential construction. Steel windows lend themselves to solid masonry construction. Since there are no wide jambs, they take a shallow space. They are usually set into a chase in a masonry wall. No interior side and head trim is normally used. Plaster or other interior finishes are usually *returned* around a corner bead (metal corner) and finished to the face of the window with the same material as inside walls. A lightweight metal frame extends around the entire window, replacing the sill at the bottom. The bottom frame is usually placed on a masonry sill and the joint between the window and sill is filled with caulking.

Aluminum Windows

All types of windows are manufactured of aluminum. This modern material lends itself to many applications in all modern construction—commerical, industrial, institutional, and residential. Until recently residential use has been limited primarily to warm climates. They do have some disadvantages for cold climates, because they conduct cold, but buyer resistance based on traditional ideas is the main reason their use is limited. Each year aluminum windows are gaining in popularity.

Plastic

Plastics are being used in window manufacture. Sheet films and spray-on coatings form protective and decorative coverings on wood, steel, and aluminum windows. Some use is being made of molded or extruded plastic parts. Much greater use is expected in the immediate future.

Window Types

To acquaint yourself with the various window types, study illustrations of each. Only common, frequently used types are shown. The illustrations are self-explanatory of the general shapes of each type. Most types may be purchased of wood, steel, or aluminum.

No two windows of the same type, purchased from different manufacturers, will be exactly the same. The size and shape of individual parts will vary slightly.

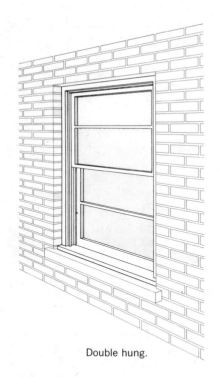

Double hung.

Casement.

Sliding or glider.

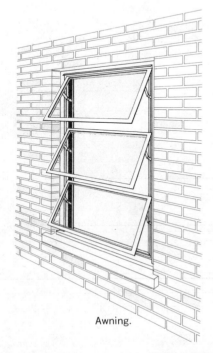

Awning.

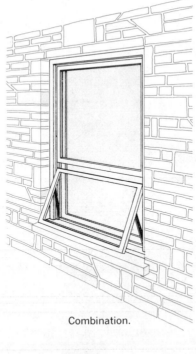

Combination.

Jalousie.

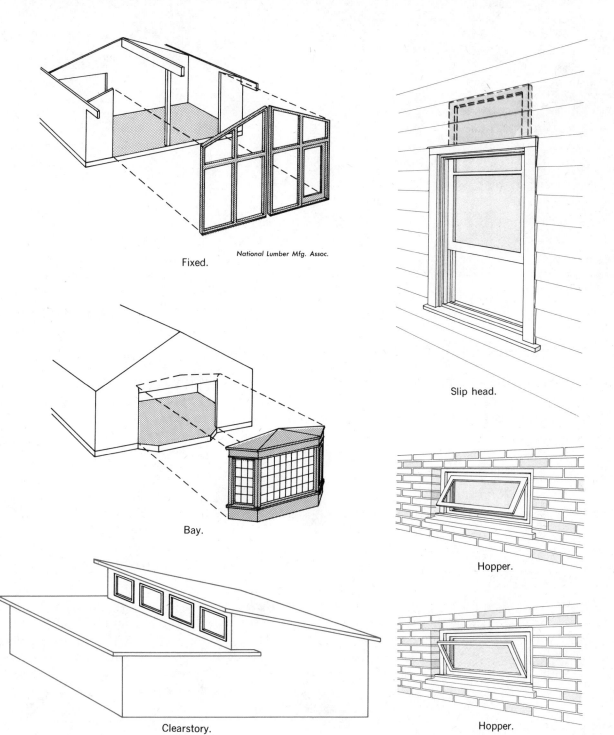

Fixed.

National Lumber Mfg. Assoc.

Slip head.

Bay.

Hopper.

Clearstory.

Hopper.

The large window on this home is called a bow window.

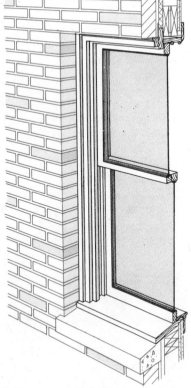

Cutaway view of double hung window and related parts.

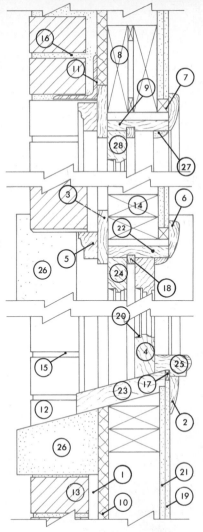

1. Air space	15. Mortar joint in elevation
2. Apron	16. Mortar joint in section
3. Blind stop	17. Ground strip
4. Bottom rail	18. Parting strip
5. Brick mold (casing)	19. Plaster
6. Interior casing	20. Putty or glazing compound
7. Ground strip	21. Rock lath
8. Header	22. Side jamb
9. Head jamb	23. Wood sill
10. Rigid insulating sheathing	24. Stile or side rail
11. Angle iron lintel	25. Stool
12. Brick in elevation	26. Stone sill
13. Brick in section	27. Stop
14. Double studs	28. Top rail

Section view of double hung window with parts identification.

That is why the illustrations represent general shapes and do not refer to specific detail. One must refer to manufacturers' data to obtain exact sizes and shapes. This information is then included in the working drawings. It will be shown as details and notes.

Window Parts, Sizes, and Elevations

Window size is usually (but not always) designated by the glass size of the individual sash units. Names of parts and typical sizes are given in the illustrations. Glass size is based on 4" increments in width and 2" in height. Typical glass sizes range from 12" to 48" in width and from 12" to 36" in height. Sash sizes, which is the wood frame enclosing the glass, are based on modules to accommodate standard glass sizes. Window stiles are approximately 2" wide. This makes the horizontal window opening 4" wider than the glass size. Top rails are 2" wide, bottom rails 3", and meeting or lock rails 1". This gives a total of 6" of wood showing. The size is sometimes increased so 7" of wood is showing. This is not the size of the actual parts; they are larger and are rabbeted to accommodate the glass. Overall window heights are also based on the 4" increment. When double hung windows are used and each size is based on 2" increments, the combined units form a modular size. Most manufacturers include more than the glass size in their window description, giving the glass size, opening or sash size, masonry or rough open-

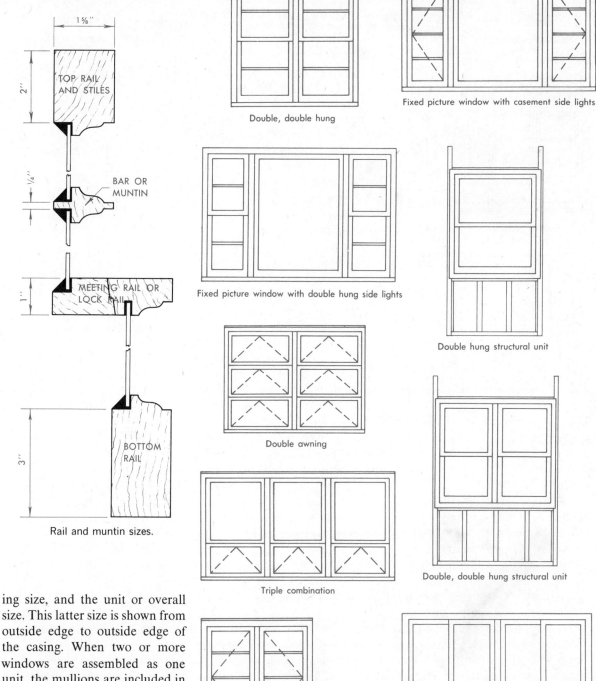

1 5/8"

TOP RAIL
AND STILES

2"

BAR OR
MUNTIN

1/4"

MEETING RAIL OR
LOCK RAIL

1"

BOTTOM
RAIL

3"

Rail and muntin sizes.

Double, double hung

Fixed picture window with casement side lights

Fixed picture window with double hung side lights

Double awning

Double hung structural unit

Triple combination

Double, double hung structural unit

Double casement

Double sliding

Window elevations.

ing size, and the unit or overall size. This latter size is shown from outside edge to outside edge of the casing. When two or more windows are assembled as one unit, the mullions are included in the overall length. Names and approximate sizes of window parts are shown in the illustrations here and on the following page.

161

Window size designations.

Window muntin designs.

Bars or Muntins

Bars or muntins (different names for the same thing) sometimes divide the glass into smaller panes. When the window is subdivided, the individual panes are not modular sizes since the glass must be trimmed because of the addition of the muntins. The muntins may form vertical or horizontal window panes, or both vertical and horizontal bars may divide a window into a larger number of panes. Early American designs use many panes. Modern design favors only horizontal divisions.

Mullions

A mullion is any post or division between individual window units. Size is variable. Side jambs are ¾″ thick; when two windows are placed side by side the smallest possible mullion is 1½″ wide. Manufacturers combine individual windows into groups, with mullions between the windows. NOTE: *Most manufacturers will not permit these to be returned if the wrong size is ordered.* The manufacturer does not normally arrange more than three windows in a group. If more are placed side by side, a wood stiffener extending from the bottom to the top plate should be used between each window. This calls for a larger mullion than if the windows are placed against each other. If more than three units are used together, a subsill is added beneath the regular sill, extending the entire length of the unit. The subsill must be notched to pass the vertical stiffeners between windows. Draw a separate detail to show this.

Note that modern practice tends to keep mullions narrow. However, as discussed here, wide mullions extend the size of a window unit. If individual units

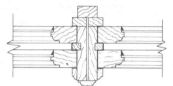

Side jambs joined to form narrow mullion

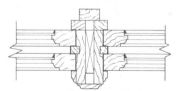

Stiffener between windows

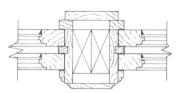

Double studs between windows

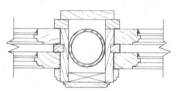

Steel post encased by jambs and trim

Mullion details.

are to be job assembled, or are not a manufacturer's standard size, working drawings include large scale details showing construction and methods of assembly.

Picture Windows

Picture windows used alone or in combination with other windows should be designed to use standard glass sizes. Many large picture windows have insulating glass, so the cost is prohibitive if standard sizes are not used. Sash may be purchased in standard width of stiles and rails. Sash with wide stiles and rails may be made for standard glass sizes. This makes the sash opening size nonmodular to accommodate custombuilt and oversize units. These parts are not constructed at the building site, so it is important for complete details to be shown; then they can be custom built.

Exterior Window Trim

Because exterior window trim (finishing boards) is applied when windows are assembled, they are a part of the window. Trim with decorative molding on its face is called *brick mold.* Flat trim is called *casing.* Brick mold is more widely used. Its name implies that it is used only with brick but this is not a proper assumption. It is also used with other masonry and wood frame construction. Size is slightly variable; it is approximately 1⅛″ thick and 2½″ wide. Exterior casing is 1⅛″ thick and the width is variable. Casing 3″ wide is most common. NOTE: When drawing elevations, the casing is drawn outside the actual window size.

Drip Cap

A drip cap as illustrated in the previous chapter is placed over the top of the casing to prevent water from standing on the flat surface and to prevent capillary action from drawing moisture behind the exterior covering. Metal flashing extends from under the siding. It is bent so it covers the top of the drip cap.

When several windows are combined into one unit, the drip cap should be continuous.

Sills

A sill is a sloping surface at the bottom of a window to drain water away from the parts. Most sills are of wood. They extend past the front edge of the window

so water will not drip on the exterior covering. Some sills have a groove in the bottom to accommodate a wood molding. If a molding is used beneath a sill, it helps block entrance of water and serves as a cover over window flashing.

As previously noted, wood windows have sills but most metal windows do not. However, wood sills and casings or brick mold are sometimes attached to aluminum windows. Even though, in addition, most windows in masonry walls have a stone sill, this is not a part of the window. It is designed and purchased separately.

When several windows are combined into one unit, the wood sill should be continuous.

Installation of Glass

Windows may be purchased glazed (with glass factory-installed) or they may be unglazed (no glass). When they are glazed, the glass is purchased as a part of the window. When they are unglazed, of course, the glass is purchased separately. Small units (as all but picture windows for a house) are usually purchased glazed. Larger ones are usually unglazed. The plans or specifications must state method of purchase and also state the method of securing the glass in the sash and the method and glazing material. This description must include whether the glass is to be *set* in putty, whether it is to be back puttied (putty placed between the face of the glass and face of rabbet on the sash), imbedded in neoprene rubber gas-

kets, placed on setting blocks, or employ some other method of installation.

Window Descriptions

Descriptions of windows refer to the window type: double hung, casement, awning, picture (fixed sash), or other kinds. It may refer to combinations of window types.

Reference is also made to the number of windows in the group. When one window is to be installed alone it is called a single (the word window is not included). When two windows are included in one unit it is called a mullion unit, abbreviated to *mull.* When three windows are included in one unit, it is called a triple, and when four windows are combined it is called a quadruple, abbreviated to a *quad.*

Window types and number of units are combined when stating a window description. There is no set form in composing window descriptions. However, one must be sure all necessary information is included. This information may or may not be used during construction, but it is vital for estimating and purchase of materials. Sample descriptions of windows follow:

A picture window with two double hung side lights, one on each side. Each double hung sash is to have two bars or muntins:
• Picture/w/DH. 2-bar Sd. Lts.

A triple awning unit:
• Mull. awning

A corner picture window with casements on each side:
• Corner picture/w/2 three-bar casements

NOTE: It is necessary to include complete size description. This is usually placed on the window schedule.

Window Hardware

There is a wide variety of hardware available to make a modern window more useful. Some of the hardware includes sash balances and tension tracks to permit sash removal. Hinged support bars are designed to hold awning and hopper windows open. Hand crank and automatic operators move and hold awning and casement sash in selected positions. There are also many lifting and locking devices. Screen and storm window combinations are sometimes built as a part of the window unit. It is not possible to discuss all available hardware. One should consult manufacturers' literature for details.

Required window hardware may be listed on a schedule of the plans or in the specifications.

For most building materials small measurements are given before large ones. *This is not true when specifying glass.* The width is always given before the height. Ordinary glass has slight waves in it; they cause less visual distortion if horizontal.

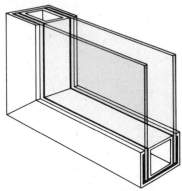

Insulating glass with metal edge.

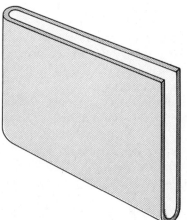

Glass edge for small units.

Window Glass

All glass used in windows is not window glass. The term window glass means the glass has had no additional finishing processes. It is used as it is *drawn*. Drawing is one of the methods of manufacturing glass into large sheets.

There are four widely used qualities of window glass:

• AA QUALITY—This is the best window glass obtainable, manufactured on special order only and priced accordingly.

• PREMIUM—Best commercial quality, remarkably free of distortion.

• A QUALITY—Has no imperfections that cause noticeable distortion.

• B QUALITY—Has some distortion but is suitable for usual small panes.

There are several thicknesses of window glass. Sizes may vary slightly with different manfacturers. The more common thicknesses are:

Classification	Approximate Thickness	Oz. per sq. ft.	Maximum size
Photo	.58 to .68	12-14	36x50″
Picture	1/16″	16	36x50″
Single strength	1/16″-3/32″	19	40x50″
Double strength	1/8″	26	60x80″
Heavy sheet	3/16″	40	120x84″
Heavy sheet	7/32″	45	120x84″
Heavy sheet	1/4″	52	120x84″

Insulating Glass

Insulating glass has two sheets of glass separated by space. Dehydrated air at atmospheric pressure is sealed into the space. There are two methods of sealing the edges. Large windows have a steel frame with gaskets to form a seal. Smaller panes have a glass edge. The two sheets are melted together to form a rolled edge. Insulating glass can be used on all window installations. Sash must be made to provide for the additional glass thickness. Standard sizes are shown in the accompanying tables.

Be exact in ordering. Do not specify the wrong trade name.

Grey Glass

When one wishes to reduce transmission of light or heat one may use special greyed glass. Vision is obscured only slightly. Looking through it reminds one of looking through sun glasses.

Insulating Glass—standard sizes

METAL EDGE

2 Pieces ¼″ Polished Plate Glass—½″ Air Space

UNIT SIZE	UNIT SIZE	UNIT SIZE
33″ x 76¾″	46⅛″ x 56½″	56½″ x 58⅛″
35½″ x 36″	47⅞″ x 50⅜″	56½″ x 66″
35½″ x 48⅛″	47⅞″ x 66⅝″	56½″ x 70⅛″
35½″ x 60⅜″	48″ x 48″	57″ x 76¾″
36″ x 44½″	48″ x 60″	58″ x 64½″
36″ x 55¼″	48″ x 72″	58″ x 72½″
36″ x 68¾″	48⅛″ x 55¼″	58″ x 80½″
36″ x 75″	48⅛″ x 68¾″	58″ x 96½″
36″ x 93″	48⅛″ x 75″	58″ x 116½″
42″ x 48½″	48⅛″ x 93″	60″ x 72″
42″ x 56½″	48½″ x 50″	60¼″ x 66⅝″
42″ x 66″	48½″ x 58″	60⅜″ x 68¾″
42″ x 72″	50″ x 56½″	60⅜″ x 75″
44½″ x 48⅛″	50″ x 64½″	60⅜″ x 93″
44½″ x 60⅜″	50″ x 72½″	64½″ x 66″
45″ x 76¾″	50″ x 80½″	66″ x 72½″
45⅜″ x 52″	50″ x 96½″	66″ x 84″
46″ x 48½″	50⅜″ x 60¼″	66″ x 96″
46″ x 64½″	52½″ x 58⅛″	72″ x 84″
46″ x 72½″	52½″ x 70⅛″	72″ x 96″
46⅛″ x 52½″	55¼″ x 60⅜″	

2 Pieces 3/16″ Window Glass—½″ Air Space

35½″ x 36″	48½″ x 42″	64½″ x 46″
35½″ x 48⅛″	48½″ x 46″	64½″ x 50″
35½″ x 60⅜″	48½″ x 50″	64½″ x 58″
42″ x 66″	55¼″ x 36″	68¾″ x 36″
42″ x 72″	55¼″ x 48⅛″	68¾″ x 48⅛″
44½″ x 36″	55¼″ x 60⅜″	72″ x 48″
44½″ x 48⅛″	56½″ x 42″	72½″ x 46″
44½″ x 60⅜″	56½″ x 46⅛″	72½″ x 50″
45⅜″ x 52″	56½″ x 50″	75″ x 36″
48″ x 48″	56½″ x 58⅛″	75″ x 48⅛″
48″ x 60″		

2 Pieces ⅛″ Window Glass—¼″ Air Space

For Wood Doors (Width x Height)	For Window Walls (Width x Height)
21¾″ x 62¾″	45½″ x 25½″
25¾″ x 62¾″	42½″ x 22½″

Glass Thickness†	Air† Space	Max. Area Sq. Ft.*	Dimensional Tolerances	Unit Thickness ¼″ Air Space	Unit Thickness ½″ Air Space	Approx. Average Net Weights Per Sq. Ft.
⅛″	¼″ or ½″	12	To 48″ +1/16″, −1/16″ Over 48″ +⅛″, −1/16″	17/32″ ±1/32″	13/16″ ±1/32″	3¼ lbs.
3/16″	¼″ or ½″	27	To 48″ +⅛″, −1/16″	1 1/16″ ±1/32″	15/16″ ±1/32″	5¼ lbs.
¼″	¼″ or ½″	70	Over 48″ +3/16″, −1/16″	13/16″ ±1/32″	1 1/16″ ±1/32″	6½ lbs.

GLASS EDGE

(DS premium)

2 Pieces ⅛″ Window Glass—3/16″ Air Space

Picture window sizes

DOUBLE HUNG WINDOWS Width x Height	AWNING WINDOWS Width x Height	CASEMENT WINDOWS Width x Height
49 3/16″ x 46″	36⅝″ x 49¼″	35 7/16″ x 36 1/16″
49 3/16″ x 50″	39⅝″ x 49¼″	35 7/16″ x 48¼″
49 3/16″ x 58″	44⅝″ x 49¼″	35 7/16″ x 60 7/16″
57 3/16″ x 46″		44 7/16″ x 36 1/16″
57 3/16″ x 50″		44 7/16″ x 48¼″
65 3/16″ x 46″		44 7/16″ x 60 7/16″
65 3/16″ x 50″		55 3/16″ x 36 1/16″
		55 3/16″ x 48¼″
		68 11/16″ x 36 1/16″
		68 11/16″ x 48¼″

GLASS EDGE (SSA)

2 Pieces 3/32″ Window Glass—3/16″ Air Space

Width x Height	Width x Height	Width x Height
16″ x 24″	21 1/16″ x 49″	36″ x 16″
16″ x 32″	21 1/16″ x 61 3/16″	36″ x 20″
16″ x 36″	22″ x 18″	36″ x 24″
16″ x 48″	22″ x 55 9/16″	36⅝″ x 14¼″
16″ x 60″	24″ x 16″	36⅝″ x 18¼″
16 9/16″ x 24⅝″	24″ x 20″	36⅝″ x 22¼″
16 9/16″ x 30 13/16″	24″ x 24″	36⅝″ x 30¼″
16 9/16″ x 36 13/16″	24″ x 32″	39⅝″ x 14¼″
16 9/16″ x 49″	24″ x 36″	39⅝″ x 18¼″
16 9/16″ x 61 3/16″	24″ x 48″	39⅝″ x 22¼″
19″ x 15″	24″ x 60″	39⅝″ x 30¼″
19½″ x 53″	24¼″ x 15¼″	40″ x 16″
20″ x 16″	27¼″ x 14¼″	40″ x 20″
20″ x 20″	27¼″ x 18¼″	40″ x 24″
20″ x 24″	27¼″ x 22¼″	42½″ x 22½″
20″ x 32″	27¼″ x 30¼″	44″ x 16″
20″ x 36″	28″ x 16″	44⅝″ x 14¼″
20″ x 48″	28″ x 20″	44⅝″ x 18¼″
20″ x 60″	28″ x 24″	44⅝″ x 22¼″
21 1/16″ x 24⅝″	32″ x 16″	44⅝″ x 30¼″
21 1/16″ x 30 13/16″	32″ x 20″	45½″ x 25½″
21 1/16″ x 36 13/16″	32″ x 24″	

Glass Thickness	Air Space	Max. Area Sq. Ft.	Dimensional Tolerances	Unit Thickness	Approximate Average Net Weights Per Sq. Ft.
⅛″	3/16″	24	±1/16″	7/16″ ±1/32″	3¼ lbs.
3/32″	3/16″	10	±1/16″	⅜″ ±1/32″	2½ lbs.

**Minimum size, 28 actual united inches. Solex®, Solargray® Solarbronze™ — maximum 50 sq. ft. †Glass thickness and air space are subject to practical manufacturing tolerances.*

This glass is not recommended where high light transmittance is desired—for example, in merchandise display windows.

Polished Plate Glass

After glass is manufactured, it may be ground and polished to true flat surfaces of great brilliance and high reflectivity. Usual thickness is from ¼″ to 1½″. There are three qualities of plate glass:
- SILVERING QUALITY—This is the best quality available; it is seldom used in sizes over 20 square feet.
- MIRROR GLAZING QUALITY—There are some small visible defects but the quality is exceptional.
- GLAZING QUALITY—This is used when ordinary glazing is required but not for mirrors. It is a very good quality.

Tempered Glass

Most sheet glass is quite brittle but can be made more shock resistant by heat tempering. Tempered glass will bend about four times as far as ordinary glass without breaking. When it does break it does not shatter; it disintegrates into small, blunt-edged pieces. The uses of this glass are practically unlimited. Its extra cost is more than offset by its many advantages.

Structural Glass

Many parts of the interior and exterior of buildings may be faced with opaque colored glass. It is usually in square or rectangular shapes of varying size and thickness. The face may be polished or embossed. This material is in-

stalled in much the same manner as ceramic tile. Large sheets may require special metal anchors to help secure them to the building.

Patterned Glass

As the name implies, decorative patterns are manufactured on the face of glass. This decoration may be on one or both faces. When one considers the number of glass manufacturers and all the decorative glass patterns of each, the variety is virtually unlimited. For specific information concerning individual patterns, consult manufacturers' literature.

Safety Glass

Safety glass consists of two or more sheets with tough, transparent plastic bonded between them. Recent development has seen foreign objects, such as leaves, fiber glass, butterflies, paper, cloth, or metal imbedded in the plastic. The plastic is so clear that it may be as much as ⅛″ thick for the inserts. Very interesting patterns may be achieved by "sandwiching" decorative inserts between several sheets of glass. Standard patterns may be purchased or panels may be custom fabricated to specifications. Any material selected for use must be inert to the plastic so as not to affect it chemically.

Glass Block

Structural glass blocks are not designed to be load supporting. When masonry is placed above them, lintels must carry the load. Wood framing above must be supported by headers.

Space must be left between the top of the blocks and lintels or headers to allow for deflection. Clearance should also be given at the sides of openings to allow for expansion and building settlement. This space should be packed with oakum, which is a fiber material similar to rope that has been soaked in oil. It serves as a cushion. The joint is then covered with caulking to give a finished appearance.

Glass blocks are modular units. Block thickness is nominal 4″ or 3⅝″ actual. Nominal face sizes are 6″x6″, 8″x8″, 12″x12″, and 4″x12″. Any actual face size is ⅜″ less for both dimensions.

The units are laid in much the same manner as other masonry and should have reinforcement between alternate courses. They must be secured to other masonry or frame with wall ties or set in metal channels which are secured to the structure.

Glass blocks are frequently used in combination with other windows. Modular windows are sometimes set in the center of the glass block area.

Decorative patterns vary slightly with individual manufacturers. The faces may be smooth, have a swirled effect, or have wide or narrow flutes running in one or both directions. Newer patterns may have a pebbled or textured surface, or sculptured designs may be created by texturing portions and leaving other glass plain. Surfaces may also be finished with colored ceramic enamel. They may have directional screens imbedded in the

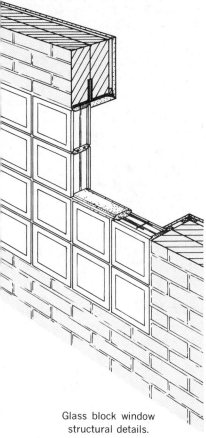

Glass block window structural details.

center cavity to control light and heat transmission.

Glass blocks are normally a very pale green but some companies make them in a variety of colors.

Other Uses

There are many other kinds and applications of glass that cannot be fully covered in a book of this nature. Some of the more common are mentioned to acquaint you with the need for further study.

- Corrugated glass
- Wired glass
- Glass brick
- Sculptured glass
- Glass mirrors
- One way glass
- Bullet resisting
- Bent glass
- Sand blasted
- Rolled edge—fire polished
- Heat grid glass
- Glass lighting panels

ter of the building so other rooms can use the exterior walls.

If windows are to be used for light or ventilation, they should still be placed following the old established rules.

Questions to Reinforce Knowledge

1. What window material is best?

2. What species is usually used for wood windows? Why?

3. Do steel windows normally have a sill and wide jambs?

4. Steel windows are most frequently used in what kind of construction?

5. What is a plaster return?

6. What is a corner bead?

7. What window types are manufactured from aluminum?

8. What is the extent of aluminum window usage?

9. What role is plastics playing in window manufacture?

10. Name and describe common window types.

11. Are windows of the same type always exactly the same? Explain.

12. What module is used for glass and sash size?

13. What is a sash?

14. Is a 30"-wide glass size one of the standard sizes? Why?

15. What is the relationship of stile width to glass width?

16. Describe the following window sizes:
    - rough or masonry opening
    - opening
    - unit opening

17. What is a muntin?

18. What is a bar?

Window Requirements

In the past, windows were needed to admit light and provide ventilation. Every room was required to have at least one window and preferably more. When more than one window was used, they were placed to provide adequate cross-ventilation. Mechanical light and ventilation have changed this somewhat. Many codes still state minimum glass and ventilating areas for each room; however, with electric lighting and mechanical ventilation, windows may never be required to serve their original purpose.

Windows still remove the feeling of living in a cubicle by expanding the line of vision, appearing to bring the outside to the inside. This is usually their most important function at the present time. If a window is not used for this reason, it is sometimes omitted. For example, when bathrooms and kitchens were always placed on outside walls, this was done so the room could have windows. Modern applications may move these rooms to the cen-

19. What is a lock or meeting rail?

20. What is a stile?

21. What is a top rail?

22. What is a bottom rail?

23. How does its size compare with a stile or top rail?

24. What is a brick mold?

25. What is an exterior casing, and what is the difference between this and a brick mold?

26. What is a mullion? Are mullions always the same size? Explain?

27. When is a vertical stiffener placed inside the mullion?

28. What is a subsill?

29. Is a stone sill a part of a window?

30. Is exterior casing or brick mold a part of the window?

31. What is a drip cap and why is it used?

32. What is meant when one says a window is to be purchased unglazed?

33. When ordering glass how are the dimensions listed? Why?

34. How does one describe several windows made into one large unit?

35. What is a mull window?

36. What is a triple window? Does it have vertical stiffeners?

37. After studying the chapter, from your own reasoning, describe a Corner picture/w/ 3-bar casement Sd. Lt.

38. What is window hardware? Explain.

39. Is all glass for windows called window glass?

40. What are the qualities of window glass?

41. What is insulating glass?

42. Why is it important to select standard sizes?

43. What is between the panes of insulating glass?

44. What are two methods of sealing the edges?

45. What is grey glass?

46. What is polished plate glass? Does it come in more than one thickness? Explain.

47. Is there more than one quality? Explain.

48. What is tempered glass?

49. What is structural glass?

50. What is patterned glass?

51. How are decorative objects placed in glass?

52. Do glass blocks support weight of the structure?

53. What are the standard sizes of glass blocks?

54. Is it necessary for all rooms to have windows? Explain.

55. What are three functions of a window?

56. Does each window always serve all three functions?

Terms to Spell and Know

prime coat	window opening	drip cap
chase	unit opening	Neoprene
trim	muntin	mull.
caulking	mullion	quad.
plastic	window stiffener	D.H.
extruded	subsill	Sd. Lt.
double hung	top rail	window operator
casement	meeting rail	distortion
awning	flute	window glass
hopper	ceramic	insulating glass
fixed sash	lock rail	grey glass
bow window	bottom rail	polished plate glass
bay window	sticking	tempered glass
stile	casing	patterned glass
rough	brick mold	sandwich glass
opening	pebbled	oakum

15

Stairs and Stair Framing

In this discussion no distinction will be made between stairs and an ordinary set of steps. The term *stairs* will include any set of steps *attached* to a building.

Wood is most frequently used in light frame construction, but steel and concrete are not uncommon. Heavy construction makes almost exclusive use of steel and concrete. Since this book deals primarily with light construction, greater emphasis will be given wood stair construction. However, any stair part may be constructed of other materials.

Stringers

Stringers are the structural parts (similar to inclined and notched floor joists) that support the stairs. Although minimum requirements permit only two stringers, one at each side of the stairs, a third stringer in the middle makes the steps more rigid and should be included except on very inexpensive construction. There are two general methods of constructing wood stringers (with many variations of each).

A *plain stringer* is a 2″x10″ or larger, with notches at each step. This is used for basements or other very inexpensive construction. The treads and risers are nailed directly to the stringers. These are sturdy stairs but do not give a finished appearance. Noise (squeaking) is likely when weight is shifting on the treads.

Treads for basement stairs are frequently made from 2″ thick dimension lumber, and risers are sometimes omitted.

A *housed stringer* is made from finished lumber; ½″ deep grooves are routed into it so the treads and risers slip into the stringers.

First Federal Savings, Berwyn, Illinois

Stairways may be the focal point of beauty for a room.

Unit Structures, Koppers Company, Inc.

Stairways may be the focal point of beauty for a room.

Stair Parts

Total Stair Rise

This is the distance from the top of one finished floor to another.

Total Stair Run

This is the total horizontal stair length.

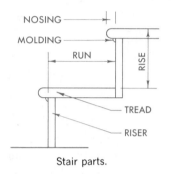

Stair parts.

Riser

A vertical member (back of step) extending from the bottom of one tread to the bottom of the tread above.

Rise

The vertical distance from the top of one tread to the next.

Tread

A horizontal member (top of step) extending from the face of one riser to the face of an adjoining one, plus nosing.

Run

The horizontal distance from the face of one riser to the face of an adjoining one.

Nosing

The portion of tread that overlaps the riser below.

The grooves are slightly larger than tread and riser thickness, to accommodate glued wood wedges which are placed in the grooves behind the risers and below the treads. This closes all joints so they are tight from the finished side of the stairs.

Three methods of framing stringers at floor openings are shown. The method shown in the third illustration is preferred by the author because the header joists are doubled, which permits the outside header to be left unattached when the floor is framed. This header may be assembled with the stairs while they are on the floor in a flat position, and raised into place. A ledger as shown in the first illustration may also be used with the third method if greater strength is desired. The method shown in the second illustration is least satisfactory because the stringer has very little surface bearing upon the header.

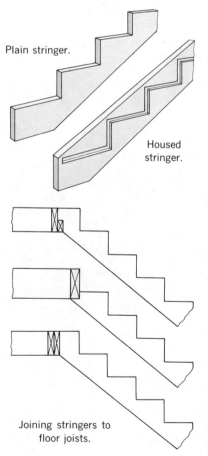

Plain stringer.

Housed stringer.

Joining stringers to floor joists.

Stair Rail

The side hand rail following the rake angle of the steps.

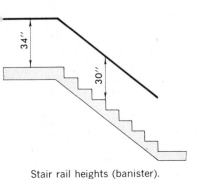

Stair rail heights (banister).

Newel Post

The large post at the foot (bottom) or head (top) of a stairs which supports the ends of the stair rail.

Typical baluster shapes.

Balusters

Small, evenly spaced posts to support the stair rail.

Straight Stairs

Straight stairs lead from one level to the next without turns. These are the least expensive to build. If the stairs are enclosed by a wall on both sides, they are called *closed string* stairs. If they are against a wall on one side, but open on the other, they are called *open string* stairs. When open string stairs are used, a stair rail is required on the open side. If both sides are open (as for basement stairs) a stair rail is needed on both sides.

L Stairs

An L stairs (sometimes called a dogleg or platform stairs) has one landing somewhere in the flight of steps. A person using the stairs must make a 90° turn at this point. When the landing is near the top or bottom of the flight, it is called *long L* stairs.

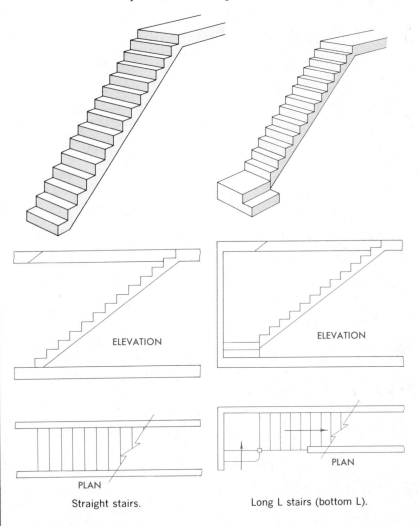

ELEVATION

PLAN

Straight stairs.

ELEVATION

PLAN

Long L stairs (bottom L).

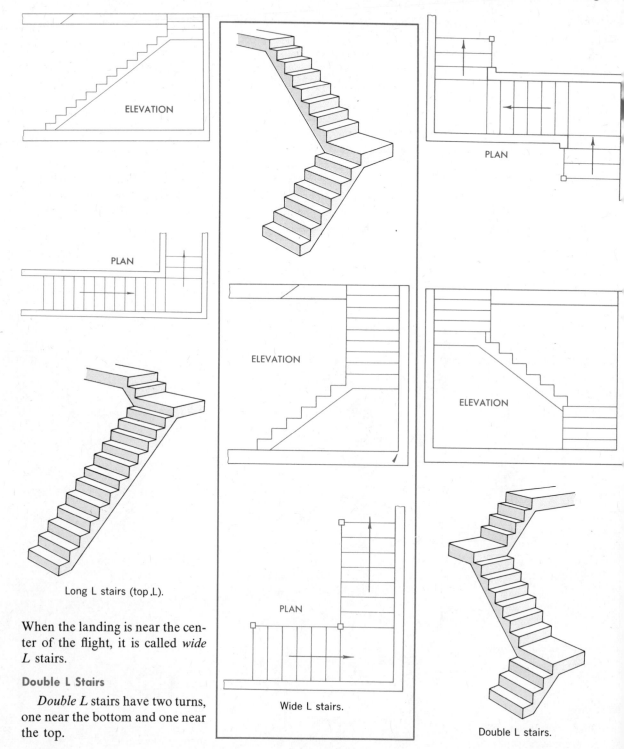

ELEVATION

PLAN

Long L stairs (top .L).

ELEVATION

PLAN

Wide L stairs.

PLAN

ELEVATION

Double L stairs.

When the landing is near the center of the flight, it is called *wide L* stairs.

Double L Stairs

Double L stairs have two turns, one near the bottom and one near the top.

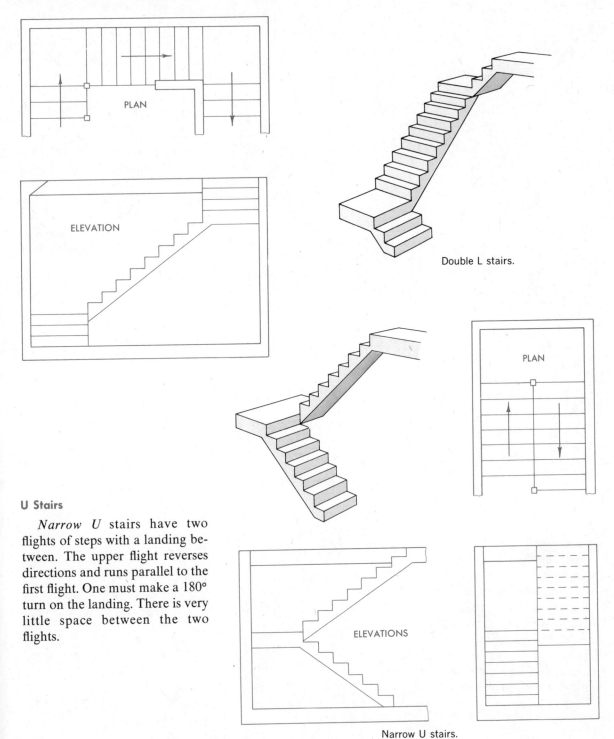

PLAN

ELEVATION

Double L stairs.

PLAN

U Stairs

Narrow U stairs have two flights of steps with a landing between. The upper flight reverses directions and runs parallel to the first flight. One must make a 180° turn on the landing. There is very little space between the two flights.

ELEVATIONS

Narrow U stairs.

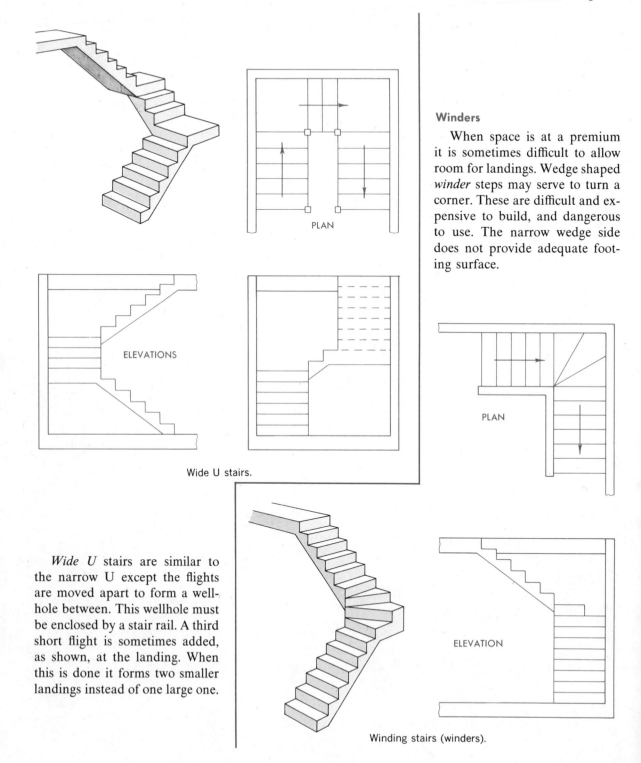

PLAN

Winders

When space is at a premium it is sometimes difficult to allow room for landings. Wedge shaped *winder* steps may serve to turn a corner. These are difficult and expensive to build, and dangerous to use. The narrow wedge side does not provide adequate footing surface.

ELEVATIONS

PLAN

Wide U stairs.

Wide U stairs are similar to the narrow U except the flights are moved apart to form a wellhole between. This wellhole must be enclosed by a stair rail. A third short flight is sometimes added, as shown, at the landing. When this is done it forms two smaller landings instead of one large one.

ELEVATION

Winding stairs (winders).

Stair Uses and Locations

- **Main stairs:** well-constructed and finished for constant use.
- **Service or basement stairs:** designed for utility uses.
- **Outside steps or stairs:** attached stairs outside the building.

Main stairs leading to upper levels should be located near the main or front entrance. When possible, one should enter the stairs from a hall (preferably the entry hall). It is not good practice to be required to walk through a room to reach a stairs. Can you see why? However, open string stairs are sometimes placed inside a room to achieve an architectural effect. Additional service stairs are usually provided elsewhere. Both open string and closed string stairs without a door at the bottom or top waste heat and allow cold drafts to descend. Warm air also ascends through

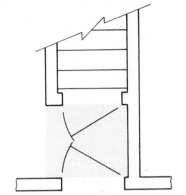

For most convenient use, service stairs are in line with an entry door. Doors should not interfere, but neither should they open directly over a stairway.

the stair well to upper levels, but this does not necessarily cause discomfort to occupants. One should carefully consider whether the beauty of an open stairs warrants the discomfort and extra heating expense that will probably result. Furthermore, drafts are a definite fire hazard. Stairs in public buildings are frequently required to be enclosed in well-

holes and have doors at the bottom or top. In a multi-story building, doors are required at each level.

Service stairs are usually located near the kitchen or other service area. Basement stairs are in the same general location. One should be able to enter a building and go to a basement without walking through another room. The method used in the illustration affords easiest access. It is not necessary to turn a corner when carrying bulky objects to the basement. This direct access also eliminates carrying items through other parts of a building.

Outside steps or stairs may lead from the ground to the building, or to upper levels. They may also lead from the ground to a basement floor. When inside access to a basement is not near a service entry, additional outside access should be provided.

Structural Details

Stair width for main stairs, as stated by the FHA, is 2'-8" minimum, plus the width of the stair rail. However, this is hardly adequate. The author considers 3'-0" a minimum width, with 3'-2" to 3'-6" much better.

Minimum stair width for service and basement stairs is 2'-6", as stated by the FHA. However, 3'-0" is better.

Outside stairs must be at least as wide as the walk leading to them and no less than 3'-0". Outside steps to a basement must be at least 2'-6" wide.

Rise

Maximum rise for main stairs is 8¼".

Maximum rise for service or basement stairs is 8¼".

Maximum rise for exterior steps or stairs is 7½".

Run

Minimum run for main stairs is 9" plus 1⅛" nosing.

Minimum run for service or basement stairs is the same as above when closed risers are used. With open risers, run is 9" plus ½" nosing.

Minimum run for outside steps or stairs is 10" plus 1" nosing. If

no nosing is used (as for concrete steps with vertical risers) the minimum is 11".

NOTE: *Every* step in a flight of stairs *must* be the same—that is, have the same rise and run. This means exactly the same!

Winder size. The rise of a winder is the same as the rise of any other step in the flight.

When possible, winders should not come to a point at the narrow end. An old rule says that the narrow end of the tread should be no less than ¾ the width of an ordinary tread, but this rule is seldom observed.

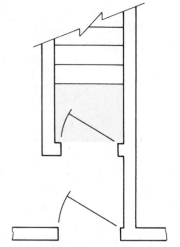

When a door opens toward the stairway a landing should be provided.

FHA prescribes that tread width, when measured 18″ from the converging end, should be the same as full treads.

A *landing* at the top of stairs is desirable. A door should not open *over* the stairs. If a door swings *toward* the stairs, a landing is required. Minimum landing width (from door to stairs) is 2′-6″, but when the door width is greater than 2′-6″, a landing at least as wide as the door is recommended.

Headroom is measured from the front corner of a tread (edge of nosing) to the closest obstruction above. This obstruction may be a door opening, a soffit (which in this reference is a sloped ceiling over the stairs), or a framed opening in a floor or ceiling above. FHA minimum headroom for a main stairs is 6′-8″, but 7′-4″ to 7′-7″ is better. Minimum headroom for basement or service stairs is 6′-4″.

A *stair rail* should be provided on at least one side of a stairway. Standard height of the stair rail is 30″ on the rake (angle following the steps) and 34″ on the landing. Three steps or fewer do not require a stair rail. Wellholes more than 30″ deep require a stair rail.

Calculating Number and Size of Treads and Risers

The following procedure was used to determine the number of treads and risers, and their sizes, for the stairs shown in the illustration. Procedure for designing your stairs would be the same.

You must know the distance between finished floors. Detail and overall dimensions for this drawing are both given. Add all detail dimensions together to verify the overall dimension. When no overall floor to floor dimension is given be sure you include *all* sizes of *all* building materials when computing this height. For example, on this plan the following sizes are included:

Finished lower floor to finished ceiling	8′-0″
Ceiling material thickness	0½″
Furring strips between ceiling and joists	0¾″
Height of floor joists	9½″
Thickness of subfloor	0¾″
Thickness of finished floor	0¾″
Total rise	9′-0¼″

Since the size of each step is computed in inches, the overall dimension should also be changed to inches. The total rise then is 108¼″. Since 7″ is an ideal step height, the total rise is divided by 7. This indicates 15$\frac{4}{7}$ risers are required. Then since rise for each step must be exactly the same, either 15 or 16 risers will be required. When 108¼″ is divided by 15, riser height is 7.22″. So far, this figure appears to be very satisfactory, so additional calculations will be based upon it.

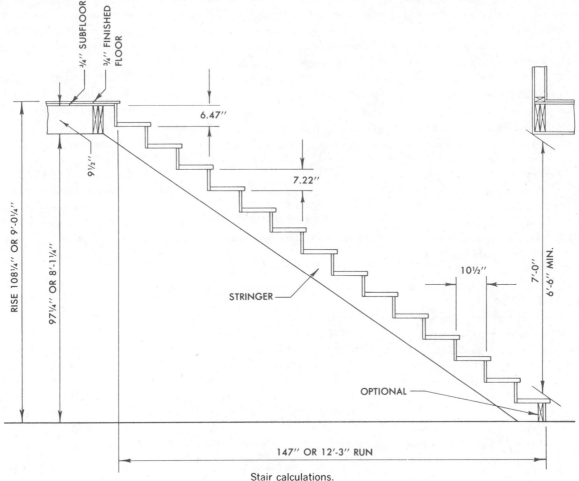

Stair calculations.

The number of treads is always one less than the number of risers, so 14 treads are required. This is because the floor or landing serves as the top tread. Since 11″ is an ideal tread width, and is a whole number, it will be used for preliminary tread calculations. Using method number 1 of checking stair slope, add the rise (7.22) to the proposed tread width (11). The sum of these two numbers is 18.22. This is larger than the number 18, which indicates the

stairs are too flat. Using method number 2, the size is also unsatisfactory. Another trial must be made, using another tread width. For the second trial 10½″ is used. If 10½″ is added to 7.22, the sum is 17.72, which indicates that the slope is satisfactory.

To find the total stair run, 10½ is multiplied by the number of treads (14). This gives a total stair run of 147″ or 12′-3″. Since these stairs give adequate headroom, they are satisfactory.

Questions to Reinforce Knowledge

1. What are stair stringers?
2. Describe plain stringers, their limitations and uses.
3. Describe housed stringers, their advantages and uses.
4. Draw sketches showing methods of joining stairs to floor framing.
5. Describe total stair rise.
6. Describe total stair run.
7. What is a riser?
8. What is rise of a step?

9. What is a tread? Does this include all of the material forming the horizontal part of a step?

10. What is run of a step?

11. What is a nosing?

12. What is a stair rail?

13. What is a newel post?

14. What is a baluster?

15. Describe a straight stairs.

16. What are *open string* stairs?

17. What are *closed string* stairs?

18. What are *L* stairs? What is the difference between a long L and a wide L?

19. What are *double L* stairs?

20. What are *narrow U* stairs?

21. What are *wide U* stairs?

22. What is a winder?

23. Where is the best location for a main stairs?

24. When the main stairs are placed in this location, why are service stairs usually provided elsewhere?

25. Why is it a good idea to have a door at the top or bottom of a stairs?

26. Why is it good to have a basement stairs directly across from a service entry door?

27. When should an outside basement stairs be provided?

28. What is recommended as a minimum main stair width?

29. From your own reasoning, why must all steps in a straight flight be the same size?

30. Do maximum rise and minimum run, as stated in the text, represent ideal step sizes? Explain.

31. What are the FHA minimum size requirements for winder treads?

32. Is it permissible to have a door open out over a stairs? Why?

33. When a door must open toward a stairs, what special provisions should be made?

34. What is the FHA minimum requirement for headroom over a stairs?

35. What is the standard stair rail height above the steps?

36. What is the stair rail height on a landing?

37. Why is the correct stair slope so very important?

38. Describe ideal tread width.

39. Describe ideal riser height.

40. How can one determine if a stairs has a proper rise-to-run ratio? Describe two methods of checking.

Terms to Spell and Know

plain stringers	stair rail	dogleg
housed stringers	newel post	U stairs
total stair rise	baluster	wellhole
total stair run	straight stairs	winder
riser	L stairs	main stairs
rise (of step)	closed string stairs	service stairs
tread	open string stairs	headroom
run (of step)	landing	soffit
nosing	flight (of stairs)	rake

16

Insulation

As used here, to insulate means to hinder or stop the transfer of heat, cold, or sound from one area to another. All building materials have some insulating value, so a structure is never without insulation. However, the term here refers to materials used exclusively for the purposes just stated.

For convenience, the three methods of heat transfer are reviewed, even though you have studied them in other courses, because they are closely connected with understanding the handling of insulation. While studying the chapter remember that insulation is to work with heating and cooling systems discussed in Chapter 19.

ducted through building parts such as floors, walls, or ceilings, and the rays of the sun may strike surfaces inside through windows. The problem is to control the transfer.

Good construction methods and weather stripping at all doors and windows help a great deal. Usually more heat and cold are transferred through windows than any other building parts. Glass is a very poor insulator. When standing near a window one may experience heat or cold transfer through the glass and mistake it for outside air entering the building, even though it is tightly closed.

The addition of storm windows or double glazing helps stop this transfer. Air space between the panes of glass is the actual retardant.

As said, walls, floors, and ceilings act as conductors. The amount of conduction depends upon the materials used. When the construction materials themselves do not have sufficient insulation value, additional materials must be used.

Methods of Heat Transfer

Heat is transferred in one of three ways. These are: (1) by conduction, (2) by radiation, and (3) by convection.

● **Conduction** is the direct passage of energy, light, or heat from one object to another, through contact. For example, you place your hand on a cold windowpane, the cold is conducted to your hand, and heat to the glass, by direct contact.

● **Radiation,** in a simplified sense, is the passage of heat rays through space or air. An object is warmed when the rays strike its surface. For example, if your hands are

held near a lighted electric bulb they are warmed by radiation.

● **Convection** is the mass movement of heated air or other particles either resistant to or caused by gravity or mechanical forces. For example, in a two-story home, heavier cool air descends along the steps of a stairway while light warm air moves toward the top of the stair well. These are convection currents.

Means of Retarding Heat Transfer

Heat or cold may be convected into a building through openings such as windows, doors, or loose construction. It may also be con-

Classifications of Insulation

There are many materials used as insulation. They may be grouped into four general categories: (1) vegetable, (2) mineral, (3) metal, and (4) plastic. Each may be processed into many different forms for special uses.

Loose Fill Insulation

This insulation is not pressed into a sheet or other solid unit and must be placed loose between framing members. It may be poured or blown into position. Loose fill insulation is usually of mineral composition, but occasionally vegetable material such as granulated cork is used. It may be either fibrous (like threads), or granular (small particles). Examples of fibrous insulation are rock wool, glass wool (spun glass fibers), and slag wool. Cork (vegetable) and expanded mica (mineral) may be granular.

It is sometimes difficult to handle loose fill insulation because it must be installed after most construction is completed.

Packaged Fill Insulation

This material is similar to fibrous loose fill insulation except it is adhered to, or contained between, sheets of kraft paper for more convenient use. The packaging permits installation while construction is in progress. Package width is designed to fit between normal stud spacings. Thicknesses most frequently used, are 1″, 2″, 4″, and 6″.

This insulation may be installed as batts, blankets, or rolls

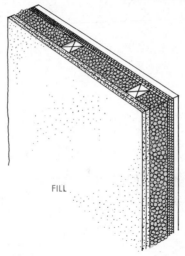

FILL

Loose fill insulation may be poured or blown between studs.

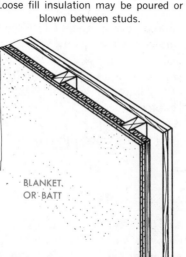

BLANKET, OR BATT

Half thick batt insulation should be fastened on the warm side of a wall to minimize condensation.

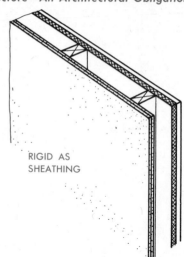

RIGID AS SHEATHING

Rigid insulation placed toward the outside of a frame wall may also serve as sheathing.

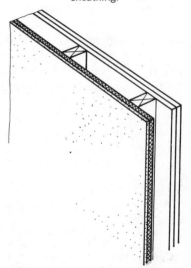

Fiberboard insulation may serve as a plaster base.

as shown. Observe that some of the insulations have paper on only one face while others are completely encased in it. Note also that some have nailing flanges while others do not. Those without provisions for fastening are held in place by forcing them between the framing members.

Rigid Insulations

These may be of mineral, vegetable, or foamed plastic, and are available in many different sized sheets, used for many specific purposes. One should consult manufacturers' literature to become acquainted with the many forms and uses. Typical rigid

180

insulations are manufactured of grass-type vegetable fiber that has been broken down from its living state and reprocessed by pressure, heat, and the addition of resins. Some are fibrous mineral materials such as spun glass or rock wool. Foamed plastic contains cells that insulate.

These are frequently dual purpose products that serve as insulation but also as wall sheathing, soffit coverings, plaster base, roof sheathing, acoustic wall or ceiling materials such as panels or tile, and similar items. See three illustrations, top left, on page 182.

Insulation (pressed) board wall sheathing is widely used. Its standard thickness is $^{25}/_{32}''$ but ½″ meets most code requirements. Standard widths are 24″ and 48″. Standard lengths are 8′-0″ and 9′-0″.

Board surfaces may be untreated and have the fibers exposed, or they may be encased in a waterproof bituminous coating.

Slab insulation is similar in appearance to insulation board with a coated surface, except the sheets are not pressed into a rigid form. Even though the exterior is rigid the interior material is usually quite soft. They are usually of mineral or foamed plastic.

Reflective Insulation

Thin sheets of high gloss metal, usually aluminum, may be used to reflect heat or cold. The sheets may be used alone or combined with other materials. When used alone they are usually secured to framing members. They may be

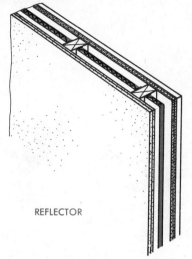

Foil reflector insulation is nailed or stapled to studs.

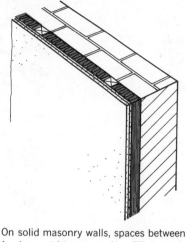

On solid masonry walls, spaces between furring strips may be filled with insulation.

flat or have folded or stamped designs to add to rigidity and increase reflective quality. Paper backing is sometimes added to the foil to increase its strength. In turn, aluminum foil is frequently added to one face of packaged insulation for increased effective-ness. As a backing of drywall or rock lath, it also serves as a fire retardant.

Reflective insulation may have a sandwich construction, consisting of two layers of foil with space and stiffeners between them as shown.

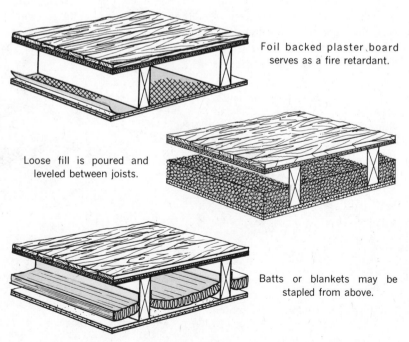

Foil backed plaster board serves as a fire retardant.

Loose fill is poured and leveled between joists.

Batts or blankets may be stapled from above.

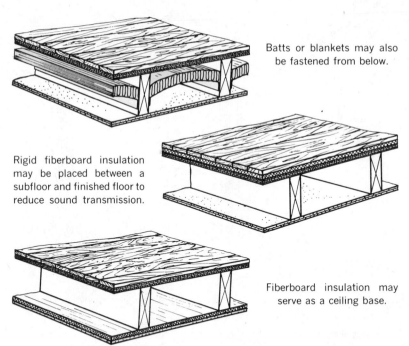

Batts or blankets may also be fastened from below.

Rigid fiberboard insulation may be placed between a subfloor and finished floor to reduce sound transmission.

Fiberboard insulation may serve as a ceiling base.

Plaster as Insulation and Sound Control

Ordinary sand plaster has very little insulating value. When insulating qualities are desired, lightweight plasters made from minerals such as expanded mica, vermiculite, or perlite are effective. Insulating plaster is frequently used for sound control. Greater insulating value as well as sound control can be obtained with a sprayed plaster, texture finished. Sprayed plaster is currently very popular because large areas can be applied quite rapidly. It is most widely used on commercial structures. Sprayed plaster gives a beautiful and interesting appearance. Its greatest disadvantage is its softness which causes it to become damaged easily.

Sound Conditioning

Special effort to sound condition homes and apartments is a relatively recent development. Livability can be greatly enhanced if sound conditioning is carefully planned.

Some surfaces absorb, while others reflect sound waves. Sound conditioning means absorbing waves as much as is possible, to prevent them from passing to other areas. Hard, smooth surfaces reflect more sound than porous textured ones. This is why a room with an acoustic plaster or tile ceiling and carpeted floor is quieter than one with a smooth

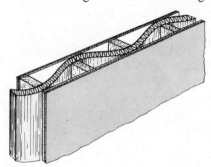

Stud arrangement for sound control wall.

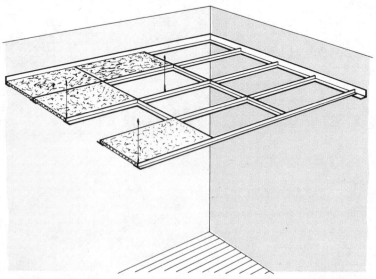

A metal channel system is used to support suspended acoustic ceilings.

Adapted from information supplied by California Redwood Association

Acoustic wood panel wall.

plaster ceiling and a hard surface floor.

Wood joists and floors permit much sound to pass through to other living areas. When this is objectionable, sound deadening insulation, as shown, can be cemented between the subfloor and finished floor. NOTE: The finished floor should not be nailed through the insulation to the subfloor because nails transfer sound.

An acoustic ceiling on the adjacent level will also improve sound conditioning. A drop ceiling, as shown on the bottom of page 182, not directly attached to the joists, provides even better sound control.

If the methods discussed do not provide sufficient control, other construction methods, such as poured concrete or concrete plank floors, may be used.

As walls between rooms allow sound transfer, two independent walls with space and insulation between them, as shown, helps reduce this.

Special metal and rubber clips may also be used to hold wallboard and other sheet materials away from framing members to reduce sound transmission.

Wood paneling similar to the one shown may be fastened to a wall, acting as a trap to prevent sound reflection. Although the paneling does not absorb the sound, it turns waves into each other.

Questions to Reinforce Knowledge

1. As used here, what is meant by the term insulation?

2. What is conduction? From your own reasoning give an example other than the one in the book.

3. What is radiation? Give an example other than the one in the book.

4. What is convection? Give an example other than the one in the book.

5. What is weather stripping and why is it used?

6. How do storm windows or double glazing help stop heat transfer?

7. From what four basic materials is insulation usually manufactured?

8. What is loose fill insulation?

9. What is meant by the term fibrous insulation?

10. What is meant by the term granular insulation?

11. What are two disadvantages of using loose fill insulation?

12. What is batt insulation?

13. What is blanket insulation?

14. In what two ways are the insulations mentioned in questions 12 and 13 held in place?

15. What is rigid insulation?

16. What are three types of rigid insulation?

17. What is insulation board wall sheathing?

18. What is its standard thickness?

19. Name two surface treatments for insulating board wall sheathing.

20. What is reflective insulation? How is it used?

21. Why is it sometimes paper backed?

22. How is reflective insulation sometimes used with other insulating materials?

23. Describe insulating plaster. How does it differ from regular plaster?

24. What is sound conditioning? Why is it important?

25. Describe some of the methods used to improve sound conditioning.

Terms to Spell and Know

heat transfer
conduction
radiation
convection
weather stripping
loose fill insulation
batt insulation
blanket insulation
rigid insulation
slab insulation
reflective insulation
sound conditioning

17

Electrical Requirements

Each year many new electrical devices are placed on the market to make life easier and more enjoyable. New homes and other buildings are equipped with as many of these devices as the budget will permit. Even modest homes include many devices that were formerly very luxurious or even non-existent. The number of electrical items included in homes is increasing, and will continue to do so.

If one tries to use all of today's conveniences with wiring designed for the past, the results can be disastrous. Inadequate wiring can cause lines to overheat, which may result in fires. Overloads cause fuses to burn out, which is very inconvenient. Wires that are too small create excessive resistance which in turn increases the electricity used. This causes an increase in the electric bill. It is necessary to plan a building's electrical features so they exceed the anticipated demand for electric current.

Electric Service

Electric service is supplied by private or publicly owned organizations that deliver current through wires to a building. This source usually (but not always) provides the lines only *to* a building. The entrance service and wiring throughout a building are usually provided by the owner.

The conventional way of running *entrance conductors* to a building—or from the power plant —is by overhead service, which means wires on poles from a source to the building. Another method is underground wiring. The first method is most often used because it is least expensive. However, it has serious drawbacks. Wires strung from pole to pole are unsightly. They are also easily damaged during storms, which can cause interruptions in service. The underground method is much more expensive to install but is more desirable because it removes these objections. Many newly planned communities have complete underground service.

Kind of Service

For the architectural draftsman, a course in electrical circuitry is valuable. Homes and other small buildings usually require three-wire, single-phase, 120-240 volt electric service. Entrance conductors up to the service entrance panel are No. 6 or heavier. Most codes require that 100 amp. service be used, but some require even greater amperage. Of course the system must be designed to meet the demand of all electrical items. A sketch of general requirements is covered here.

Units of Measure

Ampere. Amperage is the strength of an electric current. It is the quantity that can be transmitted through a wire at a given time. The larger the wire the more amperage it can transmit.

Ohm. The unit of electrical resistance in a circuit.

Volt. Voltage is the pressure that forces current through a wire. It is the force that causes one ampere to flow through a wire whose resistance is one ohm.

Watt. A watt is one ampere under one volt of pressure.

Watt hour. A watt hour is one watt used for a period of one hour.

Kilowatt. A kilowatt is 1,000 watts.

Kilowatt hour. A kilowatt hour is 1,000 watts used for one hour.

Abbreviations for Units of Measure

ampere . . . . Amp., amp., A
volt . . . . V, v
watt . . . . W, w
watt hour . . . . . watt-hr., wh., whr.
kilowatt . . . . . . KW, kw.
kilowatt hour . . . K.W.H., kwh.,
     kw-h, kw-hr

Formulas for Units of Measure

$$W = A \times V \qquad V = \frac{W}{A} \qquad A = \frac{W}{V}$$

Calculating Demand

The following table shows items of electrical equipment and the amounts of current they require. This is only a partial list. If different items or ones with different power ratings are to be used, their requirements must be secured from manufacturer's data.

Electrical Equipment Demand

	Diversified demand (KW)
General illumination	4.0
Automatic clothes washer	.6
Dishwasher	.9
Electric range	8.0
Electric oven, built-in	3.6
Electric cooking top, built-in (4 units) .	4.5
Electric clothes dryer:	
Normal	3.4
High speed	6.3
Electric water heater:	
Normal recovery	1.5
High recovery	3.4
Food freezer	.6
Food waste disposer	.4
Water pump	.4
Attic fan	.4
Electric bathroom heater (each)	1.3
Central heating system[1]	.5
Room air conditioner (each)	1.0
Central air conditioner[1]	([2])

[1] Only the larger of the heating or cooling load need be considered.
[2] Rated wattage.

F. H. A.

An example of the electric requirements for a small home might be as follows:

General illumination	4.0 KW	=	4,000 W	@ 120 V	=	33.30	amps.
Dishwasher	1.0 KW	=	1,000 W	@ 240 V	=	4.15	amps.
Electric stove	9.8 KW	=	9,800 W	@ 240 V	=	40.83	amps.
Automatic clothes washer . .	0.6 KW	=	600 W	@ 120 V	=	5.00	amps.
Automatic clothes dryer	6.3 KW	=	6,300 W	@ 240 V	=	26.25	amps.
Heating system	0.5 KW	=	500 W	@ 120 V	=	4.17	amps.
Central air conditioning	5.0 KW	=	5,000 W	@ 240 V	=	20.83	amps.
Future appliances	8.0 KW	=	8,000 W	@ 120 V	=	66.66	amps.
	35.2 KW					**201.19**	**amps.**

NOTE: *The above list does not include all items normally found in a home; the ones given are for illustrative purposes only.*

If one were to use all the electrical items listed above at the same time the entrance service would need to carry 202 amperes. However, one may safely assume that no more than $^3/_5$ of the items will be in use at the same time. To arrive at a realistic amperage then, one would provide approximately $^3/_5$ the computed amount, or 121 amps. A search of manufacturer's data reveals no entrance service panel designed for this specific amperage. However, one is listed as providing 125 amp. service, so this one may be used.

Entrance service panels may be equipped with fuses, as described earlier, containing a limited conductor that melts when excess current is passed through, or panels may be equipped with *circuit breakers* that can be reset after an overload is removed.

Distribution

From the electrical center, and passing through individual fuses or circuit breakers, branch circuits are run to equipment and lighting. Branch circuits are usually designed to carry 15 or 20 amps., depending upon the conductor wire size. For many years No. 14 conductor wire was considered adequate but, with today's increased demand, No. 12 is desirable. If circuits are to carry heavy loads as for electric stoves, air conditioners, or heavy duty motors, they may require No. 10 or larger conductor wires.

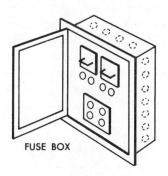

FUSE BOX

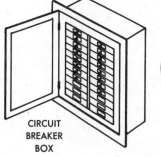

CIRCUIT BREAKER BOX

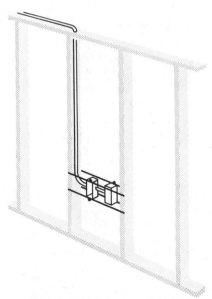

Rigid conduit and receptacle boxes back to back.

There are several methods of protecting circuits, determined by local code requirements and personal preference. The most common uses wires in metal or plastic pipe, called *conduit*. Different pipe sizes permit any number of wires to be placed inside. If many wires are to be run in the same direction they may be placed in a single conduit; it is unnecessary to have separate conduits for each set of wires. Conduit may be categorized into two classifications: *rigid* or *flexible*. On the illustration, observe how the conduit is bent so wires can turn corners.

Some codes permit wires to be run without conduit if they are considered fire safe. Two or more wires, depending upon the number needed for the circuit run, may be encased in flexible cable similar in appearance to flexible conduit, or two or more wires may have built-in protection, such as strands of wire inside a waterproof covering, or wires may be encased in plastic. The latter is frequently used for outside or underground circuits. It must be of a grade that seals out water, which can cause short circuits, and does not deteriorate from exposure.

Any of the protective methods mentioned above can be used in conjunction with low voltage systems, which are discussed later.

conduct static charges, thereby reducing danger and annoyance to the user. Many building codes require all wiring in new construction to be installed in this manner.

Wires running from an appliance or fixture to a switch are frequently colored red for easy identification.

Number of Circuits Required

As discussed earlier, each circuit should carry no more than 15 or 20 amps; so individual circuit loads must be calculated and distributed throughout the system to accomplish this. Proper distribution is very important for efficient operation.

Stoves, air conditioners, water heaters, furnaces, freezers, large motors, or any other device that requires large amperage should be placed alone on a circuit. Receptacle outlets in the kitchen, laundry, or utility room should be distributed between two or more circuits and should not be on ones used for illumination. All receptacle outlets in a room should not be placed on the same circuit. Circuits may overlap into two or more rooms.

In rooms other than the service area, lighting fixtures and receptacle outlets may be placed on the same circuit. However, no room should have *all* equipment on the same circuit. The load can be too heavy and if service is disrupted the entire room is without electricity.

Outlet Boxes

Except for low voltage systems, all wire connections, fixtures, re-

Wires and Circuits Required

Three wires are normally brought from the source to the entrance panel. Two of them are black and one is either white or uninsulated. Each of the black wires supplies 120 volts, while the white one serves as a neutral or ground wire. If branch circuits require only 120 volts, just one black wire and one white wire are needed. If a circuit requires 240 volts, all three wires must be strung. In addition to these wires a green one is sometimes included to serve as a *secondary ground*. This wire is not connected to the electrical system. One end is fastened to a water pipe or metal stake outside the building and the other end is fastened to the case of the appliance or fixture. This wire is used to siphon electricity into the ground in the event of a short circuit, and to

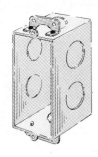

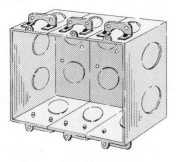

Outlet boxes.

ceptacle outlets, switches, and other devices should be joined to the electrical system in outlet boxes. Rectangular, square, and octagonal boxes are shown. The first two are used primarily for switches and receptacle outlets. Octagonal boxes are used for installing light fixtures and making wire connections. Octagonal boxes are used alone, but square or rectangular ones may be used as

individuals, or some models have removable sides so several can be joined together to form *gang boxes* to accommodate several switches or receptacle outlets. Boxes may be fastened directly to structural members, or they may be secured by a variety of fastening devices.

When installed, the open side of a box is placed flush with the finished wall.

Required Lighting Outlets and Switches

Every room except the bath should have at least three duplex (double) receptacle outlets. They are installed a maximum of 12 feet apart, but 8 feet is more desirable. Every wall large enough for placing furniture should have a receptacle outlet; this includes wall spaces between doors, below windows, or by fireplaces. Outlet location should be planned to coincide with furniture placement. That is, if a lamp or other electrical device is likely to be used at a certain location, there should be a receptacle outlet near it.

Special outlet requirements. (1) Every hall should have at least one receptacle outlet. (2) In addition to regular kitchen or utility room outlets, each permanent appliance should have a separate outlet. There should be two or more outlets above each counter top. (3) An outlet must be provided above or close to the lavatory mirror. (4) When outlets are placed in basements, garages, outdoors, or any other place where dampness is likely to occur, they must be of the grounding type. (5) If outlets are exposed to the

weather, they should be waterproof.

Living room. No permanent light fixture is usually required if switch-controlled receptacle outlets are provided.

Dining room. The dining room must have at least one switch-controlled, permanent light fixture. For best results this fixture should be near or over the dining room table.

Kitchen. The kitchen should have a permanent light fixture mounted in or near the center of the ceiling. This light should be controlled by switches near the doors. A permanent fixture should also be installed above the sink. The switch for this light may be on the wall adjacent to the sink.

Utility or laundry rooms. These rooms should also have permanent, ceiling-mounted light fixtures controlled by switches. Fixtures must also be provided near the laundry tubs or sink and other work areas.

Bedrooms. Bedrooms do not always have permanent ceiling-mounted fixtures. These may be omitted if switch-controlled receptacle outlets are provided and the client so desires.

Activity room (with any name). This room should be equipped with permanent switch-controlled fixtures. They may be simple ceiling mounts or very elaborate installations featuring light troughs, indirect lighting, accent lights, dimming devices, or other specialties.

Halls. The entry or foyer and all halls should have permanent switch-controlled fixtures.

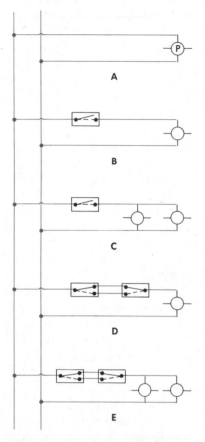

Three-way switches are recommended for a long hall. These are operated at two points, for convenience.

Bathroom. The bathroom must have at least one permanent fixture mounted above the lavatory mirror. Its switch should be near the point of use. However, if this is the only fixture in the room the switch should be near the door. If the room is larger than 5'-0"x 8'-0", an additional ceiling fixture should be provided. NOTE: One should be unable to reach any switch or receptacle outlet from the bathtub because of the electrical danger to the user.

A. Light outlet with pull switch

B. One lighting outlet controlled by a single pole switch

C. Two lighting outlets controlled by a single pole switch

D. One lighting outlet controlled by three-way switches

E. Two lighting outlets controlled by three-way switches

Switching diagram.

Suspended ceilings with luminous panels are decorative as well as functional.

Artcrest Products Co., Inc

Closets or cupboards. All closets, except very small shelving units, should have a permanent light fixture. These are usually very simple with exposed incandescent or fluorescent bulbs. All closet lights must be switch-controlled. The switch may have a simple pull chain attached to the fixture, or it may be mechanical, to turn the light on automatically as the door is opened. When closets are filled with shelves, as a linen cupboard, it is a good idea to place a simple ceiling-mounted fixture so it will illuminate the area.

Stairways. Permanent fixtures should be provided to illuminate all stairways. They may be at a point along the stair well or near the top or bottom. When illuminating basement stairs, if the light is placed at the foot of the stairs it may also illuminate part of the basement. If there is no other access to the basement this light may have a single-pole switch. If the basement has another door providing access, a three-way switch should be provided so the light can be controlled from both the head and foot of the stairs. Even though a single-pole switch fulfills the minimum requirements, three-way switches are strongly recommended for all stairs.

Basement lights. There are no special lighting requirements for the basement. However, proper illumination must be provided for safety and the tasks to be performed. Lights may be controlled by switches or pull chains as desired.

188

Exterior lighting makes this home an after-dark showplace.

Lighting for this family room and kitchen adds to both function and beauty.

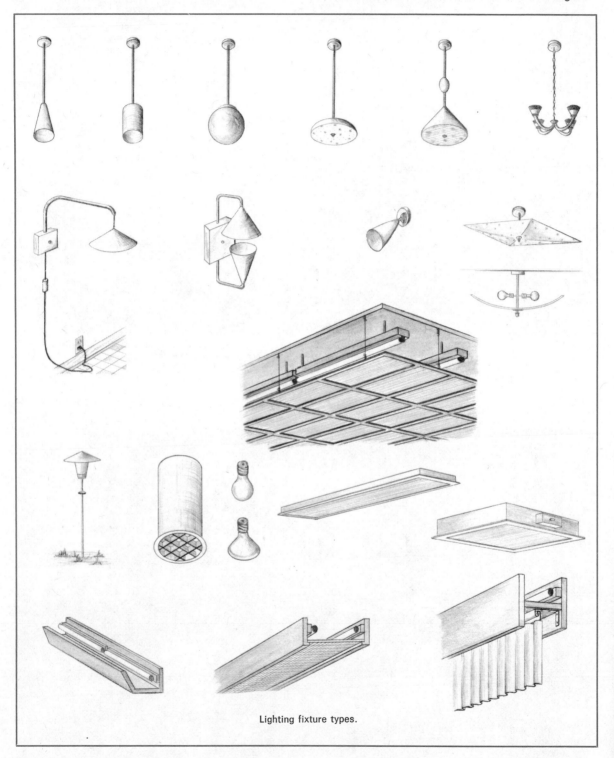

Lighting fixture types.

Garage. Permanent switch-controlled fixtures are to be included in the garage. One should be able to control them from either the house or garage.

Outside illumination. Permanent fixtures must be provided to illuminate the entrance outside each door. These are controlled by switches inside the building but next to the door opening. Additional exterior lighting is desirable but must be designed to fulfill specific needs or desires.

Special Lighting Requirements

In addition to the general illumination just discussed, it is desirable to have additional light in most rooms for reading, sewing, writing, cooking, or other uses. One may also desire light for its beauty or psychological effect.

There are so many electrical fixtures available that it is not possible to discuss or show all of them. Only general types are represented to convey an idea of the possibilities.

The accompanying diagram shows how the electrical system can be divided into two parts. The main system supplies 120 volts to fixtures and is very similar to conventional wiring. Conventional switch wires leading from fixtures have been eliminated. They are replaced by electromagnet switches actuated by the low-voltage circuit.

At the left of the diagram observe the transformer. Switch wires leading from the transformer supply 12 or 24 volts (depending upon the system). Observe also that after the switch wires leave the transformer the two sets of wiring are not connected anywhere in the building; that is, they operate independently of each other. Since they supply little voltage they may be of very light-duty bell wire. There is no danger of a hazardous short circuit in the switching system; wires need not be run in conduit nor installed in metal switch boxes.

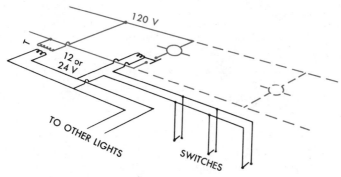

Low voltage wiring diagram.

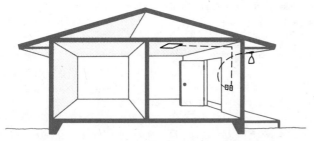

Switch locations for interior and exterior fixtures.

Low Voltage Systems

When switches must control electrical devices from a great number of locations, the installation becomes very complex and the cost may be prohibitive. Low voltage wiring and switching devices are a practical solution because they are designed for these installations.

Electrical Plans

Electrical plans for light construction are drawn to show the approximate location of the entrance service panel, all switches, receptacle outlets, and fixtures. Exact locations are seldom dimensioned, thus permitting slight variations to expedite installation.

Except for very large buildings with complicated electrical systems, conductor wires are not indicated on electrical plans. When one observes electrical floor plans and sees lines connecting switches and fixtures, these may be misinterpreted as wire locations.

These lines only indicate the proper switch to control a specific fixture; they do not indicate the exact location of conductor wires.

If space permits, electrical information may be included on a floor plan. If the plan is too complex, a separate one may be drawn to show wiring and fixtures.

Electrical information may also be required on elevation, detail, and section drawings. For example, typical and special switch and receptacle outlet heights need to be shown.

Symbols

Electrical items are drawn as symbols on building plans. For convenient reference those most frequently used are included in Chapter 38, rather than with other electrical information. Of course, symbols replace specific items. If such items must be identified, code numbers or manufacturers' model numbers may be added to the plan at a location near the symbol. When drawing symbols on your plan be sure to check the examples mentioned earlier.

run to a building? Explain the use of each.

27. What is a secondary ground?

28. Why are switch wires sometimes colored red?

29. From your own reasoning, from the preceding question, why are several colors used on the insulation of electric wires?

30. What is the recommended amperage for a typical electrical circuit?

31. Is it permissible to place an electric stove and an air conditioning compressor on the same circuit? Explain why or why not.

32. What is a receptacle outlet?

33. Should all receptacle outlets in a kitchen or utility room be on the same circuit?

34. Should light fixtures be on the same circuit as receptacle outlets in a kitchen or laundry room? Why or why not?

35. In other rooms is it permissible to place light fixtures and receptacles on the same circuit?

36. How would you advise a client on having all receptacles and fixtures in any room on the same circuit? Why?

37. What kinds of items require individual circuits? Why?

38. Excluding the items in question 37, must each room be placed on a separate circuit? Explain why or why not.

39. What are outlet boxes? What are the three most frequently used shapes?

40. What are gang boxes?

41. What is a duplex receptacle outlet?

42. How should receptacle outlets be spaced in a room? What is the minimum number for each room?

Questions to Reinforce Knowledge

1. Why does the number of electrical items found in homes today exceed the number used in the immediate past?

2. What is the anticipated trend for the future? How does this affect building wiring?

3. What is likely to happen if wiring is inadequate?

4. What is electric service? Who supplies it?

5. Who pays the cost for entrance conductors up to a building? Explain.

6. What are two methods of running entrance conductors to a building? Explain the advantages and disadvantages of each.

7. How much voltage is normally supplied to a home? Amperage?

8. What is an ohm?

9. What is an ampere?

10. What is a volt?

11. What is a watt?

12. What is a watt hour?

13. What is a kilowatt?

14. What is a kilowatt hour?

15. Give abbreviations for items 9 through 14.

16. What is the formula for finding watts?

17. What is the formula for finding volts?

18. What is the formula for finding amperes?

19. Explain how to determine the electric requirements of a home.

20. When making electrical calculations, does one presume that all equipment will be used at the same time? Explain.

21. What is an entrance service panel?

22. What is a branch circuit?

23. What conductor wire size is recommended for most circuits? When is heavier wire recommended?

24. What is conduit? Describe two kinds.

25. Are conductor wires always run in conduit? Explain why or why not. How do building codes help determine this?

26. How many wires are usually

43. What walls should have receptacle outlets?

44. If a room does not require a permanent light fixture, what special provision must be made?

45. Describe possible lighting requirements of a kitchen, utility room, or laundry room.

46. Describe the possible lighting requirements of bathrooms.

47. What kinds of closets require light fixtures?

48. Must all closet lights be operated from wall mounted switches? Explain.

49. Describe locations of fixtures to illuminate a stairway.

50. What kind of switch is recommended for stairways?

51. Describe lighting requirements at exterior doors. Where are switches for these lights located?

52. How does a low-voltage wiring system differ from the conventional one?

53. Explain why low-voltage switch wire size can be less than with conventional wiring.

54. On electric plans, does one normally dimension the location of receptacle outlets or light fixtures? Why or why not?

55. On a floor plan, what do the lines connecting switches and fixtures show?

56. Is electrical information included on the regular floor plan or is a separate one drawn to include this information? Explain.

57. Explain how code numbers or letter symbols can be used with electrical symbols.

Terms to Spell and Know

electric service	watt	flexible conduit
entrance service	watt hour	secondary ground
entrance conductors	kilowatt	receptacle outlet
overhead service	kilowatt hour	switch
underground service	entrance service panel	low-voltage plan
ohm	fuse	fixture
ampere	circuit breaker	single-pole switch
volt	branch circuit	three-way switch
	rigid conduit	

18

Plumbing

Elsewhere in this book it is pointed out that one cannot believe that everything new is necessarily good and that everything old is no longer applicable. If this were true plumbing would have been discarded a long time ago.

So-called modern history indicates that many of our immediate forebears had no plumbing conveniences. It is easy to rationalize that if they had none, plumbing had not been invented prior to this time. This is a false assumption. Study of the rise, decline, and fall of the Roman Empire shows that plumbing played an important part in their daily lives.

Great aqueducts transported water from distant mountains for use in the cities. Some of these were open channels built with a gradual slope which permitted gravity to carry the water to its destination. Others were completely enclosed by stone, brick, or concrete. Per capita water consumption was greater than that of many cities today.

Excavations of ruins also revealed interior plumbing fixtures and supply systems that are still virtually intact.

Today's Water Supply

Availability of a suitable and abundant water supply is too often taken for granted. We know that water is taken from lakes, reservoirs, rivers, deep wells, and that some is being converted from sea water to make it suitable for human consumption. Because of waste, neglect, and increased usage, an adequate water supply is becoming difficult to maintain.

leads from the city main, well, or other source to a location just inside the building. The size of this pipe is determined by the amount of water to be supplied and by local code requirements. FHA minimum requirements specify at least a ¾″ supply line. However, a larger size is more desirable. This line is usually of galvanized iron or copper, but brass alloy or cast iron pipe are also frequently used, with infrequent or experimental use of other materials.

This main line may be located in the same trench with the waste line leading from the building to the sewer. NOTE: Back fill covering water lines must not contain cinders or other debris that could have a corrosive action on the pipe.

The water supply line usually connects to a meter and/or shut-off valve. In warm climates the meter may be installed either inside or outside the building, but in cold climates it is most often installed inside. A water line may pass through a foundation wall or beneath a footing. When the pipe passes through a foundation wall it should be encased in a short length of larger diameter pipe to permit building settlement

Water Distribution System

People are familiar with plumbing fixtures because they see and use them. Almost every home has at least one kitchen sink, water closet, lavatory, bathtub, and either a laundry tub or connections for an automatic washer. Also, each house usually has either a gas or electric water heater. Each of these fixtures must be connected to a water supply source and drain. (Except that some water heaters do not connect to the house drainage system.) Plumbing fixtures and their arrangement into rooms are discussed in Chapter 27.

One large water supply line

and pipe movement. The void between pipes should be filled with a pliable waterproofing.

If city mains supply more than 80 pounds of water pressure per square inch, then a pressure reducing valve should be installed in the main before it connects to house lines. If too little pressure is supplied, one may install a booster pump and storage tank to increase pressure.

In localities where no city mains are present, the owner must connect a pump and storage tank to a well or other supply source.

Branch Water Lines

Inside the building the water line divides into two pipes called *branch lines*. One pipe supplies cold water and the other is connected to a hot water heater. Both lines then contine on toward each tap. These pipes are called primary branch lines, which frequently have ¾″ inside diameter. A smaller diameter (usually ½″) secondary branch line is used to connect each tap with both hot and cold primary branch lines.

Each branch line should have a shut-off valve before it connects to a faucet so individual fixtures can be isolated from the system without shutting off all water to the building.

Water pipes that extend vertically to each fixture are called *risers*.

Many codes require compression chambers to join branch lines with faucets. These serve as air cushioning devices to help reduce pipe noises during faucet

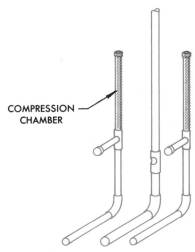

COMPRESSION CHAMBER

Pipe noises are reduced by using compression chambers.

use. The compression chambers shown in the illustration are constructed of short pipe risers with closed ends.

All water lines should be installed in an orderly manner but should use a minimum amount of pipe. Pipes are usually installed parallel to building edges with hot and cold lines running parallel to each other approximately 6″ apart. Closer spacing permits transfer of heat and cold from one pipe to the other. If closer spacing is required, pipes must be insulated to prevent heat transfer. When finances permit, insulated hot water pipes conserve hot water and reduce water heating costs.

When pipes must be installed between a floor and a ceiling they may be placed between joists, when both pipes and joist run the same direction. When pipes are at right angles to the joists their installation is more complicated.

Pipes must either be placed below the joists and the ceiling furred down to accommodate them, or joists may be notched to receive the pipe. Joists should be notched close to their top edge and the cut should be no more than ⅓ joist width to avoid weakening. It is also a good idea to place the notch in the first ⅓ of the joist length from a supported end.

The tap fixture location is shown on floor plans and no further dimensioning is usually required to show where pipes extend through a floor or into a wall. Their exact positions are usually determined by the plumbing contractor. Naturally there are exceptions to this; when specific pipe locations are necessary because of other construction features, then exact dimensions are required. In addition to the water lines for fixtures, others are also desirable. Every home should have at least one outside faucet (also called a *sill cock* or *hose bib*), and additional ones are also frequently installed. In cold climates these should be of the frost-free type. When lawn sprinkling is anticipated *freestanding types* may be installed in the lawn. These may protrude above the lawn level or be recessed so they are not visible. Permanent lawn sprinkling systems with pipes and sprinklers throughout the lawn may be installed if desired and finances permit. It is also a good idea to have a faucet in or near the garage. NOTE: Some heating and air conditioning units also require a water supply.

Waste Removal

Used water and wastes must be drained from the building through sewage disposal pipes. Those inside the building are frequently called drains. Sewage pipes or drains are composed of many individual parts.

Traps. Connecting directly to each fixture is a pipe with a sharp bend in it. This bend is called a trap. For most fixtures the trap is of a small diameter, except for the water closet, which requires a 4″ one. Other drain trap sizes are determined by the fixture opening to which they are connected. Traps are very necessary to a plumbing system. They remain full of water at all times to prevent sewer gas from backing up into the building. In addition to its objectionable odor, this gas is poisonous and, if confined in a closed space, is explosive.

Traps empty into the main house drainage system. Horizontal drains then slope gently toward the city sewer or other drainage system. Drains should slope approximately ¼″ per foot. A steeper slope causes water to drain from the building sewer too rapidly, thus leaving waste materials in the pipe. If drains in the house or those connecting to a city sewer must change levels rapidly, it is best to continue the gentle slope as described and then drop them vertically to their new level. When drains change direction of flow, as when they turn a corner, a cleanout opening must be provided.

Vents. Have you ever poured liquid from a container with one

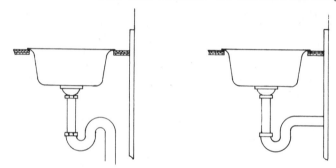

All plumbing fixtures require traps before emptying into house drains.

A properly designed water supply and waste removal system.

Anaconda American Brass Company

small opening in the top? If not, obtain a metal container with such an opening. Fill it with water and then pour the contents out. The liquid will not pour smoothly from the container because there is no air inlet. Now, puncture a small hole in the top on an edge opposite the original opening. The small air hole permits the liquid to flow freely.

This same principle is applied to a house drainage system. It was mentioned earlier that traps always contain water; therefore it is not possible for air to enter the drains from the traps. Drains must have ventilation to empty properly. Observe the cutaway photograph showing a house plumbing system. Note the large pipe extending vertically through the roof. This is a soil and vent stack. From the bathroom, pipe carries waste from the second floor to a point below the first floor; this part of the pipe is the soil stack. The vertical riser extending up from the second floor is the vent stack. Of course, in a one-story home the vent stack comes from first floor level. This large vent usually connects to the water closet drain. On the cutaway photograph observe how other fixtures are vented into this main one. If fixtures are widely separated, as those for bathrooms and the kitchen, additional soil and vent stacks are required. When only one fixture is to be vented (excluding water closets) some codes permit 2″ vent stacks. Otherwise, they are 4″ inside diameter and will not fit inside regular stud walls. Walls contain-

ing these large vents are usually framed with 2″x6″ studs instead of 2x4's.

Like water supply lines, there are many different kinds of pipe used for removing wastes. Cast iron pipe is widely used. This is a very good material because it is long lasting and its permanently sealed bell joints seldom if ever need repairs. Copper and brass alloy pipes are also frequently used. These are not only long lasting and easy to install but do not rust. Four-inch diameter pipes are most frequently used for main lines. Vitreous clay bell tile is sometimes used to connect from a building to the city sewer or other drainage system. With this material a 6″ diameter pipe is recommended. NOTE: Bell tile should not be used in areas where tree roots are present because they penetrate cemented joints between tiles and clog the system. Neither should it be used on unstable soils unless it is held

Western Wood Products Association

Vent stacks require flashing to prevent leaks.

level by additional support. Fiber, bituminous coated, and plastic pipe are also used, most frequently outside a building.

Before selecting a kind of pipe for drains or specific sizes to drain fixtures one must check local codes because some codes specify the exact kind and size required for each application.

After all interior drainage lines merge to form one line, a final trap should be installed to prevent gas and wastes backing up from the city main. This trap should be placed at a point just before the sewer leaves the house.

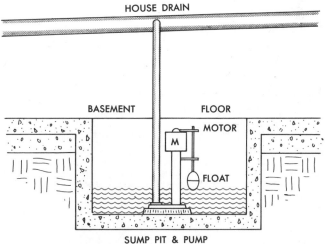

Sump pumps lift water to overhead sewers.

A vent should be installed on the house side of the trap to permit gas not exhausted by other vents to escape.

Main sewers frequently are not as deep as basements. House drains leading from living levels then cannot be concealed beneath basement floors. Attach them to basement walls or suspend them from joists in order to maintain a suitable sewer depth and slope for joining outside sewers.

It is customary to locate drains in basement floors but when the sewer is higher than floor level a gravity type drain cannot be used. A concrete pit with a cover is located in an inconspicuous location and the floor sloped slightly toward it. The pit is equipped with a sump pump that has a pipe connected to the house drain. When water fills the pit to a predetermined level, the pump turns on automatically and lifts the water to the drain.

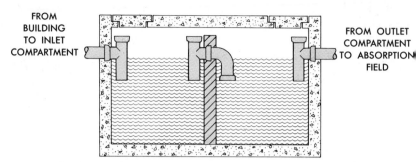

FROM BUILDING TO INLET COMPARTMENT

FROM OUTLET COMPARTMENT TO ABSORPTION FIELD

Septic tanks are used in localities not served by city sewers.

Septic Systems

As stated earlier, when there is no sewage system, it is necessary to provide other means of waste removal. The most widely used is a septic system. This removal method is favored because it purifies house wastes rather than contaminating the immediate vicinity.

House sewers empty into the upper part of an air-tight underground container called a septic tank. The tank has two compartments. The compartment closest to the building collects wastes and permits solid materials to settle. Bacterial action then decomposes the solid wastes. Near the top of the tank an opening is joined to the second compartment. Clear water drains from the first into the second. Another outlet in the second compartment permits water to overflow and drain into a septic field. The field is a series of open jointed pipes laid in gravel or crushed stone; it allows drainage water to seep into surrounding earth.

Recommended Minimum Standards for Individual Sewage-Disposal System
(To be supplemented by local code requirements)

Table 1
REQUIRED CAPACITIES AND SUGGESTED DIMENSIONS FOR SEPTIC TANKS
(Minimum size tank 750-gallons liquid capacity)

No. of Bedrooms in Dwelling	Max. No. of Persons Served	Normal Liquid Cap. of Tank in Gallons	Inside Width	Inside Length	Liquid Depth	Total Depth
2 or less	4	750	3'-6"	7'-6"	4'-0"	4'-9"
3	6	900	3'-6"	8'-6"	4'-0"	4'-10"
4	8	1,000	4'-0"	8'-6"	4'-6"	5'-5"
5	10	1,250	4'-0"	9'-6"	4'-6"	5'-5"
6	12	1,500	4'-6"	10'-0"	4'-6"	5'-6"

Suggested Dimensions for Rectangular Tanks spans the Inside Width, Inside Length, Liquid Depth, and Total Depth columns.

Table 2
Locations of Systems

Minimum Safe Distances in Feet

From	Septic Tank	Absorption Field	Seepage Pit	Absorption Bed
Well	50	100	100	100
Property Line	10	5	10	10
Foundation Wall	5	5	20	5
Water Lines	10	10	10	10
Seepage Pit	6	6	—	—
Drywell	6	20	20	20

Absorption Trench

Function: The absorption trench gives needed additional treatment to the sewage from the septic tank. In it the effluent is treated by bacteria that live in the upper reaches of the soil. Final disposal is accomplished by ground absorption. The absorption area needed is determined by percolation tests. See "Percolation Test Instructions," below.

Percolation Test

After a tentative site for the absorption trench has been selected, at least two percolation tests should be made. The percolation test determines the absorption rate of the soil. Knowing the absorption rate of the soil, the absorption area needed per bedroom can be taken from Table 3.

Percolation Test Instructions

The procedure for conducting the percolation test is as follows:

1. Dig or bore holes with horizontal dimensions of from 4 to 12 inches and vertical sides to the estimated depth of the bottom of the proposed absorption trench. On level ground this depth is usually about 30 inches. In order to save time, labor and volume of water required per test, the holes can be bored with a 4-inch auger.

2. Scratch the bottom and sides of the hole with a knife blade or sharp pointed instrument in order to remove any smeared soil surface and to provide a natural soil interface into which water may percolate. Remove all loose soil from the hole. Place about 2 inches of coarse sand or fine gravel in the bottom of the hole.

3. Carefully fill the hole with clear water. By refilling if necessary keep some water in the hole for at least 12 hours. This saturation procedure will give most soils ample time to swell and approach the conditions that prevail during the wettest season of the year. Thus the test will give comparable results whether made during a wet or dry season.

4. After the 12-hour saturation period allow the hole to empty. Remove that portion of the sand or gravel which has become coated with soil particles.

5. Pour about 12" of water into the hole and wait until about 6" of this water remains.

6. With about 6" of water remaining in the hole, establish a reference point such as a nail stuck in the side near the top of the hole. From this point obtain a measurement to the top of the water level. Record the measurement and the exact time.

7. Allow the water to seep away completely. Again record the exact time and compute the distance the water has dropped.

8. Convert the time interval to minutes and divide this figure by the number of inches of water which has seeped away to obtain the average time for one inch of water to seep away.

9. Determine from Table 3 the square feet of trench bottom area needed for each bedroom. See Table 4 for width and spacing of absorption trenches.

10. Multiply the square feet of trench bottom absorption area needed for each bedroom by the number of bedrooms in the house to get the total trench bottom area needed.

Table 3

DATA FOR DETERMINING SQUARE FEET OF ABSORPTION AREA NEEDED PER BEDROOM

Average time in minutes for water to fall one inch	Effective absorption area in square feet needed in trench bottom per bedroom
2 minutes or less per inch	85 sq. ft. per bedroom
3 minutes per inch	100 sq. ft. per bedroom
4 minutes per inch	115 sq. ft. per bedroom
5 minutes per inch	125 sq. ft. per bedroom
10 minutes per inch	165 sq. ft. per bedroom
15 minutes per inch	190 sq. ft. per bedroom
30 minutes per inch	250 sq. ft. per bedroom
45 minutes per inch	300 sq. ft. per bedroom
60 minutes per inch	330 sq. ft. per bedroom
Over 60 minutes	Unsuitable for absorption field

Table 4

SIZE AND SPACING REQUIREMENTS FOR ABSORPTION TRENCHES

Width of Trench at Bottom in Inches	Depth of Trench in Inches	Effective Absorption Area in Square Feet per Linear Foot	Minimum Spacing of Lines C to C in Feet
12—18	18 to 30	1.5	6.0
18—24	18 to 30	2.0	6.5
24—30	18 to 36	2.5	7.0
30—36	24 to 36	3.0	7.5

Material

Absorption lines may be constructed with four-inch field tile or properly perforated sewer tile. Place strips of building paper or similar material over the open joints of the field tile. Surround the pipe completely with coarse gravel or stone.

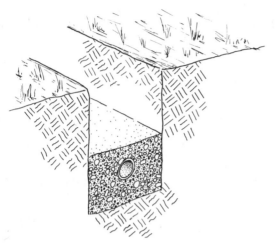

Details of Absorption Trench and Line, for Non-Perforated Sewer Pipe

ABSORPTION TRENCHES IN HILLY LAND

On rolling or hilly land each absorption line should follow approximately the land surface contour.

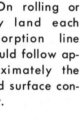

Absorption Trench for Rolling or Hilly Land.

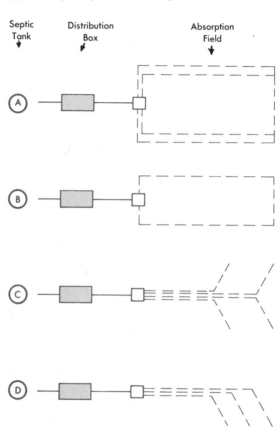

Absorption Field Patterns for Reasonably Level Land

Slope

Slope the absorption lines two to four inches per 100 feet. Progressive clogging of the absorption lines may develop if the slope of the lines is flatter or steeper.

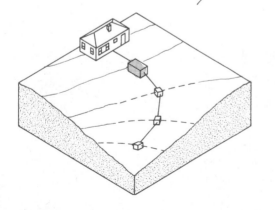

Plumbing-Heating-Cooling Information Bureau

Other Plumbing Lines

Foundation drain tiles were discussed in Chapter 3, Footings and Foundations, but are again mentioned here as a reminder that they are a part of the plumbing system.

Gas lines may also be a part of and installed at the same time as other plumbing.

Garage floor drains are frequently included as a part of the plumbing system.

Drainage for gutters and downspouts should be installed along with the plumbing system.

Questions to Reinforce Knowledge

1. Is the use of plumbing a modern development? Explain.

2. Name four sources frequently used as a water supply.

3. What is the minimum recommended size for water lines connecting from the city main to a home?

4. What two materials are most frequently used for water lines?

5. Why must cinders and debris be kept from back fill covering water lines?

6. Describe water meter locations in relationship to a home? Why are they sometimes located one place and sometimes another?

7. Why should water pipes or sewers be placed inside a pipe collar when they pass through a foundation wall?

8. What is a branch water line? How many are required? Why?

9. What is the smallest diameter pipe recommended for branch water lines?

10. What is the difference between a primary and secondary branch line?

11. What name is given to vertical water and drain pipes?

12. What is the purpose of compression chambers at faucets?

13. What is the recommended spacing between parallel hot and cold water pipes?

14. Why are water and sewer pipes usually installed parallel to building walls?

15. Describe the special provisions necessary when pipes must be concealed between floors and ceilings.

16. What is another name for outside water faucets?

17. Describe two types and reasons for their use.

18. Pipes to drain water and wastes from a building are called by what names?

19. What is a trap? Why are traps used?

20. What is the recommended amount of slope for a sewer? Why?

21. From your own reasoning, why are cleanouts necessary when sewer drains change directions?

22. Describe why vents are a necessary part of a plumbing system.

23. What is the difference between a soil stack and a vent stack? When may the same pipe be used?

24. Describe which plumbing fixtures require vents and tell why.

25. Why do walls containing vent stacks almost always have 2"x6" studs?

26. Describe the variety of different pipes available for waste lines.

27. How does one determine which one to use?

28. Why is a trap placed in the sewer pipe just before it leaves a building?

29. Which side of this trap is vented? Why?

30. What is a sump pump? Why is it used?

31. What is a septic system? Why is it used?

32. Describe the operation of a septic tank.

33. What size pipe is usually used for septic absorption fields?

34. How does this size compare with foundation perimeter drain tile?

Terms to Spell and Know

aqueduct	compression chamber	soil stack
plumbing	pipe riser	vent stack
water main	sill cock	bell tile
water meter	hose bib	sump pump
pressure reducing	trap	septic system
valve	sewer	percolation test
booster pump	sewage	absorption trench
branch water line	drain	or field
shutoff	cleanout	distribution box

Climate Control

Man's physical environment plays an important part in how he feels and reacts to situations. This chapter discusses ways of altering building temperature, air circulation, and humidity for healthful, comfortable living.

Man's primary concern in the past was to change temperature just to survive, but at the present time this is not enough. One cannot be pleasant or work at maximum efficiency when he is uncomfortable.

Chapter 16 is directly related to this discussion because insu-

lation is one of the necessary ingredients for adequate climate control. The three methods of heat transfer (1) conduction, (2) radiation, and (3) convection discussed earlier are ways mechanical equipment transfers heat, cold, and humidity from one location to another.

Heating progress evolved from an open fire to the fireplace, then to the heating stove. After the heating stove the next great step forward was the invention of a furnace capable of heating an entire building. Early models were

crude and inefficient, but recent ones are highly sophisticated, capable of heating, cooling, and humidifying buildings automatically. They are well designed, require less space, and are very efficient.

Heat Distribution Methods

There are three widely used methods of heat distribution:
1. Ducts for warm air.
2. Pipes for carrying steam or hot water.
3. Surfaces for distributing radiant heat.

A light-colored roof reflects the sun's rays and makes a home easier to cool.

National Homes

Gravity Warm Air

Warm air gravity heating systems were formerly widely used. Early warm air furnaces were merely large round stoves with an outer jacket to lead air into large round ducts radiating in all directions from the furnace top. These ducts supplied warm air to heat outlets in each room. There were no mechanical devices to move air through the ducts, hence the name gravity flow. Warm air ducts in both early and current furnaces usually terminate at inlets near outside walls. Inlets are usually located beneath windows because more heat is radiated through them than at any other point. Cold air outlets near inside walls connect with ducts that return cold air to the furnace for warming and recirculation.

Forced Warm Air

A gravity system loses considerable heat during transfer through ducts because air movement is slow. A more rapid movement could minimize heat loss. When a fan is installed in the furnace plenum chamber to speed air transfer, the unit is then called a forced warm air furnace.

The plenum is the air chamber or bonnet of the furnace used to collect warm air for distribution. It is usually on the top of the furnace because warm air rises naturally to this location. However, some furnaces have a *reversed flow* (counterflow) and the plenum is on the bottom. Homes with basements use the first type, but no-basement homes having the furnace on the main

level, with ducts below floors, require the latter type.

Appearance and operation of newer forced warm air furnaces are much improved over earlier models. Whereas early models were large, round, and hàd sprawling round ducts occupying much space, newer models are compactly designed, rectangular units with shallow, rectangular ducts that occupy little space. When ducts run the same direction as joists they may be recessed between them.

Mueller Climatrol

The plenum chamber for connecting heat ducts is placed below this counterflow, forced warm-air furnace.

Fuel

Early warm air furnaces used coal as their fuel. This required shoveling and was both dirty to handle and did not burn with a clean flame. Introduction of stokers to feed the furnace automatically removed the first objection but even better methods were sought. Oil and gas replaced coal as the most widely used fuels. Furnaces using oil or gas are fed automatically. These fuels also burn with a cleaner flame.

Advantages and Disadvantages

Forced warm air furnaces have both advantages and disadvantages when compared with other types. They are inexpensive to purchase and easy to install. They provide an adequate heat supply.

Mueller Climatrol

This upflow, forced warm-air furnace may be installed with 0″ clearance at sides and back.

Mueller Climatrol

This low forced-air furnace may be equipped with air conditioning evaporator coils at any time, thus simplifying any future air conditioning installation.

Honeywell Inc.

A thermostat is an automatic sensing device to be pre-set at a desired temperature.

Honeywell Inc.

Controlled thermostats automaticlly change desired temperature at a prescribed time.

Honeywell Inc.

Deluxe thermostat for automatic temperature change of both heat and air conditioning.

Heat ducts for warm air furnaces may also be utilized for central air conditioning, thus making air conditioning installation less expensive than when installed separately.

Heat is supplied almost instantly when automatic devices denote a need. When the temperature reaches the prescribed level the furnace ceases operation. Continual switching from heat to no heat can be objectionable.

Most disadvantages are related to the rapid air movement through ducts. Since the air moves rapidly, noise is transmitted from room to room. Rapid air flow can also create drafts in the vicinity of heat registers. NOTE: Dust in the air may be moved with the flow but furnace air filters help remedy this.

Four common ducting methods are shown in the illustrations. You should use the one that fits best with your construction.

Heat ducts are not always below floors. They may be placed in attic space or between ceiling joists. Registers then are either in the ceiling or upper walls. Some authorities feel this location gives more uniform heat distribution. However, ceilings and walls tend to become soiled around registers, thus requiring greater maintenance effort.

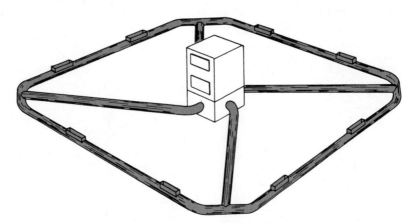

Honeywell Inc.

Deluxe multi-stage thermostat for auto-matic changeover of heating and air-conditioning systems. This thermostat raises and lowers temperature auto-matically as desired.

Perimeter loop duct system.

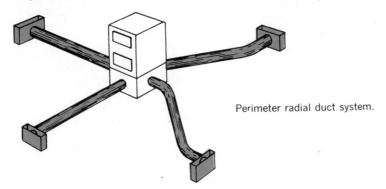

Perimeter radial duct system.

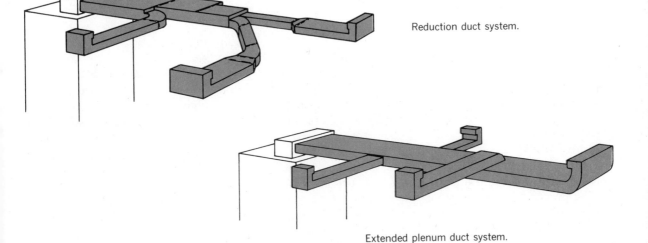

Reduction duct system.

Extended plenum duct system.

Mueller Climatrol

Hot water boiler.

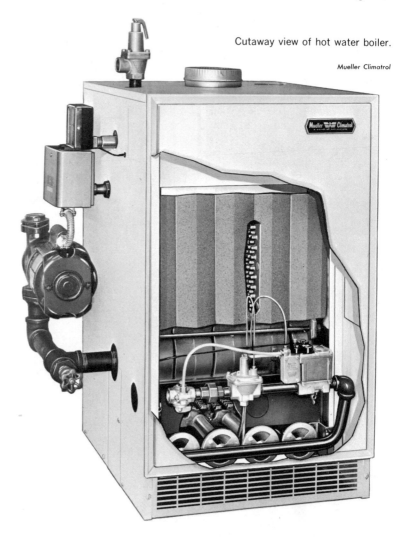

Cutaway view of hot water boiler.

Mueller Climatrol

Hot Water and Steam Heat

Furnaces supplying hot water and steam heat are very similar. When hot water is used, the water circulates in pipes and radiators; but when steam is used, only steam passes through pipes and radiators. Since the operation is similar and steam heat is most frequently used for large buildings but seldom for homes, this method will not be discussed further.

As with warm air furnaces, early models were large and unsightly. Coal was the most widely used fuel and gravity carried water through pipes and radiators. Well designed, compact, current models are most often fired by oil or gas. Pumps circulate water through pipes and radiators.

The process of circulating hot water from a furnace boiler through pipes and radiators is called *hydronic* heating.

In the following paragraphs *two-pipe* and *one-pipe* distribution systems for supplying radiators with hot water and returning cooled water to the furnace boiler are discussed. This does not imply that only one or two pipes are actually required. Each system is composed of many individual pipes.

Two-pipe system. The two-pipe system is the oldest but least frequently used. In Chapter 18 you learned that the large pipe supplying water to a building is called a *main*. Likewise, the large supply pipe distributing hot water from the furnace is also called a main. This pipe leads past each radiator so all can be supplied. The two-pipe system requires a second main to return cooled water to the furnace boiler for reheating. Two smaller branch lines connect each radiator to supply and return mains.

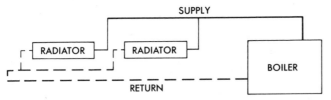

Reverse return two-pipe hot water system.

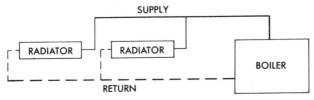

Direct return two-pipe hot water system.

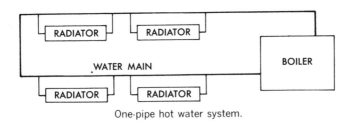

One-pipe hot water system.

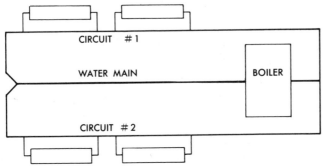

For more uniform heat distribution, a home may be zoned into separate heating circuits.

each. Automatic controls may supply different zones with varying amounts of heat as desired. A bedroom zone may require less heat than a living area.

Radiators are usually located on outside walls. The best location is beneath windows. Room size and the amount of heat loss through building parts determines the radiation surface required. Radiation surface is that part of a radiator, such as fins or tubes, that actually emits heat.

For maximum comfort heat must be distributed uniformly throughout a room. Long, low radiators spread heat more uniformly over a wider area than tall narrow ones.

Radiators may be open to view or encased by decorative covers. They may protrude into rooms or be recessed into walls so only their face is exposed. Baseboard radiators are favored for homes because of their long, low radiation surface and their pleasing appearance.

Advantages and Disadvantages

Hot water is one of the best heat distribution methods. It gives uniform spread without sudden temperature changes. It is easily controlled to supply varying amounts of heat to different rooms or zones. There is no rapid air movement near radiators.

However, hot water heating equipment is more expensive to purchase and installation costs are greater than forced warm air. For best results hot water systems should be designed and installed by experienced personnel.

One-pipe system. The one-pipe system is widely used. One main leads past all radiators and then returns cooled water to the furnace boiler for reheating. Two branch lines connect to each radiator and the main.

Circuits

If one main serves an entire building, distant radiators may not receive sufficient hot water. A building may be divided into zones (areas) with piping layout subdivided into circuits to supply

Hot water furnaces react slowly to changing needs. When radiators are cold and heat is demanded, water must be heated in the furnace boiler and pumped through the radiator until it also is warmed. If a radiator is hot and heat is no longer required, the water and the radiator still must cool, so that room temperature continues mounting for awhile. NOTE: Adjustment of the thermostat allows for this, but in extremely cold weather only efficient insulation can hold an even temperature.

Central air conditioning units cannot be built into hot water heating systems. Pipes are required for heating but ducts are needed for air conditioning. This makes combined installation costs greater than when air conditioning is installed to use forced warm air ducts.

It is possible to air condition with cold water if radiators are equipped with fans, but this system is not economically installed or maintained.

Radiant Heating

Another excellent heating method is called radiant heating, which gives a more uniform distribution than any other. With radiant heat an entire surface such as a floor, wall, ceiling, or large panel is warmed so it will radiate heat to all parts of a room.

There are several radiant systems, but two have proved most effective and widely used.

Radiant hot-water heat. This system requires a conventional furnace and boiler. Hot water distributes heat to rooms. There are no radiators, which are replaced by pipe coils imbedded in the floor, to spread heat throughout its area. The floor thus acts as a large radiator to heat the room. This system is used almost exclusively in buildings with concrete floors because pipes are easily imbedded in the material. Concrete is a poor insulator so heat spreads uniformly over the surface. When on-grade slabs are used, insulation beneath the floor minimizes heat loss to the ground. Any suitable material can then be laid over the concrete to form a finished floor; however,

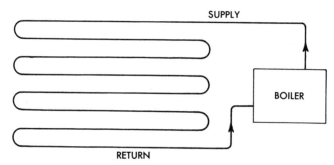

Radiant hot water coils are most often imbedded in concrete floors.

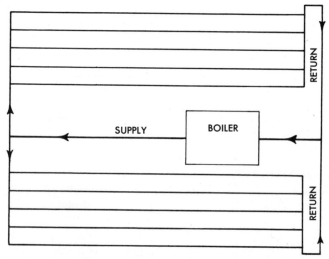

Heat distribution is most uniform when a radiant system is divided into circuits.

wood or other insulative materials partially restrict heat transfer.

A radiant hot water coil may be installed so an entire building is on a single circuit. That is, one coil serves an entire building. Using a single coil may permit the water to cool before the entire building is warmed. It is best to have a home zoned into separate circuits so water does not travel long distances. Separate circuits also permit individual temperature controls for different zones.

Radiant heat may be supplemented by auxiliary units such as radiators when large windows or other areas require additional radiation. Auxiliary units are not part of the radiant system.

As said, radiant hot water heat is very good; but it has two disadvantages over other methods: (1) It is expensive to install because much pipe is required and (2) pipes are imbedded in floors, so are difficult to service or modify.

Electric Radiant Heat

Heating by electricity has traditionally been more expensive than using other fuels. Many utility companies now give special rates for total electric homes. In some localities this fuel is more costly than others but is becoming competitive.

Electric radiant heat is usually installed in ceilings but it may also be located in walls. Most installations use coils similar to those for hot water radiant heating, except coils are of wire and are imbedded in the ceiling. Each room has an independent heating element with its own temperature controls.

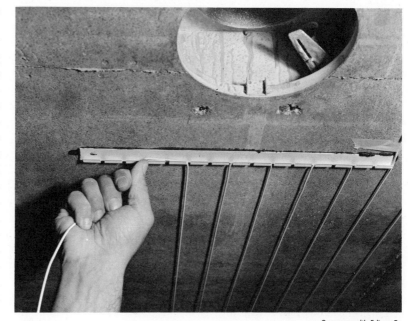

Commonwealth Edison Co.

Plastic spacer strips fastened to this concrete ceiling with a strong adhesive assure proper cable spacing.

Application of plaster completes this radiant electric cable installation.

Commonwealth Edison Co.

There are several prefabricated elements designed for rapid, economical installation. They may be single wire grids fastened to a flexible backing, or panels that fit together. After installation all form a continuous resistance element and operate in the same manner. One small wire is coiled back and forth across the ceiling and is stapled to cover the surface. The resistance wire becomes warm during use but never hot, so this is a very safe heating method. Wires extend room length and successive coils are approximately 1½″ apart. Exact spacing is determined by the amount of radiation needed. Installations should be designed by specialists. Many utility companies calculate heating requirements and design installations free of charge.

Electric radiant heat can be used with both plaster and drywall, but it does not work well with insulating ceiling tile. Plaster ceilings should have a sand base because this plaster permits heat to spread uniformly and makes a good radiation surface. Newer lightweight plasters should not be used because they insulate and do not give proper radiation.

When conventional drywall is used with electric radiant heat, two thicknesses are required. The first thickness is nailed to ceiling joists and resistance wire is stapled to it. The outer layer should be fastened to the first thickness with adhesive rather than nails to avoid damage to wires.

Radiant electric heat is very clean because no combustible materials are used. Heating elements have no moving parts, so maintenance costs are virtually eliminated. Radiation from the ceiling distributes heat uniformly.

Electric heat is widely used in warm regions but is efficient in almost any climate if proper insulation is provided. Minimum recommendations specify 6″ in ceilings, 4″ in walls, and 2″ beneath floors.

As with other heating methods, electric radiant heat has weaknesses. There are no ducts or fans for air exchange, so exhaust fans are necessary. Equipment for humidity control may be required. Air conditioning installation costs are greater than with forced warm air heat because ducts must serve only a single use.

There are other ways of heating with electricity. Forced warm air furnaces may be equipped with electric heating elements. Radiant baseboard heat may use electricity. Small electric units are designed to heat individual rooms.

Other Heating Equipment

Almost all heating equipment operates by one of the methods just described. Some combine principles from two systems. For example, conventional or baseboard hot water radiators may be heated by self-contained electric units. Specialized equipment may be designed to heat an entire building or it may be capable of heating only small areas. Because of the scope of the subject it is not possible for a book of this nature to present an in-depth study. For a better understanding of furnaces and heating systems you may study detailed specifications of many manufacturers, or books devoted exclusively to this subject. Many large heating equipment manufacturers publish engineering manuals.

Determining Heating Requirements

To calculate a building's exact heating (or cooling) requirements and then to design a system to fulfill the need is very technical and should be done by an engineer specializing in this work. However, preliminary design data must be calculated by the architect. Many building codes require the calculations to be included as a part of the working drawings or specifications. The subject cannot be discussed fully in a book of this nature; heating engineering manuals may be consulted if additional information is needed.

Necessary information includes an understanding of:

- British thermal units.
- Heat loss and heat gain.
- Conductance or thermal resistance.
- "U" factors.
- Building surfaces transmitting heat loss.
- Infiltration.
- Design temperature.

- Formulas for calculating heat loss.
- Compilation of heat loss data.
- Equipment selection based upon compiled data.

British Thermal Unit

A British thermal unit (abbreviated to BTU) is the quantity of heat needed to increase the temperature of 1 pound of water 1°. If room temperature is approximately 70°, one cubic foot of air can be warmed 1° by .018 BTU. Heating and cooling needs are computed by the number of BTU required to maintain a selected temperature within a building. Furnaces are rated by their BTU input and output. Furnace BTU *output* per hour (BTU/H) is used when sizing a furnace to BTU heat loss calculations. Air conditioners are rated by the number of BTU they *remove* per hour. Air conditioners were formerly rated in tons but this measurement is not as exact.

Heat Loss and Heat Gain

Every object conducts heat or cold, but some permit more transfer than others. As you know, materials that allow much transfer are called *conductors,* and those that permit little transfer are called *insulators.* Presence of heat does not insure warmth or comfort. To be comfortable a person must gain the exact amount of heat he loses. When it is cold outdoors but warm inside, heat transfers through walls to the outside. Your body radiates heat toward the cold wall. If the body loses more heat than it gains, regardless of temperature, you feel

cold. Since some construction materials transfer heat more readily than others, insulators are used to help balance heat loss and heat gain.

Conductance

Most individuals cannot scientifically test each building material or component part to determine conductance. Such tests have been completed by others and the information recorded for use. There are slight variations in the ways that heat transfer takes place, so information recorded on charts or tables may be called *conductance, thermal resistance,* or *resistivity.* For, in depth analysis, each has its own code designations. In this discussion all are identified by the code letter "C."

Heat Loss Data

Approximate resistances of one sq. ft. of building material of stated thickness

	"C" Resistivity		"C" Resistivity
4" concrete or stone	.32	½" fiberboard sheathing	1.45
6" concrete or stone	.48	¾" fiberboard sheathing	2.18
8" concrete or stone	.64	½" plywood	.65
12" concrete or stone	.96	⅝" plywood	.80
4" concrete block	.70	¾" plywood	.95
8" concrete block	1.10	¾" softwood sheathing or siding	.85
12" concrete block	1.25	roll roofing	.15
4" lt. wt. concrete block	1.40	asphalt shingles	.16
8" lt. wt. concrete block	1.70	wood shingles	.86
12" lt. wt. concrete block	1.88	metal roofing	.00
4" common brick	.82	tile or slate	.08
4" face brick	.45	composition floor covering	.08
4" structural clay tile	1.10	1" mineral batt insulation	3.50
8" structural clay tile	1.90	2" mineral batt insulation	7.00
12" structural clay tile	3.00	4" mineral batt insulation	14.00
1" stucco	.20	2" glass fiber insulation	7.00
plastic vapor barrier	.00	4" glass fiber insulation	14.00
building paper	.06	1" loose fill insulation	3.00
⅜" rock lath or plasterboard	.33	1" air space for brick veneer	.00
½" sand plaster	.15	2" wall air space	.50
½" insulating plaster	.75	4" wall air space	1.00
½" fiberboard ceiling tile	1.20	6" wall air space	1.50

Heat loss data.

Charts and tables giving thermal resistance of building materials designate by number which materials have the *most* resistance. The larger the number the greater the thermal resistance. For example, the thermal resistance of a 4″ common brick is .82, but 4″ of glass fiber insulation has a thermal resistance of 14.00.

Thermal resistance "C" cannot be used directly for heat loss calculations, but must be converted to a *"U" factor* which is used for calculations.

"U" factor. A "U" factor, abbreviated to "U" in actual computations, is the number of BTU transmitted in 1 hour through 1 square foot of a building material (or combined materials) for each degree of air temperature difference between indoors and outdoors. As with "C," "U" factors for building materials have been predetermined and recorded on charts and tables for convenient reference.

Converting "C" to "U." As stated, "C" cannot be used in *final* heat loss calculations, but must be converted to "U." For conversion to a "U" factor, determine the reciprocal of "C." That is, divide 1 by "C." To calculate a building's heat loss it is necessary to obtain "U" factors for all construction materials (or combined materials) that will transfer heat to the outdoors.

Building Surfaces Transmitting Heat Loss

All building surfaces (entire walls, floors, ceilings, doors, and windows) exposed to outdoors,

Reciprocals

"C" Resistivity	"U" Factors	"C" Resistivity	"U" Factors
100.00	.01	2.44	.41
50.00	.02	2.38	.42
33.33	.03	2.33	.43
25.00	.04	2.77	.44
20.00	.05	2.22	.45
16.67	.06	2.17	.46
14.29	.07	2.13	.47
12.50	.08	2.08	.48
11.11	.09	2.04	.49
10.00	.10	2.00	.50
9.09	.11	1.96	.51
8.35	.12	1.92	.52
7.69	.13	1.89	.53
7.15	.14	1.85	.54
6.67	.15	1.82	.55
6.25	.16	1.79	.56
5.88	.17	1.76	.57
5.55	.18	1.72	.58
5.26	.19	1.69	.59
5.00	.20	1.66	.60
4.76	.21	1.64	.61
4.55	.22	1.61	.62
4.35	.23	1.59	.63
4.17	.24	1.56	.64
4.00	.25	1.53	.65
3.85	.26	1.50	.66
3.70	.27	1.49	.67
3.57	.28	1.47	.68
3.45	.29	1.45	.69
3.34	.30	1.43	.70
3.23	.31	1.40	.71
3.13	.32	1.39	.72
3.03	.33	1.37	.73
2.94	.34	1.35	.74
2.86	.35	1.33	.75
2.78	.36	1.32	.76
2.70	.37	1.30	.77
2.63	.38	1.28	.78
2.56	.39	1.27	.79
2.50	.40	1.25	.80

Reciprocals.

or adjoining spaces with different temperatures, transmit heat loss or heat gain. Inside walls, floors, and ceilings between heated spaces do not transfer heat to the outdoors, so they are not used for heat loss calculations. NOTE: Ceilings adjoining attics, and floors above crawl spaces, are often considered as outside surfaces. Attics and crawl spaces have slightly different temperatures than outdoors but to consider them partially heated spaces requires additional test data. Attached garages are also usually considered as unheated spaces because doors are frequently left open.

Heat loss is computed for individual rooms rather than for entire buildings. Room losses are then combined to determine total building heat loss. NOTE: *How to calculate heat loss* will be explained step by step following discussions of infiltration and design temperatures.

Infiltration

In addition to heat loss through construction materials, wind pressure causes air to enter a building through spaces around windows and doors. Such air entry is called *infiltration.*

"U" Factors for Windows and Doors

Single thickness glass	1.13
Glassweld insulating glass	.60
Single glass with storm window	.60
Metal edge insulating glass	.54
Nominal 4″ thick glass block	.47
1⅜ wood door	.54
Above but with storm door	.34
1¾ wood door	.50
Above but with storm door	.32

An exact way of determining the amount of infiltration is called the *crack method.* To use this method it is necessary to know the size crack around all windows and doors. A locality's wind pressure helps determine the volume of air that will enter a given size crack. To use this method, consult prepared tables or charts. (Such tables and charts are not included in this text.)

The FHA permits *estimation* of air infiltration. To prepare heat loss data for a home, infiltration may be assumed to equal one air exchange per hour. For example, if a room is 10'-0"x12'-0" and has an 8'-0" ceiling, its volume is 960 cu. ft. Therefore air infiltration per hour can be assumed to equal 960 cu. ft. NOTE: Infiltration rate must be combined with other room heat losses to arrive at a total loss.

Design Temperatures

When calculating heating requirements one must know the room temperature level to be maintained. A 70° room temperature may be considered suitable for most activities in the home. However, 75° is frequently used in calculations so a higher heat level can be maintained. Desired room temperature level is called *inside design temperature.*

It is also necessary to know outdoor minimum temperatures during the heating season. NOTE: It is unnecessary to know the coldest temperature ever recorded because extreme weather conditions seldom occur. It would be almost useless to size a furnace for use at −20° if this temperature is likely to occur only once every 30 years. Averages are sought rather than coldest temperatures.

The average outdoor minimum temperature during the winter months is called an *outside design temperature* which has been predetermined for many cities and is available in heating engineering manuals. If data cannot be obtained for your community, you can compile your own. To establish an outside design temperature for your locality consult the weather bureau or other reliable source and ask for the coldest temperature ever recorded during October; also secure coldest temperatures for November, December, January, February, and March. The median of these is the outside design temperature for your locality. (To simplify later calculations round off your average to the nearest 5°.)

Heat loss calculations use the *design temperature difference* between indoors and outdoors. For example, if the inside design temperature is 75° and the outside design temperature is −10°, then the design temperature difference is 85°. The design temperature for a given locality remains constant. One must secure this information only once for permanent use on all jobs.

Calculating Building Heat Loss

Heat loss calculations are based upon the terms, definitions, and data discussed on preceding pages. One must also know facts relating to the specific room for which losses are to be computed. Data assembly and heat loss computations for one room are presented in the following logical order.

For an understanding of heat loss calculations be sure each point is understood as it is presented.

The heat loss calculations and explanations are for the room shown in the *floor plan illustration.* Additional construction data will be found on wall section "A," wall section "B," and the section through the ceiling. See drawings on the next page.

Wall "A"

• Wall "A" is an outside wall and must be used for heat loss calculations.
• This wall is 8'-0" tall by 12'-0" long. Multiply height by length to determine gross (total) wall area; so 8'-0" × 12'-0" = 96 sq. ft. of area.
• The window is 3'-0"x5'-0" and has an area of 15 sq. ft.
• From the 96 sq. ft. of gross wall area subtract the 15 sq. ft. of window area to determine the (net) wall area; so the net wall area is 81 sq. ft.
• Wall section "A" names each building material used in this frame wall.

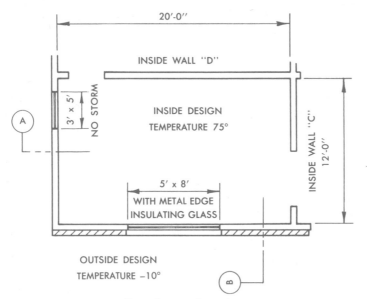

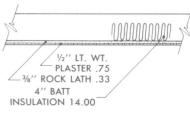

Section through ceiling.

Example room floor plan.

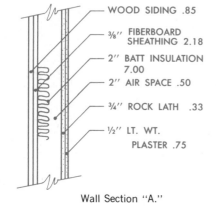

WOOD SIDING .85

⅜" FIBERBOARD SHEATHING 2.18

2" BATT INSULATION 7.00

2" AIR SPACE .50

¾" ROCK LATH .33

½" LT. WT. PLASTER .75

Wall Section "A."

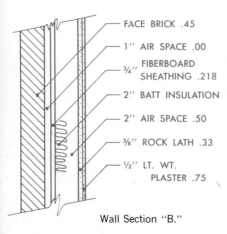

FACE BRICK .45

1" AIR SPACE .00

¾" FIBERBOARD SHEATHING .218

2" BATT INSULATION

2" AIR SPACE .50

⅜" ROCK LATH .33

½" LT. WT. PLASTER .75

Wall Section "B."

Resistivities of each building material were taken from the table on page 212 and placed adjoining each identifying name.

• Individual material resistances when added together equal 11.61 total wall resistivity.

• Resistivity must be converted to a "U" factor by dividing 1 by 11.61 to find the reciprocal. The "U" factor of 11.61 is .086.

• The window in wall "A" has no storm sash, so its "U" factor (from the table on the bottom of page 212) is 1.13.

• The floor plan shows an inside design temperature of 75° and an outside design temperature of −10°, so the design temperature difference is 85°.

To determine BTU loss per hour of net wall "A", multiply the net wall area of 81 sq. ft. by the wall "U" factor of .086 by the design temperature difference of 85; as $81 \times .086 \times 85 = 592.11$

BTU/H. Change the decimal to the closest whole number which is 592 BTU/H.

To determine BTU/H of window "A", multiply the window area of 15 sq. ft. by the glass "U" factor of 1.13 by the design temperature difference of 85°; as $15 \times 1.13 \times 85 = 1,440.75$, which is rounded off to 1,441 BTU/H.

Wall "B"

• Wall "B" is also an outside wall and must be used for heat loss calculations.

• This wall is 8'-0" high by 20'-0" long; so $8'-0" \times 20'-0" = 160$ sq. ft. of gross wall area.

• The window is 5'-0"x8'-0" and has an area of 40 sq. ft.

• From the 160 sq. ft. of gross wall area subtract the 40 sq. ft. of window area, which leaves 120 sq. ft. of net wall area.

• Note on wall section "B" also name each building material used and give resistivities of each.

• Individual material resistances, when added together, equal 11.21 total wall resistivity.

• Convert resistivity 11.21 to a "U" factor by finding its reciprocal, which is .089 "U."

• The window in wall "B" is double insulation glass with a metal edge. From the table on page 212 the "U" factor for this glass is .54.

- The design temperature difference of 85° is the same for wall "B" as it was for wall "A."
- To determine net wall "B" BTU/H, multiply the net wall area of 120 sq. ft. by the wall "U" factor of .089 by the design temperature difference of 85°, as 120×.089×85=907.80, which is rounded off to 908 BTU/H.
- To determine window "B" BTU/H, multiply the window area of 40 sq. ft. by the glass "U" factor of .54 by the design temperature difference of 85°; as 40×.54×85=1,836 BTU/H.

Walls "C" and "D"

Neither wall is exposed to outdoors; therefore neither is used for heat loss calculations.

Floor

This floor is above a heated basement and does not transmit heat loss to outdoors; therefore no heat loss calculations are required.

Ceiling

- This ceiling is below an unheated attic, so its heat loss to outside must be calculated.
- The ceiling is 12'-0"x20'-0" and has an area of 240 sq. ft.
- The drawing of the ceiling section names each building material used and gives resistivities of each.
- Individual ceiling material resistances when added together equal 15.08 total ceiling resistivity.
- The reciprocal of 15.08 is .066 "U."
- The design temperature difference of 85° is also used for ceiling computations.
- To determine ceiling BTU/H multiply the ceiling area of 240 sq. ft. by ceiling "U" factor of .066 by the design temperature difference of 85°, as 240×.066×85=1,346.4, which is rounded off to 1,346 BTU/H.

Infiltration

- The room dimensions of 12'-0" ×20'-0"×8'-0"=1,920 cu. ft.
- If air infiltration equals 1 exchange per hour; this also equals 1,920 cu. ft.
- Since room air is to be warmed and it requires .018 BTU/H to warm 1 cu. ft. of air 1°, infiltration calculations are based upon a "U" value of .018.
- Design temperature for this infiltration calculation is 85°.
- To determine room infiltration BTU/H losses, multiply the volume of 1,920 cu. ft. by the "U" factor .018 by 85; as 1,920×.018 ×85=2,937.6, rounded off to 2,938 BTU/H.

Room Heat Loss Schedule

Room name or number	Dimensions	Area or volume	X	"U" factor	X	Design Temp. Difference	=	BTU/H
Gross wall "A"	8'-0"x12'-0"	96 sq. ft.						
Window "A"	3'-0"x5'-0"	15 sq. ft.		1.13		85°		1,441
Net wall area "A"		81 sq. ft.		.086		85°		592
Gross wall "B"	8'-0"x20'-0"	160 sq. ft.						
Window "B"	5'-0"x8'-0"	40 sq. ft.		.54		85°		1,836
Net wall area "B"		120 sq. ft.		.089		85°		908
Floor	Heated basement below so there is no loss.							
Ceiling	12'-0"x20'-0"	240 sq. ft.		.066		85°		1,346
Infiltration	12'-0"20'-0"x8'-0"	1,920 cu. ft.		.018		85°		2,938

Total room heat loss in BTU per hour 9,061

Approximate B.T.U./H. Furnace Capacities and Sizes

FORCED WARM AIR			HOT WATER BOILER		
B.T.U./H. input	B.T.U./H. output	Approx. size	B.T.U./H. input	B.T.U./H. output	Approx. size
75,000	60,000	20"x28"x58"	100,000	60,000	16"x22"x32"
100,000	80,000	24"x28"x58"	130,000	80,000	16"x25"x32"
120,000	100,000	28"x28"x58"	160,000	100,000	16"x28"x32"
150,000	120,000	32"x28"x58"	200,000	120,000	18"x28"x32"
175,000	135,000	36"x28"x58"	240,000	135,000	20"x28"x32"

For detailed specifications consult manufacturer's literature.

A central air conditioner has a condenser outdoors and an evaporator indoors.

Mueller Climatrol

Air Conditioning

As with heating, some form of air conditioning has been in existence for a long time. Homes during the Roman period were often built around a courtyard having a large fountain in its center. Falling water from the fountain caused air convection currents which helped cool the home.

Mechanical air conditioning is a relatively recent development. Early models relied on air movement through water for cooling. Later equipment employs refrigeration units to manufacture cooled air.

In the immediate past only expensive homes were air condi-tioned. Because of early high costs it was truly a luxury. This is no longer so. Improved equip-ment design, mass production, and resultant lower costs have helped make it widely used. Al-most all medium priced and some inexpensive homes are air condi-tioned, and use continues to expand.

There are two main ways homes are air conditioned. For small spaces such as individual rooms, or homes formerly without air conditioning, window air con-ditioners are widely used. These small refrigeration units are equipped to blow cooled air di-rectly into rooms. NOTE: The term window air conditioner im-plies that this is the only location where such units may be used. Many window air conditioners are mounted permanently through outside walls so they do not oc-cupy window space.

Central air conditioning cools entire buildings. As stated earlier, there are two distribution meth-ods. (1) Cold water may be cir-culated through pipes to fan-equipped radiators that spread cooled air throughout each room. This is not found generally in homes. (2) Refrigeration units equipped with blowers to force cooled air through ducts are most widely used. Central air condi-tioners may be compact units serving only a single function, or they may be combined with warm air furnaces so that one circuit both heats and cools.

As stated earlier, air condi-tioners are most often rated by the number of BTU they extract per hour. Air conditioning needs are computed in much the same manner as heat loss calculations. Instead of doing computations for heat loss, air conditioning re-quirements are based upon *heat gain*. Instead of using the coldest days in each month to determine design temperature difference, the mean of warmest recorded days of the six summer months is used.

Inside design temperature for summer cooling is normally 75°. The direction a wall faces, amount of roof overhang, sunlight ex-posure, shade trees or other ob-structions in the immediate area, number of occupants, and other considerations are necessary before one can complete heat gain calculations. Because of the subject's complexity, this chapter does not attempt to present an in-depth study. For additional information, consult engineering manuals or other books devoted to air conditioning.

Humidity Control

In addition to temperature, the amount of moisture in the air affects physical comfort. Indeed, it is a serious part of air conditioning. The amount of moisture in the air is called relative humidity. Under normal circumstances the FHA recommends a relative indoor humidity of 50%. When

Mueller Climatrol

Electronic dust filters make a home practically dust free.

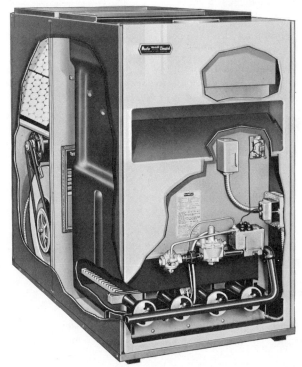

Mueller Climatrol

An air conditioner may be designed into a furnace so one unit takes care of both heating and cooling needs.

moisture is added to inside air, it is called humidification. When moisture is extracted from inside air, the process is called dehumidification. Equipment may be purchased to do either or both operations. Units may be portable or permanently installed, with some that are automatically controlled by sensing devices that register humidity level and are switched on or off as a need arises.

Ventilation

Ventilation for rooms, attics, crawl spaces, basements, garages, and spaces between walls is essential to a building to insure occupants' comfort and safety. These areas are mentioned in this chapter only as a reminder that each must be considered during building planning. Specific references for each are found in appropriate chapters.

Questions to Reinforce Knowledge

1. What does the term climate control mean to you?

2. From this and other chapters name and describe the three heat-transfer principles.

3. What are the three most widely used methods of distributing heat to rooms?

4. Describe a gravity warm-air furnace and its operation.

5. Describe a forced warm-air heating system.

6. What is a plenum chamber?

7. What is a reversed flow warm-air furnace? When is it used?

8. Name two combustible fuels that have practically replaced coal for home heating. Why are these favored?

9. Name three advantages of using warm-air furnaces.

10. Name three disadvantages of using warm-air furnaces.

11. From the illustrations, name and describe four ducting methods for forced warm-air furnaces.

12. What is hydronic heating?

13. What is the difference between a two-pipe and a one-pipe hot-water heating system? Describe each.

14. Of the two systems, which is most widely used? Why?

15. When referring to a hydronic heating system, what is a circuit?

16. What is meant by the term zone control?

17. What radiator shape is most effective? Why?

18. Name three advantages of using hot-water heating.

19. Name three disadvantages to using hot-water heating.

20. What is a radiant heating system?

21. Describe two different methods of distributing radiant heat.

22. What is a British Thermal Unit?

23. How many BTU are required to raise the temperature of 1 cu. ft. of air 1°F.?

24. How is a furnace rated?

25. What name is given to building materials that transfer much heat?

26. What name is given to building materials that transfer little heat?

27. What is thermal resistance? What are two other names closely associated with this?

28. Does a building material having a high number "C" have more or less resistivity than a building material with a low "C" number?

29. What is a "U" factor?

30. Describe how "C" is converted to a "U" factor.

31. What building materials adjacent to outdoors transmit heat loss?

32. What is infiltration?

33. What is an inside design temperature?

34. What is an outside design temperature?

35. What is a design temperature difference? What is its use in heat loss calculations?

36. Explain in detail how building heat loss is determined.

37. Is the idea of air conditioning new? Explain.

38. Name two applications of window air conditioners as the best system to install.

39. Explain another method of mounting a "window" air conditioner.

40. What is central air conditioning? Describe two distribution methods. Which is preferred? Why?

41. How are air conditioning units sized?

42. Explain what is meant by the term humidity control.

43. Under normal circumstances what indoor relative humidity is recommended?

Terms to Spell and Know

hot-water radiant heat	one-pipe hot water	"U" factor
duct	system	reciprocal
gravity warm air	pipe circuit	infiltration
forced warm air	zoned heating	inside design
inlet	baseboard radiator	temperature
outlet	electric radiant heat	outside design
plenum	resistance element	temperature
reversed flow	British Thermal Unit	design temperature
stoker	(BTU)	difference
hot water heat	BTU/H	gross wall area
steam heat	conductance	net wall area
hydronic heating	heat loss	window air conditioner
radiator	heat gain	central air conditioner
boiler	thermal resistance	refrigeration unit
two-pipe hot water	resistivity	relative indoor humidity
system	"C" number	humidity control

20

Chimneys and Fireplaces

Chimneys

The main purpose of a chimney is to provide a draft so fuel in a furnace or fireplace will burn. Of course, fumes and smoke also are conducted off. Combustion cannot be sustained without an oxygen supply. There are three common methods of constructing chimneys, with many variations and sizes for each.

(1) Solid masonry. When solid masonry is used there should be at least two wythes of masonry surrounding the flue to minimize fire danger. If one wythe fails the other will contain the fire or heat. A solid masonry chimney for either a furnace or fireplace requires a footing. It should extend at least 12″ past the sides in all directions and should be at least 12″ thick. Large footings, as for fireplaces, should include reinforcing rod or wire mesh for additional strength.

Chimney masonry should not be in contact with any wood framing material. Leave a 2″ mini-mum space between them, usually with insulation added. Some codes require its inclusion.

(2) Masonry with clay flue lining. Mortar joints deteriorate from heat; clay flue liners provide additional fire protection. When they are used, some codes permit only one masonry wythe instead of two. Except for the inclusion of the liner, construction is the same as for solid masonry.

(3) Prefabricated chimneys may be of masonry similar to flue liners or they may be of metal. Most prefabricated units are double walled with insulation in the cavity. These chimneys have advantages over conventional ones. They do not require a footing because they are lightweight and are designed so they can be suspended from framing members. They are safe because they are fully insulated. They are easy to install and do not require as much space as conventional chimneys.

NOTE: Even though they are a good product many codes do not permit their use.

In most instances the chimney is round and does not present a finished appearance from the exterior. This is because we do not identify the round shape as proper for a chimney. Therefore many companies supply covers that resemble a conventional chimney.

Flue Liners

The three most common shapes for flue liners are (1) round, (2) square, and (3) rectangular. There are many different sizes, so you should consult technical data when selecting the size to use. An 8″x8″ is adequate for most furnaces, and 8″x12″ or 12″x12″ is suitable for most fireplaces.

These are nominal modular sizes. Actual sizes are ½″ less so they can be fitted with other masonry modular sizes.

When flue liners are used, the first section of liner at the bottom of the flue should be supported by other masonry.

Prefabricated chimneys blend well with this traditional style home.

Scholz Homes Inc.

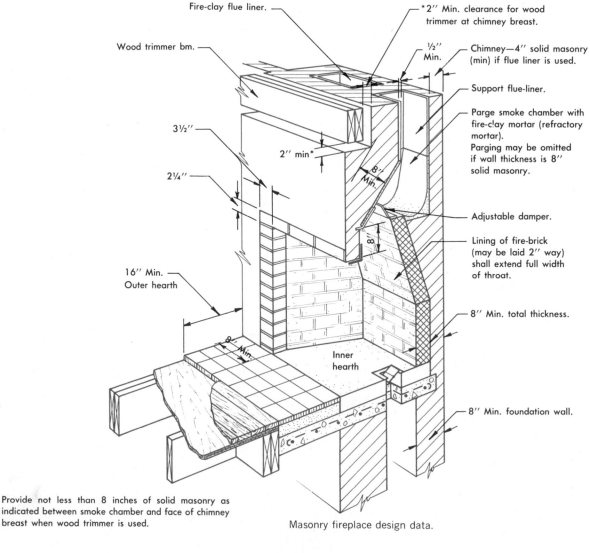

Fire-clay flue liner.

*2" Min. clearance for wood trimmer at chimney breast.

Wood trimmer bm.

½" Min.

Chimney—4" solid masonry (min) if flue liner is used.

Support flue-liner.

Parge smoke chamber with fire-clay mortar (refractory mortar).
Parging may be omitted if wall thickness is 8" solid masonry.

3½"

2" min*

8" Min.

2¼"

8"

Adjustable damper.

Lining of fire-brick (may be laid 2" way) shall extend full width of throat.

16" Min. Outer hearth

8" Min. total thickness.

8" Min.

Inner hearth

8" Min. foundation wall.

Provide not less than 8 inches of solid masonry as indicated between smoke chamber and face of chimney breast when wood trimmer is used.

Masonry fireplace design data.

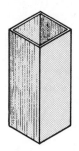
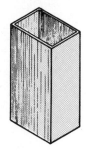

Clay flue liners may be round, square, or rectangular.

Improper chimney height reduces efficiency of a fireplace or flue.

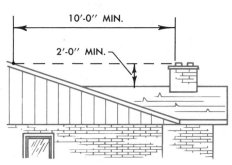

10'-0" MIN.

2'-0" MIN.

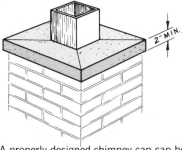

A properly designed chimney cap can be both decorative and functional.

2" MIN.

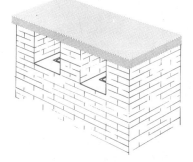

A chimney cover is frequently used in areas with abundant snow or rainfall.

The liner usually extends about 4" above the top of a masonry chimney. When determining chimney height, use the top of the liner as the terminus.

Chimney Cap

A solid masonry cap should be installed above brick or stone chimneys to prevent deterioration of the mortar joints. This cap should have a wash, or angle, so water cannot stand on it and speed deterioration. Stone or concrete is the most frequently used material. There is no standard thickness for chimney caps, but they should not be less than 2" thick. The proper thickness is dictated by local custom and personal preference.

Chimney Cover

Rain or snow can enter the opening in the chimney top and cause dampness inside the building. Covers may be placed above the chimney to prevent this.

Chimney Height

The height a chimney must extend above a roof varies with local codes. FHA requirements specify that the top of a chimney must be at least 2'-0" higher than the highest roof point within 10'-0".

Flashing

Where a chimney passes through a roof the joint must be sealed with flashing and counter flashing as shown, except when built-up roofing is used. It can be lapped continuously onto the chimney to replace the flashing. Counter flashing must be bent down to cover the edge of the roofing. See roof construction illustrations in Chapter 9.

Saddle

If a chimney can be located on a roof ridge, rain water is shed away. When the chimney passes through a single inclined roof surface, water can accumulate and back up beneath the roofing, causing leaks. This is especially true if the roof slope is low or the chimney is wide. If the chimney is more than 30" wide, a small protector with the same pitch as the main roof should be built behind the chimney. This is called a *saddle*. If the saddle is quite small, it may be covered with sheet metal. If it is large, regular roofing should be used.

Fireplaces

Fireplaces were formerly used exclusively for heating but they are now used primarily for appearance and enjoyment.

Many fireplaces are constructed of solid masonry, but other materials are also used. Double-walled sheet metal liners that warm and circulate air into a room are widely used. These units require less masonry than conventional fireplaces, are easy to install, and their design helps insure proper functioning. Prefabricated freestanding fireplaces and unusual shaped custom built units are also quite popular. The desired finished appearance—and whether or not it is to be used for heating purposes—helps determine which kind to use.

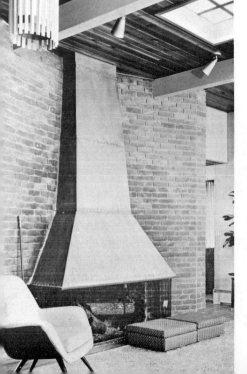

Metal is a widely used fireplace material.
Koppers Company, Inc.

One face open.

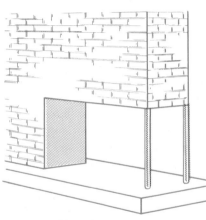

Two faces adjacent.

Two faces opposite.

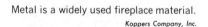

Three faces open.

Hearth

An open fire is quite dangerous unless it is properly shielded. A non-combustible hearth should extend at least 16″ in front of a fireplace and at least 8″ past each side of the opening. Stone, brick, and tile are most frequently used, but other suitable materials are available. The hearth is extended beneath the fireplace to form an inner hearth. This may be the same material as the outer hearth, but fire bricks are recommended if frequent use is anticipated. The hearth may be flush with the floor or can be raised as desired.

Ash Chamber

When space is available beneath the finished floor, an ash chamber is recommended. Any such chamber must be equipped with a metal clean-out door. A rectangular ash dump is located in the inner hearth so ash removal is simplified. When no space is available for an ash chamber, a small rectangular recess can be built into the inner hearth floor to contain the ashes.

Fireplace Opening and Liner Dimensions

1 FACE OPEN				2 FACES ADJACENT				2 FACES OPPOSITE				3 FACES OPEN			
D	H	W	FLUE	D	H	W	FLUE	D	H	W	FLUE	D	H	W	FLUE
20″	30″	30″	12″x16″	20″	30″	30″	16″x16″	28″	30″	34″	16″x20″	24″	24″	34″	16″x16″
20″	30″	34″	16″x16″	20″	30″	34″	12″x16″	28″	36″	38″	16″x16″	28″	30″	38″	16″x20″
20″	36″	42″	16″x20″	24″	42″	42″	16″x20″	30″	38″	42″	16″x20″	28″	36″	38″	20″x24″

Fireplace opening and liner dimensions.

Damper

Every fireplace should have a damper to regulate the flow of air and to block off the chimney when it is not in use.

Lintel

Masonry above a fireplace opening must be supported. A 3″x3″x¼″ lintel extending 4″ on each side of the opening is recommended.

Position of Fireplace Face

The face of a fireplace may be flush with a wall, or it may project into a room. Since a fireplace has considerable depth, special consideration must be given to the space it occupies. It could give a beautiful appearance in the room it occupies but protrude into and spoil the use of another room.

Fireplace Finish

Fireplace designs are limited only by the imagination. The exposed masonry can vary from 8″ surrounding the opening to entire walls of stone or brick.

Some period settings require the addition of wood mantels, but current design tends to eliminate them. Simplicity rather than ornateness is usually preferred.

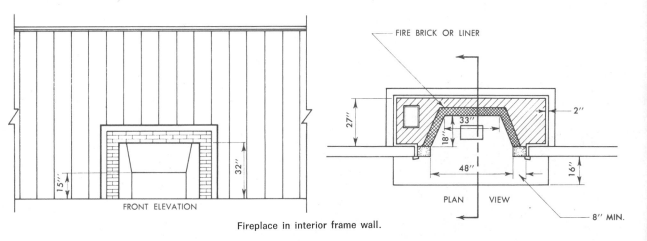

Fireplace in interior frame wall.

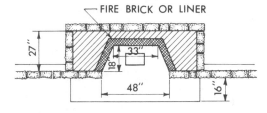

Stone fireplace in exterior frame wall.

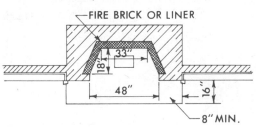

Brick fireplace in brick veneer wall.

Stone laid with wide mortar joints plus a stone mantel gives this fireplace a rugged appearance.

A double-faced fireplace serves as a room divider.

This prefabricated barbecuing fireplace helps give the home a feeling of country charm.

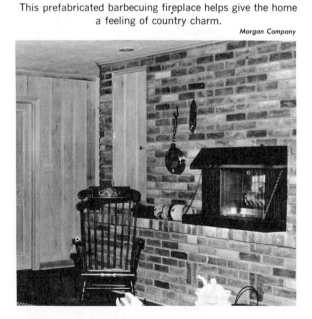

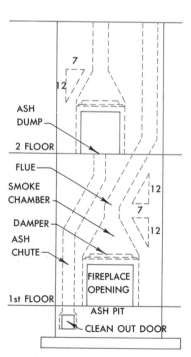

Offset fireplace flues permit one fireplace to be installed beneath another.

ASH DUMP

2 FLOOR

FLUE

SMOKE CHAMBER

DAMPER

ASH CHUTE

FIREPLACE OPENING

1st FLOOR

ASH PIT

CLEAN OUT DOOR

Large areas of stone or brick are very popular. When space permits, fuel storage compartments may be built into the fireplace wall. Book shelves, storage spaces, or built-in entertainment equipment are frequently incorporated into the fireplace wall.

Two or More Fireplaces

If two or more fireplaces are to be included, considerable savings result if they can be designed into one masonry unit. The additional fireplaces may be on the same or different living levels. Each one should have a separate flue. When they are on different levels it is sometimes possible to offset the flues, as shown, to conserve space. Observe the angle of the inclined flue on the illustration. Too sharp an angle is hazardous and also prevents proper functioning.

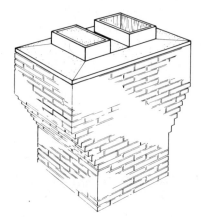

Brickwork may be corbeled to change chimney size.

Corbel

If the chimney area is small and you desire it to appear larger from outside the building, or if you wish it to be located in a different position on the roof, the chimney may be corbeled, as shown.

Questions to Reinforce Knowledge

1. Why is it very important that a chimney have proper draft?

2. Why should a solid masonry chimney have at least two wythes?

3. What are two advantages of using clay flue liners?

4. What chimneys require a footing? How large should they be?

5. What chimneys do not require a footing? Why?

6. What is meant when one says that most prefabricated chimneys are double walled?

7. Why are imitation brick shells sometimes used to cover the chimney on the building exterior?

8. What are three shapes of flue liners?

9. Why should the bottom section of flue liner be supported?

10. About how much does a flue liner protrude above other chimney masonry?

11. When determining total chimney height, where is the measurement taken?

12. What is a chimney cap? Why is it used?

13. What is a wash on a chimney cap? Why is it used?

14. What is the minimum thickness of a chimney cap?

15. What keeps rain or snow from entering the top of a chimney? Explain.

16. What is the recommended chimney height?

17. Is flashing always used between the chimney and roof? Explain.

18. What is a saddle? Why is it used?

19. Explain the variety of fireplace shapes?

20. Give three reasons why fireplace liners are frequently used.

21. What is a prefabricated fireplace? Describe the variety available.

22. What is a hearth? Should every fireplace have one?

23. Describe the minimum dimensions of a hearth.

24. What is the best material for an inner hearth if the fireplace is to be used frequently?

25. What is an ash chamber?

26. Why must a fireplace have a damper?

27. Describe a corbeled chimney.

Terms to Spell and Know

chimney	hearth
fireplace	inner hearth
flue liner	ash chamber
chimney cap	ash dump
chimney cover	cleanout door
flashing	damper
saddle	corbel

21

Roof Overhang and Exterior Trim

Cornice. The word cornice, from ancient Greek, means a horizontal molding along the top of a wall. This molding when viewed in profile is usually, but not always, curved or sculptured.

The term cornice as used in this book is more inclusive than the above definition. It includes all building materials necessary to join a wall and roof. The purpose of a cornice is to make a beautiful finished intersection to join the two parts, and to protect other building materials from the weather.

There are many different methods of enclosing a cornice, so they must be designed to suit regional or personal preferences.

Rafter tails. As stated earlier the part of a rafter extending past an outside wall is called a rafter tail. Its outside end may be perpendicular to the ground or at right angles to rafter edges. The first method is normally used when metal gutters are desired. The second method permits a wider variety of styles and is normally used when built-in gutters are desired. NOTE: It is difficult

to mount conventional gutters on a surface unless the surface is perpendicular to the ground.

Open cornice. An open cornice

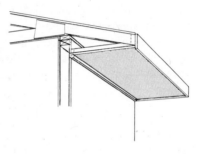

Rafter tails and fascia are usually perpendicular to the ground when attached gutters are to be installed.

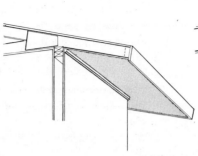

If no gutters are required, or if they are to be the built-in type, rafter ends and fascia may be square with joist edges.

is the simplest kind. On this style rafter tails are exposed. The back of roof sheathing serves as the exterior finishing material. A sim-

National Lumber Manufacturers Assoc.

Short overhangs and vertical fascia are often used with traditional designs.

Flat roof overhangs may have soffits parallel to the ground, or they may be tapered toward rafter ends. The fascia may be at right angles to joist-rafter edges or at any desired angle.

ple molding covers the joint where the wall and sheathing meet. Rafter ends may be left exposed or a board called a *fascia* may partially or fully cover them. A fascia may be flat or of elaborate, molded shapes. However, simple shapes are more practical when gutters are to be installed.

Economy construction using conventional framing, with rafters spaced 16″ or 24″ o.c., sometimes employs this open cornice method. Post and beam construction with structural parts exposed is also a popular and widely used application of an open cornice.

This open cornice has false rafter tails with finished lumber exposed to view on the under side.

This open cornice has brick veneer extending up to the roof sheathing. When planks form the finished overhang the rafter tails may conform to spacing requirements for plank and beam systems shown in Chapter 11.

Rafter tails shown on this wall section are notched to receive roof planks above the exposed rafters.

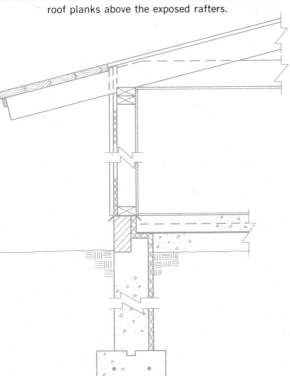

Closed Cornice

Rafters are encased—not visible—in a *closed* or *box* cornice. Variations are used for much light construction.

A closed cornice may have finishing materials attached to rafters so the overhang follows the roof slope; or an overhang may be finished so its lower surface is parallel to the ground.

Soffit

A soffit is a covering for the lower edge of rafters. It may be of wood, metal, fiberboard, drywall, plaster, plastic, or others. The proper material to use depends upon personal or regional preference.

Nailers for Soffit Materials

Most soffit materials are only semi-rigid and must be nailed or fastened to each rafter and along all edges. Materials should be installed according to the manufacturer's directions.

The lower edges of rafters are usually below the top edge of wall sheathing and there are no exposed structural parts that permit nailing the back edge of a soffit. A *nailer strip* must be fastened to the sheathing, flush with the lower edge of rafters, so the soffit can be nailed securely.

Fascia

A closed cornice has at least one finishing board nailed to cover rafter ends. This board is called a fascia. A fascia is also used as a nailer for the front edge of the soffit. Study the four common methods of joining a wood

fascia and soffit, shown in the illustrations. The first illustration shows a butt joint with the soffit fastened to the bottom edge of the fascia. This is the poorest method because it leaves an unfinished exposed edge. It is not only unsightly but may permit moisture to enter the soffit material and cause deterioration.

The second illustration shows the fascia extending below the rafter ends the same amount as the soffit thickness. The edge of the fascia is rabbeted to permit nailing and to form a tight joint between the two materials.

The third illustration shows the fascia protruding below the soffit any desired amount within limits. The back of the fascia is grooved

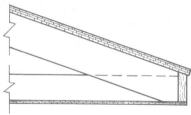

An exposed soffit edge is undesirable because water may enter between it and the fascia.

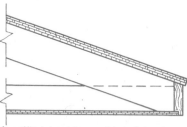

A soffit joined to a rabbeted fascia requires perfect alignment to insure a close fitting joint.

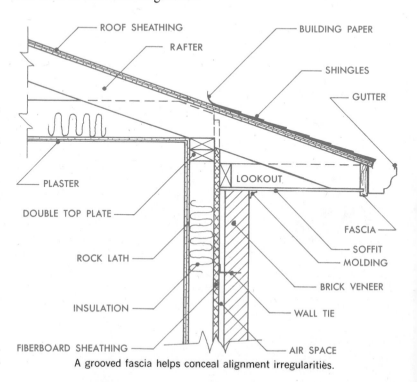

A grooved fascia helps conceal alignment irregularities.

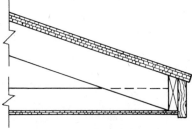

A double fascia increases nailing surface at the soffit edge.

to receive the soffit. This method is very desirable because it permits slight discrepancies but the joint appears closed.

The fourth illustration shows a double fascia. Naturally only the exposed one on the outside needs to be of fine quality materials. Although the double fascia requires more material than the first three, it is frequently used because it is easy to construct and looks very good. The small molding covering the joint can be any desired shape. If materials fit without open spaces between them, this molding may be omitted.

Relationship of Ceiling Joists and Fascia

One cannot assume that all fascias are on the same level as ceiling joists. When rafter ends protrude beyond a wall as continuations of the rafters, the fascia is lower than the ceiling joists. Roof slope and amount of overhang determine how much the fascia is below the ceiling joist line. Of course, a fascia can be at the same level as joists, but special construction is then required. The illustrations show two ways the problem may be solved.

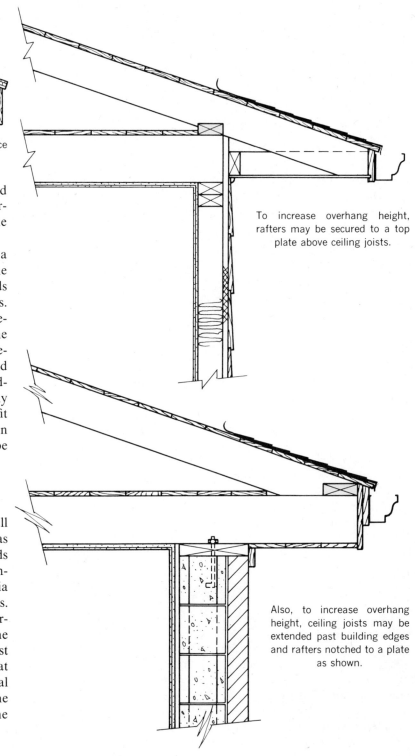

To increase overhang height, rafters may be secured to a top plate above ceiling joists.

Also, to increase overhang height, ceiling joists may be extended past building edges and rafters notched to a plate as shown.

Molding for Soffit

A small molding of your choice is used to conceal the joint between a soffit and exterior wall covering. Study the illustrations and observe that the soffit is installed before exterior wall coverings.

A *frieze board* is sometimes used to join wood siding and a soffit. This is flat with the lower edge rabbeted to receive the siding. The wood molding described earlier is then placed to cover the joint between the frieze board and soffit.

Lookout

When a soffit is to be level an additional framing member, a lookout, is required. Fastened between the rafter ends and wall sheathing as shown in the illustrations, the lookout serves as a nailer for the soffit.

Cornice Return

A cornice is sometimes returned around the end of a building. This is done for improved visual effect. When a box cornice is used, the entire box may be returned. When an open cornice is used, a simple single-piece re-

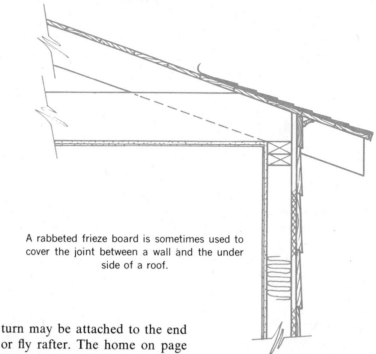

A rabbeted frieze board is sometimes used to cover the joint between a wall and the under side of a roof.

turn may be attached to the end or fly rafter. The home on page 2 has cornice returns.

Gable End Overhang

A gable end may be finished so it has little or no overhang, or it may extend any desired amount. When designing an overhang it must be appropriate to the rest of the building style.

Molding for Fly Rafter

A fly rafter, sometimes called the rake, gives outside finish at a gable end. This rafter is fastened to the lower face of roof sheathing, and sheathing ends are exposed unless covered with a molding. The molding can be a 1"x2" rectangular board or a more elaborate molding of your choosing. The same molding shape as used between the wall and soffit is frequently chosen.

Attic Ventilation

Insulation applied between ceiling joists causes a temperature difference between the attic and rooms below. This results in condensation; therefore the attic must be ventilated so air can circulate and remove moisture. Ventilators may be provided beneath the roof overhang, in the gable ends, in the roof ridge, or on the roof surface. They may be pre-manufactured or custom built units. All ventilators must be equipped with screens. Screens with 8 squares per running inch are recommended by the FHA. For specific ventilation requirements, consult the illustrations and their accompanying data.

Louvers

A louver is a ventilator with fins or slats to allow air to pass through. Fins may be fixed (sta-

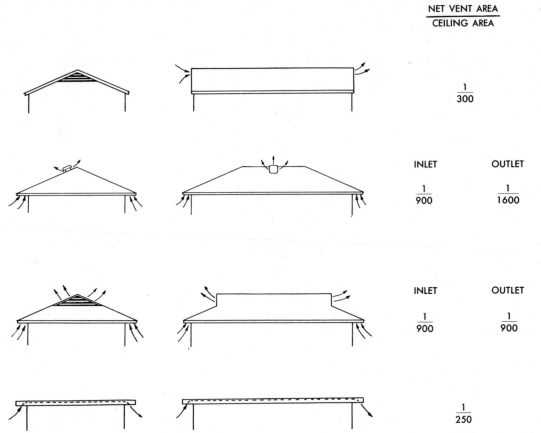

NET VENT AREA / CEILING AREA

$\dfrac{1}{300}$

INLET $\dfrac{1}{900}$ OUTLET $\dfrac{1}{1600}$

INLET $\dfrac{1}{900}$ OUTLET $\dfrac{1}{900}$

$\dfrac{1}{250}$

National Lumber Manufacturers Assoc.

Methods of ventilating roof spaces and amount of ventilation required.

tionary) or adjustable so they can be opened or closed. Expansible metal ventilators are available so they can be adjusted to fit varying roof slopes.

The amount of net free ventilating area is usually stamped or printed on a purchased ventilator. One must secure sizes to meet calculated ventilating requirements, as discussed earlier. For job or custom built units one must measure and calculate the net ventilating area. To determine actual ventilating area one must deduct the amount of space occupied by wires in the screen.

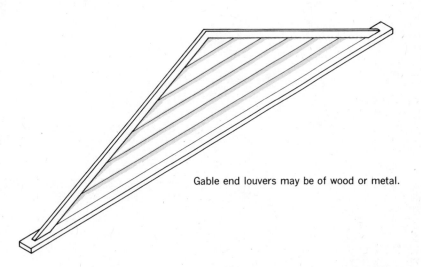

Gable end louvers may be of wood or metal.

231

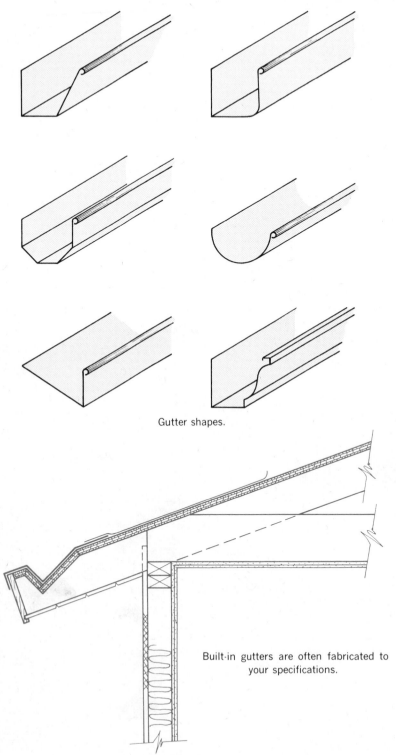

Gutters

Gutters are troughs attached to the edge of a roof to carry water away. They may be of metal, wood or plastic, and are available in a wide variety of styles and sizes. Metal is most frequently used, commonly galvanized iron because it is less expensive. Molded wood gutters are not as popular as formerly. Most wood gutters are of the built-in type and may be custom designed for each specific application. These are lined with sheet metal or other material to make them waterproof.

Some of the more common gutter shapes are shown. The proper one to use depends upon building style and amount of water to be drained away. A 4″ or 5″ gutter is usually adequate for small structures such as homes. For most beautiful results simple styles are recommended.

The FHA permits gutters to be installed perfectly level if the material is rigid and pockets or low spots do not develop. However, for best results they should slope slightly toward downspouts.

Leaders or Downspouts

Leaders or downspouts are pipes that carry water from a gutter to the ground. They should be of the same material and size as the gutter. If a gutter is 4″ wide its downspout should be 4″ across. Hangers must be used to secure both the gutter and downspout to the building. NOTE: Gutter hangers should be installed before roofing to prevent nail holes from causing leaks.

Gutter shapes.

Built-in gutters are often fabricated to your specifications.

Coarse screens over all gutters, and basket strainers at downspout heads where they join the gutter, catch and help prevent clogging by leaves or other foreign matter that is washed down.

Water must be drained away from the bottom of downspouts. They may empty into a sanitary sewer when building codes permit, but preferably a storm sewer, a drain tile field, dry well, or—for an economical installation—onto a splash block and then onto the yard.

In localities with little rainfall and only traces of snow, as Arizona or northern desert regions, water may be trapped for special uses. Drainage is generally not a problem. Heavy precipitation areas such as the Northwest Coast, New England, the Great Lakes region, and parts of the Gulf Coast may have rigid water drainage codes.

Questions to Reinforce Knowledge

1. As used in this book, what does the word cornice mean? How does this compare with the older definition?

2. What is the purpose of a cornice?

3. How does one determine exact cornice style and construction?

4. What is a rafter tail?

5. Why are some rafter tails perpendicular to the ground while others are at right angles to rafter edges?

6. What is an open cornice?

7. Describe two widely used applications of open cornices.

8. What is a closed cornice? A box cornice?

9. What is a soffit?

10. What is a nailer strip?

11. Describe materials suitable for soffit construction. How does one determine the proper one to use?

12. Describe two relationships of soffits to roof slope?

13. Why are nailers frequently installed before soffits are applied?

14. What are fascias? Why are they necessary?

15. Describe four methods of joining a soffit and fascia.

16. Why are fascias usually placed below the ceiling joist line?

17. Describe two methods of constructing a cornice so it is on the same level as ceiling joists.

18. Why are moldings used where a soffit joins a wall?

19. What is a frieze board?

20. What is a lookout?

21. What is a cornice return?

22. What is a fly rafter?

23. What is a gable rake?

24. Why is a molding frequently applied along the top edge of a fly rafter?

25. Why is attic ventilation necessary?

26. How does one determine the number, size, and location of attic ventilators?

27. Why must ventilators be equipped with screens?

28. Describe a louver.

29. Why do louvers sometimes have movable fins?

30. What is a gutter? From what materials are they frequently made?

31. What is a leader or downspout?

32. How does one determine downspout size?

33. Why should gutters and downspout heads be equipped with screens?

34. Describe a built-in gutter.

35. Describe ways of draining water from downspouts. Why do you think codes must be designed and enforced for different regions?

Terms to Spell and Know

cornice	rake
rafter tail	louver
open cornice	gutter
closed or box cornice	leader
	downspout
fascia	gutter hangers
frieze board	basket strainer
lookout	downspout head
cornice return	storm sewer
fly rafter	drain tile
	dry well

22

Exterior Wall Coverings

Exterior coverings are used to protect buildings from the elements, afford a degree of permanence, and to add architectural beauty. Use should conform to elements of good design, "line, form, color, texture, etc.," see Chapter 25.

Some materials suitable for exterior wall coverings are discussed in other chapters because they are also structural materials. These will be mentioned briefly here so as to give a complete picture. Actually, because of the large number of materials that are available, no lengthy discussion of any will be given. When selections are being made, one must refer to manufacturers' literature, specifications, or samples for best results.

Cost of materials often has an influence on those selected. But you must consider more than the initial cost. *Permanence* should be given careful consideration. A good building is designed to require a minimum of maintenance. An inexpensive material may require continual maintenance to retain its serviceability and beauty. This will make its overall cost greater than another material which has a greater initial cost but requires no maintenance. For example, a painted wood wall may require repainting every three to five years, while a brick wall will require virtually no maintenance. *Ease* and *speed* of installation also affects the choice, when cost is a factor. Materials requiring little maintenance often keep a good appearance longer. Many factors must be considered when selecting exterior building materials.

Wall Sheathing

Wall sheathing is placed between a building frame and exterior covering. It adds rigidity, serves as a backing for exterior coverings, and may also serve as insulation.

Lumber is the traditional sheathing material. Traditionally, this may be one of three selections—*S4S, tongue and groove,* or *ship lap.* There are two methods of installation. It may be placed horizontally across the studding, or it may be applied diagonally at a 45° angle to the studs. The latter is preferred because it gives more rigidity to the building. When diagonal sheathing is used, most codes permit elimination of the "let-in" diagonal bracing at corners as discussed in Chapter 7. A note on the plans or specifications must state the *size* of lumber to be used and the *method* of installation.

Sheathing grade plywood and *fiberboard* are also suitable for walls. Large plywood panels permit rapid erection. Panels are applied with the face grain vertical for maximum strength. When 16″ or 24″ studding spacing is used, ½″ plywood is adequate. Some codes permit less thickness, but this should be avoided on quality construction.

Fiberboard wall sheathing may be purchased with the faces untreated, or the sheets may have a bituminous coating. Of course, when the latter is used it is not necessary to cover the sheathing with building paper because the surface is already protected. Treated fiberboard is moisture resistant but does not act as a vapor barrier. It will allow the wall to "breath" (permit transfer of vapor). Therefore sheathing should not be covered on the outside with a vapor barrier because this will trap condensation within the wall.

Most common fiberboard sheet sizes are 24"x96" and 48"x96". However, a wide variety of sizes is available. The 24"x96" sheet is installed with the long dimension across the studding. Sheets are staggered so adjoining ones do not end on the same stud. The 48"x96" sheets are installed with the long dimension vertical.

The two most frequently used thicknesses are ½" and $^{25}/_{32}$". The ½" thickness meets most minimum code requirements but $^{25}/_{32}$" is preferred because of its greater strength and added insulation value.

When solid lumber is used as wall sheathing a diagonal installation is most satisfactory.

Omission of Wall Sheathing

When frame buildings are in warm climates, or when they are used for unheated garages and other utility structures, sheathing is sometimes omitted. If wall sheathing is not required, building paper is applied to the walls and the exterior covering is applied.

Wall sheathing and exterior covering are frequently incorporated into a single prefabricated product.

Wall coverings may be structural or non-structural.

Horizontal Siding

Horizontal siding is made of thin, narrow, uniform-width strips of material. It is usually installed with the strips overlapping. This produces interesting horizontal shadows at the intersections. Wood is the traditional material used. When solid wood is used, the boards taper in a wedge, angled down from top to bottom. It is called "bevel siding," or in some areas of the country "lap siding" or "weather boarding." The first is more descriptive.

The thick bottom edge "butt" is used when specifying thickness. Nominal thicknesses are ½", ⅝", and ¾". Nominal widths are 4", 6", 8", 10", and 12". Bevel siding will cover much less surface than one might anticipate from the nominal size. Regular bevel siding will cover 1½" less height than its nominal size. For example, the exposed face of 10" bevel siding is 8½". Rabbeted bevel siding will cover 1" less width than the nominal size; therefore the exposed face of 10" rabbeted bevel siding is 9".

Boise Cascade

Bevel siding can be incorporated into beautiful designs.

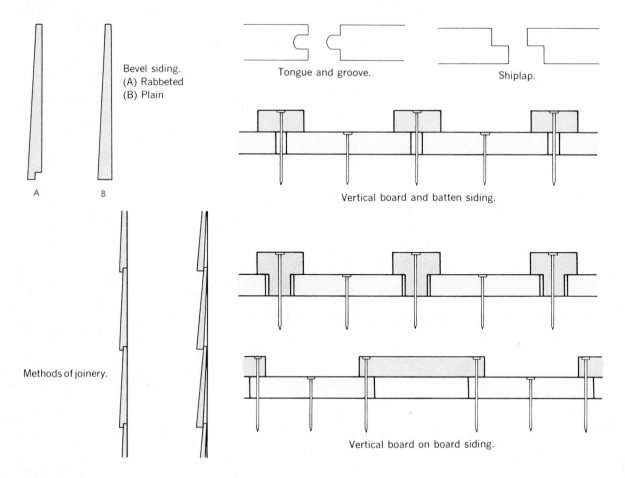

Bevel siding.
(A) Rabbeted
(B) Plain

A   B

Tongue and groove.

Shiplap.

Vertical board and batten siding.

Methods of joinery.

Vertical board on board siding.

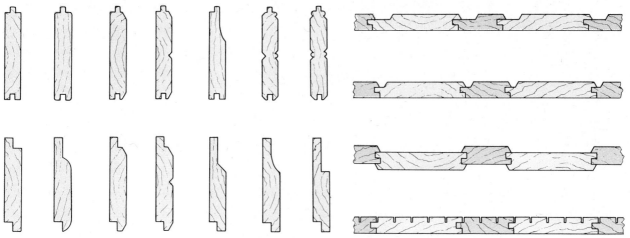

Tongue and groove siding patterns; shiplap siding patterns.

Plank patterns.

Lumber with good weathering characteristics should be used. Redwood is considered best. There are two common patterns of wood bevel siding—plain and rabbeted. Cross-sections of each are shown.

The finished surface may be smooth or saw textured.

Other Horizontal Siding

Horizontal siding may also be of plywood, hardboard, or reconstructed wood. The latter is made of small sections which have been jointed and glued to form large boards.

The above materials may be purchased with unfinished surfaces, or a variety of surface finishes applied. They may be overlaid with resinous paper, prefinished with paint, or covered with colored plastic film.

Horizontal siding is also manufactured of pre-finished steel, aluminum, and plastic. These may have rigid backing panels or the backs may be covered with insulation. Pre-finished siding is usually applied with special fasteners to avoid face nailing.

Wood siding patterns. Two methods of edge joining lumber siding are shown—shiplap and tongue and groove. *Cove* and *drop* siding are designed to be used horizontally. The other patterns are usually applied vertically. Examples of exterior siding patterns include only those most frequently selected.

Boards and battens. S4S boards may be applied vertically and the joints between boards covered with narrow strips of wood called *battens.* In the illustrations, notice the spaces between each board. These spaces permit expansion and contraction. Notice also that wide boards are nailed in the center, but not at the edges. This minimizes warping. Narrow boards may be nailed along one edge, with the other edge "floating" free.

Board-on-board. Board-on-board installations are very similar to boards and battens. The main differences are that the first boards applied have much more space between them, and the board replacing the batten is much wider.

Edges of this tongue and groove siding are beveled to form a "V" which conceals joints and produces shadow lines for vertical emphasis.

Olympic Stain

Early American style cedar plywood siding.

"Planktex" siding.

Plywood siding. Large sheets of exterior grade plywood may be used as a finished covering, or vertical wood strips may be added to simulate battens. Plywood may be purchased with saw-textured or other decoration cut into the outer surface. Some of the more common are shown.

When large sheets are used the face grain is vertical.

Shingles or shakes. Wood shingles or shakes, described in Chapter 10, may also be used as exterior wall covering. Because wood shingles are quite narrow, they are sometimes manufactured in assembled widths on a solid backing board. Coverings simulating wood shingles are also manufactured of asbestos, bituminous composition, hardboard, or aluminum. Their surface is machined to resemble sawed or hand split shingles. A great many sizes, shapes, and colors are manufactured, so it is necessary to consult manufacturers' literature when making selections.

Stucco

Stucco is a thin plaster used primarily on the outside. It must be waterproof. Stucco may be similar to interior plaster in that it takes a three-coat application—one brown scratch coat, one brown coat, and one lime finish coat. Or it may be made entirely of cement plaster. However, this is quite brittle; it may crack because of expansion and contraction of base materials, unless control joints are used. Lime stucco is less brittle, although its surface is not as hard.

Curtain walls with sandwich panels between vertical members have long-lasting beauty and require no maintenance.

The modern design of this brick apartment complex is aesthetically pleasing.

The beauty of this apartment structure is enhanced by its stucco finish.

Stucco may have a smooth or textured surface. Most stucco is a brilliant white and may be left this color. Pigments or decorative aggregates may be added to the finish coat for a built-in permanent finish. Stucco also paints well and is easy to maintain.

Stucco is sometimes plastered directly on masonry surfaces. However, wire reinforcing (frequently with paper backing) is usually secured to the building first and then the stucco is plastered. Minimum recommended thickness is ¾".

Rohm and Haas Co.

Plastic panels are a popular covering material for commercial installations.

Questions to Reinforce Knowledge

1. What functions do exterior coverings perform?

2. How does maintenance affect selection?

3. Why might one choose to cover a building with large plywood sheets instead of boards?

4. What is wall sheathing?

5. What materials are used for wall sheathing?

6. What are the two directions in which solid wood sheathing may be applied?

7. Which of the two methods is better? Why?

8. What is the face-grain direction of plywood sheathing?

9. What is the correct application of 48"x96" fiberboard sheathing?

10. What is the sheet direction of 24"x96" fiberboard sheathing?

11. What is an advantage of using bituminous-coated fiberboard sheathing?

12. What is likely to happen if plastic film is placed between the sheathing and the exterior wall covering?

13. What are the two most frequently used fiberboard sheathing thicknesses?

14. When may sheathing be omitted from wood frame walls?

15. What is meant by the statement, "Wall sheathing and exterior covering are frequently incorporated into a single product"?

16. What is horizontal siding?

17. What is bevel siding?

18. What is the name for the thick edge of bevel siding? How does its meaning differ from its meaning in other joints?

19. What are the nominal widths of bevel siding?

20. What are three methods of pre-finishing wood siding?

21. What other materials may be used as horizontal siding?

22. What is shiplap siding?

23. Is it applied vertically or horizontally?

24. What is drop siding?

25. What is board and batten siding?

26. Why are wide boards only nailed in the center on this siding?

27. What is board-on-board siding?

28. What are some advantages of using plywood for exterior walls?

29. What is the purpose of backing boards?

30. What is stucco?

31. What is the normal color of stucco?

32. What may be done to change the color?

33. What are the two common types of stucco?

34. What is a control joint?

35. Which is more brittle, lime or cement stucco?

Terms To Spell And Know

wall sheathing
tongue and groove
shiplap
taper
bevel siding
rabbeted bevel siding
boards and battens
board-on-board siding
stucco
lime

Part Two

FUNCTION
AND BEAUTY—
ESSENTIALS OF
PLANNING

23

The Architect

An architect is a designer or builder of anything, including golf courses, but the term is most frequently used to describe a person who designs, draws plans for, and supervises building construction. The term comes from ancient Greek, meaning "master builder."

As is true in other professions, architecture is becoming very specialized. Individual architects usually confine their activities to small areas of the field. In addition to designing buildings, architectural professions include such specialties as city planning, landscape architecture, and naval architecture. Architects engaged in designing buildings frequently specialize in designing one kind —homes, churches, schools, hospitals, or others. The main reason for this specialization is because the building industry is so large one cannot hope to become proficient at designing all building types. Thus the architect concentrates on one kind of design to become more expert.

Need for an Architect

Architects usually do not design very small or simple buildings such as garages or other utility structures unless they are a part of a large project. For personal satisfaction buildings as complex as homes or larger should be designed by an architect. This is not to imply that one should not avail oneself of a plan service or prefabricated structures, because these are usually designed by professionals.

It is sometimes difficult for people to realize that they need the services of an architect. They may think that they know exactly what they want and how the building should be constructed. This may or may not be true; usually it is not. They may not even be aware of many design and construction problems which may be encountered.

One of the most frequently used excuses for not commissioning an architect is that their services cost too much. However, the architect's fee is often less than the amount saved by the architect's efficient use of building space and good utilization of building materials and construction methods. An individual may not keep abreast of new products

and building trends but the competent architect must always do so.

Many states and communities have building standards and laws that practically require an architect, except for utility structures. Even in residential areas, this can be true. Of course any building must meet state and local code requirements.

Architect's Training

To register as an architect today, one almost must have a college degree. Accelerated courses, with limited general education, may allow completion in three years. However most accredited colleges will require at least four and many five years for graduation.

Two types of curricula may be offered (not all schools offer both). One may study architecture as it relates to design, or a more technical course is offered in architectural engineering.

Most colleges require a broad liberal education, as well as professional study. The reason for this is that architects must be fluently aware of the cultural aspects of society.

Graduation from a four or five year course earns the student a bachelor's degree. If additional formal education is desired, he or she may do advanced study for a master's or doctor's degree.

In addition to formal education, the prospective designer must also serve under the guidance and supervision of a competent architect in much the same manner as a doctor serves an internship. The length of time one must serve is not exactly the same everywhere but it is usually about three years.

After the training period one may take examinations to qualify and become a registered architect in the state of residence. It is then possible to secure a license in other states.

It is still possible in some instances to become a registered architect without attending college. However, because one must have so much more knowledge than was formerly necessary, it is becoming increasingly more difficult. After serving under an architect for a period, one must take and pass the same qualifying tests as those with college training.

The Architect's Duties

An architect has many duties and responsibilities which require thorough familiarity with the total building industry. To discuss all of the specific duties would result in much repetition of information presented elsewhere in the book; therefore only broad categories are listed to suggest the extent of the work.

The architect must be responsible for the following, whether he or she does all the work or not:

• Determine the needs and wishes of the client.
• Determine the financial status of the client and the amount of money the client desires to spend so the building plan is within reasonable bounds.
• Draw preliminary plans until a suitable one is achieved.
• Draw all working plans for the building, no matter how complicated.
• Determine all materials to be used.
• Draw up contract documents between the client and architect, and also between client and contractors.
• Write specifications for the building.
• Make cost estimates so the owner will know approximate cost and whether or not bids are within reason.
• Supervise the letting of bids.
• Know responsibility and financial ability of individual contractors.
• Audit the contractors' accounts and analyze receipts and statements. The architect must be certain that all bills for material and labor are paid.
• Make payments to contractors.
• Supervise construction and see that plans are followed accurately. In cases of errors or omissions on the plans, or misinterpretation by contractors, the architect corrects or explains them.
• Inspect and pass upon the quality of all material and of labor performed, and secure all guarantees.

The Architect's Fee

Successful architects are well paid for their services, but it is difficult to say how much one may be expected to earn per year. It is like any other profession. Some architects become very expert or well known and earn large sums of money while others do not. Average income is about the same as that of a good doctor, lawyer, or other professional person. Again, as in any other work, one does not become rich the first year of employment. In fact, during early years one may be paid less than many persons in less glamorous lines.

An architect usually works on a commission basis, the fee being a percentage of the total building cost. This fee is variable but is frequently between 5% and 8% of the building cost. This seems like a large fee, but one must realize that it is not all clear profit. Business relations and office upkeep, taxes, plus payment of drafters and supervisory personnel, consume a large percentage of the fee. Expensive maintenance must continue through all seasons. Much of the architect's success depends on good business management.

If an architect has a flourishing business with several commissions at the same time, it is not possible to do all supervisory work at each of the construction sites. Most large construction projects require that the architect have a full-time representative at the site. When this is true, the architect's representative has direct authority over construction.

Questions to Reinforce Knowledge

1. Who may be called an architect?

2. Name four different kinds of architects.

3. Why do architects frequently specialize in designing predominately one kind of building?

4. Why does one need the services of an architect?

5. Are buildings always designed by architects? Explain.

6. In what way is one required to obtain the services of an architect? Explain.

7. What are the normal educational requirements for an architect?

8. What are the two different curricula offered?

9. Why do colleges also require the architect to have a liberal education?

10. What advanced degrees are offered in the field of architecture?

11. From your reading and your own reasoning, why is it necessary for a prospective architect to serve a period of time working for a competent architect?

12. After formal and informal training is completed, how may one secure an architect's license?

13. Is it always necessary for an architect to attend college? Explain.

14. Why must an architect be familiar with all phases of the building industry?

15. What services does the architect perform for the client? There are 14 major items listed in the text. You should be able to list 10 or more. They need not be in any given order.

16. How does the architect's income compare with earnings in other well known professions?

17. On what basis is the architectural firm paid for its services?

18. What is required of the successful architect besides the ability to attract clients? Discuss.

19. What are the duties and responsibilities of an architect's representative?

Terms to Spell and Know

architect's commission
registered architect

architectural engineering
architect's representative

24

The Draftsman

Very briefly, this chapter merely identifies the particular work of the architectural drafter. As you know, a drafter is a person who draws pictorial and working plans for any structure—buildings, equipment for buildings, and other items. He or she works for and under the supervision and direction of an architect. Duties and responsibilities vary with experience and ability.

Beginning duties frequently include distribution of supplies to other drafters, reproduction of prints from tracings, and other routine assignments. The first actual drawing will probably consist of copying or tracing small details from other drawings.

Later, the drafter will develop working drawings from information supplied him or her. After more experience, when he or she knows the materials and construction methods used by the employer, the drafter will handle much of the detailed planning, such as the size of structural parts and

methods of joining them. After becoming a master drafter, he or she can become responsible for the work of other drafters as well.

If one is extremely ambitious and talented, the drafting position may be used as a stepping stone to other positions. One may through further work and study become an estimator, specifications writer, architect's representative, or an architect.

There is no prescribed amount of formal education one must have to become a drafter. One may secure a position upon completion of high school, but many firms require at least two years of college. Many young architects, upon completion of their formal education, begin their careers as drafters.

It is impossible to say exactly how much a drafter can be expected to earn per year. Wages are variable throughout the country. Even in the same city, all drafters do not earn the same wage. Beginning salaries are not high. They may be compared to other types of office work, but as one remains in a position the salary increases are usually better than the average of other office workers. After several years of experience, a good drafter can reasonably expect to earn as much as an office manager or service department head in other types of business. One may have a flair for advertising layout or sales work that will lead to work in product promotion not connected with architecture.

Questions to Reinforce Knowledge

1. Explain the difference between an architect and an architectural drafter.

2. Investigate the opportunities in your community for the drafter in architecture, manufacturing firms, city planning departments, and legal work such as producing site drawings.

25

Design for Today's Living

Architecture, in its truest sense, is shelter from the elements. It may serve many purposes. It may be a home or permanent shelter. It may be a place to work, play, or worship. All *great* architecture is a solution to a building problem, using the best building materials and construction methods available. Architecture must fulfill three obligations:

(1) **function**
(2) **structure**
(3) **beauty**

The three are interdependent. The function is the reason for a building's existence. The structural materials and methods of construction must enhance the function. When a selection of structural systems must be made, the main consideration is, how can the building best be built to fulfill its function? For example, at the present time thin-shell concrete dome structures represent the latest building fashion. Yet one does not build a concrete dome unless this represents the best solution to the problem.

Architectural Merit

In this period of rapidly changing technology, one sometimes gets the impression that everything new is good and everything old is poor. Nothing could be farther from the truth. Only time, continued use, and acceptance can determine true worth.

Building has seen a continual evolution from the beginning of recorded history to the present; however, there have been setbacks and periods of regression. Progress cannot be constant. More progress is made at some times than at others.

As is true today, buildings of the past which we regard as great were built using the best materials and methods of the time. Some examples of this great architecture are the Egyptian pyramids, Greek and Roman works, Gothic cathedrals, classic homes, and the forerunners of modern skyscrapers. Each of these represents an expression of their times and the way of life of the people.

Style

During each period of history, style has evolved when individual groups developed basic architecture to suit their own needs, using construction materials available in their own locality. For example,

people living in forest regions built mostly of timber, while those in volcanic regions made extensive use of stone, and available clay resulted in brick structures. Architecture took materials at hand and used them to solve building problems. However, with today's modern transportation, all materials are readily available, although the fact that transportation costs add to the building cost must still be given consideration.

Since this book is primarily concerned with drafting, rather than a course in architecture, no lengthy discussion of individual styles or their merits will be presented. It is the author's opinion that architecture of today should not be *copies* of building styles from the past. They should have straightforward designs taking advantage of today's materials and construction methods.

Beauty

Beauty pleases or satisfies. It may give the beholder a feeling of awe and inspiration. It is important for one's inner enrichment. This may be stated as an esthetic quality or feeling. Beauty is not a simple thing. Total architectural beauty will rely upon building lines, form, proportion, harmony, balance, color, and texture.

Beauty is directly related to past experience. If one has seen only ugly things, one may think the least ugly is beautiful! Architecture is, or at least should be, a work of art. Yet a building considered beautiful by some may provoke feelings of disgust in others. No two people have the same feeling of beauty for a given object or experience. An untrained individual may like a great, complicated musical composition; however, this is doubtful because it is not within his or her realm of experience. This person will probably gain greater pleasure from the music of the street because it is familiar. The same is true of buildings. One may like a building style because it represents the familiar, having complete disregard for other merits. Likewise, a building of unusual form (but of good design) may be disliked only because it represents the unfamiliar or unknown. It is easier to rely upon the security of the past (the tried and true) than to explore the unknown.

Pseudo Beauty

When one observes the shiny embellishments of an industrial society, one sometimes confuses gaudiness with design and beauty, especially in judging buildings. This is not to say that no decoration is to be used, because decoration plays a very strong role. Applied or "stuck on" decoration without a purpose is to be avoided.

It also dates a building. The decoration should naturally and logically go with the building materials. The designer does not want the building to appear monotonous and drab. The building should express one's feeling for beauty. The designer must rely on functional design and an honest use of materials to support the desired artistic effect. He or she should not rely upon gimmicks or unusual uses to bring attention to the structure. This false idea is the basis for much of the poor architecture one sees. Not to imply that all of today's architecture is poor, it is not; much is very good. In most of today's good design the architect employs an honest use of materials and simplicity as primary guides.

Elements of Beauty and Design

Line

Building *lines* (do not confuse with earlier definition of building line, meaning the location where the building is to be placed) represent the border, boundary, or outline of the building or its parts. They may be described as a connected *series* following each other in time or space. For example, a building with horizontal lines is one that is usually low and has a profile that closely follows the ground plane. Or the building lines may be emphasized by horizontal shadow lines of bevel siding. Vertical lines may also make the points of emphasis.

Form

The total of all lines, when combined or enclosed, creates the building form. Form may be described as the solid *mass* of the building. Form was best analyzed by America's great architect, Frank Lloyd Wright, when he stated the principle that *form follows function.*

Proportion

Proportion is the relationship of one part, item, or area to another. All structural units, or visual spaces, must contribute to a feeling of total architectural unity. The Greek Golden Rec-

tangle is approximately 5 units wide and 8 units long, or has a width to length proportion or ratio of 5 to 8. This rectangle is considered the most pleasing proportion obtainable. It is used extensively when designing room sizes and building shapes.

Greek golden rectangle.

Horizontal line emphasis.

Vertical line emphasis.

Massive structure contributes to the beauty of this luxury home.

Windows of the second story balance with those on the lower level. "Borrows" from both Georgian and Colonial styles.

Balance

Balance is the ability of one mass or area to equal or counteract another *visually*. An example of balance is large windows on a first and second story placed directly in line with each other, or a 2-story unit balanced with a long, low extension, such as a garage.

Rhythm

Rhythm is the visual artistic relationship of individual building parts and their arrangement in the total building pattern. It is enhanced by a visual flow or movement of regularly recurring elements or features such as placing tops of all windows and doors at the same height, or repetition of parts to unite the structure visually.

Color and Texture

Color—or patterns of color—and texture, which is the degree or pattern of roughness of a material, can be used to emphasize all of the elements of design and beauty.

A plain (also plane) surface can be made interesting by their use. Since color is part of the surface finish and texture is in the surface of the material, these are not applied decoration.

Good architecture incorporates these elements of design into an integrated whole. An adequate designer has a knowledge of all design principles and knows how to unite them into a structure of esthetic appeal.

The previous discussion of the *elements of beauty and design* only serves as an introduction to a broad topic. For those with special interest, further study is recommended.

Choosing the Form

As mentioned, the building form should follow the function. Quite frequently a building could take any one of a number of forms and still adequately perform its function. When this is true the designer must choose the most satisfactory form to fulfill the obligations of function and structure, and still create a pleasing and beautiful building.

Application of Design

After the needs and wishes of the client have been determined and recorded—see Chapter 26—actual design is begun. The discussion of planning problems and solutions will be confined to house construction because this is typical of all light construction. When other structures are to be designed the principles are the same.

Since a building is planned for the function it is to perform, this suggests the interior should be planned first. Still, the exterior must contribute to a harmonious and unified structure. A home may follow any of a variety of forms. Therefore the designer must choose one that is suitable.

Chapter 27 discusses elements of planning individual rooms and areas. From the wishes of the client, and using details learned concerning planning individual rooms, tentative room and area sizes may be determined for the entire plan. For example, the client may have previously decided that 10'-0" x 12'-0" is the minimum size of children's bedrooms and the master bedroom must be at least 14'-0" x 20'-0". The plan must contain and conform to these requirements.

Room Cutouts

A beginner may use lightweight cardboard and a ¼" = 1'-0" scale, then cut rectangles representing tentative room and area sizes. The cutouts might well follow the 5 to 8 proportion of the Golden Rectangle previously described. Two or three alternate shapes and sizes should be suggested for each room. The room and its size should be labeled on each cutout. The cutouts may be arranged and rearranged until the most suitable room arrangement is achieved.

It will not be possible to make all the cardboard rooms fit together perfectly. Some may overlap slightly, or the plan may have insufficient or too much area allowed for halls and closets. Minor adjustments will naturally have to be made. When a good tentative room arrangement is achieved, a quick sketch of the floor plan should be made (not drawn with instruments).

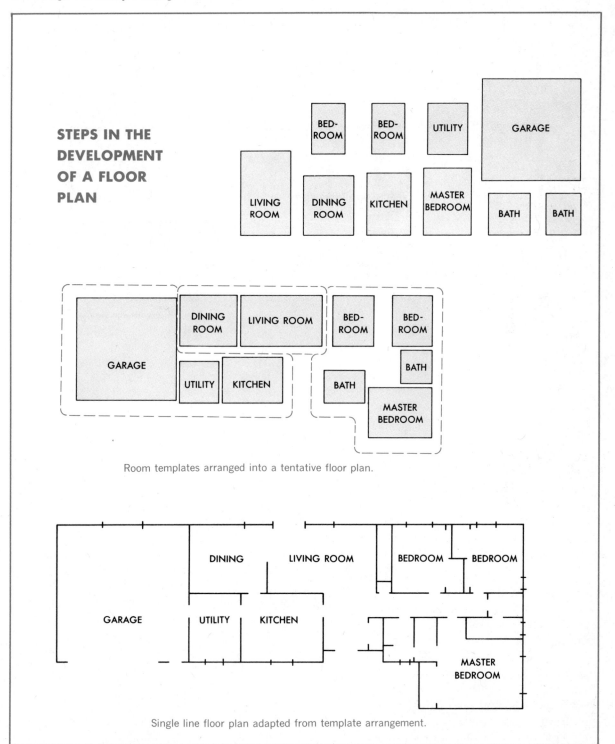

STEPS IN THE DEVELOPMENT OF A FLOOR PLAN

Room templates arranged into a tentative floor plan.

Single line floor plan adapted from template arrangement.

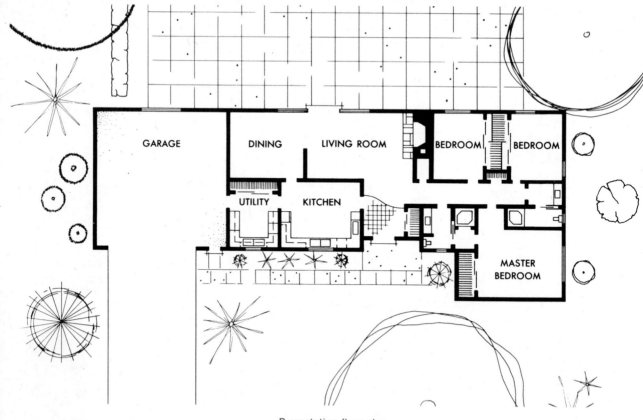

GARAGE   DINING   LIVING ROOM   BEDROOM   BEDROOM

UTILITY   KITCHEN

MASTER BEDROOM

Presentation floor plan.

Before an originally styled building takes its final form, many tentative plans are made and the final selection is taken from the best one. The cardboard cutouts should be saved for future use.

Requirements of a Good Home

A good home expresses the way of life of its occupants. A design for an active family will be different from one for a family which spends much time reading and listening to good music. This fact creates a problem for the development home because it is not designed for specific individuals. An attempt is made to design for a relaxed atmosphere but still provide for many physical activities. This has led to the inclusion of multi-purpose rooms (with many names) and has contributed a tendency to the isolation of living rooms. In the past the living room was the focal point of activity, but it is gaining popularity as a retreat or company room similar to the turn-of-the-century parlor.

Well-planned Details

The home and each room in it should be well planned including all necessary features in each room, arranged in a logical and orderly manner. The arrangement of rooms and location of walls, doors, windows, and all building parts should make best use of all building materials so the house will be economical to build. One house (or any building) which is almost identical to another may cost hundreds of dollars more because it does not make maximum use of building material sizes. One method of framing may cost more than another, when the less expensive one might actually perform the job better.

Flexibility

The house should be flexible.

254

The use of certain rooms might change in the future and this must not restrict the use of other rooms. If the house is expansible, provide for additions which do not interfere with present rooms or look as though they were stuck on when viewed from the inside or outside. A well planned addition blends so well with the rest of the building that an observer should not be able to tell an addition has been made.

Privacy

A good house should afford privacy for the occupants. This means privacy for the individual family members or visitors, and also those within must have privacy from those outside. Many things are done to afford privacy. One of the recent trends has been to place the kitchen near the front and place the living room in the rear. This arrangement also gives the living room access to patios in the rear, which contributes to relaxed outdoor living. Even more recent is the use of high privacy walls across the front enclosing open courts, or omission of all windows across the front. Omission of windows on any wall where complete privacy is desired is becoming accepted practice. The rebirth of the atrium, which is an enclosed garden, or inner court, and the division of living areas into separate structural units are popular means of gaining privacy.

Limiting Influences

As population increases, as cities grow in size, as land becomes scarce, as labor costs rise and the value of money goes down, average size homes have become smaller. It is necessary for planning to be much better than it was in the past. This smaller size has also contributed to the popularity of multi-use rooms. (For minimum housing, sizes are still small. Middle and upper income housing is beginning to feature more and larger rooms.)

Size and Type Home To Be Considered

A home must be compatible with its surroundings. It should look as though it fits or belongs in its location. Another of the truths expressed by Frank Lloyd Wright is that architecture should be *organic*. He believed nature is beautiful and one should use as many native materials as possible. One should make maximum use of the natural terrain and the home should approximately follow its contour. Naturally this does not imply that floors slope to follow the ground. Floor levels may be stepped so they conform.

Other Homes in Area

Besides blending harmoniously with its surroundings, the home must look well with other homes in the area. If all the other homes are large one should not build a small home, or if all homes are small one should not build a large one. If the area contains older homes of questionable value, it is usually poor economics to construct a large expensive home in their midst. A person must carefully study an area's property values to see whether they are increasing or decreasing before deciding to build.

Solid walls facing a street, separated living areas, and an atrium give privacy to this home's occupants. P.M. Bolton Assoc.

Practical Considerations

Client's Financial Ability

The home designer must know the financial status of the client. Many people have wants that are completely out of proportion to their ability to finance them. One must decide what is luxury and what is necessity. Sound use of the prospective home owner's credit may determine whether or not the proposed building is constructed.

Rule-of-thumb estimates say a home should not cost more than 2½ to 3 times the individual's annual salary. Such a rough estimate is not reliable in all instances. One must consider the individual's prospects for the future. The amount of current outstanding debt and how obligations are fulfilled must be considered. The amount spent on luxury, travel, social activities, and family education also affect one's ability to pay. Of course, only the family head can decide, but the designer may suggest ways of adjusting.

Number of Stories

Whether a home is to have one, two, or possibly more stories changes with current fashion and from locality to locality.

Four general classifications are:
• Single story
• One and one-half story
• Two story
• Split level

Single Story

The single story home has been most popular in recent years. All low, sprawling homes have become known as ranch-house style. This label is not properly used. The true ranch house is an outgrowth of the warm climate southwest. It presents a low profile, wide overhangs to keep out the sun, and large sliding glass areas which open so the evening breeze will enter. Extensive use is made of outdoor living areas and patios. Post and beam construction lends itself to this design.

The single story home is most expensive to build, per square foot. More footing and foundation length, outside wall area, and roof materials are required than for other classifications of equal area.

One and One-half Stories

One and one-half story houses usually have a steep roof slope so the attic space can be utilized. Ceilings usually follow the roof slope over part of a room. Dormers admit light and air. Shed dormers are frequently placed on the back of the house to give additional flat ceiling area. The style is prevalent in Cape Cod and other early American designs.

Two Story

Two story homes make maximum use of limited ground area. They are less expensive to build than single story homes of an equal area. The two story home is enjoying a new popularity in many parts of the country, but it is not as widely used as the one story designs.

Split Level

The split level home has been much abused and misused. The purpose of a split level is to permit the floors to follow the natural ground contour. Thus the split level can be placed on irregular lots totally unsuitable for homes with one or two stories. Portions of the garage, basement, or recreation room may be placed below the ground. When the ground slopes from the front of the lot toward the back, it is common practice for the house to appear as a single story dwelling from the front and a full two stories from the rear.

Rows of suburban split levels placed on level ground are an unrealistic use. Other designs would afford more house for less money and would be more harmonious with their surroundings.

Floor Plan Shapes

Shape of the floor area also affects the cost. A square or rectangular building is less expensive than one of an irregular shape. However, if finances will permit, homes have two or more rectangles adjoining each other to relieve monotony of appearance. These rectangles may form L, U, or T shapes. Again, when finances permit, and one desires nonconformity, still more irregular and unusual designs may be adopted. Unusual designs take care and expert knowledge.

Areas of a Home

A home is divided into three *areas* (groups of rooms). The divisions are based upon the functions to be performed. These areas are:

- **Public:** Living rooms, dining rooms, front entry, or any other place entertaining is to be done.
- **Private:** Bedrooms, den or study, any room used as a retreat.
- **Work:** Kitchens, utility rooms, laundries or any room where the business of running the household is performed.

Baths or powder rooms may be placed in any area. Some rooms are designed with overlapping functions. For example, a master bedroom may also be used as the owner's sitting room or retreat (same area). A kitchen may also be used as the only planned dining area in the home, or a family room may be used for informal entertaining (different areas).

Traffic Pattern

As stated earlier, privacy is important to the individual. Each room or area should allow privacy when it is desired.

One should be able to walk from one room or area to another, without passing through a third one. Living and dining rooms are considered the same, when fulfilling this requirement. It is permissible to walk through a dining room to go from a living room to a kitchen. One may also pass through a kitchen to reach a utility room or laundry. One should not pass through a bedroom to reach any other room.

The three areas of a home (1) Public, (2) Private, and (3) Work.

Family room of a prefabricated home, adjoining a kitchen and patio, contributes to gracious informal living.

Scholz Homes Inc.

Halls

Front entry and bedroom halls are necessary to fulfill the above requirements. A central entry, similar to the ones in the floor plan layouts illustrated earlier, permits greatest design flexibility.

Many inexpensive or poorly arranged homes do not have a front entry space. One must step directly from the outside into the living room, bringing the rain, snow, dust, and wind with them. The living room must also serve as a corridor to reach other rooms. If space and finances permit, this is to be avoided.

All homes and apartments should have at least two entries. Besides the front entry, most codes require a side or rear service entry. In addition to providing for service deliveries, the additional entry gives an alternate means of leaving the building for convenience and in case of fire or other disasters.

Planning the Exterior

"Organic" architecture has led to a reduction in building height. Heat and cold may be controlled better than in the days of high ceilings and big attics. Not all buildings emphasize low horizontal lines, but they tend to do so. Building cost is another factor leading to height reduction. Less material is required if height is reduced.

Combination of Wall Materials

As stated earlier, simplicity should be the designer's guide. When combinations of building materials are used they must have a look of belonging together. For example, it is generally poor practice to build a brick structure and then insert a few stones at random, or to build of brick and then place a triangular section of stone at each of the lower outside corners. One does not put on ornamentation such as this just to make the building different or eye catching. One must rely upon the building's good design to bring attention to it. For the beginner this is very difficult to believe. One sees buildings oddly constructed and thinks it is acceptable and good. Just because a thing is done by some does not make it good or acceptable. It is not being done by leading architects and designers.

Mixing Architectural Styles

One should not use different architectural styles on different parts of the same building.

Roof Slope

Roof slopes on a building should all be the same. Changing pitch does not add to the design

Economically used brick and vertical siding skillfully combined to complement the total design.

Scholz Homes Inc.

and will also require additional labor. Shed dormers were mentioned earlier as a means of gaining added flat ceiling area; these roofs do have a roof slope that is different from the rest of the building. When these are used they must not have a stuck-on appearance.

Changes in Exterior Wall Coverings To Reduce Height Visually

Since horizontal lines are usually emphasized, common practice calls for two exterior wall covering materials, divided horizontally to visually reduce building height by adding horizontal lines. When this is done, the lower portion is built of one material, and another material is added above. If masonry is to be used, it is placed on the lower portion because it must be supported by the foundation and footing. If other masonry, or a dissimilar material is used, a stone sill serves as a cap (water table) and a division between materials. The sill may be of stone similar to ones used on the lower part of the building, or cut stone of a contrasting color may be used. If brick covers all of the exterior or only the lower part, rowlock brick sills may be used. If materials other than masonry are used on the lower part, the sill may be wood.

Location of Changes in Coverings

Changes in materials are usually made in line with the lower edge of windows, or at least are kept at a uniform height. When changes in height are desired, this change is usually made at door or window openings.

Stone and brick can be combined if it is done with care, adds to the appearance, and the designer can justify this practice. The combination must improve the design. Generally speaking it is more desirable to use dissimilar materials when more than one exterior covering is planned. For example, brick and redwood can be a very harmonious combination. Aluminum siding goes very well with light-colored limestone, especially on remodeling jobs. Red brick does not go well with yellow brick. Upper wall covering is generally lighter than the lower one, to keep the building from looking top-heavy.

Questions to Reinforce Knowledge

1. What is architecture?

2. What are the three obligations of architecture?

3. What is the primary purpose of a building?

4. What determines the structural system one should use?

5. If an idea is new, does that mean it is good? If it is old, does that mean it is no longer usable? Explain.

6. What makes great architecture great?

7. From your own reasoning, what is a period of architecture?

8. How does style evolve?

9. What should be the basis for planning today's buildings?

10. What is beauty? What determines it?

11. Why is beauty important?

12. What is meant by the term pseudo-beauty?

13. What is meant when one speaks of an honest use of materials?

14. What is applied decoration?

15. What is a "gimmick"; what is wrong with it when used on a building?

16. If something is modern, does that mean it is bare of all decoration? Explain.

17. When speaking of design, what are the lines of a building?

18. What lines are emphasized in ranch-house design?

19. When referring to a building, what is form?

20. What is proportion?

21. What is the Greek Golden Rectangle; what are its proportions?

22. What is balance?

23. What is rhythm?

24. What is texture?

25. Which is planned first, a building interior or exterior?

26. How may cardboard cutouts be used as an aid in planning?

27. What problems of design does the development house present that a custom house does not?

28. What is a multi-purpose room?

29. In some homes, why has the living room been placed away from other rooms and out of the traffic pattern?

30. Why must one make maximum use of building material sizes?

31. What is meant when one speaks of a flexible house?

32. What is an expansible house? How does one provide for this?

33. What does it mean to say that additions should not look stuck on?

34. A home must provide two kinds of privacy. What are they?

35. Why have average homes become smaller?

36. What is *organic* architecture?

37. How do other homes in an area affect one that is to be built?

38. Do people always desire homes in keeping with their financial ability? What are some of the financial factors that must be taken into consideration?

39. Is it absolutely safe to say one can afford to buy a house worth three times one's annual income?

40. What is ranch-house design?

41. When considering the amount of area, is a single story home economical to build?

42. What is a 1½ story home?

43. How do shed dormers make such a house more usable?

44. For area received, is a two story home economical to build?

45. What is a split level home? What should determine the floor levels?

46. What floor plan shapes are most economical to build?

47. What are the three *areas* of a home?

48. What area is a bathroom in?

49. Why is traffic flow important?

50. How do halls aid this?

51. What are two reasons why height of homes has decreased?

52. From your own reasoning, what is likely to happen if a building has several architectural styles?

53. Does a variety of roof slopes add interest to a building? Explain.

54. How may changes in exterior wall coverings *visually* reduce building height?

55. Where are these changes usually made?

Terms To Spell and Know

timber	interior	overhang
form (building)	sketch	patio
proportion	multi-purpose	dormer
rhythm	retreat	attic
harmony	parlor	areas of the home
balance	flexibility	public
applied decoration	atrium	private
building lines	organic	work
"form follows function"	profile	corridor
Greek Golden Rectangle	rowlock	ornamentation

26

Determining Needs and Wishes of the Client

There are literally thousands of items and ideas to be given consideration when planning a building. Any one item, if not properly resolved, can cause errors or misunderstandings. Therefore it is necessary to keep a written record of all planning. This can be in the form of organized notes, check lists, or data compiled on charts. Samples of these are included.

Many items mentioned briefly here are discussed at greater length in other chapters. This chapter only indicates some of the important items that must be given consideration before the design is begun, so discussion is limited.

Financial Ability of Client

Before planning begins, the architect must know the financial status and ability of the client. He or she must know exactly how much can be spent on the total building project. People have a tendency to overstate their financial ability. If the building is too costly, it may work hardships on the family for a long period of time, perhaps over several years.

Necessities vs. Luxuries

Most individuals have no real idea of the combined cost of all the beautiful items they desire to incorporate into their home. They usually visualize a rosy picture of a spacious, near-perfect home completely filled with convenient gadgets, fine furniture, and lovely accessories. One must keep the budget in mind during all planning stages. The client, with the architect's help, must decide what items are necessities and what ones are luxuries.

Adapting Client's Ideas

Every person desiring to build a home (or other structure) has many ideas he or she wishes to incorporate into the plan. This is as it should be. However, if the ideas are so inflexible that the architect is allowed no design freedom, a poorly designed building will probably result.

General Appearance of

One of the first things an architect should know about the client is the architectural style preferred. Buildings designed by the same architect tend to have certain identifying features. He or she is usually commissioned because the client is impressed with previous structures. However people's ideas vary, so they must reach an agreement as to the style to be used. NOTE: This is why presentation drawings are submitted before detailed planning is done.

The architect must also determine the type home the client desires; for instance, is it to be a single story, two story, split level, or tri-level? He or she should also inquire whether the client prefers compact homes or ones that use a large area. The client's preference as to construction methods should also be sought. For example, does the client prefer wood frame, solid masonry, masonry veneer, steel, or some other? The architect must also know the client's preference of exterior covering materials. The roof shape and degree of slope should also be discussed.

The Lot

The architect should examine the lot before planning is begun.

If a large scale map of the plot is not available a survey may be made at this time. The size, shape, and terrain must be known. Consultation with the client will determine what existing features such as trees, shrubs, boulders, earth, or others are to be retained or removed.

Orientation

Preliminary examination of the lot will also help determine problems and solutions of orientation. Major problems to be given consideration at this time are:

- Location of other structures in the immediate vicinity.
- How to design the structure so it is harmonious to the permanent features of the terrain.
- The relationship of the front elevation and entries to the street.
- How to secure the best view.
- Orienting the structure to take advantage of prevailing winds.
- Orienting the structure to take best advantage of the sun.

Specific Information the Architect Must Know

- Number of people in the family: Is the home being designed for a young family that is likely to increase or is the number rather permanent? Will it be necessary to accommodate the client's parents at a later date?
- What is the age of each member of the family: Are children each to have separate bedrooms or are two or more boys or girls to share a room? If rooms are to be shared, are separate storage facilities to be provided for each person?
- Number of rooms desired—number required.
- Functions each room must perform—how to accomplish them?
- Approximate size of rooms: How much can these sizes vary? What are the minimums and maximums for each room?
- Special interests: Are space and facilities provided for activities such as painting, photography, sewing, reading, woodwork, music, or others, when these represent the client's interests?
- Storage facilities: List all of the items the family needs to store. Categorize according to use.
- What is the family's living pattern? Is the home to have a formal or informal atmosphere?
- Open or closed plan: Are rooms to be open to each other? Which ones? Or are all to be separate rooms?
- Number and location of bathrooms, half baths, or powder rooms. Equipment desired in each.
- Room finishes: What are the client's preferences as to wall, floor, and ceiling finishes?
- Basement: Is the home to have a basement, or shall utility services be provided by a utility room, laundry, or other?
- Garage: Is a garage or carport to be included; if so, for how many cars? Is the garage or carport to be used for storage?
- Equipment desired: List all mechanical items to be included. Is there a preference for any brand or specific models?
- Color: What are the client's (entire family's) preferences and dislikes in colors?
- What kind of heating and cooling is desired?
- Special features for interior: What special features are desired such as fireplaces, bookcases, planters, dividers, or others?
- Special features for exterior: What special features are desired such as pools, terraces, patios, outdoor fireplaces, fences, gardens, or others?
- Can all of the proposed features be incorporated into the client's actual budget?

27

Room-by-Room Planning

Entries and Halls

Most buildings *should* have at least one entry hall. However, they are sometimes omitted because of space and cost limitations. Entry size should be in proportion to the scale of other rooms. For example, if a spacious building is being designed, a spacious entry should be included. If the building serves only basic needs, then the entry would be minimum size. The FHA minimum width of all halls in homes is 3'-0". It is measured from the face of walls and not from framing members. NOTE: This width is too narrow for convenient use and beauty, and should be used only for minimum installations. Wider halls are much more desirable, if space and cost permit.

Entry doors leading to the central hall should be covered by a porch or roof overhang.

A recessed entry gives the door protection from the weather.

263

Additional protection from the elements can be gained by recessing the doors into an alcove as shown.

The front entry hall is usually given special architectural emphasis. The entry sets the mood or feeling of the entire building. It extends an invitation to enter.

Halls should be located so they give access to all rooms.

To give maximum service with a minimum of care, entry halls should have hard-surfaced floors that are easy to clean. Composition and plastic tile or roll flooring, ceramic tile, or flagstone lend themselves to contemporary installations. Carpet and exposed hardwood floors are to be avoided in entries because they are more difficult to maintain.

Inclusion of furniture makes this spacious, luxurious tiled entry even more inviting.

The Mosaic Tile Co.

Contemporary design makes frequent use of large glass areas in a spacious entry. A feeling of uninterrupted space may be further enhanced by adding small gardens, rocks, plants, small trees, pools, or fountains. Any of the above may be further emphasized by mood lighting. A variety of wall treatments, if combined with good taste, can also create interest. Another trend is to make the entry spacious vertically (tall) by having it extend to a two-story height. However, ceiling height in entries or other halls may be lower than in other rooms so one has a feeling of greater space when he steps from the hall.

Hall use can be improved if it is large enough to accommodate some furniture.

Doors leading from an entry hall (foyer) to other rooms tend to conserve heat, but are sometimes eliminated in the interest of beauty. Recent trends sometimes omit a solid wall between an entry and an adjoining room and replace it with dividers, planters, screens, or free-standing divider closets. When closets serve as room dividers they are not always built with conventional framing. Closets with thin walls are frequently constructed of hardwood plywood or of less expensive plywood and covered with decorative materials such as hardwood paneling, plastic laminate, fiber glass, vinyl, or resinous coated fabric.

FHA regulations state that a home *must* have a closet to serve the front entry. Minimum inside size is 2'-0" x 3'-0". If possible

The Mosaic Tile Co.

Large glass areas appear to increase entry size.

A loggia is an outside entry used primarily in warm climates.

P.M. Bolton Assoc.

264

Two-story height adds to the impressiveness of a foyer.

Scholz Homes Inc.

this closet should open into the hall.

As mentioned earlier, a service entry hall is usually placed near the kitchen; if a basement is required, frequently the hall is used for entering the basement. A service entry hall is not always included, but should be when possible. Available space and finances do not usually permit a spacious service entry. It is designed to be utilitarian. The service entry is sometimes enlarged and called a mud room.

It is very desirable to have a

closet near the rear entry. This closet is frequently designed with special storage places for outdoor wearing apparel and equipment.

Living Rooms

A living room usually has direct access to the entry hall. When the living room is used as a focal point of family activity it should be quite large. The author's minimum recommended size is 12'-0" x20'-0", but if the room is to be used only as a retreat it is frequently no larger than 12'-0"x 14'-0".

Each living room should have a special center of interest such as a fireplace, lighted mural, or entertainment center around which furniture may be grouped.

There is no required equipment for this room; however, fireplaces, bookcases, planters, built-in storage areas, special window emphasis or high ribbon windows, and built-in furniture add to beauty and use. Living rooms may be given an added feeling of spaciousness by designing them sunken two or three steps, or by having the ceiling a different height from that of other rooms.

Interior masonry walls are also quite popular. Floor surfacing materials are influenced by regional preference. Carpet, exposed hardwood, tile, and terrazzo are all very popular. See illustrations on the next page.

Dining Rooms

If a dining room is the only eating area in a home, the room size and surface treatments are different from those of homes with other eating areas provided.

Metal grilles may serve as open dividers between an entry and living room.

Scholz Homes Inc.

265

Scholz Homes Inc.

Large glass areas and a massive fireplace wall add to the interest of a living room.

Scholz Homes Inc.

A dining room may be open to the kitchen.

A sunken living room and an open stairway in the entry give a feeling of luxury.

Scholz Homes Inc.

One end of a living room may be set aside for formal dining.

Scholz Homes Inc.

For example, if the room is used only for special occasions you might want to carpet and equip the room with fine furniture. If used daily by the family, the room might have hard surfaced floors and durable, plastic-surfaced furniture. China, silver, and linen storage would be entirely different to meet the needs of the two uses mentioned. Room size would probably be about the same for either use. Size is determined by the anticipated number to use the room. There is no established minimum size, but 11'-0"x13'-0" or 12'-0"x14'-0" is satisfactory for modest dwellings.

A dining room is not always separated and closed off from other rooms. It may be partially open to a living room, family room, or kitchen. When the dining room is open to another room, both rooms will appear larger. Walls between the dining room and one of the other rooms are frequently omitted, or may be replaced with partial walls, fireplaces, planters, screens, counters, or cabinets to define the areas. Of course, the view into other rooms is limited by these devices.

A living room and dining room should be adjoining. It is very poor practice to have the two rooms separated by a foyer or hall. This tends to separate people into small groups when you need the extra space rather than uniting everyone. Also it divides the home into cells, losing a sense of spaciousness. A dining room and kitchen should be adjoining for convenience of use.

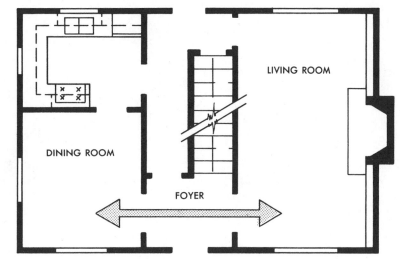

If possible, avoid living and dining rooms separated by a hall.

Den or Study

Such a room is usually quite small. It is used as a specialized retreat for work or relaxation. Small homes frequently use it as an auxiliary guest room. It may be equipped with a fold-out bed or couch. Both dens and studies may have a desk or bookcases. These rooms may be located so they adjoin a living room, or they may be in the bedroom area. When in the latter, they are usually close to the entry hall. Since such rooms serve as guest bedrooms they should have a closet.

This study provides an individualized learning center that can be easily changed by readjusting movable shelves.

Knape & Vogt Mfg. Co.

They may convey a masculine feeling by using deep wood tones for room finishes. Wood paneling is frequently used for walls. Ceilings are frequently of acoustic material for sound control. Any floor surfacing material may be used, with personal preference dictating choice.

Bedrooms

The number of bedrooms required is determined by the needs of the occupants. Moderate sized homes usually include at least three. It is customary to have all bedrooms in a separate wing or on a separate living level to insure privacy. They should be near the front entry and connected by a hall so occupants are not required to walk through other rooms to reach them. Bedrooms may be separated and placed in other locations if there is a good reason for it. For example, the master bedroom may be separated from children's bedrooms so all will have maximum privacy.

FHA minimum area is 100 sq. ft. but 120 sq. ft. is more desirable. The author's minimum recommendation for children's and guest bedrooms is 10'-0"x 12'-0". The master bedroom is usually larger; if space and finances permit, 12'-0"x16'-0" is a desirable size.

Every bedroom must have at least one closet, and master bedrooms frequently have two. Size is determined by the items to be stored but a minimum of 8 sq. ft. of area is recommended. Minimum depth is 2'-0". Combination chest, drawer, and wardrobe units

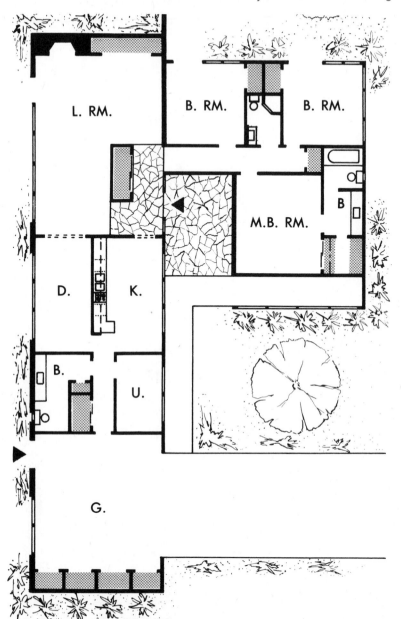

Closet and storage space locations.

are a welcome addition to any bedroom. When bedrooms have private baths the closets should be close to the bath. If a separate dressing area is provided, the closets are in this area.

Size and location of doors and windows determine where furniture may be placed in a room. Remember that bedrooms are designed for convenient use. See the drawing above.

Bathrooms

Size, number, and location of bathrooms. The minimum 5'x8' bathroom is rapidly disappearing. In both moderate priced and luxury homes, bathrooms are becoming quite large. It is not uncommon for them to be 10'x10' or larger. Both custom and manu-

Gerber Advertising Agency

Bathrooms must be beautiful as well as utilitarian.

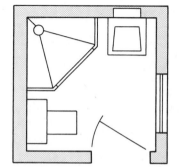

A half-bath frequently occupies a small space and does not have all major fixtures.

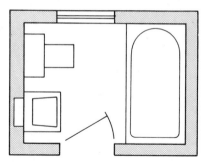

Typical fixture placement for a small bathroom with a bathtub.

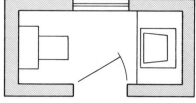

Typical fixture placement for a small bathroom with a shower.

factured homes are including spacious baths and feature many built-ins. Buyers are no longer content with the minimum fixtures in a simple, rectangular room.

The number of bathrooms per home is also increasing. Every home is required to have at least one, but most have a minimum of one and one-half or two. It is not uncommon for a home to have three or more. Each does not have to include all major fixtures but may serve only specialized needs. The term *half-bath* denotes rooms that do not include all three major fixtures.

If a home has only one bath, it *must* be entered from a hall. It is not permissible or convenient to walk through a bedroom to reach this bath. Full baths are frequently located between bedrooms and doors lead to the bath from each room. This is permissible if the home has other bathrooms for general use. Additional bedrooms cannot use this bath. They must have their own or use a bath in an adjoining hall.

It is very appropriate to have a bathroom near the main entry and living room for convenience of guests. If a bath in this location must also serve bedrooms, it is placed so that occupants of bedrooms can reach it without being visible from other areas.

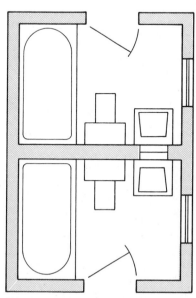

Bathroom fixtures placed back to back conserve space and money.

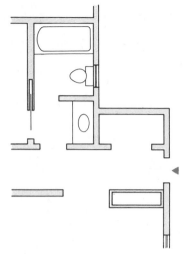

This bathroom arrangement for a master bedroom also serves as a guest powder room.

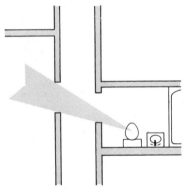

Water closets should not be visible from other rooms.

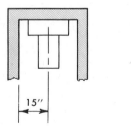

Space must be provided at both sides of a water closet.

It is also very desirable to have a bath near the kitchen and rear entry. Many homes also have half-baths in finished basements.

Bathroom doors are usually hinged, but when space is at a premium pocket or sliding doors may be installed. Swing of hinged doors should not interfere with fixtures or their use.

Water closets are usually located so they are not directly in line with the door. They are usually partly shielded by other fixtures or partial walls. Water closets are usually placed farthest from the door. They may be placed in alcoves, or separated from the rest of the room by divider screens.

Original water closet styles had a separate base and water tank. Many are still manufactured as two-piece models. Newer designs are one-piece. The tank on two-piece models is quite tall. One-piece units have low tanks. Conventional water closets are floor mounted. Some later designs are wall hung for ease of cleaning.

Minimum wall area for a water closet is 30″. It must be 15″ from an adjoining wall or object to the center of the fixture. However, 36″ is more desirable. Water supply pipes frequently go straight from the tank, through the floor. Quality installations should have a shut-off valve on this supply line.

Early rules implied that a water closet should not be against an outside wall because of freezing, and also the need for space inside the wall for a vent or soil stack. However, if the vent can be placed inside a closely adjoining wall it is permissible to place the fixture on an outside wall.

Lavatories. There are many beautiful wall-mounted lavatories. However, when space permits, general preference is for built-in units. These may be simple, containing only the lavatory, or they may have elaborate storage and dressing facilities. Many occupy an entire wall. They may include soiled clothing storage, space for linens, space for medicines and toilet supplies, and elaborate make-up areas.

It is not uncommon for long lavatory cabinets to have two lavatory bowls. Double lavatories may be one single fixture, or separate fixtures may be mounted in the counter top. The lavatory is frequently located close to the bathroom door for convenient use, on the wall opposite the direction of door swing.

Lavatory units can be purchased in standard manufactured sizes or, at slight additional cost, they may be custom fabricated for any style or requirement. When custom made, recommended door width should not exceed 18″. Drawers on rollers are included on quality installations.

Lavatory cabinets are manufactured in many depths (distance from wall to cabinet front). Most frequent is 22″. Counter tops usually project 1″ more than the cabinet. This gives a standard counter top depth of 23″. Minimum depth for special lavatories is 16″. Custom-built counter tops may vary between these two sizes.

Lavatory height is also variable, but 32″ is most frequently used.

Lavatory cabinets may be covered with fine hardwoods, plastic laminates, ceramic tile, metal, or translucent plastic panels. Design is limited only by the imagination, but you must remember the function is the most important consideration.

Bathtubs. Common shapes and typical installations of bathtubs are shown. They may be of enameled cast iron or pressed steel, or plastic. They may also be custom built of tile, marble or other stone, or terrazzo. Cast iron is still most frequently used.

Standard length of rectangular tubs is 5′-0″, but 5′-6″ is frequently used. Lengths of 4′-6″ and 6′-0″ can be obtained on special order. Tub width, height, and design are not standardized. Specific sizes and styles must be determined from manufacturers' literature. Later design makes extensive use of sunken tubs. Most manufacturers offer tubs for recessed installations. Although custom-built tubs add only slightly to total building cost, they contribute a definite feeling of luxury. They are used in both modest and luxury homes.

Tub and shower. Combination tub and shower installations are common. These require shower curtains or doors. Glass or plastic doors may be of the folding or sliding type. NOTE: A bathtub-shower door in small bathrooms makes the rooms seem even smaller. Shower curtains, which can be left open when not in use, do not give this feeling.

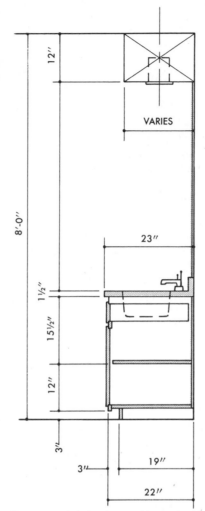

Recommended lavatory cabinet sizes.

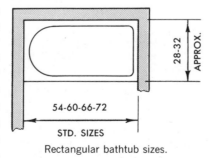

STD. SIZES

Rectangular bathtub sizes.

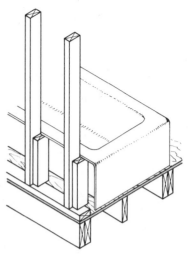

Blocking beneath a bathtub helps minimize cracking.

Showers in large bathrooms are usually given separate enclosures. Bathtubs or showers are frequently built into alcoves. The ceiling may be lowered and a soffit used so the enclosure appears as a unit when you step inside.

Walls extending up from a bathtub must be waterproof. Special attention must be given the joint between the tub and wall material.

Blocking, as shown, should be provided under the back edge of the tub for additional support. Because the bathtub and walls are of dissimilar materials their rate of expansion and contraction is not the same. This makes it difficult to avoid cracking at this line. Pliable caulking which adheres to both materials reduces the problem. The only permanent solution is the fiber glass tub which has the enclosure itself built as an integral part. This eliminates the joint or line.

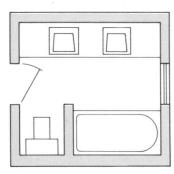

A long lavatory cabinet is frequently placed on a wall opposite other fixtures.

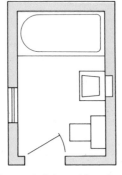

Plumbing materials cost is reduced if all fixtures are located on a common wall.

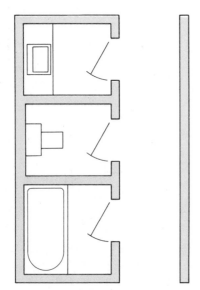

A compartmented bathroom places each main fixture in a separate room.

P.M. Bolton Assoc.

To create a feeling of spaciousness bathrooms may have an enclosed garden.

Bathtubs are frequently placed on walls opposite the lavatory. The least expensive installations place all three fixtures (water closet, lavatory, and the head of the bathtub) and their plumbing along the same wall. This may cause the tub to be under the window. It is a poor location and should be avoided if possible. When the tub must be under a window, aluminum framed or glass block units are recommended.

Prefabricated metal showers are sometimes used for minimum

Luminous ceilings and soffits may replace bathroom windows.

Artcrest Products Co., Inc.

installations. Luxurious showers are usually built on the job. Minimum size is 30″x30″; however, 30″x36″ is better. Luxury installations may be 36″x48″ or even larger.

It is more desirable to have the shower and tub separated than to have them together because footing is better in a regular shower. When a home has two bathrooms, the tub and shower are frequently placed in different rooms.

Compartmented bathrooms which have each fixture in a separate room are very popular.

Bathroom floors may be of any durable material; most frequently used is ceramic tile, terrazzo, composition tile, or roll goods. Carpet is sometimes used. Exposed wood floors are not recommended because of moisture.

Suspended and luminous ceilings are very attractive in bathrooms.

Combination bathrooms and dressing rooms, with built-in fixtures, vanity units, closets, and storage drawers, are frequently used. When placed so they are entered from a master bedroom, the dressing area sometimes is not closed off from the bedroom.

As mentioned earlier, some provision should be made for soiled clothing and clothes bins may be incorporated into lavatory or other cabinets. One large compartment may be included, or several small compartments may provide for clothing sorts as it is used. Inclosed clothes chutes for storage on other levels are convenient. Doors to clothes chutes should be self closing to prevent drafts. Modern design sometimes includes laundry facilities in a bathroom. Washers and dryers may be placed in alcoves or behind doors. Occasionally these appliances are installed free-standing.

Imaginative use of accessories can improve both appearance and function of any bathroom. Medicine cabinets above a lavatory were once standard. Many beautiful medicine cabinets are still available, but current design may replace them with large mirror areas, sometimes covering entire walls. Medicines formerly stored in a cabinet above a lavatory may be stored in a locked drawer. All medicine should be locked away from children. Cosmetics formerly stored in the medicine cabinet are easier to use if space is designed for them in a make-up unit.

The following common accessories, and others, may be included in bathrooms. When included, they should be shown on the plans, and additional descriptions given in the specifications.

Towel bars
Soap and grab
Soap dishes
Toilet tissue holders
Toothbrush and glass holders
Clothes hooks
Facial tissue holders
Magazine racks or book shelves
Retractable clotheslines
Telephones
Divider screens
Intercommunication systems
Auxiliary heaters
Exhaust fans
Built-in scales

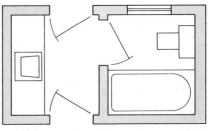

A bathroom serving two areas may be partially compartmented.

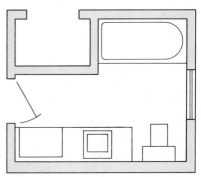

This common bathtub alcove arrangement adjoins a closet of another room.

Combination bath-dressing rooms are very popular.

Scholz Homes Inc.

273

Kitchens

Since the kitchen is the most used room in a home, not only by the housewife but others as well, prospective owners demand inclusion of many labor-saving devices. These may be arranged in convenient and pleasing patterns. Items that were luxuries a very short time ago are now demanded even in very inexpensive homes. More attention must be given to planning the kitchen than any other room.

There are five basic kitchen layouts:

- **"U" shaped**
- **"L" shaped**
- **Corridor**
- **Straight line**
- **Island**

An example of each of these layouts is shown. The proper one to use is determined by the room size and arrangement of doors and windows, and by personal preference. A **"U" layout** is best because it permits efficient use of all equipment with a minimum of steps or movements. An **"L" layout** is the second choice. A **corridor layout** can be very satisfactory

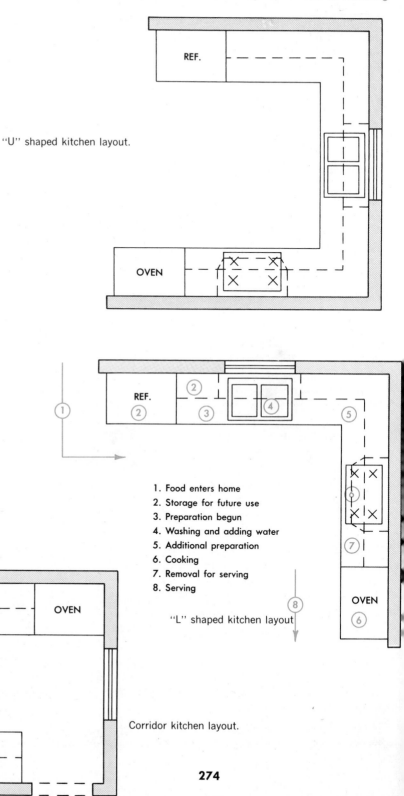

"U" shaped kitchen layout.

1. Food enters home
2. Storage for future use
3. Preparation begun
4. Washing and adding water
5. Additional preparation
6. Cooking
7. Removal for serving
8. Serving

"L" shaped kitchen layout

Corridor kitchen layout.

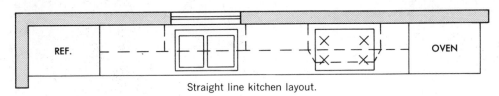

Straight line kitchen layout.

if adequate room is provided for people to pass. Recommended minimum corridor width is 4'-0''. For most convenient use a corridor should not exceed 5'-0'' in width. A **straight line kitchen** is least convenient because much walking must be done during use. An **island layout** is an adaptation of any of the above, with some of the equipment placed in the center of the room.

After the basic layout is determined, cabinets, appliances, and the sink are arranged for convenient use. Adequate planning includes counter space near each item of equipment. The basic items are arranged according to their order of use during food preparation. For example, the refrigerator is usually placed near the service entry so food can be stored without walking across the room. (NOTE: All equipment is not always furnished as a part of the building; stoves and refrigerators may be added later. When they are not included, space must be provided for their installation.) Kitchens in the accompanying drawings are arranged for efficient use. The plan for the "L" layout is numbered, indicating logical order of use. The numbered circles on the drawing, page 274, show the orderly use of space allowed by this arrangement.

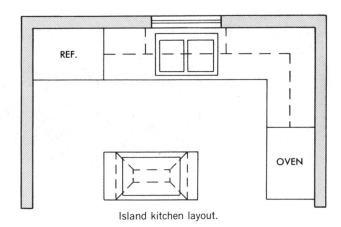

Island kitchen layout.

This built-in kitchen features concealed laundry equipment behind large folding doors.

General Electric Co.

This kitchen features an island for equipment storage and food preparation.

Note the corner sink in this L-shaped kitchen.

A built-in planning area is a welcome addition to any kitchen.

This kitchen design is an adaptation of a corridor layout.

When basic items are drawn on a plan, their size and shape must conform to the general shape of the item. Most are drawn as symbols but, when no standardized symbol is available, they are drawn to conform to the shape of the object. When you draw your plan you should (1) consult the sample floor plans, (2) study sizes and shapes from manufacturers' literature or actual objects, and (3) study sample working drawings in the text and elsewhere.

After preliminary design is complete, specific conveniences or appliances not found in every kitchen—storage cabinets, racks, holders, trays, special drawers, etc.—are located for best use. For example, refrigerator containers would be located close to the refrigerator; dishwashing supplies

are placed near the sink or dishwasher; seasonings are placed near the stove and also near the eating area.

All appliances and equipment should be selected before the final kitchen layout is determined.

Appliance styles and some sizes change slightly each year. (This may be planned obsolescence.) Nevertheless, specific selections must be made so they will fit with the cabinet arrangement. For example, you must know the exact size of a built-in oven before an oven cabinet can be selected.

Built-in appliances are favored over free-standing models. Current designs feature square corners which eliminate spaces between appliances and other items such as cabinets. Square designs also help avoid a cluttered ap-

pearance because of smooth transitions between objects.

Traditional kitchen appliance color was formerly white. Today, appliances may be almost any color, or they may be of brushed chrome, copper, or stainless steel.

Because of the extreme variety of appliances available, only the more common are shown. Later, when large scale plans are drawn, you must include exact sizes, so consult manufacturers' specifications.

Modern *kitchen cabinets* look like fine furniture. They appear best as part of an open plan.

Many choices of decorative materials are available as cabinet facings. Inexpensive cabinets built on the job are sometimes of fir plywood. Birch plywood is most frequently used for standard cabinets.

This material has a close grain structure, beautiful pattern, and lends itself to many finishing methods; it is also reasonably priced. Oak is also quite popular but slightly higher priced. Other hardwoods are sometimes used for custom installations, as are plastic laminates, but they cost slightly more than wood. Thin laminate for vertical surfaces only makes the price about the same as wood. Plastic laminate may be used as an exterior covering only or, on luxury installations, cabinets may be surfaced throughout.

Particle board is being used extensively for cabinet parts. When used, it may be faced (covered) with wood veneer, plastic laminate, or plastic film. On inexpensive cabinets, particle board interiors are sometimes painted.

Metal cabinets are used extensively in commercial, institutional, and large apartment projects, but less in homes today.

Most cabinets are prefinished with lacquer, plastic, or baked-on finishes. However, some are finished after cabinets have been installed on the job. Brush-applied finishes *can* be satisfactory but it is difficult and costly to duplicate the quality of factory applications.

There are three general ways of mounting cabinet doors, (with many variations of each). They are: (1) rabbeted (sometimes called inset or offset doors), (2) surface mounted, and (3) flush mounted. Study the illustrations to determine the relationship of each door type to cabinet face frames and other necessary structural parts.

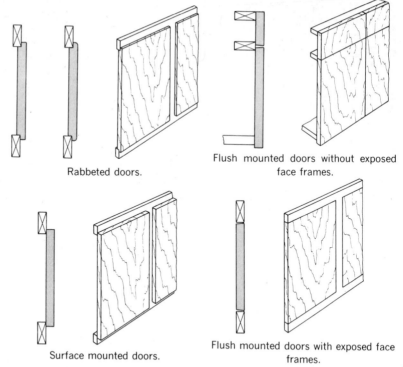

Rabbeted doors.

Flush mounted doors without exposed face frames.

Surface mounted doors.

Flush mounted doors with exposed face frames.

Designing the Kitchen

To design kitchens you must know cabinet and equipment sizes. The accompanying small scale drawings of kitchen cabinets show standard sizes of individual units. These represent selections from only one manufacturer, but others are similar. Study these sizes carefully. Also, study the code system for designating cabinet selections. See page 279. Now find the cabinet that is coded W-3930. The W indicates this is a wall cabinet (upper); the 39 is the cabinet length; the 30 indicates height. Notice also that there are two additional codes on the cabinet; this indicates that the cabinet is available in two additional sizes. Identification of other codes is given in accompanying notes.

Observe the assortment of filler strips for joining cabinets at corners and to fill space between cabinets and end walls. Kitchens should be designed with a minimum of filler strips because the strips may appear to be added on. They may be eliminated by designing the kitchen so it conforms to modular cabinet sizes.

When several cabinets are made for combining, unlimited arrangements may be ordered. Some manufacturers offer only individual units which must be combined at the construction site, while others manufacture large units containing more sections.

The large scale cabinet detail on page 282 shows additional structural parts and typical sizes.

WALL UNITS

SCALE ¼" = 12"

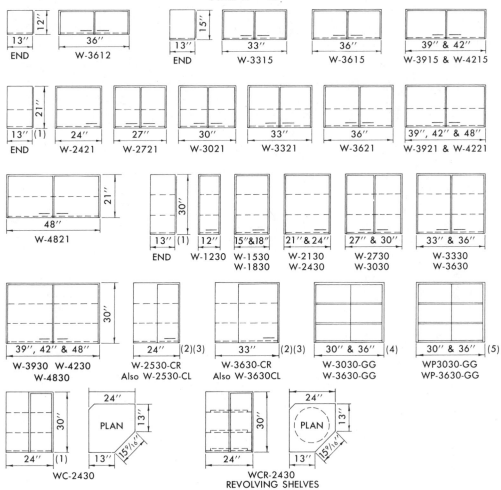

END 12" 13"
W-3612 36"

END 15" 13"
W-3315 33"
W-3615 36"
W-3915 & W-4215 39" & 42"

END 21" 13" (1)
W-2421 24"
W-2721 27"
W-3021 30"
W-3321 33"
W-3621 36"
W-3921 & W-4221 39", 42" & 48"

W-4821 48" 21"

END 30" 13" (1)
W-1230 12"
W-1530 W-1830 15"&18"
W-2130 W-2430 21"&24"
W-2730 W-3030 27" & 30"
W-3330 W-3630 33" & 36"

W-3930 W-4230 W-4830 39", 42" & 48" 30"
W-2530-CR Also W-2530-CL 24" (2)(3)
W-3630-CR Also W-3630CL 33" (2)(3)
W-3030-GG W-3630-GG 30" & 36" (4)
WP3030-GG WP-3630-GG 30" & 36" (5)

WC-2430 24" (1) 30"
PLAN 24" 13" 15⁹/₁₆"

WCR-2430 REVOLVING SHELVES 24" 13" 30"
PLAN 24" 13" 15⁹/₁₆"

COOKING TOP OR SINK UNITS

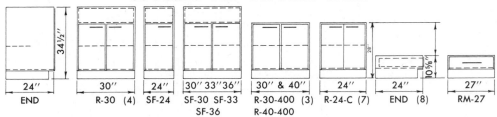

END 24" 34½"
R-30 (4) 30"
SF-24 24"
SF-30 SF-33 SF-36 30" 33" 36"
R-30-400 R-40-400 30" & 40" (3)
R-24-C (7) 24"
END (8) 24" 28" 10⁵/₈"
RM-27 27"

Standard cabinet sizes.

BASE UNITS

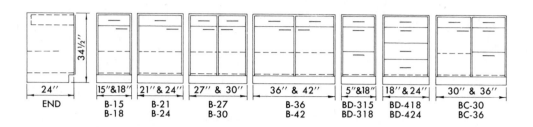

24″	15″&18″	21″ & 24″	27″ & 30″	36″ & 42″	5″&18″	18″ & 24″	30″ & 36″
END	B-15 B-18	B-21 B-24	B-27 B-30	B-36 B-42	BD-315 BD-318	BD-418 BD-424	BC-30 BC-36

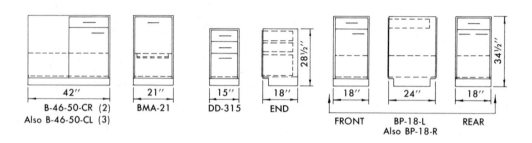

42″	21″	15″	18″	18″	24″	18″
B-46-50-CR (2) Also B-46-50-CL (3)	BMA-21	DD-315	END	FRONT	BP-18-L Also BP-18-R	REAR

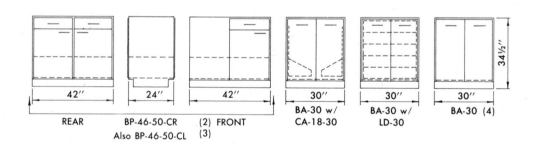

42″	24″	42″	30″	30″	30″
REAR	BP-46-50-CR Also BP-46-50-CL	(2) FRONT (3)	BA-30 w/ CA-18-30	BA-30 w/ LD-30	BA-30 (4)

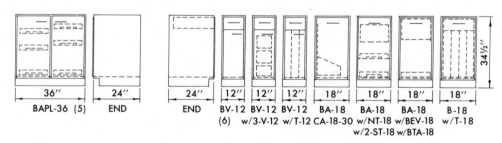

36″	24″	24″	12″	12″	12″	18″	18″	18″	18″
BAPL-36 (5)	END	END (6)	BV-12 w/3-V-12	BV-12 w/T-12	BV-12 CA-18-30	BA-18 w/NT-18 w/2-ST-18	BA-18 w/BEV-18 w/BTA-18	BA-18 w/T-18	B-18

Standard cabinet sizes.

BASE UNITS (continued)

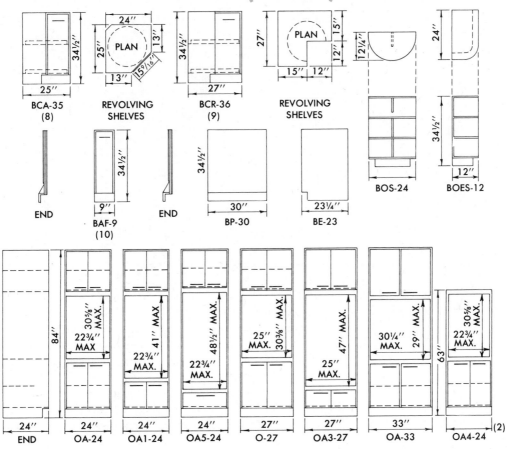

BCA-35 (8) REVOLVING SHELVES BCR-36 (9) REVOLVING SHELVES BOS-24 BOES-12

END BAF-9 (10) END BP-30 BE-23

END OA-24 OA1-24 OA5-24 O-27 OA3-27 OA-33 OA4-24 (2)

UTILITY AND PANTRY UNITS

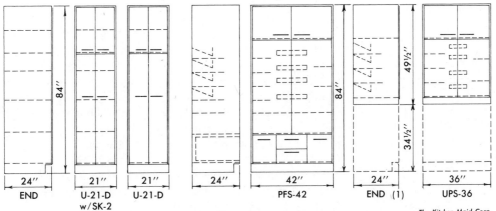

END U-21-D w/SK-2 U-21-D PFS-42 END (1) UPS-36

Standard cabinet sizes.

The Kitchen Maid Corp.

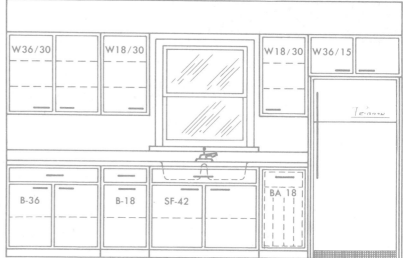

Kitchen cabinet elevation detail with code designations.

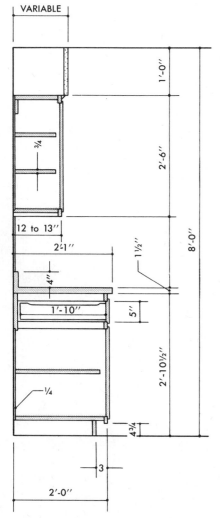

Approximate kitchen cabinet dimensions.

FHA Minimum Kitchen Standards

The following *minimum standards,* as established by the FHA, should be included in any kitchen planning.

Each kitchen shall have accessible storage space for food and utensils, and space for such activities and equipment as needed to perform the intended functions.

Minimum Shelf and Counter Top Area

• Total shelving in wall and base cabinets, 50 square feet, with not less than 20 square feet in either wall or base cabinets.
• Minimum counter top area 11 square feet.
• Minimum drawer area 11 square feet.
• Area occupied by sink basin and by cooking units shall not be included in minimum counter top area.
• Storage space in ranges, when provided in the form of drawers or shelving may be included in the minimum shelf area.

• Shelf area of revolving base shelves (lazy susan) may be considered as twice its actual area in determining required shelf area provided clear width of opening is at least 8½″.
• Drawer area may be substituted for not more than 25% of required base shelf area.

• If a range is not provided, provide at least a 40″ space for range.

Height of Shelving and Counter Top

• Wall shelving above 74″ cannot be included in required area.
• Maximum height of counter top is 38″. (Standard 36″)
• Counter top space below 30″ above floor shall not be included in required area.
• Height between counter top and wall cabinets shall be at least the following:

Over range and sink cabinets, 24″.

Over other base cabinets, 15″.

Depth of Shelving and Counter Top

● That portion of shelving and counter top space less than or exceeding the following dimensions shall not be included in the required area:

	MIN.	MAX.
Wall shelving	4″	18″
Base shelving	12″	24″
Counter top	15″	30″

Spacing of Shelving

Clearance between shelving shall comply with the following to be included in required area.

DEPTH OF SHELF	MINIMUM SPACING
4″ to 6″	5″
6″ to 10″	6″
10″ to 15″	7″
15″ to 24″	10″

Mechanical Ventilation

Air shall be exhausted from kitchens in a range hood, or by a wall or ceiling fan through a grilled opening located (a) in the ceiling above the range, (b) in the wall close to the ceiling above the range, or (c) in the wall immediately above the range. When located in the wall immediately above the range, the wall fan shall be located approximately at the centerline of the range and a metal hood of the size and height shown below shall be installed above the fan. All fans shall discharge to outdoor air.

Range hood shall be at least as long as range, shall be at least 17″ wide, and the bottom of the hood rim shall be not more than 30″ above the range top.

Scholz Homes Inc.

This kitchen-family room features a built-in barbecuing grill with exhaust hood for all-weather use.

Cores for counter tops are usually made of plywood or particle board. They may be covered with plastic laminate, vinyl (or other plastic), ceramic tile, or stainless steel. Stone or manufactured stone is also sometimes used. Edge-grain maple or birch is suitable for chopping tops and cutting boards.

Methods of construction and standard sizes are shown.

Floor coverings should be hard surfaced for easy cleaning. Wood surface floors for kitchens are not recommended. When ceramic or plastic tile or roll flooring is specified over wood subfloors, a plywood, particle board, or hardboard underlay is required.

Wall surfacing should be washable for easy cleaning.

Soffits are usually placed above kitchen cabinets to enclose the space between the top and the ceiling. They may be finished flush with the face of upper cabinets; extend slightly so a wood molding can be applied over the joint between cabinets and the soffit; or they may extend in front of the cabinets to accommodate recessed lighting.

Upper cabinets are not usually placed closer than 6″ to a window. When they are required on both sides of a window, the soffit is usually continued across, above the window. This visually unites the cabinet structure.

A **valance** usually extends between the cabinets. It is placed flush with the face of the cabinets, with its upper edge against the soffit. When a valance is required it is built of the same material as the cabinets and in the same design.

"Multi-purpose Rooms"

Family rooms, recreation rooms, activity rooms, rumpus rooms, play rooms, learning centers and others with similar names, have much in common. They give the family a place for informal living without disrupting other parts of the home. These are designed to serve the specific needs of occupants. Such rooms may be on main or upper levels, or in a basement.

There are two approaches to locating activity rooms. They may be (1) close to or opening from the living room, to give additional area for entertaining; or (2) they may be isolated in an area of their own for privacy. In this way parents and children can have a retreat while others are entertaining or perhaps watching a different TV program in the living room. The extra room usually is placed close to the kitchen and may not be closed off.

Activity rooms are usually quite large. There is no minimum size but for modest homes 12'x20' is popular.

They are designed for easy maintenance, usually with hard-surfaced floors, washable walls, acoustic or suspended ceilings, and specialized built-in storage. Equipment sometimes includes hi-fi, stereo, television, intercommunication, refrigerators, bars, or a small food center. Fireplaces may be included for atmosphere.

Utility Rooms or Laundries

Main-floor utility rooms and laundries are required in homes that do not have basements. There are exceptions of course, as when individual functions such as heating and laundries are included as parts of other rooms. They are placed near the kitchen, sometimes with no wall between. Individual needs of the client determine equipment to be included. Utility rooms were formerly unsightly catch-alls because furnace, water heater, and laundry facilities did not have unified design or pleasing appearance. Since design improvements have been made on equipment, the areas are frequently given a glamour treatment and finished in the same style as kitchens.

To design, you must analyze the functions to be performed and the order in which they are done. All cabinets, equipment, and appliances are then arranged in their order of use.

It is permissible to walk through utility rooms from the kitchen to reach the rear door.

The services may be located elsewhere as said. For example, it was mentioned earlier that laundry facilities are sometimes placed in a bathroom. They may be located at the end of an all-purpose kitchen of the proper size and arrangement. They may also be placed in a closet off a hall. Furnaces and water heaters may also be placed in closets if proper ventilation is provided. Combustible fuels require oxygen. Local codes must be consulted to determine fire wall requirements for furnace rooms. Specific directions for designing firewalls are provided by Underwriters' Laboratories.

There is no minimum size for utility rooms or laundries, but ample work space must be provided. Storage for supplies must be included.

Hard surfaced materials make this utility room easy to maintain.

The Mosaic Tile Co.

Garage or Carport

A garage is an enclosed unit which may be separate or attached to another building. A carport is an open shelter (on at least one side) which also may be either free-standing or attached.

Both garages and carports provide storage space for items in addition to automobiles. This storage should be designed to make maximum use of all available space. Equipment and supply storage in a garage may be in separate compartments, as closets, or wall shelves and hooks may be utilized. Storage areas in carports are usually enclosed units with doors extending across one side.

Garages and carports attached to a home are preferred over free-standing units. However, this usually raises insurance rates slightly. When attached, provide a fire wall between the two structures. Many codes permit a wall with a one-hour fire rating.

When unattached they may be of lightweight construction, with the interiors frequently left unfinished. When attached to a home their construction is the same as for the rest of the building. No footing is needed for strength across the garage door opening; however, in cold climates, a frost wall must extend as deep as the rest of the building foundation.

When the unit is attached to a home, it should have a direct connection, preferably to the basement or kitchen. It is not only inconvenient to connect only from the outside, it defeats the purpose of the idea.

Garage or carport design should harmonize with the house. **Minimum inside size** for each car is 10'-0"x20'-0". However, a larger size is preferred. Recommended inside size is 12'-0"x 24'-0" for each.

Garage door sizes are given in Chapter 13.

Hard-surfaced floors, as concrete or asphalt, are required. If in a damp region, or if cars are to be washed in the garage, floor drains should be provided.

Since many families have two or more cars, double-car garages or carports are recommended for all new construction of homes that exceed a basic, low-cost plan.

Many garages are designed so they can be heated to provide a play area for children, and to make the car easier to start during cold weather.

An additional outside door (besides ones for cars) should be provided. It should be located for most convenient use. A 2'-8"x 6'-8" or 7'-0" size is satisfactory.

A window or windows conforming to the style used in the house should be provided.

Driveways should be at least as wide as the garage door. When a hard-surfaced driveway is not included, a concrete apron is to be provided in front of the garage doors.

Basements

Many homes, especially in warm climates, or areas with unfavorable terrain, do not have basements. However, when physical conditions are favorable, or if in congested urban or suburban areas where land values are high, basements provide inexpensive additional living and utility space.

Basements may be unfinished, or finished into auxiliary living areas. Note, however, that some codes will not permit permanent habitable rooms in basements if the floor is more than half the total ceiling height below grade.

As stated and illustrated in Chapter 3, FHA minimum ceiling height in basements is 6'-10", but 7'-6" or 8'-0" is more desirable, if finances permit.

It is not permissible to place wood columns (posts) in direct contact with the basement floor. They must be raised on a concrete base as shown.

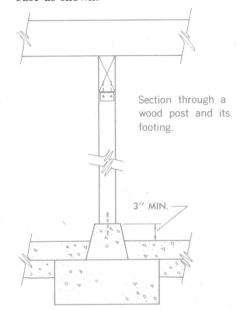

Section through a wood post and its footing.

3" MIN.

Concrete floors must be at least 3″ thick, with wire mesh as described in Chapter 5. Under-floor fill and waterproofing are recommended. Drain tile, as used around the outside perimeter of the footing, may also be placed around the inside under the floor if surface water is a problem.

If sewers in the area are deeper than the basement floor, floor drains may be used. If sewers are shallow (overhead type) sump pumps as shown in Chapter 18 may be required. If floor drains or sumps are installed, the floor should be sloped slightly toward them.

Questions to Reinforce Knowledge

1. Why should a home have a front entry? Is it always possible? Why?

2. What determines the size of an entry hall?

3. What is the minimum width of entries and other halls? Is this usually adequate? Explain.

4. Why are entry doors sometimes recessed into an alcove, or covered by a wide roof overhang or porch? Explain the desirability of this.

5. Why should a front entry hall be decorated and furnished artfully?

6. Why should entry halls have hard-surfaced floors? What materials are recommended; what materials are not? Why?

7. What are some of the things which can be done to give an entry architectural emphasis?

8. What is meant when one says an entry is spacious vertically?

9. Why should all homes have a closet near the front door? What is its minimum size?

10. What is a service entry hall? Why is it usually placed near the basement or kitchen?

11. What is a mud room?

12. Why is it desirable to have a closet near the service entry?

13. From study of this chapter and your own reasoning, why is it a good idea to have a half-bath near the service entry?

14. What is the relationship of the living room to the front entry?

15. What is a special center of interest for a living room? Explain.

16. What special features can be included to make a living room appear more spacious and beautiful?

17. What are two major factors which help determine dining room size?

18. What determines the room finish to be used, and type of furniture and built-ins to be included in a dining room?

19. What is the desired relationship of a living room and dining room?

20. Why should they not be separated by an entry or other hall?

21. What is the relationship of a dining room and kitchen?

22. Why should they not be separated by a hall?

23. Why is a den or study frequently a multi-purpose room?

24. If such a room must serve as a guest bedroom, what special provision should be made?

25. Are dens or studies usually designed as quiet places? Explain.

26. Moderate sized homes usually have how many bedrooms?

27. Why are bedrooms normally placed in a separate area from other rooms?

28. When may they be placed in another location?

29. What is the minimum area for children's bedrooms?

30. What is the recommended size for a master bedroom?

31. What is the minimum number of closets for a bedroom?

32. Is it true that bathrooms should occupy as little space as possible? Explain.

33. How does today's bathroom size compare with the common size in the past? Why?

34. Do new homes tend to have one or more than one bathroom?

35. What is a half-bath?

36. If a home has only one bathroom, why must it be located in a central hall?

37. When is it permissible to attach a bathroom to a bedroom?

38. From your own reasoning, what are the most frequent bathroom locations?

39. Why are pocket doors sometimes used on bathrooms? If space permits other types, are they recommended? Why?

40. Why are water closets sometimes placed in alcoves or separated from the rest of the room?

41. What is the minimum wall area at the back of a water closet? What amount of wall area is better?

42. Is it permissible to place a water closet on an outside wall?

43. What are the possible objections to this? How are they overcome?

44. From your own reasoning, what is the difference between a lavatory and a sink?

45. Which is most popular today, wall hung or built-in lavatories?

46. Describe the variety of lavatory cabinet designs (items of equipment frequently included in lavatory cabinets).

47. Describe three methods of mounting lavatories or kitchen sinks.

48. What are the most frequently used materials for counter tops?

49. What is the standard depth of lavatory cabinets? Of counter tops? Why are they different?

50. What is standard lavatory height? Is this the only height used? Explain.

51. Describe the different materials used for bathtubs.

52. What is the standard length for rectangular bathtubs? What other stock sizes are common?

53. What is a sunken or recessed bathtub?

54. Why are shower doors not recommended for bathtubs in *small* bathrooms?

55. Why is a drop ceiling or soffit sometimes built over a bathtub or shower stall?

56. Why is it difficult to avoid a crack where the bathtub joins a wall?

57. Why are all three main bathroom fixtures frequently placed along the same wall?

58. What is a compartmented bathroom? Explain.

59. What kinds of materials are recommended for bathroom floors? Why?

60. Are combination bathroom and dressing rooms very popular? Explain.

61. What is the major disadvantage of clothes chutes? How is this disadvantage remedied?

62. When may a typical medicine cabinet be omitted above a lavatory? What replaces it? Explain.

63. From your own reasoning, why are bathroom accessories important?

64. Why must kitchens be more than just functional? Explain.

65. Describe *five* basic kitchen layouts.

66. Of these five, which is most convenient? Why?

67. Explain what is meant by logical order of use.

68. Why should one not place a refrigerator and oven next to each other?

69. If there is no conventional symbol for an appliance, what determines how it is drawn?

70. Are appliances selected before or after kitchen planning is completed?

71. Why must one select specific equipment rather than relying upon general size and shape?

72. Which are most popular, free standing or built-in appliances?

73. Is it true that it is difficult to obtain colored kitchen appliances?

74. What wood is most frequently used for kitchen cabinets? What other woods or materials are also frequently used? Explain.

75. What is particle board? How and with what finishes may it be used as a cabinet exterior?

76. Why are factory or shop-applied finishes usually more satisfactory than job-applied ones?

77. Describe three kinds of cabinet doors.

78. When referring to a kitchen cabinet, what do the letters and numbers in the following code represent—W-3930?

79. What is a filler strip?

80. How may the number of required filler strips be reduced?

81. From previous reading, what is the size of a module for kitchen cabinets?

82. What is a toe board? Kick board?

83. What is the standard depth of a lower base cabinet?

84. What is the standard height of a base cabinet?

85. What is the standard height from the floor to the top of the counter top?

86. What is standard backsplash height?

87. What is the depth of an upper cabinet? Why is this variable?

88. What is the greatest standard height of an upper cabinet?

89. Why is more than one standard upper cabinet height necessary?

90. What is a range hood? What determines its size and capacity?

91. What is the standard kitchen counter top width (distance from wall to front of counter)?

92. What type of floor surfacing is preferred in the kitchen? Why?

93. How is a soffit used in a kitchen?

94. What is a valance? Why is it used?

95. What are two different ideas concerning the location of activity rooms?

96. Why are activity rooms desired?

97. When are utility rooms or laundries usually placed on the main living level? Explain.

98. Are these rooms ever open to or part of a kitchen? Explain.

99. If no basement or utility room is included, how may the normal services of these rooms be provided?

100. What equipment is usually included in these rooms?

101. What is the difference between a garage and a carport? Explain.

102. How will their construction differ if they are attached or unattached from a house?

103. Why are attached units preferred?

104. Except in basic, low-cost housing why should one try to avoid a single-car garage or carport?

105. What is the minimum size for a single-car garage or carport? Two-car garage? What is a more suitable size for a single-car garage? Two-car garage?

106. What is the minimum ceiling height for a basement? Is this adequate? Explain.

107. From your own reasoning, why is it inadvisable to have wood walls in a basement? If they are desired, what precautions should be taken?

108. Is a sump pump always required in a basement? Explain.

Terms to Spell and Know

porch	shower enclosure	filler strip
alcove	shower stall	utensil
flagstone	caulking	lazy susan
foyer	bathtub	range
hardwood	plumbing	grill
plastic laminate	compartmented	chopping top
fiber glass	bathroom	cutting board
vinyl	luminous ceiling	soffit
focal point	suspended ceiling	valance
fireplace	vanity	intercommunication
terrazzo	kitchen	utility room
built-in	cabinet	laundry
half-bath	appliance	water heater
water closet	refrigerator	garage
lavatory	planned obsolescence	carport
self-rimming	brushed chrome	frost wall
fabricated	stainless steel	urban
translucent plastic	veneer	suburban
cast iron	lacquer	sump pump

28

Furniture

To function adequately a home —or any other building—must have furnishings that contribute to its total efficiency and please our taste. Many periods in history have given us furniture styles that remain popular to the present time. Personal preference determines whether an individual selects French Provincial, Early American, Contemporary, or some other furniture style. Naturally, the one selected should conform to or fit well with the building in which it is to be used.

Furniture scale (its size and mass) should be compatible with the building's size. For example, if rooms are small, furniture should seem less massive and lightweight in appearance. If rooms are large, massive furniture can give a feeling of strength and dignity.

The collection of furniture sketches shown is not intended as actual furniture styles. However, the sketches and plan view drawings may serve you in five ways:

1. The sketches represent furniture items most often used in homes. They will serve as reminders to plan for their inclusion.

2. Even though individual items do not represent furniture styles, the sketches show general furniture shapes.

3. The stated dimensions accompanying each sketch represent standard or frequently used sizes.

4. The plan view drawings may be used as guides for drawing templates to be cut out and arranged and re-arranged to determine furniture placement within rooms.

5. The plan view drawings may also be used as guides when furniture outlines are required on presentation or working drawings.

1. Studio couch
   length 88″
   depth 32″
   height 29″
   as fold out bed
   length 60″

2. Occasional chair
   width 28″
   depth 32″
   height 29″

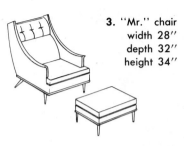

3. "Mr." chair
   width 28″
   depth 32″
   height 34″

4. Ottoman
   length 24″
   width 19″
   height 16″

5. "Mrs." chair
width 28"
depth 32"
height 30"

9. Step table
length 27"-30"
width 15"-19"
height 21"

13. Hi-fi or stereo
length 48"-60"
depth 20"
height 30"

6. Cocktail table
length 48"-60"
width 16"-22"
height 15"
or diameter 34"-48"

10. Corner table
length 30"
depth 30"
height 15"

14. Organ or piano
variable sizes
approx. 48"x26"

7. Lamp table or night stand
width 21"
depth 17"
height 22"

11. Desk
length 36"-55"
depth 20"
height 29"

15. Buffet
length 48"-60"
depth 18"-20"
height 30"

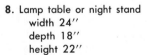

8. Lamp table or night stand
width 24"
depth 18"
height 22"

12. Television
length 24"-60"
depth 20"
height 30"

16. China cabinet
length 56"
depth 18"-20"
height 70"

17. Rectangular dining table
    length 60''-72''
    width 40''-42''
    height 29''

18. Round dining or breakfast table
    diameter 36''-44''
    height 29''

19. High back chair
    seat 17''x17''
    seat height 17''-18''
    height 34''

20. Chair
    seat 17''x17''
    seat height 17''
    height 30''

21. Beds—mattress sizes
    twin 39''x75''
    long twin 39''x80''
    double 54''x75''
    long double 54''x80''
    Queen 60''x80''
    King 75''x80''

22. Chest
    length 38''
    width 19''
    height 46''-50''

23. Double dresser
    length 48''-62''
    depth 20''
    height 30''

24. Triple dresser
    length 60''-72''
    depth 20''
    height 30''

25. Refrigerator or freezer
    width 30''-36''
    depth 26''
    height 60''-72''

26. Single oven range
    width 24'' or 30''
    depth 25''
    height 36''

27. Double oven range
    length 40''-42''
    depth 25''
    height 36''

28. Drop in range
  length 24'' or 30''
  depth 23''-25''
  fits with 36'' counter height

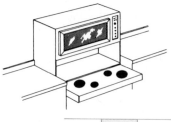

30. Drawer range with oven above
  length 30''-40''
  depth 25''
  height 30''-34''

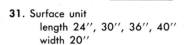

31. Surface unit
  length 24'', 30'', 36'', 40''
  width 20''

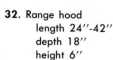

32. Range hood
  length 24''-42''
  depth 18''
  height 6''

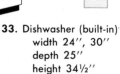

33. Dishwasher (built-in)
  width 24'', 30''
  depth 25''
  height 34½''
  Portable dishwasher
  width 24''
  depth 25''
  height 36''

34. Automatic washer
  width 27''
  depth 25''
  height 36''

29. Built-in oven
  width 24''-34''
  depth to fit 25'' oven cabinet
  height 24''-42''

35. Clothes dryer
  width 27''
  depth 25''
  height 36''

29

Community Factors To Be Considered

When it is necessary to change location of residence, whether you rent, buy, or build, examine the new community to determine if it fulfills your specific needs.

Sometimes a job or position may dictate where one lives, without regard for likes or dislikes. However, if a community is completely unfavorable, one may be required to seek another job elsewhere.

A majority of the people now live in or near a large city. This concentration of population around major cities is increasing, while it is decreasing in small, isolated or poorly developed communities and rural areas. All predictions indicate this trend will continue.

Four Kinds of Communities

Urban. An urban community is a large city, perhaps with a population of 100,000 or more. This is an arbitrary figure; an urban area may have fewer or greater numbers of people. The highly congested central city or inner city is usually considered the urban area.

Suburban. A suburban community is a smaller one on the fringes or outskirts of a large city. It is frequently primarily residential, and owes its existence to the large city.

Small town. This is a small community with a distinct business center, independent of an urban area. Most residents work here rather than commuting to the city.

Rural. In a rural area there is no organized, built-up community of homes; each one is separated from others. Rural areas are usually associated with agriculture, and present a quiet, isolated atmosphere.

Utility Services

Utility services may be provided by public or private corporations, or by government agencies. Services in most communities are provided by both corporations and government. Telephone service is supplied by private corporations. Water, gas, and electricity may be either private or community-owned services. Sewers, garbage removal, streets and roads, curbs, gutters, storm sewers, street lights, and sidewalks are provided by government agencies.

Private corporations ("public service" companies) operate under a franchise, or agreement with government, which gives them sole permission or authority to operate in a community without competition from similar companies. These legal monopolies have close governmental control and supervision—federal, state, and local. Even though rates are regulated by government, cost of services rendered vary widely from community to community.

If services are not available in rural areas, the owner may provide them himself or as part of a cooperative system. If one is contemplating living where some services are not provided, the extra cost of obtaining them must be considered.

Utilities supplied by government. Even though government agencies furnish some utility services, they must be paid for by the property owner through taxes or special assessments. These charges must be taken into consideration when selecting a community.

For example, streets, sewers, water mains, curbs, sidewalks, street lighting, and others, as mentioned earlier, must be paid for by property owners. Sometimes real estate taxes cover the costs and maintenance. Individuals may also be assessed for improvements which adjoin their property. When the latter is true, the charges are usually paid as time payments, due annually or semi-annually until the debt is retired. However, in some instances the costs must be paid upon completion of the improvement, or within a short time limit afterward.

When a person is interested in buying in a new development the charges for existing and future utilities or services must be checked carefully. It is not uncommon for property to be advertised at a very low selling price; then the prospective owner discovers several assessments that were not included in the purchase price.

Real Estate Taxes

Real estate taxes may be a determining factor in selecting a building location. Comparisons of taxes in neighboring communities and city areas should be evaluated prior to purchase. Both present and anticipated future values should be considered. Generally speaking, local real estate taxes are less in communities with many large industries. Real estate taxes of large industries usually relieve the burden of the individual tax payer and make the overall tax rate much lower. Areas that are primarily residential, as many suburban areas, usually have a high real estate tax. Taxes in old established areas may be higher or lower than in recently developed areas. It is not always possible to determine the exact amount of tax to be paid, but a close estimate can be made. Personal property tax should also be investigated because this can affect cost of living. Some communities have none, while others have quite a severe tax.

Transportation

Transportation plays an important part in modern life. If it will be necessary to commute to work, available transportation facilities will help determine where you live.

If an automobile is the only means of transportation, you must be concerned with the streets and roads. Road improvements and how well they handle traffic are very important. The location of expressways, how close they pass to your place of employment, their accessibility to your home, location of entrances and exits, and how well they handle traffic at peak rush hours may be determining factors. Parking facilities at your place of employment and in downtown areas, as well as their cost, also become important considerations.

If local public transportation must be used, check the availability of rail and bus services, and their cost. If one is interested in flying, either as a hobby or as transportation, then an available airport is a necessity. If one must fly frequently to other cities, reason says his home should be convenient to the airport.

Stores and Shopping Centers

A beautiful little home in the country may be just what a person would like to have. However, it may be very inconvenient when shopping must be done. You should consider the location of stores and shopping centers, their distance from the home, the amount of time required to reach them, whether one can walk to them or whether other transportation must be used. Adequate parking facilities should be present. You may also want to consider availability of shopping areas in larger nearby cities. If so, their location and time needed to reach them are important.

Fire Protection

When selecting a community you should inquire about fire protection. In large cities this service is taken for granted. Most cities have adequate equipment and personnel to meet most emergencies. No direct charge is usually made for this service. Small communities may have only minimum equipment, manned by volunteer firemen who either donate their services or receive a nominal fee for each fire call. Many rural areas have no organized fire protection. Residents must rely upon their neighbors for help, or call firemen from nearby cities. When outside firemen must be called, individual property owners pay for the service.

A good community must have adequate shopping facilities.

There are usually no water mains in rural areas. It is necessary to rely on wells and pumps, or water may be conducted or even trucked from central sources.

Insurance rates are usually greater in areas with little or no fire protection.

Schools

There are several important factors you must consider when checking the schools in a community. The quality of education offered is most important. Education is not the same everywhere. Some schools are very good while others have lower standards. You can at least check the facilities—buildings and equipment.

The distance of schools from home is also very important. If one has small children he will be interested in elementary schools that are within walking distance of home or have bus transporta-

tion provided. If there are high school or college students in the family, one will be interested in transportation to these schools. Unless private or parochial schools are available, a small community may have only one high school. Large consolidated schools can usually offer a wider variety of courses. Teachers are better paid. Many large communities also offer local or area junior college programs.

The direct and indirect costs of attending each school must be considered. Also the amount of money spent by a community on its schools has a greater influence on the local tax rate than any other single factor. Amount of tuition, book purchase or rental, and other charges vary widely.

Churches

The spiritual life of the individual and a community is a

major consideration. When one is a long-time resident of a locality he frequently takes his church for granted. But when moving, you should check to see if your specific denomination is represented. Note the distance of the church from your home.

Parks, Recreation, and Cultural Opportunity

As the nation becomes more urban in character it is increasingly difficult for the individual to "feel" the beauty, solitude, and comfort once achieved by spending a quiet moment in the splendor of undisturbed natural surroundings. The serene landscape has given way to commercialization and "progress." In many localities there is no undisturbed countryside to enjoy. Fortunately, a new interest in preserving and re-establishing natural beauty is emerging.

Conveniently located schools that are both beautiful and offer a fine education are an asset to a community.

The Ceco Corp.

We have had national, state, and local parks for a long time, but a new emphasis is being placed on their creation and use. Some projects are primarily conservation measures, while others are devoted to beauty.

In areas where poorly planned development has marred a riverfront or hillside, steps are being taken for renewal. This need for natural beauty is expressed in other ways. Many residential areas have restrictions which are designed to preserve natural beauty by requiring existing trees and terrain to be left undisturbed when new building is being done. This need is also expressed by the inclusion of trees, shrubs, other plantings, and open areas when new projects are planned.

Many citizens are not aware of the parks and recreation facilities available in their own locality or surrounding area. Make it a point to notice these things.

Many communities provide additional facilities, for swimming, shuffleboard, tennis, ice skating, golf, baseball, and bowling. Check to see if your specific interest is included. In addition to the public programs, the YMCA and many business establishments or other private organizations provide centers for your enjoyment. Of course, a private club is expensive.

You may desire cultural enrichment. Libraries, theaters, music centers, art galleries, museums, and sports are usually available in larger communities.

Zoning Regulations and Building Codes

As mentioned earlier, you must check all local zoning ordinances and building codes. Prior discussion was directed toward design-ing a building to fulfill or conform to all established requirements. This is an absolute necessity if difficulty with local authorities is to be avoided. Check the requirements before a location is chosen, because they greatly affect both the kind of building that may be erected and the total cost.

If zoning regulations or building codes are unrealistic—a hindrance to good construction, or good land use—or if they discriminate in favor of certain building materials and against other accepted ones, dictate building design, or are not compatible with your ideas, then you will wish to choose another building location. This is not to imply that all codes and regulations are bad, because they are not. The primary purpose of codes and zoning regulations is to *protect* the rights of individuals.

Questions to Reinforce Knowledge

1. Name some reasons for examining a community before moving there.

2. What are the population trends at the present time?

3. Describe the four basic kinds of communities—urban, suburban, small town, and rural.

4. What are some of the services usually provided by government or private utility companies?

5. Are the same services available in all communities? Explain.

6. Are utility costs constant throughout the country? Why or why not?

7. What are two different kinds of organizations that supply utility services?

8. Who pays for utility services?

9. What is a real estate tax? Personal property tax?

10. How do industries in a locality affect the tax rates?

11. Why do suburban areas frequently have a high tax rate?

12. How may transportation facilities affect your choice of building location?

13. Why should you be concerned with location of stores and shopping centers?

14. How does living in a rural area affect fire protection? Why?

15. How do small communities that cannot hire fulltime firemen solve the problem?

16. Is it true that all schools in all communities are equally good? Explain.

17. Why does one usually want to live close to elementary schools or determine if bus service is provided?

18. Why is this not so important for high schools and junior colleges?

19. Why and when may churches affect where you live?

20. Do zoning ordinances and building codes always fulfill their intended purpose? Explain.

30

Site Planning

As emphasized in Chapter 25, a building should be related to its site so the two appear to belong together and to the neighborhood. For this reason a plot should be selected before the building is designed. Of course, when doing classroom problems or other assignments it is necessary to *assume* a hypothetical or imaginary site, terrain, and related conveniences.

Many people feel that an ideal building lot should be almost level. Building on flat ground does help reduce costs and requires little imagination. When building on flat ground it is not usually necessary to coordinate the building plan with the terrain.

Near large cities much of the desirable flat land is already occupied. To find an ideal, level plot it may be necessary to look farther out. Some clients may prefer to use less desirable land closer in. The available city land is generally in congested areas, lots are frequently odd shaped, they may be quite small, may need clearing and filling, or the terrain may have undesirable features such as irregularity.

The fact that a plot seems to present serious problems should

be analyzed. Actually the problems and striving for solutions to them may result in better design, construction, and land use, because of conveniences overlooked at first glance.

A fully developed housing area has many advantages because of services already "built in." A small site or irregular terrain can be offset by clever design in two-story or split level style.

Most important, the site should fit the client's needs best.

Site Divisions

A lot is divided into three areas according to their use. These are: (1) The approach, (2) service area, and (3) living area.

The Approach

Remember, this area is most noticeable to the general public and must be designed to present a pleasing appearance. It is the building's "showcase."

The Service Area

This area includes the driveway and parking facilities, when they are to be included in the plan. Of course, the area should adjoin the service door for convenience of deliveries. It may in-

clude space for gardening and play.

The Living Area

The *outdoor* living area may include not only the lawn but spaces for flowers, shrubs and trees, terraces, a patio, reflecting or swimming pool, or a game court. It may also contain elaborate food service facilities. The outdoor living area should be designed to fulfill the individual family's needs. It is frequently shielded from the public by a screen, wall, or fence, especially in a closely settled neighborhood and dry, warm climate where privacy is needed because of regular outdoor living.

Formal vs. Informal

One must decide whether the building and its surroundings are to be formal or informal in character. In the past much emphasis was placed on formality, which was often achieved by symmetrical balance of the building and its landscape. For instance, if one is designing a duplicate of a stately colonial mansion both the structure and its surroundings should be very formal, is the way the originals were designed.

The driveway of this home leads to both the living and service entries.

This home is especially designed for outdoor living.

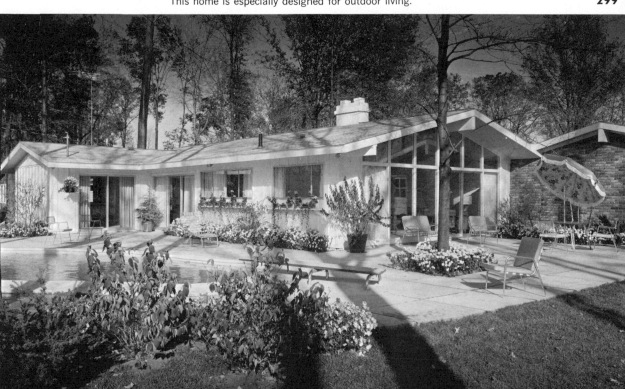

Window and door arrangements of this home present a formal balance.

Generally, current design favors relaxed informality but with an interesting, livable atmosphere. Lack of formality does not mean a hodgepodge of outdoor features.

Landscaping, like building design, should be restrained and simple. For smaller homes and lots, this means making use of the same area for different occasions.

Orientation

To properly orient a building to the site, one must consider many things. The terrain has been discussed in other chapters, as was location of other buildings. Planning must also consider prevailing wind direction. Large glass areas should be avoided on a side exposed to a cold north wind, or wind blowing in from a lake or bay.

The sun can be made to work for you. Both wind and sun can be partially controlled by the proper placement of trees, wide overhangs, and shading devices. When properly designed, wide overhangs or shading devices take advantage of the low winter sun and admit its warming rays, but they block out hot summer rays when the sun is near its zenith and its heat is most intense.

The illustration—which includes pertinent data and the table accompanying it—shows how a building can be oriented to take advantage of the sun. To use this information in a drawing, place a small scale plan in the center circle, draw a line from the center perpendicular to each wall, and extend each line beyond the circumference of the circle, as in the example. Read about the recommended wall treatment and sunshading in the quadrant that each wall faces. Naturally, these suggested sunshading devices apply whether or not you plan to install air conditioning (cooling) equipment. (See caption.)

Determining Landscape Requirements

As with some building designs, landscape developments frequently just seem to happen. For maximum beauty and use, the designer's job is to make them happen in an organized manner.

Orientation*

1. Sun exposure very brief, if any.
2. Little sunshading needed.
3. Overhang can be minimum.

1. Sun exposure is short and intensity is partly relieved by cool air.
2. Overhang and reflective screens ineffective.
3. Low trees or hill give valuable shade.

Solutions (in order of effectiveness)

A. Sunshading by walls, trellis, lattice, high fences, low trees, etc.

B. Awnings.

1. Sun exposure is short but intensified by high air temperature and low angle.

Solutions (in order of effectiveness)

A. Sunshading by walls, trellis, lattice, high fences, low trees, etc.
B. Porch or veranda.
C. Attached carport or garage.
D. Awnings.
E. Minimum Glass Area.

1. Sun exposure is sustained and intense.
2. Both tall and medium trees are needed for shade.

Solutions (in order of effectiveness)

A. Porch or veranda.
B. Awnings.
C. Reflective screens.
D. Recommended overhang.

1. Sun exposure is sustained and intensified by day's hottest air.
2. Both tall and medium trees needed for shade.

Solutions (in order of effectiveness)

A. Attached carport or garage.
B. Porch or veranda.
C. Glass area fully shaded.
D. Storage cabinets in wall.
E. Awnings or reflective screening.
F. Avoid slab reflecting heat against wall.

1. Sun is almost overhead and wall absorption is moderate.
2. Exposure is sustained and intense.

Solutions (in order of effectiveness)

A. Recommended overhang.
B. Reflective screens.
C. Large glass area (if used) under recommended overhang.
D. Awnings.
E. Avoid slabs reflecting heat against wall.

Recommended Roof Overhang*

Latitude	\ 24"	30"	36"	42"	48"	54"	60"	66"	72"	78"	84"	90"	96"	102"
					Height of Eaves Above Window Sill									
25°...	9	12	14	16	18	21	23	25	27	30	32	34	37	39
30°...	12	15	18	21	24	27	30	33	36	39	42	45	48	51
35°...	14	18	22	25	29	32	36	40	43	47	50	54	58	61
40°...	17	22	26	30	35	39	43	37	52	56	60	65	69	73
45°...	20	25	31	36	41	46	51	56	61	66	71	76	82	87
50°...	25	31	37	43	50	56	62	68	74	80	87	93	99	105

Dimensions below staggered line generally not practical as an overhang unless used as porch due to added cost and structural problems. Figures apply to wall facing south.

"Reprinted from National Association of Home Builders' Research Institute publication entitled RESIDENTIAL AIR CONDITIONING— A Summary Report of the Austin Air-Conditioned Village Project."

NOTE: Differences in latitude affect the overhang required to minimize heat gain. For that reason a house having an overhang designed for one area will not be effective in another.

To give you some idea of approximate locations at various latitudes, the southern tip of Florida and Texas are at 25°, New Orleans 30°, Charlotte, N. C. and Santa Maria, Calif. 35°, Philadelphia and Denver 40°, Bangor, Me. and Portland, Ore. are at 45°, and the 50° line crosses lower Canada.

As stated earlier, it is a good idea to retain as many natural features—such as earth contour, trees, shrubs, and native top soil—as possible. The method of landscaping by removing all natural features and replacing them with symmetrically clipped shrubs was once the fashion, but is no longer so popular. This method of landscaping requires very little imagination but a lot of work, and the lack of variety may be monotonous. This is not to imply that one cannot use foundation and other plantings; it is only urging imaginative use.

If plantings are used near a building they should complement it. For example, if the foundation is high, strategically located shrubs can help hide it; they may also help visually tie the building to the ground. Tall plants help emphasize vertical lines, while low spreading plants help accent horizontal lines. Therefore, if a building is rather tall, as a two-story house, tall shrubs will complement it, or if the building has long, low horizontal lines, spreaders are preferred.

When selecting plantings, one should express his individuality. One does not have to be a conformist and have landscaping like all others in the vicinity. Choose flowers, shrubs, and trees that are your favorites, regardless of what others are using. NOTE: Harmony with neighboring 'scapes is appropriate, especially on an inside lot. A corner lot gives more freedom.

An avid gardener may choose items that require a lot of care, but if a client has greater interests in other activities, he should be warned that any elaborate plan will require much attention. If lawn mowing is a chore, ground covers such as pebbles, crushed stone, or a leafy spread such as myrtle may be used at selected intervals with plantings. Slow growing plants or ones that look best without trimming can also reduce care. Remember that most small plants grow: a yard may be beautiful now but one must consider how it will look in a few years. Many new buildings look barren for many years. By making economical selections one may obtain partially grown trees and shrubs so the yard can be enjoyed soon rather than late. Two or three broad leaf trees are better than none at all.

Plot plan showing building outlines plus approximate planting locations.

PLOT PLANS

Preliminary landscape planning should be done on paper so changes can be made at little cost until the desired results are in mind. These can be in the form of rough sketches. The final layout is drawn on a plot plan.

Plot plans, as shown earlier in the text, may contain technical data such as building location, contour lines, and ground heights. Information concerning the landscape may also be included on technical plans, or other plot plans may be drawn. The accompanying illustrations show different methods of drawing and labeling items to be included. Observe that some plans give the names of each item while other drawings are for illustrative purposes only. These drawings are rendered in color but may be done in black and white.

Rendered plot plan showing roof outlines. Identification may be labeled directly on the trees and shrubs.

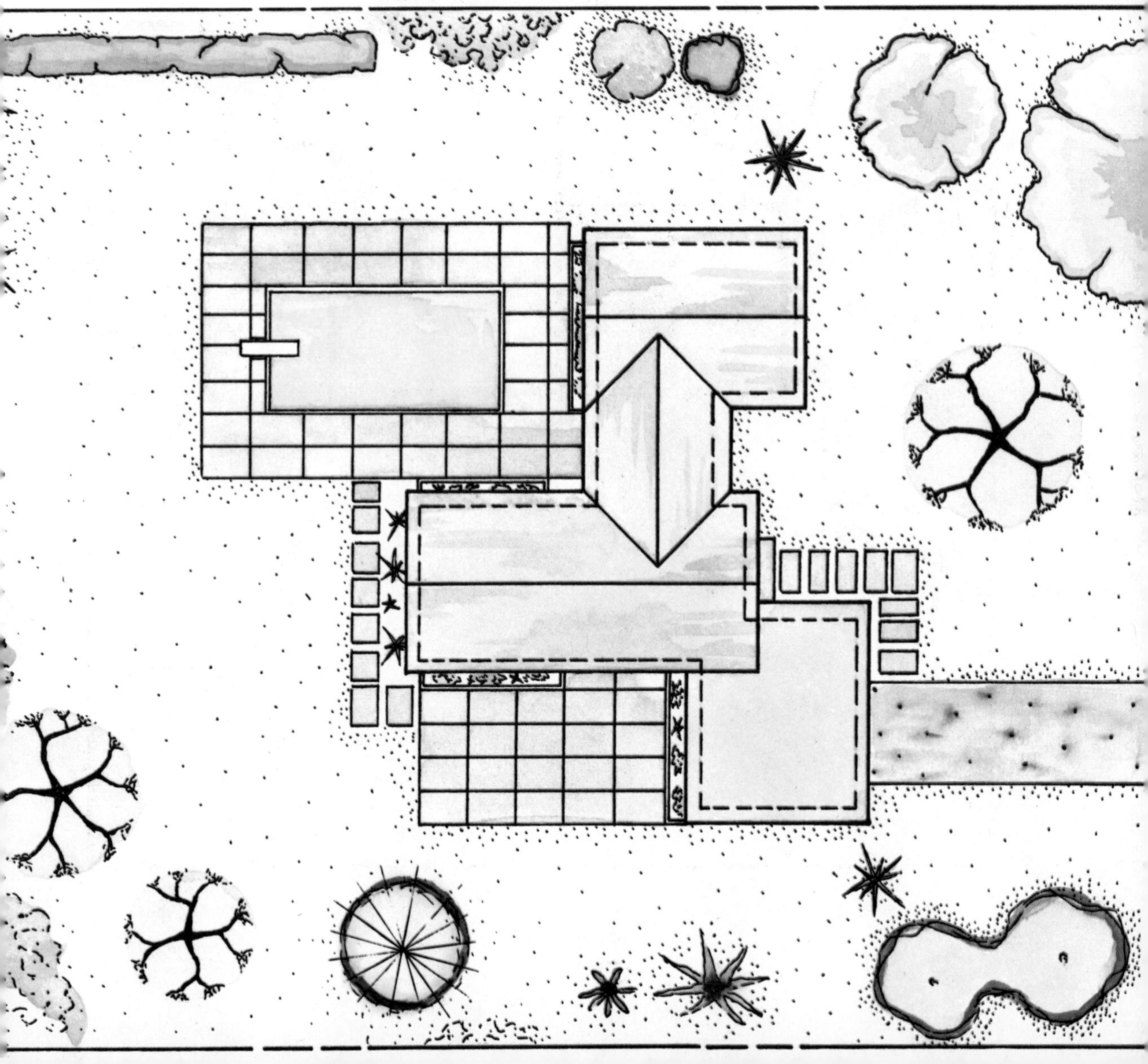

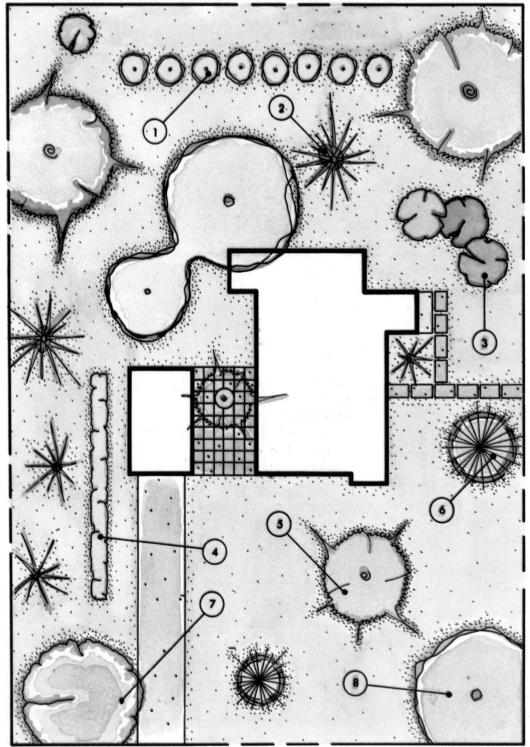

Plot plan showing building outlines. Code numbers refer to a schedule of plant species. You may decide what the numbers represent when you draw your plans. They may identify any planting that you desire.

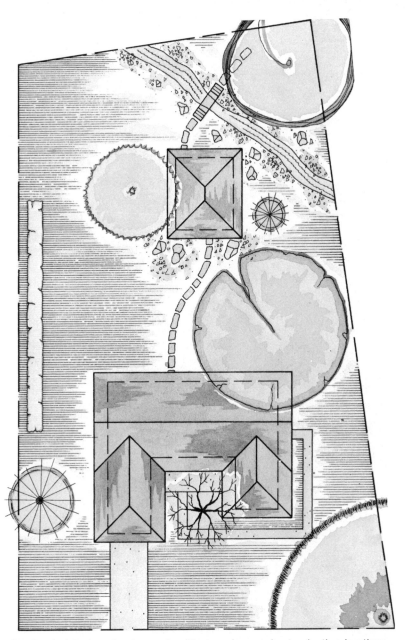

Rendered plot plan showing roof outlines and approximate planting locations.

Questions to Reinforce Knowledge

1. Why should a lot be selected before a building is designed?

2. Having no actual lot how may you proceed with your design?

3. What are the advantages of a level lot?

4. How do built-up city neighborhoods affect land availability?

5. What are some of the results that are likely to develop?

6. Do small lots have good landscape possibilities? Why?

7. What are the three divisions of a lot? From previous reading, how do these compare with the three divisions of a home?

8. What is the approach? Describe.

9. What is the service area? Describe.

10. What is the living area? Describe.

11. How does one determine whether a landscape plan is formal or informal in character? Describe each.

12. From your own reasoning, why is a simple, unified landscape best?

13. What is meant by the statement that the building and the terrain must have proper orientation?

14. How do prevailing winds affect orientation?

15. How does the sun affect orientation?

16. What are four items used to block the sun's rays?

17. How does one use the circular orientation illustration shown in the text?

18. From the table in the text, how does latitude affect the width of an overhang? Why?

19. Is it wrong to use foundation plantings as your only landscaping? Explain why or why not.

20. When is it best to use tall plants? Low ones?

21. Why does the author recommend individuality when planning the landscape?

22. How might the landscape of a home for a botanist and a professional golfer differ? Why?

23. What are the advantages of planting grown or partially grown trees and shrubs? What are the disadvantages?

24. Why are preliminary landscape plans done as sketches?

Terms to Spell and Know

orientation
quadrant
plot plan

Part Three

FROM IDEAS TO REALITY

Quality of work produced is improved when you use a good drafting table.

31

Drafting Tools and Techniques for Developing Skill

Drafting skill is dependent upon the mastery of many small details, any of which when considered alone may seem relatively unimportant but, when combined into a finished drawing, can make the difference between an average or a superior result.

Before you can draw a plan you must have a knowledge of the materials to be used and how they fit into the total building. You must understand something of the manipulative skills required in construction work. You must also know how parts are represented (shown) on a working drawing (plan), and then you must develop skill and techniques for communicating these ideas through drafting.

This chapter discusses the tools of drafting and offers guides on developing skill in using them.

Since a draftsman spends quite a long time on each individual drawing (some large drawings may take several days to complete), great care must be taken to keep the drawing clean. Dirty drawings present an unsightly appearance, emphasize erasures and changes, and cause poor reproduction. Since working drawings are made to be used, but an original drawing would soon be spoiled if it were taken on the job or into a shop, the quality of the reproduction is very important because it shows how to build the actual object. Sloppy drawing usually produces a poor print, but a neat, beautiful drawing with improper line weights also makes a poor reproduction.

Cleanliness

To keep your drawing clean you must first keep yourself clean! If you are neat and orderly in your appearance, this will reflect itself in your drawing. Your hands must be clean at all times. Even if no dirt is visible, your hands should be washed frequently. Oil or perspiration will cause a drawing to collect dirt; this is especially true when you are working on a very complicated plan and if you have a high degree of nervous tension.

The desk top and items to be handled while you are drawing must also be kept clean.

The drawing board must be clean before the paper or other drawing medium is placed upon it. A dusting brush is needed to remove loose particles of dust, eraser crumbs, or lint, but the surface should also be rubbed thoroughly with a clean cloth. *All* drafting instruments must be clean. Even if they appear clean, they should be wiped vigorously with a clean cloth. If they appear soiled before use, it may be necessary to wash them with a mild solution of soap and water. Then they should be dried with a clean cloth to prevent water damage. Do not submerge the instruments in water. Use a cloth that is only slightly damp.

During use, all tools and equipment should be wiped off frequently to remove any new accumulation of dirt and perspiration. Particles of graphite and eraser should be constantly removed, by brushing, from your drawing.

Drawing Tables and Boards

Since architectural plans may be quite large, it is necessary to have large tables and boards to accommodate them.

A drafting table should have a slanted top to make it easier to reach the work. Large firms, with adequate finances, may equip you with combination tables and boards, that are power-operated to change table height or angle. However, if finances are limited, height may be stationary and only the angle adjustable—usually by mechanical means. Drafting rooms frequently use custom-made tables. An inexpensive type can be provided by mounting a flush door or heavy plywood on a simple framework.

It is common practice to provide a flat table for the draftsman's books, papers, tools, and other supplies.

Gum, birch, or basswood is preferred for drawing board surfaces because of their close grain structure and smooth surface.

Unattached drawing boards are usually much smaller than table models, for easy handling. They are generally constructed of basswood. Two methods of crossbanding on the ends to minimize warping are shown. See the drawing, center of this page.

A drawing board should be handled with care; true lines cannot be drawn if the face or edges are damaged.

Drawing Pad

It is well to place padding between the drawing board and the

Drafting table with attached work surface and storage space.

Wood crossbands.

Metal crossbands.

paper. If a wood board is used, and a pad is not, the pencil tends to follow the grain, thus making the lines slightly irregular. Drawing across the hard and soft grain structure also keeps lines from being uniform. If a hard surfaced board is used (such as a plastic laminate table top), a pad prevents the pencil point from wearing as rapidly as it would otherwise. Any clean, heavyweight paper may serve as a pad.

Plastic-coated, paper or vinyl board covers make a pad unnecessary.

Board cover with printed grid lines eliminates much measuring on the drawing.

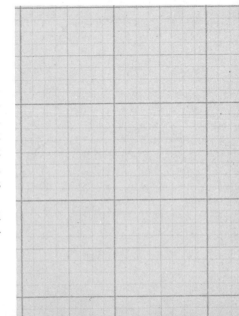

Instruments

T Square

For architectural drafting a T square measuring from 36″ to 42″ in length is recommended. The beginner frequently uses an all-wood T square, but it is not suitable for professional quality work. A clear plastic edge is needed so adjacent work is visible. Also, the plastic edge is smoother than wood. The *blade* may be of hardwood with clear plastic on both edges, or it may be entirely of plastic. The blade is fastened to a *head,* which is used to guide the blade on the drawing board. The head may be mounted permanently at right angles to the blade, or it may be adjustable as shown. Good quality T squares have the plastic along the blade slightly recessed to prevent ink from running under it. A T square with the head secured to the blade with bolts is more satisfactory than one secured with glue and small wood screws.

NOTE: The T square should not be longer than the drawing board because this causes the blade to arch off the paper in the center of the drawing.

Triangles

Large 30°–60° and 45° triangles are needed for architectural drawing. They should be large enough that all vertical lines can be continuous. When only small triangles are used, lines must be spliced, and it is very difficult to keep the splice from showing. A 12″ triangle is suitable for most work but the 18″ size is recommended.

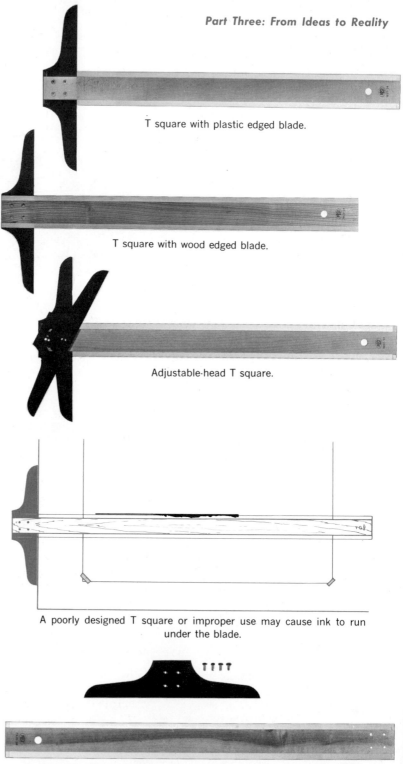

T square with plastic edged blade.

T square with wood edged blade.

Adjustable-head T square.

A poorly designed T square or improper use may cause ink to run under the blade.

On the better T squares the head and blade are held together by bolts.

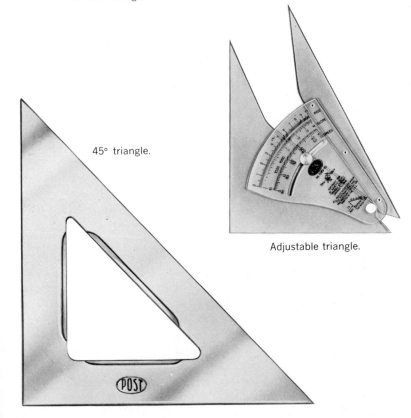

30°·60° triangle.

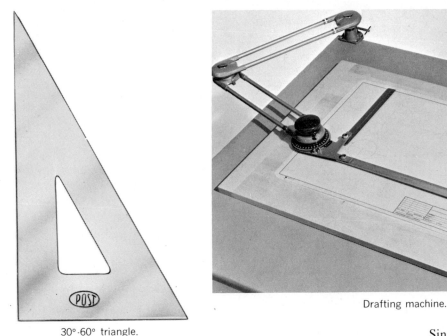

Drafting machine.

45° triangle.

Adjustable triangle.

Since large triangles are inconvenient for short lines, many draftsmen prefer to have two sets. The second set is usually 4″ or 6″ size.

An *adjustable triangle*, as shown, is very convenient for architectural drawing. It should be marked in degrees and also divided for rise, run, and roof pitch.

The quality of plastic is very important. Inferior plastic will become very brittle and the edge will chip and wear easily. A good triangle, even though more expensive, will give much longer and better service.

Drafting Machines

Drafting machines, as shown, have become widely used. Their chief advantage is the combining of T square, triangles, protractor, and scales into one unit.

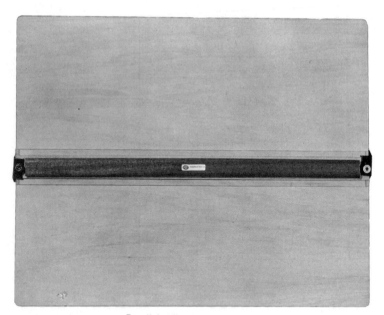

Parallel ruling straightedge.

to break, and graphite from the extreme pencil wear can cause a drawing to become smudged and dirty.

Parallel Ruling Straightedges

Parallel ruling straightedges, as shown, are very convenient for drawing long, continuous lines. However, it is difficult to keep the edges of the paper from being torn unless it is taped around the entire perimeter. These devices also rub continuously on the drawing paper, so the work is more difficult to keep clean.

Automatic Drafting Machines

Computer operated machines are a very valuable aid for variations in production drawing, but are not as well suited to custom architectural drafting which requires individual work. The machines may be controlled by commands placed on magnetic or punched paper tape, or commands may be read directly from punched cards through a computer.

This eliminates most of the tools that normally must be kept on or near the drawing table.

Drafting machines have two disadvantages: (1) Since the pen or pencil is guided by the scale edge, when long, continuous lines are desired they must be spliced. (2) When drawing near the end of the scale, the arms of the machine are not rigid and the line tends to drop or be forced out of the desired position.

Scales with transparent edges allow the draftsman to observe the work as it is done, and a smoother line can be drawn along this kind of scale. Metal scales are not so smooth, tend to wear the pencil lead causing the point

Handling Paper and Pencil

Placing Paper on Drawing Board

The size of your T square and triangles or your drafting machine helps determine paper location. *(Note: All directions are for right-handed draftsmen; if you are left handed, you will reverse procedures.)* If the sheet size permits, the paper should be placed about 6″ from the bottom of the

drawing board. If the bottom edge of the paper is closer than this it is difficult to hold the instruments and draw accurately. In using the T square the left edge of the paper should be 3″ or 4″ from the left edge of the board. This is variable, of course, but you do not want to draw too near the right (free) end of the

T square because it tends to "give" near the unsupported end. Drawing near the free end also makes the instruments hard to hold in place while working. With a *drafting machine* the paper is usually placed near the center of the board.

To position the drawing paper, place the head of the T square firmly against the left edge of the drawing board and slide it down to locate the bottom of the drawing paper. Place the paper so it is against the T square. Slide the paper to the right or left as desired. Then when the paper is parallel to the T square (or straightedge of the drafting machine) it is fastened to the drawing board.

Fastening the Paper to the Drawing Board

Thumbtacks were formerly used to secure the paper, but they made holes in the drawing board which interfered with accurate drawing. Drafting tape is much preferred. There are two kinds: (1) Conventional drafting tape has adhesive on only *one* side. A small amount is needed to hold a drawing in place. Strips approximately ¼″ x 1″ are placed diagonally across each corner. Note: Tape should be firmly pressed down because it has a tendency to curl and roll up when instruments are rubbed over it. **Caution** must be observed when tape is removed to prevent tearing the paper. (2) Drafting tape is available with adhesive on both sides. This can be placed between the drawing board and paper so as not to interfere with instrument use or mar the paper surface when removed.

If a drawing will take several days to complete, some draftsmen prefer to put tape around the entire drawing sheet to prevent damaged edges by the instruments. Beginning students should check with their instructor to see

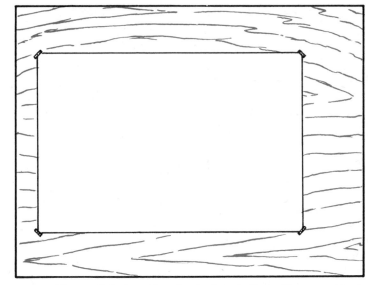

Paper is most frequently fastened to a drawing board with drafting or masking tape.

if this is necessary for a specific drawing.

Drawing Pencils and Lead Holders

Drawing pencils for line work are usually of the H series. There are nine gradations in this series. They range from a plain H, which is quite soft and makes a dark line, to a 9H, which is very hard and makes a very light line.

Some draftsmen do all their drawing with one pencil. However, this is not recommended. At least two pencils are required, one a fine grade, such as for construction lines, guide lines, extension lines, dimension lines, and equipment lines. Either a 3H or 4H is recommended, although some draftsmen prefer a very hard pencil such as a 6H for guide and construction lines. A 2H or H is recommended for heavy lines. A third softer pencil,

such as an F or HB, is frequently used for lettering.

Drawing pencils of the B series are used for architectural rendering but are not recommended for working drawings.

If wood pencils are used the wood should be sharpened to a long conical point as shown. The best sharpening is done on a draftsman's pencil sharpener.

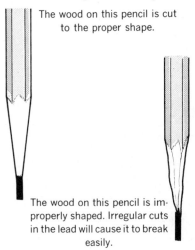

The wood on this pencil is cut to the proper shape.

The wood on this pencil is improperly shaped. Irregular cuts in the lead will cause it to break easily.

Lead holder.

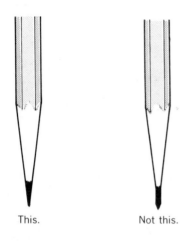

This.   Not this.

This is similar to a regular one except only the wood is removed while the lead is left intact. Wood pencils may also be sharpened with a knife if no sharpener is available, but care must be taken to prevent nicking or cutting the lead because this weakens the point and it is likely to break. The wood should be cut away from the lead until ⅜″ to ½″ is exposed. Pencil pointers, fine files, or fine sandpaper can then be used to shape the point.

Lead holders are preferred by many experienced draftsmen. The holder maintains a constant lead length so it can always be held in the same position during use. It is not necessary to take time to sharpen the wood away, and lead can be extended quickly to any desired length. Lead hold-

ers are also easier to use in automatic pointers.

Regardless of which is used, wood pencils or automatic lead holders, the lead should be sharpened to a long conical point as shown. Short tapers on the cone require more frequent sharpening.

Every time the point is reshaped the excess graphite *must* be removed before the pencil is used; otherwise the particles will be deposited on the drawing. A small cloth or facial tissue serves to wipe off and burnish the point. Then it is a good idea to condition the point by drawing a few lines on a scrap of paper. Rotate the pencil so the point will be uniform. It makes the point slightly blunt so it will not break when pressure is placed on it.

Beginning to Draw

Holding the T square. A T square is used to draw *all* horizontal lines. Lay the blade across the paper that you have attached, so the head is against the left edge of the drawing board. Remove both your hands from the drawing area. Lay the heel of your left hand on the blade of the T square at about a 45° angle and exert slight pressure toward the right. The fingers of the left hand are not placed on the T square because they must be free to hold and manipulate your triangle.

Holding the triangle—right handed. Standard triangle position places the trademark so it

is readable; that is, toward the bottom of the drawing board with the words facing you. This places the vertical edge so it is to the left of the triangle. With the heel of the left hand still firm on the T square blade, hold the triangle with your fingers of the left hand so they are over the center of it. Do not let your fingers touch the paper where the triangle is cut away. Now, using just your fingers, move the triangle back and forth without moving the heel of your left hand. Keep the base of the triangle firmly against the T square. *Left-handed* procedures are reversed of course.

Holding the pencil. The pencil should be held firmly as for writing, but the fingers should not be cramped. Stand the pencil perpendicular to the paper.

Line Weights

Lines to represent different details are drawn to different widths. The widths for each kind of line are to be the same on each drawing you do. Sample sets of lines are shown, identified, and described. They are drawn in ink; the same thickness as you are to draw them on your drawings.

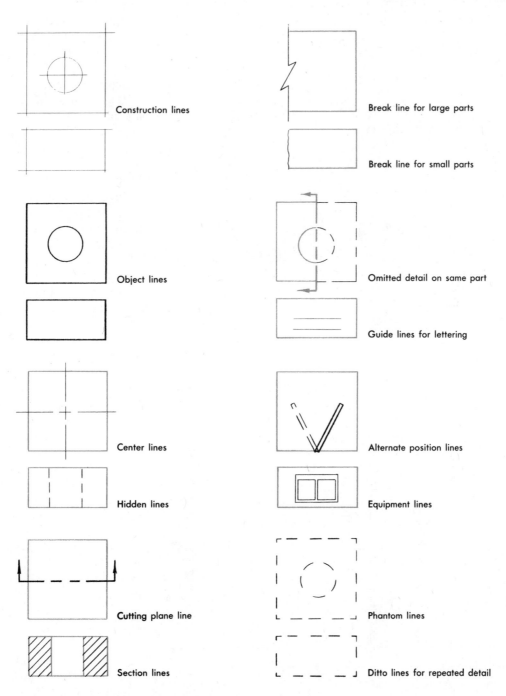

Construction lines

Break line for large parts

Break line for small parts

Object lines

Omitted detail on same part

Guide lines for lettering

Center lines

Alternate position lines

Hidden lines

Equipment lines

Cutting plane line

Phantom lines

Section lines

Ditto lines for repeated detail

Kinds of lines—inked in with India ink.

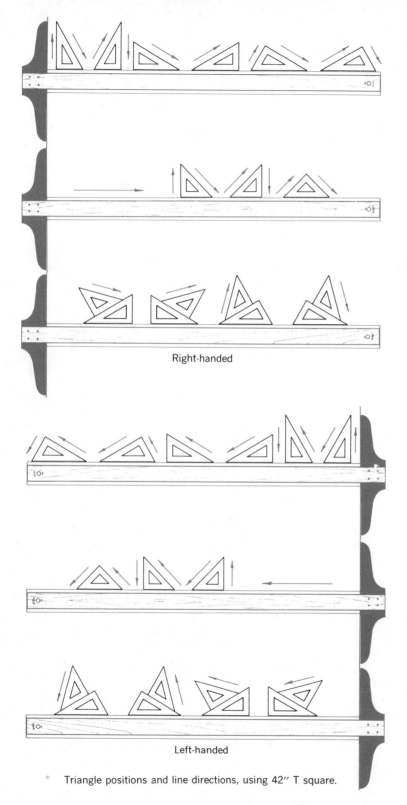

Right-handed

Left-handed

Triangle positions and line directions, using 42″ T square.

Tilt the top about 30° *in the direction the line is to be drawn.* The wrist should be held rigid and the entire arm moved when drawing lines. Your work will not be smooth if you use only your fingers or wrist.

Line direction. Horizontal lines are drawn from left to right along the top edge of the T square.

Vertical lines are drawn from bottom to top along the left edge of the triangle.

Inclined lines along the left edge of the triangle are drawn from bottom to top.

Inclined lines along the right edge of the triangle are drawn from top to bottom.

All lines are drawn by pulling the pencil. Pushing may cause a line to be uneven or skip. Also, the sharp point may injure the paper, tear or punch holes in it. These difficulties are emphasized more when drawing with ink. Note that even if you see no apparent objection to pushing the pencil you should use the proper technique to avoid problems and to develop good drafting habits.

Guide lines are very light pencil lines (barely visible) drawn with a hard pencil. They are drawn for the bottom and top of *all* lettering and figures (numbers). Since these lines are very light, they do not reproduce; therefore it is not necessary to remove them from the finished drawing. The lines are drawn by "floating" the pencil along the T square or triangle without pressure. Practice making many lines which you can barely see. They should appear shadow-like.

Construction lines are drawn in the same manner and the same weight as guide lines. The only difference between the two is that construction lines are used for laying out the drawing. These might be described as "insurance lines," because the object is first represented with them and then, when everything is correct, they are all redrawn, using the proper line weights. Since these lines are shadow-like and do not reproduce it is also unnecessary to remove them.

As mentioned earlier, you may have noticed that corners on architectural drawings do not always meet perfectly. This is because the lines are drawn quite hurriedly by professionals. Time is very valuable. They cannot take time to form all corners precisely. It also gives the drawing an artistic freedom which can make a pleasing appearance, if expertly done. As a beginner, you should not do this. Your drawing will look as though you are trying for an effect that doesn't "come off." As your speed increases you will do this naturally.

Practice for skill. Following the techniques set down on previous pages, practice line work. Draw horizontal lines first, then vertical lines. After horizontal and vertical lines have been mastered, draw inclined lines on both the right and left sides of the triangle. Try joining vertical and horizontal lines so the corners are square without overruns or spaces between. Practice making each *kind* of line, such as construction lines, dimension lines, equipment lines, and object lines. Remember that all except construction and guide lines are to be solid so no light will pass through when they are reproduced. Examine the lines carefully; if they are fuzzy on the edges they are not suitable. Hold the paper to a strong light to get a better idea of opacity. Your teacher may have you draw practice lines on a scrap of tracing paper so they may be reproduced to help determine the quality of your work.

Architect's Scales

Building parts tend to be large. Since they must be represented on a set of plans it is obvious that all parts cannot be drawn their true size. Sizes must be shown reduced. An ordinary ruler could be used to make reductions but it would be very time consuming and mathematically involved. For example, if a part needs to be reduced from full size to $\frac{1}{4}'' = 1'\text{-}0''$, then each $\frac{1}{4}''$ on the ruler would equal 12" or 1'-0"; if a wall is 10'-0" long, then it requires ten $\frac{1}{4}''$ spaces or $2\frac{1}{2}''$. One could easily become overwhelmed by the number of calculations. An *architect's scale* has the reductions already calculated. A *triangular scale* has regular dimensions with each inch divided into 16ths, plus ten (10) additional scales. Naturally the scales are those most frequently used in architectural drawing. It is necessary to learn to *read* and *use* the scales.

An architect or draftsman does not think of the divisions on his scale as representing fractions or parts of an inch; they are considered as lengths in feet and inches, at a reduction suitable for drawing.

Reading a scale. Examine a scale carefully. Note that measurements do not begin at the end. This space is reserved for identifying each scale; also, as scales and rules become worn they may not be accurate near the ends, so divisions are placed back, away from points of wear. Turn *your* scale so the #1 at the end of the scale is in reading position. Compare yours with the first illustration on page 318. The #1 means the divisions for this scale are 1" long. Each 1" division represents 12" or 1'-0". Notice that the scale is read from right to left. Now look immediately to the left of the #1; here you find a 1" space divided into 48 equal parts. Imagine the 1" as being a foot ruler that has been reduced to this size.

Architect's triangular scale.

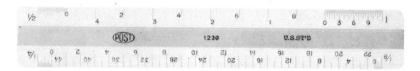

Flat architect's scales.

The 3″, 6″, and 9″ divisions have been marked so the scale is easier to read. Notice the smaller divisions for 1″, ½″, and ¼″.

The scale in the illustration is "open divided." This means the small divisions are not continued the full length of the scale; the remainder of the divisions are open, or free of measurements. Other scales may be "full divided," which means the small divisions, as those to the right of the 0, are marked the full length of the scale.

Notice the 0 at the left end of the small divisions. This is the starting point for measuring. The first number to the left of the 0

is 8; disregard this number, it is part of the scale measuring from the other end. The next number to the left is a #1. This is 1″ (actual size) from the 0, so it represents 1′-0″. Likewise it is 2″ from the #2 to the 0, so this represents 2′-0″. These ratios

continue the length of the scale.

The left end of the scale has a #½ in the space before the graduations. This means the ½″ divisions represent 1′-0″. Since a foot must fit into a ½″ space, it is not possible to divide the scale into as many subdivisions or fractions as the one just discussed. However, except for the size reduction and fraction divisions, all architect's scales are read exactly the same.

Triangular architect's scales are manufactured of boxwood, other hardwoods, and high impact plastic. Plastic has the hardest surface and the divisions are more distinct than wood scales.

Graduations are placed on the scale by two different manufacturing methods. On inexpensive scales they are printed or stamped all at one time into the surface. Better scales have the graduations engine divided. This is done by a machine that makes each division mark individually in exact steps.

Flat scales. Except for shape and number of scales, a flat scale is the same as a triangular one. Many draftsmen prefer them because of their handy shape and ease of locating measurements.

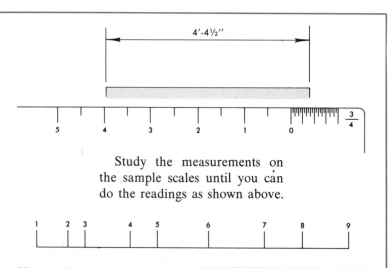

Study the measurements on the sample scales until you can do the readings as shown above.

Using different scales and the numbered vertical lines above, determine full-scale measurements between lines which you select. For example, using a ½″ scale, the distance from 3 to 9 is 5′-8½″.

Do several practice measurements so you will master use of the scale.

Some Practice Problems
Scale

½″	2 to 8 = ?
¼″	5 to 7 = ?
3″	4 to 1 = ?
1½″	3 to 6 = ?
⅜″	8 to 4 = ?

Tools for Curved and Irregular Forms

Protractor

Horizontal and vertical lines and lines at 15° increments are drawn using a T square and triangles, as shown on page 316. When other angles are required they are laid out with a protractor. It may be a simple one as shown or it may be included as a part of a template, adjustable triangle, or drafting machine.

Compasses

A bow compass, either large or small, is easiest to adjust and holds its position best. A drop compass is used for a radius of one and a fraction inches or less. A beam compass is used for larger diameters. Compasses are available to do either pencil or ink lines. Combination compasses have interchangeable ruling pens and lead holders.

The stem of a compass is held between the thumb and forefinger; and is inclined slightly to the right. Circles and arcs are drawn clockwise with a steady, continuous motion. When drawing with a pencil, use a slightly softer lead than for straight lines because less pressure is exerted.

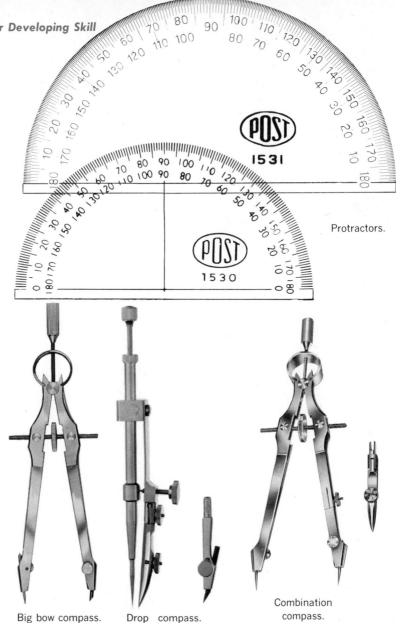

Protractors.

Big bow compass. Drop compass. Combination compass.

For Expert Work

1. When a circle is completed, do not stop abruptly; this causes the splice to show. Instead, gently lift the pen or pencil as the circle is continued.

2. Do not continue tracing around the circle, as this widens the line.

3. Both the lead and needle points of the compass are extended approximately the same distance so the compass can be held vertically. When the legs of an adjustable compass must be extended, or when a lengthening bar is attached, as shown, the lead or ruling pen and the needle point should be vertical.

4. The compass lead is sharpened to a long, chisel point as shown.

5. If several circles have a common center, the point soon drills a hole in the paper. A *compass horn* can be placed over the center and the point placed on the plastic or metal.

6. When arcs or circles are drawn *tangent* to straight lines, the arcs or circles should be drawn first and then the straight lines constructed tangent to them. It is much easier to impose a straight line on an arc or circle than it is to impose an arc or circle on a straight line.

Dividers

Dividers are very similar to the compass except they have two needle points and no marking lead or pen. They are used for quick, true measuring. A compass may be converted to dividers by replacing the lead with a metal point. Dividers are available in bow styles. Fine (small) measurements can be made very quickly and accurately if they are stepped off with dividers. It is much more accurate than marking directly from a scale. This is because a pencil cannot be controlled free

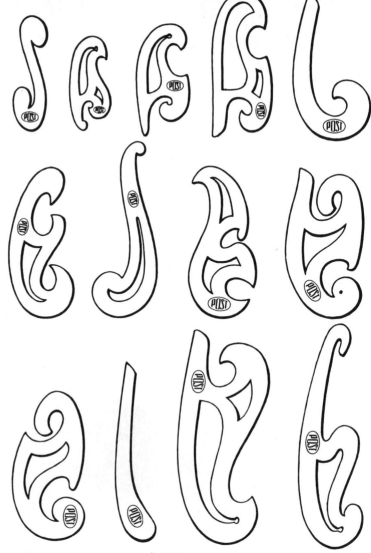

Irregular curves.

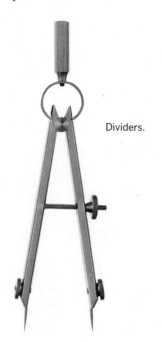

Dividers.

hand closely enough for very fine measurements.

When dividers are used to *step off* equal distances both points are never removed from the paper at the same time. Rotate the divider from one point to the other. If both points are removed from the paper and put back again, it is no more accurate than measuring from the scale. It also makes the job much slower.

Proportional dividers, shown on page 326, can be used to enlarge and reduce.

Irregular Curve Templates

An irregular curve template is a clear plastic sheet with curved line shapes cut in. A pattern of desired curves is traced onto the working drawing. Examples of irregular curves are shown in the accompanying illustration.

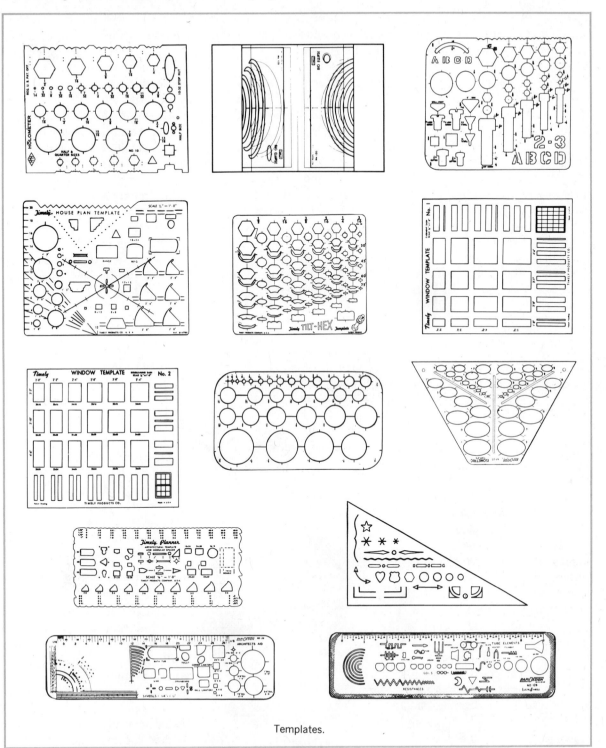

Templates.

Other Templates

Much of the drawing of small circles, ellipses, conventional symbols such as doors, windows, shrubs, trees, appliances, bathroom and kitchen fixtures, and many more, that were once laboriously constructed with instruments, is now done with clear plastic templates. Examples of frequently used architectural templates are shown on the preceding page, 321.

Details that must be repeated, but are not available on standard templates, may be carved by the draftsman to fill his particular need. Soft vinyl Lucite, or Plexi-glass is frequently used. If a template is needed on the spur of the moment and no sheet plastic is available, the required shape may be carved on the edge of a standard template. Shapes may also be cut into a soft plastic can lid.

Caution About Using Templates

Some quality is usually sacrificed for speed when templates are used because they are not always smooth and accurate. However, since most firms are interested primarily in production, this slight loss of quality is not usually considered important.

For Expert Work

When templates are used with technical fountain pens, ink may seep under the plastic. This can be avoided by placing drafting tape under the parts or the template near the pattern to be traced. This leaves space between the paper and the plastic. Incidentally, this practice works equally well on triangles and Other instruments. NOTE: High-quality, heavyweight templates frequently have the pattern undercut slightly to remedy this problem. Good quality templates are not brittle and thus keep their uniform edges longer.

Drawing Aids

Erasers

Selection of erasers is very important. *Pencil erasers* are available in many qualities. A poor quality product tends to leave a film of the eraser's color on the paper. Several should be on hand. Only trial and error will determine which is most suited for the job and paper. *Ink erasers* have an abrasive added to the rubber. Care must be exercised to prevent damage to the drafting surface while erasing.

Art gum is a soft eraser used primarily for cleaning the drawing and removing light lines. It is available in solid pieces or as a fine powder, contained in a shaker can. The powder may also be enclosed in a mesh cloth sack and be used as a cleaning pad. When they are used on pencil drawings, some of the graphite is removed, thus reducing the quality of your work.

Both ink and pencil erasers are available in block form or are encased in wooden holders, the same as ordinary pencils.

Erasing Machines

Erasing machines, as shown,

Dry cleaning pad.

are used by many draftsmen. The chuck on the bottom of the machine allows the draftsman to select the proper eraser.

Erasing Shield

An erasing shield is a thin plate of plastic or metal with slots of different sizes and shapes cut for use on limited areas. A slot is placed over the part to be erased and the rest of the shield protects other areas.

Underlays and Tracing Sheets

Drawing intricate details such as section lines and symbols is very time consuming. Many are repeated constantly. To increase drafting speed and insure greater accuracy, underlays with typical patterns and parts printed on paper or plastic film may be positioned beneath the drawing and used as copying guides.

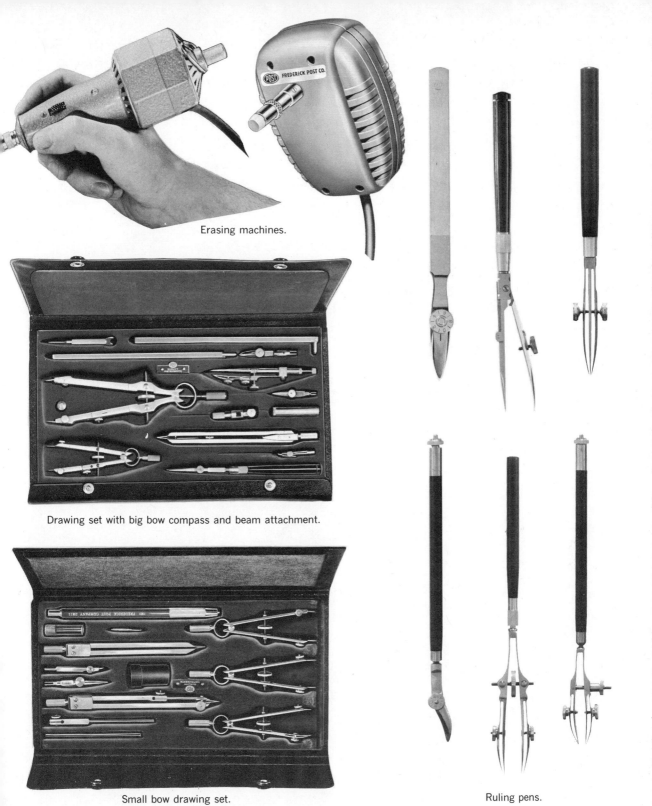

Erasing machines.

Drawing set with big bow compass and beam attachment.

Small bow drawing set.

Ruling pens.

Morgan Company, Oshkosh, Wisconsin

SCALE ½″ = 1′-0″

Tracing sheets.

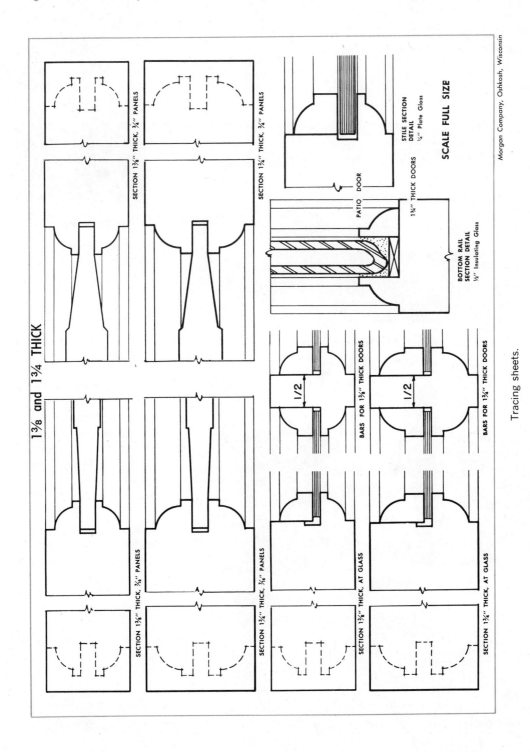

Tracing sheets.

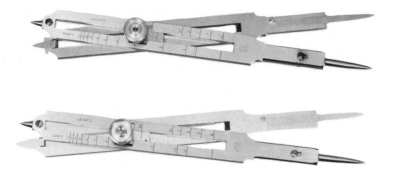

Proportional dividers.

Technical fountain pens.

Tracing sheets of specific parts —such as doors, windows, structural metal, and others—are available without charge if requested from the manufacturers of such building items.

Sandpaper pad for pointing pencils.

Overlays

A draftsman may be required to make temporary suggestions on a drawing, show alternate ideas and proposals, or show relationships of traditional and new materials. Such work imposed on an original drawing can destroy its value. Instead, clear plastic film may be placed over the original drawing and the changes or proposals drawn on the film. When a copy is reproduced, both drawings (old and new) appear as one, but the original has not been damaged or changed.

Pencil pointer.

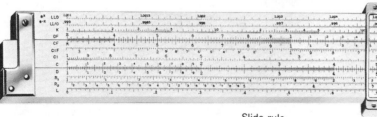

Slide rule.

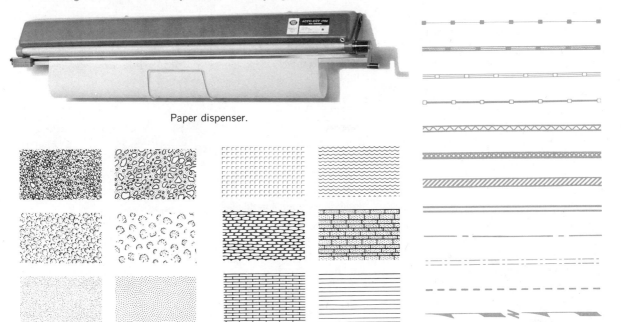

Paper dispenser.

Pressure-sensitive overlays.

Paratone, Inc.

Pre-printed symbols on pressure-sensitive tape.

Symbols on Film

Much of the tedious work of drawing symbols, shading, etc., can be avoided by purchasing and applying adhesive backed plastic film with symbols printed on the surface. This is especially valuable for architectural renderings.

Rubber Stamps

Notes and individual symbols that are used frequently on different sets of plans may be represented on rubber stamps so they can be stamped instead of drawn on a plan.

Unusual Drafting Equipment

A good draftsman needs to be ingenious; he is often required to draw many unusual shaped objects, some of which may be quite difficult with conventional instruments. Ordinary objects such as buttons, washers, tin cans, strips of plastic, hollow core solder, or pieces of string can become valuable drafting aids.

(All photographs of drawing instruments in this chapter courtesy Frederick Post Co.)

Questions to Reinforce Knowledge

1. Explain the purpose of a set of building plans.

2. Why is cleanliness essential to good drafting?

3. Do neat drawings always reproduce well? Explain.

4. When should drawing equipment be cleaned?

5. What is the danger of washing instruments with soap and water?

6. What three kinds of wood are suitable for drawing surfaces? Why?

7. Of what material are portable drawing boards usually constructed? Why are they usually cross banded?

8. Why must a drawing board be used with care?

9. Why are pads placed between the board and drawing paper?

10. When can they be omitted?

11. From your own reasoning, why do board covers sometimes have 1/8″ grid lines imprinted upon them?

12. What is the disadvantage of plastic laminate as a drawing board surface?

13. Why is a long T square recommended for architectural drawing?

14. Why should a T square have a plastic edge?

15. Why is this strip sometimes not as thick as the wood blade?

16. What is a satisfactory arrangement for securing the head and blade? Why?

17. Why are large triangles a necessity for architectural drawing?

18. Why is it desirable to also have a set of small triangles?

19. What is an adjustable triangle?

20. Describe the advantages and disadvantages of using a drafting machine.

21. What is a parallel-ruling straightedge?

22. Why should you avoid placing drawing paper too near the lower edge of the drawing board?

23. Why is the drawing paper placed near the left edge of the drawing board?

24. Explain how to position paper on the drawing board and align it with the T square.

25. Describe fastening drawing paper to a drawing board.

26. Why are thumbtacks not recommended?

27. Which pencil is the hardest, a 2H or 4H?

28. Which pencil draws the darkest line, a 2H or 4H?

29. Guide and construction lines may be drawn with a harder or softer pencil than those discussed above. Why?

30. How much lead should be exposed on a drawing pencil?

31. Why must care be taken if a wood drawing pencil is sharpened with a knife?

32. Why is the lead shaped to a long conical point?

33. Why are lead holders preferred by some draftsmen?

34. Describe different methods of pointing a pencil lead.

35. Why must the lead be wiped off after it is pointed. What else may be done to condition the lead?

36. Draw samples of the following lines:

    Object line
    Construction line
    Hidden line
    Long break line
    Short break line
    Leader
    Extension line
    Dimension line
    Equipment line
    Cutting plane line
    Phantom or alternate position line
    Section line
    Center line

37. Describe how a T square and triangle are held to draw vertical lines.

38. Describe how a drawing pencil is held during use.

39. In what direction are horizontal lines drawn?

40. In what direction are vertical lines drawn? Along which edge of the triangle?

41. How can you tell if the triangle is right side up or upside down?

42. Why does one *always* pull the pencil or pen?

43. Describe how to draw guide lines and construction lines their proper weight.

44. Describe why and when lines sometimes cross at corners.

45. Excluding the foot ruler, how many scales are there on an architect's triangular scale?

46. Why are flat scales sometimes preferred?

47. What is an open divided scale?

48. What is a full divided scale?

49. You should never draw along the edge of a scale. From your own reasoning give reasons why.

50. From what three materials are scales frequently manufactured?

51. What are two methods of putting graduations on a scale? Which is best? Why?

52. Describe five kinds of compasses.

53. Why may a compass require a softer lead than a pencil on the same drawing?

54. What shape is recommended for a compass lead? Can you think of a good reason why?

55. What is the purpose of a compass horn? Describe two kinds.

56. What is the main difference between a compass and a divider?

57. Describe ''stepping off'' measurements with a divider.

58. What is an irregular curve?

59. Why are templates widely used in architectural drawing?

60. When drawing with ink, why should the working edge of a template not be touching the paper?

61. Why would a draftsman make a template himself?

62. What is the disadvantage of using a cleaning pad on pencil drawings?

63. What does art gum usually remove?

64. Why is an erasing shield a valuable instrument?

65. What is an underlay? Describe.

66. What is an overlay? Describe.

67. Why are symbols available printed on adhesive-backed plastic film?

68. Describe how a draftsman might use each of the following as a drafting aid?

    A button   Hollow core solder
    A tin can   String

Terms to Spell and Know

technique	pencil pointer	bow compass
graphite	object line	beam compass
basswood	construction line	chisel point lead
board cover	hidden line	conical point lead
T square	break line	compass horn
30°-60° triangle	leader	irregular curve
45° triangle	dimension line	template
adjustable triangle	equipment line	art gum
drafting machine	phantom line	cleaning pad
straightedge	section line	erasing machine
drafting tape	guide line	erasing shield
drawing pencil	architect's triangular scale	underlay
H series	architect's flat scale	overlay
lead holder	graduation	printed symbol

32

Drafting Mediums

You may have the idea that all drawing paper is pretty much alike. This is not true; there are literally hundreds of papers to choose from. A satisfactory finished drawing depends partially upon the selection of the proper paper medium for the job to be done. A medium that is very satisfactory for one use may be totally unacceptable for another. You are probably already familiar with heavyweight drawing papers. These are widely used in schools because of ease in handling. Drawing paper is available in many weights and qualities, the poorest sometimes being classified as school quality. Least expensive varieties are soft and porous, suitable only for pencil. Since they are porous, it is difficult to keep them clean during use. Better grades have a smooth, dense surface, suitable for both pencil and ink. Even the better papers have a slight surface matte to hold lines in shape. This is called *tooth*. If a surface is very smooth, with no tooth, lines widen and spread.

Most frequently used paper colors are white, green, and yellow. The specific job and personal preference dictates choice.

Even though heavy papers are seldom used in a professional drafting room, their use by beginners is justified because they seldom complete a drawing without making errors and corrections, and these are best made on heavyweight stock. After the drawing is in final form, it may be copied onto tracing paper.

Since this paper is seldom used for finished drawings even inexpensive butchers paper, without a wax surface, or the back of used copy paper is suitable for preliminary drawings.

Tracing Paper

Tracing paper is also available in different weights and qualities. Inexpensive sulfite papers may be made of wood pulp, while better grades are 100% rag content vellum. The latter are more transparent and so make better copies. They can also be run at faster speeds for reproduction work. Tracing vellum may be white or have a slightly blue color.

Tracing Cloth

If more permanent, durable drawings are required, they may be done in either pencil or ink on tracing cloth. Some cloths are designed specifically for pencil, some only for ink, and others for both.

Analysis of tracing cloth shows one side to be rather dull and the other glossy. Draw on the dull side.

NOTE: Manufacturers advertise that ink can be erased on tracing cloth, and it can, but it is very difficult to do so without the correction showing.

Tracing Film

Plastic film has advantages found in no other medium. It is very durable and its dimensional stability is excellent. There are two types of tracing film; one is acetate and the other is a polyester base film. The latter is one of the toughest substances known and so is very durable. It is almost impossible to tear this material. Acetate film is not quite so indestructible, but it is also superior to paper or cloth.

Both materials are suitable for use when a high degree of permanence or accuracy is called

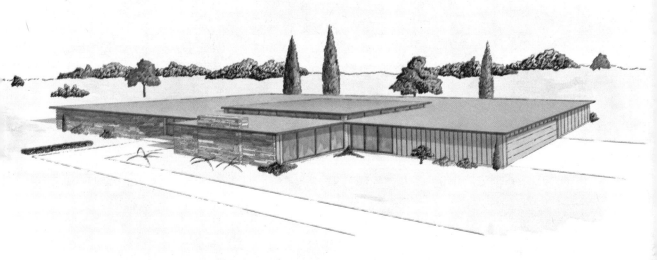

Student rendering combining water color and airbrush techniques on cold press medium surface illustration board.

for. Both are available in clear form, or they may have one or both surfaces roughened to form a matte surface. A matte surface allows the film to hold ink or pencil lines better than a glossy surface. The matte causes film to be only translucent, but almost all light from developing passes through, so exceptionally fast developing speeds and very clear prints are obtained.

Objections: Since ink does not penetrate the material, plastic is more difficult to use than other media. Even on a matte surface lines have a tendency to widen because of a lack of real tooth. Standard India ink is likely to chip off the surface. Special acetate inks should be used because they adhere better.

Matte surfaces on this tough material are very abrasive and wear pencils or other instruments quickly. Specially hardened or jewel-tipped pens are sometimes used for their long wearing qualities.

Graphite pencil lines do not always reproduce well when used on film. This is especially true when reduced to microfilm. Parts of lines may reproduce while others do not, or the metallic graphite surface may cause reflections and distortions. These phenomena, called "ghosts," must be avoided. When one draws on film, pencils with a wax core are popular. The degrees of hardness are the same as for the H series.

Grids

Any of the drafting media previously discussed is available with pre-printed, blue grid lines. Major grids are spaced both vertically and horizontally. Intermediate grids, preferably a lighter shade of blue, may be spaced at 8 or 10 per inch. These serve merely as guide lines that do not copy onto reproductions because they are engulfed by white light.

Packaging

Paper, cloth, or film may be purchased in rolls, loose sheets, or sheets bound into pads.

Printed Borders and Titles

Cut sheets of any of the materials can be imprinted with borders or titles to fit your requirement. This insures uniform line and border widths, reduces drafting time, and have the same prestige value as a fine letterhead.

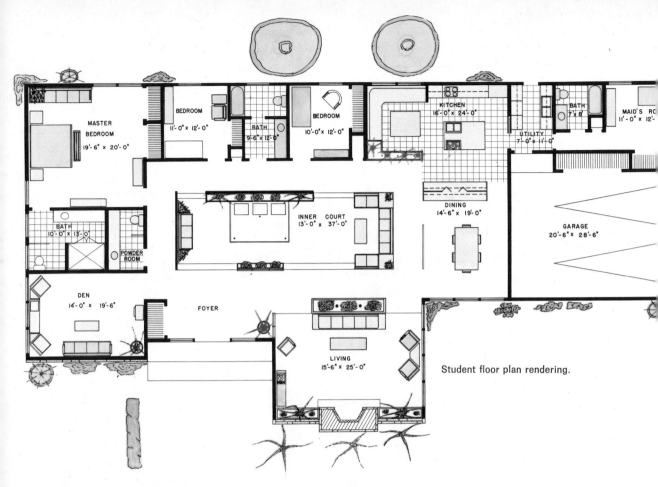

Student floor plan rendering.

Water Color Paper

Water color paper is relatively soft, pliable, and usually rough textured. It may be manufactured either by the hot or cold press method. The method used affects the texture of the surface, as explained later. Most popular colors are white and parchment (yellowish white), but it is available in a wide range of other colors. It may be purchased in a great number of different sheet sizes, as loose sheets or bound into pads for greater convenience.

When water is spilled on an ordinary sheet of paper, the fibers stretch and wrinkle it permanently. The fibers of water color paper also stretch while it is wet, but when it dries they return to their original form.

Poster Board

Poster board is semi-rigid, about 1/16″ thick. As the name implies it is ideally suited for posters rather than for drafting. Subjects are usually sketched lightly and then painted in with opaque water color. Board is not so good for heavy line work because the fibers are loosely pressed. However, the surface is very smooth; one can obtain satisfactory results with ink provided very little pressure is exerted on the drawing instrument.

Boards are available in a wide range of colors, some of which are subtle in tone while others have much brilliance. Patterned surfaces such as marble or wood grain imprints are also available, on one side only. The other is unfinished.

Illustration Board

This board is used for a majority of all architectural renderings. There is a thickness for almost every requirement. Thickness is determined by the number of plies, or layers of paper pressed together to form the board. Very thin boards may be single ply, or heavyweights may be seven or more ply. Interior plies are of inexpensive sulfite but the finished surface is of very high quality. Of course quality from some manufacturers is better than from others. Only experience will determine which is best for your specific rendering, or you may rely upon the advice of an experienced person.

Boards may be finished with only one working surface or they may be double mounted and have two good surfaces. Generally speaking, boards with cotton fiber faces are better than those made from other substances.

There are two standard finishes. One manufacturing method presses the board while the paper is hot, so the finished board is called *hot press* illustration board. This is also sometimes referred to as *high surface* board because the face is very smooth. The other method presses the board when the paper is cold and is called *cold press* or, sometimes, regular illustration board. Its surface is slightly grained or textured.

White is most frequently used but others are available.

Matte Board

This material is similar to illustration board except the surface is more *pebbled* or textured. It is used primarily as a base for mounting other pictures or drawings so they can be stood or hung for viewing. It is cut larger than the original drawing to make a backing and border. After constructing guide lines for positioning the original it is mounted with wallpaper paste, rubber cement, or contact cement or laminating machines.

Renderings on heavy illustration board also look better with matte borders. Frames are frequently cut from large sheets of matte board and placed over the face of the rendering.

Questions To Reinforce Knowledge

1. Explain the variety of drawing media available and how one determines which to use?

2. What is school quality drawing paper? How does this compare with other qualities? Why is it used?

3. What is tooth on a drawing medium?

4. Why are heavyweight drawing papers used by the beginner but seldom by a professional draftsman?

5. Can less expensive materials be substituted for this paper? Why? What materials?

6. What are two kinds of tracing paper? Which is best? Why?

7. Are different thicknesses of tracing paper available?

8. Are different colors of tracing paper available? Explain.

9. Why is tracing cloth sometimes used?

10. How does one determine which side of the material to use for drawing?

11. What are the advantages of plastic tracing film?

12. What are two kinds available? Describe each.

13. What is a matte surface? Why is it necessary on plastic film?

14. How does the translucence (rather than transparency) of the matte surface affect reproduction?

15. What is likely to happen if regular India ink is used on plastic film? Why?

16. How can the above be remedied?

17. How does the surface of plastic film affect drawing instruments? How is this sometimes remedied?

18. When using pencil lines on plastic film, why do pencil lines not always reproduce well?

19. When parts of lines reproduce and others do not, or when some lines appear like shadows, what is this phenomenon called?

20. What kind of pencil core is sometimes used instead of graphite?

21. Why might one purchase tracing media with blue grid lines on it? How do these show on reproductions?

22. What are the reasons for purchasing paper with titles and borders already printed?

23. Is water-color paper smooth or textured? Why?

24. Is it available in only one or more than one color?

25. Why is poster board not ideally suited for ink work? Can it be used for this? Explain.

26. Describe the colors available.

27. Most architectural renderings are done on what kind of material?

28. What determines the thickness of illustration board?

29. Is illustration board the same all the way through?

30. What is double mounted illustration board?

31. What is hot press illustration board? Describe its surface. What is another name for the surface of hot press illustration board?

32. What is cold press illustration board? Describe its surface. What is another name for the surface of cold press illustration board?

33. From what materials are the best boards manufactured?

34. What kind of surface does matte board have?

35. How may matte board be used with architectural renderings?

36. Describe how they are mounted.

Terms To Spell and Know

drawing paper	tracing film	illustration board
tooth	matte surface	hot press
tracing paper	ghosts	high surface paper
tracing vellum	water color paper	cold press
tracing cloth	poster board	matte board

33

GOOD LETTERING *is needed on architectural drawings. The most important reason is to include information such as names, dimensions, or lettered notes. The secondary purpose is appearance, to impress the client. This is especially true for presentation type drawings that are done for public exhibition.*

Architectural Lettering

Lettering Styles

Architectural lettering is not as mechanical in appearance as the style for ordinary working drawings. The *basic* shape of each letter is the same, but a top-flight draftsman perfects his own free-flowing style. You may see ex-

amples of architectural lettering and gain the impression that letters can be formed any way you may choose; this is not true.

To do good lettering you must first develop a permanent visual picture of the basic shape of each

letter and figure. These shapes are shown on the large scale lettering illustrations. To help you achieve good, uniform shapes, both illustrations have numbered arrows indicating a suggested procedure for forming the letters.

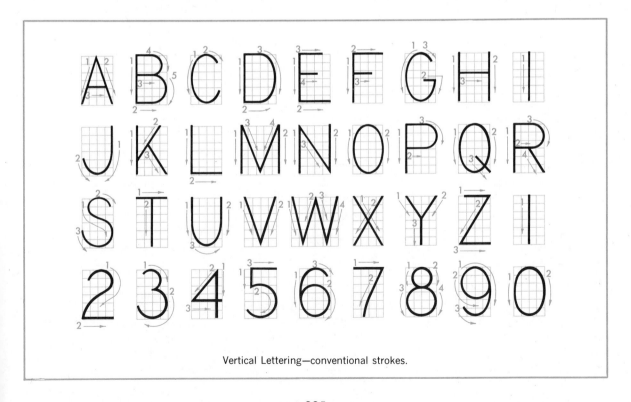

Vertical Lettering—conventional strokes.

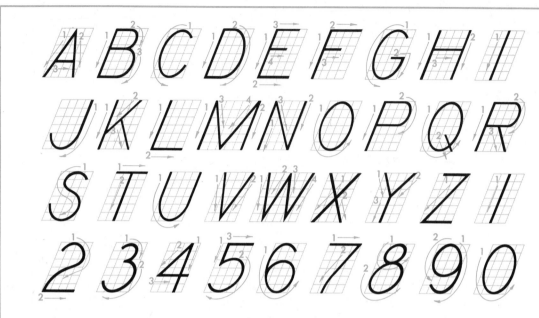

Inclined Lettering—abbreviated strokes.

The first illustration, showing vertical letters, includes the strokes that are recommended for mechanical drawing. The second illustration showing inclined letters, presents simplified strokes recommended for architectural lettering. The novice should use the recommended strokes until a satisfactory lettering technique has been acquired.

After you have acquired a visual image of exactly what each letter is to look like, practice until you can reproduce the lettering on your drawings.

Vertical vs. Inclined Lettering

Either vertical or inclined lettering may be used. The instructor or the employer and—if policy allows—personal preference determine the choice. If vertical letters are used, each letter must be really vertical, or if they are inclined they must all slope at the same angle; otherwise, the lettering will not be neat in appearance. Decide on an angle such as 60°, 67½°, or 75°; then stick to it.

Height of Lettering

Large letters take longer and are more difficult to form neatly than small ones; but since many sizes are required on a drawing you must be able to master all. Practice on ⅜″ characters until you have mastered the strokes and shape of each letter and figure. NOTE: Even practice lettering must be placed between guide lines.

Leave a minimum space of ⅔ the lettering height between lines (rows) of lettering. After you have become proficient at doing ⅜″ lettering, practice should be devoted to smaller and larger lettering. You must become especially proficient at quick rendering of characters about ⅛″ size, because it is most used for names and dimensions.

Detail lettering height must be appropriate to the size of the drawing; that is, it must neither dominate the drawing nor be so small you must hunt to find it or it is hard to use.

Recommended Heights

Identifying names and dimensions on body of drawing . ⅛″
Lettered notes . . . . ³/₃₂″
Sub-titles . . . . ¼″
Indication of scale used . . . ³/₁₆″

Study samples on actual building plans and note that fractions are about 1⅔ the height of lettering.

Width of Letters

The amount of space available helps determine lettering width. In a wide space, lettering may be expanded so it looks appropriate; or if there is little space the letters may be condensed to fit. Both individual letters and spaces between may be adjusted by expanding or condensing.

To add to appearance, draftsmen frequently use condensed lettering but use expanded spaces between them as shown.

Lower Case Letters

Lower case letters are seldom used on architectural drawings, so they are not shown in this book.

Changing Height of Letters in Words

All letters of a word or group of words are normally the same height because only capitals are used; however, the first letter of words or phrases may be slightly extended in height. Some draftsmen believe this adds to appearance and clarity. NOTE: Avoid tendency to broaden the stroke on extended caps.

Guide Lines

All lettering and dimensions are placed between accurately measured guide lines, so individual characters can be kept in line, and to keep words parallel to other lettering in the same direction. Failure to use guide lines will result in lettering that does not follow straight rows. If you have difficulty maintaining the proper slant, or the letters are not vertical when they should be, use additional guide lines to set a standard for the up-and-down strokes. Since guide lines are shadow lines that will not reproduce when copies are made, they should not be removed from the finished drawing.

Consistency

As mentioned earlier, lettering cannot be done any way you choose. Be sure individual letters fit together appropriately. Some should not be done in a straight line style while others are very elaborate; they must be consistent. The same lettering style must be maintained throughout a set of drawings. For best results, master one style and then use it for *all* drawings. One must really be an expert to do lettering satisfactorily in many styles.

Expanded vertical architectural lettering.

Bold expanded inclined architectural lettering.

Condensed lettering with expanded space.

Architectural lettering for titles.

THERMOPANE   REFRIGERATOR   SURFACE UNIT   SINK   CABINET   BATHROOM
LINEN CLOSET   HAMPER   QUARRY TILE   SPLIT FACE   ROCK LATH
INTERIOR   EXTERIOR   SHEATHING   ROOFING   FLASHING   SADDLE   HIP
BALLUSTER   STRINGER   TREAD   RISER   WEDGE   NOSING   LANDING   LANDING
DISHWASHER   LAUNDRY   FURNACE   WATER HEATER

Rapid free style architectural lettering for notes.

Lettering Hints

Speed of Strokes

While practicing and learning shapes and strokes, do not hurry. Strive for perfection; however, if letters are formed too slowly they will appear shaky, as shown. After techniques have been mastered, gradually increase speed, but *do not sacrifice quality*. It takes much practice before good lettering can be done rapidly, but you can achieve it if you try seriously. It gives you professional prestige.

THIS IS AN EXAMPLE OF POOR ARCHITECTURAL LETTERING

Do not attempt to draw each letter slowly.

Pencil for Lettering

Use a soft lead pencil so you can obtain a firm stroke without exerting much pressure. Of course, hard lead requires much pressure to obtain an opaque line. Excess pressure also dents the paper and makes the pencil hard to control. An HB or No. 2 writing pencil is recommended. The pencil should be sharpened as for drawing. Be sure the point is slightly rounded; this makes it easier to control.

Ink for Lettering

Lettering with ink is more difficult than with pencil. Do not letter with an ordinary dip pen; it has a sharp point and is difficult to guide. It must be held delicately and it is difficult to use in obtaining uniform lines. Use a round tip lettering pen, a broad-point regular fountain pen, or a large-size technical fountain pen.

Width of Strokes

Do not try to make strokes too fine and delicate; letters with broader, more positive strokes are easier to read.

Positioning Lettering

Do not letter over lines of the drawing. Place the lettering so it is in an open space, easy to find and read. For names of rooms or building parts, center the lettering in the space available. In congested areas it may be necessary to omit part of a line or symbol to accommodate the lettering.

Letters may be spaced apart, as said, so they fill better between lines of the drawing.

When lettering dimensions, they should be placed above the dimension line about $1/16''$.

Freehand Lettering vs. Mechanical Aids

Lettering and dimensioning on the body of architectural working drawings is almost always done freehand, so it can be executed quickly.

Lettering for presentation drawings, title blocks, and subtitles is frequently done using lettering templates or other devices. Speed is sacrificed for quality.

Frederick Post Co.

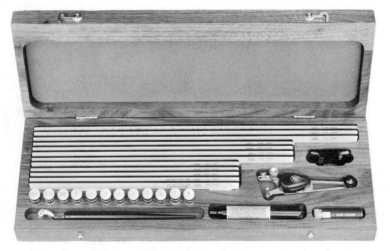

Mechanical lettering set.

LETTERING DONE WITH A LETTERING DEVICE

Mechanical lettering sample.

APPLIQUÉ LETTERING

Drawing guide lines for lettering.

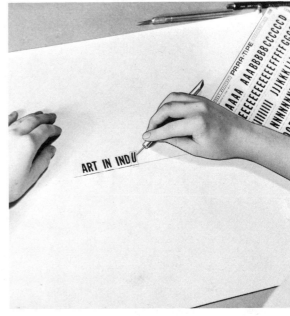

Positioning the letter.

Paratone, Inc.

Cutting letters from plastic film.

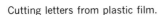

Removing guide lines.

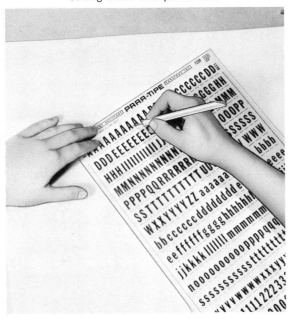

PRESSURE SENSITIVE LETTERING

Positioning letter on drawing sheet.

Burnishing the letter with any smooth hard instrument.

Spraying fixative to permanently set letters.

Paratone, Inc.

Remove backing sheet and place letter in transferring position—**rub** letter with any smooth instrument. After transferring, place backing sheet over letter and rub with a harder pressure. In case of error, letter can be removed by using any soft pencil eraser.

ARTWORK
BLUEPRINTS
COMPS
DISPLAYS
LOGOTYPES
MOCK-UPS
PRINTING
SIGNS
SLIDES and many other uses

Sample of pressure-sensitive lettering styles and uses.

Questions To Reinforce Knowledge

1. Give two reasons why neat lettering is important on architectural drawings.

2. How does freehand architectural lettering differ from other types?

3. Why must you memorize the shapes of letters and figures?

4. Why should you learn the recommended strokes?

5. Will your strokes be exactly the same as for mechanical lettering? Why?

6. How do you determine whether to use vertical or inclined lettering?

7. Why must you use guide lines for all freehand lettering? Why are they also sometimes added for up-and-down strokes?

8. Why is a clear space left between rows of lettering?

9. Why should much practice be done at the ⅛″ height?

10. What is meant by the term expanded lettering?

11. What is meant by the term condensed lettering?

12. Why do some draftsmen extend the first letter of words or notes above other letters?

13. Why must you use a uniform lettering style on a set of drawings?

14. Why is it recommended that you follow the same style for all your lettering?

15. How should experience affect speed with which freehand lettering is done?

16. What pencils are recommended for lettering?

17. What kinds of pens are recommended for ink lettering?

18. Why are ordinary dip pens not recommended?

19. How do you determine where to place required lettering on a drawing? Explain.

20. Why is most architectural lettering done freehand?

21. When are lettering templates or other devices recommended?

Orthographic Projection and the Architectural Drawing

Since most beginning architectural drawing students have had introductory mechanical drawing courses, this discussion is limited to a review of basic principles and their application to architectural drawing. If you have not had previous drawing experience, you should obtain a good book on beginning mechanical drawing and study this background material further.

This can be considered a review of main points for quick reference.

Problems of Projection

There are several pictorial methods of representing solid objects on paper which are discussed in Chapter 36. These methods have serious drawbacks; they are either time consuming or, because of visual distortion, do not give a true representation of the object.

When one views an actual object, it is three dimensional; that is, it has thickness, width, and length. Since a sheet of drawing paper is flat and is in one plane, some method must be employed to represent the sides of this three-dimensional object on the flat paper so that each view shows in full, if required for dimensioning. NOTE: Sometimes all views are necessary.

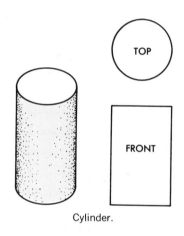

Cylinder.

Orthographic Projection

The basis for representing solid objects in working drawings is called orthographic projection. Working drawings view only one side of an object at a time. This keeps each surface in the same plane as the paper. To understand orthographic projections it is necessary to learn how to "swing" other sides around so they are all in the same plane as the front view.

The most simple object to describe using a working drawing is a sphere, as shown. Since a simple sphere is completely round it appears the same regardless of how it is viewed. Therefore, it requires only one view to describe its outlined shape.

A simple cylindrical object can be described with only two views,

Sphere.

one to show its height and one its diameter.

Most objects, even the simple rectangular block shown below, require a minimum of three views to describe their dimensions adequately. Objects with *offsets* or *projections* on several surfaces may require additional views for clarity.

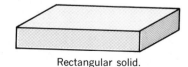

Rectangular solid.

The illustrations below show how the observer must look at each side of an object to obtain individual orthographic views. On each of the sides shown, the black dot farthest from the object represents the viewer's eyes. The black dot on the corresponding surface and connected to the first dot by a hidden line represents the viewer's center of vision. The color area on the pictorial drawing represents the only part seen in that particular view. The color shaded orthographic view—labeled the same as the pictorial drawing—shows the true shape of the individual side.

Notice that three surfaces are shown; the FRONT, TOP, and RIGHT SIDE. These three views are most

frequently shown on working drawings. However, as mentioned, other views may be needed for complete description of an object.

If your center of vision is not in the center of the side being viewed, you will not see an orthographic plane. The view observed may appear similar to the one shown below. NOTE: An orthographic view *cannot* show depth; everything *must* appear in a single flat plane.

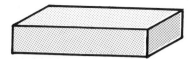

Individual faces of this rectangular solid do not appear in a single plane (wrong way of viewing for orthographic projection).

Workmen need to know where to look to find individual views of an object. Therefore views are usually arranged following a set pattern of placement.

A front view is usually the one that shows the most detail, and is the key to all other views. Also, it usually shows the largest horizontal dimension. For this reason a part may frequently be used as a front regardless of its actual position when constructed. This is especially true for small details on complicated surfaces. *Building elevations are usually labeled according to their actual position on the building.*

How Projection Is Done

For determining the proper relationship of views, imagine a rectangular block suspended in

the center of a glass box as shown below, outlines of the views have been projected onto the "glass." The next illustration shows the other surfaces and right side hinged into the same plane as the front view. See the first drawing on the next page. This rotating of the views into the same plane causes space between the views. The space is used for placing dimensions as discussed in Chapter 39.

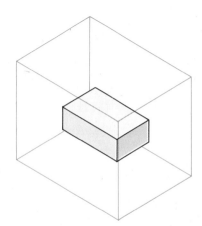

Object suspended inside glass box.

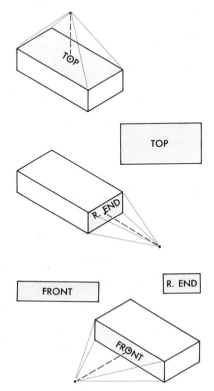

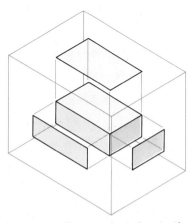

Surface outlines projected onto the "glass".

(The box on the preceding page opened flat.)

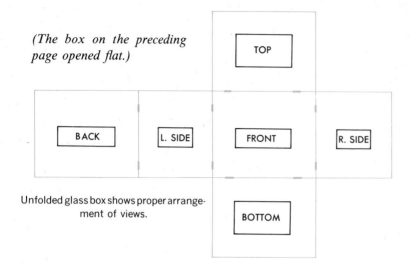

Unfolded glass box shows proper arrangement of views.

When additional views are necessary to describe the object they are arranged as shown in the following illustrations.

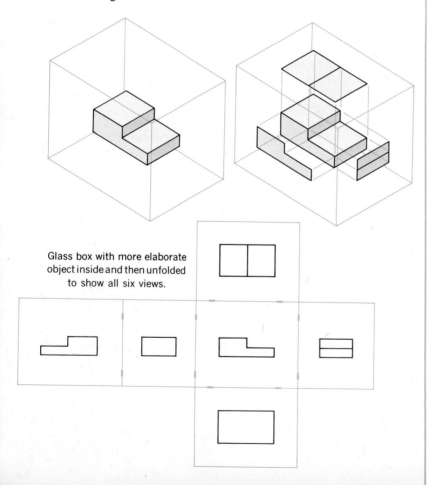

Glass box with more elaborate object inside and then unfolded to show all six views.

Very few designs can be represented by three flat surfaces. Most objects have holes, offsets, or other irregularities. Viewing and drawing irregular shaped objects in flat planes is considerably more difficult. The object shown in the following illustration has simple offsets. The accompanying drawing shows how the top and side are rotated into the same plane as the front view. See illustrations top of facing page.

Another method of showing relationship of views is found at the bottom of the page.

Three pictorial drawings of rectangular objects with simple offsets are shown. Three orthographic views accompany each pictorial. Surfaces on each pictorial and its orthographic views have corresponding letters. To check your knowledge, even if you have studied drawing, compare them until you understand why each individual view appears as it does. See Figs. 1, 2, and 3.

Foreshortened Lines and Surfaces

When an object has a slanting surface, as on the one shown, lines or surfaces on the orthographic views may appear shorter than their true dimensions. Lines or surfaces that are *viewed from an angle* and appear shorter are called *foreshortened*. The slanting surface "F" is indicated with a black tint on the pictorial drawing. The same surface is shown on the top and right side orthographic views, and is also indicated with black tint. This surface appears only slightly foreshortened on the top view, but has much foreshortening on the side view.

344

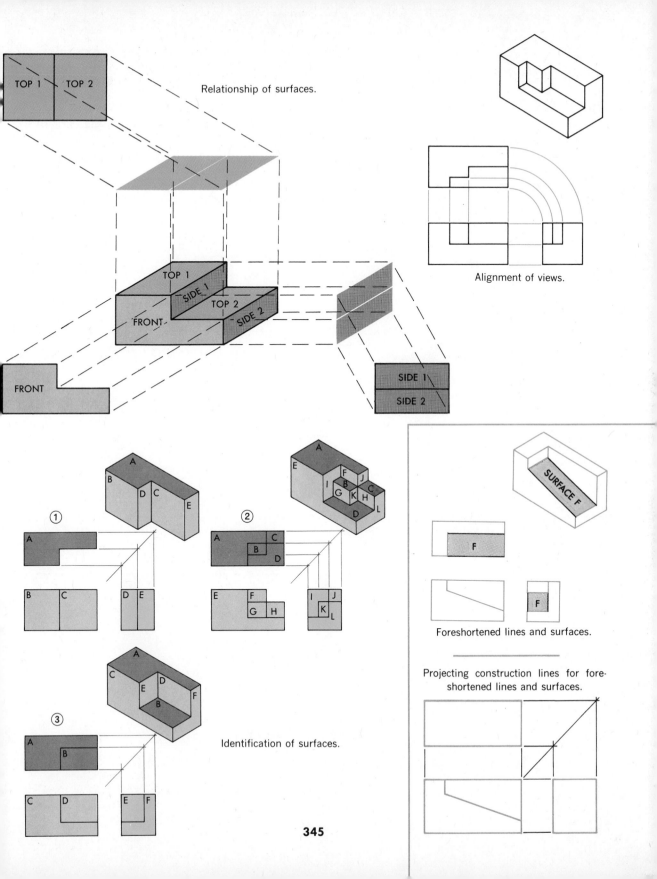

Relationship of surfaces.

Alignment of views.

① ② Identification of surfaces.

③

Foreshortened lines and surfaces.

Projecting construction lines for fore-shortened lines and surfaces.

The object lines shown in black on the orthographic views are also foreshortened and therefore do not indicate true length.

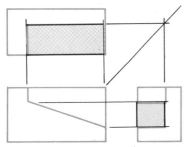

Projecting lines to side and top views.

After the angle of the foreshortened plane has been measured and established on the front view, one can project extension lines from both ends of the foreshortened line to the top and side views as shown.

Hidden Edge Lines

Offsets, surface irregularities, or holes may not be visible in a view because they are hidden by a solid portion of the object. Complete description usually requires these parts to be shown. Since they cannot be "seen" but still must be represented, they are included as hidden lines.

When a hidden line terminates either perpendicular or at an angle to an object line, the hidden line touches the object line.

When a hidden line is a continuation of an object line they do not touch.

When two hidden lines form a corner they should meet so the corner is closed.

When hidden lines cross, no consideration is given as to how they meet.

Some hidden lines may be omitted if this will add to drawing clarity.

Use of Hidden Lines Example

Study the illustration until you see why the hidden lines are located as they are, and observe that they are drawn to conform to the rules discussed earlier.

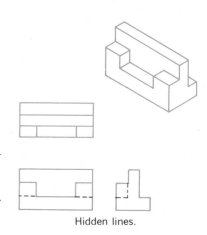

Hidden lines.

NOTE: The hidden lines on the front orthographic view to represent the offset at the back of the object. Also, the side view shows hidden lines to represent the outline of the lower portion of the front. Observe also that all offsets are visible as object lines on the top view, so no hidden lines are required.

Curved Parts

As mentioned earlier, individual views do not always show true shape. Curved edges cannot be shown on all three views. The illustration describes the true shape of the front view, but the top and right side views do not. The arc at the upper right corner cannot be described on either view. Observe the omission of lines on both views. Even though the surface changes direction, this cannot be shown because there is no edge where two planes meet.

The curved side is described on the front view. Without the front view the object could represent a rectangle.

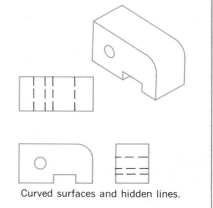

Curved surfaces and hidden lines.

Auxiliary Views

As said, since slanting surfaces and lines appear foreshortened on some orthographic views, it is not possible for every view to show true shape. To clarify the shape an auxiliary view may be used. This view is drawn as though the draftsman were looking directly *toward* and *in the same plane as* the slanting surface, permitting it to be drawn its true shape.

The auxiliary view may be included with other views or it may replace some views if it makes them unnecessary. The first two illustrations indicate that all surfaces viewed on the inclined plane are included on the auxiliary view. Yet they may or may not be. Surfaces in the horizontal and vertical plane may be omitted on the auxiliary view if they do not help clarify the shape. The third illustration shows the auxiliary view as it is frequently represented.

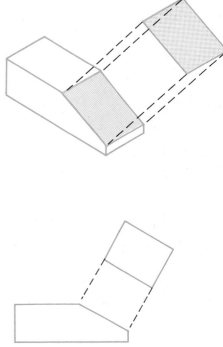

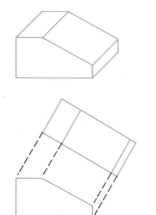

Auxiliary view showing adjoining surfaces.

Auxiliary view with adjoining surfaces omitted.

Orthographic Views and Building Plans

Even though building plans show little resemblance to the multi-view orthographic projections just discussed, they are based upon the same drawing system. Elevations, floor plans, and details do not look like orthographic drawings partly because building parts are so large, and all views cannot be placed on the same drawing sheet. Also, buildings are complex; *many* views of individual areas and parts are necessary, but *every* part cannot be drawn. The small scale floor plan and elevation drawings with lines showing projections illustrate that these are really orthographic drawings.

The drawing scale does not permit individual parts to be shown on floor plans and elevations because they are drawn to a scale of ⅛″ or ¼″ = 1′-0″. Therefore the drawing must be simplified by the use of conventional symbols representing materials and construction methods. NOTE: If a part needs to be drawn because a conventional symbol is not available, it is drawn as a *simplified version* of the actual object. Conventional symbols are shown in Chapter 38.

Intricate parts must be shown in exact detail, so they are drawn to a scale of ½″ to 3″ = 1′-0″, depending upon the complexity of the part. It is sometimes necessary to draw extremely complicated parts full size.

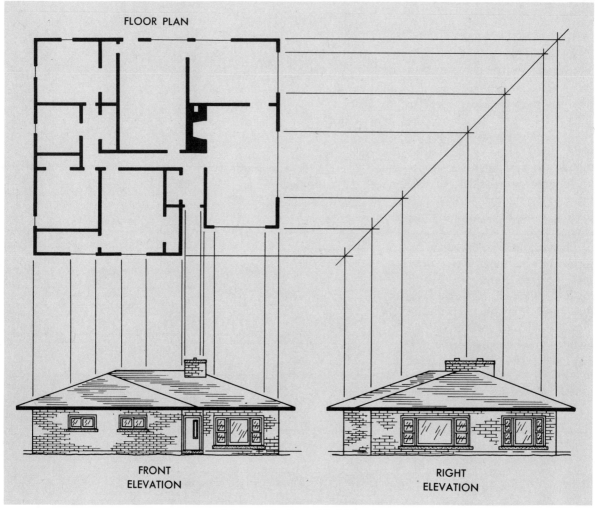

FLOOR PLAN

FRONT
ELEVATION

RIGHT
ELEVATION

Orthographic views of building plan.

Questions To Reinforce Knowledge

1. Why are pictorial drawings impractical as working drawings for building plans?

2. Describe the method of projection most frequently used for working drawings.

3. What is meant by the term orthographic projection?

4. What shape is easiest to describe using orthographic drawing? Why?

5. How many views are required to describe a cylinder? Why?

6. How many views are usually required to describe a rectangular solid?

7. What views are most frequently shown? Why?

8. What happens if you do not view directly toward the surface to be drawn?

9. Describe the arrangement of views. You may do a sketch.

10. How does one decide which view is to represent the front?

11. What is meant by the term foreshortened?

12. What are auxiliary views? Why are they used?

13. Is an auxiliary view included with other views or may it substitute for them? Explain.

14. Explain why and when hidden lines are used.

15. When a hidden line terminates perpendicularly or at an angle to an object line, does the hidden line touch the object line? Explain.

16. When a hidden line is a continuation of an object line, does it touch the object line? Why or why not?

17. When two hidden lines form a corner, how are they drawn?

18. When hidden lines cross, how do they intersect?

19. Are all hidden lines always included? Explain.

20. Explain why it is impossible to show curved edges on three views of a part.

Terms To Spell and Know

orthographic
projection
pictorial
three
  dimensional
single plane
sphere

cylinder
rectangular
  solid
center of vision
flat planes
foreshortened
auxiliary

35

Sections

In the preceding chapter, details concealed by solid parts were drawn as hidden lines. This method is satisfactory if the object is solid or its shape simple. However, if the object has a complicated shape or is composed of several individual parts the large number of hidden lines required for complete description becomes confusing.

Interior views, called sections, eliminate some hidden lines and give better shape description.

Imagine the concrete block in drawing A as being cut with a masonry saw at the line where the grey shade penetrates the block; *this is the cutting plane.*

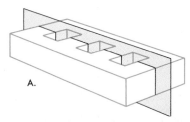

A.

Now remove the front half as at B so the interior is visible; *this is a pictorial section.* The ortho-

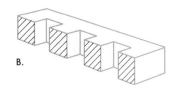

B.

graphic top view of drawing C has a *cutting plane line* with ar-

rowheads to indicate viewing direction of the *frontal section.*

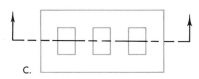

C.

Drawing D shows the completed frontal section. Observe that the crosshatching of the cut areas is drawn in black and all other lines of the front view are drawn in blue. This is done for emphasis only. On working drawings all lines are the same color.

D.

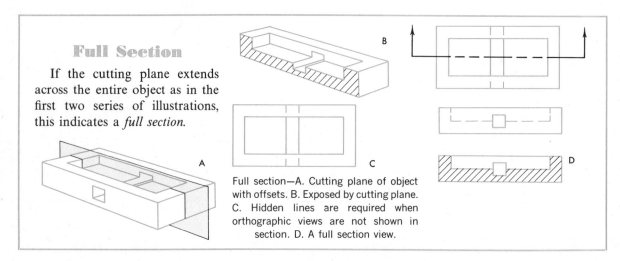

Full Section

If the cutting plane extends across the entire object as in the first two series of illustrations, this indicates a *full section.*

A

B

C

D

Full section—A. Cutting plane of object with offsets. B. Exposed by cutting plane. C. Hidden lines are required when orthographic views are not shown in section. D. A full section view.

Half Section

The following series of illustrations here shows an object with the cutting plane extending only halfway across. This is called a *half section*. Observe that the arrowhead or indicator is placed only on the end of the cutting plane line that shows viewing direction. The opposite end does not indicate viewing direction, so no indicator is required.

Symmetrical objects are often drawn as half sections so an outside and interior view can both be included on the same drawing. Hidden lines need not be included in the outside portion of the view, since the interior shape is shown on the sectioned area.

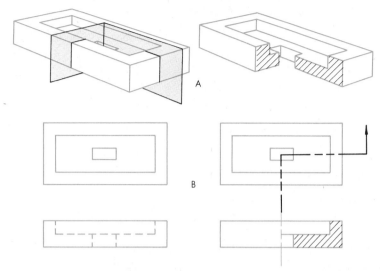

A. Half section pictorial. B. Comparison of orthographic drawing with hidden lines and a half section.

Offset Cutting Plane

If an object is symmetrical, the cutting plane is placed on the central axis. However, if details not in the center need to be shown, the cutting plane may be offset to include them. The two illustrations—one of a simple object and the other of a more intricate shape—do not have any portion of the cutting plane on the central axis.

Broken Section

If both exterior and interior details need to be shown, the cutting plane can be offset to include both. The first illustration on the next page shows a cutting plane passing through a square hole; then it is offset so it crosses outside the front view to show the horizontal hole; then it is offset again to pass through the center of the vertical circular hole.

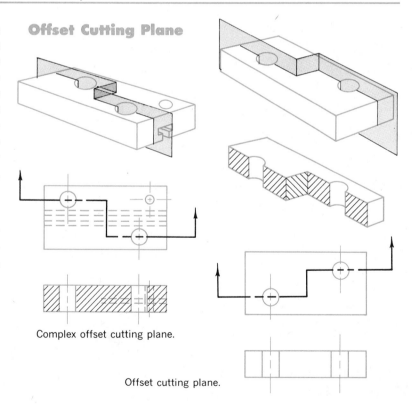

Complex offset cutting plane.

Offset cutting plane.

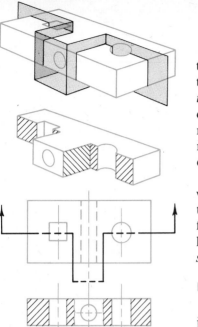

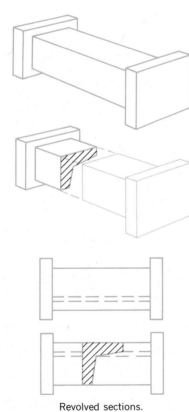

Offset cutting plane with broken section.

Revolved sections.

Observe that the direction of the cutting plane is indicated on the top orthographic view. On *this* top view the cutting plane is drawn as one continuous line. It might also be drawn as two separate offset sections which are not connected outside the view.

On the illustration observe where the cutting plane extends through the front surface of the front view. It is shown as a broken line; hence the name *broken section*.

Revolved Section

The illustration shows an object with three distinct units—two end pieces connected by a center unit. The shape of the center unit is concealed from view by the solid ends. Instead of either including hidden lines on an end view or drawing a separate complete section to describe the center part, its shape may be "revolved" and superimposed upon an existing view as shown. Revolved sections are valuable for showing profiles of round, elliptical, or unusual shaped parts. Since a view of this nature may appear to be something extending toward the viewer, the part should be labeled as a revolved section.

Opaque Section

Small, thin parts—such as aluminum or steel extrusions, flashing, waterproofing, or window glazing—may become lost in a maze of lines. To make them stand out or be more clearly visible they may be drawn as *opaque sections* similar to the one shown.

I beam revolved section.

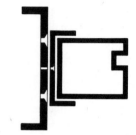

Opaque section of door detail.

Window detail shaded section.

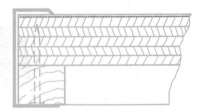

Counter top edge with symbols in section.

When adjacent parts are to be opaque they are separated slightly so the shape of each is defined.

Opaque sections may be used alone or in combination with conventional section drawings.

Shaded Section

Parts to be emphasized may be given a light shade by using very fine pencil lines about 1/32″ apart. Or an even tone can be obtained by darkening freehand with a blunt pencil or graphite dust. Care must be taken to avoid unintentional smudging of other areas. Samples should be made first to insure the effect desired.

Section Lines

Section lines are fine, unbroken, firm lines drawn at a 45° angle and spaced ¹⁄₁₆″ apart. They are not measured with a ruler. They are estimated by eye or may be matched to a line drawn on the triangle as described earlier. Examples of section lines are included on many drawings for this chapter.

When two or more parts are included on the same drawing, the section lines for each part should be placed at different angles or spacing.

Because of the large variety of materials such as wood, metal, concrete, stone, glass, and others that must be represented on architectural drawings, it is not desirable to have all materials shown as diagonal section lines. Each material has its own symbol, so it can be easily identified. Symbols for architectural materials are shown in Chapter 38.

Questions To Reinforce Knowledge

1. What is a section drawing?
2. What is a cutting plane?
3. What is a cutting plane line?
4. What is a pictorial section?
5. What is a full section?
6. What is a half section?
7. Why are arrowheads or indicators not always placed on both ends of all cutting plane lines?
8. Are hidden lines included on half section drawings? Explain.
9. What is an offset cutting plane?
10. What is a broken section?
11. What is a revolved section?
12. What is an opaque section? Why is it used?
13. Why are adjacent parts of opaque sections drawn as though the parts were separated by space?
14. Must opaque sections be used by themselves? Explain.
15. What is a shaded section? Describe two techniques for shading.
16. Describe how to draw typical section lines.
17. From your own reasoning, why are section lines on adjacent parts drawn in different directions or at different spacings? Do you think this means they can be drawn at angles other than 45°?
18. Why are typical diagonal section lines not used for all architectural drawings symbols?
19. What other methods of showing sectioned materials are used?

Terms To Spell and Know

cutting plane	half section	revolved section
pictorial section	interior view	opaque section
frontal section	offset cutting plane	shaded section
crosshatching	central axis	adjacent parts
full section	broken section	section lines

36

Pictorial Drawings

Since orthographic drawings do not show a complete picture on a single view, they are difficult for the layman without drafting knowledge to understand. Yet information from drawings must frequently be conveyed to people not familiar with drafting. Pictorial drawings serve this purpose very well. As stated in Chapter 34, all pictorial drawing methods are not perfect solutions to every drawing problem.

Four kinds of pictorial drawings are explained briefly. They are: (1) isometric, (2) oblique, (3) cabinet, and (4) perspective.

Isometric Drawing

Isometric drawings present a picture effect with a minimum of drafting time, effort, and experience. The view seems strange because visual distortion is caused by the receding lines. When viewing an actual object the eye sees parallel sides as though they converge in the distance. Parallel lines on isometric drawings are actually drawn parallel; so they appear to spread apart at the back of the object.

The illustration shows how a simple rectangular solid is drawn

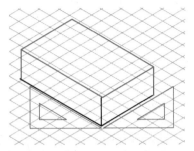

Isometric axes.

in isometric. Observe that both the front and end (in this drawing the right end) are drawn at a 30° angle from horizontal, and of course, all perpendicular lines are drawn vertical. Observe the three black lines of the drawing, two on the base and the vertical line at the closest corner. These lines form the *isometric axes*. Isometric lines are always parallel to one of these lines, receding at 30° from horizontal.

Note the blue isometric background lines on this and succeeding drawings. They are not part of the drawing but serve only as additional guide lines for the beginner. Paper with 30° lines, similar to this is sometimes used, especially when doing isometric sketches.

Non-isometric Lines

Lines of an object are not always at right angles to each other and cannot be drawn as isometric lines. Lines not parallel to the isometric axes are called *non-isometric lines*. To establish and draw these lines, first draw the object with construction lines as though it is a rectangular solid, similar to the ones shown in the two illustrations. Along the edges of this solid locate dimension points for the non-isometric lines. It is necessary to locate positions for each end of such lines. The illustrations show how they are located and drawn. Observe the construction lines, shown here as fine black lines parallel to the isometric axes that are superimposed on the rectangular shape previously drawn. The ends of the non-isometric lines are located at the points where the construction lines cross.

After all lines of the object have been established, the entire drawing is given the proper line weight. NOTE: If the construction lines were drawn as light "shadow" lines, they need not be removed from the finished drawing.

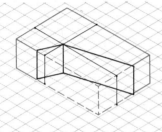

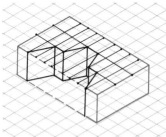

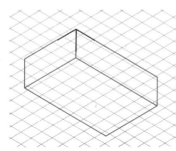

Isometric Arcs and Circles

Carefully study the isometric circle illustrations for an understanding of their construction. An isometric circle is really four connected arcs that form an ellipse. Each arc is based on the same principle even though the ones at 90° angles to each other do not match.

Directions for Drawing an Isometric Arc

1. Using construction lines, draw an isometric solid to the overall sizes of the desired object. NOTE: For irregular shaped objects, more than one isometric solid will be required.
2. Set the compass to the stated dimension of the arc.

   NOTE: Two construction lines form an angle in which the arc is to be drawn. If the arcs are to be constructed on the top view, both lines will be 30° isometrics. If the arc is on the front or side view, one of the lines will be in isometric and the other will be vertical.
3. Place the needle point of the compass at the vertex (corner) of the angle where the arc is desired.

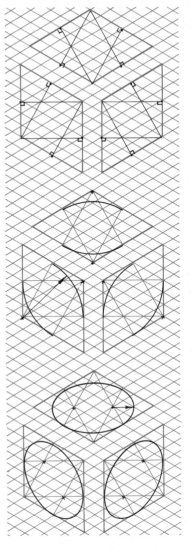

Isometric arc and circle construction.

Reversed Axes

Isometric drawings may show the front, end, and bottom (instead of the top) as shown. This is called a reversed axis isometric. The procedure is the same as for other isometric drawings except the isometric lines are drawn 30° *below* horizontal from the isometric axes.

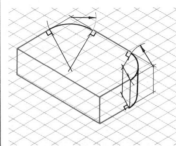

Isometric arc application.

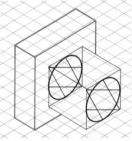

Isometric circle application.

355

4. Using construction lines, draw an arc so it crosses the two lines forming the angle. These are the points of tangency of the isometric arc to be constructed.

NOTE: Place your 30°-60° triangle so the hypotenuse is against the blade of your T square, and line it up with the object previously drawn. Observe how the T square forms right angles to the vertical lines of the object and the 60° angle of the triangle forms right angles with the isometric lines of the object.

5. Draw perpendiculars to both legs of the angle through the points of tangency previously established.

6. Place the needle point of the compass where the perpendiculars cross and adjust it so it touches one of the points of tangency.

7. Using an object line, draw an arc to connect the two points of tangency.

8. If other arcs are required, repeat the above steps; then draw object lines tangent to the arcs as required to complete the shape.

Curved Lines in Isometric

Curved lines in isometric are only a close approximation. Observe the curved line on the orthographic drawing. The black lines superimposed over the object divide it into many small squares. To duplicate this curved line in isometric you must draw the same grid lines on the isometric layout as shown in the second illustra-

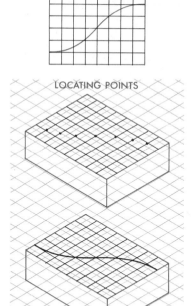

TOP VIEW

LOCATING POINTS

LINE CONNECTING THE POINTS

Plotting curved lines in isometric.

tion. Using dividers, calculate where the curved line crosses each of the parallel grid lines on the orthographic drawing and step these measurements onto the grid lines of the isometric drawing.

On the second illustration observe how the located points indicate where the line is to be. Using construction lines, sketch the proposed curved line so it passes through each of the points previously located. *Do not* draw the curved object line freehand. The results will be unsatisfactory. Find a segment of an irregular curve that is the same shape as the freehand line and draw the object line using the irregular curve as a guide. If the line cannot be drawn as a continuous one, exercise care to prevent the splice from showing.

The third illustration shows how the finished line should appear. It appears to be continuous with no splices showing.

OBLIQUE DRAWING

Oblique drawing is very similar to isometric, except that one of the axes is parallel to the plane of the paper as shown, instead of both receding at 30°. Oblique drawing has three axes; they are shown on the illustration as black lines. This drawing method permits everything in the frontal plane to be drawn its true shape.

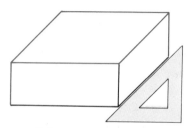

Oblique rectangular solid.

It is very good for objects that have considerable detail on one face and very little on the others. It is also very good for objects having little depth or thickness because they appear quite realistic. Drawings of objects with considerable depth appear too distorted for the oblique method.

The oblique illustrations here show the sides receding at a 45° angle, but they may recede at *any* desired angle.

Two important points to remember when drawing oblique pictorials are to: (1) Use the side that shows the most detail as the front. (2) Use the longest side as the front to minimize distortion.

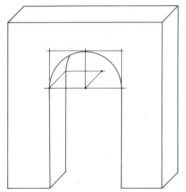

Curved surfaces of oblique drawing are most frequently shown on the frontal plane.

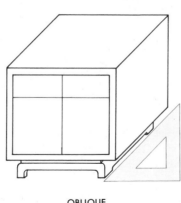

OBLIQUE

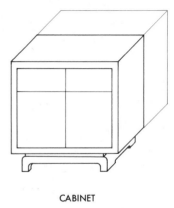

CABINET

Comparison of oblique and cabinet drawing.

CABINET DRAWING

Cabinet drawing is exactly the same as oblique except that lines receding toward the back are drawn only half their actual length. This helps to minimize distortion. The two illustrations of the small cabinet—the first done with an oblique and the second with a cabinet drawing—show how foreshortening the receding lines gives the latter drawing a more realistic appearance.

Perspective Drawing

Perspective drawing is a close approximation of what one sees when viewing an actual object. It is the most realistic of the pictorial drawing methods. However, drawing perspectives is more time consuming, so they are used only to show what a proposed object looks like when other details have been planned.

When viewing an actual object, all horizontal lines, or continuations of them, appear to converge in the distance and vanish toward the horizon. The size of the object determines how soon these lines appear to converge.

There are several different methods of drawing perspectives, but all are very similar. This discussion is limited to the common or office method because it is most frequently used, and other methods expand upon it. After you have mastered the office method, you may desire further study and experimentation with others.

The biggest problem of drawing perspective is capturing an illusion of depth and space on the flat plane of the paper. One must *always* think of the paper as having depth, or as space. The problem then is to project the different planes of the object into their proper relationship with this space. The following instructions tell how to accomplish this.

Two-point perspective rendering.

Items You Will Need

• A large drawing surface.
• All common drafting instruments.
• A long straightedge.
• Three thumbtacks to use as points for radiating lines. This will be discussed at length later.
• Tracing or drawing paper. Any drawing paper or illustration board may be used, but very satisfactory results may be obtained by drawing a preliminary perspective on tracing paper and then, when all lines are complete, graphite paper similar to carbon paper may be placed between the tracing paper and the final drawing sheet. If this paper is not readily available a soft pencil may be used to cover the back of the tracing with graphite. When transferring the perspective to the final sheet a stylus or hard pencil should be used.

NOTE: Do not use carbon paper when tracing the perspective. It smudges easily and the lines do not cover well when traced.

• A floor plan drawn to an appropriate scale. The plan should include locations of all windows and doors, an outline of the roof overhang, the location of all ridges and valleys, chimneys, and other items on the roof.

• An elevation at the same scale as the floor plan showing details and heights to be included on the perspective.

DIRECTIONS FOR TWO-POINT EXTERIOR PERSPECTIVE

Since there are a large number of new terms to become familiar with, perhaps the easiest way to master perspective is by drawing one under a carefully controlled learning experience. In order to check results for accuracy it will be essential for your sample drawing to conform exactly to the illustrated drawing upon which this problem is based. It is suggested that the floor plan and elevations shown in the accompanying illustration be used for the initial project. It will be necessary to use a drawing scale of ¼"=1'-0", and redraw the sample floor plan and elevations

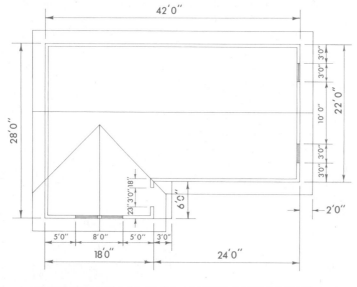

Building plan to be used while following directions for two-point perspective. The following series of illustrations is marked to indicate which steps of the directions the drawings accompany.

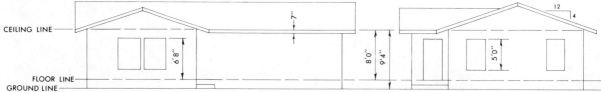

to the sizes given. The drawing should be laid out very accurately for best results. If this proposed large drawing size presents a problem, it is possible to cut all stated sizes in half and use a ⅛"=1'-0" scale instead. However, all directions refer to the larger drawing size. After you have mastered perspective techniques, drawings of your own choosing can be done.

Secure a large sheet of drawing paper, whose dimensions are 30" high and 42" wide, to the drawing board. Be sure the edges of the paper are parallel to the edges of the board. NOTE: To complete the drawing satisfactorily, it is essential that the directions be followed very carefully.

1. Picture Plane Line. Using a regular ruler, measure down from the top of the paper 10⅝" and make a small horizontal dash at this location. Through this dash draw a horizontal line all the way across the paper and label it *picture plane line*. Repeat the name of this line over and over because it is essential that it be remembered.

2. Horizontal Plane. The area above the picture plane line represents a horizontal plane; that is, a plane that is parallel to the ground. The floor plan, which is a horizontal section through a building, will be located in this space. It is to be used as an area from which lines for the perspective picture will be projected.

3. Vertical Plane. The area below the picture plane line represents a vertical plane, which must be considered as having depth. Imagine the drawing board surface as a window you are looking through, into space.

4. Positioning Floor Plan on Horizontal Plane. The illustrations accompanying these directions show the floor plan positioned at a 30°-60° angle to the picture plane line. However, any angle could be used. Because the angle helps determine what the finished perspective will look like, it must be selected with care. It is sometimes necessary to draw several partial perspectives to determine the best building viewing angle. The most frequently used

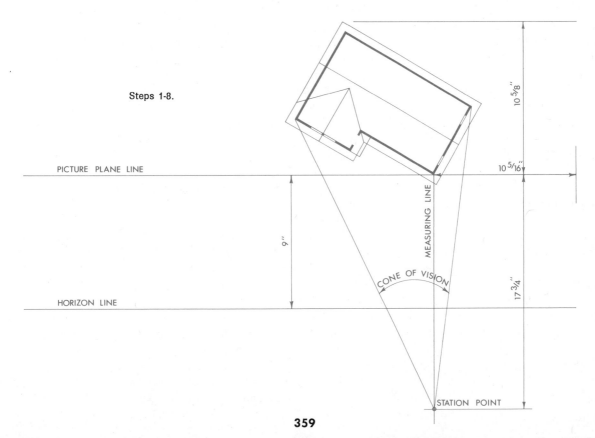

Steps 1-8.

angles are 30°-60°, and 45°, because triangles may then be used easily to set up the perspective.

The illustrations show a building corner touching the picture plane line. The building does not have to touch this line, but when it does, drawing procedure is simplified. Therefore the beginner will probably achieve best results with the floor plan placed in this position.

Perspectives can be drawn with the floor plan behind the picture plane line. This, however, makes the perspective picture small. The plan can also extend in front of, or below, the picture plane line, but this creates distortion.

Place the ruler on the picture plane line and measure 10⅝₁₆″ from the *right* edge of the paper, toward the *left*. Make a dot on the picture plane line at this location.

Place the lower right-hand floor plan corner on the picture plane line at the location previously marked with a dot. Using a 30°-60° triangle, adjust the plan location until it conforms to these angles. Be extremely accurate in the positioning. Tape the floor plan in place, but do not cover any of the building corners.

A portion of the overhang now covers the picture plane line. Redraw the picture plane line across this small portion of the floor plan.

5. Measuring Line. From the point where the building corner touches the picture plane line, *drop* a perpendicular line to the bottom of the paper. Near the bottom of the paper, label this line as the *measuring line*. Repeat

the name of this line until you remember it, because it is an essential term in perspective drawing.

Remember that the space below the picture plane line, where the perspective picture is to be drawn, may be compared to a window glass with distance behind it and that the building only touches this plane on the measuring line. Therefore this line is the only place where sizes may be measured to their true scale. *All* vertical measurements for the entire building *must* be made on this line, even though some will need to be projected back into space.

6. Station Point. The *station point* is the location from which the observer is viewing. In a lifelike situation, the closer an observer is to an object, the larger it appears. In perspective drawing the reverse is true. As the distance from the picture plane line to the station point increases, the picture becomes larger.

For best results the novice should place the station point *on* the measuring line.

For this drawing, begin at the picture plane line and measure down the measuring line 17¾″. Make a heavy dot at this location and label it *station point*. Repeat the name of this dot over and over. It is an important term in perspective technique.

7. Cone of Vision. The cone of vision is the scope of what an observer sees without moving his eyes from side to side. The cone begins at the station point and should not exceed approximately 30°. If a much greater angle is

used, the perspective will be somewhat distorted. Observe the cone of vision illustration in the text to be sure you understand what it is.

Now draw two lines connecting the station point to both the extreme left, and extreme right, building floor-plan corners (not overhang corners). Notice on the illustrations that these lines enclose the cone of vision.

8. Horizon. The *horizon* is a line in the distance where the earth seems to meet the sky. It can be located at any convenient drawing position below the picture plane line. On this drawing place the horizon 9″ below the picture plane line, and extend it from the left to the right edge of the paper. Label the line *horizon*. Repeat this name to yourself until you remember it. Later, when projecting new lines, it is very easy to confuse this line with the picture plane line.

9. Locating Vanishing Points. Beginning at the station point, draw a line parallel to the front of the floor plan and extend the line until it meets the picture plane line near the left edge of the paper. Again beginning at the station point, draw a line parallel to the side of the floor plan and extend it to the picture plane line. Mark two dots where these diagonal lines intersect the picture plane line. From these two dots draw two vertical lines down to the horizon. The vanishing points are located where these vertical lines cross the horizon. Make dots to locate the two vanishing points. Then draw a small freehand circle around them so they will be easy to locate. Label the left vanishing point VPL, and the right vanishing point VPR. Repeat these names until they are permanently in mind.

On some drawings, the lines from the station point and those lines parallel to building edges extend off the drawing board before they intersect with the picture plane line. In such cases it is necessary to reposition the floor plan, move the measuring line, and also relocate the station point.

The following can be used as a general guide for determining the placement of the floor plane on future drawings: (1) If it is to be positioned at a 45° angle to the picture plane line, the corner of the floor plan that touches the line should be centered on it. (2) When the corner is at a 30°-60° angle to the picture plane line, it should be located approximately one-third the board width from the edge closest to the 60° angle. Observe that the floor plan of the perspective layout illustration is positioned in this manner.

10. Preparing Permanent Points for Radiating Construction Lines. Thumbtacks may be placed upside down over the two previously drawn vanishing points and the station point, and taped in place to serve as permanent positions for these points. Because thumbtacks can scratch or puncture, they must be used with caution. Small bits of pencil eraser may be placed on the points for protection. Map tacks are also sometimes used. They are pressed into the drawing surface. However, such devices leave holes and permanently damage the board; so they are not recommended.

Whether one merely lines up with the points previously marked on the paper or uses some device as a marking aid, these points are very important because they are used for radiating a large number of construction lines.

11. Eye Level. The eye-level illustration in this unit shows three rectangular solids: one above, one below, and one at eye level.

The relationship of eye level to ground determines whether one

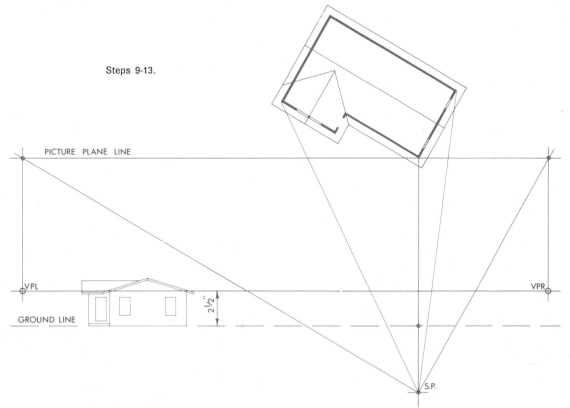

Steps 9-13.

PICTURE PLANE LINE

VPL

VPR

GROUND LINE

2½"

S.P.

looks up, down, or straight at the perspective picture. The angle from which the object is to be viewed is a matter of personal choice, to be determined by the way you desire the completed picture to appear.

Assume that, when standing, the average person's eye level is 5'-6" above the ground. Therefore if the perspective is to be exactly at eye level, the ground line would be placed 5'-6" below the horizon, on the measuring line. When the drawing is complete, the viewer would be looking directly at the building.

On this sample drawing, however, a slightly different measurement is to be used. With an ordinary ruler, measure 2½" down from the horizon anywhere along its length. Then draw a light, broken line all the way across the paper. This is the ground line.

The ground line is now 10'-0" below the horizon, using the ¼"=1'-0" scale used for drawing the original floor plan and elevations. Label this *ground line,* near the left edge of the paper.

12. Positioning an Elevation. Using the right side elevation previously drawn, position it so that the bottom of the drawing, which also represents the ground, is on the ground line of the partial perspective. Move the elevation horizontally until it is approximately 3" to the right of the left vanishing point. Now carefully tape the elevation to the drawing surface, again being certain that no building corners are covered by tape.

13. Place a small dot on the drawing paper where the ground line intersects the measuring line. This intersection is the location where the building perspective is begun.

NOTE: All measurements, from now until the drawing is completed, will be drawn at the original building plans scale of ¼"= 1'-0", unless otherwise specified.

This perspective will be accomplished in three stages:

- The basic building outlines will be drawn.
- The roof and its overhang will be laid out.
- To complete the picture, details, such as window openings, doorways, and steps will be added.

Compare your drawing with the one in the text before proceeding. Be sure that everything drawn up to this time is correct.

Beginning the Building Outlines

14. Using a straightedge, position it on the drawing paper so that its edge passes through the measuring line at the ground line, and also through the right vanishing point. Beginning at the measuring line and drawing from left to right, draw a very light construction line to the right vanishing point.

15. Now position the straightedge so that it passes through the left vanishing point, and also through the intersection of the ground line and measuring line. Drawing from right to left (which is backwards), make a light construction line approximately the same length as the front wall of the floor plan (the wall that touches the picture plane line).

16. The location where the building corner touches the ground at the measuring line has now been established. Make a

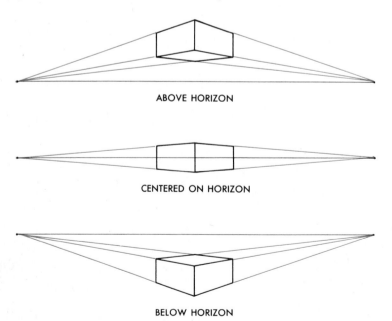

ABOVE HORIZON

CENTERED ON HORIZON

BELOW HORIZON

The relationship of the object to the horizon is a matter of personal choice.

dot to indicate where the two lines, vanishing to the right and to the left, intersect the horizon line. These two vanishing lines are where the building front and right side touch the ground. Erase the left half of the original ground line previously drawn, for it is no longer needed. The position from which the lines vanish at the bottom of the building will now be referred to as the ground, since this is where the building touches the ground in the drawing.

17. Position the straightedge to pass through the station point and also to touch the right rear floor plan building corner. If the straightedge was positioned correctly, it will be on the right cone of vision line previously drawn.

Make a dot on the paper where this cone of vision line intersects the picture plane line. Using the point just located, drop a light perpendicular construction line to the ground at the bottom of the building.

18. Place the point of a pencil on the building corner where the floor plan touches the picture plane line. Lift the pencil slightly, following the front wall until the corner by the doorway is reached. Make a dot to emphasize this corner. Position the straightedge so that it passes through this dot and also through the station point. Beginning at this building corner by the doorway, draw an inclined construction line to the picture plane line.

19. From the intersection of the inclined construction line and the picture plane line, drop a light perpendicular to the ground. Make a small dot where this perpendicular touches the ground.

20. Position the straightedge so that it touches both the dot just drawn, and the right vanishing point. Beginning at the dot and drawing to the left, make another construction line slightly longer than the wall containing the door on the floor plan.

21. Align the straightedge so that it passes through the front corner by the door on the floor plan, and through the station point. Drop an inclined construction line to the picture plane line, and make a dot where the two

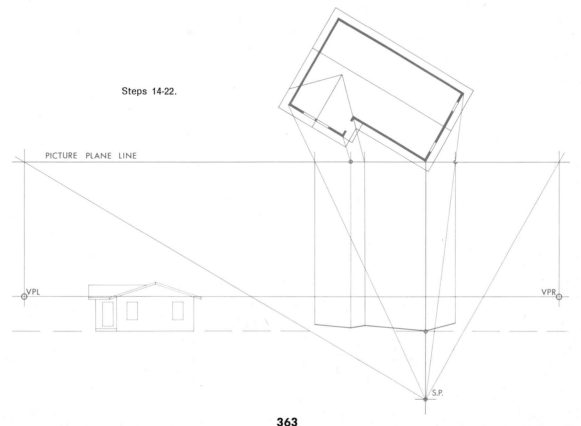

Steps 14-22.

PICTURE PLANE LINE

VPL

VPR

S.P.

lines intersect. From this intersection drop a perpendicular to the line that represents the wall containing the door. This forms a building corner. From this corner project left toward the vanishing point with another construction line.

22. Position the straightedge so that it passes through the left, front corner of the floor plan and the station point. The straightedge should now be aligned with the left cone of vision line. Mark the point where this line intersects the picture plane line and drop a perpendicular to represent the location of the left building corner.

Drawing Building Ceiling Lines

23. Use the ¼″ scale and the right side elevation previously

drawn, now taped to the left of the drawing paper. Measure the distance from the ground line to the underside of the overhang where it touches the right building wall. This distance should measure 9′-4″. From the lower building corner on the measuring line in the perspective, measure this 9′-4″ and make a dot at this height.

24. Position the straightedge to pass through the dot just drawn, and through the right vanishing point. Make another dot where the straightedge crosses the right building wall. Draw a light construction line to connect the dot on the measuring line with the dot on the right wall (back corner of the building).

NOTE: When any remaining lines to be drawn are to be projected toward the vanishing points, the lines need to be extended only to the corner where they terminate on the building, or slightly beyond an anticipated edge.

25. Reposition the straightedge so that it passes through the left vanishing point, and also through the 9′-4″ measurement on the measuring line. Drawing from right to left, project a construction line from the measuring line to the wall by the doorway.

26. Position the straightedge to cross the doorway corner, and also the right vanishing point. Now draw a construction line to

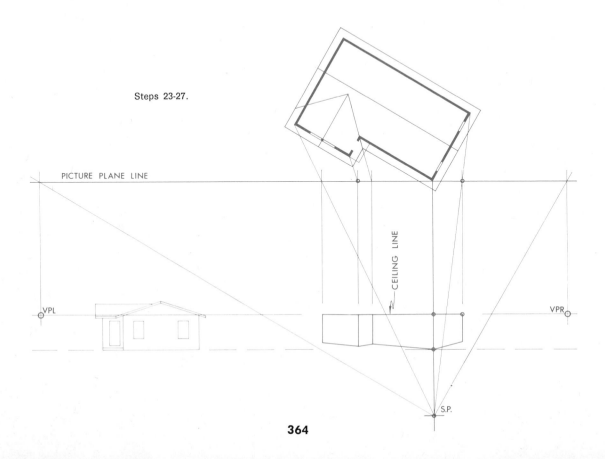

Steps 23-27.

PICTURE PLANE LINE

CEILING LINE

VPL

VPR

S.P.

represent the wall above the doorway.

27. Place the straightedge at the upper right-hand corner of the wall offset and also on the left vanishing point. Then draw a line connecting the right-hand to the left-hand corner.

If all lines have been drawn correctly, the ceiling line drawn on the perspective is complete. Compare your ceiling line just drawn with the illustration in the text, to check for accuracy.

Drawing a Roof Outline

28. On the right side elevation, place a parallel rule, T-square, or drafting machine at the underside of the roof overhang peak. Make a dot on the measuring line at this same height. Position the straight-

edge so that it passes through this dot on the measuring line, and also through the right vanishing point. Draw a line from the dot on the measuring line to the right-hand wall.

29. Position a straightedge to pass through both the station point and the location on the floor plan where the roof ridge crosses the right-side wall. NOTE: This is against the outside wall and not against the overhang. Draw a line from the intersection of the wall and roof ridge to the picture plane line. Drop a perpendicular from this intersection to the uppermost line on the perspective that vanishes to the right (the line drawn in the preceding step). Mark this location with a dot.

30. Place the straightedge or triangle so that it passes through the dot just drawn, and also through the intersection of the ceiling line and measuring line. Draw a construction line between these two points. Repeat this step by placing the straightedge on both the dot at the roof peak, and on the ceiling line at the right building corner. Draw a line between these two dots.

31. Darken the following:

- The wall on the front picture plane line from the ceiling line to the ground.

- The rear wall line from the ceiling line to the ground.

- The building ground line

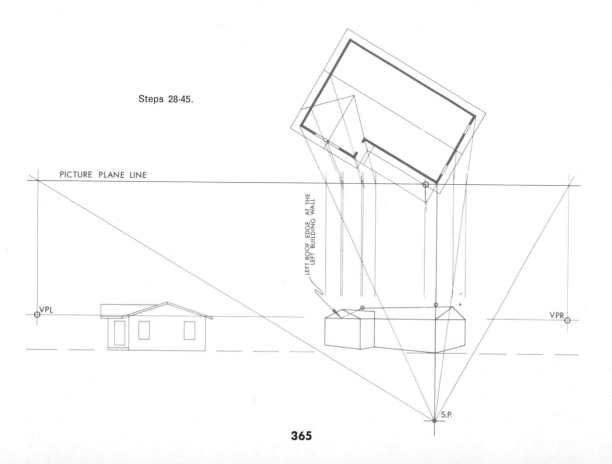

Steps 28-45.

PICTURE PLANE LINE

LEFT ROOF EDGE AT THE
LEFT BUILDING WALL

VPL

VPR

S.P.

from the measuring line to the rear wall.

- The two inclined lines representing the roof. If all procedures were followed correctly, an outline for the right end of the building is now complete.

Projecting the Front Gable Wall Outline

32. Place a straightedge on the floor plan from front to back, so that its edge is aligned with the right building wall. If aligned properly, it should pass through the point at which the building wall intersects the picture plane line and measuring line. Extend this outside, end-wall line so that it protrudes into the vertical plane approximately the length of the front building offset containing the doorway. This is a distance of about 2″ on an ordinary ruler. On the floor plan, align the straightedge with the front wall containing the windows, and project the wall line until it intersects the right-side wall projection, previously drawn.

33. Align the straightedge with the point where the two wall projections intersect, and with the station point. Now draw a line from the intersection to the picture plane line. Draw a circle around this picture plane intersection, because this point will be used for dropping the next vertical line. Now, using the front elevation, measure the distance from the ground line to the underside of the roof overhang at the peak. This distance should measure 12′-5″. Transfer this height di-

mension to the perspective measuring line.

34. Place the straightedge through the point just located and also through the right vanishing point. Using the intersection where the straightedge crosses the front roof slope, draw a light construction line from right to left, to a point approximately 1″ left of the measuring line. From the point on the picture plane line with the small circle drawn around it, drop a perpendicular until it crosses the last vanishing line drawn. Mark this location with a dot. Place the straightedge on the paper through this dot and through the left vanishing point. Project a line, from the dot toward the left, past the vertical wall furthest to the left.

35. Position the straightedge on the floor plan, at the intersection of the front wall containing the windows and roof ridge line of the front building offset, and also on the station point. Then drop a construction line to the picture plane line. From this picture-plane line intersection, drop a perpendicular to the last line drawn (that vanished to the left), and mark their intersection with a dot.

Using this dot, and the ceiling line at both building offset corners, draw two inclined lines to complete the front gable. Now darken the outlines to enclose this front gable section. NOTE: If the building perspective were to immediately include an overhang, it would not be necessary to complete the steps for the roof outline at this time. These outlines are

placed on this perspective only to enclose the picture and show what the basic structure would look like.

36. Hold the straightedge so it passes through the left vanishing point, and also through and along the ground line where it meets the building corner at the measuring line. Darken the ground line from the measuring line to the corner by the doorway.

37. Now position the straightedge so it passes through the right vanishing point and along the ground line below the doorway, and darken this short ground line. To darken the two ceiling lines, repeat the procedures for the two steps just completed.

38. Place the straightedge on the right roof peak, and also on the left vanishing point. Draw a vanishing line from the peak to a location beyond the left building wall. From the location on the floor plan where the longest roof ridge crosses the left-hand wall, place the straightedge so it passes through this location and the station point. Working along the straightedge, make a small dash where it crosses the picture plane line. (It is only coincidence that this dash falls near a line drawn earlier.) From the dash on the picture plane line, drop a perpendicular line until it passes the vanishing roof-ridge previously drawn. Make a dot at this location.

39. Position the straightedge on the floor plan so it follows the front wall that touches the picture plane line. Observe that the straightedge also touches the location where the left roof valley crosses the left outside wall. Using this intersection on the left wall, align the straightedge through it and also through the station point. Make a small dash on the picture plane line where the straightedge crosses it. From this intersection, drop a perpendicular line down to the perspective picture to touch the ceiling line. On this perspective, the ceiling line is almost straight, because it is close to the horizon. On other drawings, however, the ceiling line would not necessarily appear almost straight. In such cases, the ceiling line that touches the measuring line would need to be projected left, to connect with the wall at the valley line.

40. The straightedge should be held so it passes through the left vanishing point, and also through the ceiling line at the building measuring line. Make a dot where the straightedge crosses the last perpendicular line drawn. This dot represents the bottom of the left-hand roof slope. Position the straightedge on the perspective picture so it passes through this dot, and also through the point of intersection of the roof line with the line previously dropped down for the roof ridge at the left building edge. Draw a construction line connecting the two locations just determined. Label this line *left roof edge at the left building wall.*

41. Align the straightedge so it passes through the left-hand roof peak on the perspective, and through the right vanishing point. Draw a construction line from the roof peak toward the right, until it crosses the vertical line connected to the back corner of the roof ridge at the building offset on the floor plan. Make a dot to mark this intersection. Place the straightedge on the perspective picture, so it passes through this dotted intersection, and also through the intersection of the front-wall ceiling line and the doorway wall ceiling line. Then darken a line between these two intersections.

42. Position the straightedge so it passes through the left-hand roof peak, and also through the right vanishing point. This is aligned with the roof ridge line previously drawn. Now, darken this line to form a roof ridge.

43. Relocate the straightedge along the line previously labeled: *left roof edge at the left building wall.* Darken this line, from the roof ridge of the front building offset, to the roof line of the longest roof ridge.

44. Now align the straightedge through both the left vanishing point and the right roof peak and darken this roof line.

45. Draw a perpendicular for the inside building corner by the doorway. If the directions have been followed exactly, the building outline is now completed.

The Roof Overhang

46. The original building outline was previously enclosed with dark lines. It is suggested that you use a soft eraser to lightly erase the roof outline and the upper ¼" of all walls so that they will not interfere with subsequent lines to be drawn. These lines should not be completely erased, only lightened because it will be necessary later to make some projections associated with these former lines. (See illustration on next page).

47. On the floor plan, place a straightedge along the right end wall, and lightly extend the wall line until it touches the rear overhang.

48. Using the right side elevation, which is attached to the drawing paper, align the instrument used for drawing parallel lines so it touches the top of the roof peak. Place a dot on the measuring line the same height as the roof peak. Using the ¼" scale, and measuring on the measuring line, this dot is approximately 7" above the dot formerly made to locate the original roof height. Position the straightedge through this upper dot, and also through the right vanishing point. Make a new dot on the perspective directly above the original roof peak. This dot will be on a perpendicular previously drawn.

49. Slide the parallel instrument down until it crosses the roof directly above the side walls in the elevation. Mark this location on the measuring line. This dot should also be 7" above the corner formed by the original ceiling line and roof. Position the straightedge through this dot, and also through the right vanishing point, and place another dot directly above the rear wall.

50. Place the straightedge on the front sloping roof of the right building end of the perspective, and extend the existing line approximately 1" downward and to the left. This projection is in the space below the ceiling line, and to the left of the measuring line. Now slide the straightedge upward so it is aligned with the dot on the measuring line that is 7″ above the ceiling line, and also with the dot at the roof ridge. Project a construction line through these two dots, extending to the left past the ceiling line approximately 1″ (the same distance as the inclined line previously drawn).

51. Align a straightedge with the rear roof line on the perspective, and extend the line into space approximately 1″. (This is to the right of the existing drawing.) Realign the straightedge so it is touching both the dot above the right wall, and the dot above

the original roof peak. From this new, upper, roof peak extend a construction line into the space to the right of the rear wall.

52. Align the straightedge so it passes through the station point and also through the floor plan intersection of the front roof overhang and the right side wall extension. Make a small dash where the straightedge intersects the picture plane line. From this dash on the picture plane line, drop a perpendicular until it crosses the roof overhang and is even with the right building wall. Draw a vertical construction line to connect the *top* sloping roof line to the *lower* sloping roof line.

53. Position the straightedge through the station point, and

also through the intersection on the floor plan where the rear sidewall extension crosses the rear overhang. Make a small dash where the straightedge crosses the picture plane line. From this dash, drop a perpendicular and darken the distance between the *upper* sloping roof line and the *lower* sloping roof line at the back of the building perspective. This line, along with the one that was drawn at the front of the building, represent the fascia location, which is exactly even with the building end. If these two short, vertical lines were drawn with accuracy, a straightedge placed at the top of the short vertical line to the left and through the right vanishing point will also pass through

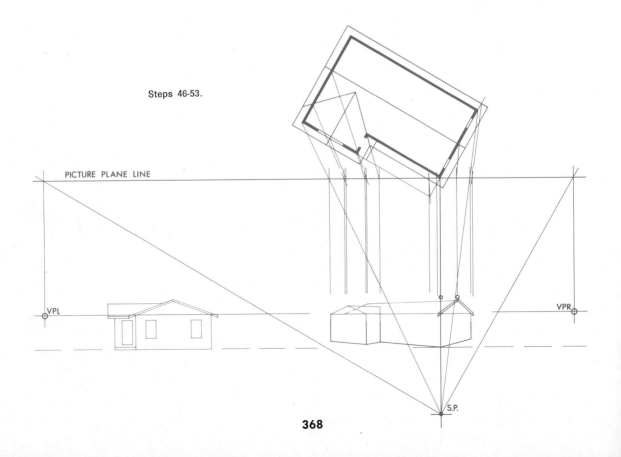

Steps 46-53.

PICTURE PLANE LINE

VPL

VPR

S.P.

the top of the vertical line to the right. This happens because both the front and rear overhangs are at the same roof slope, equidistant from the ground. The same is true for the two lower ends of the short vertical lines.

54. Align the straightedge through the left vanishing point and through the top of the short vertical line closest to the measuring line. Beginning about 1" on a regular ruler to the right of the measuring line, project a vanishing line to the left until it extends about ½" past the building corner by the doorway.

Realign the straightedge so it passes through the left vanishing point, and also through the bottom of the short vertical line.

Draw another line approximately the same length as the vanishing line just drawn.

Relocate the straightedge through the left vanishing point, and through the top of the short line on the right representing the back roof edge. Starting at the end of the sloping roof line, project to the right about 1" with a light construction line.

Realign the straightedge through the left vanishing point and through the lower end of the short vertical line. Begin at the rear building wall on the perspective, and draw a construction line to the right, approximately the same length as the one previously drawn.

55. Align the straightedge with

the station point and the roof overhang corner that is on the floor plan and below the picture plane line. Then make a small dash where the straightedge crosses the picture plane line. From this dash, drop a perpendicular to the two lines that vanished left. Darken the corner for the roof overhang.

56. Now, with the straightedge through both the station point and the rear overhang corner on the floor plan, make a dash where the straightedge crosses the picture plane line. In the space to the right of the rear wall, two short vanishing lines were previously drawn toward the right vanishing point. Drop a perpendicular from the last dash placed on the picture

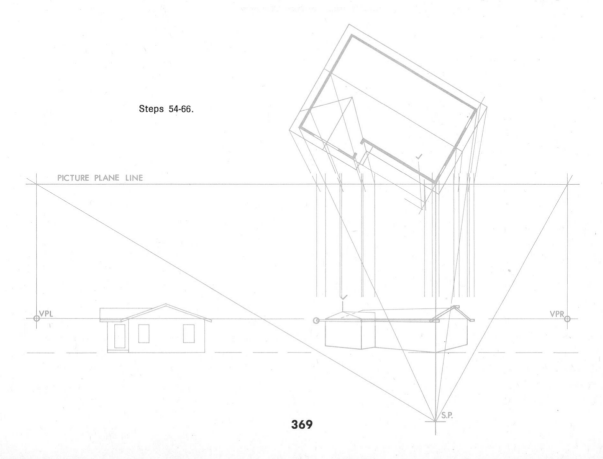

Steps 54-66.

PICTURE PLANE LINE

VPL

VPR

S.P.

plane line, and darken the distance between the upper and lower lines.

57. Hold the straightedge so it passes through the left vanishing point, and through the uppermost roof peak. Draw a construction line from the peak to a point approximately 1″ to the left of the existing left roof end. Locate the straightedge so it passes through both the station point and the roof ridge at the left building overhang of the floor plan. Place a dash on the picture plane line where the straightedge crosses it. From this dash, drop a perpendicular to the new roof line just drawn, and make a dot where the two lines intersect. Draw a small, light circle around this dot so that it can be easily located later.

58. Lay the straightedge on the drawing through the left vanishing point, and also through the upper edge of the front fascia line. Here, the fascia line is near the ceiling line: this is only coincidence and one should not assume that the ceiling line always aligns with the upper fascia line. Observe also that the straightedge passes below the dot drawn earlier to represent the lower edge of the left end roof. From below the dot representing this lower corner, project a construction line to the left, until it almost touches the sloping line for the front gable.

Now, on the floor plan, project the left roof-valley line until it crosses the roof-overhang line. Using this intersection, and the station point, align the straightedge through these two points,

making a small dash where the straightedge crosses the picture plane line.

From this picture plane intersection, drop a perpendicular until it crosses the left vanishing line just drawn. Make a dot at the new intersection. Align the straightedge through this intersection and the upper dot with the small circle around it; then draw a light construction line to connect the two. This is the roof edge at the left overhang.

59. Position the straightedge so it passes through the station point, and through the overhang corner that is closest to the doorway (on the floor plan), near the front wall that touches the picture plane line. Observe that this corner is in line with the right roof valley, and with a construction line previously dropped to the picture plane line. A perpendicular was later drawn to the building corner on the perspective picture. This is another coincidence due to the floor plan position on the drawing sheet: these corners are not always aligned in this manner.

Using the perpendicular just referred to, darken a short vertical line across the corner to represent the fascia end.

60. Hold the straightedge so it passes through the right vanishing point, and through the upper fascia corner just drawn. Project a line from the corner toward the left, until it extends past the corner building wall approximately ½″. Repeat this process for the lower fascia edge that is above the doorway.

Now position the straightedge so it passes through the station point, and through the outside overhang corner at the building offset on the floor plan. (The straightedge is again by coincidence placed on the line representing the offset corner.) Drop a perpendicular, and darken the left fascia end over the doorway.

61. Align the straightedge through the left vanishing point, and also through the upper edge of the just drawn dark, vertical line, representing the upper fascia corner. Beginning ½″ left of the left building wall, project a construction line to the left approximately ¾″ long. Realign the straightedge through the left vanishing point, and through the lower fascia corner, and project another line similar to the vanishing line previously drawn.

62. Position the straightedge through the station point, and through the left, front overhang corner on the floor plan. Mark a dash where the straightedge crosses the picture plane line. From this dash, drop a perpendicular and darken the distance between the two vanishing lines most recently drawn. This short, dark, vertical line represents the left overhang corner, in space.

63. A roof peak for the left building offset was previously drawn on the perspective. From this peak on the front building wall, extend a vertical construction line upward into space (on the drawing) approximately ½″. Place a small check at the top of this vertical line so it will be easy to identify later.

64. Lay your straightedge on the floor plan so it is on the overhang line in front of the front windows, and make a dash on the line that was projected forward on the floor plan from the right end wall. Observe that this intersection is in the space below the picture plane line. Place a straightedge through this intersection, and through the station point. Make a dash where the straightedge crosses the picture plane line. Place a small check mark above this dash, so it will be easy to locate for future reference.

65. Align the straightedge with the left vanishing point, and with the *original* long roof line. (This is the original roof that was darkened, and then lightly erased before the overhang was begun.) Now extend this line approximately 1″ to the right of the right roof peak at the right building end wall. Realign the straightedge through both the left vanishing point and the upper roof peak, and extend this line approximately 1″ to the right.

66. Position the straightedge on the floor plan to pass through the intersection of the long roof ridge at the right overhang, and through the station point. Mark a dash on the picture plane line where the straightedge crosses it, and drop a perpendicular to the two extensions of the roof ridges on the perspective. Darken the space between these two lines.

67. There are now three vertical dashes to the right of the original roof outline. With the straightedge passing through the upper end of the line immediately to the right of the measuring line, and through the upper line to the right of the original roof peak, darken the distance between these two short, vertical lines. Move the straightedge to the lower end of these two lines, and draw a new, inclined dark line to connect the lower corners.

68. Position the straightedge so that it is at the top of the short, vertical line at the roof overhang peak, and the top of the short vertical line farthest to the right. Now darken the distance between the two lines. Move the straightedge to the bottom of the two

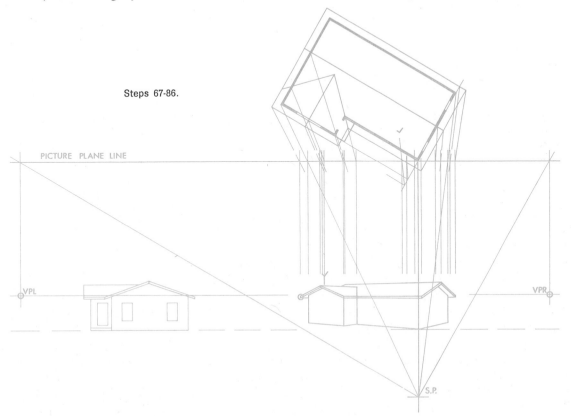

Steps 67-86.

PICTURE PLANE LINE

VPL

VPR

S.P.

short, vertical lines, and draw the bottom edge of the roof overhang.

69. Use the parallel drawing instrument on the right side elevation and align it with the top of the horizontal roof line of the offset. Make a dot on the measuring line where the straightedge crosses it. Since the fascia width is 7″, measure down this 7″-distance, and make another dot on the measuring line. Although the fascia does not show on the side elevation at this peak, it does show on the front elevation.

70. Position the straightedge through the right vanishing point, and through the upper dot just drawn. Beginning where the straightedge crosses the front roof edge at the fascia, draw a line to the left until it is approximately 1″ left of the measuring line. Again place the straightedge on the right vanishing point, and through the lower dot that was previously drawn. From the intersection of the straightedge with the lower, front fascia line, project approximately 1″ to the left of the measuring line.

71. Earlier, a small check mark was placed above a dash that crossed the picture plane line. This dash represents the overhang corner in space, and is in the same plane as the right building end. From the check mark, drop a perpendicular to the perspective, and connect the two vanishing lines last drawn.

72. Position the straightedge so it passes through the left vanishing point, and through the top of the short, vertical line last

drawn. A small check mark was earlier placed on the vertical line at the wall offset building peak. Beginning about ⅛″ to the left of the vertical line with the check, project a construction line to the left about ⅝″.

73. Reposition the straightedge so it passes through the left vanishing point, and also through the lower edge of the short vertical line last drawn (approximately 1″ to the left of the measuring line on the perspective). Again beginning about ⅛″ to the left of the vertical line with the check, project to the left approximately ⅝″.

74. Position the straightedge so it passes through the roof ridge of the front building offset, on the floor plan, at its intersection with the front roof overhang line, and also through the station point. Make a small dash on the picture plane line, and drop a perpendicular to connect the two vanishing lines just drawn. Darken this short, vertical line that represents the upper building overhang peak at the fascia edge.

75. Now position the straightedge so it passes through the top of the line just drawn and the short, vertical line to the left of the left building wall. Darken the distance between them. Move the straightedge to the bottom of the two short vertical lines, and again darken between them.

76. Place the straightedge through the upper corner of the highest vertical line, and the vertical line representing the front overhang corner by the doorway. Connect between them with a

dark line. Reposition the straightedge through the lower ends of these two vertical lines, and darken the lower edge of the fascia.

77. Position the straightedge through the new roof peak of the building offset, and through the right vanishing point. Beginning at this roof peak, project a 3″ construction line to the right.

78. Position the straightedge through the intersection of the two valleys and roof ridge on the floor plan, and through the station point. (Once again, the straightedge is aligned with a line previously drawn, an event which would not likely occur in other drawings.) Where the straightedge crosses the picture plane line, drop a perpendicular until it crosses the last drawn roof ridge on the perspective, and make a dot at this location.

79. Align the straightedge through the dot just drawn, and through the fascia intersection of the front, and side overhang above the doorway. This is a valley line. It should be drawn as a dark line.

80. Draw a dark line following along the roof ridge of the front building offset.

81. A small circle was formerly drawn around a dot at the left roof-ridge end. Position your straightedge through this dot, and also through the right-end building peak. Draw a dark line connecting these two points, to complete the final roof ridge.

82. Beginning at the small dot with the circle around it, align the straightedge with the left roof overhang. Most of this line is now covered by building, but a small portion next to the left roof edge remains. It should be darkened in.

83. Position the straightedge so it passes through the right vanishing point, and also through the left lower corner of the front fascia at the building offset. Working from left to right, darken a line to connect to the left building edge.

84. Position the straightedge through the left vanishing point, and through the lower fascia corner to the right of the building end. (This is the line farthest to the right that has been drawn.) Now draw a line connecting to the right, rear building corner.

85. Vanish to the right vanish-ing point, and darken the two fascia lines above the doorway wall. Now align the straightedge through the left vanishing point, and darken the two fascia lines that are parallel to the front wall without windows. Position the straightedge through the right vanishing point, and through the bottom of the fascia beyond the left wall, and darken from the bottom of the short dark vertical line, back to the wall.

86. The original building out-lines were darkened during the early part of this assignment, and then subsequently lightened with an eraser. The upper portion of wall lines, and the intersections of soffits with building walls, are still probably partially visible through the erasures. These lines should be redarkened to complete this stage of the perspective drawing.

Window and Door Outlines

87. Before you begin to draw the window and door outlines, erase all construction lines pre-viously projected down to the perspective. Also, erase the con-struction lines between the eleva-tion and the perspective.

88. The third stage of this perspective drawing consists of drawing the window and door openings. To simplify the draw-ing, only the openings are to be drawn. As you become more pro-ficient, you can show these items in detail.

To begin the windows and doors, place your T square or

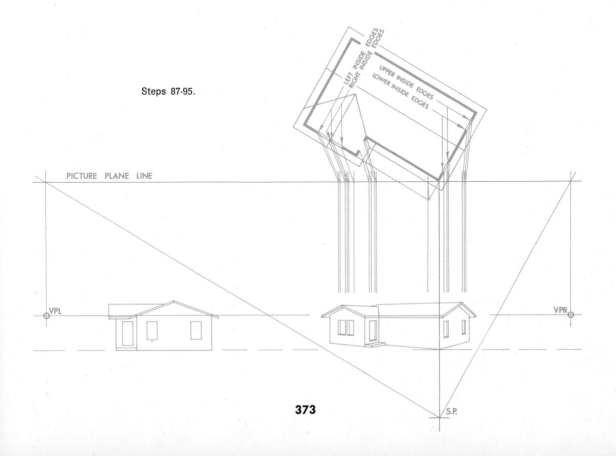

Steps 87-95.

drafting machine in position for drawing horizontal lines. Project construction lines from the tops and bottoms of all windows and doors shown on the elevation over to the measuring line. Make small dashes on the measuring line to indicate these locations.

89. From the dashes just marked on the measuring line draw light construction lines vanishing to the right for the top and bottom of the windows on the right building end.

90. Align the straightedge through the station point and the rear window edge on the floor plan. Drop a construction line to the picture plane line. Repeat this step five more times—once for each visible window corner. Please observe the six construction lines shown on the last drawing in this series. These show how they were projected from the windows to the station point.

91. Each of these six inclined construction lines terminates at the picture plane line. From the ends of these lines drop perpendiculars onto the right building end.

92. Locate the construction lines for the top and bottom of the two windows and also the two outside vertical lines of each window. Darken each window outline.

93. Each window still has a vertical construction line that has not been darkened. These were projected from the floor plan at the locations marked *upper inside edges*.

Align the straightedge so it passes through the left vanishing point and the lower rear window corner. Draw a short dark line from the construction line to the darkened window outline. Now darken the construction line from the top of the window down to the vanishing line previously drawn. This represents the inside edge of the window. Repeat this process for the other window.

94. Align the straightedge through the inside window corners just drawn and also through the right vanishing point. Draw two lines to show the inside lower window edges.

95. The longest front wall has no windows or doors. To be able to draw the windows and doors in the two walls of the building offset, it is necessary to vanish left from the heights previously marked on the measuring line and then remark these locations on the first wall line to the left of the measuring line.

Position the straightedge so it passes through the new heights just located and also through the right vanishing point. Draw the door, following exactly the same procedures as were used for drawing the windows on the right end of the building.

To draw the windows in the front building offset, transfer the height measurements to the corner in front of the door. Then vanish these heights to the left vanishing point and draw construction lines for the horizontal window lines. These windows are to be completed following the same procedures that were used for the right building end.

96. The front step is the final item to be drawn. Position the straightedge so that it passes through the station point and the front edge of the step where it touches the longest front building wall. Make a small dash where the straightedge crosses the picture plane line. Drop a perpendicular onto the perspective and draw a light construction line

Step 96.

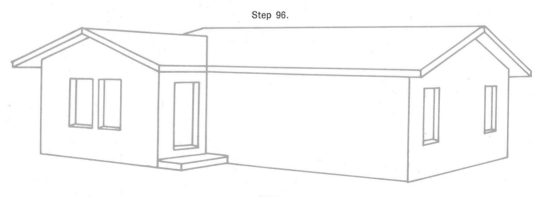

slightly longer than the step height as shown on the building elevation. Repeat this process for the front corner of the step. Make a small horizontal dash on the measuring line that is the same height as the front step shown on the elevation drawing.

Position the straightedge through the height just located and also through the left vanishing point. Draw a dark line to represent the top of the step.

Repeat the above procedure for the step end that is even with the front building edge. Darken the two vertical lines to the corners of the step. Vanish to the right and darken the top and bottom of the step.

97. Erase all construction lines

Two-point interior perspective.

and touch up any object lines as needed so that your completed perspective is identical to the last two-point perspective illustration shown. If your drawing is not exactly the same as this drawing, check through the procedures and make any necessary corrections.

PERSPECTIVE FOR ONE-POINT

One-point perspective is very similar to two-point except the plan view placed above the picture plane line is positioned so one side is parallel to the line. Drawing procedure is simplified if the front edge of the plan view is placed on the picture plane line. This permits the front perspective outline to be drawn at the same scale as the elevations and floor plan. When the front outline is parallel to the picture plane line and all horizontal lines are drawn parallel, it provides an opportunity for one to use any horizontal line in this plane as a measuring line.

All vertical lines are drawn vertical on one-point perspective. All lines of the plan view that are at right angles to the picture plane

line vanish toward a single vanishing point. The vanishing point can be located in any position. If it is in the center of the perspective drawing, you are looking directly toward the object.

The four illustrations showing interior perspectives and the four illustrations showing exterior per-

spectives let you see how objects would appear when they vanish at different angles.

The procedures for drawing one-point perspectives are almost identical to those for two-point except that only one vanishing point is used. The most important thing to be aware of is that one

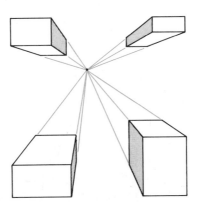

One-point exterior perspectives.

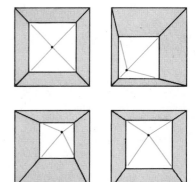

One-point interior perspectives.

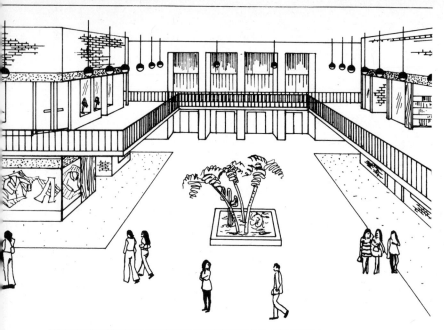

can measure only on the frontal plane and that all measurements must be transferred back to their proper locations.

One-point perspective is especially valuable when it is necessary to show an object with three sides visible. The accompanying illustration emphasizes the vanishing lines. It also shows the great illusion of depth that is possible with this perspective method.

Patrick McFall

One-point pen-and-ink perspective.

Questions To Reinforce Knowledge

1. Describe isometric drawing.

2. What is the main objection to isometric drawing?

3. What is an isometric axis?

4. What are non-isometric lines?

5. How do you determine where to draw non-isometric lines?

6. Why is an object drawn first using construction lines and then re-drawn with object lines?

7. Is it necessary to remove construction lines? Explain.

8. What is a reversed axis isometric drawing?

9. Draw an example of an isometric circle and explain briefly how it was done.

10. Explain how curved lines are drawn in isometric.

11. What is an oblique drawing?

12. What are two advantages of using this drawing method?

13. What is the chief disadvantage of this drawing method?

14. What is cabinet drawing? What are its advantages?

15. What is perspective drawing?

16. Are perspective drawings used as plans? Explain.

17. What is the major difference between two-point and one-point perspective?

18. What is a picture plane line?

19. When referring to perspective, what is the horizontal plane?

20. What is the vertical plane?

21. Is it necessary to place a floor plan so it touches the picture plane line? Explain.

22. Explain how the angle is determined when positioning the floor plan.

23. What is a measuring line? Explain its use.

24. What is a station point? What determines its location?

25. What is a cone of vision?

26. What is the horizon?

27. What are vanishing points?

28. What is the relationship of the vanishing points to the horizon?

29. In two-point perspective, how are the vanishing points established? Explain.

Terms To Spell and Know

isometric
oblique
cabinet drawing
perspective
isometric axes
non-isometric lines
reversed axes
isometric arc
isometric circle
needle point
office method—perspective
angular perspective
two-point perspective
one-point perspective
picture plane line
horizontal plane
vertical plane
measuring line
station point
cone of vision
vanishing point
eye level
ground line
non-perspective lines

Sketches and Renderings

Preliminary Sketches

As you know, building plans must be approved by the prospective client, and verbal discussions do not always communicate the ideas of all persons involved in the planning.

While a project is in the formative stages, the architect makes several tentative plans based upon information supplied by the client and through conferences. These beginning drawings probably will combine freehand and quick instrument sketches. Usually the floor plan is worked out first and then principal elevations. During formation of the design, floor plan drawings may be done as a heavy single line, or wall thickness can be added if desired.

Very little detail is included—walls, door and window openings, locations of major equipment, and the name and approximate size of each room.

Elevations are also sketched or drawn in outline while ideas are being developed, with very little detail information. It is frequently necessary to sketch dozens of preliminary plans before a final design is developed. Samples of ten-tative floor plan and elevation sketches are shown.

There is no specific drawing scale that must be used; the size of the structure determines the scale. But for the average home plan $\frac{1}{8}'' = 1'-0''$ is usually satisfactory.

Determining Need for a Rendering

After a tentative plan has been decided upon, architectural renderings of the proposed building may be required. Large, elaborate structures such as schools, churches, hospitals, or office buildings require elaborate renderings to be put on public display or for making reproductions to accompany newspaper or magazine articles, or literature to be given to interested persons. Renderings are also usually done for tract or development homes, or homes with stock plans, so brochures can be made available to prospective clients. One-of-a-kind or custom homes may have only simple renderings, or none at all, if of conventional size and appearance. On luxury-class homes, the client can well afford complete renderings so as to judge details.

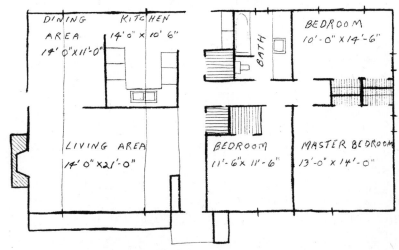

Preliminary floor plan pencil sketch.

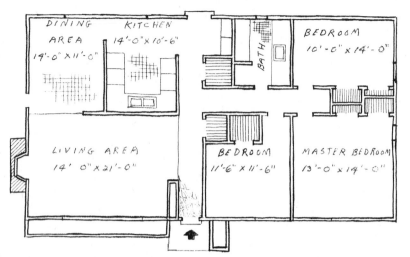

Pencil sketch with walls drawn as solid lines.

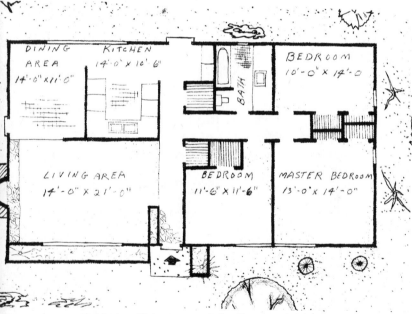

Finished preliminary presentation for plan sketch.

Pencil sketch of a front elevation.

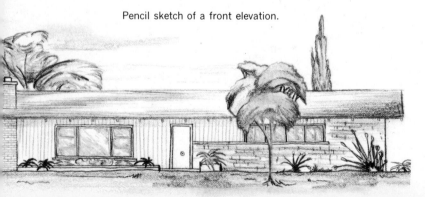

Who Does the Rendering

Renderings may be done by the architect, or he may have them done by studios or individual architectural illustrators specializing in this work.

Scope of the Chapter

The discussion of renderings here does not treat the subject fully. It serves as an introduction to the topic.

Quality of Materials

If he had to pay for them, the learning student could not always afford the best equipment and materials. However, even a modest school budget should permit stocking of most supplies and equipment of satisfactory range and quality. All materials should then be handled with great care.

Rendering Mediums

Nine different rendering mediums are discussed on the following pages, some in detail while others are simply identified. Careful study of the illustrations accompanying the discussions will help show you how to develop specific skills.

Transparent Water Colors

Transparent water colors are available in cake or tube form. Cakes in metal trays are economically packaged and sold as sets, with color replacements available. Tube colors can be purchased individually or in packaged sets.

You may feel you should use cake colors because they are less expensive. However, they are harder to tone with water to just the right mixture, they can ruin

378

a delicate brush, and therefore are less desirable than tube colors.

To pick up color from the cakes the brush must be dipped in water and rubbed on the paint. This is very hard on the brush. Cake paint is convenient for doing small areas but is difficult to use for large-spread, even tones.

Standard procedure for using tube color: A small dab of paint is placed in a mixing tray, dish, or jar so water can be added. Mixing in jars with tight lids permits storage for future use. You should mix slightly more color than you think you will need because it is very difficult and time consuming to match colors previously used.

You should have two water containers—one for mixing paint, and one for cleaning brushes. Two half-pint or pint jars are recommended.

Water color brushes must have soft, fine bristles for flowing or washing the paint. One should have at least three to five sizes of wide and narrow flat brushes and a similar range of conical shapes. Good brushes are expensive, so they must be handled with care. Never allow paint to dry in them; always wash them immediately after they are used. They must also be washed when you change colors, so other hues do not become discolored. Brushes must be stored so the bristles do not become bent. They can either be stored flat or inverted with the handles standing in a tall container.

Handling color tubes. If tubes of water color are to be used they must be handled with care because they are of soft material. Don't squeeze the tube while the cap is on because this builds up pressure. When the cap is removed, more paint than is desired will come from the tube.

If excess color is taken from the tube don't try to hold or force it back in by placing the cap over extended paint. This paint accumulation between the cap and tube threads makes it difficult to remove for subsequent uses. If the cap does become sealed on the tube it may be loosened by soaking in warm water. Dried paint can also be picked from between the cap base and threads with a sharp instrument.

The best practice is never to allow paint to fill the cap or threads.

To unscrew the cap, hold the tube near the rigid top (where the sides meet the cap) and turn gently. Do not hold the tube where it is flexible or you might twist the top off.

Use of colors. Water colors are seldom used full strength, generally, only as accents to brighten the rendering. For example, shrubs, flowers, or foliage on foreground trees are sometimes accented in very intense colors.

Four Ways of Applying Water Color

1. Flat wash.
2. Graded wash.
3. Laid-on color.
4. Wet into wet.

Flat Wash

The term flat wash means that color is deposited uniformly over an entire area. To do a flat wash, mix the desired color with water in the mixing tray or jar. Brush a sample onto a scrap of the same kind of paper as being used for the rendering. This is very important because paint does not look the same on all papers. If the color is satisfactory, you are ready to apply the wash.

NOTE: Color on a large finished rendering *will appear darker* than on a small sample.

Strong colors do not usually flow on smoothly in a flat wash. Therefore, if a strong color is desired, several light washes should be applied until the right effect is achieved. For best results, a wash should be dry before another one is placed over it. Also, if two different colored washes are to be placed side by side, one should be dry before the next one is applied.

Flat washes can be applied to small or large areas and a smooth color achieved. If the area is large, the color can be controlled better if the area is "painted" first with clear water.

Try several sample flat washes before doing your permanent rendering.

Albert Benda

Diluted water-color wash rendering.

Strong pigmented water-color wash rendering with accents of flowers, shrubs, and exterior trim of opaque water color.

Erwin H. James, Architect

Steps for Painting a Flat Wash on a Drawing

1. Select a flat brush of an appropriate size for the area to be washed.
2. Lay the drawing flat on a table. In light pencil, outline carefully the space to be washed. Paint with water only.
3. Next, be sure the paint and water are mixed thoroughly.
4. Dip the brush in the middle of the paint and fill it. It should not be necessary to wipe the brush on the side of the container to remove part of the paint.
5. Hold the brush at the same angle as you would hold a pencil for writing. Place the tip of the brush in one of the upper corners of the area to be washed.
6. Observe the puddle of paint beneath the brush. To do a flat wash you must always have a puddle.

7. Following the top outline of the part, stroke the brush horizontally to the other side of the area. Be sure to follow the outline very carefully so the paint covers only the desired area. With only a little practice you should be able to paint up to a line without leaving spaces or lapping over. If the paint consistently runs over the top line, you have too large a puddle.
8. Following the side outline of the area, and without lifting the brush, move it slightly down so the tip touches and barely laps into the wet paint from the first stroke.
9. Check the puddle beneath the brush; if it is about used up, refill your brush from your paint tray. You must do this quickly because the first stroke cannot be allowed to dry before the second one is made or the splice will show a darker shade.

10. Continue making strokes back and forth across the paper, always moving the puddle beneath the brush, until the entire area is filled. NOTE: On the last stroke, turn the brush so the tip follows the area outline.
11. When the area is completely washed, you should still have a puddle at the bottom of the painted area. This must be removed. Either touch a blotter to the puddle or wipe your paintbrush on a clean cloth to partially dry it and then lift the puddle with the brush. Regardless of the method used, do not touch the paper because this may pick up more color than desired and a light area may result.

While the color is still damp it may not appear smooth; this is no cause for alarm if the surface is only slightly uneven. When it dries the paint should level out to an even tone.

Graded Wash

A graded wash is very similar to a flat tone except that the color gradually changes from light to dark, dark to light, or alternates from one tone to another. The allover size of the area and how gradually the tone must change determines the number of different shades required. Note that each shade or tint must be mixed separately and tested before you start.

Steps for Painting a Graded Wash

1. Determine the number of shades required. Trying them out will help you achieve this.
2. Using a mixing tray or a series of containers prepare the shades required. Trying them out will help you achieve this.
3. Paint samples of each color to ascertain if they are correct.
4. Divide the area to be painted into the number of required spaces. Make short dashes at both sides of the area. *Do not draw a guide line* across because it will show through the finished wash.

5. Using the same technique as for a flat wash, paint the first area with the lightest color. If a large puddle remains at the end, pick up most of it.
6. While the first wash is still wet, apply the second one in the same manner. Lap slightly into the first wash so there is no pronounced line.
7. Repeat the process in each succeeding space, using the color mixed for it.
8. After the last area is painted, remove the excess puddle.

Laid-On Color

This technique requires much less water than a wash. The color tends to be much stronger, of course, except when very light tints of pigment from the tube are employed.

Areas to be painted should be outlined very lightly with a pencil so colors can be confined to their proper areas. Since the paint is transparent, items such as trees, shrubs, and fences cannot be added over wash areas or any other color because the color underneath will show through. It is necessary to leave shapes blank and unpainted for the laid-on effect.

To apply paint, the brush is filled and then laid or *touched* onto the paper repeatedly to form a pattern. Also, by moving the brush slightly as it is laid on, short *strokes* can be formed. The brush can also be stroked farther to form lighter accents. With this method an uneven tone, such as for a shrub, may be achieved. Do not scrub at a spot in an attempt to make the paint smooth. All strokes should be made with a flowing motion. Before beginning a rendering, practice until you are sure that you have mastered this technique.

Wet-Into-Wet

This method is entirely different from those just discussed. The colors are literally dropped into water on the drawing surface. The surface must be extremely wet so the paint will spread in all directions to form designs. By varying (1) the amount of water on the paper, (2) the quantity and color of the paint, (3) the location where it is dropped, and (4) by tilting the drawing slightly, one can guide the pattern.

Steps for Painting Wet-Into-Wet

1. Mix the color or colors. The mix must be stronger than desired on the rendering because the paint is thinned by the water on the paper.

2. Determine how the pattern is to appear.

3. Using a brush of an appropriate size apply clean water to the area. (The amount of water determines how much the paint will spread.) For only slight spreading, the surface should have only a thin film of water washed over it. For medium spread, apply more heavily by using closer puddles. For a wide spread, apply puddles so close they touch each other. Then smooth lightly. Less water may be applied close to the edges of an area so the paint won't spread into other areas. NOTE: Prolonged soaking may damage the paper, so one must work quickly and know what he plans to do.

4. Paint may be placed on the drawing in several ways: (1) It may be dropped from a loaded brush so it falls into the water. (2) A loaded brush may be touched lightly to the water without touching the paper. (3) It may be brushed lightly across the surface of the water.

5. To stroke color from one point to another or to spread it into designs, you may brush deposited paint without touching the paper or you may tilt the paper so the paint runs to the desired point.

6. If water accumulates at edges of areas it causes lines of paint where none are desired. Excess water may be lifted with a blotter, brush, or other absorbent material. This must be done with great care to prevent disrupting the paint pattern.

7. The rendering should remain stationary until the water dries and the paint becomes set. When there is no longer any water standing on the surface, drying may be completed by applying heat to speed the process. NOTE: If illustration board is painted by this method, it may buckle from the water. The back surface may be pre-dampened to counteract this.

NOTE: The clouds for the opaque water color rendering at the bottom of page 369 are an example of this painting method.

Kramer and Engstrom, Architects, Park Ridge, Ill.
Rendering by Forest Studios, Park Ridge, Ill.

Professional opaque water-color rendering.

Opaque Water Colors

Several different names are used for opaque water colors. The most common are tempera, poster paint, and show-card paint, or polymer plastic. Many qualities are available, packaged in glass jars of graded sizes. Some manufacturers also package small quantities in tubes.

Opaque water color makes a heavy bodied paint similar in appearance to rubber-base wall paints.

This medium is a favorite with many professionals because it accurately duplicates colors that are used on building surfaces. Many times photographs of opaque water color renderings are mistaken for actual photographs of a building because of their life-like colors, and the realistic small details possible with this medium.

These are very strong colors, seldom used full strength except as accents to brighten the rendering. To obtain natural, lifelike effects, they are usually cut with white. When mixing colors, begin with the lightest one required.

Student opaque water-color rendering.

383

Voyta-Hagood

Opaque water-color rendering done in tones of grey.

Erwin H. James, Architect

If mixing is begun with a strong color, an entire jar of white may be needed to lighten it sufficiently! One could add so much white that the rendering might become chalky.

As with transparent water colors, a mixture is very difficult to match, so one should prepare enough to complete the entire rendering and still have some left over for touch up.

Mixed paint must be stored in air-tight containers so it does not dry between uses.

Before removing paint from the original container it should be well stirred, because heavy pigments settle and leave only colored water at the top of the jar. Paint should be dipped not poured from the original container so the mouth of the jar will not become caked. Always clean the object being used so colors do not become contaminated.

NOTE: If the threads in the lid or on the jar get paint on them it must be cleaned off so the cap will screw on properly.

Since this material is heavy bodied, water must usually be added so it will spread properly. However, if good coverage is not obtained, too much water is being used. When mixing or adding water use a stiff bristled mixing brush or a wood paddle; never use a paintbrush.

One-point interior kitchen perspective rendered with opaque water-color.

Morgan Company

Two-point interior kitchen perspective rendered with opaque water-color.

Opaque water color is applied with a stiff brush so paint can be spread thin. Different sized large and small brushes are needed for different sized areas to be painted. Since the paint covers well, it is not necessary to have a heavy coat. Too much paint will cause air bubbles, uneven texture, and it will check and flake off. During application the brush should contain very little paint and should be spread as though this is all you have. A painted area should be perfectly smooth with no visible brush marks or unevenness in coverage.

After one becomes expert at using this medium it can be washed on, graded, or dropped in; but best results are obtained with flat, solid colors.

Since colors are opaque, it is possible to paint items and then repaint them another color without the first one showing through. To prevent paint build-up, a damp brush may be used to remove paint so a new coat can be applied. For example, if a tree or shrub is to be painted in front of a building, the building may be painted and then the area occupied by trees or shrubs removed so they can be painted without build-up. Not all opaque paints are water soluble so some cannot be removed after they have dried.

Airbrush

An airbrush is a small paint sprayer manufactured exclusively for art work. It ranges from inexpensive to very expensive, depending upon the quality of the equipment. Good equipment is recommended for school use.

Paint or lacquer is placed in a container attached to the gun and it is forced out and onto the rendering by compressed air. The gun has adjustments to regulate the air pressure and the size of the nozzle opening (orifice). The paint consistency also helps determine how well it sprays and whether or not it is atomized into consistently fine particles. Generally speaking paint or lacquer must be very thin to spray well. Since the paint is thin, only a limited amount can be sprayed onto a rendering at one time. If a large quantity is deposited it will form bubbles or drops which will run and cause streaks. Water color is the conventional material used, but it is very slow drying, which makes it time consuming. The most important advantage of using lacquer is that it dries very rapidly.

When using water color it is important to clean the gun after use, but with lacquer it is much more important. Lacquer should not be allowed to dry in the gun because it is very difficult to remove. If only lacquer is to be used, it is a good idea to clean it and then spray lacquer thinner through the gun to clean the nozzle inside. After cleaning is complete, one may leave a little thinner in the gun's tank so there is no possibility of residual lacquer's drying and clogging the nozzle.

When storing, clean all equipment, including hose from the air tank, thoroughly.

Airbrush rendering.

385

Erwin H. James, Architect

Items for Consideration in Airbrush Rendering

- Before the actual rendering is begun, do a preliminary color study on inexpensive paper. This is usually a rapidly executed pencil sketch tinted with water colors.
- Make a very light pencil drawing on drawing paper showing the outlines of all items.
- If a rendering is held in a vertical position while it is sprayed, the danger of color dripping from the airbrush during use is minimized. Most paint tanks have an air hole in the top; when the brush is tilted, paint runs out.
- If water color is used the paint is transparent. If lacquer is used it may be either transparent or opaque depending upon the quantity sprayed on.
- Completely mask off all areas of a rendering that are not to be sprayed a given color to prevent them from being tinted by overspray (paint sprayed where you do not wish it to be).
- Masking: Large areas may be covered with any paper and then masking tape used at edges of the part being sprayed. NOTE: Gummed or plain frisket may be used instead of masking tape.
- Frisket is very thin transparent or translucent paper or plastic that is placed over the drawing. The part to be painted is cut out with a knife while it is on the drawing. One must cut through the frisket without damaging the rendering. This requires patience and delicacy for accurate cutting. Use a straightedge, when possible. Cut exactly on outlines, and do not cut past lines at corners. *After all cutting is complete,* the frisket is removed from the area to be sprayed.
- When masking tape is used, do not cut ends off flat against the surface of the rendering, because this will cut through the tape and damage the drawing. Hold tape end clear while cutting it. Even a small cut is very pronounced after paint is applied.
- Since all parts must be masked or have frisket applied at some time during the rendering process, it is sometimes applied over painted surfaces. Broad strips of masking tape should never contact painted surfaces. The paper covering should extend almost to the area where paint is to be applied, and then the tape lapped onto it so only about a 1/16″ to 1/8″ strip is exposed for adhering to the drawing.
- Careful tape or frisket removal is important so previously painted surfaces and edges of new paint are not damaged when the material is lifted. NOTE: Some masking tape has a heavy adhesive coat while others do not. Tape with light adhesive works best.
- When applying the color medium only experience will indicate the distance to hold the air brush away from the drawing. Air pressure, how much the orifice is open, the coverage desired, the viscosity of the paint, and the rate of movement of the brush all help determine how much is applied.
- The brush should be held a constant distance from the rendering and should be moved across the area at a uniform rate of speed. If these are varied the color will not be uniform.
- Make the first pass or swath across the top of an area beginning on the masking at one side and ending on the masking at the other side. Do not stop at the edge of the masked area or a dark spot will result.
- After the first pass, the gun should be moved down so the spray pattern laps about halfway into the first pattern pass. Then spray back across onto the masking at the other side.
- This process is repeated until the entire area to be painted is filled.
- It is not always possible to spray enough paint to achieve the desired density in one application. When greater coverage is desired, additional coats must be applied in the same manner as described. For a more even appearance, the second coat can be applied up and down at right angles to the first coat.
- Sometimes one desires graded tones with some areas darker than others. Instead of moving constantly back and forth as

previously described, the airbrush may be used in a tight circular motion to apply additional paint to some areas.

- It is difficult to judge exactly how much paint is applied. After masking is removed, colors usually look much darker than anticipated. It is a good idea to apply only about half as much paint as one feels necessary, then lift a corner of the masking and check the color with areas already rendered before continuing.

India Ink

There are two different ways the beginner may render with ink, (1) for line work or (2) as a wash, or render an entire drawing in a single color (usually black). Ink is applied as solid lines of different lengths and widths to form objects, or as shading.

Pens used may include ruling pens, technical fountain pens, and crow quill pens, which are either sharp pointed or flat or rounded in different sizes.

Since there are so many kinds and sizes of pens one must check manufacturer's descriptions or rely upon the judgment of an experienced person when selecting the proper pen to use for a desired effect.

Long, straight lines are usually drawn or sketched along a straightedge, while irregular lines may be drawn or sketched freehand. Broad areas may be filled in with a brush.

Renderings may be either in the form of very simple line drawings or may include much intricate detail such as individual leaves, blades of grass, textures, and shadows.

Colored inks may also be used as a wash similar to water color, although it is rather difficult and requires much practice for satisfactory results.

Pen-and-ink rendering.

Kramer and Engstrom, Architects, Park Ridge, Ill.
Rendering by Forest Studios, Park Ridge, Ill.

EIGHT — UNIT APT.
BUILDING

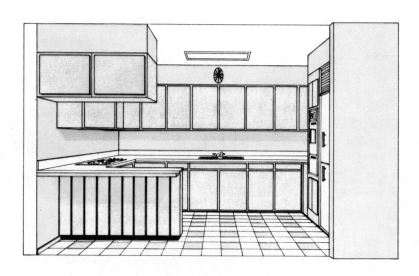

Robert Borlik

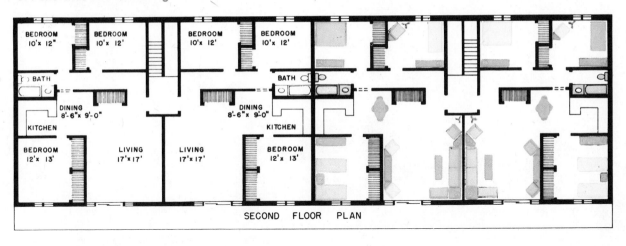

SECOND FLOOR PLAN

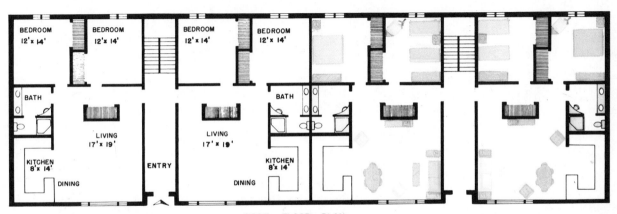

FIRST FLOOR PLAN

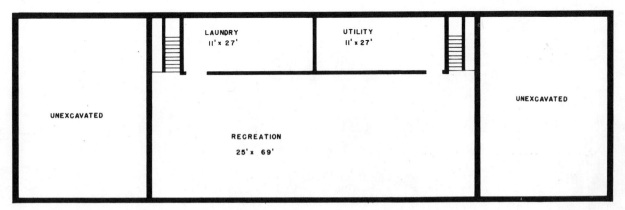

BASEMENT PLAN

Robert Borlik

Ink line drawings with water-color washes.

Robert Borlik

Pen-and-ink rendering combined with water-color washes.

Pencil rendering.

Erwin H. James, Architect

390

Interesting and beautiful results can be obtained by combining the two ink methods, or by substituting water colors or colored pencils for the ink wash.

Pencil Renderings

When renderings are done in pencil, ones from the B series are normally used; however, for delicate lines one may desire H series drafting pencils. The pencil lead may be pointed, flat, or chisel shaped depending upon the kind of line desired. Pressure can be varied to obtain different degrees of shading.

Colored pencil. Colored pencils can be used to add highlights or small amounts of color to other mediums such as pencil or ink renderings, or they can be used for doing an entire rendering. Colors may be shown as distinct lines or they can be applied as even tones by rubbing the pencil lightly over the entire area to be colored.

This medium is seldom satisfactory when strong or opaque colors are desired. However, some colored pencils are water soluble. After applying color, the drawing may be washed with water to dissolve and spread the tone, which gives a water-color effect.

Charcoal and Pastels

These two mediums remind one of blackboard chalk because of their soft texture. They are applied dry by rubbing directly on the rendering. Charcoal is black, while pastels are available in a wide range of colors. Very beautiful results, though not natural or life-like, can be obtained with them. Since both mediums are so soft they are difficult to handle and smear easily. Extreme care must be taken while using them. After a rendering is completed, it should be sprayed with a lacquer fixative to hold the colors in place.

Scratch Board

This medium produces a rendering with a dark background and white lines. A finished rendering reminds one of a photographic negative or a pen and ink rendering that has been done in reverse.

With this material, one is able to show very intricate detail.

The basic material is heavy white paper coated with a chalklike substance and then burnished to a very smooth finish. The coating is about $1/32''$ thick. Before rendering is begun the surface is painted with India ink (usually black) and allowed to dry completely. The ink can be spread with a paint brush or an airbrush.

Scratch board rendering.

Ink rendering combined with pressure-sensitive appliqué.

Alan Clemons

Both methods are satisfactory but a smoother finish can be obtained with the latter.

After the ink is dry, outlines to be rendered are traced or drawn onto the inked surface. Do not exert a great deal of pressure when penciling the drawing, to avoid damaging the coating. Using a sharp instrument—and a straightedge where required— scratch all lines of the subject. NOTE: A slight burr on the scriber will make the line "peel" out smoother. Line width can be varied by exerting different pressures on the scriber. If large areas must be removed, the ink can be scraped away with a knife, chisel, or other suitable instrument.

Small corrections of errors will scarcely be noticed. It is difficult to keep large corrections from showing through. To remove un-wanted lines one must re-coat them with ink and allow it to dry before doing them over.

Appliqué

Continuous or broken lines, repetitious patterns, or colored surfaces need no longer be laboriously drawn or painted. One may purchase adhesive-backed clear plastic appliqués with lines or patterns pre-printed on them. Both transparent and opaque solid colors are also available. Individual lines and narrow patterns are available in rolls, while large patterns or even tones are available with either gloss or matte surfaces to fill almost any drafting need.

Appliqués are easy to use. With only a little practice professional-looking results can be obtained. Rolls from dispensers are laid along a straightedge for accurate straight lines. Curves may be laid either with instruments as guides or freehand.

When sheet material is to cover any area, the sheet is positioned and partially adhered by rubbing where the pattern is to remain. Using a straightedge as a guide, square-cut around the pattern with a sharp knife or scriber. Curves may either be cut with instruments as guides or freehand.

The rest of the sheet is then removed leaving the cut-out section in place. One must burnish the surface (rub with a smooth instrument) to remove air bubbles and seal the appliqué to the drawing.

Entire drawings can be done in this medium, but it is most practical as an accessory item.

Procedure for Rendering

There are two opposing views on the order of rendering a picture. Some artists prefer to render the building first because it usually includes the most intricate detail. Then after the building is rendered the *entourage* or landscape is done. The reason they feel the building should be done first is because your most careful work is done when you begin a job, and the building is the most important part of the rendering.

Other artists feel that best results can be obtained by beginning the rendering at the top and progressing down the sheet until the entire work is complete.

The best way for you can be determined by experimentation.

Beginning the Rendering

Decide how the building is to be viewed; then draw a perspective on tracing paper at a suitable scale. Also draw all required floor plans, interior views, elevations, or other items to be included.

Plan the composition of the entire rendering. If several drawings and their titles are to fit upon one sheet, you must determine the most effective layout for the entire presentation. For example, an exterior perspective, interior views and a floor plan may be included.

After an arrangement has been decided upon, all drawings must be traced or copied onto the sheet. This should be done very lightly in pencil so corrections can be made.

If the composition is made up of several individual drawings as described above, it requires a long time to complete a rendering. For maximum cleanliness cover the drawing and then uncover only the section where work is to be done. For example, in a composition including a pictorial view and a floor plan, the floor plan should be covered while the pictorial is being done. Keeping drawing clean is important to its final appearance.

Introduction to Rendering Details

Scope of Discussion

This book does not contain a lengthy discussion of colors, their relationships to each other, or how colors are mixed to achieve additional hues. Neither does it give specific instructions for painting individual items such as exterior wall coverings, roofs, shrubs, trees, and others using the different media, but rather it gives a broad overview of items to include. For detailed information consult a good artist's guide or architectural rendering book.

Planning the Entourage for Perspective Rendering

If a landscape plan is available use it as a guide for adding the entourage. Very lightly sketch all landscape items such as trees, shrubs, pools, rocks, or others. Slight changes from the proposed landscape are frequently later made to enhance the visual image. The outlines of these items should be exactly as you desire to paint them, but do not add intricate details. These are added when painting.

Remember that the farther one is from an object the less distinct it becomes. Trees are a good example of this. Ones in the background will be only general outlines, while ones in the middle distance show some of the limb and trunk structure. Foreground trees show much trunk and branch detail and may even include individual leaves or leaf clusters. Bushes and shrubs are usually shown in some detail because they tend to be close to the observer, near the front of the plan.

A SUGGESTED ORDER FOR RENDERING

Wall Surfaces

Since most walls have straight outlines, it is a good idea to outline them with the background color of paint to help confine it to the proper area. The medium being used helps determine how they are outlined but most paint, if thinned slightly, can be used effectively in a ruling pen, with a straightedge. A paintbrush is also frequently used.

After outlining, the base color should be applied. If you show details such as individual bricks, stones, or boards, the base coat need not be perfectly smooth. If these are not to be included, walls should be smooth.

Using a ruling pen or brush, add lines for mortar or individual boards as required. Then add details such as wood grain, texture, or shadow. NOTE: Remember that sometimes paint media require leaving open spaces so other transparent paints can be used over the areas later.

Glass

If glass is to be transparent it is treated as though it did not exist. In other words, paint in objects such as draperies and ignore the glass. In normal daylight it is darker inside a building than it is on the outside. When viewing an exterior this causes windows to reflect light and appear dark. They are usually shown as black, dark grey, dark blue, or dark green. For very realistic renderings, items such as clouds, trees, people, or any other object nearby may show in the glass as reflections—not often required.

Curtains

The outline of curtains should be sketched lightly with a pencil. They may be painted with alternate light and dark shades to obtain an illusion of folds in the material. Folds should be uniform and are usually vertical, unless the curtains are closed at the top and tied back near the bottom. Then the folds follow the outline of the tieback. It is very

difficult to add designs unless the drawing scale is quite large.

Doors

Solid doors may be painted a single color to match or contrast with the building. If they are to have a natural finish, grain may be added by drawing or painting fine lines using a pencil, colored pencil, pen, or brush. Glass, wood panels, divisions, moldings or hardware are added when desired.

Posts, Mullions, and Beams

These are best added after walls, windows, and doors are complete because it is very difficult to paint up to or around them. Their edges are also usually straight and may be ruled to cover or straighten previous edges. Since their sides are usually parallel they should be drawn or painted using instruments as guides. After all edges are painted flat surfaces should be filled in. Since both a face and a side are usually shown one will be in shadow and should be slightly darker than the other. They may be wood color, metal (usually silver or shades of grey), or painted to match other trim.

Roof Surfaces

The same techniques are used for roof surfaces as described for walls. On roofs, different surfaces are usually painted slightly different shades to emphasize changes in direction. Composition roofing may be painted with even or graded tones, or horizontal lines can be added to give an indication of shingles. Textures and designs are sometimes added to

simulate both horizontal and vertical lines on wood shingles, clay tile, slate and others. Stippling is frequently used to indicate pebbles applied to built-up roofing.

Items such as soil pipes, ventilators, and chimneys are shown if the drawing scale and the client's need for detail warrant their inclusion.

Medium or dark roof surfaces highlight and emphasize the building and make it stand out on the rendering.

Fascia and Trim

Like posts and mullions, outlines of fascias and other trim are usually done first as straight lines and then their surfaces are painted. Fascias and trim on different building sides should be in slightly different tones so corners are easily recognizable. They are frequently light toned to contrast with the rest of the rendering. However, they are seldom painted white, even though this is a popular trim color. White makes them appear too brilliant. When they are to appear white, they are usually painted a light cream or light grey.

Overhangs and Their Shadows

The underside of a roof overhang is usually in shadow and shows darker than its true color. Overhangs appear quite small on a rendering and are usually painted a uniform color. However, if drawing scale and client's needs warrant, individual boards may be drawn, ruled, or painted.

Since overhangs protrude past the building, they may cast shad-

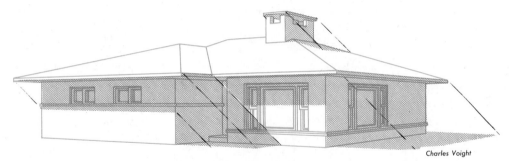

Charles Voight

Shadows projected 45° from the left.

ows on walls. A detailed study of shadows is very complex, so a simplified method of drawing them, suitable for most renderings, is discussed briefly:

To determine where shadows will fall on a wall one must know the position of the sun in the sky. Since the sun is many miles from the earth, its rays are considered parallel. For convenience in plotting shadows, the sun rays are frequently drawn at 45° either right or left of vertical. This simulates mid-morning or mid-afternoon in the northern hemisphere, with the sun midway between the horizon and zenith.

One must know the overhang width so the rays can be plotted onto the wall. Study the illustration carefully. Observe the rays striking the wall and how the shadow is formed by the overhang. Note also that one wall is completely in shadow while the adjoining wall is not.

NOTE: Shadows formed by overhangs radiate either right or left toward the same vanishing points as the building.

Steps, Sidewalks, Driveways, and Streets

These items are usually sketched lightly before the remainder of the entourage is added. They may be rendered before or after other items of the entourage, depending upon which items are to show in front of others. Colors may be light or dark, varying with the material represented and the desired appearance.

Sky

The sky can be rendered in blue using any of the media or techniques described at the first of the chapter. It may remain unpainted, or it may have only clouds added.

When planning clouds, the total rendering and its finished effect must be kept in mind. If trees or other items protrude above the horizon, cloud formations should be planned to fit with or around them. If trees lap over clouds, it may be distracting.

Trees and Shrubs

As stated earlier, background trees usually show general outlines, while some details are included on middle distance trees, and much detail may be shown on foreground trees or shrubs.

To obtain realistic results, one should study many species of trees in their natural surroundings to ascertain their shapes and general characteristics.

Perhaps the two greatest errors the beginner makes are his failure to interpret tree shapes properly, and a tendency to draw more detail than required. Generally, one should only suggest their shapes and not try to capture every intricate detail. For example, draw only a few branches to indicate their general shape and direction. When adding foliage draw only enough to suggest general shapes.

Background trees should not form a straight line or have their height taper toward the edge of the rendering because this leads the observer's eyes away from the building, which should be given the most emphasis. Uneven heights, or tall trees near the edge of the rendering, can lead the eyes back to the building. Clusters of trees behind and above the roof near the center of the building can also detract.

Foreground trees can add much interest and give the rendering greater perspective depth. These should be placed so large areas of foliage do not block the view.

Pen and ink presentation elevation.

Alan Clemons

If the building is predominately straight lined, gently curving trees help relieve monotony, or if the building has curved outlines such as a domed or arched roof, straight, tall trees will emphasize this.

Locations of trees and shrubs should balance with and complement the rest of the rendering. In other words, an area could look too vacant without them.

Trees or leafy shrubs are seldom painted as a solid mass. That is, they have spaces in them, and other objects show through. Small, heavy-needled, evergreen shrubs may be in more solid form. Except for background trees, foliage is seldom a single color. Sunlight makes the tops appear to be very light. Sides are usually a medium color and undersides, in shadow, are dark.

Background trees may have a subdued color, while those in the foreground are usually very vivid.

Bare-limbed, winter foliage is not represented except for very special renderings.

Grass

Grass may be added before, after, or while trees and shrubs are being done, depending upon how items fit together. Careful analysis of the renderings shown in this chapter will indicate different ways grass can be represented. Observe that on some renderings it appears smooth and flat, while on others the colors are graded. Contrasting tones with bold, distinct edges are also used.

For realistic appearance, trees, shrubs, and other items should have shadows included.

People

Most professional renderings include drawings of one or more persons to help emphasize perspective and to give an idea of the drawing scale. If only one or

two people are included they are usually close to the building. People should be engaged in some activity and appear to have a reason for being there. Only general shapes are shown. Do not try to capture minute features; they may prove to be distracting.

Automobiles

Since automobile styles are constantly changing, their inclusion dates a building. Avoid especially on art that may be hung in the office of a corporation for years. If they must be included, use stylized shapes instead of specific details.

Presentation Elevations

Presentation elevations are sometimes substituted for perspective drawings.

Landscape features are added to create a pictorial effect. The drawing is rendered with any of the media or techniques used for perspectives.

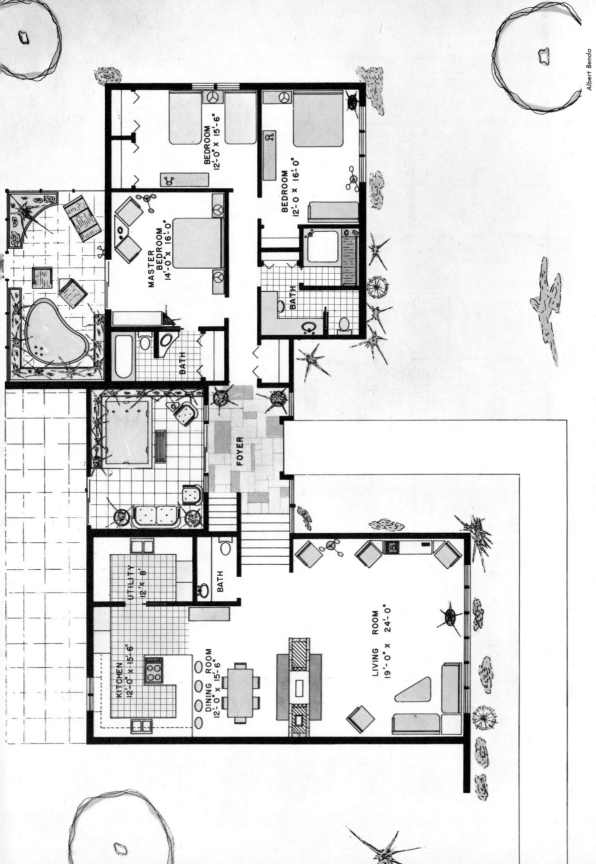

BEDROOM
12'-0" x 15'-6"

BEDROOM
12'-0 x 16'-0"

MASTER
BEDROOM
14'-0" x 16'-0"

BATH

BATH

BATH

FOYER

UTILITY
12' x 8'

BATH

KITCHEN
12'-0" x 15'-6"

DINING ROOM
12'-0" x 15'-6"

LIVING ROOM
19'-0" x 24'-0"

Albert Benda

Presentation floor plan rendered with water-color washes.

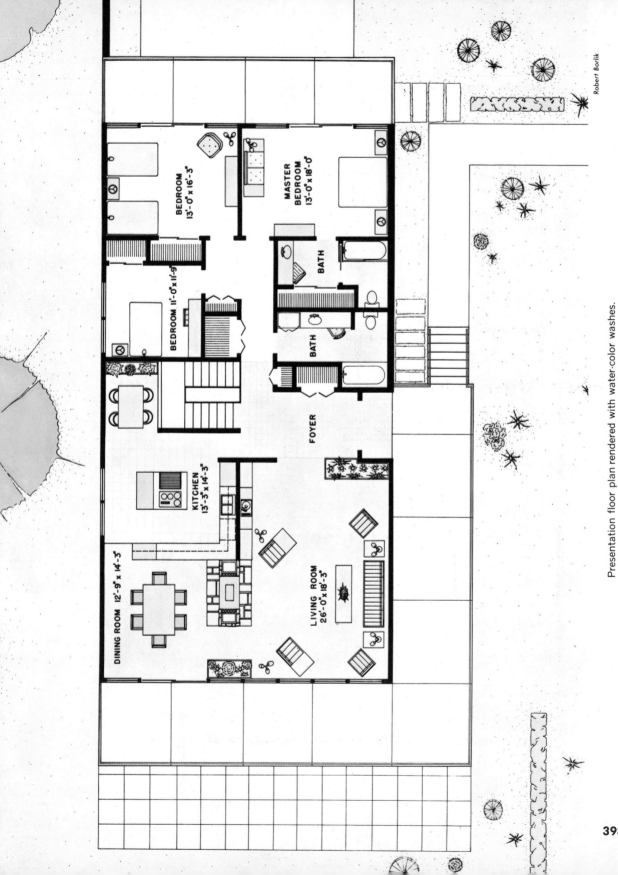

BEDROOM
13'-0" x 16'-3"

MASTER
BEDROOM
13'-0" x 18'-0"

BATH

BEDROOM 11'-0" x 11'-9"

BATH

FOYER

KITCHEN
13'-3" x 14'-3"

DINING ROOM 12'-9" x 14'-3"

LIVING ROOM
26'-0" x 18'-3"

Robert Borlik

Presentation floor plan rendered with water-color washes.

Growth patterns for trees and shrubs.

Presentation Floor Plans

Presentation floor plans are used for illustrative purposes and not as building plans. They may show only wall outlines and major items plus approximate room sizes, or they may be very detailed and include furniture, floor coverings, shading in open closets, outside details such as garages, patios, pools, complete landscaping, or other items as desired. Any parts may be rendered in any media. The examples here show some of the different items that may be included and different ways of rendering them. (See pages 397 and 398.)

Questions To Reinforce Knowledge

1. Why are preliminary sketches or drawings necessary?

2. How detailed are these drawings? Describe.

3. What are two ways walls may be shown on preliminary floor plans?

4. Does an architect ever need to make several drawings for one client? Explain.

5. How does one determine the drawing scale to use? What scale is frequently used?

6. What determines how elaborate a rendering should be?

7. Who does the rendering? Explain.

8. What does one mean by the term transparent water color?

9. What are two forms in which it is available?

10. What are the advantages of cake water colors? Disadvantages?

11. What are the advantages of tube water colors? Disadvantages?

12. Why are two water containers recommended?

13. What kind of bristles should water color brushes have?

14. What are their two recommended shapes?

15. When should brushes be washed? Why?

16. Why must water color tubes be handled with care? Explain.

17. What is a flat wash? How is it applied?

18. What sized areas can be done with a flat wash?

19. Which work best, strong or diluted colors? Why?

20. How may dark colors be applied smoothly?

21. How may the size of your brush affect the wash?

22. What is the position of the drawing surface while applying a wash?

23. From your own reasoning, why should a brush be dipped in the middle of the diluted color before applying a wash?

24. Explain how to apply a flat wash.

25. Why is a puddle necessary?

26. What are two ways it may be removed when it is no longer needed?

27. What happens if one paints across an area and it dries before the next stroke is applied?

28. What is a graded wash?

29. How is a graded wash applied?

30. What is laid-on color?

31. Explain how laid-on color is applied.

32. Why should one lightly draw in the outlines of objects before painting?

33. What is the wet-into-wet method of applying water color?

34. Explain how to apply wet-into-wet.

35. Why must excess water sometimes be removed?

36. What is likely to happen if the drawing surface is moved excessively before the paint is dry?

37. What is opaque water color?

38. How is opaque water color usually packaged?

39. Why is this medium a favorite with many professionals?

40. Why are these colors seldom used full strength? When may they be?

41. How does one make a color less intense?

42. When mixing two colors together why is the dark color added to the lighter one?

43. Why is it advisable to mix more paint than is needed?

44. What are two difficulties encountered if mixed paint is allowed to accumulate at the top of the container?

45. Why is water usually added to this paint when stored?

46. How can one tell if too much water has been added?

47. What are two devices that may be used for mixing paint?

48. Why should one not use a regular paintbrush for mixing?

49. What kind of brush is used for applying opaque water color? Why?

50. What determines the size of brush to use?

51. What happens if too much paint is applied to a surface?

52. Is it possible to repaint a surface with opaque water color?

53. How can one prevent paint from becoming built up when repainting?

54. What is airbrush rendering?

55. What are two kinds of colors that are widely used for airbrush rendering? Which works best? Why?

56. Why is compressed air necessary?

57. What are three factors that help determine the amount of paint deposited on the drawing?

58. What is an orifice?

59. What is the desired consistency of the paint? Why?

60. What happens if too much is applied?

61. When doing renderings, why should preliminary color studies be made?

62. Why is it advisable for the beginner to have the rendering in a vertical position while spraying?

63. Why must the entire drawing, except the part being rendered, be masked with paper and tape, or frisket?

64. Why are edges masked?

65. Why is only a small edge strip of masking adhered to the rendering? What is likely to happen if more is applied?

66. What is frisket?

67. Explain how frisket may be cut and applied. What are the dangers of using this material?

68. Why must one remove tape or frisket very carefully?

69. For even tones, why should the airbrush be moved across the drawing at a constant speed? What happens if speed is not constant?

70. Why is it difficult to tell how much color is being applied?

71. What are two ways India ink is used as a rendering medium?

72. How much detail can be shown using this medium?

73. When renderings are done in pencil, what series is usually used? Why?

74. What are the principal ways colored pencils can be used as a rendering medium?

75. What are the advantages and disadvantages of using charcoal or pastels?

76. What is scratch board?

77. How is color applied to scratch board?

78. How are lines placed on scratch board?

79. Is it possible to correct small errors? How?

80. What is appliqué?

81. Why must it be burnished?

82. Is this medium used for entire renderings? Explain.

83. Which is usually rendered first, a building or the entourage?

84. What is the entourage?

85. Why is it necessary to plan the main features of the entire rendering before any of its details?

86. What are two methods of transferring drawings to the rendering sheet?

87. While rendering is in progress, why should parts of the drawing be protected?

88. Is the landscape of a rendering always exactly like the actual landscape plan? Explain.

89. Why are wall outlines sometimes drawn with paint before it is applied to surfaces?

90. If glass is to show transparent, how is it rendered? Explain.

91. What effect does light have on glass? Explain.

92. Describe the colors suitable for rendering glass in bright sunlight.

93. Are glass surfaces always painted perfectly smooth? Explain.

94. Why are adjoining walls or roof surfaces that are to be the same color on the actual building sometimes painted in slightly different tones?

95. Are individual wall or roof covering materials ever indicated? How?

96. Why are roof surfaces sometimes painted darker than they actually will be on the building?

97. Which is usually painted first, windows or their trim? Why?

98. Why are the undersides of roof overhangs usually darker than other sides that are the same color?

99. Why are fascias frequently painted a light color?

100. Is white often used for fascias on renderings? Explain.

101. For adding shadows, why are the sun's rays considered parallel?

102. Why is 45° frequently used for the sun direction?

103. What is the zenith? (This is not answered directly in the book.)

104. What are the vanishing points for shadows that are parallel to sides of the building?

105. How does one determine which items of the entourage to draw first?

106. How much detail does one render on trees? Explain.

107. Why should background trees not taper to the very edge of the rendering?

108. How may building shape affect the shape of foreground trees? Explain.

109. Is there one best way to render grass? Describe how it may be done.

110. Are shadows included for items of the entourage?

111. Why is a person or persons usually included in perspective renderings?

112. Are automobiles usually included? Explain.

113. How may one render presentation elevations?

114. Describe the amount of detail usually included on presentation floor plans. How does one determine what information it is absolutely necessary to include?

115. Is information concerning exterior items ever included? What kinds of information?

Terms To Spell and Know

rendering	airbrush	scratch board
transparent water color	lacquer	appliqué
flat wash	orifice	burnish
paint puddle	nozzle	entourage
graded wash	color study	media
laid-on color	overspray	stipple
wet-into-wet	frisket	zenith
opaque water color	viscosity	background
tempera	B series pencil	foreground
poster paint	H series pencil	middle distance
chalky	charcoal	foliage
pigment	pastel	stylized
	fixative	

38

Architectural Symbols

Variations of earth in section.

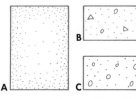

Concrete: (A) in elevation, (B-C) in section.

Cast stone: (A) in elevation, (B) in section.

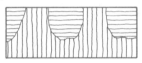

Rock in section.

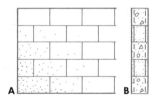

Concrete block: (A) in elevation, (B) in section.

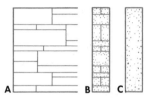

Cut stone: (A) in elevation, (B-C) in section.

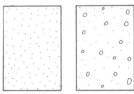

Sand.   Gravel.

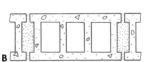

(A) Small scale concrete block.
(B) Large scale concrete block.

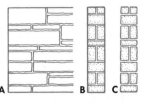

Rough cut stone: (A) in elevation, (B-C) in section.

Cinders.   Aggregate
              fill.

(A) Concrete plank. (B) Reinforced concrete plank.

(A) Random flagstone. (B) Patterned flagstone.

Part 1

STRUCTURAL

DETAILS

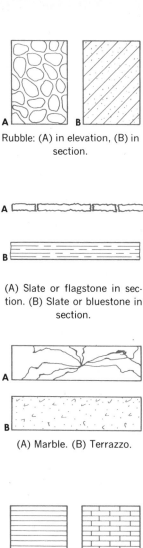

Rubble: (A) in elevation, (B) in section.

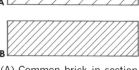

(A) Common brick in section. (B) Face brick in section.

Facing tile: (A) large scale, (B) small scale. Structural tile: (C) small scale, (D) large scale.

(A) Slate or flagstone in section. (B) Slate or bluestone in section.

Face brick on common: (A) small scale, (B) large scale.

(A) Glazed or unglazed ceramic tile in elevation, (B) large scale, (C) small scale.

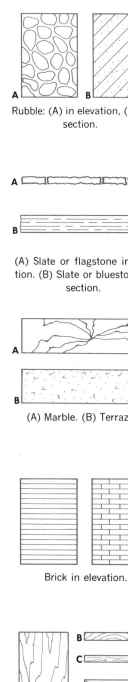

(A) Marble. (B) Terrazzo.

(A) Fire brick on common. (B) Fire brick. (C) Fire brick on common.

Lightweight gypsum block: (A) in elevation, (B) in section.

Brick in elevation.

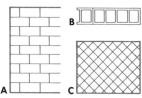

Terra cotta: (A) in elevation, (B) large scale section, (C) small scale section.

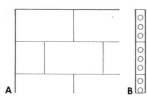

Plaster: (A) in elevation, (B) in section. (C-D-E) Plaster and metal lath in section.

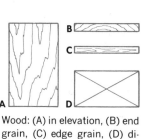

Wood: (A) in elevation, (B) end grain, (C) edge grain, (D) dimension lumber, end grain.

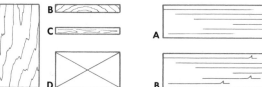

(A-B) Composition shingles.

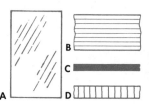

Glass: (A) in elevation, (B) large scale in section, (C) small scale in section, (D) structural.

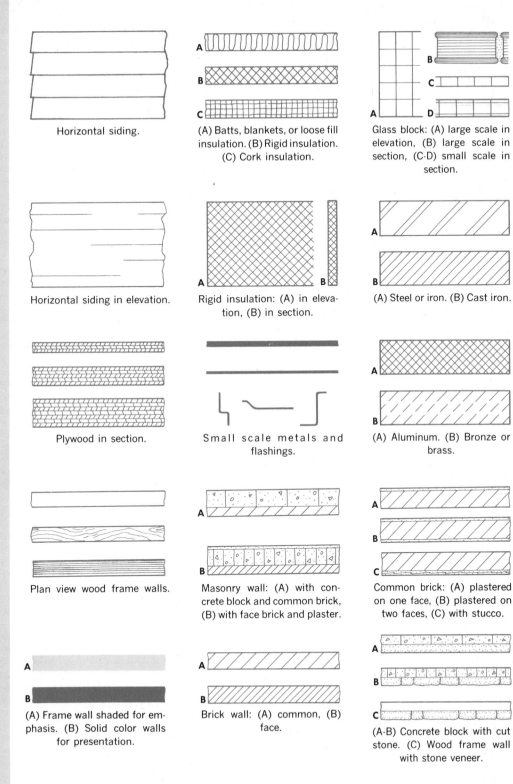

Horizontal siding.

(A) Batts, blankets, or loose fill insulation. (B) Rigid insulation. (C) Cork insulation.

Glass block: (A) large scale in elevation, (B) large scale in section, (C-D) small scale in section.

Horizontal siding in elevation.

Rigid insulation: (A) in elevation, (B) in section.

(A) Steel or iron. (B) Cast iron.

Plywood in section.

Small scale metals and flashings.

(A) Aluminum. (B) Bronze or brass.

Plan view wood frame walls.

Masonry wall: (A) with concrete block and common brick, (B) with face brick and plaster.

Common brick: (A) plastered on one face, (B) plastered on two faces, (C) with stucco.

(A) Frame wall shaded for emphasis. (B) Solid color walls for presentation.

Brick wall: (A) common, (B) face.

(A-B) Concrete block with cut stone. (C) Wood frame wall with stone veneer.

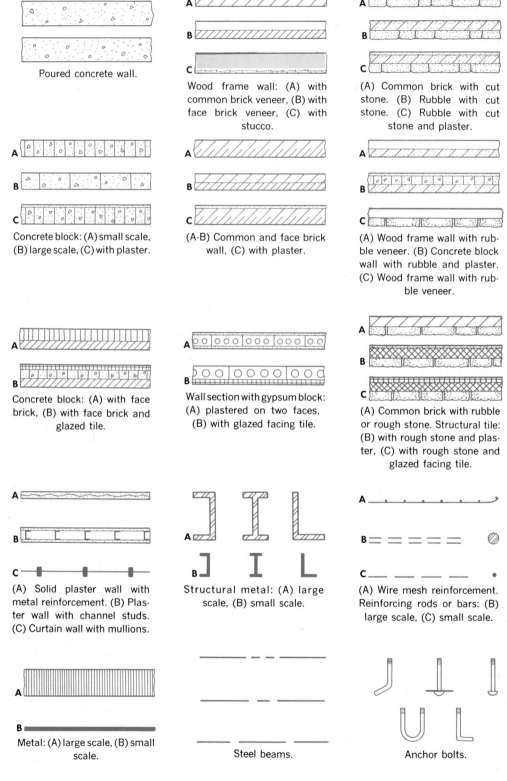

Poured concrete wall.

Wood frame wall: (A) with common brick veneer, (B) with face brick veneer, (C) with stucco.

(A) Common brick with cut stone. (B) Rubble with cut stone. (C) Rubble with cut stone and plaster.

Concrete block: (A) small scale, (B) large scale, (C) with plaster.

(A-B) Common and face brick wall, (C) with plaster.

(A) Wood frame wall with rubble veneer. (B) Concrete block wall with rubble and plaster. (C) Wood frame wall with rubble veneer.

Concrete block: (A) with face brick, (B) with face brick and glazed tile.

Wall section with gypsum block: (A) plastered on two faces, (B) with glazed facing tile.

(A) Common brick with rubble or rough stone. Structural tile: (B) with rough stone and plaster, (C) with rough stone and glazed facing tile.

(A) Solid plaster wall with metal reinforcement. (B) Plaster wall with channel studs. (C) Curtain wall with mullions.

Structural metal: (A) large scale, (B) small scale.

(A) Wire mesh reinforcement. Reinforcing rods or bars: (B) large scale, (C) small scale.

Metal: (A) large scale, (B) small scale.

Steel beams.

Anchor bolts.

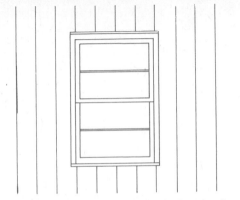

Elevation of double hung window in frame wall
(vertical siding).

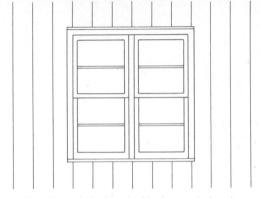

Elevation of double double hung window in
frame wall.

Plan view of double hung window in frame wall.

Plan view of double double hung window in
frame wall.

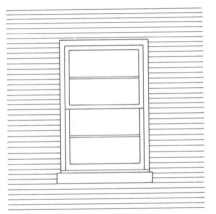

Elevation of double hung window in masonry
wall (brick).

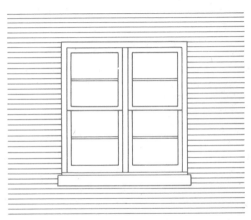

Elevation of double double hung window in
masonry wall.

Plan view of double hung window in brick
veneer wall.

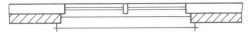

Plan view of double double hung window in
brick veneer wall.

Plan view of double hung window in solid brick
wall.

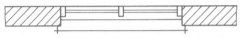

Plan view of double double hung window in
solid brick wall.

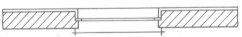

Plan view of double hung metal window with
plastered returns.

Plan view of double double hung metal window
with plastered return.

407

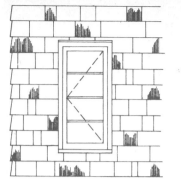

Elevation of casement window in frame wall
(shake or shingle siding).

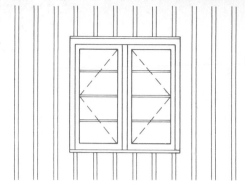

Elevation of double casement window in frame
wall (board and batten siding).

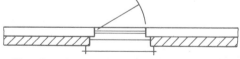

Plan view of casement window in frame wall.

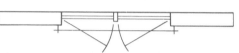

Plan view of double casement window in frame
wall.

Elevation of casement window in brick wall.

Elevation of double casement window in brick
wall.

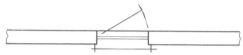

Plan view of casement window in brick veneer
wall.

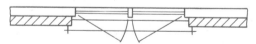

Plan view of double casement window in brick
veneer wall.

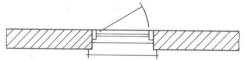

Plan view of casement window in solid brick wall.

Plan view of double casement window in solid
brick wall.

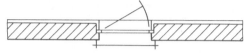

Plan view of metal casement window with plastered returns.

Plan view of metal double casement window with plastered returns.

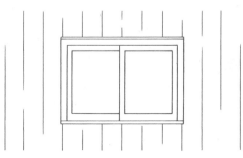

Elevation of sliding window in frame wall.

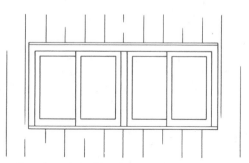

Elevation of double sliding windows in frame wall.

Plan view of sliding window in frame wall.

Plan view of double sliding windows in frame wall.

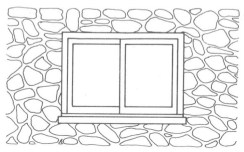

Elevation of sliding window in masonry wall (rubble or rough stone).

Elevation of double sliding windows in masonry wall.

Plan view of sliding window in masonry veneer wall.

Plan view of double sliding windows in masonry veneer wall.

Plan view of sliding window in solid masonry wall.

Plan view of double sliding windows in solid masonry wall.

Plan view of metal sliding window with plastered returns.

Plan view of metal double sliding windows with plastered returns.

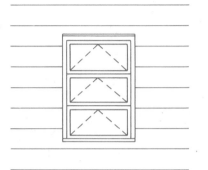

Elevation of awning window in frame wall.

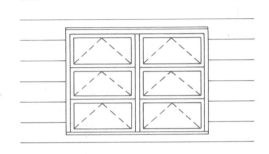

Elevation of double awning window in frame wall.

Plan view of awning window in frame wall.

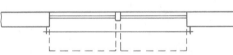

Plan view of double awning window in frame wall.

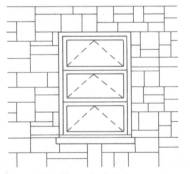

Elevation of awning window in masonry wall (cut stone).

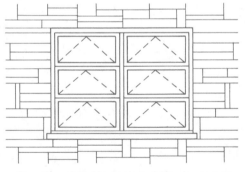

Elevation of double awning window in masonry wall.

Plan view of awning window in masonry veneer wall.

Plan view of double awning window in masonry veneer wall.

Plan view of awning window in solid masonry wall.

Plan view of double awning window in solid masonry wall.

Plan view of metal awning window with plastered returns.

Plan view of metal double awning window with plastered returns.

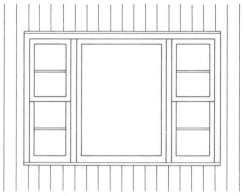

Elevation of fixed picture window with double hung side lights in frame wall.

Plan view of fixed picture window with double hung side lights in masonry veneer wall.

Plan view of fixed picture window with double hung side lights in solid masonry wall.

Plan view of metal fixed picture window with side lights and plastered returns.

Plan view of fixed picture window with double hung side lights in frame wall.

Simplified Methods of Drawing Windows in Plan View

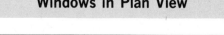

Single window in frame wall.

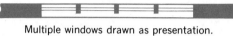

Multiple windows drawn as presentation.

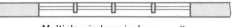

Multiple windows in frame wall.

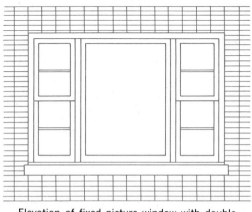

Elevation of fixed picture window with double hung side lights in masonry wall (brick, stack bond).

Picture window with side lights in solid masonry wall.

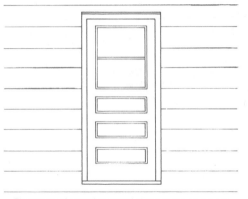

Elevation of exterior panel door in wood frame
wall.

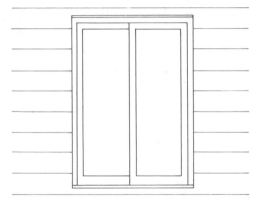

Elevation of exterior sliding door in wood frame
wall.

Plan view of exterior door in wood frame wall.

Plan view of exterior sliding door in wood frame
wall.

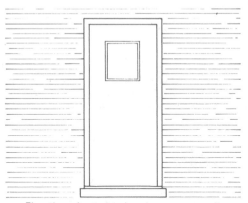

Elevation of exterior door in masonry wall.

Elevation of exterior sliding door in masonry
wall.

Plan view of exterior door in masonry veneer
wall.

Plan view of exterior sliding door in masonry
veneer wall.

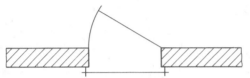

Plan view of exterior door in solid masonry wall.

Plan view of exterior sliding door in solid masonry wall.

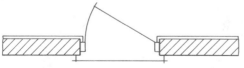

Plan view of exterior door in solid masonry wall with plastered return.

Plan view of exterior sliding door in solid masonry wall with plastered return.

A

E

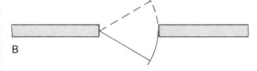

B

F

C

G

D

H

Plan view of interior doors: (A) hinged; (B) double action hinged; (C) double or French; (D) bypass sliding; (E) pocket; (F) double pocket; (G) bi-fold; (H) folding or accordion; (I) plastered or cased opening.

I

413

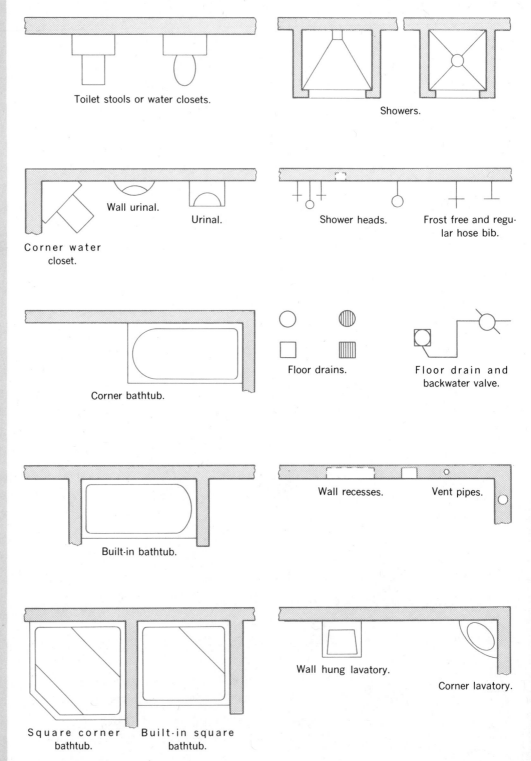

Toilet stools or water closets.

Showers.

Wall urinal.

Urinal.

Shower heads.

Frost free and regular hose bib.

Corner water closet.

Corner bathtub.

Floor drains.

Floor drain and backwater valve.

Built-in bathtub.

Wall recesses.

Vent pipes.

Square corner bathtub.

Built-in square bathtub.

Wall hung lavatory.

Corner lavatory.

Part 4

PLUMBING

SYMBOLS

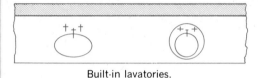

Built-in lavatories.

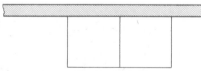

Freestanding and built-in dishwashers.

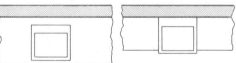

Built-in lavatories.

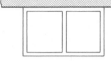

Washer and dryer.

Single bowl sink.   Double bowl sink.

Laundry tubs.   Water heater (designate capacity and fuel).

Double drainboard sink with cabinet.

Shallow bowl sink.

Part 5

RADIATORS

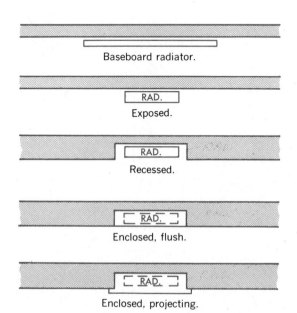

Baseboard radiator.

RAD.

Exposed.

RAD.

Recessed.

RAD.

Enclosed, flush.

RAD.

Enclosed, projecting.

Part 6

SUPPLY PIPES

HOT WATER HEATING SUPPLY
HOT WATER HEATING RETURN
LOW-PRESSURE STEAM
LOW-PRESSURE STEAM RETURN
MEDIUM-PRESSURE STEAM
MEDIUM-PRESSURE STEAM RETURN
HIGH-PRESSURE STEAM
HIGH-PRESSURE STEAM RETURN
AIR-RELIEF LINE
BOILER BLOW OFF
COMPRESSED AIR
FUEL-OIL FLOW
FUEL-OIL RETURN
FUEL-OIL TANK VENT

SOIL, WASTE AND LEADER (ABOVE GRADE)
SOIL, WASTE AND LEADER (BELOW GRADE)
VENT
COLD WATER
HOT WATER
HOT WATER RETURN
GAS
VACUUM
PNEUMATIC TUBE
SPRINKLER BRANCH AND HEAD
SPRINKLER DRAIN
SPRINKLER SUPPLY LINE

Part 7

HEAT DUCTS AND REGISTERS

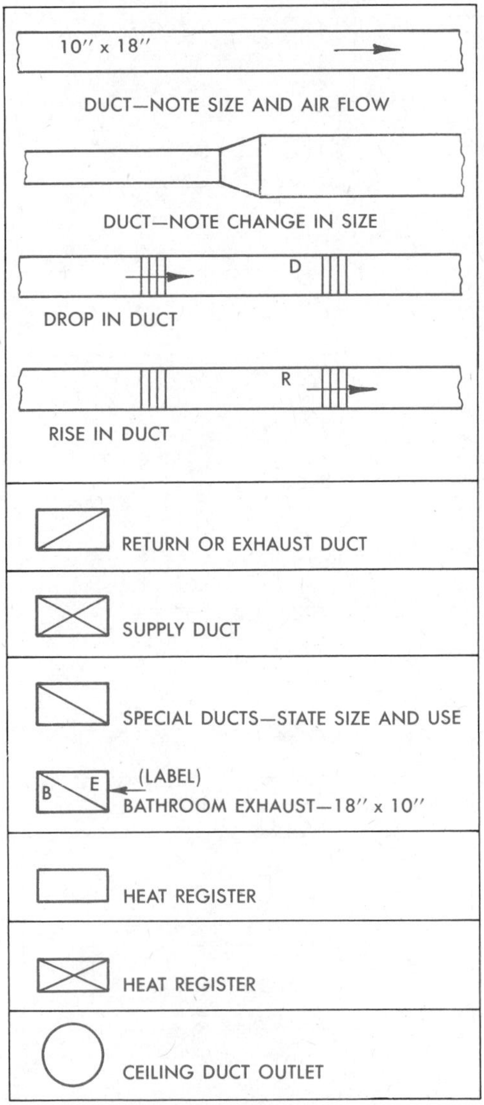

10" x 18"

DUCT—NOTE SIZE AND AIR FLOW

DUCT—NOTE CHANGE IN SIZE

D

DROP IN DUCT

R

RISE IN DUCT

RETURN OR EXHAUST DUCT

SUPPLY DUCT

SPECIAL DUCTS—STATE SIZE AND USE

(LABEL)
B E
BATHROOM EXHAUST—18" x 10"

HEAT REGISTER

HEAT REGISTER

CEILING DUCT OUTLET

Part 8

ELECTRICAL SYMBOLS

S	SINGLE POLE SWITCH
S	SINGLE POLE SWITCH
S_3	THREE WAY SWITCH
S_4	FOUR WAY SWITCH
S_D	AUTOMATIC DOOR SWITCH
S_P	SWITCH WITH PILOT LIGHT
S_{WP}	WEATHERPROOF SWITCH
S_2	DOUBLE POLE SWITCH
S	SWITCH FOR LOW VOLTAGE SYSTEM
— — —	LOW VOLTAGE WIRE
MS	LOW VOLTAGE MASTER SWITCH
 R	RELAY EQUIPPED LIGHTING OUTLET
	DUPLEX RECEPTACLE OUTLET
 3	RECEPTACLE OUTLET OTHER THAN DUPLEX
	SPLIT WIRED RECEPTACLE OUTLET
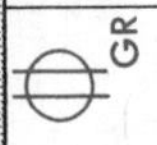 GR	GROUNDING TYPE DUPLEX RECEPTACLE OUTLET

ELECTRICAL SYMBOLS (continued)

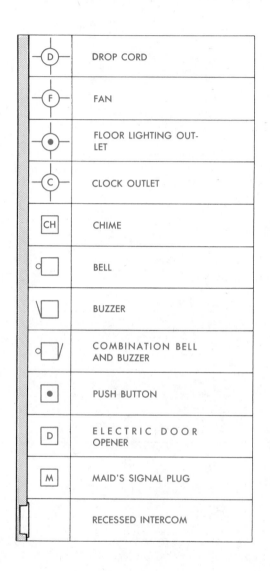

WP	WEATHERPROOF DUPLEX RECEPTACLE OUTLET
GR WP	GROUNDING TYPE WEATHERPROOF DUPLEX RECEPTACLE OUTLET
S	RECEPTACLE OUTLET WITH SWITCH
R	RANGE OUTLET
220	220 VOLT OUTLET
DW	SPECIAL—MUST BE EXPLAINED IN THE KEY TO THE SYMBOLS
J	JUNCTION BOX
	LIGHTING OUTLET
	SQUARE RECESSED LIGHT (SIZE VARIES)
	RECTANGULAR RECESSED LIGHT (SIZE VARIES)
	ROUND RECESSED LIGHT (SIZE VARIES)
	FLUORESCENT LIGHT
	FLUORESCENT LIGHT
L	LAMPHOLDER
L PS	LAMPHOLDER WITH PULL SWITCH
P	PULL SWITCH LIGHT (SAME AS ABOVE)

D	DROP CORD
F	FAN
	FLOOR LIGHTING OUTLET
C	CLOCK OUTLET
CH	CHIME
	BELL
	BUZZER
	COMBINATION BELL AND BUZZER
•	PUSH BUTTON
D	ELECTRIC DOOR OPENER
M	MAID'S SIGNAL PLUG
	RECESSED INTERCOM

ELECTRICAL SYMBOLS (continued)

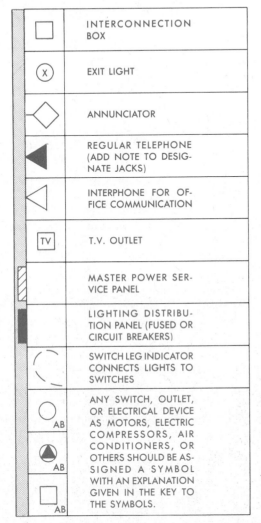

☐	INTERCONNECTION BOX
Ⓧ	EXIT LIGHT
◇	ANNUNCIATOR
◀	REGULAR TELEPHONE (ADD NOTE TO DESIGNATE JACKS)
◁	INTERPHONE FOR OFFICE COMMUNICATION
TV	T.V. OUTLET
	MASTER POWER SERVICE PANEL
	LIGHTING DISTRIBUTION PANEL (FUSED OR CIRCUIT BREAKERS)
⌒	SWITCH LEG INDICATOR CONNECTS LIGHTS TO SWITCHES
○ AB ▲ AB ☐ AB	ANY SWITCH, OUTLET, OR ELECTRICAL DEVICE AS MOTORS, ELECTRIC COMPRESSORS, AIR CONDITIONERS, OR OTHERS SHOULD BE ASSIGNED A SYMBOL WITH AN EXPLANATION GIVEN IN THE KEY TO THE SYMBOLS.

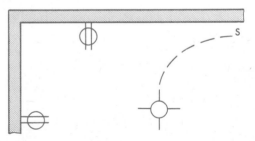

ONE SINGLE POLE SWITCH TO CONTROL ONE LIGHT FIXTURE

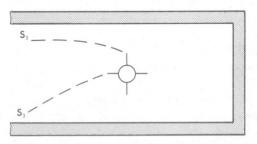

THREE-WAY SWITCHES TO CONTROL ONE LIGHT

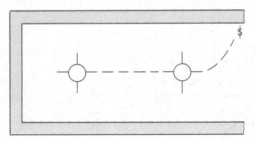

ONE SINGLE POLE SWITCH TO CONTROL TWO LIGHT FIXTURES

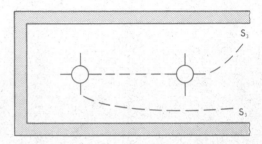

THREE-WAY SWITCHES TO CONTROL TWO LIGHT FIXTURES

39

Dimensioning and Notes

Dimensioning states the sizes of an object and its parts. This is the only reason dimensions are placed on a drawing. Dimensions must explain all sizes so well there is no chance for mistakes when interpreting them. In a building plan, they should be so complete that no additional mathematical calculations are necessary to understand the sizes.

Dimensions are placed on a drawing only if they are needed to construct the object. For example, if a window is placed 10'-0" from one end of a building, a dimension is needed from only one end. The amount of distance remaining is not important.

Dimensions Based on Understanding of Construction

An understanding of building materials, methods, construction, and sizes of parts is important for locating dimensions on a drawing. Dimensions are placed so they measure from parts that are completed first to those that are completed later. For example, if one is dimensioning a floor plan of a brick veneer building, the dimensions are placed from edge to edge of the wood frame because brick veneer is added after the building shell is complete. Since it is added later, an overall dimension from outside edges of the brick would require calculations to determine frame length.

Basis of Dimensioning Rules

There are many rules of dimensioning. It is not always possible to observe every rule because following one may cause a violation of another. One must select the best solution for each individual situation. The most important rule of dimensioning is to *use good judgment*.

Extension and Construction Lines

An extension line is a fine, dark line that extends at a *right angle* from the object or part to be dimensioned.

An extension line begins about 1/16" from the object and extends about 1/8" beyond (past) the last dimension line. One must know how many dimension lines are needed before it is possible to draw an extension line its correct length, and it is necessary to have the extension lines before one can draw the dimension lines their proper length. Both kinds of lines may be drawn as very fine, light construction lines; then darken the portion needed. Construction lines are drawn by "floating" the pencil along the instruments without applying any pressure. Construction lines are not removed from the working drawing.

Estimating Space in Dimensioning

Since the 1/16" space between the object and the extension line is estimated rather than measured, care must be taken to avoid placing the extension line either too

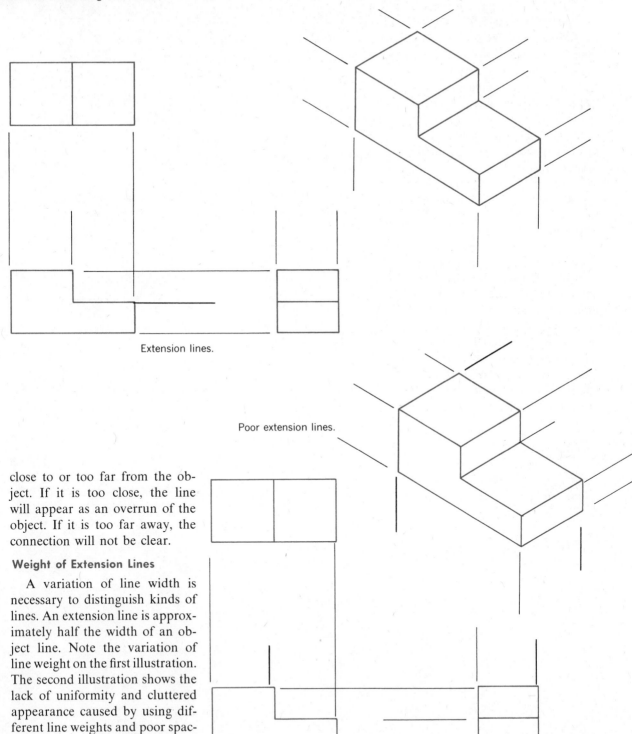

Extension lines.

Poor extension lines.

close to or too far from the object. If it is too close, the line will appear as an overrun of the object. If it is too far away, the connection will not be clear.

Weight of Extension Lines

A variation of line width is necessary to distinguish kinds of lines. An extension line is approximately half the width of an object line. Note the variation of line weight on the first illustration. The second illustration shows the lack of uniformity and cluttered appearance caused by using different line weights and poor spacing at extensions of object lines.

Dimension Lines and Dimensions

A dimension line is a fine dark line, the same width as the extension line. It is parallel to the section being measured. On architectural drawings this is continuous from extension line to extension line. Dimension lines are usually spaced ⅜″ to ½″ from the object and are ⅜″ to ½″ apart. Spacing of dimension lines is determined by the size and complexity of the drawing. They should not be placed so close together that the drawing looks cluttered or dimension figures are crowded. Dimensions should not be too far removed from the section measured.

When possible, dimensions are placed outside of the views. If more than one view is shown, dimensions are placed between views. This permits the same dimension to serve for more than one view.

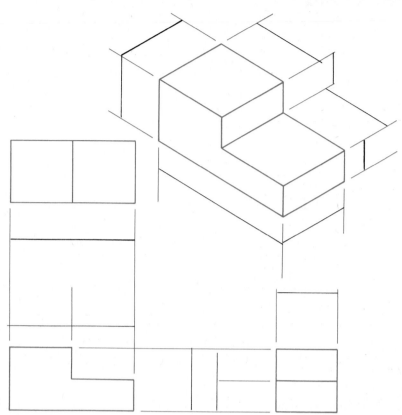

Poor application of dimension lines.

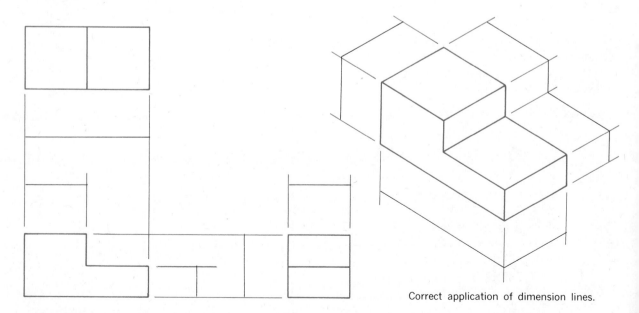

Correct application of dimension lines.

Kinds of Dimensions

There are two kinds of dimensions. *Location dimensions* tell how far something is from something else. *Size dimensions* tell the actual size of an object. The same dimension may show both a size and a location.

A dimension for a small part is called a *detail* dimension. The dimension showing the total length of an object is called an *overall* dimension. When dimensions are placed above or between views, the overall dimension is placed above detail dimensions. When the dimensions are below the view, the overall dimension is below the detail dimensions. When the dimensions are *between* the front and side views, the overall dimension is often put to the *right* of the detail dimension.

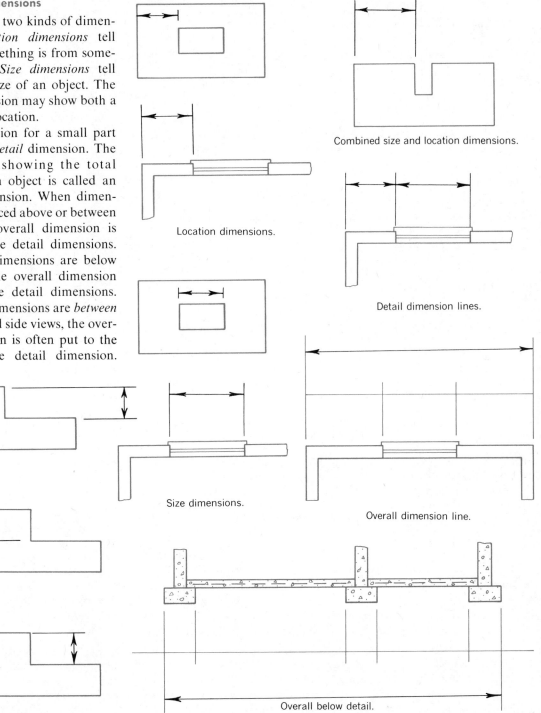

Location dimensions.

Combined size and location dimensions.

Detail dimension lines.

Size dimensions.

Overall dimension line.

Overall below detail.

Variations of dimension placement.

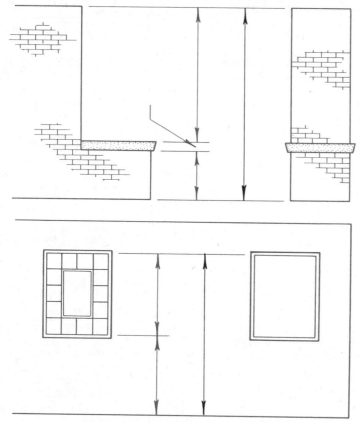

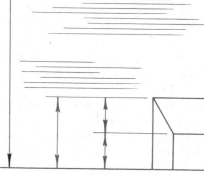

Overall dimension line to left of detail dimension.

Overall dimension line to right of detail dimension.

When the dimensions are to the *left* of a view, the overall dimension is usually to the left of the detail dimensions.

A dimension line may end at an extension line, object line, hidden line, or center line. Keep its purpose in mind, to understand this.

A center line, hidden line, cutting plane line, or object line may not be used as a dimension line. No figures may be placed upon these lines which must be kept clear to show other information.

It is poor practice, and confusing to dimension hidden parts. This should not be done if the dimension can be drawn from visible parts.

Relationship of Extension and Dimension Lines

When two dimension lines join end to end, they are separated by an extension line. Even though both dimension lines may be drawn at the same time they are distinct.

The extension line is considered as passing between the two lines rather than crossing a line. If extension lines were to cross dimension lines, one would not be able to tell where lines were ending. However, extension lines *may*

cross other extension lines; dimension lines *may* cross dimension lines. If extension lines *must* cross dimension lines (no other way it can be done), one may break the extension line where it crosses or the line weight may be varied slightly.

Dimensions for Interior Parts and Voids

Dimensions for interior parts and voids are sometimes placed outside the views. This requires the extension line to cross an object line. Old established practice called for a break in the extension line where it crossed the object

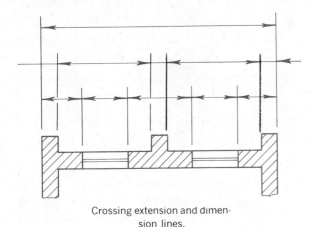

Crossing extension and dimension lines.

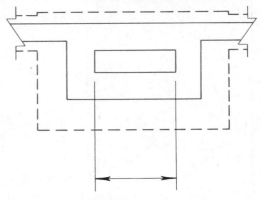

Extension lines crossing object lines.

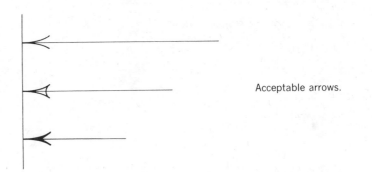

Acceptable arrows.

line. Architectural draftsmen usually cross the object line with the extension line, leaving no break.

Identifying Ends of Dimension Lines

An identifying mark is used to terminate dimension lines when they end at extension lines. An arrow is the conventional symbol. The arrow may be either the open or closed type. Arrow size is determined by the size and complexity of the drawing. It is usually drawn about $1/16''$ wide and $1/8''$ long. The sides of the arrow should be symmetrical. However, one cannot waste time when drawing it. Arrows in architectural drawing are usually free flowing in character.

Because of the time required to form arrows, architectural draftsmen frequently replace them with a diagonal dash at intersections of extension and dimension lines.

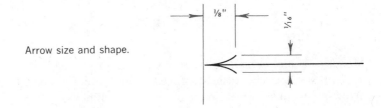

Arrow size and shape.

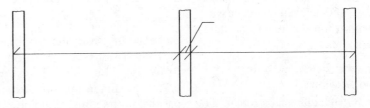

Diagonal dashes replacing arrows.

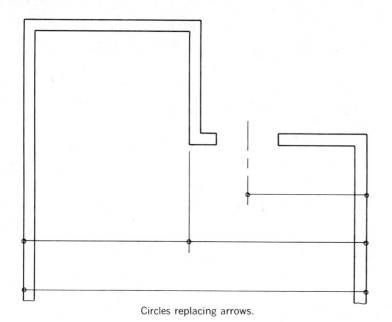

Circles replacing arrows.

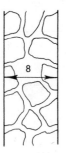

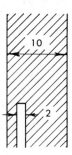

Dimensions on symbols.

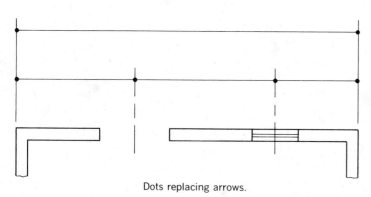

Dots replacing arrows.

Modern practice sometimes uses dots or small circles instead of arrows. In modular dimensioning, combinations of dots and arrows are used. The arrows show all modular measurements; all fractions and uneven inch measurements (non-modular) are shown with dots.

Dimensions on Symbols and Sections

When a dimension is placed on a symbol or in a sectioned area, symbol and section lines *do not* cross the figure. It is good practice to add all dimensions before section lines are placed on the views.

Extension lines and dimension lines *may* cross a sectioned area.

Dimensioning Systems

There are two systems of placing dimensions on a working drawing. The *aligned* system places the dimensions so they are parallel to the dimension line. All horizontal figures are read from the *bottom* of the drawing sheet. All vertical dimensions are read from the *right side* of the drawing. When pictorials are used, the dimensions are parallel to the dimension lines. Architectural drawings employ the aligned system.

The *unidirectional* system places all dimension figures so they are read from the bottom of the drawing sheet. Thus all dimensions are parallel to the bottom of the sheet. This system is used primarily in the aircraft and some automotive and ship building industries.

Figures for Dimensions

Dimensions show the length of the section. These figures must not be crossed by other lines. They must be lettered so well there is no possibility of workmen mis-reading them. Lettering size is determined by size and complexity of the drawing. Guide lines are drawn for *all* lettering. One never becomes so experienced that they are no longer needed. Professionals always use them for standard plans. The only exception is if one is using very thin tracing paper placed over a grid paper, as described in Chapter 31, or if heavy guide lines are on a sheet from which a tracing is being made.

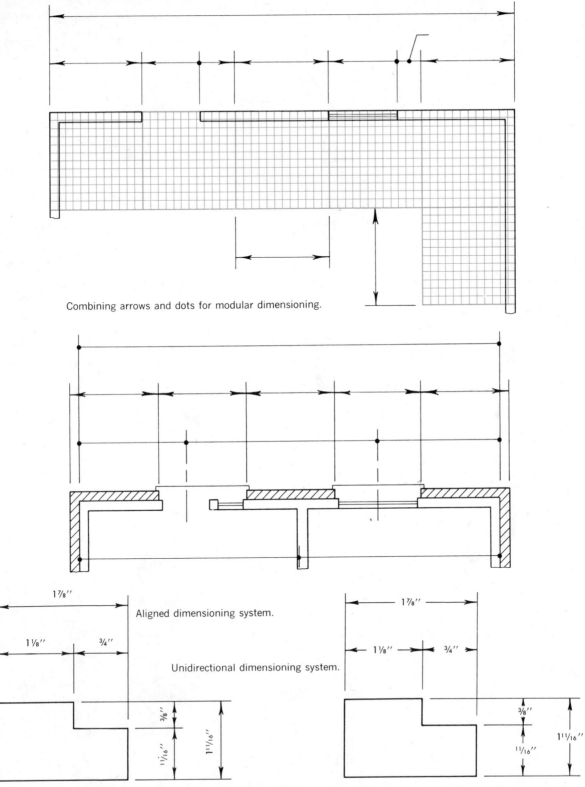

Combining arrows and dots for modular dimensioning.

Aligned dimensioning system.

Unidirectional dimensioning system.

1⅞″

1⅛″ ¾″

⅜″

1⅐/16″ 1¹¹/16″

1⅞″

1⅛″ ¾″

⅜″

1¹¹/16″

¹¹/16″

427

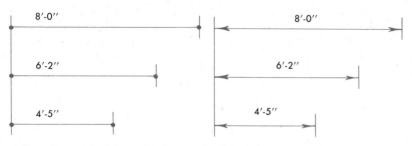

| Poor placement of dimension figures. | Better placement of dimension figures. |

The lower edge of the figure is about $1/16''$ above the dimension line. Standard size of dimensions is $1/8''$, however, on a complex working drawing such as a floor plan, $3/32''$ may be more suitable for crowded areas. Names of rooms should be at least $1/8''$. A beginner may measure these distances, but after experience is acquired they are estimated.

When two or more dimension lines are closely parallel, dimensions are placed so they are not directly in line with each other. This makes them easier to read and helps avoid reading errors.

As mentioned earlier, dimensions are not placed on a drawing unless they are needed. Manufactured and pre-assembled parts are dimensioned only where and when necessary. If a size is important in relationship to something to be built, the size is added.

On architectural drawings, measurements over $12''$ in length are shown in feet and inches, as $7'-3\frac{1}{4}''$, $8'-0''$ or $6'-0\frac{1}{2}''$. If the measurement is less than $12''$, the dimension is shown as $0'-8\frac{1}{4}''$. (If space is limited the $0'$ may be omitted.)

If dimension lines are on isometric, perspective, or other pictorial drawings, of course, dimensions are made in the same manner.

Dimensioning Circles

When parts of an object are circular, the overall dimension is given *to the center* of the circle. The circular part is dimensioned separately.

Location of circles is also di-

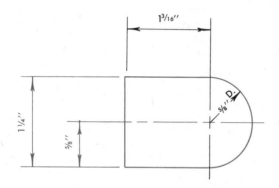

Dimensions for an object with one circular part.

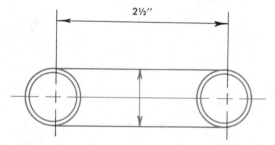

Dimensions for an object with two circular parts.

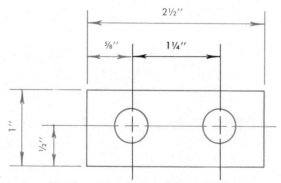

Location and center-to-center dimensions.

mensioned to the center of the circle. When two or more circular forms are shown, such as holes, center-to-center dimensions are given.

When the *size* of a circle (solid or void) is dimensioned, the diameter is shown. If the circle is large enough to place the dimension inside the circle, the dimension line should pass through its center. Figures are added above the line and are read from the bottom or right side. If the dimension cannot be placed inside the circle, outer dimension lines penetrate toward the center.

If there is more than one circle on an object and only one is dimensioned, all other circles are the same size. If there is more than one circle on an object and only one location dimension is given, the other circles are equally spaced.

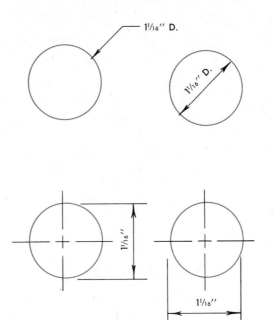

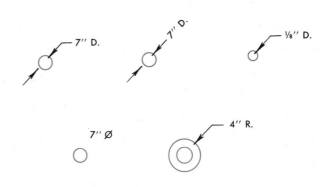

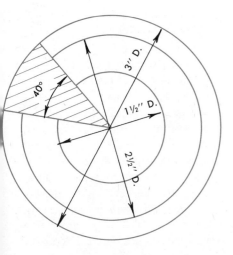

Dimensions for circles.

Dimensions for equally spaced circles.

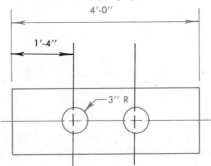

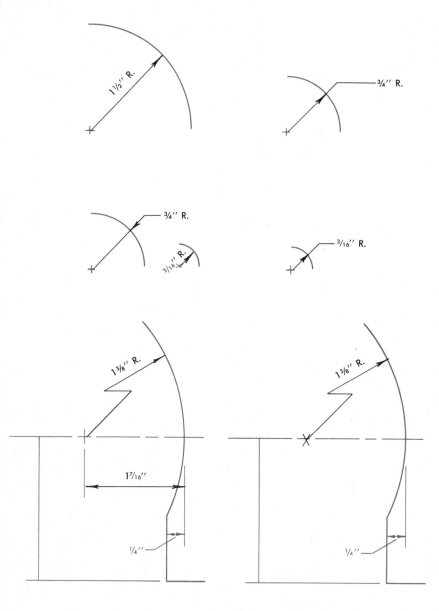

tween the object and extension line as on rectangular objects), and a dimension arc radiating from the vertex is drawn. Angles may also be dimensioned to show the ratio of rise to run. This is used to show roof slope.

Leaders and Notes

All information cannot be presented graphically. Some must be presented as lettered notes and symbols. If space permits or if a note applies at only one location, the note may be placed adjacent to the part. A pointer called a *leader* shows the part being discussed.

There are two kinds of leaders. One is drawn freehand and the other is drawn with instruments. When drawn with instruments, all leaders in a given area are drawn at the same angle. No prescribed angle is used; however, 30°, 60° and 45° are common because triangles have these angles. Lettering from different leaders is uniform.

A leader is a fine dark line the same thickness and weight as an extension or dimension line. If a leader is pointing to a line, it should touch the line. If it is pointing to a surface, it should end on the surface. The leader is leading the eye from the note to the part. The end of the leader (at the part) should terminate with an arrow or, if dots are being used, with a dot. There is no arrow on the other end. There should be ⅛" to 3/16" space between the leader and the lettering.

Horizontal guide lines are drawn for lettering the note. The

Arcs

An arc is dimensioned by showing its *radius*. The dimension line should terminate at the center of the arc. If the dimension line (or a "leader") is placed outside the arc, it must point toward the center of the arc. To make the center (vertex) more clearly visible, it is common practice to make an + crossing the center of the arc.

Dimensioning Angles

When angles are dimensioned, extension lines are projected from the angle (1/16" space is left be-

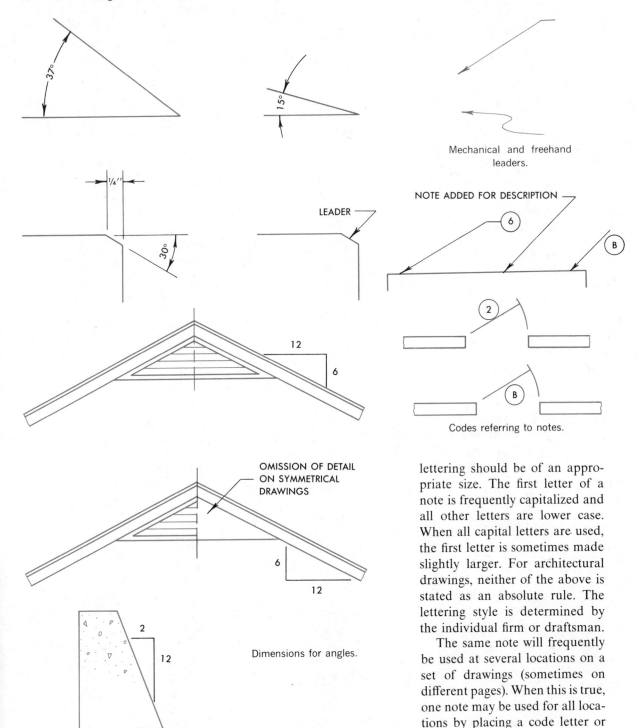

Mechanical and freehand leaders.

NOTE ADDED FOR DESCRIPTION

Codes referring to notes.

LEADER

OMISSION OF DETAIL ON SYMMETRICAL DRAWINGS

Dimensions for angles.

lettering should be of an appropriate size. The first letter of a note is frequently capitalized and all other letters are lower case. When all capital letters are used, the first letter is sometimes made slightly larger. For architectural drawings, neither of the above is stated as an absolute rule. The lettering style is determined by the individual firm or draftsman.

The same note will frequently be used at several locations on a set of drawings (sometimes on different pages). When this is true, one note may be used for all locations by placing a code letter or figure near the end of the leader.

If clearly understood, the leader may be omitted and the code placed near the part. These codes usually refer to a series of notes that have all been grouped in one convenient location, or they may refer to charts and schedules of building parts, sizes, or patterns (styles). The code letter or figure is usually placed inside a circle, square, rectangle, or triangle. This is done to bring attention to the coded part.

For example, if code letters are placed on doors, all door codes might use letters and all might be in squares. Or if windows were being coded, all codes might use figures and be in circles. Circles are not always used to code windows and squares are not always used to code doors, this is an example. Whether to use a square, rectangle or other shape, and whether to use letters or figures, is the draftsman's decision.

Application of Dimensioning Rules

Statement of a dimensioning rule does not always insure its proper use on a working drawing! If rules are not followed or if omissions of dimensions are made because of an inadequate understanding of them, an incomplete plan will result. As stated earlier, the reason dimensions are placed on a drawing is so workmen can build the object. If you omit any dimensions or have them wrong, the work will be in error. This is in effect telling men to build the part any size they choose. Workmen must follow the building plans; they are not responsible for correcting your errors. Chances are they won't know you made an error. For example, if you dimensioned a pier as 24" square and it should have been 16" square, the workmen have no way of knowing this. Extra care must be taken to be sure that all sizes are correct and that detail dimensions, added together, equal the total or overall dimension involved.

A complete set of working drawings concludes this chapter. Each item discussed on the following pages is shown on the completed plans. To gain an understanding of the items being discussed, one should study and make constant reference to the completed plans. It is not possible to cover all situations or all methods of drawing and dimensioning on one set of plans. Other plans in the text show additional items and other ways parts may be drawn and dimensioned.

DIMENSIONING FLOOR PLANS

Rules state that dimensions are placed outside of the views, if possible. However, reason says that a floor plan must have many of the dimensions inside the view. It is common practice to place dimensions for windows and exterior doors outside the view (floor plan). These are usually placed on the first dimension line.

Dimensioning Windows and Doors on Floor Plan

Wood windows and doors in typical frame construction are dimensioned from an outside wall to the center of the window or door. When several windows make one large unit (as a picture window with double-hung side lights, or three awning windows in one unit), the dimension is to the center of the group. This does not imply windows or doors may be placed anywhere one desires. Pre-planning places one edge of the window or door on normal stud spacing. The window and door manufacturer and specific units must be selected before the finished and rough opening sizes can be determined. For the beginner, an instructor may suggest approximate window sizes rather than have you select a specific window. This saves time and still teaches the way it is to be done.

Windows and doors in modular construction (solid masonry, masonry veneer, and modular panels) are dimensioned from an outside wall to the edge of the window or door opening. All wall and opening sizes are dimensioned.

Dimensioning Offsets in Exterior Walls

The second exterior dimension line usually shows the irregular shape of the outside walls. All offsets must be dimensioned. If the exterior wall is straight for its entire length, of course, a second dimension line is not needed.

On frame construction the first dimension is drawn from the edge of the studding and not from the face of the exterior wall covering. Solid masonry is measured from the outside corner. Masonry veneer over wood frame is measured from the corner studding. One may show the distance from the edge of the studding to the outside face of masonry as a separate detail dimension.

Other Outside Dimension Lines

The overall dimension line is for the last dimension (farthest from the view). It terminates at the same location as detail dimensions of offsets, or if one desires to show overall dimensions of masonry veneer over wood frame, two overall dimension lines may be used.

Porches or landings, steps, and areaways may require an additional set of dimension lines. These are usually placed between the window dimension lines and wall dimension lines. Exact location will depend upon shape.

Floor plans usually require only two overall dimensions, one for length and one for width. Occasionally, for reference, four overall dimensions are shown, one on every side of the floor plan. This is not to be done unless one has a good reason for it.

Overall dimension lines may be placed on *each* floor plan to save workmen time during construction.

Since the scale of working drawings is small, it is not always possible to tell exactly where extension lines are pointing. Then a note must be placed in a conspicuous place stating where dimensions are taken. For example, on a frame building with masonry veneer, as described earlier, the note might read:

NOTE: ALL DIMENSIONS ARE FROM OUT-SIDE EDGE OF STUDS.

Or it might read:

NOTE: EXTERIOR DIMENSIONS ARE FROM

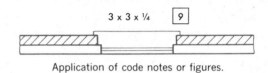

3 x 3 x ¼   9

Application of code notes or figures.

OUTSIDE EDGE OF STUDS; INTERIOR DIMENSIONS ARE TO CENTER OF STUDS.

Code and Code Key for Windows and Doors

In a previous paragraph on leaders and notes an example was given of placing notes on windows and doors. A code letter or figure system to identify each window may be used on the floor plan or elevations. Or, for reference purposes, it may be placed in both locations. This saves estimators and workmen from turning pages to find necessary information. *All* windows and doors that are the same size and style have the same code number or letter. If a window or door is the same size as another one, but a different style, the code is different. Use of door and window codes is shown on the dimensioned floor plan accompanying this chapter.

If the building is small and there is not a large variety of sizes and styles, and no specific manufacturer is desired, the window and door sizes are sometimes lettered on the plan. This information is placed next to the part and replaces the codes. Details are much better than just putting the size on the plan.

Interior and exterior doors are all coded and keyed to the same door schedule. *All* doors for *all* stories are placed on the same door schedule. *All* windows are

placed on one window schedule. Examples of door and window schedules are shown in Chapter 40 and on the dimensioned plans in this chapter.

Lintel Code and Schedule

If an opening in a masonry wall has masonry above it, lintels are required. For small structures, the lintel size may be lettered by the opening as in the illustration. For larger structures, or if several lintel sizes are required, a code letter or figure on each opening refers to a lintel schedule. A complete lintel schedule is shown in Chapter 40.

Interior Dimensions

Every room or enclosed space must have width and length dimensions. All offsets in rooms must be dimensioned. The length of all stub or partial walls must be shown. Distances across plastered or cased openings are shown if lengths of rooms and stub walls do not give an adequate description.

Dimensions for adjoining rooms or spaces should be kept *in line* (even) with each other when it is possible. The dimension lines should be placed in a relatively open space. Considerable pre-planning and trial placement are necessary to avoid conflict with symbols and names of rooms and parts.

Dimensioning Interior Doors

If dimensions for interior doors are measured to the door centers, a center line is used. If the dimension is to the edges of the door, or the rough opening, a regular extension line is used. A note should be placed on the floor plan to designate how dimensions for door openings are measured (rough opening, finished opening, center of opening). One must remember to place all codes, as described earlier.

Dimensioning in Halls

Since a hall is quite narrow, the drawing can easily become cluttered with extension and dimension lines and figures. If at all possible, only one row of dimension lines should be used. Generally it is not necessary to have an overall dimension for the hall. However, the width must be shown. Note how dimensioning has been accomplished on the sample first-floor plan.

Names of Rooms and Spaces

Each room and space (closet, hall, dining area, etc.) must be prominently identified. This is usually done near the center of the room or in the center of its largest open space. Size of lettering depends upon the complexity of the part. Names of rooms are usually ⅛″, but may be ³⁄₁₆″ or larger if space permits. Dimension notes and figures in a small area may be as small as ¹⁄₁₆″.

Equipment not recognizable by its shape must have the name lettered on or near the object. If outside the object, a leader points to it.

Dimensioning Equipment

Show *location* dimensions for *all* equipment, cabinets, bathroom fixtures, or any other item to be installed, unless previous dimensions (as for windowed walls) make their location obvious. *Detail* dimensions for the above are shown only if they are not given on detail drawings. When possible, it is much better to prepare large-scale detail drawings.

Electrical Symbols

Electrical symbols show the *general* (approximate) location of all electrical items. These are not dimensioned on a floor plan. If the exact location is required, or if wiring diagrams are needed, a separate electrical plan is drawn.

Wall Thickness

Wall thickness is usually shown on the view, rather than outside it.

Illustrations on page 435 show different ways of dimensioning walls. These should be studied carefully so you can select the most appropriate method for dimensioning your own plans.

Overhead Joists

If the working drawings are to include a complete set of framing diagrams, it is not necessary to show floor and ceiling joists on the floor plans. However, since conventional framing today usually does not have framing plans, it is necessary to show joist size and spacing. The symbol is placed and noted as shown on the sample floor plans accompanying this chapter. Each plan shows the overhead joists.

For example, a basement plan indicates the first floor joists; a first floor plan shows the ceiling joists over it. If all joists on each level are the same size, run the same direction, and have the same spacing, they need to be indicated only once. If they are not all the same on each story, every change needs to be noted.

Cutting Plane Lines

Cutting plane lines, as described and shown in Chapter 35, are drawn on the floor plan to indicate where sections and details will fit into the completed plan. Remember that the part is to be viewed from the cutting plane line, toward the arrow or "code key" circle. This same code key is also placed on the detail or section drawing. Examples are shown on the sample floor plan.

Heat Registers and Radiators

The general location and the outline of all heat and return sources are indicated on floor plans. These are not usually dimensioned. If complete heat plans are required they are drawn separately.

Plumbing Lines

Except for very small structures, these are usually placed and dimensioned on a separate plan. Examples of plumbing lines shown on the regular working drawing may be seen on the sample footing and foundation plan.

Designation of Scale

The name and scale of each drawing must be clearly indicated. See plans, pages 499-527.

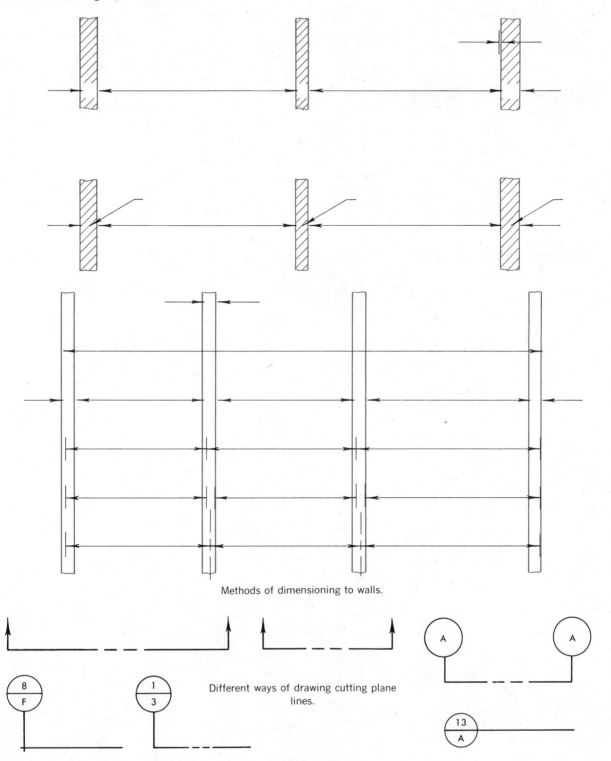

Methods of dimensioning to walls.

Different ways of drawing cutting plane lines.

Title blocks with this information are included. If not in the title block, name and scale must be shown on the plan.

DIMENSIONING AND NOTES FOR ELEVATIONS

Overall dimensions are not shown on elevations, since they are given on floor plans.

Since section and symbol lines do not cross a dimension figure, they may be omitted until all dimensions and notes are placed on the drawing. Otherwise considerable pre-planning for dimensions and notes is necessary.

Dimensioning Footings, Foundations, and Special Details

When footings and foundations are drawn on the plan (they are not always), total footing depth below grade must be shown. When the building is to have several footing depths, each must be shown. One must also show the height (depth) and width of all footings. If most footings are the same size but some are different, the typical size is shown and a note added stating that all are this size unless dimensioned differently. Each foundation thickness (width) must also be shown. Only one dimension is required if all are the same size. If more than one thickness is required, the typical one is noted and all different sizes are shown. These dimensions may be repeated on two adjoining elevations when all elevations are not on the same drawing sheet.

The thickness of a basement or crawl space floor is also shown.

Pier heights are measured from the top of the pier to the bottom of the footing. Complete sizes are usually shown on separate details. If they are not shown elsewhere, complete sizes must be dimensioned on the elevations.

Location and detail dimensions are required for all areaways, porches, landings, steps, and other exterior parts.

Height and width (length) of all changes in wall covering materials must be shown unless their location is obvious because of their relationship to some other part. For example, if stone veneer ends at the side of a door, and the door location is dimensioned on the floor plan, a dimension is not needed on the elevation. Vertical location dimensions for parts may be taken from grade line or floor line, whichever is more applicable. Horizontal dimensions are taken from an outside wall or offset (not necessarily the same one).

The top of foundations or bottom of joists are dimensioned from grade. Basement or crawl space height is dimensioned from the bottom of the floor joists to the face of the floor below. In addition, a combined thickness of floor joist and subfloor is shown.

Ceiling height is usually measured up from the top face of the subfloor to the bottom of the ceiling joists. If it is measured from some other point, a note should state this. NOTE: When typical 8'-0" ceilings are to be used, the measurement is not exactly 8'-0". Allow also for the finished floor and ceiling material thickness.

Additional stories are dimensioned the same as the first story. They also require ceiling joist and subfloor dimensions.

Window, Door and Sill Dimensions

Window and door heights are dimensioned from the face of the subfloor to the top of the sash or door and not to the top of the casing.

When the tops of all windows and doors are a uniform height, only one height dimension (from the subfloor) is required. If heights vary from the standard used, each window or door that is not the same height as others is dimensioned separately.

Actual window height and distance from the floor to the bottom of the window are not usually shown. If these dimensions are needed when laying masonry walls, or to give the size and location of stone sills, they must be shown. Height of stone sills and their distance above the subfloor are shown.

Horizontal location dimensions for windows and doors are not shown on elevations because this information can be found on the floor plan.

Glass size may be indicated on each window. The width is shown first and then the height. A code letter similar to the one placed on the floor plan may also be shown on the window.

A note is needed to show the size and style of window and door casings unless detailed elsewhere.

Chimney Dimensions

It is not necessary to show horizontal location dimensions for a chimney because these are shown on floor plans. One must include detail and overall dimensions for the chimney.

Total height is shown from the ridge to the top of the flue liner.

Roof Covering

Notes are placed on roofs to describe the kind and weight per square of roofing material. Special features such as ridge finish and flashing are also indicated. If flashing is used in other locations and is not shown on separate details, it is noted on the elevations.

Louvers or Ventilators

When louvers or other ventilators are required, these are dimensioned or notes are added if not shown on separate details.

Other Items Requiring Dimensions and Notes

The following items are found on almost every plan. Your elevation should be checked for their inclusion, when they apply:

- Size and kind of downspouts and gutters.
- Fascia and soffit materials.
- Amount of overhang on each side of each roof.
- Name and notes of all wall covering materials.
- Indication of roof pitch. Only one is required unless different roof slopes are used on the same building; then each slope must be indicated.
- Names of all masonry bonds or siding patterns and reference to detail drawings of same.
- Height of steps and offsets of floor and ceiling levels, or reference to details.

- Name of each elevation.
- Check plan carefully for unusual items and methods of construction that may need additional dimensions.
- A note on omissions and errors, as described in Chapter 51.
- Scale used when it is not included in the title block.

DIMENSIONING

Heating Plans

Heating plans should include the following dimensions and notes, when they are applicable:
- Fuel storage size and location, when required.
- Location dimensions for supply lines. Notes describing size (diameter), I.D. or O.D.
- Location dimensions for heating-cooling source (furnace and air conditioning).
- Information about the heating-cooling source. Notes describing name, model, kind of fuel, system used (forced air, hot water, steam, heat pump, or other) and the output in btu's.
- Runs for all pipes or ducts; notes stating sizes used.
- Location and size dimensions where pipes, ducts, registers, or radiators fit into or pass through a wall.
- Location and size dimensions for all pipe chases and recesses. These may need to be shown on regular floor plans.
- Check the plan carefully to be sure all heating-cooling details are fully described.

NOTE: Study carefully the sample footing and foundation plan. Also study the heating diagrams in Chapter 48.

Electrical Plans

Electrical plans should include the following dimensions and notes when they are applicable:

- Location of entrance service. Note for voltage, amperage, and whether the system uses fuses or circuit breakers. Number of circuits to be accommodated. One may list the manufacturer and model number.
- Plans for large buildings may require details of entrance service. If they do, describe required parts.
- Location of all convenience outlets, boxes for lights and switches. All other electrical equipment such as motors, pumps, fans, disposers, and mixers must be shown and dimensioned when required.
- Lines (as on a regular floor plan) connecting switches and convenience outlets or lighting outlets do not describe actual wire location and are not dimensioned.
- When wires are placed in conduit, its location is shown if the exact location is necessary.
- One should add notes describing size of all wires used, size, type, and location of all junction boxes, and descriptions of electrical connections.
- Identification of individual circuits.
- Location of low voltage transformers and relays.
- Location of door chimes and transformers.
- Telephone or jack locations when they are to be installed during construction.

- Check the plan carefully to be sure all electrical details are fully described.

REMEMBER: Only partial electrical plans are usually shown for small buildings and the detail information is incorporated with the floor plans.

Plumbing Plans

Plumbing plans should include the following dimensions and notes, when they are applicable:
- A note is used to indicate direction and distance from edge of building to water main and sewer.
- Location of water line entering building. Size of collar required where it passes through exterior foundation or basement wall.
- Location of water meter.
- Location and size of water heater; capacity and type of fuel used. Manufacturer and model number may be shown.
- Indication of size for all water and drainage lines.
- Location and size of soil stacks and vents.
- Sizes of all pipes and kinds of connections noted on schematic diagram.
- Location of all pipes passing through floors or walls and the size collars, when required. This is especially important when concrete floors or walls are to be used.
- Note special traps and drains.
- Note, describe, and dimension size and location of cisterns, drywells, catch basins, or septic tanks.
- When drainage fields are required, the size tile and methods of installation are noted.
- Check the plan carefully to be sure all plumbing details are fully described.

REMEMBER: Only partial plumbing plans are usually shown for small buildings and the detail information is incorporated with the floor plans.

Dimensioning Details

Small-scale plans do not adequately describe or allow space for dimensioning intricate parts. Therefore the details are enlarged separately. Since there are infinite possible details, no attempt will be made to show where each dimension on every drawing is to be placed. One must follow good dimensioning practice when placing *all* location and detail dimensions. The detail is usually set in with adjacent parts. As mentioned earlier, manufactured parts are not usually dimensioned unless size or shape affects other items to be constructed. Only the actual part being emphasized, or its location and relationship to other parts, is dimensioned and names of parts lettered or noted on the drawing. This is arbitrary. If the

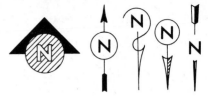

North point indicators should be attractive but simple.

designer or draftsman feels dimensions or names of other parts are necessary for an adequate description, they are added.

The code key on each detail *must* refer to the location of the detail on other parts of the plan. Examples of the code on small-scale drawings keyed to the detail are shown in the illustrations. When a plan includes many details, it is necessary to have several letters and figures for each code. Notice the numbering system on the illustrations.

Careful study of these illustrations and the sample plans will help you gain an understanding of dimensioning and coding details. When studying a detail, find the same detail as shown on all other parts of the plan.

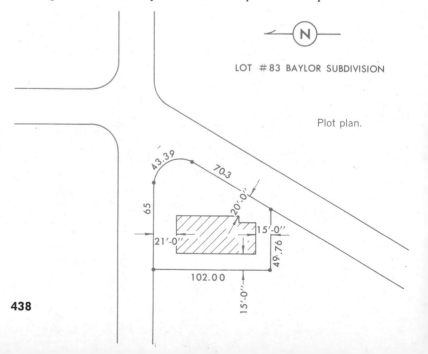

LOT #83 BAYLOR SUBDIVISION

Plot plan.

METRIC MEASUREMENT

About 90% of the world's countries have adopted the metric measurement system (Système International d'Unités), frequently referred to as SI. After much study, Congress has initiated necessary legislation to establish a 10-year metric conversion program for the United States.

Much headway has already been made by business and industry toward complete or partial metric conversion. Many firms are now using a dual dimensioning system for their working plans, specifications, and operating manuals. Dual dimensioning means that both metric and customary units are shown. In many businesses the dual system will probably be replaced by complete metric conversion.

When established ways of doing things are discarded and new procedures adopted, the new almost always appears more difficult. It is true that conversion from one system to another is difficult, but the metric system itself is much simpler than the customary system. The metric system is based on multiples of 10. For example, the *metre* is the basic unit of length. A *centimetre* is 1/100 of a metre; a *kilometre* is 1000 times a metre. Conversion from one unit to another is easy. Compare this to the customary system, in which there are 12 inches in a foot, 3 feet in a yard, and 1760 yards in a mile.

The best method for learning the metric system is to think in the new terms rather than to attempt to equate metric units to customary. However, during the transition it will be necessary to make conversions. This chapter

Metric Decimal Prefixes

Multiplication Factors	Symbol	Prefix
1 000 000 000 000 $= 10^{12}$	tera	T
1 000 000 000 $= 10^{9}$	giga	G
1 000 000 $= 10^{6}$	mega	M
1 000 $= 10^{3}$	kilo	k
100 $= 10^{2}$	hecto	h
10 $= 10^{1}$	deka	da
1	(Units)	
0.1 $= 10^{-1}$	deci	d
0.01 $= 10^{-2}$	centi	c
0.001 $= 10^{-3}$	milli	m
0.000 001 $= 10^{-6}$	micro	μ
0.000 000 001 $= 10^{-9}$	nano	n
0.000 000 000 001 $= 10^{-12}$	pico	p
0.000 000 000 000 001 $= 10^{-15}$	femto	f
0.000 000 000 000 000 001 $= 10^{-18}$	atto	a

Metric
UNITS OF MEASUREMENT

Quantity	Unit	Symbol	Relationship of Units
Length	millimetre	mm	1 mm $=$ 0.001 m
	centimetre	cm	1 cm $=$ 10 mm
	decimetre	dm	1 dm $=$ 10 cm
	metre	m	1 m $=$ 100 cm
	kilometre	km	1 km $=$ 1000 m
Area	square centimetre	cm^2	1 cm^2 $=$ 100 mm^2
	square decimetre	dm^2	1 dm^2 $=$ 100 cm^2
	square metre	m^2	1 m^2 $=$ 100 dm^2
	are	a	1 a $=$ 100 m^2
	hectare	ha	1 ha $=$ 100 a
	square kilometre	km^2	1 km^2 $=$ 100 ha
Volume	cubic centimetre	cm^3	1 cm^3 } $=$ 0.001 l
	millilitre	ml	1 ml }
	cubic decimetre	dm^3	1 dm^3 } $=$ 1000 ml
	litre	l	1 l }
	cubic metre	m^3	1 m^3 $=$ 1000 l
Mass	milligram	mg	1 mg $=$ 0.001 g
	gram	g	1 g $=$ 1000 mg
	kilogram	kg	1 kg $=$ 1000 g
	metric ton	t	1 t $=$ 1000 kg

includes conversion charts as well as tables of metric units. Study these tables to become familiar with the terms used. As they relate to building construction two linear measurements are most frequently used. These are: millimetres (mm) and metres (m). (In technical practice, centimetres are seldom used.) The following list gives an initial approximate size comparison of these units (but not accurate enough to be used for calculations).

1 mm = approx. 0.04" (3/64")
1 cm = approx. 0.4" (13/32")
1 m = approx. 3.3' (3'-3 3/8")
1 m = approx. 1.1 yd. (39 3/8")

Metric Measurement

BASIC AND DERIVED UNITS

Quantity	Unit	Symbol	
BASIC UNITS			
Length	metre	m	
Mass	kilogram	kg	
Time	second	s	
Electric current	ampere	A	
Temperature	kelvin	K	
Luminous intensity	candela	cd	
Amount of substance	mole	mol	
DERIVED UNITS			
Area	square metre	m^2	
Volume	cubic metre	m^3	
Force	newton	N	$(kg \cdot m/s^2)$
Pressure	pascal	Pa	(N/m^2)
Work, energy, quantity of heat	joule	J	$(N \cdot m)$
Power	watt	W	(J/s)
Electric charge	coulomb	C	$(A \cdot s)$
Voltage, electromotive force	volt	V	(W/A)
Electric field strength	volt per metre	V/m	
Electric resistance	ohm	Ω	(V/A)
Conductance	siemens	S	(A/V)
Electric capacitance	farad	F	$(A \cdot s/V)$
Luminance	candela per square metre	cd/m^2	
Illumination	lux	1x	$(1m/m^2)$
Thermal conductivity	watt per metre kelvin	W/m K	
Radiant intensity	watt per steradian	W/sr	
Activity (of a radioactive source)	1 per second	s^{-1}	

Approximate Conversions from Metric Measures

Symbol	When You Know	Multiply By	To Find	Symbol
		LENGTH		
mm	millimetres	0.04	inches	in
cm	centimetres	0.4	inches	in
m	metres	3.3	feet	ft
m	metres	1.1	yards	yd
km	kilometres	0.6	miles	mi
		AREA		
cm^2	square centimetres	0.16	square inches	in^2
m^2	square metres	1.2	square yards	yd^2
km^2	square kilometres	0.4	square miles	mi^2
ha	hectares (10,000 m^2)	2.5	acres	
		MASS (weight)		
g	grams	0.035	ounces	oz
kg	kilograms	2.2	pounds	lb
t	tonnes (1000 kg)	1.1	short tons	
		VOLUME		
ml	millilitres	0.03	fluid ounces	fl oz
l	litres	2.1	pints	pt
l	litres	1.06	quarts	qt
l	litres	0.26	gallons	gal
m^3	cubic metres	35	cubic feet	ft^3
m^3	cubic metres	1.3	cubic yards	yd^3
		TEMPERATURE (exact)		
°C	Celsius temperature	9/5 (then add 32)	Fahrenheit temperature	°F

Approximate Conversions to Metric Measures

Symbol	When You Know	Multiply By	To Find	Symbol
		LENGTH		
in	inches	*2.5	centimetres	cm
ft	feet	30	centimetres	cm
yd	yards	0.9	metres	m
mi	miles	1.6	kilometres	km
		AREA		
in^2	square inches	6.5	square centimetres	cm^2
ft^2	square feet	0.09	square metres	m^2
yd^2	square yards	0.8	square metres	m^2
mi^2	square miles	2.6	square kilometres	km^2
	acres	0.4	hectares	ha
		MASS (weight)		
oz	ounces	28	grams	g
lb	pounds	0.45	kilograms	kg
	short tons (2000 lb)	0.9	tonnes	t
		VOLUME		
tsp	teaspoons	5	millilitres	ml
tbsp	tablespoons	15	millilitres	ml
fl oz	fluid ounces	30	millilitres	ml
c	cups	0.24	litres	l
pt	pints	0.47	litres	l
qt	quarts	0.95	litres	l
gal	gallons	3.8	litres	l
ft^3	cubic feet	0.03	cubic metres	m^3
yd^3	cubic yards	0.76	cubic metres	m^3
		TEMPERATURE (exact)		
°F	Fahrenheit temperature	5/9 (after subtracting 32)	Celsius temperature	°C

METRIC MEASURE BUILDING PLANS FOR A SMALL HOME

The drawings in this set of plans are for illustrative purposes only. Standard metric dimension sizes have not been established for construction materials. When such standards are adopted, materials sizes may be slightly different from those shown here.

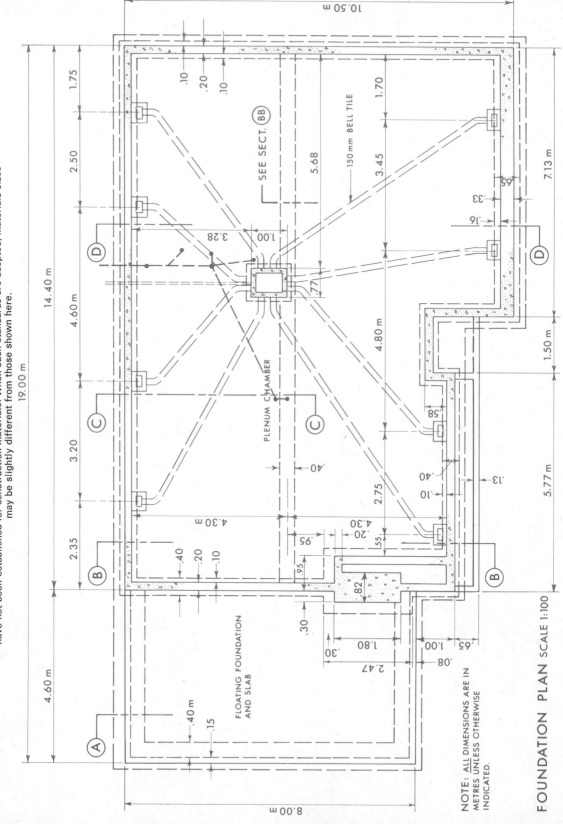

FOUNDATION PLAN SCALE 1:100

NOTE: ALL DIMENSIONS ARE IN METRES UNLESS OTHERWISE INDICATED.

442

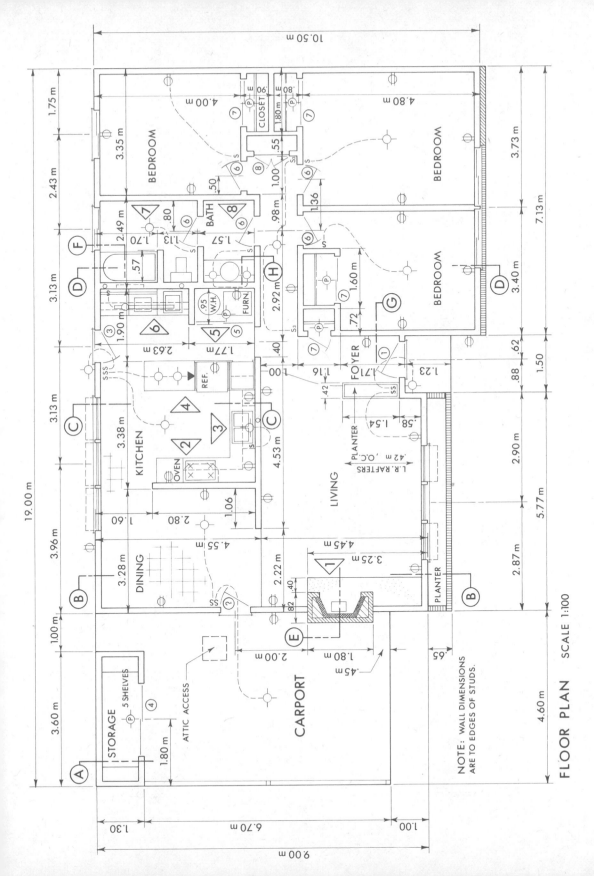

FLOOR PLAN   SCALE 1:100

NOTE: WALL DIMENSIONS
ARE TO EDGES OF STUDS.

443

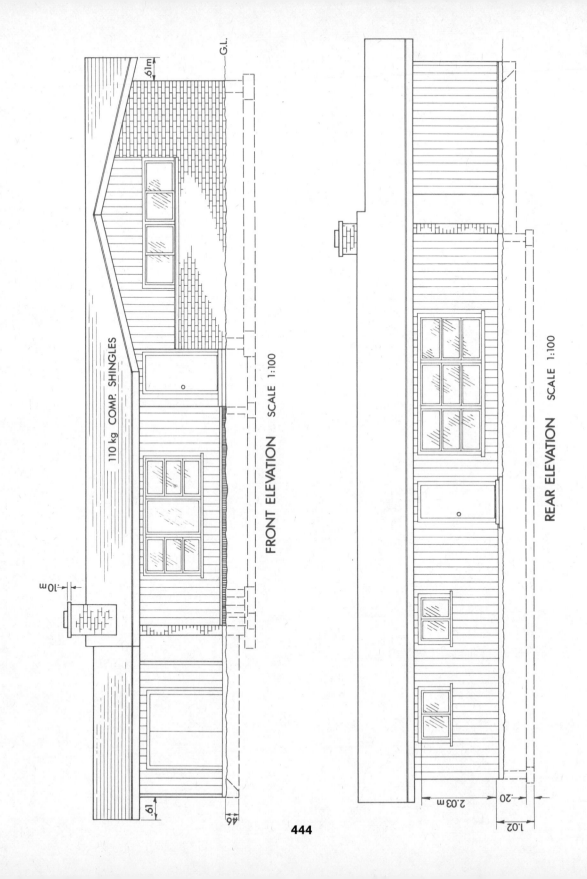

FRONT ELEVATION   SCALE 1:100

110 kg COMP. SHINGLES

.61m

G.L.

.10 m

.91

46

REAR ELEVATION   SCALE 1:100

2.03 m

.20

1.02

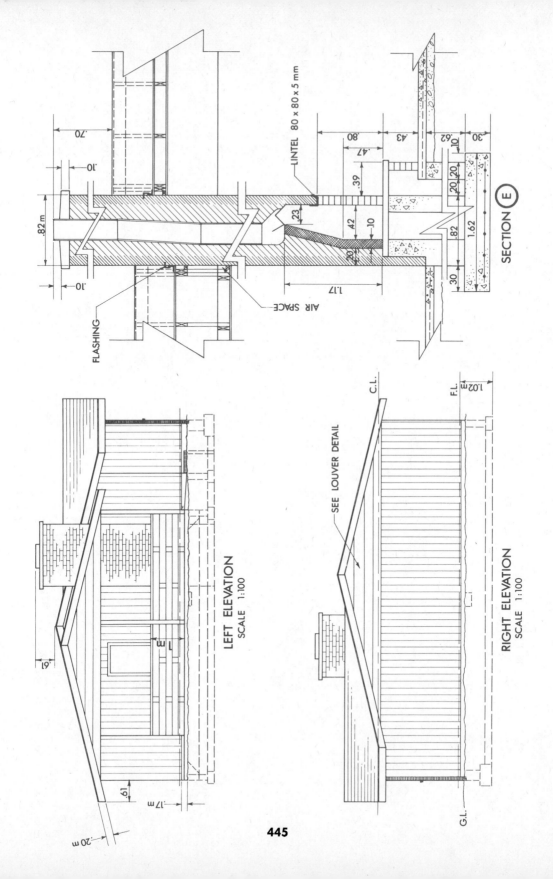

LINTEL 80 × 80 × 5 mm

SECTION E

AIR SPACE

FLASHING

.70

.10

.82 m

.10

.10

.39

.23

.42

.10

.20

1.17

.80

.47

.43

.62

.10

.20 .20

.82

1.62

.30

.30

1.62

LEFT ELEVATION
SCALE 1:100

.61

.17 m

.61

.20 m

RIGHT ELEVATION
SCALE 1:100

SEE LOUVER DETAIL

C.L.

F.L.

1.02 m

G.L.

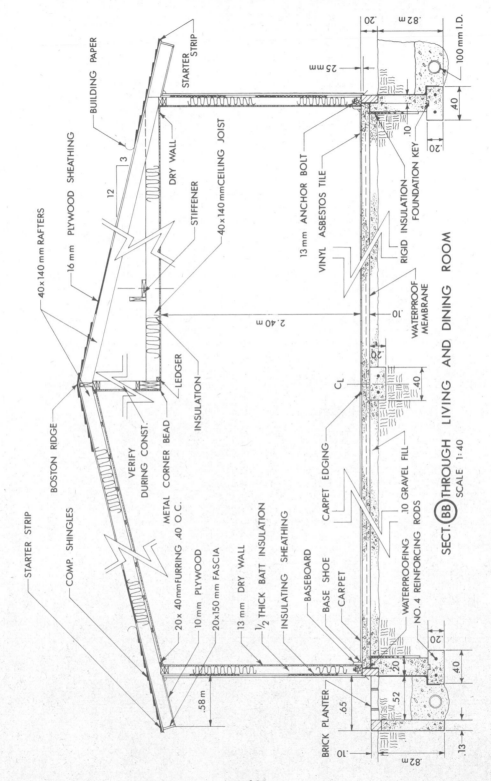

SECT. (BB) THROUGH LIVING AND DINING ROOM

SCALE 1:40

BUILDING PAPER

STARTER STRIP

16 mm PLYWOOD SHEATHING

DRY WALL

40×140 mm RAFTERS

STIFFENER

40×140 mm CEILING JOIST

BOSTON RIDGE

VERIFY DURING CONST.

METAL CORNER BEAD

LEDGER

INSULATION

STARTER STRIP

COMP. SHINGLES

20 x 40 mm FURRING 40 O.C.

10 mm PLYWOOD

20x150 mm FASCIA

13 mm DRY WALL

½ THICK BATT INSULATION

INSULATING SHEATHING

BASEBOARD

BASE SHOE

CARPET

BRICK PLANTER

CARPET EDGING

WATERPROOFING

NO. 4 REINFORCING RODS

.10 GRAVEL FILL

Cʟ

13 mm ANCHOR BOLT

VINYL ASBESTOS TILE

RIGID INSULATION

FOUNDATION KEY

WATERPROOF MEMBRANE

100 mm I.D.

.82 m

.20

25 mm

.40

.20

.10

2.40 m

.10

.20

.40

.20

.20

.40

.52

.65

.82 m

.10

.13

.58 m

12

3

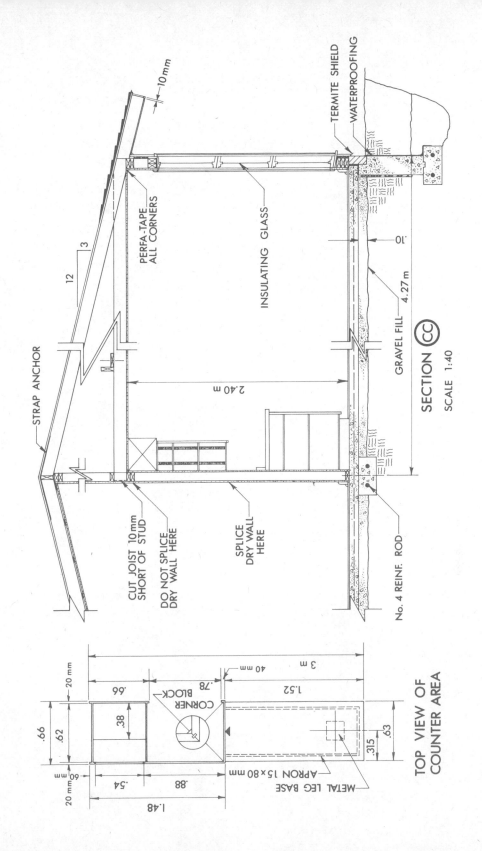

10 mm

TERMITE SHIELD

WATERPROOFING

STRAP ANCHOR

PERFA-TAPE
ALL CORNERS

INSULATING GLASS

12

3

2.40 m

.10

GRAVEL FILL

4.27 m

CUT JOIST 10 mm
SHORT OF STUD

DO NOT SPLICE
DRY WALL HERE

SPLICE DRY WALL
HERE

No. 4 REINF. ROD

SECTION CC

SCALE 1:40

20 mm

.66

.78

40 mm

3 m

CORNER
BLOCK

1.52

.38

.66

.62

.315

.63

60 mm

20 mm

.54

.88

METAL LEG BASE

APRON 15 × 80 mm

1.48

TOP VIEW OF
COUNTER AREA

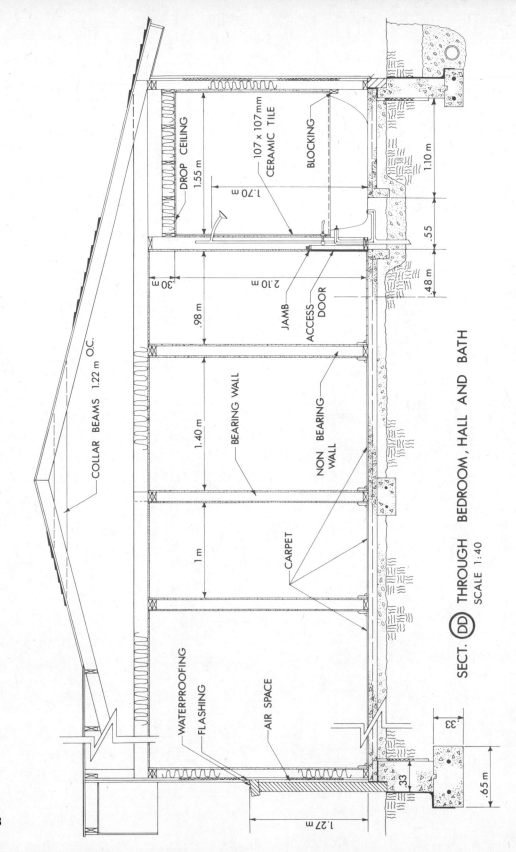

SECT. (DD) THROUGH BEDROOM, HALL AND BATH
SCALE 1:40

COLLAR BEAMS 1.22 m O.C.

DROP CEILING
1.55 m
1.70 m
107 x 107 mm CERAMIC TILE
BLOCKING
1.10 m
.55
.48 m

.30 m
2.10 m
.98 m
JAMB
ACCESS DOOR

BEARING WALL
1.40 m
NON BEARING WALL

1 m
CARPET

WATERPROOFING
FLASHING
AIR SPACE

.33
.33
.65 m
1.27 m

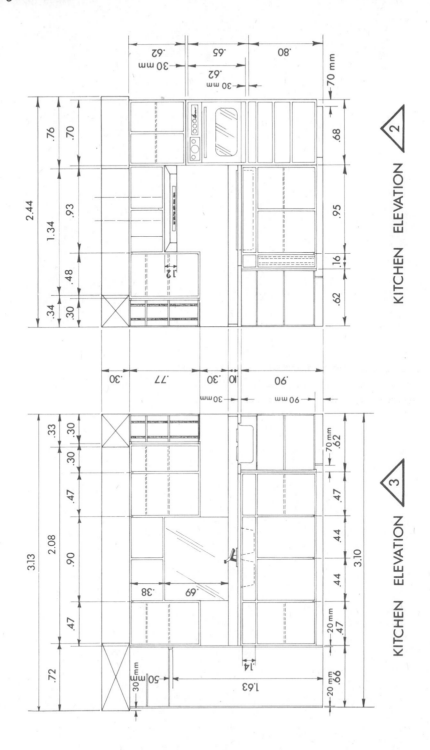

KITCHEN ELEVATION 2

KITCHEN ELEVATION 3

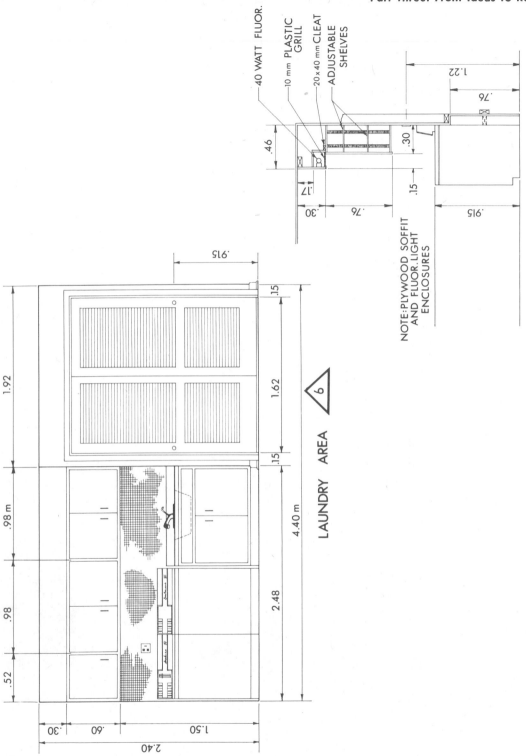

40 WATT FLUOR.

10 mm PLASTIC GRILL

20 x 40 mm CLEAT

ADJUSTABLE SHELVES

1.22

.76

.46

.30

.17

.30

.76

.15

.915

NOTE: PLYWOOD SOFFIT AND FLUOR. LIGHT ENCLOSURES

.915

.15

1.92

.98 m

.98

.52

1.62

.15

2.48

4.40 m

LAUNDRY AREA

6

.30

.60

1.50

2.40

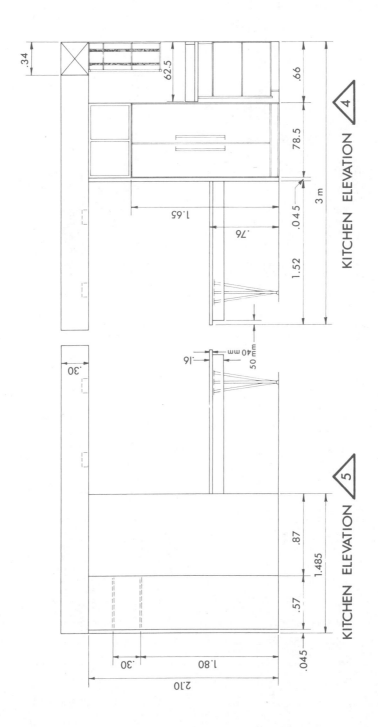

KITCHEN ELEVATION △4

KITCHEN ELEVATION △5

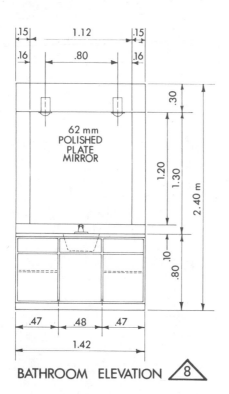

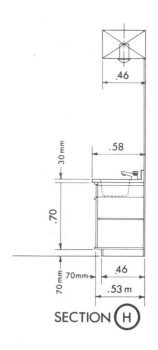

.15 | 1.12 | .15
.16 | .80 | .16

62 mm
POLISHED
PLATE
MIRROR

.30

1.20
1.30
2.40 m

.10
.80

.47 | .48 | .47

1.42

BATHROOM ELEVATION 8

.46

30 mm
.58

.70

70 mm | 70 mm
.46
.53 m

SECTION H

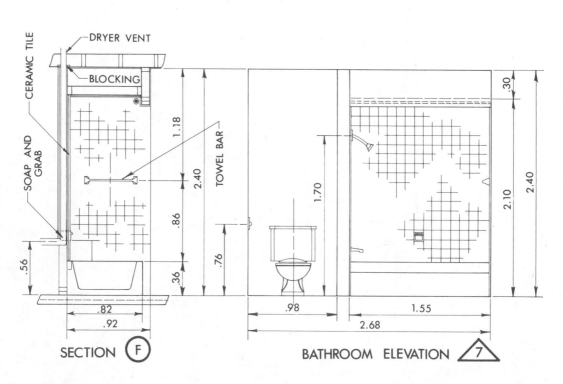

CERAMIC TILE

DRYER VENT

BLOCKING

SOAP AND
GRAB

TOWEL BAR

1.18

2.40

.86

.76

.36

.56

.82

.92

SECTION F

.30

2.10

2.40

1.70

.98

1.55

2.68

BATHROOM ELEVATION 7

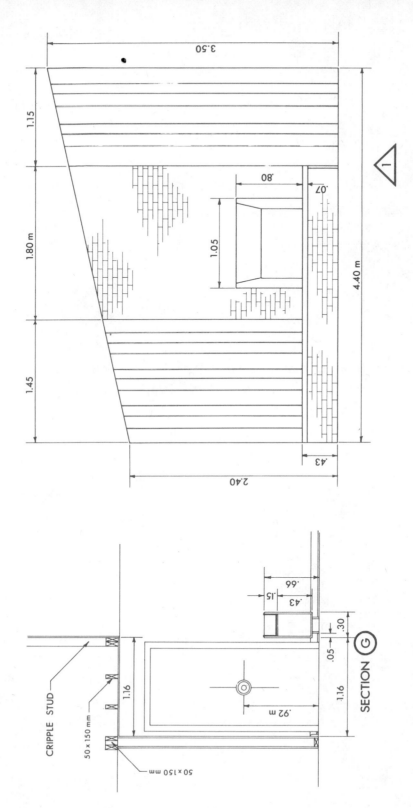

3.50

1.15

1.80 m

1.45

4.40 m

2.40

.43

.80

.07

1.05

1

.66

.15

.43

.30

.05

1.16

.92 m

1.16

SECTION G

CRIPPLE STUD

50 × 150 mm

50 × 150 mm

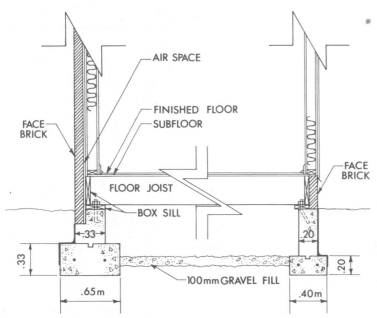

AIR SPACE

FINISHED FLOOR
SUBFLOOR

FACE
BRICK

FACE
BRICK

FLOOR JOIST

BOX SILL

.33

.33

.65m

.20

.20

100 mm GRAVEL FILL

.40m

ALTERNATE FLOOR CONSTRUCTION

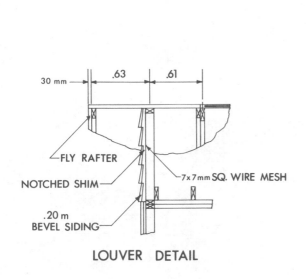

30 mm

.63

.61

FLY RAFTER

NOTCHED SHIM

7 x 7 mm SQ. WIRE MESH

.20 m
BEVEL SIDING

LOUVER DETAIL

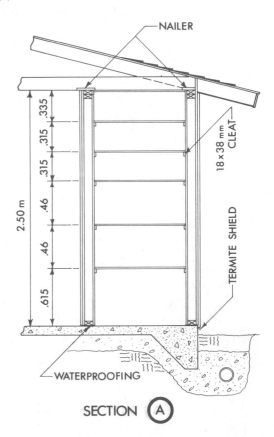

NAILER

.335

.315

.315

.46

.46

.615

2.50 m

18 x 38 mm
CLEAT

TERMITE SHIELD

WATERPROOFING

SECTION Ⓐ

Questions To Reinforce Knowledge

1. Why is an understanding of building construction methods important for placing dimensions on a working drawing?

2. What is the most important rule of dimensioning?

3. What is an extension line?

4. How much space is allowed between the outline of the object and the extension line?

5. What determines the length of an extension line?

6. How much does an extension line extend past the outside (overall) dimension line?

7. What is a dimension line? Is it drawn the same for architectural and machine drawings?

8. On architectural drawings, what is the approximate spacing of adjacent dimension lines? What controls their spacing?

9. Describe the weight of dimension lines.

10. Which is drawn first, an extension line or a dimension line?

11. Why are construction lines drawn for extension and dimension lines?

12. Are construction lines removed from a drawing?

13. Does one measure the spacing and line length of extension and dimension lines?

14. What is a location dimension? What is a size dimension?

15. What is an overall dimension? Describe. Is it a size or location dimension?

16. What is a detail dimension?

17. May one use an object line as a dimension line? Explain.

18. Dimension lines may end at what kinds of lines?

19. Are dimensions measured from hidden parts? Explain.

20. May extension lines cross extension lines? Explain.

21. May dimension lines cross dimension lines?

22. May extension lines cross dimension lines?

23. Are there exceptions to the three questions above? Explain.

24. Explain placement of dimensions inside and outside of the views. Which is preferred?

25. What are four methods of marking ends of dimension lines?

26. Approximately how large is an arrow on the end of a dimension line?

27. Explain some of the ways it may be drawn.

28. May an extension or dimension line cross a symbol or sectioned area?

29. Do symbol or section lines cross a dimension figure or note?

30. What is the aligned system of placing dimensions?

31. What is the unidirectional system of placing dimensions?

32. Which system is used on architectural drawings?

33. What is the standard size of lettering on a working drawing? When may this vary?

34. When are guide lines used for letters and figures?

35. What is the difference between a guide line and a construction line?

36. Are guide lines removed after lettering is complete?

37. Are dimension figures placed directly above each other?

38. Circles are dimensioned showing their _____.

39. Arcs are dimensioned showing their _____.

40. A dimension line inside a circle passes through the _____ _____ of the circle.

41. If the dimension line is outside the circle, it points toward the _____.

42. The vertex of an arc is marked with an _____.

43. Dimension lines for arcs terminate at the _____.

44. What is a leader and when is it used?

45. What are two methods of drawing leaders?

46. At what angle are leaders drawn? Explain.

47. Describe the line weight used for leaders.

48. How are leaders terminated?

49. Explain dimensioning for wood windows and doors in wood frame construction.

50. In modular construction, how is dimensioning done?

51. What dimensions are usually placed outside the view on a floor plan?

52. Why are overall dimension lines farthest from the view?

53. Small size of floor plans makes it impossible to tell exactly where an extension line is pointing. How is this remedied?

54. What is a code letter or figure? Explain use.

55. How many window schedules are there on a complete set of working drawings? How many door schedules?

56. What is a lintel schedule? What information is included?

57. What dimensions are required in each enclosed space?

58. Explain two ways interior doors may be dimensioned.

59. What notes or codes are placed by each door?

60. Why are only minimum dimensions placed in a hall?

61. Explain lettering sizes to be placed on floor plans.

62. Are exact equipment sizes usually shown on a floor plan?

63. How are joists indicated and noted on a floor plan? What information is included?

64. What is a cutting plane line? How is it drawn? How are the codes used with these lines?

65. Are heat registers or radiators indicated and dimensioned on a floor plan?

66. Are plumbing lines placed on a first floor plan? Explain.

67. Where may the scale of a drawing be shown? Explain.

68. Are overall dimensions placed on elevations? Why?

69. How many times is footing or foundation width shown on an elevation? Footing thickness or height?

70. Are all ceiling heights shown on elevations? Explain.

71. Window and door heights are dimensioned to what location?

72. Are vertical window dimensions usually shown? When are they?

73. How is glass size indicated on an elevation?

74. How is roof pitch (slope) indicated?

75. How is roof covering indicated?

76. How is exterior covering for walls indicated? How are changes in materials indicated?

77. What chimney dimensions are required on elevations?

78. Is roof overhang shown on elevations? Explain.

79. How does one determine what dimensions to place on individual detail drawings?

80. How are details coded?

Terms To Spell and Know

dimension	detail dimension	modular construction	arc
dimension line	overall dimension	modular dimensioning	vertex
extension line	object line	symbol	leader
building shell	center line	section	note
overrun	hidden line	unidirectional	schedule
line weight	cutting plane line	grid	sphere
location	code key	perspective	cylinder
dimension	symmetrical	pictorial	rectangular solid
size dimension	arrows	center-to-center	prism

Organization of Building Plans

Building plans will not always fit onto standard sized sheets. Therefore sheets are sometimes made to fit the drawings. Naturally, all sheets in a set of plans are the same size.

Use standard sizes if possible. They permit more economical purchasing and also aid in handling and filing.

Standard Sheet Sizes

Sheet sizes are standardized by numbers. The smallest is a No. 1, the next larger size a No. 2, and so on. The untrimmed No. 1 size is 9"x12". After the drawing is complete, it is trimmed to a final size of 8½"x11". All standard untrimmed and trimmed sheets are multiples of these two sizes. Every standard sheet size is twice as large as the one preceding it. On the diagram of sheet sizes, the numbered rectangles list the smaller or trimmed sizes first and then give the larger, untrimmed sizes.

Trim Lines

Regardless of which is used—standard or non-standard sheets—trim lines must be added to show the final size. These are drawn light and fine. The page is later trimmed along them.

Borders

Borders are used to frame the drawings and give them a finished appearance. Their marginal width is variable, but they are usually drawn between ¼" and ½" wide, except for the left border which is from 1" to 1½" wide to permit binding individual drawings into sets. Of course, all borders in a set of sheets should have the same ratio.

Border Lines

There is no standard border line width. The size of the drawing sheet helps determine it. The larger the sheet the wider the border line. Note that border lines are more prominent than other lines on the drawing. Naturally, in a set of plans they should all be the same width.

When one measures and draws trim and border lines on each sheet, the slightest misjudgment can cause them to be different. For best results, do one sheet layout and then trace all others from it.

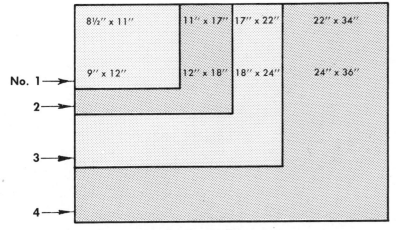

8½" x 11"	11" x 17"	17" x 22"	22" x 34"
9" x 12"	12" x 18"	18" x 24"	24" x 36"

No. 1 →
2 →
3 →
4 →

Standard trimmed and untrimmed sheet sizes.

Titles

Every sheet should have an appropriate title. There is no one best way all titles should be drawn. The information to be included in the title and description is variable, but some firms use the same conventional title for all their drawings. The three most common locations for titles are: (1) the lower right-hand corner of the sheet, (2) across the bottom of the entire sheet, or (3) at the right end of the sheet.

The sample titles show a variety of ways they may be drawn and information to be included. The samples with much information are from plans for large buildings. Plans for small buildings frequently have abbreviated titles which contain little information.

On large, elaborate sets of plans, each sheet has a full title. Simple sets may have a formal title on the first sheet only.

Both complex and simple sets have all their sheets numbered. On large sets the number is included in the title block. On small sets the numbers are inserted at the lower right-hand corner of each sheet, as in the illustrations on the right.

For a professional appearance, the main body of a title is seldom lettered freehand. When pre-printed titles are not readily available, they may be lettered with a mechanical lettering device or template. Information concerning the individual drawing—such as the name of the client, his address, or the name of the project—may be lettered freehand.

STEVEN'S GENERAL HOSPITAL		
4423 RIVERSIDE DRIVE TAMPA, FLORDIA	REVISED ON	
A. R. JONES, ARCHITECT 1357 SUNVIEW AVENUE TUCSON, ARIZONA	SHEET NO. 1	
PLAN NO. 357	DATE	

DRAWN BY	HOUSE FOR	
CK'D BY		
DATE	THOMAS CAVANAUGH	
DRAWING NO.	701 INDEPENDENCE BOULEVARD CHICAGO 24, ILLINOIS	
REVISIONS	JOHN DUMBKOWSKI, ARCH. 2016 HICKORY DR. CHICAGO, ILLINOIS	SHEET NO.

REVISIONS – DATE		BY
	JOB NO. DR. BY TR. BY CH. BY DATE APPROVED	DESCRIPTION
	C.W. HEATH, ASSOC. 216 NORTH PARK AVE. MONTEREY, CALIF.	SHEET NO

HOUSE FOR	SAMUAL WARNER 470 61st COURT SAN DIEGO, CALIFORNIA	
DRAWING NO. 927-43	FRONT ELEVATION	MADE BY RJM CK'D BY K.F.H.
REVISIONS	SCALE ¾" = 1'	DATE
	DELUXE PLAN SERVICE	PAGE NO. 7 of 12

HOUSE FOR		
	MR. & MRS. J. PRIBBEN	
ARCHITECT	EDWARD P. DIETER 370 DATON STREET ATLANTA, GEORGIA 767-0193	PLAN NO. 56
		SHEET NO. 9

Titles for building plans.

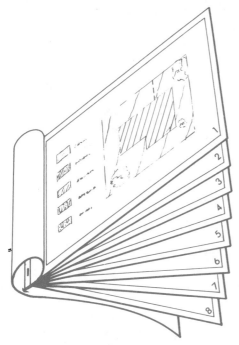

Arrangement of sheets.

Arrangement of the Plan

There are seldom exactly the same number and kinds of sheets in a set of plans, so one cannot establish an absolute order. Nevertheless, plans may be categorized so all similar information is grouped properly. The illustration showing a set of plans has sheets numbered in the following order:

1. Schedule of symbols and plot plan.
2. Footing and foundation or basement plan.
3. Floor plans.
4. Elevations.
5. Sections
   and
6. Details.
7. Framing plans.
8. Mechanical plans.

Sections and details are not always placed on separate pages. If these plans are simple, they may be placed on the same sheets as other drawings. For example, floor plan sheets may contain all related detail drawings, or elevation sheets may contain details pertinent to them.

Sheet Layout

Every drawing sheet must be organized to make good use of its space, but information should be as clear as possible. When a sheet contains only one drawing, it is centered on the page. If more than one drawing is included, they should be related. For example, if a front and rear elevation are above one another, their extremities should be in line. Spaces above, between, and below them should be the same.

Remember that all drawings have auxiliary information that must be included. Dimensions, notes, titles, indication of drawing scale, leader lines, and lettering all require space, and must be considered when planning the sheet.

If different drawing scales are used on an individual sheet, each must be indicated near the appropriate drawing. If the sheet contains only one drawing scale, it need be indicated only once. The indication may be in a prominent place on the body of the drawing or it may be placed in the title block, but one should use the same method of indicating the scale which he is using, throughout the set of plans.

Schedules

Since most building plans are drawn to a very small scale and most items are only symbolized, it is not possible to include all necessary information. Chapter 39 discusses how to identify and use code letters and figures. These codes frequently refer to schedules where detailed information about items such as doors, windows, lintels, room finishes, and others are organized into lists which give specific details about each item.

When plans are drawn for a specific building, the items to be included determine what schedules are used. No two different building plans would call for exactly the same schedules or direct information.

Good schedules are an important part of any building plan.

LINTEL SCHEDULE

		STEEL LINTELS		PRECAST CONCRETE LINTEL REINFORCING PER 4" WALL			
CLEAR SPAN	LINTEL LENGTH	STEEL LINTEL SIZES		CLEAR SPAN	LINTEL LENGTH	LINTEL HEIGHT	REINF. TOP, BOT.
		8" THICK WALL	4" THICK WALL				
2'-0"	3'-4"	2—3½"x3½"x⁵⁄₁₆"	3—3½"x3½"x⁵⁄₁₆"	2'-0"	3'-4"	7⅝"	1—#3
4'-0"	5'-4"	2—3½"x3½"x⁵⁄₁₆"	3—3½"x3½"x⁵⁄₁₆"	4'-0"	5'-4"	7⅝"	1—#3
6'-0"	7'-4"	2—3½"x3½"x⁵⁄₁₆"	3—3½"x3½"x⁵⁄₁₆"	6'-0"	7'-4"	7⅝"	1—#4
8'-0"	9'-4"	2—5"x3½"x⁵⁄₁₆"	3—5x3½"x⁵⁄₁₆"	8'-0"	9'-4"	15⅝"	1—#4
10'-0"	11'-4"	2—6"x3½"x⅜"	3—6x3½"x⁵⁄₁₆"	10'-0"	11'-4"	15⅝"	1—#5
12'-0"	13'-4"		8I-18.4+12"x⅜"	12'-0"	13'-4"	15⅝"	1—#6
14'-0"	15'-4"		8I-18.4+12"x⅜"				

DOOR SCHEDULE

KEY	QUAN.	SIZE	MTL.	DESCRIPTION	FRAME
A	2	3'-0"x7'-0"	ALUMINUM	EXTRUDED ALUMINUM	ALUMINUM
B	4	3'-0"x7'-0"x1¾"	WOOD	1 LT. BIRCH SOLID CORE	WHITE PINE
C	1	3'-0"x7'-0"x1¾"	"	" " " " "	BIRCH
D	2	2'-6"x7'-0"x1⅜"	BIRCH	BIRCH HOLLOW CORE	WHITE PINE

ROOM SCHEDULE

AREA	WALLS	CEILING	FLOOR	BASE	TRIM	REMARKS
ENTRY	PLASTER	ACOUST.	ASPHALT	RUBBER	W.P.	
CORRIDORS	"	"	"	"	"	
EQUIP. RM.	BLOCK	RF. DECK	"	"	"	

ELECTRICAL

KEY	DESCRIPTION
⊕	CEILING OUTLET
⊖	DUPLEX CONVEN-IENCE OUTLET
◄	TELEPHONE OUTLET

Sample schedules.

Like details, they may be shown on sheets with other details when they apply, or they may all be grouped in one location. Several sample schedules are included to illustrate the kinds of information found on them. However, they are to serve only as a guide to formulating necessary schedules and information for your plans, and are not to be considered an absolute way an individual schedule must be handled.

Binding

A building plan should have a cover page to enclose the set and protect it. This may be an expanded version of a title block or it may also display a copy of a rendering. After necessary prints are reproduced and assembled into sets of plans, they are bound or stapled (usually along the left edge) together and distributed to those who are to use them.

Questions to Reinforce

Knowledge

1. Are all building plans drawn on standard sized pages? Why or why not?

2. As a rule, all sheets in a set of plans are made the same size. From your own reasoning, do you suppose there is ever an exception to this?

3. What are the advantages of using standard sized drawing sheets?

4. What is the size of a No. 1 untrimmed sheet? A No. 1 trimmed sheet?

5. How are other standard sizes based upon these sizes? Explain.

6. Explain what is meant by the term trim line.

7. Why are borders not the same size on all four edges of a sheet?

8. What are the minimum and maximum recommended border widths?

9. Why does the author recommend that you measure trim and border layouts on one sheet and then trace other pages from it?

10. What are the most frequently used locations for title strips?

11. Are they always drawn exactly the same way? Explain.

12. From your own reasoning why must all sheets be numbered?

13. Why are pre-printed or mechanically lettered titles more desirable than those done freehand?

14. List an order in which plans may appear in a set. Is this an absolute order that cannot be changed? Explain.

15. When sections or details are placed on sheets with other drawings, what determines their location?

16. Explain how one determines where to locate drawings on a sheet.

17. Explain the different ways the drawing scale may be indicated.

18. Why are schedules of information necessary? Explain how one determines what schedules to include and what information should be in them.

19. What are two reasons why a bound set of plans should include a cover page?

The following nine chapters are designed to serve as a guide and check list while drawing your building plan. The chapters do not give *complete* step-by-step explanations for drawing all items because building plans differ and do not require exactly the same information. However, the chapters do set forth procedures to guide you.

Chapters 41 through 48 include very few illustrations because they are to serve only as a drawing guide and are not intended for presentation of information relating to building parts. Such explanations and illustrations are presented in other chapters.

Chapter 49 is a set of working plans for a split level home. It may be used as a guide for drawing your plans. Another set of plans is included in Chapter 39. These should also be consulted.

Drawing Plot Plans

This chapter presents a description of plot plans and explains how they are drawn. It is to be used as a check list and guide for drawing your plot plan. The chapter cannot be all-inclusive because it is concerned with special factors, only applied to plot plans. Likewise it is probable that some information included here may not be required on your plan.

As with other chapters, you cannot expect to read the entire unit and then put it aside and remember every item to include on your plan. Study small sections at a time and then draw each item required. Naturally, after you become proficient you will modify the procedures to suit your own needs.

The Plot Plan

Plot plans for presentation purposes are discussed elsewhere in the text. Featured in this chapter are working drawings and technical information required during actual construction. These plans are aerial-type views showing the entire building plot, all building outlines, and related features influencing construction.

Drawing Scale

The plot-plan drawing scale is determined by the property size and building complexity. Plans for small buildings may be drawn as large as ⅛″ = 1′-0″ but larger buildings are usually drawn to a scale of 1″ = 20′ or smaller. Drawing sheet size is also an influencing factor because each sheet in a set of plans must be the same size yet property has many sizes and shapes. If the property and/or building are extremely large, two plot plans may be necessary. When two are drawn, one is to a very small scale, showing the entire property and the building location upon it. Uniformly spaced grid lines are drawn and identified to pinpoint locations. The second plot plan includes only those grid sections occupied by the building. It is drawn to a large scale so detailed information can be included.

Determining Plot Plan Shape

Plot plan size and shape can be determined from a legal description or from a plat of the area. NOTE: A student draftsman may not have an actual building site, so specs are frequently assumed or supplied by an instructor.

Positioning a Plot Plan on a Drawing Sheet

If a plot plan is to be drawn approximately the same size as a drawing sheet, it may be centered on the page. However, if it is to occupy less space it may be positioned to one side so other data, as a key to all symbols used, can occupy the sheet.

Beginning the Drawing

Secure a drawing sheet and draw the tentative page layout. Determine the plot plan location on the sheet and then draw all property lines. Verify all symbols to use because many could be new to you. Draw all adjoining streets, roads, alleys, and *public* sidewalks. Also draw lines representing all utility easements. Then draw the center lines of all streets or roads.

Building Lines (See page 464)

Local ordinances frequently state where a building may be located on a lot. For example, an ordinance may require buildings to be at least 30′ from a street and 10′ from side property lines.

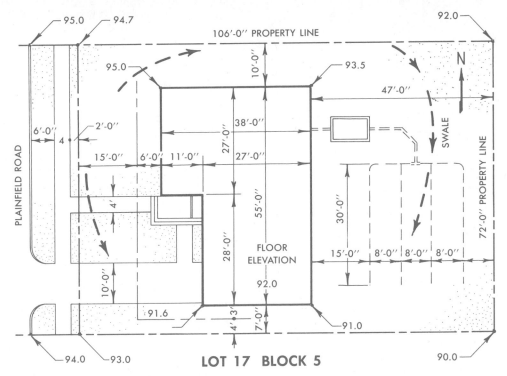

LOT 17 BLOCK 5

MANCHESTER GROVE—ELIOT, WISCONSIN

Plot plan with proposed elevations at building corners.

These established minimums are called *building lines*. Draw them first as construction lines; then after all building outlines are drawn in, superimpose hidden lines near building corners to show that the building fits within the prescribed limits. Such lines are shown on the accompanying plot plans.

Building Outlines (See page 464)

You may draw your building outline on scrap paper or cardboard and cut a template to this shape. The template can then be positioned and re-positioned on the plot plan until a suitable location is achieved. Of course, there are other influencing factors such as contour and other buildings or obstructions. These must also be given consideration. After building location is determined draw all corners on the plot plan. Then remove the template and draw all building outlines.

There are several ways to describe building outline shape:

1. Exterior wall outlines may be drawn to show all wall thicknesses. These are filled in as solid color. Doors, windows, and all interior walls are omitted. This method usually omits all roof overhangs. NOTE: If the overhang influences building location, draw it as a hidden line.

2. Another frequently used method describes exterior wall outlines with hidden lines and describes roof outlines with object lines. Construction features, such as ridges, valleys, dormers, chim-neys, and all roof surfaces, are drawn on the plan. Symbols for roofing add to appearance and help define building shape.

3. Building outlines may also be drawn with object lines and the entire structure shaded as in section. This procedure is frequently used as a supplement to other methods to distinguish between existing and new construction.

Construction Outside the Building

If sidewalks, driveways, fences, carports, walls, patios, outdoor fireplaces, or other features are to be included as part of the building construction, or if they *influence* construction in any manner, they should be drawn on the plot plan. If these items are not influencing factors omit them.

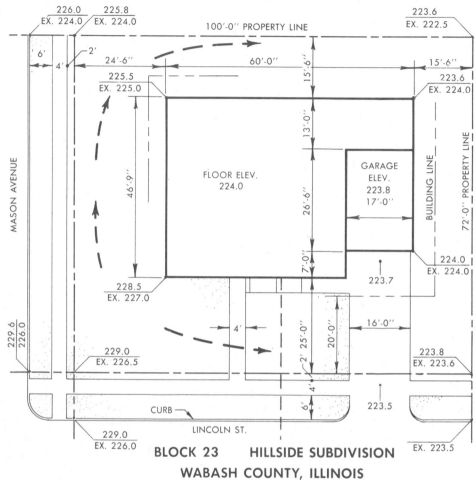

BLOCK 23   HILLSIDE SUBDIVISION
WABASH COUNTY, ILLINOIS

Plot plan with existing, and proposed, elevations at building corners.

The same is true for trees, shrubs, or other plantings; these may or may not be shown depending upon their relationship to actual construction.

Contour Lines

If the terrain is flat or has a gentle slope, contour lines may be omitted. However, when the plot is irregular or has steep grades, contour lines should be included. Vertical grades of one foot are usually shown. Later when lettering the plan, vertical relations to sea level should be indicated. If the terrain changes elevation abruptly, as at opposite sides of a retaining wall, only the highest and lowest contour lines are drawn. *Closely spaced* contour lines are hard to read and detract from the drawing.

Since buildings require surface water drainage, the lot must be graded to provide it. Observe the swales shown on the sample plot plans designed to deflect or guide water away from the building.

Utilities

Each utility line—for water, gas, sewer, septic tank and its field, and others—should be drawn with their proper symbol. These lines extend from the building to the corresponding utility in the street, alley, or easement. Exact locations of all such connections to public utilities should be dimensioned. NOTE: The city or other branch of local government and public service companies usually provide connecting points.

464

It is seldom possible to select your own points of entry into the available utilities.

Elevations Above Sea Level

In addition to the contour heights discussed earlier, other elevation notes are needed. Indicate the elevation at each building corner, each property corner, and at either the curb or crown of the street at both lot edges. A *corner lot* requires three such elevations.

If *existing* grade level and *finished* grade level are to be different, both elevations must be indicated on the plan. Plot plan #2 shows both elevations at building corners.

Observe also that *all* floor heights are shown.

Dimensions for Plot Plans

Place overall dimensions for property lines. Place the dimension adjacent to the property line. (It is not necessary to draw extension and dimension lines for this.) If the lot is rectangular only two such dimensions are required. If the lot is irregular in shape, each side must be dimensioned.

Dimension the distance from the street edge or curb to the outside edge of all public sidewalks. Then dimension sidewalk width. Also dimension the distance from the sidewalk to the property line.

Using good dimensioning practices, describe the building's size, shape, and position on the property. Then add dimensions for sidewalks, driveways, patios, walls, screens, or other exterior features.

Wells and drainage systems must also be described with dimensions.

Lettering

Information on plot plans is variable, so you should study samples to observe the kinds of information frequently included.

The following list may serve as a guide for lettering to include:
• Complete title block, as on other pages in the set of plans.
• Name of the drawing, as PLOT PLAN.
• The drawing scale.
• Identification for property lines.
• Identification for building lines.
• Names of streets or roads. (Indicate center lines when drawn in.)
• Major building parts—as first floor, garage, fence, or terrace.
• Legal description, including lot number, block number, name of the addition or subdivision, name of the city or town when applicable, name of the county, borough, or parish, and name of the state.
• Other technical data unique to this building, if any.

North Point Indicator

For orientation purposes draw in a North point indicator. For working drawings this should be functional rather than artistic. Keep it simple.

Condensed Outline to Reinforce Knowledge

The following statements present a brief outline or system that may be used when drawing plot plans. Statements in this list may not apply to all plot plans. Likewise, some required items on individual plot plans may not be presented in this list. These statements are only to aid you in establishing an orderly drawing procedure.

After you have drawn the item being discussed, check it lightly on the list and move on to the next one.

1. Secure your drawing sheet and fasten it to a drawing surface.
2. Using construction lines, draw your border and trim lines. Be sure to include the title block.
3. Calculate the overall dimensions of your building and the lot; then choose an appropriate drawing scale.
4. In the lower center of the sheet, or in the title block, letter the drawing name and scale used.
5. Either center the drawing on the sheet or determine its best location elsewhere.
6. Using construction lines, draw all property lines.
7. Draw all streets, roads, alleys, *public* sidewalks, and easements.
8. Draw a center line for all streets and roads.
9. Draw all building lines as established by local ordinances.
10. If necessary, cut a template to your building shape.
11. Mark the building's location on the plot plan.
12. Using one of the prescribed methods, draw building outlines on the plot plan.
13. Draw in symbols, roof features, section symbols, and other required items to complete the building.
14. Draw outside features that are a part of, or influence, construction.
15. If the terrain is irregular, draw in contour lines.

42

Drawing Floor Plans

This chapter presents a system of procedures for drawing floor plans. It is to be used as a guide and check list for items to include on your plan. It cannot be all inclusive, other features not discussed might be required on some drawings.

One cannot expect to read the entire chapter and then lay it aside and remember how to draw a completed floor plan. You may skim-read to gain an overall idea of its content. Then, starting at the first and reading one sentence at a time, perform the indicated operations—or simply hold some information for future use. Repeat this process for each succeeding sentence. NOTE: The beginner is advised to lightly check off all drafting steps as they are completed. This will prevent you from becoming lost as you proceed down the list of things to do. Naturally, after you become proficient you will modify the procedures to suit your own needs.

How a "Floor Plan" Is Viewed

Imagine you are observing a completed one-story building from the top. Also, imagine a plane

surface parallel to the ground cutting through all walls so the windows and doors are cut in half. When the top half of the building is removed, the remaining lower half will reveal the floor plan to the observer. As with other orthographic sections discussed earlier, one must imagine himself directly over the part being viewed. (A floor plan is a modified orthographic section drawing, with most construction details shown in symbol form rather than fully drawn.) It is necessary to draw parts for the upper half of the building even though it has been removed. All items above the cutting plane are shown as hidden lines or symbols.

Drawing Scale

Floor plans for average-size homes or other small buildings are usually drawn to a scale of $\frac{1}{4}'' = 1'-0''$. However, if the building is larger, a scale of $\frac{1}{8}'' = 1'-0''$ is used. The scale must be indicated on the drawing, either beneath the floor plan or in the title block.

Drawing Page

Your building size determines

how large the drawing sheet must be. Be sure it is large enough to include an appropriate border and title block.

After your drawing paper is positioned and secured to the board, draw construction lines for the border and trim lines. To do this it may be necessary for you to refer to sheet layouts and page sizes in your text. Make it a point of referring back to find needed information.

Using your rough sketches and preliminary sizes, calculate exact building dimensions and decide its best location on the drawing sheet.

Technical Data

Before you can draw a floor plan you must know the construction method of the outside walls; that is, whether exterior walls are solid masonry, masonry veneer, frame, post and beam, curtain, or any other. You must also know the construction method for all interior walls. It is a good idea to note each wall type and thickness on the preliminary sketch or drawing. Determine exact wall thicknesses so they are available for future reference. These will be required when placing dimensions on the plan.

Many draftsmen allow 10″ (full scale size) when drawing exterior masonry wall thickness and 6″ for both interior and exterior frame walls. These are not exact measurements; they represent close approximates. If this rounded-off wall thickness is used, the slight error must be compensated for when showing dimension figures on the plan. Dimensions must state true sizes and not these approximates.

Drawing Wall Outlines

Using the wall thicknesses and approximate room sizes as noted on your rough sketch or drawing, draw construction lines representing all exterior and interior walls. Draw these as continuous lines; *do not* leave spaces for door, window, or other openings. These are drawn as construction lines; they *are not darkened* until later.

Drawing Door, Window, and Opening Locations

Select each door, window, or opening from catalogs, manufacturers' literature, the text, or from information supplied by your instructor. List all information about each item on a separate sheet of paper and keep this. It is needed now and will be used again later. NOTE: It is a good idea to keep *all* information relating to your building plan in an organized folder so it is readily available when needed.

Draw construction lines across appropriate walls to represent opening sizes for each required item. *Do not* draw window or door symbols at this time; show only their locations.

Other Openings in Walls

Draw construction lines for all soil stacks, vents, heat registers—when required on this plan—pipe chases, and all other items that are to be recessed into walls.

Wall Object Lines

Using good drafting techniques and satisfactory line weight, broaden object lines for both faces of all walls. *Do not* draw object lines across door openings. They may be drawn across windows on the wall interior when the jambs are flush with the wall. *Do not* draw object lines across the window exterior unless the simplified non-standard symbol is going to be used, or unless the window face is flush with the wall exterior.

Drawing Window, Door, and Opening Symbols

To help you establish an accurate visual memory of each symbol to use, look them up in the text and draw yours exactly as shown. Beginners should draw window and door symbols first as construction lines; then, when all are correct, redraw to their proper line weight. Be certain doors have the proper swing for most convenient use. Lap sliding doors so the door edge is not visible from the most used portion of the room. Draw lines for thresholds, sills, and differences in floor materials when needed. Identify with notes when lettering the drawing.

Drawing Stairs

Before drawing stairs, consult stair data to be sure yours conform to one of the accepted types and that all sizes are satisfactory. Draw a break line across the stair well in the middle of the stair run. Using actual tread width, and equipment line weight, draw in steps from the head of the stairs to the break line. Then add an arrow to indicate either up or down. Using either a very hard pencil, or a blue one that will not reproduce, roughly *note* up or down direction. Do not letter it at this time. All lettering will be done later.

Drawing the Chimney or Fireplace

The chimney and fireplace outlines should be completely drawn in. All details such as the hearth, ash dump, liners, fire brick, common brick backing, fireplace facing material, and all other parts are added. Outlines should be drawn as construction lines and then darkened, but very intricate details may be drawn their proper line weight the first time.

Information about chimneys and fireplaces is very technical and should be studied carefully before any drawing is begun.

Drawing Closet Parts

Closet wall outlines and all doors are drawn later with other walls and doors. However, if some are not to be complete, they may be drawn in now. Identify the shelves, rods, drawers, compartments, or other special features. Study sample drawings showing these drawn as symbols.

Many draftsmen make a chart showing all shelf lengths and the number of each required. When this is done, a reference must be made directing attention to the chart. You are *not* to letter the note at this time. Write yourself a reminder and put it in your folder so the note can be completed when other lettering is done.

Drawing Kitchen Equipment

Kitchen items such as all cabinets, refrigerator, stove, sink, and all special equipment should be selected from manufacturers' literature, catalogs, or other sources, and the pertinent information recorded in your folder so it can be added to the drawing later.

Draw all kitchen equipment using construction lines and then, when all details are complete, trace as equipment lines.

Utility or Laundry Rooms

If such rooms are included on this living level, all equipment outlines should be drawn in. A furnace and its chimney flue may be located in a utility room. These are frequently concealed behind louvered doors for a neat appearance. A ceiling opening for access to the attic, or a floor opening for access to a crawl space, may also be included.

Bathrooms

After careful study of bathroom fixtures and their functions draw symbols for each item required.

Built-in Storage

If storage cabinets, bookcases, or other similar items are to be included in any room their outlines should be drawn on the floor plan. Such items are usually drawn using equipment lines. If conventional symbols are not available, items should be drawn to show an orthographic top view.

Room and Area Lighting

For large buildings, it is customary to draw a separate electrical plan. For the average-size home or other small structure, indicate electrical items on the floor plan.

Calculate amperage of entrance service and the number of circuits required. Add to your folder for inclusion as notes on the plan when doing the lettering. Draw outlines and fill in the symbol for the entrance service panel. Draw in the electric meter at a convenient location. Check local codes to determine the code for interior and exterior installations.

Actual wiring placement is usually decided by the electrical contractor. Symbols for receptacle outlets and fixtures refer only to their approximate location. All desired locations of electrical items should be drawn in. Do not mistake these symbols for actual electrical fixtures, which are not shown on the floor plans. If selection of individual fixtures is made, their symbol may be keyed to a separate schedule, noted on the floor plan close to the symbol, or electrical fixtures may simply be listed in the specifications.

Draw in all special symbols for chimes, chime buttons, fans, intercom, stereo or high fidelity systems, built-in television, special appliance centers, built-in mixers, or any other electrical item not of a portable nature. Each of these is to be identified by abbreviations or special notes.

Draw in all switches and add notes to designate special ones.

Draw lines connecting switches to their appropriate outlets. Lights or switches that have points of origin or termination on another floor plan should be drawn as continuing from this other plan. For example, if a stairway has a light in the center of the stairwell and switches both at the top and bottom, only one switch is included on this plan. A line connects the switch with the light and then continues on to the break line across the stairs, but the switch on the other living level is not shown.

You must include a schedule of electrical symbols, showing those used throughout the plan. The schedule may be placed on another page, if a note is added to indicate where it is located.

SPECIAL NOTE: When work is completed to this point, a careful study of dimensioning is required. Dimensions should be added to the drawing, based on the principles set forth in Chapter 39. If you have already studied dimensioning, the principles should be reviewed before you proceed.

There are still many symbols and all lettering, such as names of rooms, parts, and special notes to be added to the floor plan. Their inclusion must not crowd or make dimensions difficult to read.

Lettering

Using lettering of a size appropriate to the space in which it is to be located, letter the names of all rooms and areas of the plan. (Appropriate lettering sizes are established in the chapter on lettering.) *Each room or other space is to be identified.* Abbreviations are permitted for small areas such as closets, entries, halls, and stairs. It is difficult to locate the name of a room not placed in a prominent position. The favored location is in the center of an open area. Be sure to draw *guide lines* for all letters, and follow good lettering practice. Remember that the only reason lettering is placed on a drawing is to convey information to others. It must be so legible that there is no possibility of it being misread.

Symbols

Many symbols have already been added to the drawing. However, at this time, you must be sure all symbols for *all materials* to be used are included on the plan. Symbols for floor materials have been omitted to this point, to accommodate equipment and resulting lines, dimensioning, and lettering. All wall symbols, except for recessed items such as medicine cabinets, vents, and others, have been omitted for the same reason. Using the proper symbol for each material, these must now be added. Be sure to compare your symbols very carefully with those shown elsewhere in the text. Symbols for floor finish materials *may* be omitted, provided a separate room schedule is used, indicating all finishing materials for each.

The amount and complexity of dimensions and linework can give the drawing a cluttered appearance. In this "maze," *masonry walls* are easily distinguished only because of the addition of appropriate symbols. *Frame walls* are not as prominent because a symbol is seldom used. To remedy this, one may use a very hard, sharp pencil to draw a series of parallel lines in the wall area. An example of this is shown in "wall symbols" in the left column on page 405.

Another method of making walls more clearly identified is to reverse the plan and coat the wall with a light application of graphite on the back of the sheet. NOTE: A fixative should be placed over the graphite to prevent smudging. Pressure-sensitive or appliqué line screen may also be used for wall shading.

The symbol for finished lumber was formerly used to represent frame walls. This practice is rarely followed today. It is time consuming and costly. Artistic extras of this nature have been replaced with clean-lined simplicity.

Exterior Items on Floor Plan

Porches, patios, garages, outdoor fireplaces, fences, pools, and trees—when they affect or become a part of the building—are to be included on your floor plan. Be sure they are a part of the actual construction.

Room Heat Source

For larger buildings, it is customary to draw a separate heating plan. For an average-size home or other small structure, draw in the location of registers or radiators on the floor plan and leave placement of heat ducts and piping to the heating contractor. Use notes to identify the kind and size of each heat source. Of course, these additions to the floor plan do not represent a true heating plan, but furnish only minimum information.

Ceiling Joists

It is necessary to include the ceiling joist size, direction, and spacing on the floor plan. Examples are shown on the featured plans in Chapter 49. If the ceiling joist size is the same for the entire building, and all joists run this same direction, the indicator need be shown and noted only once. If the ceiling joist size or direction is not the same for the entire building, the symbol and note is repeated for each change. See page 504.

Access to Attic or Crawl Space

Attic access is placed in an inconspicuous area. When access is by ladder only, hidden lines are used to outline the opening size. Add a note or reference to a detail to explain actual construction features. When a disappearing stairway or ladder leads to this space it should be indicated on the floor plan by a note, calling attention to it.

Elevation Indicators

Study the sample building plans in Chapter 49 to see how elevation indicators are used.

They are shown as triangles with one obtuse angle slightly rounded. Each indicator has a code number that refers to an elevation elsewhere in the plans that is similarly marked.

Cutting Planes

Cutting plane lines are required to show where each section drawing is located in the building. Each cutting plane has a code number or letter and the corresponding section drawing has the same code. This is shown on the building plans mentioned above. On these plans, the code circle touching the ends of cutting plane lines are divided into two equal parts. The number in the upper half circle refers to the page number in the set of plans, as "1", "2", or "3". The letter in the lower half circle refers to the drawing location on the page, as "A", "B", or "C". Drawings lettered "A" are at the tops of the pages, while "B" is below or to the right. See Chapter 39 for example on plans.

Condensed Outline to Reinforce Knowledge

The following statements present a condensed order or system for drawing building floor plans. Items presented in this list may not be found on all floor plans. Likewise, items not mentioned here may be required on other floor plans. The list is to aid you in establishing an orderly drawing procedure.

To use this list most effectively, draw the part discussed and then check it lightly when drawn.

1. Secure your drawing sheet and fasten it to the board.
2. Using construction lines, draw your border and trim lines. Also make a layout of your title block.
3. Calculate the overall dimensions of your building and choose an appropriate floor plan drawing scale.
4. Letter the name of the drawing, and the scale used, in the lower center of the drawing sheet, or in the title block.
5. Center your drawing on the sheet or determine the best location elsewhere.
6. Using construction lines, draw all wall outlines.
7. Draw door and window *openings* but not their symbols.
8. Draw construction lines for items located in the walls: A, soil stacks; B, vents; C, exhaust fans; D, heat registers or radiators; E, pipe chases; F, medicine cabinets, and other items that must be recessed into walls.
9. Excluding door openings, broaden object lines for both faces of all walls.
10. Draw the proper symbol for each window or door.
11. Draw thresholds, sills, and changes in floor coverings.
12. Draw the symbol for stairs or steps and roughly indicate up or down.
13. Draw chimney or fireplace outlines and fill in all details of construction.
14. Using construction lines, draw in all kitchen cabinets and equipment. Broaden these lines as equipment lines.
15. Draw in bathroom fixtures and cabinets. Draw other accessory items as mirror, screens, linen closets, or others.
16. Draw built-in storage units for all rooms, where used.
17. Draw the electrical entrance service panel and the electric meter.
18. Draw the gas meter and all gas outlets, if required.
19. Draw all receptacle outlets, including weatherproof outside ones. Then add necessary code letters to identify special outlets.
20. Draw locations of all lighting outlets and code them.
21. Draw all special electrical items and add appropriate code letters.
22. Draw all electrical switches and code to designate special ones.
23. Draw in all telephone outlets.
24. Draw hidden lines from switches to lights.
25. Add dimension lines, figures, and notes. Follow good dimensioning practice, using the plans in your text as a guide.
26. Draw in symbols for wall materials.
27. Add appropriate notes for all symbols shown.
28. Letter in the names of all rooms or other areas.
29. Draw and designate all floor covering materials and finishes.
30. Shade frame walls.
31. Draw all porches, patios, garages, carports, or other exterior items to be constructed.

32. If a furnace, water heater, washer, dryer, and other utility items are to be included on this living level, draw them in.

33. Draw the locations and add appropriate notes for all heat registers or radiators unless a separate heat plan is to be drawn.

34. Indicate the ceiling joist direction and add appropriate notes.

35. Draw in hidden lines for access to the attic and add appropriate notes or codes.

36. Add code letters or figures for doors, windows, lintels, and header schedules.

37. Add hidden lines and a special note for plastered openings.

38. Unless a separate ceiling framing plan is to be drawn, draw in all overhead beams or girders and necessary supporting posts.

39. Draw cutting plane lines to refer to all section drawings. Code to identify.

40. If your building has required items that are not included in this list, draw each and identify.

41. Check your drawing carefully for omissions and errors; make all necessary corrections.

42. Clean your drawing.

43. Broaden border and title strip lines and trim the drawing on your trim lines. Letter in all information in the title block.

43

Drawing Basement or Footing and Foundation Plans

This chapter is to serve as a guide and check list of items to draw on your plan. All building plans do not include the same items, so the information here can serve only as a general guide.

To make most effective use of this chapter, draw a building part and then check off each item from the list as you proceed. This will let you know when all items have been drawn.

Basement, footing, and foundation plans are viewed the same way as a first floor plan, except that when walls are visually cut halfway between the bottom and top some features are hidden below the ground. All such are drawn with hidden lines or symbols.

Drawing Scale

These plans should be drawn to the same scale as the floor plan for your building. That is, if the floor plan was drawn to a scale of ¼″ = 1′-0″, then this plan should be drawn to that scale.

Drawing Sheet Size

Draw on the same size sheet as others in the same set of plans.

Construction Materials and Methods

Before you can draw the plan you must know all required building materials and their sizes. NOTE: For convenience, beginning draftsmen may use approximate sizes supplied by others.

Beginning the Drawing

Re-position and fasten your first floor plan to the drawing board. Be sure it is aligned perfectly.

Place a new sheet of tracing paper or vellum over the floor plan and fasten it to the drawing surface. This permits you to see through and trace from the first floor plan.

Using building outlines shown on the first floor plan, draw construction lines for all building outlines. (That is, draw only the outside face of each exterior wall.) Then calculate *all* foundation or basement wall thicknesses and draw them to their proper size. When a garage is attached to the building draw a foundation wall between the main structure and the garage. If interior basement walls are required, draw them as construction lines.

Drawing Wall Footings

For conventional construction, all exterior walls and each load-bearing interior wall require a footing. Using data obtained in other parts of the text, calculate the size of each, and then draw construction lines to show all footing widths. NOTE: The sample building plans in the text show these as hidden lines, but you are not to broaden them in this manner until after other construction features are drawn in.

Wall Openings

Draw the *location* of each window, door, foundation vent, or other wall openings. Then look up the appropriate symbol for the item and draw it in its proper location. Broaden symbols to the breadth of equipment lines to make them clearly visible. Then draw a code symbol near each opening. Be sure that code letters, figures, or their enclosures do not interfere with proposed extension and dimension line locations, to be added later.

While searching through manufacturers' or other literature for information about doors, windows, or other building parts, record pertinent information in your notebook for inclusion on schedules and specifications. When arranging schedules, information about doors from all living levels is combined and included on the same schedule. Information to be included on window or other schedules is also done in this manner.

Pilasters

If exterior walls require pilasters and their footings, draw them in their proper locations.

Areaways

When areaways are required, design and draw them in their proper sizes and locations.

Chimney or Fireplace

Study about chimneys and fireplaces; be sure yours are properly designed. Then draw construction lines to outline the chimney or fireplace. Also draw all footing or foundation outlines. If descriptive notes are needed, letter them in. Lines may be broadened as object, equipment, or hidden lines; use the plans in the text as a guide.

Stairway

If a stairway is needed draw it in its proper location. The first floor plan, previously drawn, included several steps (if a basement was required) leading down to the lower level, but they were drawn only to the break line. Copy the break line onto this plan and then complete the stairs to the bottom of their run. You must then indicate stair direction in the same manner as on the first floor plan. If the stairwell is enclosed by walls and they were not previously drawn, do this now. If your stair design requires footings, be sure they are properly drawn.

Access to Crawl Space

If your plan is to include an access door to crawl space, through the first floor, draw it with hidden lines.

If an access door is to open through a foundation wall, draw it using equipment lines. Consult manufacturers' literature and select an appropriate one. If workmen are to build this door, you should refer to detail drawings or explain its construction with notes.

Broaden Wall Outlines

To make walls or other structural outlines more prominent, all construction lines previously drawn are broadened as object, equipment, or hidden lines. Be sure to study the sample building plans in the text and use them as your guide.

Floor Supports

When a basement has a masonry wall below a bearing wall on the first floor level, supporting beams, girders, or posts are seldom required. Bearing walls on upper living levels that are not supported on basement or crawl space masonry walls usually require beams or girders for support. Each beam or girder must then be supported by posts, piers, pilasters, or foundation walls.

Using data found in your text, or supplied by others, calculate the sizes of these parts and draw them in their proper locations. Add notes to describe each part, or refer to detail drawings. (Naturally, if several identical parts are required, the descriptive note is used only once.) When lettering notes, be sure they do not interfere with future extension and dimension line locations.

Furnace

If you specify a furnace located in the basement, be sure it is drawn to the proper size and location. Draw lines to connect the furnace and chimney. If a fuel supply pipe or fuel vent is needed, draw them as pipe symbols. If the furnace requires footings, a raised concrete base, or other concrete work, draw as hidden lines when parts are below floor level or hidden from view. If parts have visible outlines, draw them as equipment lines.

Add a descriptive note to describe the furnace type, size, fuel required, and the number of *British thermal units* the furnace will produce. This information can be obtained from manufacturers' literature.

Water Heater

If your water heater is in the basement, its outlines should be drawn as equipment lines. Obtain descriptive information from manufacturers' literature and note it on the plans. Be sure to include the fuel required and the tank's capacity in gallons.

Draw exhaust vents on water heaters that burn combustible fuel. Vents extending through the roof are usually required by building codes. Air venting into chimneys used for other purposes is seldom permitted. Include notes to describe vent material and size.

Laundry Facilities

If laundry equipment is located in the basement, draw outlines for each required item, such as a washer, dryer, laundry sink or tubs, cabinets, water softeners, or others. If the items are not identifiable by shape, include descriptive notes or explanations.

Plumbing

If plumbing fixtures such as water closets, showers, lavatories, or others are desired, they should be drawn in their proper size and location. Vents for fixtures should be drawn inside the walls in the same manner as on your first floor plan. Drains or vents from upper levels extending below the first floor should be drawn on this plan.

If your building needs floor drains (in the basement or crawl space) water meters, or sump pumps, they should be drawn and identified by notes.

If you are to draw a separate plumbing plan, no additional plumbing information is required here. However, if this plan must also serve as a plumbing plan (and it usually does for small buildings), all waste lines should be drawn as symbols and identified with notes as described in Chapter 48.

When local building codes require catch basins, grease traps, or other special equipment, draw them in an inconspicuous location outside the building. Waste lines lead to and through these items and then continue to city sewers, septic tanks, drainage fields, or other disposal systems. Drains for heavy wastes frequently bypass catch basins and connect to the sewerage system beyond them.

If your building plan is a hypothetical problem and you have no actual building lot with all utilities in place, then sewer and other utility locations must be assumed.

Perimeter foundation drain tile discussed in earlier chapters may be required. If so, draw it on your footing and foundation plan with hidden lines. Draw them about 6″ outside the footing line so they will be clearly visible. Since footings are also drawn as hidden lines, draw these double length (approx. ¼″ long) so they will be different from those previously drawn. Damp locations—requiring foundation drain tile around the inside perimeter or beneath the floor or crawl space—should be drawn when needed.

Many building codes do not permit a person to connect foundation and floor drains to a city sewer. If city storm sewers are available, connect your drain tile to them. Foundation drain tile may also terminate at dry wells (lined pits to contain water), or lead into drain fields similar to those used for septic systems.

All supply or drain pipes passing through concrete floors or masonry walls should have a larger diameter collar around them to permit expansion, contraction, and pipe movement. All collar sizes should be noted on the plan.

Electrical Outlets

Electrical items are shown in the same manner as on first floor plans. Be sure to add notes or code letters to indicate special electrical equipment. Also, specify individual circuits for items requiring large power loads, such as clothes dryers, furnaces, water heaters, or heavy power tools.

Lighting and receptacle outlets should be provided in crawl spaces so the area can be illuminated if repairs are necessary.

Indicate on your plan whether flush or surface mounted receptacles or lighting outlets are required.

If telephones, telephone extensions, intercom units, or other electrical devices are to be included, be sure they are drawn in their proper location and that appropriate notes or code symbols are added.

Dimensioning

Dimensioning practices for footing and foundation or basement plans are similar to those followed for other floor plans. However, there are slight differences, so you should review dimensioning procedures and study sample plans in the text. Be sure to include *detail* and *overall* dimensions for *all* structural parts.

Lettering

Use the same procedures for

lettering this plan that you used on the floor plan. Include names of rooms or other areas, and all equipment and special features such as closets, shelves, or others. Throughout this chapter many notes have been mentioned; be sure each of these is lettered on the drawing as needed.

Symbols

Draw wall symbols, using the sample plans as your guide. Then draw symbols for floor covering materials and/or the surface finish. If a vapor barrier is to cover the earth in a crawl space, indicate the material used.

Room Heat Source

Unless you have a separate heating plan, draw the locations of all heat registers or radiators. Include notes to indicate their type and size. It is not necessary to draw steam or hot water lines or air ducts on this plan.

Floor Joists

You should show the floor joist direction (or directions) and add notes to indicate joist size and spacing. NOTE: If your set of plans is to include separate floor framing diagrams, do not indicate floor joist direction on basement or footing and foundation plan.

Checking the Plan

Study your drawing carefully to be sure special items not included in the discussion are shown.

Cutting Planes and Identifying Codes

Add cutting plane lines to re-fer to section drawings. Code and identify these to correspond with the same ones shown on the floor plans or elevations. Draw elevation indicators to show where and how elevation detail drawings are viewed. Chapter 49 shows elevation indicators numbered and lettered to key them to individual elevation drawings in the set of plans.

Finishing the Drawing

Clean your drawing and broaden all border lines. Fill in the title block; letter in the name of the drawing and the scale used. Then trim your drawing to size.

Condensed Outline to Reinforce Knowledge

The following statements present a condensed list of procedures for drawing basement or footing and foundation plans. Items presented in this list may not be required on every plan. Likewise, other items not discussed in the chapter may be required. The list is to aid you in establishing an orderly drawing procedure.

To use this list most effectively, draw the item or items mentioned, check them lightly on the list, and then proceed to the next item.

1. Obtain a sheet of tracing paper or vellum the same size as other sheets in the set of plans.
2. Re-position and fasten your first floor plan to the drawing surface.
3. Align and fasten the new tracing sheet over the floor plan.
4. Calculate all basement or foundation wall thicknesses. Copy exterior wall outlines from your first floor plan.
5. Using construction lines, draw in wall thicknesses.
6. Draw interior and garage walls as required.
7. Calculate the width of all wall footings and draw them as construction lines.
8. Draw construction lines across walls just to locate all door, window, or other openings.
9. Using the proper symbol and appropriate line weight, draw symbols for door, window, or other openings.
10. Draw a code symbol near each opening and fill in appropriate identifying letters or figures.
11. Draw all pilasters and their footings.
12. When areaways are necessary, draw them in their proper locations.
13. Draw all chimney or fireplace outlines and their footings.
14. If a stairway to this level is required, draw it on the plan. Include surrounding walls and all necessary footings.
15. Foundation or floor access doors opening into a crawl space should be drawn and identified with notes.
16. All construction lines previously drawn should be broadened as object, equipment, or hidden lines.

17. Using the proper symbol, draw all beams or girders and indicate their sizes with notes. If additional detail drawings are necessary, refer to these.

18. Draw each post or pier required to support the beam. Then draw footings for each. If beam ends are recessed in pockets in the foundations, be sure these are shown.

19. Draw furnace outlines; then show necessary footings or other required concrete work.

20. Draw pipes, vents, or other equipment necessary for furnace operation, and identify each.

21. If a water heater is on this level, draw it to size and add appropriate lettering.

22. Draw and identify all laundry equipment.

23. Draw all other plumbing fixtures.

24. If you do not intend to draw a separate plumbing plan, draw all waste lines, using appropriate symbols.

25. Draw all foundation or floor drains, and connect them to a storm sewer or other disposal system.

26. Draw all electrical items as described for the first floor plan.

27. Dimension the entire drawing.

28. Add all of the necessary lettering to the drawing.

29. Draw all floor covering materials and show where changes in materials occur. Add identifying lettering or notes.

30. If the floor is to be of reinforced concrete, or has a vapor barrier, indicate this. (This item may be omitted if the set of plans is to include a concrete reinforcement detailing sheet.)

31. Draw all radiators, heat registers, or other room heat sources and identify with notes.

32. Draw joist direction indicators and add notes to show joist size and spacing.

33. Check your plan carefully for other items requiring inclusion. Also, check it carefully for errors and make all necessary corrections.

34. Add cutting plane lines for reference to section drawings.

35. Draw elevation indicators to show how elevation detail drawings are viewed.

36. Add border lines, title blocks, and complete all lettering.

37. Clean your drawing and trim it to size.

Drawing Exterior Elevations

This chapter presents a system of procedures for drawing building elevations. Also, the topics presented may be used as a check list of items to include on your plan.

What Are Elevations?

Elevations are separate drawings of each exterior building side. Like those described in the two preceding chapters, they are modified orthographic drawings with many of the details shown in symbol forms.

A simple house plan usually requires four elevations, one for each side. However, this depends upon the building's shape and opening arrangements in exterior walls. All exterior wall surfaces must be shown on a completed set of plans, unless there are two identical building sides. Then, they do not require duplication. The fact that they are identical should be clearly stated on the plans.

Drawing Scale

As with floor plans, elevations are usually drawn to a scale of ¼″ = 1′-0″, or if the building is large, a scale of ⅛″ = 1′-0″ may be used. The scale must be indicated on the drawing in the same manner as on the floor plan. When drawings of different scale are located on the same sheet, the scale should be indicated beneath each.

Locating Elevations on Drawing Sheet

If your drawing board is large enough, the floor plan may be positioned above the elevation drawing sheet. This permits construction lines to be projected from the floor plan onto the extra drawing sheet. Lines for building edges, offsets, windows, doors, or other parts may be projected onto the extra sheet without measuring.

If the floor plan is too large to fit above the elevation drawing sheet, lines must be transferred with dividers or by measuring. Naturally, sizes shown on an individual drawing must correspond with those of the same item shown elsewhere in the plans. Always keep a close check.

If drawing sheet size permits, all elevations may be placed on the same sheet. Then the front and rear elevations should be drawn stacked and in line with each other. The same is true of the side elevations, which are also in line with the front and rear elevations. If the left side elevation is placed with the front elevation, it is drawn to the left. If the right side elevation is drawn with the front, it is drawn to the right. If the left side is drawn with the rear elevation it is drawn to the right. If the right side is drawn by the rear elevation, it is placed to the left. The reasons for this will be clear if you study a set of drawings.

If elevations are placed on more than one sheet, the drawings on any one sheet may be aligned either vertically or horizontally. Adequate space must be allowed between views and adjoining borders to prevent the sheet from having a cluttered appearance.

Note: Remember, the title block, which is added later, occupies space at the bottom or lower right-hand corner of the sheet. Allowance should be made for this when spacing the views.

Beginning the Drawing

When front and side, or rear and side, elevations are placed horizontally in line at the same time, drafting procedure is simplified. Measurements and construction points can be transferred directly from one elevation to the other.

Floor Line

The floor line at the foundation level is a good reference point from which drawing may proceed. Drawn as a center line, it extends past the edges of each elevation. It should be labeled F.L. on each. This line ordinarily represents the top surface of the subfloor.

Ceiling Line

Determine all desired ceiling heights, if they vary. Calculate the actual distance from your subfloor to the bottom of the ceiling joists. Draw a center line to represent the finished ceiling and label it C.L. The ceiling line extends past the edges of the elevations, similarly to the floor line described earlier.

First Floor Joists

Using the predetermined floor joist size (this was decided when developing the floor plan), draw a horizontal center line to represent the lower edge of the joists. If different sizes are required because of changes in joist height due to different joist spans, be sure this is shown. Label the end of the line with a descriptive abbreviation. For example, for a basement, this line is labeled B.C.L. because it represents the basement ceiling.

Grade Line

Determine the distance from lower edge of the floor joists to the finished grade (ground). NOTE: Minimum standards and elements of good design discussed in previous chapters should be the determining factors for this height.

If the ground is irregular—rough or sloping—the grade line may be drawn with instruments, as a construction line. Then, when broadening lines, draw this freehand to show irregularities. Extend the line past the walls similar to a floor line, and label G.L.

Footings

Determine the depth of all footings, using directions given in Chapter 3. If no basement is planned, standard minimum depths or local codes will govern. For a basement, determine the desired clearance from the basement floor to the bottom of the first floor joists. Then draw construction lines representing the basement floor and the top and bottom of all footings. If footings are at different depths, or if they must be stepped to conform with uneven terrain, drawings of these must be included on the appropriate elevation.

Walls in Elevation

Location of construction lines representing visible outside walls are determined from the floor plan and placed vertically on the appropriate elevation. Above grade, only visible edges are shown for wall corners, except that basement and foundation wall thicknesses are drawn as hidden lines to the lower edge of floor joists. Below grade, hidden lines are placed on the drawing to show the foundation width and the interior basement walls. These too, are drawn to meet the lower edge of the first floor joists. Lines showing footing widths are drawn beneath all bearing walls.

Areaways, piers, posts, pilasters, chimney and fireplace foundations, stairways, and their footings are drawn on the nearest two elevations. For example, a stairway in the exact center of a building is shown on the elevation which is next to the stairway landing when the observer is facing the stair opening. The rise and run of stairs are shown as hidden lines on one adjacent elevation.

Determining Which Roof Elevation to Draw First

As stated earlier, drawing elevations is simplified if two adjacent views are drawn at the same time. Layout work should begin on the largest gable end, if you have a choice. Gable ends must be drawn on elevations before roof height can be determined on adjacent views. Study the illustration showing how this is done.

Beginning to Draw the Gable End

Locate and mark the points where the ceiling line meets the outside walls. Then measure toward the inside of the building the width of the bird's mouth (notch) in the rafter that permits it to rest on the top plate. For example, on a frame building, stud width is 3⅝″, sheathing might measure ¾″ thickness, and

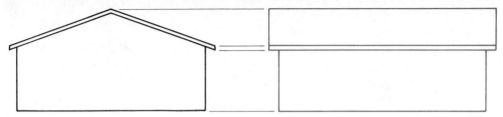

Projecting lines from gable end to show roof height on an adjoining elevation.

exterior covering might be ¾″ thickness. If building parts equaling these sizes are used, their total dimensions would be 5⅛″, so measure from the outside walls toward the center of the building this distance and mark the points on the ceiling line.

The lower edge of the rafters will pass through these points. Using each point established, measure along the ceiling line toward the building center a distance of 12′-0″. Do this even if the building is less than 24′ wide. This represents the proportion of the run. At these points, construct a perpendicular above the ceiling line equal to the rise per 12′-0″ of run. (If you do not understand these terms consult the chapter on Roof Construction where drawing examples are shown.) For example, if the roof pitch is 5/12, make perpendicular lines 5′-0″ high. Draw the bottom edge of the rafter so it touches the upper end of the perpendicular and passes through the point representing the inside edge of the top plate and rafter intersection. Extend the line past the outside wall slightly more than the anticipated

overhang width. The opposite end of the line should extend past the building center.

Repeat the above procedure for the bottom edge of the rafter on the opposite side of the building. NOTE: These lines *do not* represent roof lines. Calculate the combined thickness for the rafters, sheathing, and roofing. Then draw lines parallel to those just established, to represent the upper roof edge. Using the gable elevation, repeat the amount of the roof height on the adjacent elevation and draw construction lines for roof height. If more than one gable is required, locate and draw additional construction lines and transfer heights to adjacent elevations.

If the gable is perpendicular to the ground, the outlines just drawn complete the roof. If the gable is not perpendicular, measure the additional overhang at the ridge and connect this with the outer edge of the overhang at the lower roof edge.

Hip Roof

A simple hip roof is one with four slopes and one ridge. All

surfaces normally slant at the same angle. When viewing a single elevation one cannot tell whether a roof is a gable or a hip. Two views are required to show that roof surfaces are slanted in different directions. NOTE: A hip roof for an irregular shaped building requires more than four surfaces.

All roof outlines should be drawn as construction lines on each of your elevations before continuing to other building parts.

Drawing a Chimney Terminating on the Roof

Using local codes or recommended standards, decide upon the chimney height—including liner or pot—and draw horizontal construction lines on *each* elevation. On views showing gable ends, draw your chimney sides as shown in the illustration. Observe that one chimney face touches the roof before the other because the roof slants.

Transfer a line from the lower edge of the chimney onto the adjoining elevation, as shown, to find where the chimney passes through the roof surface.

Projecting lines for chimney layout.

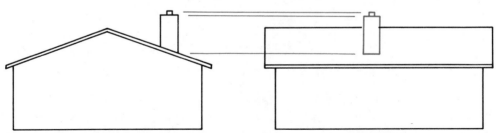

Chimney Pot, Liner, or Cap

The chimney height must represent its actual highest point, including a liner or pot. The chimney cap is below the liner. Construction lines are added to all elevations for these parts.

Saddle

As previously said, a saddle is like a miniature roof in the acute angle formed by the main roof and chimney. It leads water away from the chimney. Study the illustration to see how it is drawn.

Flashing details at the chimney and roof intersection must be drawn on each elevation.

Other Items on the Roof

Dormers, ventilators, and soil stacks should be drawn as construction lines simultaneously on adjacent elevations.

Gutters and Downspouts

Determine the size and style required. Locate high points of the gutter on the fascia. Then locate low points. Draw the tops and bottoms of gutters through these points. Gutters extend around some roofs. For example, a hip roof might have a gutter around the entire perimeter. Also, on gable roofs, when a cornice return is used the gutter may extend around the return.

Downspouts are angled from the gutter to the face of the building. Then they follow the wall to grade. If a splash block is used, the downspout ends at the grade line. If the downspout drains into a sewer pipe or dry well, hidden lines are used to show the below-grade drain. NOTE: When locating downspouts, they must not interfere with a window or door opening.

Object Lines for Parts Previously Drawn

It is well for the beginner to broaden object lines for all parts previously constructed, except vertical wall lines. This will help eliminate later confusion of lines and parts.

Gable Louver or Ventilator

Determine the size, material, location, and style required. Then draw the layout with construction lines and broaden as equipment lines. Follow the manufacturer's description and draw all parts as accurately as possible. For example, the size of fins and surrounding trim should be drawn to an accurate scale.

Additional drawings will be needed when doing the building details. Study the sample illustrations to see how these are drawn.

Window and Door Line

Since most framing methods place tops of windows and doors at the same height, the easiest way to secure this alignment is to make a horizontal construction line across each elevation at the desired height. The lower face of a head jamb is considered the window or door height. (*Do not* use the top of casing as your height.) All casings and exterior trim are above the window or door line. This line is sometimes broadened as a center line.

Door and Window Openings

When you are drawing an elevation, show only visible window and door parts; do not draw hidden parts. Study sample window elevations before drawing yours. Indicate the finished opening size of the door or window sash by drawing a rectangle at the correct scale. Individual door and window parts, and mullions between units, are then added. Casings or brick mold are usually placed at the sides and above openings; sills are drawn below. If a drip cap or flashing is required above, draw it in. NOTE: Glass block windows do not normally have the wood trim described above.

Small details such as width of stiles, rails, muntins, mullions, and glass are drawn as described in manufacturers' literature. If you do not understand all technical terms consult the index at the back of this book, and then look them up in their appropriate chapter.

Templates are frequently used for drawing doors and windows. CAUTION: One cannot copy blindly from a template, but must keep the object's shape clearly in mind.

Since much detail must be drawn in a relatively small space, broaden all window and door lines as equipment lines.

Object Lines for Walls and Sills

Construction lines for walls and all other parts previously drawn should be broadened as object or equipment lines. All other structural parts, such as covered patios, terraces, or posts —should be drawn as construction lines and then broadened to desired width. Add footings and foundations for the above, when required.

Roofing Symbol

Draw in the appropriate symbol for your roof covering. NOTE: Be sure to provide open space in the symbol for adding a note to describe the roofing material.

Dimensions for Elevations

Only a minimum number of dimensions are drawn on elevations. Eliminate unnecessary duplications. Follow good dimensioning practice as shown and discussed in Chapter 39. Also, study the building plans following these chapters.

Place a dimension on at least one elevation to show each different ceiling height. Of course, if all ceiling heights are the same, only one dimension is required. Letter a note stating points used for your measurements. For example, the note might read:

CEILING HEIGHTS MEASURED FROM SUB-FLOOR TO BOTTOM OF CEILING JOISTS.

Or if it applies, the note might read:

CEILING HEIGHTS MEASURED FROM FIN-ISHED FLOOR TO FINISHED CEILING.

Basement ceiling height is dimensioned and noted in the same manner. When both dimensions are on the same elevation, place them in line with each other, to follow good practice. NOTE: One dimension may be used to denote combined thickness of floors and joists.

Dimension the distance from the grade line to the finished floor line. (If the ground is not level,

of course, more than one dimension is required.) At all wall offsets, dimension the distance between the grade line and finished floor line. If a wall is long but has no offsets, place dimensions at both ends of the building as described earlier, and another near the building center.

The depth and size of footings and foundations are dimensioned. If steps in footings or foundations are required, dimension these. Basement floor thickness must also be dimensioned.

Areaways, piers, posts, pilasters, chimney and fireplace foundations, and their footings, are dimensioned only if not detailed elsewhere in the set of plans.

Show location dimensions for louvers or ventilators.

Roof pitch must also be indicated on at least one elevation, using the symbol. The amount of rise and run is indicated as shown on the sample elevations.

Dimension the distance from the floor line to the lower edge of the head jambs of doors and windows.

Indicate overhang width and thickness of fascia. If a gutter is used, add a note to specify the material, its size and shape. Also, add a note to describe the shape and size of downspouts.

Chimney height is dimensioned from the highest roof ridge. Both width and depth of the chimney are indicated. Dimension the amount of exposed flue liner height and the thickness of the chimney cap. The amount of wash on the chimney cap should be shown.

The distance from the floor line to the bottom of sill may be shown.

Symbols of Wall Materials

Place the appropriate symbol on each surface or item shown on the drawing. NOTE: These are usually drawn as a finished symbol the first time you draw them. It is not necessary to draw each minute detail as a construction line and then be required to draw them again. Use the symbols in the text, and the sample plans, as your guide. Add notes for each material symbolized. If a note is not on the surface of a part, add a leader line pointing to the material described.

Cutting Planes

Add cutting planes to correspond with those on the floor plan.

Check your drawings carefully for omissions and errors; make all necessary corrections.

Condensed Outline to Reinforce Knowledge

The following statements present a condensed check list for use in drawing building elevations. Items presented in this list may not be found on all elevations. Likewise, other items not mentioned here may be required on a specific elevation. The list is to aid you in establishing an orderly drawing procedure.

To use this list most effectively, draw the item or items discussed and then lightly check them off the list as you complete them.

1. Secure your drawing sheet and fasten it to the board.

2. Using construction lines, draw your border and trim lines. Also, make a layout of your title block.

3. Choose an appropriate drawing scale for your elevations.

4. Letter the drawing scale and the name of the drawing either in the lower center of the drawing sheet or in the title block.

5. Decide how many elevations can be drawn on each sheet.

6. Determine the best location for each elevation.

7. Position the floor plan above the proposed location of the first elevation, or place it nearby.

8. Using construction lines, draw lines on the first elevation to show building edges, offsets, door and window sides.

9. Re-position your floor plan and draw the same kinds of items on the other elevations.

10. Draw floor lines on each elevation; extend them past building edges about 5/8''. Letter the abbreviation F.L. at an end of each line.

11. Draw all ceiling lines, and letter to identify.

12. Draw a center line for the bottom of the floor joists and letter to identify.

13. Draw grade lines on each elevation and identify with an abbreviation.

14. Draw construction lines for the bottoms and tops of all footings.

15. Draw steps in footings and foundations when required.

16. Draw the basement floor, if your building has one.

17. Draw footings and foundations for all areaways.

18. Draw footings and piers as required.

19. Draw footings and posts as required.

20. Draw pilasters and their footings as required.

21. Draw chimney and fireplace footings and foundations as required.

22. Draw stairways on two adjacent elevations if needed.

23. Draw roof gable ends.

24. Transfer roof heights onto other elevations.

25. Draw the roof overhang on appropriate elevations.

26. Draw the chimney on elevations showing gable ends.

27. Transfer the chimney height to other elevations.

28. Transfer a line from where the chimney passes through the roof to adjacent elevations.

29. Draw in the chimney liner, cap, or pot, if required.

30. Draw chimney saddles.

31. Draw roof dormers.

32. Draw roof ventilators for exhaust fans or attic ventilation.

33. Draw all soil pipes or other items protruding through the roof.

34. If your building has gutters, draw them in.

35. If you have gutters, draw downspouts for them.

36. Door and window openings still do not have bottoms or tops; other construction lines should form completed parts. Broaden outlines for all parts whose shapes are completely defined with construction lines. Use object, equipment, or hidden lines,

and draw as shown on the building plans in Chapter 49.

37. If ventilators or louvers are required, draw them in their proper location.

38. Draw a center line to establish all window and door heights. If some heights are different, be sure all are drawn.

39. Draw all window and door details following manufacturers' literature or other information.

40. Broaden all object or equipment lines not previously completed.

41. Draw all sills and drip caps, plus their flashings when required.

42. Draw the roof pitch symbol and indicate the pitch.

43. Add the proper symbol for the roof covering.

44. Add all dimension lines, figures, and notes. Follow good dimensioning practice and use the plans in Chapter 49 as a guide.

45. Draw symbols for all wall materials.

46. Letter the notes for all symbols used.

47. If your building has required items not included in this list, draw and identify each one.

48. Draw cutting plane lines to correspond with those shown on the floor plan.

49. Check your drawing carefully for omissions and errors; make all necessary corrections.

50. Clean your drawing.

51. Broaden border and title strip lines and trim the drawing to final size. Check the title block to be sure it is completely lettered.

Drawing Building Sections

Methods of viewing and drawing sections were discussed in Chapter 35. This chapter does not attempt to describe how building parts are drawn, but rather it prescribes necessary sections to include. Of course, before you can draw building sections you must be familiar with materials and construction methods. If you are not so informed, specific information may be obtained from earlier chapters or other reference sources.

Drawing Scale

There is no one suitable drawing scale for all building sections. Each section through a building shows the arrangement of many building parts. The size and complexity of these parts help determine the scale. Each drawing should describe the parts in question and make their construction understood. The drawing scale may vary from $\frac{1}{4}'' = 1'\text{-}0''$ to $1'' = 1'\text{-}0''$, as you have learned, and in rare instances may be drawn full scale or larger.

Minimum drawing scale for most sections is $\frac{3}{8}'' = 1'\text{-}0''$, however, a larger scale is usually more desirable. For maximum clarity a suggested size for wall sections is $\frac{3}{4}'' = 1'\text{-}0''$.

SECTIONS TO INCLUDE

Section Through a Typical Wall

A building plan should include a section through a typical wall. The drawing should show all items from the bottom of the footing to the upper face of the roof. However, a large scale drawing that presents entire walls may extend higher than the drawing sheet. It is permissible to use break lines and omit middle portions of walls. Drawings in the set of plans shown in Chapter 49 are done in this manner.

If drawing size permits, include the proper symbol for each material used. Major building parts, such as studding, sheathing, joists, or others—may be identified with leaders and notes. Minor items, such as flashings, floor coverings, interior trim, and others may be identified if their inclusion is deemed necessary for the specific situation. Some system of dimensions is recommended. The story you are telling with the section drawing determines which ones to include. Study the sample set of plans to see the kinds of dimensions likely to be required.

Other Wall Sections

If any wall is to be constructed in a different manner from the typical one, each variation must be drawn. For example, if part of a dwelling is to be entirely frame construction and another section is to be covered with brick veneer, then two wall sections are required. If this same dwelling has an attached garage with footings, floors, or other construction different from those of the house, additional section drawings are required.

Sections for Different Levels

If a structure contains more than one living level or a difference in floor level between the home and a garage, then additional section drawings are required to show how the materials at each level change are joined or assembled. If footings are required below walls joining different levels they should be drawn in.

Sections for a Finished Attic

A section through a finished attic should include locations, and methods of joining knee walls to other structural parts. Floors, ceilings, wall coverings, and insulation should be drawn in. Include dimensions to show size and locations of all walls and other parts.

Stairwell

Chapter 15 presents detailed information about different kinds of stairways and their construction. Your plan should include information pertinent to your stairway.

Draw a section through the stairwell showing structural framing plus rise and run of individual steps. Dimensioning should include both total rise and run as well as individual step rise and run. But since all steps in a typical set are the same size, you need to dimension only one.

If footings are required below the stairs or at side walls, be sure they are included on the plan.

Draw a ceiling line above and include dimensions to show the amount of head room. NOTE: Be sure to consult minimum standards when designing such parts. When landings are required, be certain they are properly drawn and dimensioned. Also, draw and dimension the stair rail (bannister). A second duplicate rail need not be drawn in detail.

Fireplace

Your plan should include a section through the fireplace, if you have one. This plan extends from the bottom of the footing to the top of the chimney. The drawing should include adjoining framing for floors, ceilings, and the roof. Indicate materials used and show methods of joinery. The plan should include the hearth, complete with all its dimensions.

Kitchen Cabinets

A section through a typical kitchen cabinet is to be included. If manufactured cabinets are called for it is unnecessary to show all construction details; only general outline shapes need to be drawn. Be sure to include all shelving. Dimensions for all individual cabinet heights, distances between upper and lower cabinets, and soffit heights should be shown. Dimension all shelf spacings. NOTE: This plan should also include an overall floor-to-ceiling dimension.

If custom-built cabinets are called for, they usually require the inclusion of all construction details, such as for face frames, doors, drawers, toe boards, and all other parts. These require complete dimensioning. Custom kitchen cabinets usually require additional section views because several different items are involved. For example, in addition to the typical cross-section, plans may also be required for the sink cabinet, oven cabinet, surface unit and hood arrangement, drawer units, or others.

Bathroom Cabinets

All bathroom cabinets should be drawn as was explained for kitchens. Include section drawings of lavatory cabinets, built-in clothes hampers, linen cabinets, dividers, or any other special items. Sections through lavatory cabinets should show mirror or medicine cabinet locations.

Built-in bathtubs requiring door enclosures, drop ceilings, soffits, or other special features should be shown in cross-section.

Other Cabinet Work

All other cabinets or shelving in the building should be drawn as described for kitchens and bathrooms.

Closets

Draw a section through a typical closet to show the width and height of all shelves. Also, draw and dimension the clothes pole location. Letter a note describing the materials to use, such as particle board shelving or iron pipe for the clothes pole. Then draw in support members for shelves and rods and identify the parts. Show clothes hooks when they are to be included.

Sections Through Doors and Windows

Plans for large buildings almost always include sections through each different type of door and window. Little information except general shape and an identifying number is usually included. Door and window types may be omitted from plans for small structures unless the information is necessary for actual construction. When these must be shown, one may copy their shapes from the manufacturers' detailing sheets which are supplied for this purpose.

Miscellaneous Section Drawings

Working plans should include construction details of all important or critical framing members, showing how they are joined to other building parts. These may include built-up girders, box beams, steel beams, supporting posts, framed openings, or any other basic structural part.

A working plan frequently includes large scale section drawings of millwork items. The ones most frequently shown are baseboards, base shoe, ceiling molding, moldings at soffits, all door and window trim, and exterior moldings.

Condensed Outline to Reinforce Knowledge

The following presents a brief resumé of section drawings to include on a set of working plans. Every item in the list may not apply to all plans. Likewise, some items required on a specific plan may not be included in the list.

1. It is necessary to determine an appropriate drawing scale for each section to be done. Try to keep as many drawings the same scale as you can.
2. Draw, letter, and dimension a typical cross-section through an exterior wall. (Most are drawn as longitudinal sections showing roof slope.)
3. Draw sections through each exterior wall that is different from the typical one.
4. Draw wall sections through changes in floor levels, as for split levels, garages, or second stories.
5. Draw a wall section through a finished attic.
6. Draw a section through the stair well, showing all construction features.
7. Draw a section through the fireplace.
8. Draw a section through a typical kitchen cabinet, including lower cabinets, upper cabinets, and a soffit if specified.
9. Draw sections through each kitchen cabinet that is different from the typical one.
10. Draw sections through each bathroom cabinet or special feature.
11. If the building contains cabinets or shelving in other rooms, draw sections through these.
12. Draw a section through a typical closet to include shelves, clothes poles, and other special features.
13. Draw sections through doors and windows when their construction needs to be shown.
14. Draw sections through each critical construction point, such as built-up girders, framed openings, or post and beam connections.
15. Draw sections through millwork items such as baseboards, moldings, and other trim.
16. Include a name, the drawing scale used, and an identifying code for each section drawn.

46

Drawing Elevation Details

Elevation details are similar to exterior building elevations except they usually show features inside rooms. They show facings. They are drawn to a larger scale than exterior elevations so more information can be included. Since these elevations describe specific items in an individual building it is impossible to give exact instructions for drawing them. As discussed in the previous chapter, one must be familiar with building materials and construction methods. There are many elevation details shown in the sample set of plans; study them before drawing yours.

Drawing Scale

There is no one suitable drawing scale for all elevation details. Each drawing must be large enough to give a complete description. Elevations with uncomplicated parts may be drawn to a small scale but those with intricate construction features must be drawn larger. The scale is usually between $\frac{1}{4}'' = 1'-0''$ and $1'' = 1'-0''$. For best appearance, all drawings on a sheet should have a uniform scale. If they do

not, page layout requires more careful planning to give an orderly appearance. For a better understanding of appropriate elevation sizes and scale, study those shown in Chapter 49.

WHAT TO INCLUDE

Plans for large buildings have many elevation drawings; almost every detail is drawn. However, plans for small structures such as homes frequently include only a few elevation detail drawings.

Kitchen Elevations

A working plan should contain elevation drawings of each wall containing kitchen cabinets or appliances. Manufactured cabinets require only general outlines plus those for shelves, drawers, and doors. Custom cabinets are drawn in detail.

If appliances are to be included as part of the construction, their outlines should be drawn and dimensioned. If they are to be supplied by others, their outlines should not be drawn, but rather the space they are to occupy should be shown and dimensioned.

Walls containing doors and

windows, but having no cabinets, are seldom drawn in elevation. Include only information necessary for construction; do not clutter the drawing with trivia.

Bathroom Elevations

Smooth walls with nothing on them need not be shown. All walls requiring cabinets, fixtures, mirrors, medicine cabinets, wall tile, or accessories should be drawn and dimensioned. Be sure to include heights and locations of accessories such as soap dishes, towel bars, paper holders, or others.

Shelves or Cabinets

Every wall requiring shelves or cabinets should be drawn and dimensioned. This statement excludes closet shelves and walls because these are not always drawn. The closet cross-section usually supplies adequate information for their construction.

Fireplace Walls

Fireplace walls usually include much detailed information. In addition to showing all visible construction features, fireplace or chimney elevations also include

486

hidden lines to outline all flue shapes. If a fireplace is open on more than one face, each must be shown.

Special Construction Features

Each wall containing special features such as planters, screens, dividers, soffits, alcoves, or similar items must be fully drawn and dimensioned.

Roof Framing

A working plan should contain an elevation detail showing truss design and construction, if these are to be used. Conventional roof framing systems should also be drawn as elevation details. These should show how framing members are fitted and connected together. If metal connectors are used for joining structural parts, large scale drawings showing their shape may be included. Dimensions and technical data necessary for construction should be given.

Structural Elevation Details

Working plans should include elevation details of all critical framing members, showing how they are joined to other building parts.

NOTE: The elevation details of roof framing and other structural parts may be shown with section views.

Exterior Elevation Details

Chapter 44 discussed exterior building elevations. As stated, most of these are drawn to a small scale. This cannot include intricate detail necessary for the construction of complicated parts. Therefore it is sometimes necessary to draw special items to a large scale to show their construction. Screens, fences, planters, entrance door details, outside fireplaces, and similar items are frequently done in this manner.

Condensed Outline to Reinforce Knowledge

The following statements serve as a reminder of elevation drawings to be included on building plans. Some elevations called for may not be required on every plan. Likewise, some plans may require items not included in the list.

1. It is necessary to determine an appropriate drawing scale for each elevation to be included. Try to keep the scale consistent for similar drawings. That is, if several kitchen elevations are required, draw them to the same scale.
2. Remember that each drawing is to give a complete description of work to be done and that necessary dimensions and technical notes are extremely important.
3. Draw elevations of each kitchen wall containing cabinets or appliances. Island or peninsula cabinets not fitted to walls also require elevation drawings.
4. If laundry or utility room cabinets or fixtures are required, draw all walls to show these.
5. Draw each bathroom wall containing cabinets, fixtures, medicine cabinets, or accessories. Blank walls may be omitted.
6. All other shelves or cabinets throughout the structure (including the basement and attic) are to be shown as elevation details.
7. Draw fireplace elevations; show all flues as hidden lines.
8. Draw elevations of all special features such as dividers, planters, screens, or similar items.
9. Draw details to describe roof framing or truss systems.
10. Draw elevations of all critical construction features.
11. Draw necessary exterior elevations of items not fully described by other views.

47 ── Drawing Framing Plans

This chapter describes framing plans frequently included in a set of working drawings. It does not attempt to describe construction methods; construction details are discussed in other chapters.

Sets of plans for large structures almost always include framing plans (or diagrams, as they are sometimes called) but they are frequently omitted from plans for small buildings. NOTE: Their inclusion is always an asset to construction.

These drawings, as the term *framing plan* implies, simply describe the shape, location, and method of joining structural parts.

Drawing Scale

Framing plans may be drawn to the same scale as the building floor plan or, if little detail is to be included, they can be drawn to a smaller scale.

Drawing Sheet Size

These plans should be drawn on the same size sheets as others in the set.

Floor Framing Plan

If a floor framing diagram is to be the same scale as other floor plans in the set, preliminary linework can be copied from a finished basement or footing plan. Naturally, if it is to be drawn to a different scale, a new layout must be made.

Using construction lines, first draw all exterior walls; then draw interior bearing walls, plus all posts or piers. Broaden wall outlines as hidden lines, or they may be shown as equipment lines. When solid lines are used to represent walls, they are usually not added until after all structural framing is drawn in. This permits omission of wall lines through structural members.

Using recommended spacings for framing (as 16″ o.c.), draw all structural members. These may be shown with heavy center lines or, if the scale is large enough to permit it, their thickness may be drawn in. When the first method is used, all double framing must be indicated with notes. When the second method is used, all double framing beneath walls and at openings should be drawn in.

Framing plans include very few dimensions. However, critical locations, such as positions of double framing that must fit beneath walls from above, should be dimensioned. Locations of framed openings, and their sizes, should also be dimensioned.

Ceiling Joist Framing Plan

A ceiling joist framing plan is drawn in exactly the same manner as a floor framing plan. In addition, it is also necessary to show non-bearing walls when they require special framing to hold them in position.

Roof Framing Plan

The major difference between a roof framing plan and those previously discussed is that the roof overhang must be shown as a solid line. If the framing on this plan is drawn with double lines to show thickness, then the roof edge framing (fascia) should also be shown in this same manner.

When describing post and beam roof construction, both the beams and their supporting posts and all roof planks should be shown.

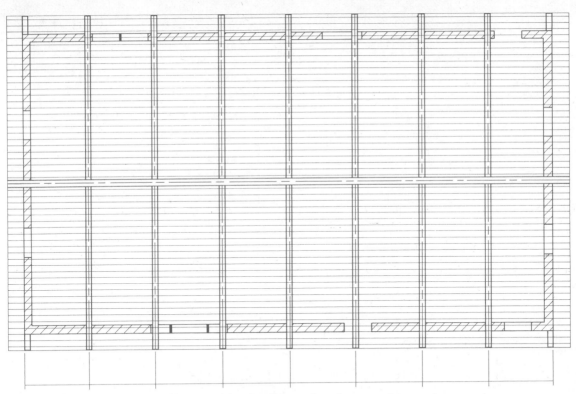

Plank and beam roof framing diagram for a transverse beam system.

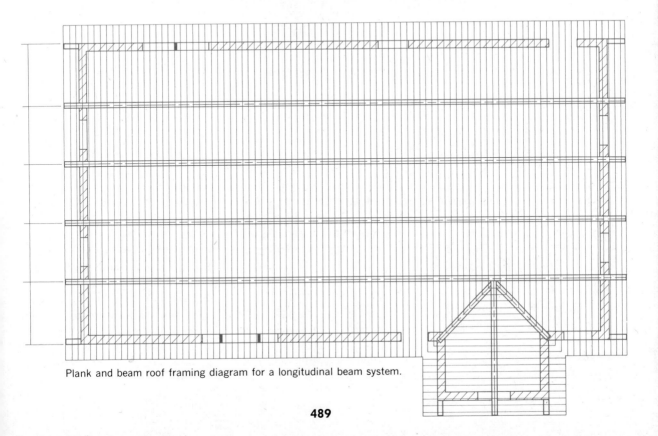

Plank and beam roof framing diagram for a longitudinal beam system.

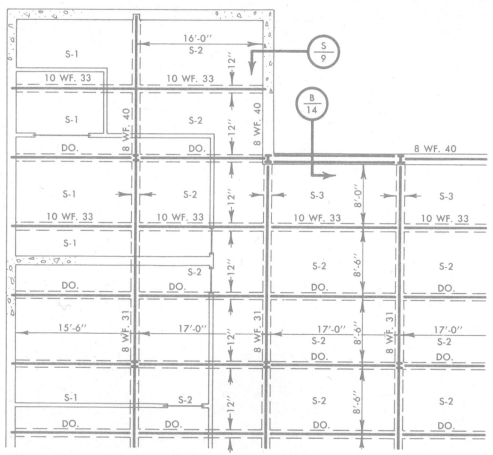

Steel beam floor framing plan with beams encased in concrete for fireproofing. Addition of hidden lines at beam edges indicates concrete fireproofing.

Steel or Concrete Framing Plans

When any of the above are to be of metal or concrete, or a combination of both, the framing plan is slightly different. To illustrate this difference, a sample framing plan showing steel beams with concrete fireproofing is shown.

Wall Framing Diagrams

Wall framing diagrams of conventionally framed buildings as shown in Chapter 7 that include all structural members are a definite construction aid. However, because of costs, complete framing plans for such buildings are seldom drawn. Persons experienced in building framing can do studding layouts without them. Only walls requiring special framing are usually included in a set of plans.

Condensed Outline to Reinforce Knowledge

The following statements are to serve as a reminder of framing plans frequently included on working drawings. It is improbable that all framing plans mentioned would be included on any one set of drawings. Use only those needed and omit all others.

1. Determine an appropriate drawing scale for each framing diagram to be included.
2. Remember that each diagram is to give a complete description of work to be done or parts to be assembled and that necessary dimensions and notes are very important.

3. Floor framing plan
- Draw exterior and bearing walls as construction lines.
- Draw all posts, piers, or other supports.
- Using suitable framing spacing, make layouts for all structural parts. Be sure to include all double framing.
- Draw center lines for, or outlines of, all framing.
- Broaden lines for walls, using either hidden or equipment lines.
- Add necessary extension and dimension lines.
- Add necessary dimension figures, notes, or other lettering.
- Indicate the scale used and name the drawing.

4. Ceiling joist framing
- Draw as described for floor framing plans.

5. Roof framing plan
- Draw exterior and bearing walls with construction lines.
- Draw other walls if they influence roof construction.
- With construction lines, draw all outlines of the roof overhang.
- Draw all ridges, gables, and valleys with construction lines.
- When roof beams are required, draw them.
- Make layouts of all structural framing.
- Draw all framing including the roof edge, using either center lines or showing framing thickness.
- If roof planks are required, draw them.
- Add necessary extension and dimension lines.
- Add necessary dimension figures, notes, or other lettering.
- Indicate the scale used and name the drawing.

6. Steel or concrete framing plans
- Using the proper symbol for each material required, draw structural framing as described for other plans.

7. When wall framing diagrams are required, draw all structural parts in their proper locations. Use notes, lettering, and dimensioning to give a complete description.

48

Mechanical Plans

Mechanical plans are drawings presenting information and installation instructions for electrical, plumbing, heating, air conditioning, ventilating, vacuum cleaning system, compressed air, or other similar needs. Each mechanical plan usually contains drawings relating to only one such installation; however, such plans may be combined if space permits.

As stated elsewhere in the text, comprehensive mechanical plans are very specific and complex. Drawing each one requires a thorough knowledge about the specific trades involved.

Mechanical plans for each type installation are always drawn for large structures, but only limited mechanical plans are drawn for homes. General information is most often shown on other drawings already included in the set; then technical problems are solved by the contractor responsible for each installation. Yet, even though only limited mechanical information is included, specific information is always more desirable because it leaves less chance for mistakes and misunderstandings.

ELECTRICAL PLANS

Electrical information is presented in Chapter 17, and symbols for individual electrical items are shown in Chapter 38. Chapter 42 sets forth electrical items that may be included on a floor plan.

This discussion is to serve as a reminder for including electrical items on your plan. There are three different ways electrical information may be presented in house plans. The first two are widely used, but the third is seldom used for homes and is most often reserved for use on plans for large buildings.

1. Electrical information is most often included on regular house floor plans as described in Chapter 42 and shown in Chapter 49. (The lower level floor plan has electrical items shown in this conventional way.) Study it carefully as a guide for drawing your own electrical plan if you are including electrical information.

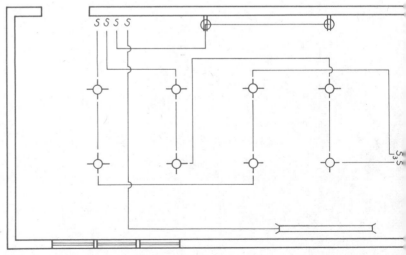

Electrical wiring circuits. Wires leading from switches represent individual circuits.

2. Floor plans often become difficult to understand when much information is drawn in a small space. To remedy this it is permissible to trace the original floor plan to show only wall outlines and major features, and then add all electrical information to this tracing. In Chapter 49, the middle and upper level floor plans were traced and electrical information added. Compare the two drawing methods to determine which is best for your plan. Regardless of the one chosen, follow the steps for items to include as outlined in Chapter 42.

3. Also as described in Chapter 42, lines connecting switches and outlets indicate only which switch controls a given fixture; they do not actually show wire placement. If your electrical system is quite complex, complete diagrams for each electrical circuit may be drawn on a traced floor plan. Such a partial plan is shown. NOTE: This method is almost always required for large buildings but seldom for homes.

Electrical items to include. Since step-by-step procedures for including electrical information on floor plans are given in Chapter 42, and the same information is included with all three methods described earlier, the steps are not restated in this chapter.

PLUMBING PLANS

As you know, horizontal plumbing lines are most often installed beneath a building or between its floors. Plumbing information (called a plumbing diagram) is drawn on the floor plan

that such plumbing lines serve. That is, if lines are beneath a first floor they serve this living level.

Plumbing information may be drawn on footing and foundation, basement, or floor plans. Or if inclusion of such information will result in overcrowding, it is more desirable to trace the plan and add plumbing information.

Drawing Tips

Chapter 18 presents plumbing information and Chapter 38 shows pipe symbols for different uses.

Plumbing fixtures, such as bathtubs, sinks, or lavatories, need not be drawn. Naturally, if any plumbing fixture diagrams are drawn on an existing floor plan, they will remain.

Study each plan in your set to determine if the inclusion of plumbing lines will result in overcrowding. Trace the plans, if necessary, for this.

Indicating drains through floors. For each footing and foundation, basement, or floor plan, draw pipe size circles (approximately same diameter to scale as the pipe required for the drain) at all locations where vertical drains extend through floors.

Indicating drains in walls. Draw pipe size circles in walls for all soil or vent stacks. Examine each wall to be certain its thickness is designed to accommodate the pipe diameter.

Branch supply lines. For each hot and cold branch supply line serving *all* fixtures, draw vertical pipe size circles where they extend through floors. When such

pipes extend (usually in walls) from one *living* level to another, note this on the plan. If shutoffs are to be provided at fixtures, indicate this on the plan.

Notes. Add notes to all supply and drain pipes, as indicated earlier, to describe their diameters and materials used.

Gas pipe. If a vertical gas pipe extends through a floor, draw an appropriate sized circle and add a note to describe. If the gas line terminates at this point with a valve and supply to an appliance, indicate this with the gas symbol rather than a circle.

Water heater. Draw a top view of the water heater in its appropriate location, and add a note to describe its fuel and capacity. If *vents* are required for combustible fuels, draw and describe.

Sillcock or hose bib. If standard or frost-free hose bibs are required, draw the symbol for these in their proper locations. Add explanatory notes when necessary.

Sprinkler systems. If outside stationary sprinklers are to be installed, draw these on a large-scale plot plan.

Floor drains. If floor drains for a basement or garage are required, draw them in their proper location.

Sump pump. If your building requires a concrete pit and sump pump, draw these. Both size and location dimensions should be given for the pit. Describe the cover if one is required. Unless your specifications contain a description of the sump pump, add notes to describe.

Water meter. Draw the water meter and/or shutoff valve.

Water softeners. If water softening equipment is required, draw it in and add notes to describe or refer to specifications.

Pressure reduction or booster devices. If pressure reduction or booster devices are to be installed, draw these to conform to manufacturers' descriptions and add appropriate notes.

Protective devices. If your plan requires a catch basin, grease trap, cistern, dry well, or similar device, draw it on your footing and foundation plan (or tracing) in its proper location to conform to local code requirements.

Plumbing lines. Each of the items previously drawn must be connected to supply or drain lines. Study the symbols of plumbing lines in Chapter 38. Study your plan to determine how all lines can best be located to use a minimum of pipe and conform to good plumbing practices.

- Draw construction lines to connect all hot water supply pipes.
- Draw construction lines to connect all cold water supply pipes.
- Draw construction lines to connect all building drains.

Broaden all lines with their appropriate symbol.

On your plot plan draw lines connecting from the building to the city sewer main, water main, and gas main, if required. If your plan requires a septic tank, draw this in its chosen location and connect to distribution boxes and the absorption field.

Perimeter drain tile. Using the appropriate symbol, draw foundation drain tile as required. If this connects to a dry well, storm sewer, or sanitary sewer, draw the connecting lines.

Check your plans carefully for omissions and errors and make corrections as needed.

Heating and Air Conditioning Plans

Heating and air conditioning information is presented in Chapter 19, and symbols for individual items are shown in Chapter 38. As was true for electrical plans, heating and air conditioning plans for homes may be limited, or elaborate information may be presented. The information may be added to regular footing and foundation, basement, or floor plans. If existing plans are too congested to permit inclusion of additional information, a plan may be traced and the information included on the tracing.

First this discussion covers information almost always included on house plans. Then detailed information sometimes included on house plans, but almost always included on plans for large buildings, is given.

The furnace. Drawing the furnace outline was described in Chapter 43 and is mentioned here as a reminder for its inclusion if the heating plan is being drawn on a tracing.

Radiators or registers. On each floor plan requiring registers or radiators, draw all such items to size. If chases or recesses are required in walls, draw and dimension these. Location dimensions for radiators or registers are not required unless their exact placement is critical to other construction features. Either notes, code letters, or figures may be added at each to describe.

Air conditioning condenser. If a central air conditioner is planned, draw the outline of the condensing unit on the plot in its desired location. Letter descriptive notes, code letters, or figures.

Air conditioner evaporator. Draw the outline of the air conditioner evaporator. This may

either be a part of the furnace or it may be a separate unit. Include descriptive information.

Window air conditioners. If these are to be installed permanently through walls, draw their outlines and add appropriate notes. If they are window mounted but not permanently installed do not draw them in, or draw them as hidden lines and include a note stating that they are supplied by the owner. (Be sure electrical connections are included on the electrical plan.)

If fuel lines connecting to a supply source were not drawn with the plumbing plans, draw them now.

Thermostats. For each heating or cooling zone draw a thermostat in an appropriate location. Add descriptive notes, model numbers, or identifying codes.

Other items. As stated earlier,

all air ducts or supply pipes may be drawn on house plans if deemed necessary, and they are almost always drawn on plans for large buildings. Symbols for these items are shown in Chapter 38. If all required valves, fittings, or mechanical accessories are also to be shown on the plan, further study of technical books and manufacturers' descriptive literature is necessary.

SCHEMATIC DIAGRAMS

Since separate mechanical plans are drawn for footing and foundation, basement, and floor plans, it is often difficult to determine how such information shown on separate sheets fits with or is a part of similar information on other sheets in the set of plans. To show this relationship clearly, schematic diagrams—in the form of simplified pictorial drawings of individual building mechanical systems—are often drawn. These omit all structural building parts to more clearly describe the system being explained.

Condensed Outline to Reinforce Knowledge

The following statements review items to include on mechanical plans. Even though discussions of how to draw furnaces, water heaters, electrical symbols, and other mechanical items were presented in other chapters, they are restated briefly here to help avoid omissions when you wish to include them on separate mechanical plans.

1. Decide what mechanical plans are required for your building.
2. Determine the scope of the information to be included.
3. For detailed information to include on electrical plans, refer to Chapter 42.
4. Determine which drawing sheets in your set require plumbing plans.
5. Trace sheets as required.
6. Draw pipe size circles for all drains through floors.
7. Draw pipe size circles for all soil or vent stacks in walls.
8. Draw pipe size circles for all branch supply lines extending through floors.
9. Draw gas pipe extending through floors or use gas outlet symbol.
10. Draw the water heater.
11. Draw sillcocks or hose bibs.
12. Draw heads for sprinkler systems when required.
13. Draw floor drains as required.
14. Draw sump pit and pump.
15. Draw the water meter and/or shutoff valve.
16. Draw water softening equipment.
17. Draw all other pumps or motored apparatus related to the plumbing system.
18. Using the appropriate symbols, draw all drain and supply lines.

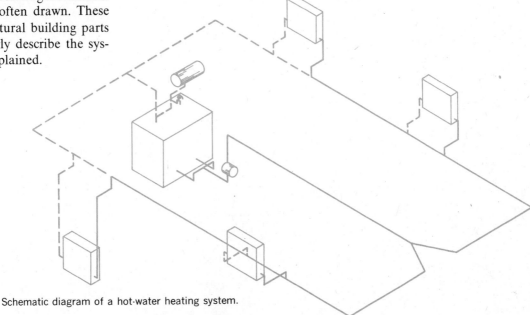

Schematic diagram of a hot-water heating system.

19. If your system requires a septic tank and absorption field, draw them.
20. Draw perimeter foundation drain tile and related items, such as catch basins, cisterns, storm sewer connections, or lines to the sanitary sewer.
21. Add all necessary descriptive notes to describe the system.
22. Check your plan for omissions and errors, and make necessary corrections.
23. Determine which sheets in your set of plans require heating or air conditioning information.
24. Trace the sheets as required.
25. Draw your furnace outline and connect supply line to its source.
26. Draw all chases or recesses for radiators or registers.
27. Draw all radiators or registers.
28. If required, draw the air conditioning condenser.
29. If required, draw the air conditioner evaporator.
30. Draw window air conditioners, if specified.
31. Draw symbols for all thermostats.
32. Draw all ducts or hot water supply pipes to be included on your plan.
33. Add necessary descriptive notes and code designations.
34. Check your drawing for omissions or errors, and make all necessary corrections.
35. Draw schematic diagrams of plumbing, heating, or other systems if clarifications are necessary.

49

Working Plans for a Contemporary Home

Much of this book has been devoted to information necessary for building planning and design. Construction features have also been discussed and drawn as they should appear on working plans. Additional emphasis has been placed upon methods of communicating ideas to others through working plans. Such verbal descriptions, or drawings of individual construction features of items requiring inclusion on working plans may not always be clearly understood by the novice. He may not know how to visually show the required technical information by lines, symbols, and notes. A set of plans for a contemporary home *(the same home shown and described in Chapter 53, Architectural Models)* therefore is included in this chapter. These plans are to supplement the printed text and individual drawings in the book to help clarify by illustration the separate drawings required, the information to be included, and to show how the finished drawings should appear.

This set of plans is not exactly the same as any you may draw because each building requires plans different from others. Yet these plans can be used as a general guide for information or kinds of lines to include on yours. Careful analysis of the plans may also serve as a standard by which you may judge the quality of your work. Compare this set to those shown at the end of Chapter 39. Observe that the plans here are much more elaborate in detail than the previous set. Naturally, the building complexity determines the amount of detail required. On small structures, only the most important detail is shown, but on large commercial structures or expensive, custom-built homes almost every detail is included.

498

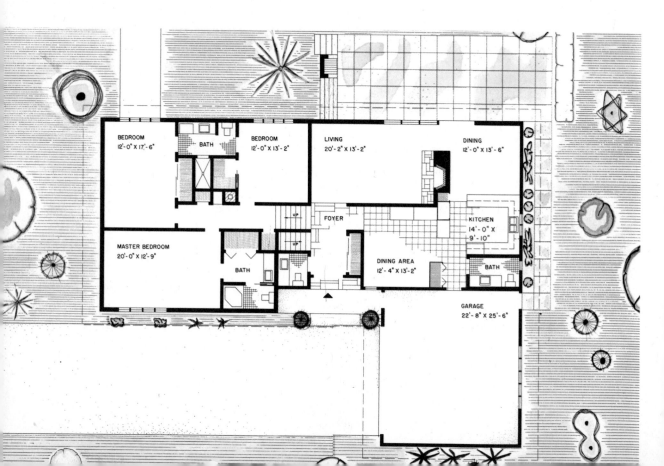

BEDROOM
12'-0" X 17'-6"

BATH

BEDROOM
12'-0" X 13'-2"

LIVING
20'-2" X 13'-2"

DINING
12'-0" X 13'-6"

FOYER

KITCHEN
14'-0" X
9'-10"

UP

MASTER BEDROOM
20'-0" X 12'-9"

BATH

DINING AREA
12'-4" X 13'-2"

BATH

GARAGE
22'-8" X 25'-6"

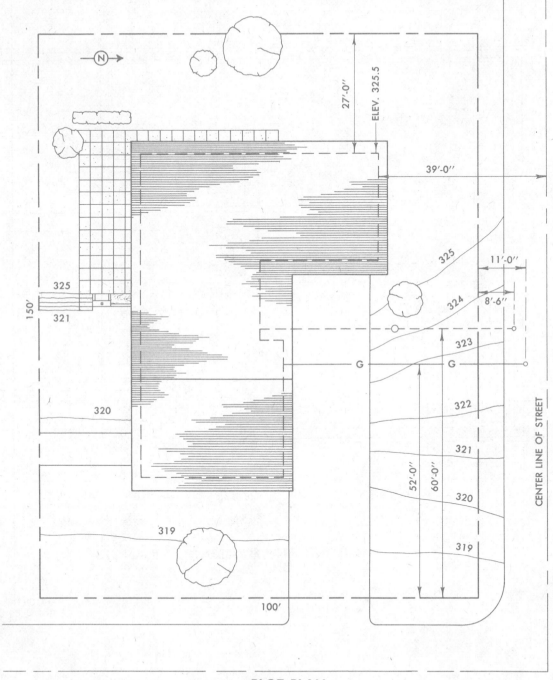

PLOT PLAN

SCALE $^3/_{64}$" = 1'-0"

499

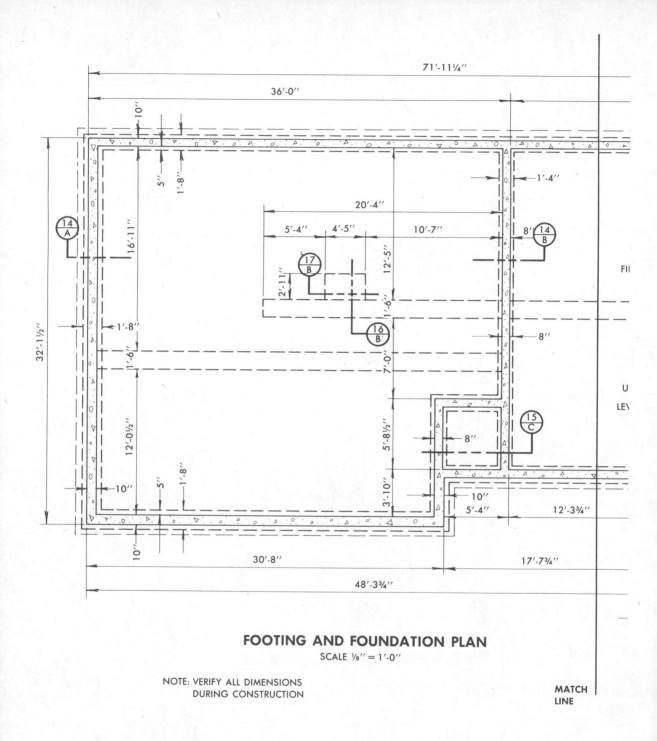

FOOTING AND FOUNDATION PLAN

SCALE 1/8" = 1'-0"

NOTE: VERIFY ALL DIMENSIONS
DURING CONSTRUCTION

MATCH
LINE

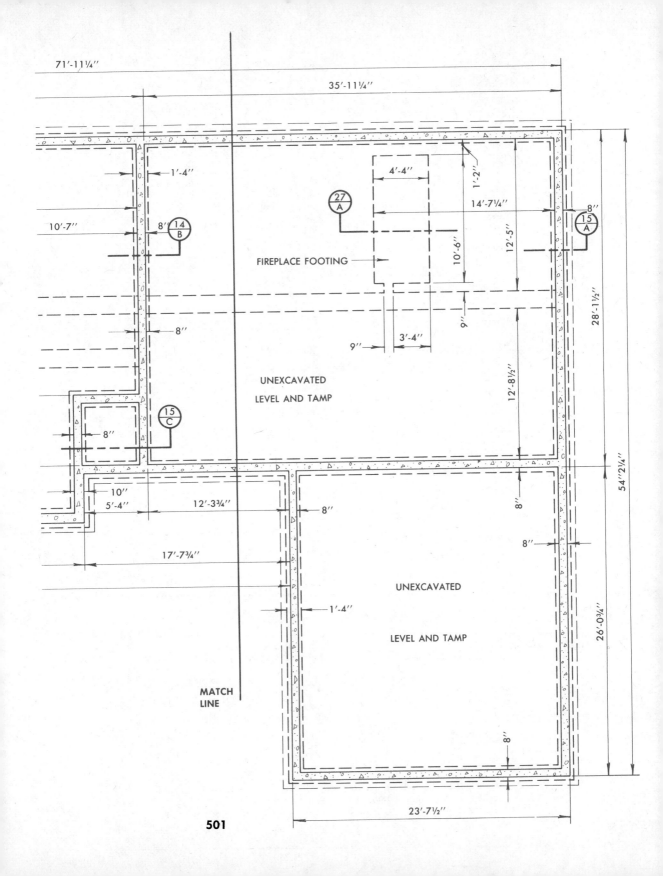

71'-11¼"

35'-11¼"

4'-4"

1'-2"

1'-4"

14'-7¼"

8"

27
A

10'-7"

8"

14
B

15
A

12'-5"

FIREPLACE FOOTING

10'-6"

28'-1½"

8"

9"

3'-4"

9"

12'-8½"

UNEXCAVATED

LEVEL AND TAMP

54"2¼"

15
C

8"

8"

10"

5'-4"

12'-3¾"

8"

8"

17'-7¾"

8"

UNEXCAVATED

1'-4"

26'-0¾"

LEVEL AND TAMP

MATCH
LINE

8"

23'-7½"

501

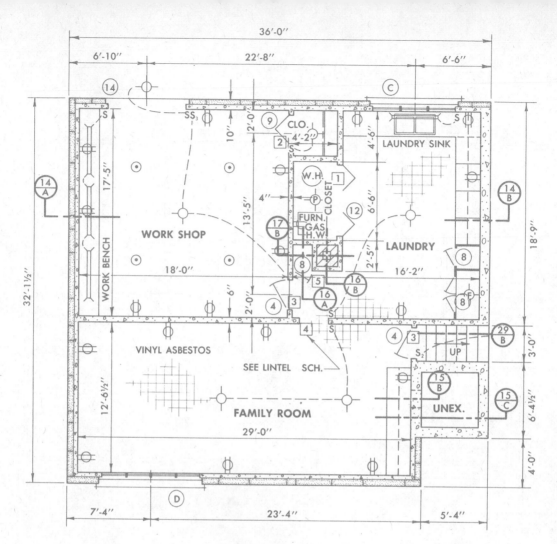

BASEMENT PLAN
SCALE ⅛″ = 1′-0″

KEY	QUAN.	MODEL NO.	DESCRIPTION	REMARKS
			WINDOW SCHEDULE			
A	1	1N4	CASEMENT W/AL STORM & SCREENS	D/S GLASS
B	1	2N4	CASEMENT W/AL STORM & SCREENS	D/S GLASS
C	3	W3N5	CASEMENT W/AL STORM & SCREENS	D/S GLASS
D	2	W4N5	CASEMENT W/AL STORM & SCREENS	D/S GLASS
E	1	W5N4	CASEMENT W/AL STORM & SCREENS	D/S GLASS
F	1		CUSTOM—SEE PLANS	½″ INS. GLASS
G	1		CUSTOM—SEE PLANS	½″ INS. GLASS
H	1		CUSTOM—SEE PLANS	1″ INS. GLASS

DOOR SCHEDULE

KEY	QUAN.	SIZE	MATERIAL	DESCRIPTION	FRAME
1	3	2'-6" x 7'-0" x 1¾"	WOOD	SOLID CORE BIRCH	WHITE PINE
2	1	2'-6" x 6'-8" x 1¾"	WOOD	SOLID CORE BIRCH	WHITE PINE
3	4	3'-0" x 6'-8" x 1⅜"	WOOD	HOLLOW CORE BIRCH	WHITE PINE
4	10	2'-6" x 6'-8" x 1⅜"	WOOD	HOLLOW CORE BIRCH	WHITE PINE
5	2	2'-6" x 6'-8" x 1⅜"	WOOD	HOLLOW CORE WALNUT	WHITE PINE
6	1	2'-2" x 6'-8" x 1⅜"	WOOD	HOLLOW CORE BIRCH	WHITE PINE
7	2	2'-0" x 6'-8" x 1⅜"	WOOD	HOLLOW CORE BIRCH	WHITE PINE
8	4	1'-6" x 6'-8" x 1⅜"	WOOD	HOLLOW CORE BIRCH	WHITE PINE
9	1	2'-10" x 6'-8" x 7⅜"	WOOD	HOLLOW CORE BIRCH—FOLDING	WHITE PINE
10	1	5'-0" x 6'-8" x 1⅜"	WOOD	HOLLOW CORE BIRCH—BI-FOLD	WHITE PINE
11	2	1'-10" x 6'-8" x 1⅛"	WOOD	HOLLOW CORE WALNUT—CUSTOM	WHITE PINE
12	1	6'-0" x 6'-8" x 1⅜"	WOOD	LOUVER—BI-FOLD	WHITE PINE
13	1	6'-0" x 6'-8" x 1⅜"	ALUM.	LEFT PANEL FIXED—RIGHT PANEL SLIDING. ¼ CRYSTAL	ALUMINUM
14	1	7'-0" x 6'-8"	WOOD	3 PANEL OVERHEAD	WHITE PINE
15	1	18'-0" x 7'-0"	WOOD	4 PANEL OVERHEAD	WHITE PINE
16	1	4'-0" x 8'-0" x 1⅜"	WOOD	PARTICAL BOARD—PLASTIC LAMINATE COVERED	POCKET ASSY. NO FRAME
17	1	2'-0" x 6'-8"	GLASS	FROSTED GLASS SHOWER DOOR	ALUMINUM

☐ LINTEL SCHEDULE

PRECAST CONCRETE LINTELS

KEY	QUAN.	CLEAR SPAN	LINTEL WIDTH	LINTEL HEIGHT	LINTEL LENGTH	REINF. TOP & BOT.
1	1	6'-0"	4"	7⅝"	7'-4"	1-#4
2	1	2'-10"	4"	7⅝"	4'-2"	1-#4
3	2	2'-6"	4"	7⅝"	3'-10"	1-#4
4	1	2'-6"	6"	7⅝"	3'-10"	1-#4

STEEL LINTELS

KEY	QUAN.	CLEAR SPAN	SIZE	LINTEL LENGTH	
5	1	1'-6"	3" x 3" x 3/16"	2'-2"	
6	1	1'-8"	3" x 3" x 3/16"	2'-4"	
7	1	3'-6"	3" x 3" x ⅜"	4'-2"	
8	1	2'-3"	2½" x 1½" x 3/16"	2'-3"	

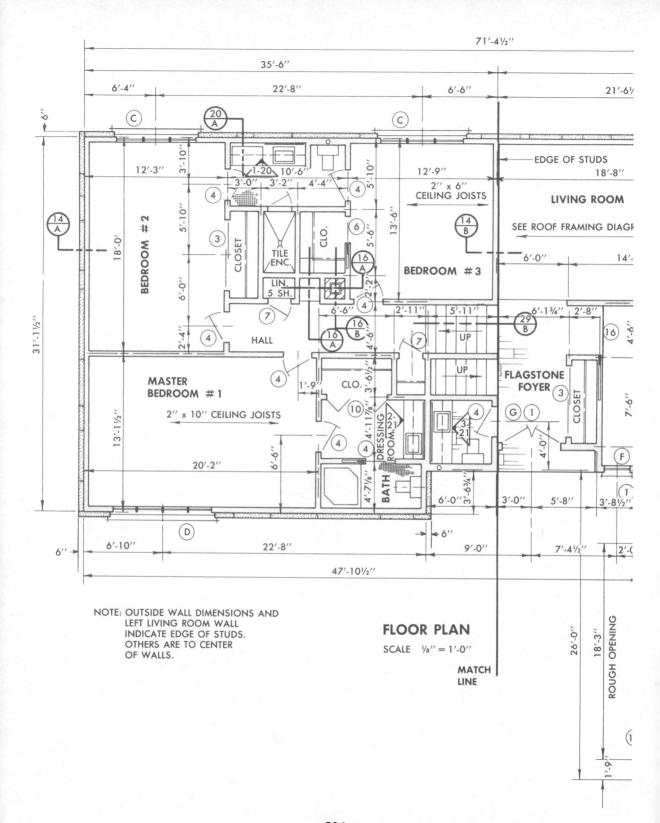

NOTE: OUTSIDE WALL DIMENSIONS AND
LEFT LIVING ROOM WALL
INDICATE EDGE OF STUDS.
OTHERS ARE TO CENTER
OF WALLS.

FLOOR PLAN

SCALE ⅛″ = 1′-0″

MATCH
LINE

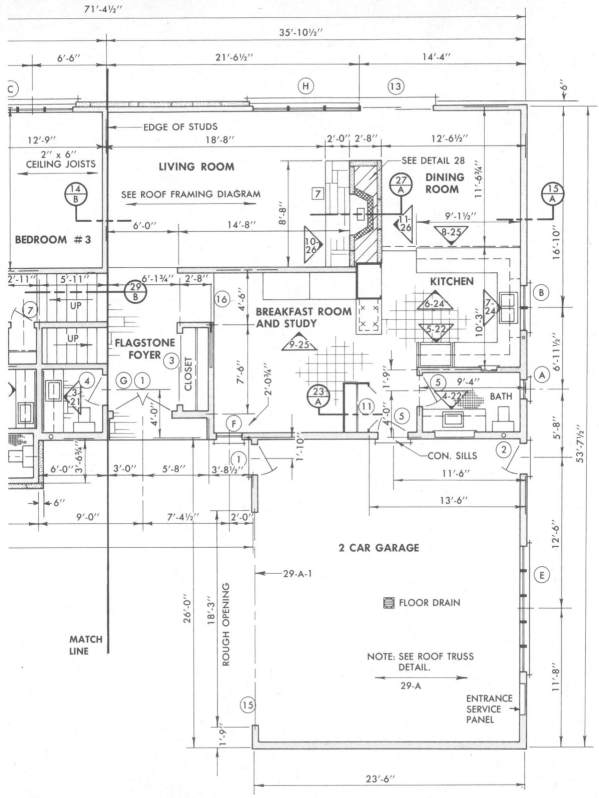

71'-4½"

35'-10½"

6'-6"   21'-6½"   14'-4"

6"

C   H   13

EDGE OF STUDS

12'-9"   18'-8"   2'-0" 2'-8"   12'-6½"

2" x 6"
CEILING JOISTS   LIVING ROOM   SEE DETAIL 28

SEE ROOF FRAMING DIAGRAM   27
A   DINING
ROOM

14
B   11'-6¾"

15
A

7   8'-8"   9'-1½"

6'-0"   14'-8"   10
26   11-
26   8-25

BEDROOM # 3   16'-10"

2'-11" 5'-11"   6'-1¾" 2'-8"   KITCHEN

29
B   16   4'-6"   6-24   7-
24   B

7   UP   5-22   10'-3"

UP   FLAGSTONE
FOYER   3   CLOSET   7'-6"   2'-0¾"   9-25   6'-11½"

4   G 1   4'-0"   23
A   11   5   9'-4"
4-22   BATH   A

3-
21   5   5'-8"

F   1'-10"   4'-0"   5   CON. SILLS   2   53'-7½"

3'-6¾"   1   11   13'-6"

6'-0"   3'-0"   5'-8"   3'-8½"   11'-6"

6"   12'-6"

9'-0"   7'-4½"   2'-0"   2 CAR GARAGE   E

26'-0"
18'-3"   29-A-1

ROUGH OPENING   FLOOR DRAIN   11'-8"

MATCH
LINE   NOTE: SEE ROOF TRUSS
DETAIL.

29-A

15   ENTRANCE
SERVICE
PANEL

1'-9"

23'-6"

505

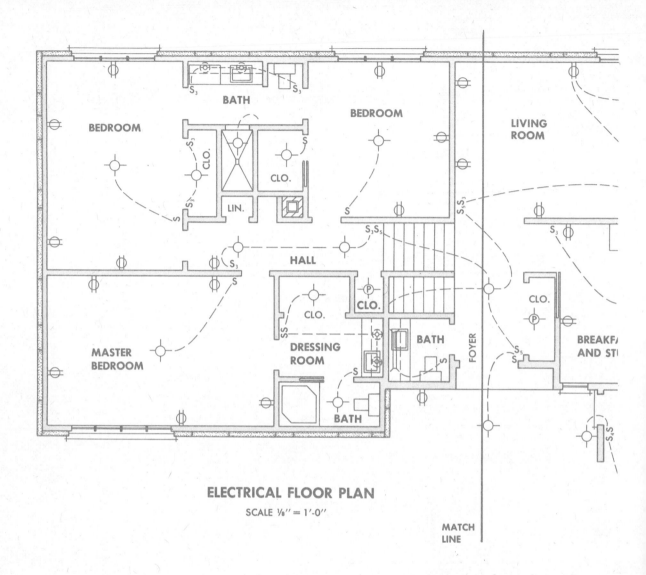

ELECTRICAL FLOOR PLAN

SCALE ⅛″ = 1′-0″

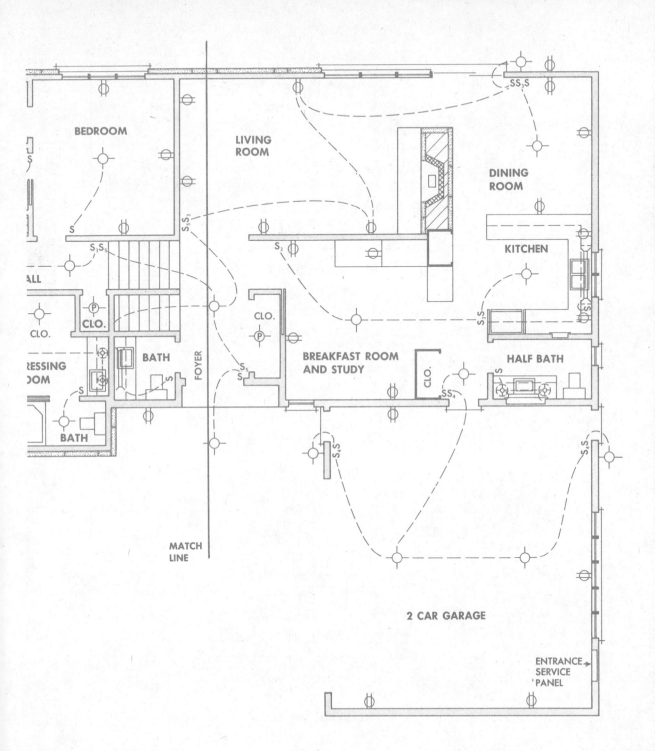

BEDROOM

LIVING
ROOM

DINING
ROOM

KITCHEN

ALL

S₃S₅

S₅S₃

S₃

S₃S

CLO.

CLO.

CLO.

P

RESSING
OOM

BATH

FOYER

BREAKFAST ROOM
AND STUDY

CLO.

HALF BATH

S₅
S₅

SS₄

S

BATH

SS₃S

S₄S

S.S

MATCH
LINE

2 CAR GARAGE

ENTRANCE
SERVICE
PANEL

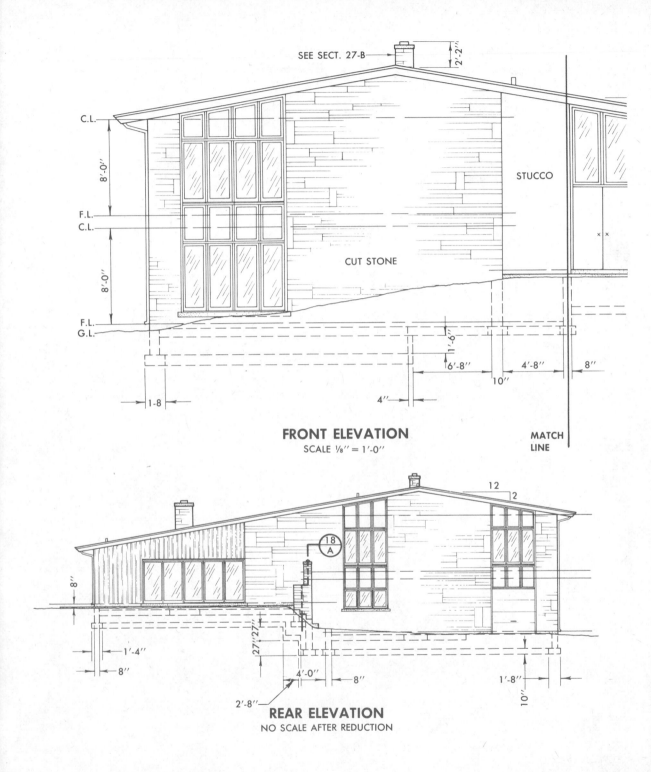

SEE SECT. 27-B

2'-2"

C.L.

8'-0"

F.L.
C.L.

STUCCO

8'-0"

CUT STONE

F.L.
G.L.

1'-6"

6'-8"

4'-8"

8"

10"

1-8

4"

FRONT ELEVATION
SCALE ⅛" = 1'-0"

MATCH
LINE

12
2

18
A

8"

27" 27"

1'-4"

8"

4'-0"

8"

1'-8"

10"

2'-8"

REAR ELEVATION
NO SCALE AFTER REDUCTION

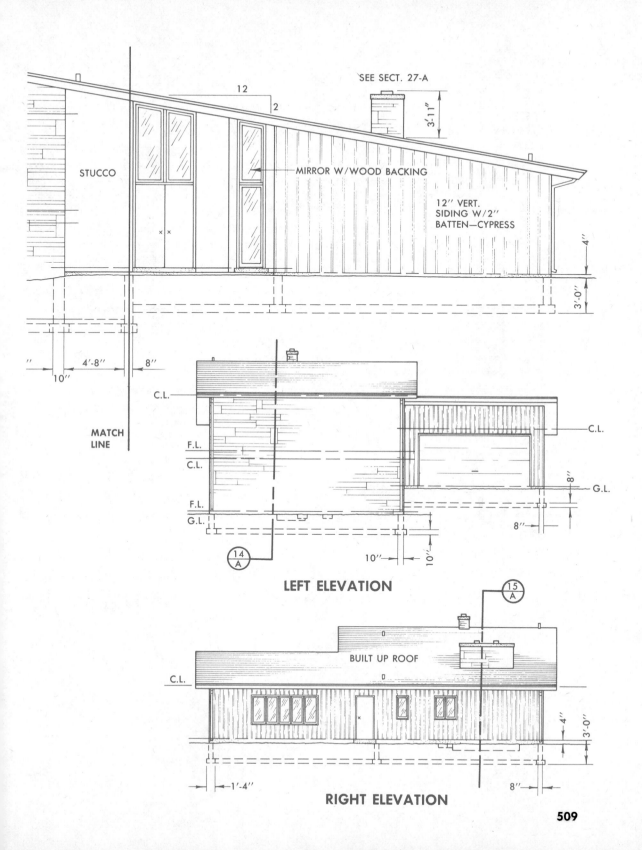

SEE SECT. 27-A

3'-11"

12
2

STUCCO

MIRROR W/WOOD BACKING

12" VERT.
SIDING W/2"
BATTEN—CYPRESS

4"

3'-0"

10"
"
4'-8"
8"

MATCH
LINE

C.L.

F.L.
C.L.

F.L.
G.L.

C.L.

8"
G.L.

8"

14
A

10"
10"

LEFT ELEVATION

15
A

BUILT UP ROOF

C.L.

4"
3'-0"

1'-4"
8"

RIGHT ELEVATION

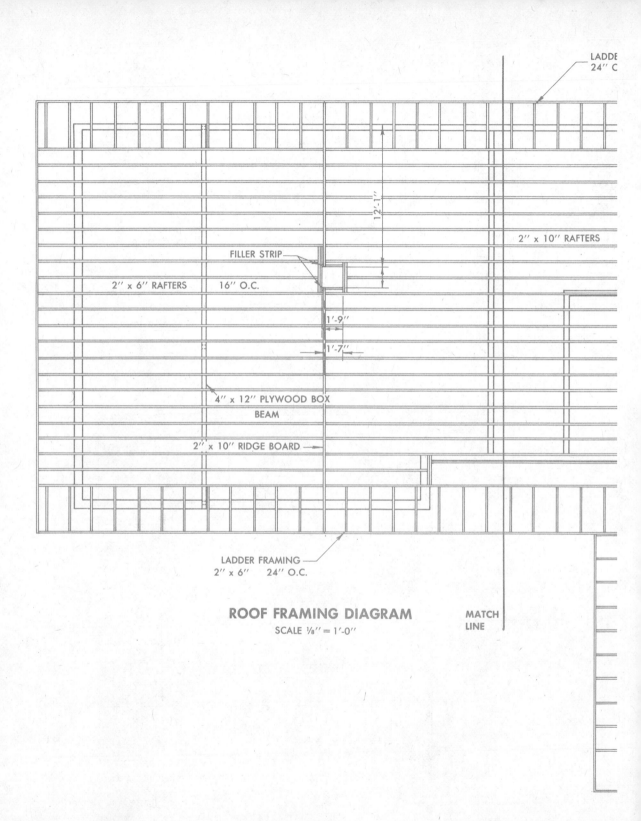

LADDE
24" C

2" x 10" RAFTERS

12'-1"

FILLER STRIP

2" x 6" RAFTERS   16" O.C.

1'-9"

1'-7"

4" x 12" PLYWOOD BOX
BEAM

2" x 10" RIDGE BOARD →

LADDER FRAMING
2" x 6"   24" O.C.

MATCH
LINE

ROOF FRAMING DIAGRAM
SCALE ⅛" = 1'-0"

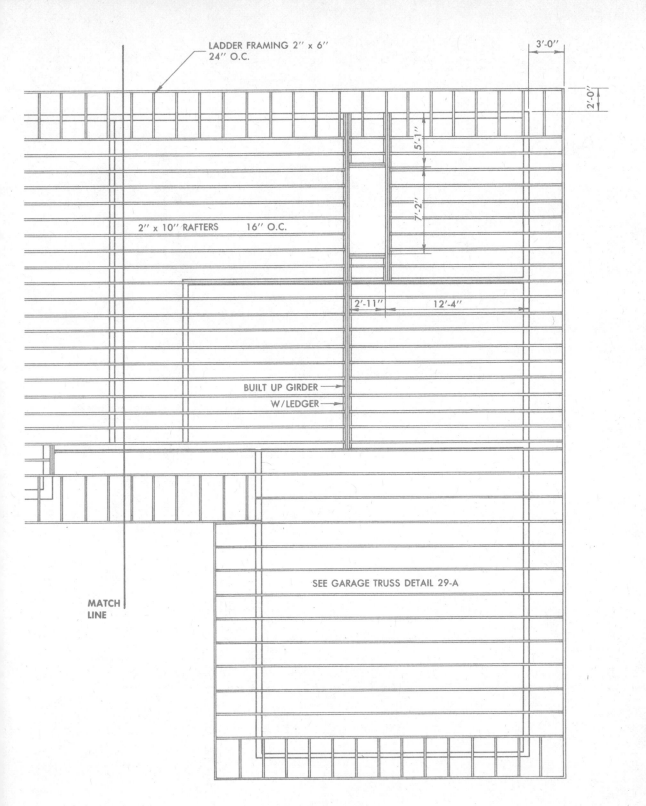

LADDER FRAMING 2″ x 6″
24″ O.C.

3'-0″

2'-0″

5'-1″

7'-2″

2″ x 10″ RAFTERS   16″ O.C.

2'-11″   12'-4″

BUILT UP GIRDER
W/LEDGER

SEE GARAGE TRUSS DETAIL 29-A

MATCH
LINE

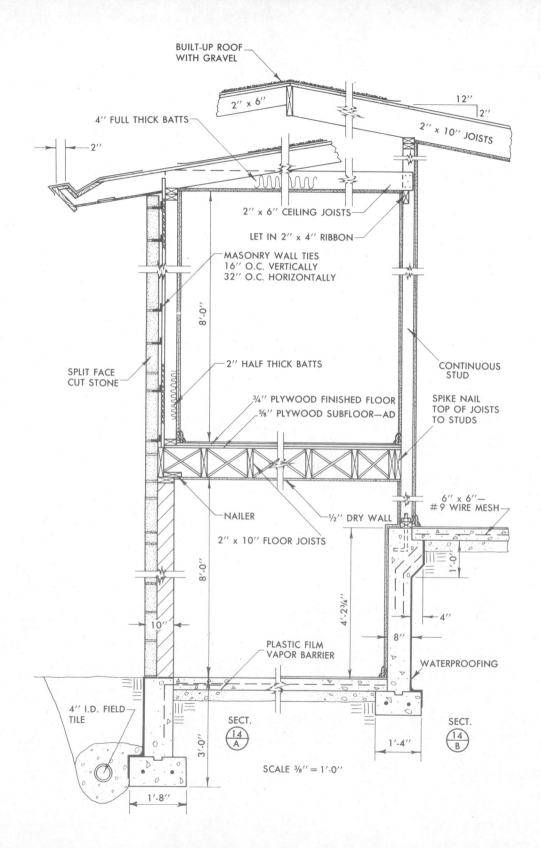

BUILT-UP ROOF
WITH GRAVEL

2″ x 6″

12″

2″

2″ x 10″ JOISTS

4″ FULL THICK BATTS

2″

2″ x 6″ CEILING JOISTS

LET IN 2″ x 4″ RIBBON

MASONRY WALL TIES
16″ O.C. VERTICALLY
32″ O.C. HORIZONTALLY

8′-0″

SPLIT FACE
CUT STONE

2″ HALF THICK BATTS

CONTINUOUS
STUD

¾″ PLYWOOD FINISHED FLOOR

⅝″ PLYWOOD SUBFLOOR—AD

SPIKE NAIL
TOP OF JOISTS
TO STUDS

NAILER

½″ DRY WALL

6″ x 6″—
9 WIRE MESH

2″ x 10″ FLOOR JOISTS

1′-0″

4′-2¾″

4″

8″

8′-0″

10″

PLASTIC FILM
VAPOR BARRIER

WATERPROOFING

4″ I.D. FIELD
TILE

3′-0″

SECT.
14
A

SECT.
14
B

1′-4″

1′-8″

SCALE ⅜″ = 1′-0″

512

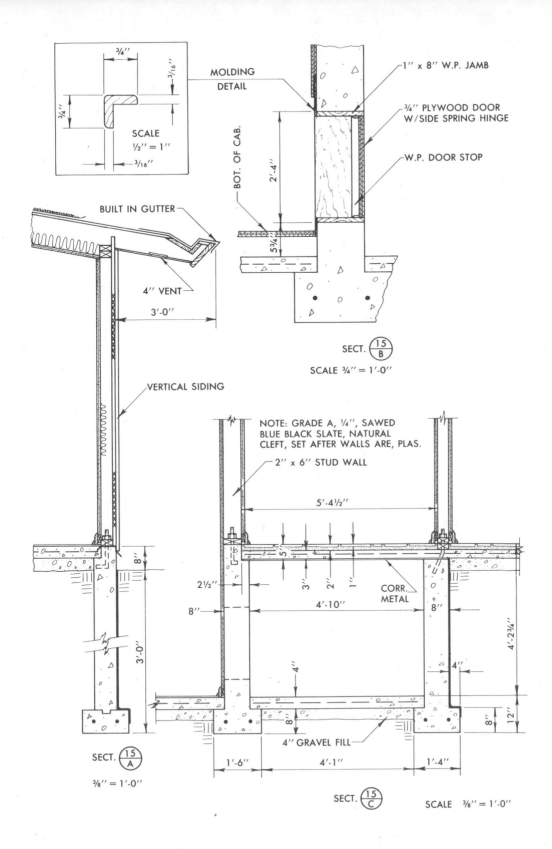

MOLDING
DETAIL

¾″

³⁄₁₆″

¾″

SCALE
½″ = 1″

³⁄₁₆″

1″ x 8″ W.P. JAMB

¾″ PLYWOOD DOOR
W/SIDE SPRING HINGE

W.P. DOOR STOP

BOT. OF CAB.

2′-4″

5¾″

BUILT IN GUTTER

4″ VENT

3′-0″

VERTICAL SIDING

SECT. $\frac{15}{B}$

SCALE ¾″ = 1′-0″

NOTE: GRADE A, ¼″, SAWED
BLUE BLACK SLATE, NATURAL
CLEFT, SET AFTER WALLS ARE, PLAS.

2″ x 6″ STUD WALL

5′-4½″

5″

2½″

3″ 2″ 1″

CORR.
METAL

8″

4′-10″

8″

8″

3′-0″

4″

4″

4′-2¾″

4″ GRAVEL FILL

8″

8″

12″

SECT. $\frac{15}{A}$

⅜″ = 1′-0″

1′-6″

4′-1″

1′-4″

SECT. $\frac{15}{C}$

SCALE   ⅜″ = 1′-0″

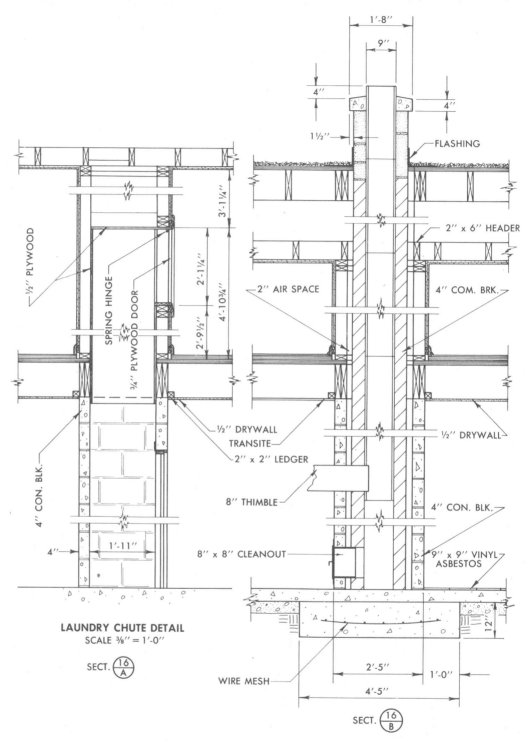

½'' PLYWOOD

SPRING HINGE

¾'' PLYWOOD DOOR

3'-1¼''

2'-1¼''

4'-10¾''

2'-9½''

4'' CON. BLK.

4''

1'-11''

LAUNDRY CHUTE DETAIL
SCALE ⅜'' = 1'-0''

SECT. 16/A

1'-8''

9''

4''

4''

1½''

FLASHING

2'' x 6'' HEADER

2'' AIR SPACE

4'' COM. BRK.

½'' DRYWALL

½'' DRYWALL
TRANSITE

2'' x 2'' LEDGER

8'' THIMBLE

8'' x 8'' CLEANOUT

4'' CON. BLK.

9'' x 9'' VINYL
ASBESTOS

12''

WIRE MESH

2'-5''

1'-0''

4'-5''

SECT. 16/B

**BASEMENT LAUNDRY
CHUTE DOOR DETAIL**
SCALE ½'' = 1'-0''

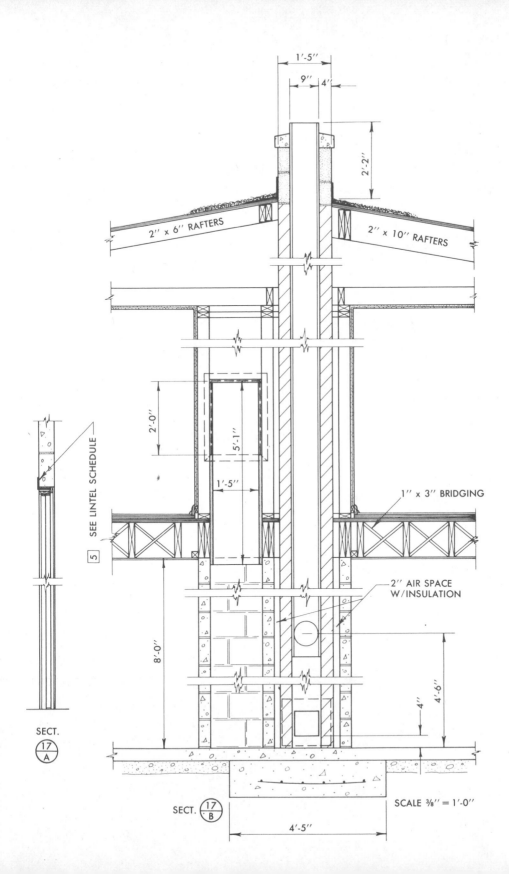

1'-5"

9" 4"

2'-2"

2" x 6" RAFTERS

2" x 10" RAFTERS

SEE LINTEL SCHEDULE

5

2'-0"

5'-1"

1'-5"

1" x 3" BRIDGING

2" AIR SPACE
W/INSULATION

8'-0"

4'-6"

4"

SECT.
17
A

SECT. 17
B

SCALE ⅜" = 1'-0"

4'-5"

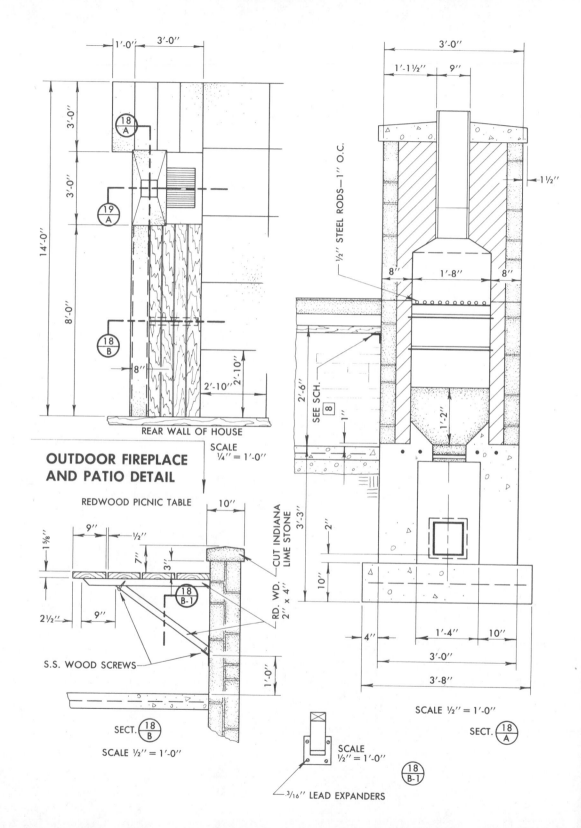

1'-0'' 3'-0''

3'-0''

18
A

3'-0''

19
A

14'-0''

8'-0''

18
B

8''

2'-10'' 2'-10''

REAR WALL OF HOUSE

SCALE
¼'' = 1'-0''

OUTDOOR FIREPLACE
AND PATIO DETAIL

REDWOOD PICNIC TABLE   10''

9''   ½''

1⅝''

7''

3''

18
B-1

2½''

9''

S.S. WOOD SCREWS

1'-0''

SECT. 18 B

SCALE ½'' = 1'-0''

RD. WD.
2'' x 4''

CUT INDIANA
LIME STONE

3'-0''

1'-1½''   9''

½'' STEEL RODS—1'' O.C.

1½''

8''   1'-8''   8''

2'-6''

SEE SCH. 8

1''

1'-2''

3'-3''

2''

10''

4''   1'-4''   10''

3'-0''

3'-8''

SCALE ½'' = 1'-0''

SECT. 18 A

18
B-1

SCALE
½'' = 1'-0''

3/16'' LEAD EXPANDERS

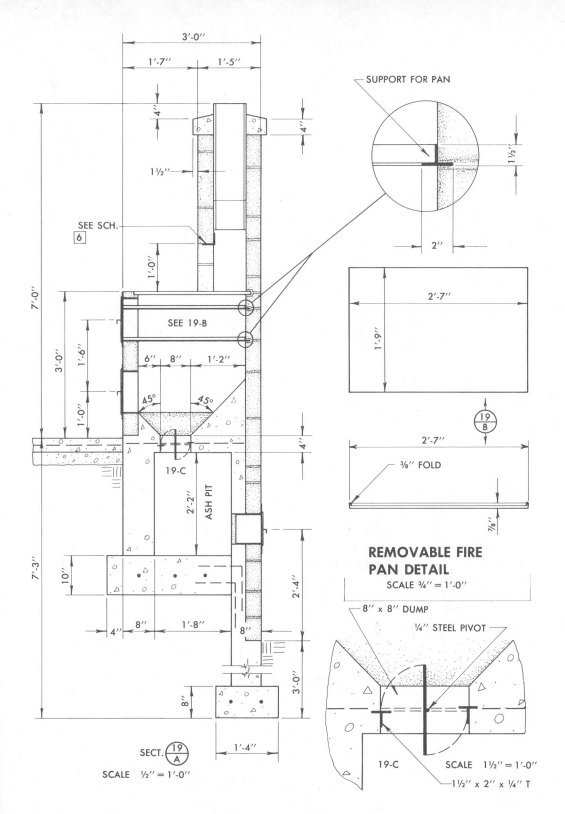

SUPPORT FOR PAN

SEE SCH. 6

SEE 19-B

45° 45°

19-C

ASH PIT

SECT. 19/A

SCALE ½″ = 1′-0″

19/B

⅜″ FOLD

REMOVABLE FIRE PAN DETAIL

SCALE ¾″ = 1′-0″

8″ x 8″ DUMP

¼″ STEEL PIVOT

19-C

SCALE 1½″ = 1′-0″

1½″ x 2″ x ¼″ T

517

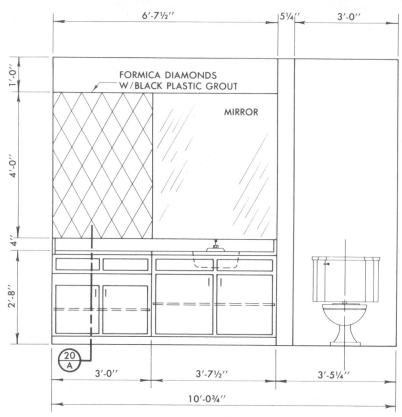

6'-7½"   5¼"   3'-0"

1'-0"

FORMICA DIAMONDS
W/BLACK PLASTIC GROUT

MIRROR

4'-0"

4"

2'-8"

20
A

3'-0"   3'-7½"   3'-5¼"

10'-0¾"

ELEV. 1

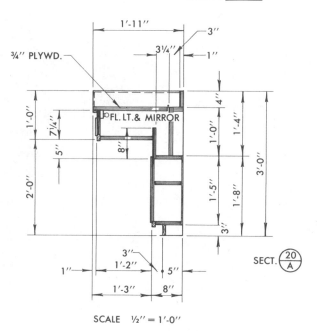

1'-11"

3"

¾" PLYWD.

3¼"   1"

4"

1'-0"

7¼"

FL. LT.& MIRROR

1'-0"

1'-4"

5"

8"

2'-0"

1'-5"

3'-0"

1'-8"

3"

3"

1'-2"

1"

5"

1'-3"   8"

SECT. 20
A

SCALE ½" = 1'-0"

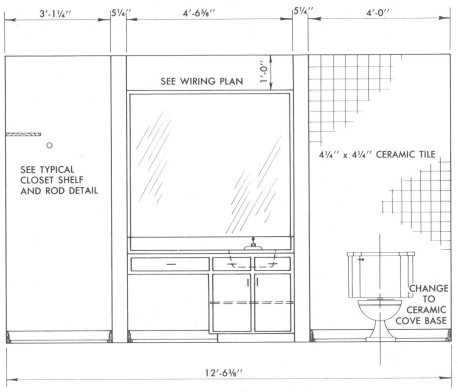

3'-1¼'' 5¼'' 4'-6⅝'' 5¼'' 4'-0''

1'-0''

SEE WIRING PLAN

SEE TYPICAL
CLOSET SHELF
AND ROD DETAIL

4¼'' x 4¼'' CERAMIC TILE

CHANGE
TO
CERAMIC
COVE BASE

12'-6⅜''

ELEV. △2

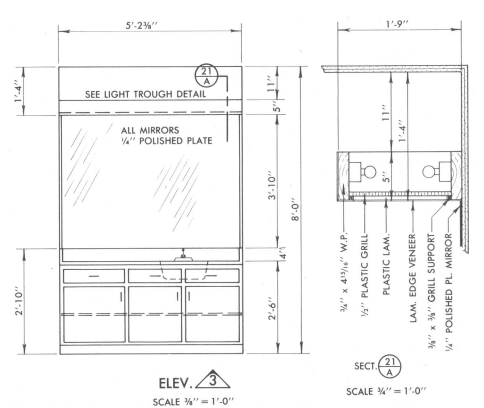

5'-2⅜''

1'-9''

1'-4''

21
A

SEE LIGHT TROUGH DETAIL

11''

5''

ALL MIRRORS
¼'' POLISHED PLATE

3'-10''

8'-0''

11''

1'-4''

4''

5''

2'-10''

2'-6''

¾'' x 4¹⁵/₁₆'' W.P.

½'' PLASTIC GRILL

PLASTIC LAM.

LAM. EDGE VENEER

⅜'' x ⅜'' GRILL SUPPORT

¼'' POLISHED PL. MIRROR

ELEV. △3

SCALE ⅜'' = 1'-0''

SECT. 21
A

SCALE ¾'' = 1'-0''

519

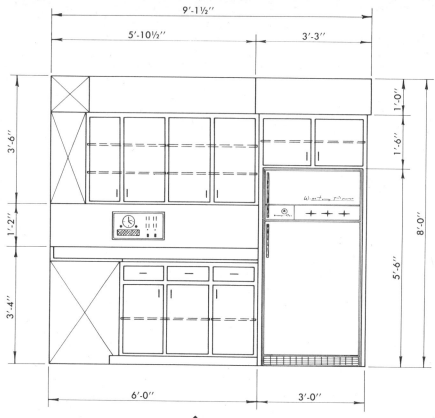

9'-1½''
5'-10½''
3'-3''
1'-0''
1'-6''
8'-0''
5'-6''
3'-6''
1'-2''
3'-4''

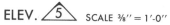

6'-0''
3'-0''

ELEV. 5   SCALE ⅜'' = 1'-0''

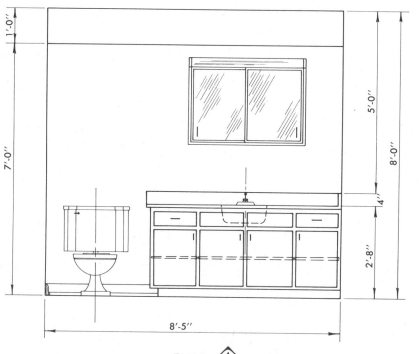

1'-0''
7'-0''
5'-0''
8'-0''
4''
2'-8''

8'-5''

ELEV. 4   SCALE ⅜'' = 1'-0''

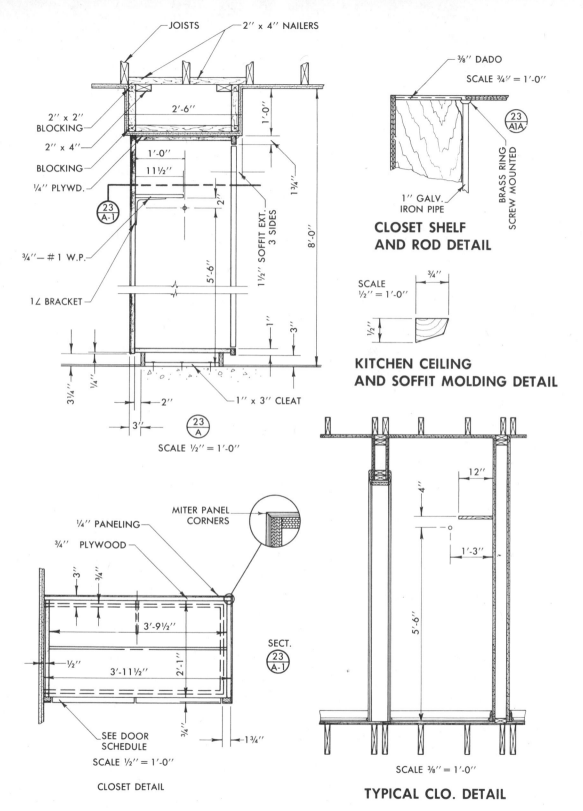

JOISTS

2'' x 4'' NAILERS

2'' x 2''
BLOCKING

2'' x 4''

BLOCKING

1/4'' PLYWD.

2'-6''

1'-0''

1'-0''

11 1/2''

2''

1 3/4''

8'-0''

5'-6''

1 1/2'' SOFFIT EXT.
3 SIDES

23
A-1

3/4'' — # 1 W.P.

1 ∠ BRACKET

3 3/4''

1/4''

2''

3''

1''

3''

1'' x 3'' CLEAT

23
A

SCALE 1/2'' = 1'-0''

3/8'' DADO

SCALE 3/4'' = 1'-0''

23
A1A

1'' GALV.
IRON PIPE

BRASS RING
SCREW MOUNTED

CLOSET SHELF
AND ROD DETAIL

SCALE
1/2'' = 1'-0''

3/4''

1/2''

KITCHEN CEILING
AND SOFFIT MOLDING DETAIL

MITER PANEL
CORNERS

1/4'' PANELING

3/4'' PLYWOOD

3''

3/4''

3'-9 1/2''

1/2''

3'-11 1/2''

2'-1''

3/4''

1 3/4''

SECT.
23
A-1

SEE DOOR
SCHEDULE

SCALE 1/2'' = 1'-0''

CLOSET DETAIL

12''

4''

1'-3''

5'-6''

SCALE 3/8'' = 1'-0''

TYPICAL CLO. DETAIL

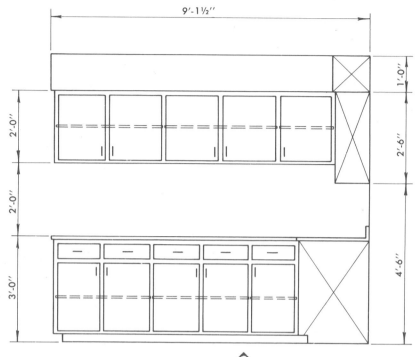

ELEV. 6
SCALE 3/8" = 1'-0"

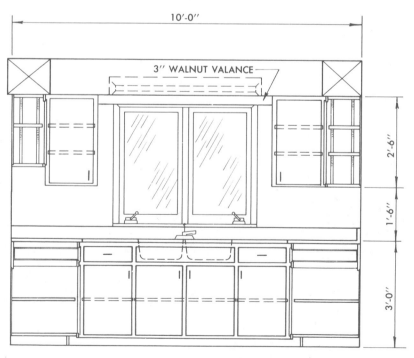

3" WALNUT VALANCE

ELEV. 7

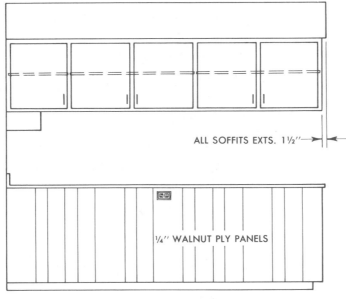

ALL SOFFITS EXTS. 1½″ →

¼″ WALNUT PLY PANELS

ELEV. △8△

SCALE ⅜″ = 1'-0″

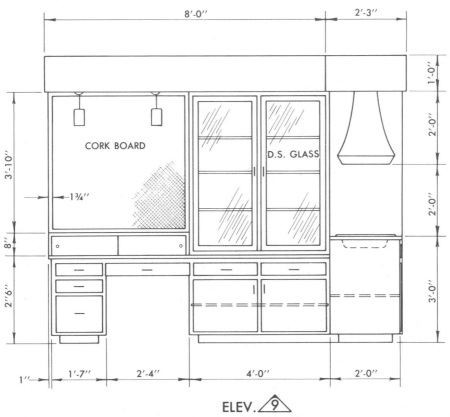

8'-0″   2'-3″

1'-0″

2'-0″

CORK BOARD

D.S. GLASS

3'-10″

2'-0″

1¾″

8″

2'6″

3'-0″

1″   1'-7″   2'-4″   4'-0″   2'-0″

ELEV. △9△

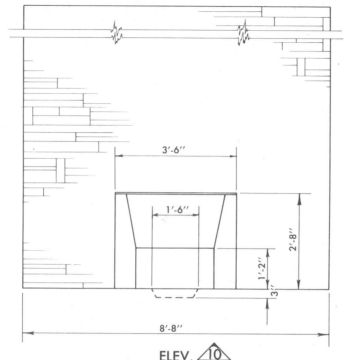

3'-6''

1'-6''

2'-8''

1'-2''

3''

8'-8''

ELEV. △10

SCALE ⅜'' = 1'-0''

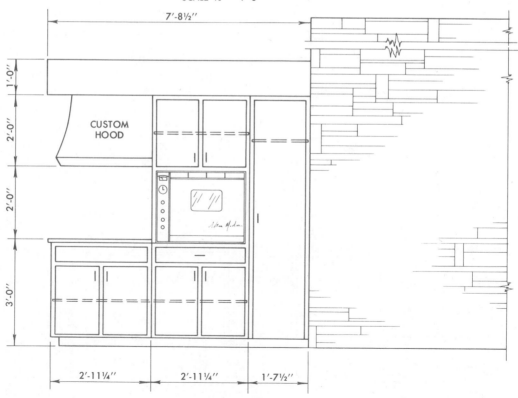

7'-8½''

1'-0''

2'-0''

CUSTOM
HOOD

2'-0''

3'-0''

2'-11¼''

2'-11¼''

1'-7½''

ELEV. △11

SCALE ⅜'' = 1'-0''

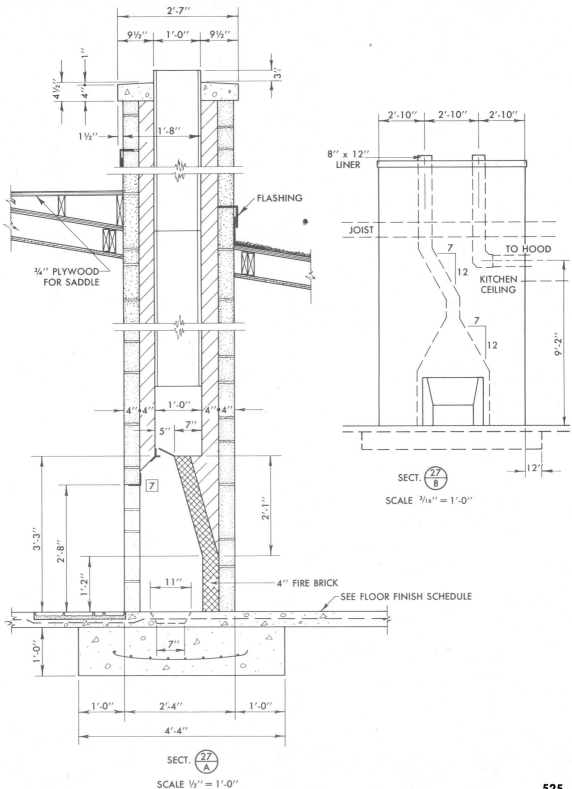

2'-7"

9½"   1'-0"   9½"

1"

4½"

4"

3"

1½"

1'-8"

FLASHING

¾" PLYWOOD
FOR SADDLE

4"   4"   1'-0"   4"   4"

5"   7"

7

2'-1"

3'-3"

2'-8"

1'-2"

11"

4" FIRE BRICK

SEE FLOOR FINISH SCHEDULE

7"

1'-0"

1'-0"   2'-4"   1'-0"

4'-4"

SECT. 27/A

SCALE ½" = 1'-0"

8" x 12"
LINER

2'-10"   2'-10"   2'-10"

JOIST

7

12

TO HOOD

KITCHEN
CEILING

7

12

9'-2"

SECT. 27/B

SCALE ³⁄₁₆" = 1'-0"

12"

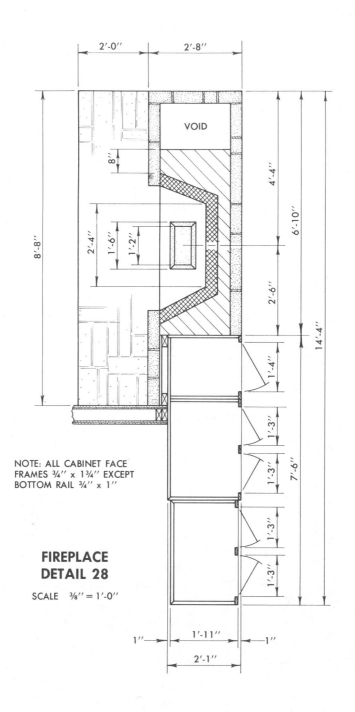

VOID

NOTE: ALL CABINET FACE
FRAMES ¾" x 1¾" EXCEPT
BOTTOM RAIL ¾" x 1"

FIREPLACE
DETAIL 28

SCALE   ⅜" = 1'-0"

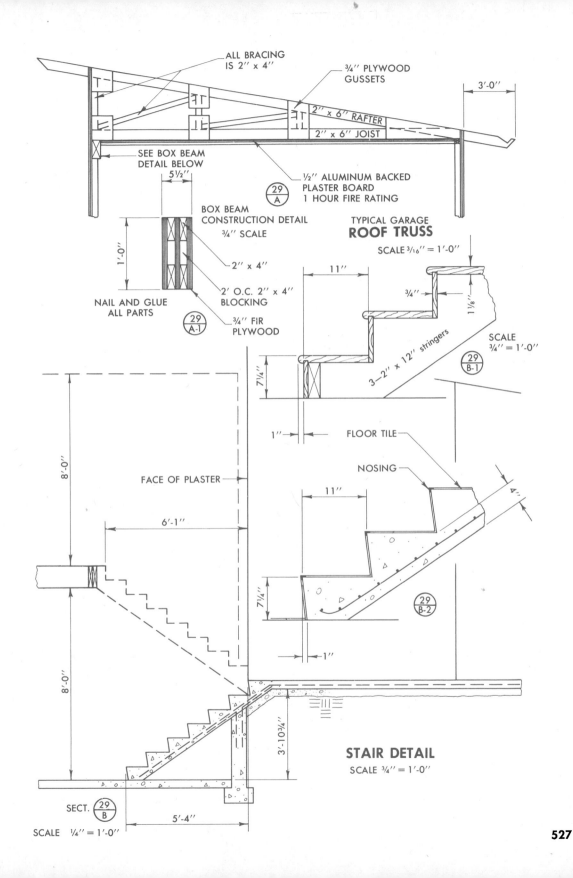

ALL BRACING
IS 2" x 4"

¾" PLYWOOD
GUSSETS

3'-0"

2" x 6" RAFTER

2" x 6" JOIST

SEE BOX BEAM
DETAIL BELOW

½" ALUMINUM BACKED
PLASTER BOARD
1 HOUR FIRE RATING

5½"

$\frac{29}{A}$

BOX BEAM
CONSTRUCTION DETAIL
¾" SCALE

Typical Garage
ROOF TRUSS
SCALE ³⁄₁₆" = 1'-0"

1'-0"

2" x 4"

2' O.C. 2" x 4"
BLOCKING

NAIL AND GLUE
ALL PARTS

$\frac{29}{A-1}$

¾" FIR
PLYWOOD

11"

¾"

1⅛"

SCALE
¾" = 1'-0"

3—2" x 12" stringers

$\frac{29}{B-1}$

7¼"

1"

FLOOR TILE

NOSING

FACE OF PLASTER

8'-0"

6'-1"

11"

4"

7¼"

$\frac{29}{B-2}$

1"

8'-0"

3'-10¾"

STAIR DETAIL
SCALE ¾" = 1'-0"

SECT. $\frac{29}{B}$

SCALE   ¼" = 1'-0"

5'-4"

50

Since many different people are involved in the planning, bidding on, and constructing a building, copies of plans must be reproduced from the original drawings.

Reproduction of Drawings

Blueprints and Semi-dry Prints

Blueprinting was for many years the only method of reproducing working drawings. It became such an important and widely used process that when other systems were later developed many people called every drawing reproduction a blueprint, even though some other reproduction method was used. Although this is not technically correct, it is accepted practice.

The quality of a blueprint is very satisfactory but it has disadvantages that frequently make it less desirable than newer methods.

About the print. Chemically treated, light-sensitive paper is placed beneath a tracing and exposed to light, either natural or artificial. Most exposures are made by machine so the intensity and exposure time can be controlled. Pencil or ink lines prevent light from passing through the tracing, so areas under them are not exposed.

After exposure, the blueprint paper must be developed in much the same manner as a photograph. After development the paper must be washed with water and dried. Older methods relied upon hanging the copy and air-drying it. This is very time consuming and not in keeping with today's ideas of speed and progress. Air-dried prints are always wrinkled and must be flattened before use. Automatic machine drying may be employed. However the size, complexity, and cost, of automatic blueprint machines has led to widespread use of other methods.

A blueprint is a reverse print. The background is blue and all lines and lettering are white. The intensity of the white lines on the blue background makes them very easy to read.

Blueprints have permanent quality, so they are very good for prints that must be used over a long period of time. If they are handled with care they may still be satisfactory after twenty or more years.

Semi-dry print. Introduction of the semi-dry method made print-making much easier than by the blueprint method. The tracing and sensitized paper are exposed in the same manner, but the developing process is greatly simplified. A roller in a long tray is immersed in the solution and another roller is in contact with it. The lower roller becomes coated with developer; the exposed, sensitized paper is fed between the rollers, and the solution is deposited onto the paper, thus developing it. The paper is only dampened slightly so it does not wrinkle as it dries. This method can produce clear, sharp prints but they have a tendency to turn yellow and the lines fade with age. Aging is gradual and does not interfere with legibility for several months. Prints stored in a dark place when not in use, should be legible for years.

Ammonia Vapor Machines

The ammonia vapor process is the most widely used method of reproducing working drawings. The tracing and sensitized paper are exposed to an ultraviolet light source and then the sensitized paper is developed with ammonia vapor.

The versatility of the many machines designed to use this process, and the relatively low cost of basic models, make them available for any business establishment.

Simple machines consist of a light source and a metal container with a heating element to vaporize the ammonia and develop the print. Larger machines permit very rapid development. Some machines automatically develop any specified number of prints from one original tracing.

These machines have many desirable features. The prints are dry and are ready to use as soon as they are ejected. Use of large rolls of developing paper permit any sheet length. New copies are clear and sharp, and lines are intense. Developing papers are available in many colors. Some of the more common are blue, black, red, brown, and green. Prints can be developed onto many different mediums such as different weights of paper, transparent paper, plastic coated paper, transparent and opaque plastic. Beautiful overlays can be obtained by printing parts of a drawing on different sheets of plastic with different colored lines.

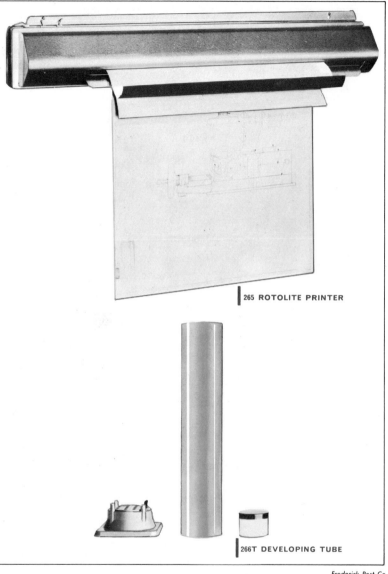

265 ROTOLITE PRINTER

266T DEVELOPING TUBE

Frederick Post Co.

A developing tube and separate light source can be used when only a limited quantity of prints is required.

There are two principal objections to this process. One is a human objection. Many persons familiar with blueprints simply cannot or will not change to the use of the newer method. Then, too, these prints tend to discolor and fade with continual exposure to light. However, they can be preserved for several years if they are stored in a dark place when not is use.

This white printer is ideal for offices or other institutions that require a small number of large size prints.

An automatic white printer can produce letter or legal size prints in any desired quantity.

Sepia Masters

An intermediate print called a sepia master—which is a brown line print on a special translucent paper—can be developed and used as a tracing instead of the original. Sometimes so many prints must be made from one original tracing that the excessive handling could damage it. Equipment is sold by many companies under various trade names. Sepia masters are also very useful when tracings must be forwarded to other departments or companies. For example, there are several large companies that specialize in designing homes and developing plans for them. They sell these plans to individual builders. Frequently a builder desires to have the name of his own company on all the drawings. Instead of buying regular prints he obtains sepia masters and then inserts his own business name on the titles before having them printed.

Plastic Film

Sometimes sepia masters cannot produce the quality of print that is desired. There are many plastic films that produce photographic negatives suitable for making prints. On some, the lines are permanent, while on others they can be removed or washed off so changes or corrections may be made.

Some films must be exposed in direct contact to the original, while others permit reductions or enlargements. Some are transparent while others have a matte or frosted surface to make addition of lines easier.

Films are especially useful for combining information from several drawing sheets. Information can be assembled and photo-

A production machine is capable of high-volume output.

graphed; then when printed it appears as one drawing.

Photo-copying

When very fine quality copying is required, as for reproduction of legal documents and other important papers, photo-copying is frequently used. This process is similar to the film copies just described except the copy is reproduced upon opaque paper. Since it is a one-exposure process, the copy is reversed from the original; that is, everything on the original that is white is black on the print, and everything that is black on the original is white on the print. If the final copy must look exactly like the original, it is necessary to make another print from the reproduction.

Printing on Anything

Sometimes it is necessary to make prints on unusual materials such as wood, metal, glass, or plastic. This can be done by spraying a light-sensitive solution onto the item and then placing a tracing over it to be exposed. Application of developing solution then completes the print.

Electrostatic Machines

Small electrostatic copying machines are very popular for a wide variety of reproduction jobs. Sheet size is limited. Maximum width is usually about 9″. Some machines are belt driven which permits additional sheet length, while others require a fixed exposure over a glass plate. The biggest advantage of these machines is that almost any drawn or printed matter can be copied, regardless of the kind of paper the original is on. However, many machines will not reproduce blue lines, as from a ball point pen.

They also may not copy photographs or other materials produced by similar methods. In other words, you cannot always make a copy of a copy. Printed or drawn subject matter in both pencil and ink reproduces well.

Some machines will make spirit process masters for duplicator copying, masters for offset printing, or reproduce on plastic film for overlays and projection.

Line quality and permanence are often not as good as when ammonia vapor is used.

Direct Copying

Temporary prints such as shop drawings may be produced without developers. Exposure of special paper through a tracing produces the finished print. This print is a kind of blueprint; that is, it is a reverse print with a blue background and white lines.

Storage and Retrieval

When an organization needs many tracings, their storage for future use becomes a problem. They occupy considerable space; and they must be accessible for use without being damaged.

Rolling tracings and storing them in tubes makes them very accessible but it damages the fibers of the paper. When they are unrolled, they wrinkle easily which reduces their quality. They soon become unsuitable for use.

Tray Storage

Tracings may be stored in flat trays or drawers. This preserves them in good condition if the compartments are kept orderly. Trays are not always orderly, especially if several people must use them; then it is necessary to hunt through many drawings to find the one desired.

Folders

Giant size folders are frequently used for storing tracings vertically. These protect the tracings but are cumbersome to handle.

Storage on Film

Since tracings may be large and difficult to store and use without damaging them, other storage-and-use systems have been developed. Many firms record their tracings on film and then use the film for reproduction purposes. There are several film systems in general use.

Very simple systems use contact film, as described earlier, which makes the negative the same size as the original tracing, but more durable and easier to store and use.

A non-contact system copies the tracing so the film is only ½ the original size. Copies are the same size as the negative.

Miniaturization is also being used for copying and reproducing drawings. The best known system is called microfilm. The tracing is photographed onto a very small film, sometimes less than ½" square. When it is to be used, an image is projected onto a screen or a large size copy is made. There are automatic machines available that project the desired image onto a TV-like screen for easy viewing. Some of the more sophisticated machines are combination reader-printers. If a copy is desired the machine will automatically reproduce one.

There are two basic systems. In one system using roll film in cartridges, the film is passed through a projector until the desired frame (individual picture) is reached. The other system has negatives mounted in key punch cards, called aperture cards. They are run through a sorter for retrieval, projection, and copying. Many companies have developed systems that are variations of the above.

Questions to Reinforce Knowledge

1. Why must many sets of building plans be reproduced from the original tracings?

2. For many years what was the best method of reproducing working drawings?

3. Why are some prints that are not blueprints called by this name? Do you feel this is permissible?

4. What are some of the disadvantages of blueprints?

5. What are some of the advantages of blueprints?

6. Why do blueprints wrinkle and require flattening before use?

7. What is meant when a blueprint is called a reverse print?

8. What advantages does a semi-dry print have over a blueprint?

9. Does this method produce clear prints? Explain.

10. Describe the permanence of these prints.

11. What is the most widely used reproduction process for making copies of building plans?

12. What is the capacity of ammonia vapor machines?

13. Describe a very simple ammonia vapor machine.

14. How much drying time is required for ammonia vapor prints?

15. Is it true that only blue and white prints can be made on these machines? Explain.

16. What is an overlay print?

17. What are the two principal objections to ammonia vapor reproductions?

18. What are sepia masters? Why are they used?

19. Describe some of the ways that plastic films can be used as intermediate prints. What is an intermediate print?

20. What is photo-copying? Is this an important process? Why?

21. How can a print be made on wood, metal, glass, or plastic?

22. Describe two kinds of heat-light machines.

23. What are some of the advantages of these machines?

24. What are some of the disadvantages?

25. Explain how a reproduction may be made and finished without being developed.

26. What are the disadvantages of rolling tracings for storage?

27. What is an advantage of rolling tracings for storage?

28. What are two disadvantages of storing tracings in large trays or drawers? Any advantage?

29. Why are many firms recording copies of their tracings on film?

30. What is miniaturization?

31. What is microfilm?

32. How may it be projected for viewing?

33. What is a reader-printer?

34. How are key punch cards used for reproductions?

Terms to Spell and Know

copy or reproduction	sepia master	light sensitive
blueprint	intermediate print	electrostatic
reverse print	photographic negative	storage and retrieval
sensitized paper	wash-off film	miniaturization
developer	contact negative	microfilm
ammonia vapor	matte	reader-printer
ultraviolet light	photo-copying	aperture card

51

Specifications

A set of building plans cannot communicate all incidental ideas, detail analysis, quality conditions, and materials such as nails or paints required for the construction of a building. This additional information is included in the specifications. Specifications are seldom written by the professional draftsman but he must be acquainted with them.

Every set of building plans should be accompanied by a set of specifications. Large architectural firms have employees who devote all their time to writing them. In small firms the architect is responsible for their compilation. Large firms frequently have them compiled, and then printed by a spirit duplicator or office size offset press. Small firms may type them on 8½"x11" tracing paper and then print them with the same process as used for the building plans. They are bound in booklets and accompany the working drawings. They are a legal part of a contract, as are the official plans, and are binding upon all parties involved.

Specifications for large, complicated structures include much

SPECIFICATIONS—GENERAL COVERAGE

Title page

Titled as; Specifications for _____. (Name kind of building as school, church, residence, or factory.)
Name of owner.
Complete address of the proposed building.
Name of architect.
Official title of architect.
Complete address of architect.
Seal of official registration of qualifications.

Table of contents

This is usually quite specific as to where items appear in the specifications.

Instructions to bidders

Location of building to be constructed.
Explanation of how bid is to be made and presented.
Allowances for alternate materials or methods of construction.
Qualifications of bidders.
Time for receiving bids.
Responsibility of successful bidder for insurance, social security, workman's compensation, fees, taxes, bonds, labor, and materials.
Proof of payment of the above items from successful bidder.

Contract between owner and contractor(s)

Scope of work included.
The contract price.
Signed, sealed, and witnessed.

General specifications applying to all trades

Explanation of how detailed specifications for individual trades are subdivided into different groupings.

detailed information. They may have 75 to 100 typewritten pages. For small, simple structures the specifications are much briefer, containing only "stock" information. However, if full information is included, there is less chance for disagreement or misunderstanding between the owner and contractor as to exactly what is to be done.

Many firms use standard printed forms, filling in the blank spaces with the appropriate information.

Space does not permit a book of this nature to include a complete set of long, involved specifications. The outline given here covers many of the key details that are a general coverage—usually included in a standard form:

Specifications (continued)

Statement that a contractor may or may not subcontract part of the construction.

Responsibility of a contractor for the work he subcontracts.

State the necessity of consultation with the architect if there are errors or omissions from the plans or specifications.

Statement that the architect is the legal representative of the owner and the contractor is responsible to him.

Statement that all manufactured items are to be installed according to the manufacturers' specifications. They automatically become a part of this contract.

Statement that the contractor may not substitute materials or construction methods other than those specified, without a written request and approval.

Statement that damaged work must be repaired.

How payments for labor and materials will be made.

Shop drawings to be furnished by the contractor and approved by the architect before any work is begun.

Construction schedule:

Amount of time allowed.

Penalties for failure to maintain schedule.

Amount of cleanup required.

Guarantees on work performed.

Detailed Specifications—Short Form

Work to be performed by each contractor or subcontractor is outlined in the detailed specifications. So you can see how they are written, an excerpt from a set of specifications for a small residence follows:

Excavating and grading

This contractor shall excavate for all work as required by the plans, and shall keep all excavations dry during progress of the work. Bottoms of all trenches are to be kept level and free from loose earth. Scrape away all topsoil from the area to be excavated and pile separately for use in grading. All earth is to be piled so it does not interfere with material deliveries or construction.

Concrete

This contractor shall install all footings, foundation walls, concrete floors, sidewalks, and driveway to street.

Shall waterproof outside of all basement and foundation walls from the grade line to the bottom of the footing using sprayed-on asphalt waterproofing.

All concrete floors must have a trowel smooth finish. Driveway and walks are to have a broom finish and are to be finished with an edger at all joints and edges. Basement side of the foundation is to be dampened and smoothed with a cement and sand mix using a wood float finish.

All concrete to be ready-mix 1:3:5.

Basement and garage floors are to be poured on 4" of gravel fill.

Visqueen film with sealed joints and all damaged areas repaired shall be placed over the gravel fill.

Masonry

This contractor shall furnish and install all masonry. Construct fireplace as shown with_____ No. _____ liner. Install all flue liners and flues as shown.

Structural steel contractor shall furnish all steel angle lintels but this contractor shall install same above each opening.

Face brick: Entire building to be faced with $65.00 M, face brick, color and pattern to be selected by architect.

Backup for all stone and face brick is concrete block.

Overhead doors: Set $\frac{3}{8}$" x 8" threaded bolts 24" o.c. on each side of door for wood plate.

Sash: This contractor shall furnish and install all aluminum casements. _____ aluminum or equal.

Plate anchors: Install $\frac{1}{2}$" x 18" anchor bolts around perimeter of building, spaced 8'-0" o.c. All sill plates shall have at least two anchor bolts regardless of their length.

Cleaning: All stone and face brick are to be washed with diluted acid or cleaning solution. No discoloration of the cut stone is permitted.

Carpentry

This contractor shall do all wood framing. All framing lumber shall be #2 Southern Yellow Pine or Douglas Fir. Wall sheathing is to be bituminous coated, 25/32" insulating board siding. Roof sheathing is to be $\frac{1}{2}$" sheathing grade, unsanded fir plywood. Subfloor is to be $\frac{5}{8}$" sheathing grade, unsanded fir plywood, of _____ quality.

Install all necessary ground and furring strips. Install 3" wood bridging following F.H.A. recommendations.

This contractor shall install all millwork, wood frames, windows, doors, and trim. Furnish and install $1\frac{3}{4}$" thick white pine overhead garage door as shown on the plans complete with necessary hardware.

All floors are to have $\frac{5}{8}$" BD fir plywood on saturated felt, nailed securely with ringed nails to subfloor, except where composition floors are required; these are to be screwed with $1\frac{1}{4}$" #8 flat head steel wood screws spaced 6" o.c. except at edges of sheets, where the screws are to be spaced 3" o.c.

Insulation: Furnish and install 4" full-thick rockwool bats on all ceilings. All exterior walls are to have 2" half-thick bats.

Caulking: Caulk all steel and wood frames at all exterior openings.

Closets: Install 1" steel pipe for clothes pole in all closets. All closet shelves are to be $\frac{3}{4}$" of_____ quality. All edges are to be filled and sanded. Linen closet shelves and divisions in double closets are to be of $\frac{3}{4}$" AA fir plywood, all edges are to be veneered with Weldwood wood trim, secured with one coat of contact cement on the tape and two coats on all plywood edges.

Doors and trim: All inside doors are to be Weldwood white birch, Stay Straight, book matched, hollow core, flush doors. All baseboards, jambs, and other trim are to be select white birch. Front door is to be solid core white birch. Kitchen cabinets are to be select white birch, prefinished with frost white lacquer. Counter top is to be White Spindrift, postformed Formica.

Bathroom vanity is to be select white birch, prefinished with smoke grey lacquer. Counter top is to be Pink Nassau Formica with self edge.

Hardware: Install aluminum interlocking thresholds on front and rear doors. Allow $200.00 for finish hardware, not including the above items. Use sterling track for all sliding doors.

Windows: Windows are to be Pella casements with wood brick molding, complete with screens and storm panels. Window and door openings on inside of building are to be finished with metal corner bead.

Structural Metal

This contractor shall carefully examine the General Conditions.

This contractor shall furnish and erect all structural beams and columns.

Furnish all steel angle lintels for window and door openings. Masonry contractor will set all angle lintels.

All steel must be primed with red lead or equal.

This contractor is to furnish the fireplace liner.

Sheet metal

This contractor shall furnish and install all sheet metal work as shown on the plans. All sheet metal work is to be 26 gauge galvanized iron. All gutters and downspouts are to be aluminum. Furnish and install galvanized duct for kitchen hood as shown on plans.

Install metal roof vents as shown.

Install metal vent in basement for clothes dryer.

Install_____ 36" exhaust fan with motorized louvers in bedroom hall.

Roofing

All roofing is to be 235 lb. 3 tab, self sealing, asphalt shingles installed over 15 lb. felt, with Boston ridge and hips.

All shingles are to be white, of_____ quality.

Lathing and Plastering

This contractor shall check all grounds and furring strips before lathing.

All ceilings on first floor are to have rocklath and three-coat plaster.

All walls on first floor to have rocklath and three-coat plaster.

Garage ceiling to have metal lath and three-coat plaster, with one hour fire rating.

All inside corners are to have 9" wide metal lath reinforcing bent to lay flat in the corner.

All arches or outside corners are to have Expanded Cornerite, metal corner bead.

Expanded metal lath is to be applied diagonally above each corner of all windows and doors. Expanded metal lath stripping is to be nailed to the ceiling, centered under all beams and built-up girders.

All doors are to have metal bull nose trim, mitered and soldered at corners.

All windows are to have corner bead on three sides.

Glazing

This contractor shall furnish and install all glass as required on the plans. All glass shall be D.S.A., except glass areas larger than 24" x 30" are to be Thermopane or equal.

Glazing compound must be the best for metal or wood sash.

Replace all broken glass after construction work is completed.

Ceramic tile

Install 4" x 4" ceramic tile in master bath as shown on the plans. Install ceramic mosaic tile floor in master bath.

All colors and patterns are to be selected by the architect.

Composition floors

Kitchen is to have vinyl tile, of _____ quality. Stairs

to basement are to have standard grade linoleum treads
and risers, edged with aluminum bullnosing.
   All colors and patterns to be selected by the architect.

Plumbing

   This contractor is to install complete plumbing, sewer,
water, and gas services in the building. Install 1½" water
service to the building. All sewer lines are to be
cast iron.
   This contractor is to install and connect the clothes
washer and dishwasher.
   Install 4" field tile around the perimeter of the
building leaving ⅜" joints between each tile. Joints are
to be covered with 15 lb. saturated felt strips 4" x 12"
and covered with 8" of clean washed gravel.
   Gas service is to be provided at two locations in the
basement.
   All bathroom fixtures and kitchen sink are to be of
_____ quality.

Electrical

   This contractor shall install a complete electrical
system as per these plans and specifications.
   All receptacles as shown shall be duplex. Install
telephone outlets and television jacks as shown. Connect
dishwasher, surface unit burners, built-in oven, clothes
dryer, clothes washer, exhaust fan, furnace, and others
as shown.
   Furnish and install 16 circuit, circuit breaker box. All
equipment described above, and the refrigerator, deep
freeze in the basement, air conditioning unit, and
calcinator, are to be on separate circuits.
   Each room shall have receptacles and lights on at least
two separate circuits.
   All switches are to be of the mercury, silent type.
   Provide 100 amp., 230-115 volt entrance service.
   Make alternate bid for underground neoprene entrance
service.
   Allow $300.00 for electrical fixtures, excluding
installation.
   All fixtures to be selected by the architect.

Heating

Install electric radiant heat in ceilings of all rooms and basement according to Westinghouse layout. Each room is to have an individual thermostat.

Contractor must guarantee system to heat all rooms to 75° when the outside temperature is −10°.

NOTE: *The following specifications are of the long-form type, used when you wish to be quite specific.*

Painting and decorating

Scope of work: A finish is to be applied to all surfaces not factory pre-finished, throughout the building.

This contractor shall supply all labor, materials, tools, scaffolding, and other equipment necessary for completion of this work.

Materials used are to be exactly as hereinafter specified in brand and quality. No claims by the painting contractor as to the unsuitability or unavailability of any material specified, or his unwillingness to use the same, or his ability to produce first class work with them will be entertained unless such claims are made in writing and submitted with his bid.

Paints, enamels, and similar materials must be delivered in the original containers, with seals unbroken and labels intact.

Use materials only as specified by the manufacturer's directions on the container.

Do all necessary puttying of nail holes and cracks after the first coat, with Swedish putty of a color to match the finish. Strike putty flush with adjoining surfaces in a neat and workmanlike manner.

Tint priming coat on plaster to approximate shade of final coat. Touch up suction spots or ''hot spots'' on plaster or cement after application of first coat to produce an even result in the finish coat.

Tint undercoats of paint and enamel to the approximate shade of the finish coat; each coat is to be slightly darker than the preceding one unless otherwise directed.

Each coat must be inspected and approved by the architect before application of the next coat; otherwise no credit for the coat applied will be given and the contractor automatically assumes responsibility to recoat the work in question. The architect is to be notified when each coat is applied.

Clean all paint or other finishing materials from other finished surfaces.

Before painting, remove all hardware, accessories, plates, lighting fixtures, and similar items or provide ample protection of these items.

Secure color schedules for rooms from the architect before priming the walls. All colors are to be selected and approved by the architect.

Questions to Reinforce Knowledge

1. Why are building specifications necessary?

2. What building plans should have a set of specifications?

3. Who writes the building specifications? Explain.

4. Are printed and bound specifications superior to simpler kinds? Discuss.

5. What is meant when one says the specifications are legal?

6. Explain why some sets of specifications are written to include much detail and others may contain only limited information.

7. How may standard printed specifications be used for different buildings?

8. What information is to be included on the title page of the specifications?

9. Why is the table of contents usually quite specific?

10. What kinds of information may be found in the instructions to the bidders?

11. From your own reasoning, why is a contract between the owner and contractor a necessity when building even a small home?

12. What are general specifications?

13. What are detailed specifications?

14. What is the difference between a long form and a short form detailed specification?

15. From your own reasoning and your study of the sample specifications, why are the detailed specifications subdivided according to the different trades?

16. From your study of the sample specifications, try writing a specification for one of the trades using a building plan you have developed or one provided by the instructor.

Terms to Spell and Know

specifications
contract
general specifications
long form detailed specifications

subcontract
construction schedule
short form detailed specifications

52

Estimating

The term estimating is used in this book to mean an organized method of determining required amounts of materials, labor, or money necessary to construct a building.

Construction estimating can be a full-time occupation. To become proficient at it, one must be thoroughly familiar with building materials and their costs. One must also be familiar with different construction methods and the labor required. This book can only give a summary to show the problems of estimating.

Approximate Methods

There are two quick methods of estimating approximate building costs.

Square foot method. The method most often used relies upon the number of square feet of floor area. To find an approximate building cost, multiply the number of square feet by the estimated cost per square foot. Of course, the cost per square foot varies with the construction method and degree of luxury desired. To use this method effectively one must base the square foot price upon *known local costs* for buildings that have used similar construction.

One might use the following scale:

	per sq. ft.
Low-cost economy building	$10.00
Good, sturdy construction	$15.00
High quality construction	$20.00
Maximum luxury features	$25.00

If the building has a basement, garage, or carport with storage shelter, calculate them at one fourth the square foot cost used for the living area.

Example: The following estimating example—using the above method—is based upon the small home plan is Chapter 39. This house is 28'-0" x 50'-0", so it has 1,400 square feet of floor area. Observe that the total area is included, not just the actual room areas. If $10.00 per square foot economy construction is used, its estimated price is $14,000.00. The carport is 15'-0" x 22'-0" so it has 330 sq. ft. At ¼ the regular price, which is $2.50 per sq. ft., its total price is $825.00. The combined cost then is $14,825.00. The lot, its preparation, and landscaping is about 20% of the home cost, or $2,965.00, which gives a combined total cost of $17,790.00.

Variation of square foot method

Many appraisal agents use an extension of this method. They determine a price based upon the number of square feet and a national average price per square foot as scaled earlier. Then, since building costs vary in different localities, they add or deduct the percentage variance from the norm. For example, if a city's building costs are 10% above the national average, this amount must be added to the base price.

ABBREVIATIONS of LUMBER TERMS

AD . . . . . . Air-dried.
AST . . . . . Anti-stain treated.
B1S . . . . . Beaded one side.
B2S . . . . . Beaded two sides.
bd. . . . . . Board.
bd. ft. . . . Board foot.
bdl. . . . . . Bundle.
Bev. . . . . . Bevelled.
B/L . . . . . Bill of Lading.
b. m. . . . . Board (foot) measure.
Btr. . . . . . Better.
c. i. f. . . . Cost, insurance and freight.
c. i. f. e. . . Cost, insurance, freight and exchange.
Clg. . . . . . Ceiling.
Clr. . . . . . Clear. Also Cl.
Com. . . . . . Common.
C. M. . . . . Center matched; i. e., the tongue and groove joints are worked along the center of the edges of the piece.
Csg. . . . . . Casing.
Ctg. . . . . . Crating.
cu. ft. . . . . Cubic foot.
*D&CM . . . Dressed (one or two sides) and center matched.
*D&M . . . . Dressed and matched; i. e., dressed one or two sides and tongued and grooved on the edges. The match may be center or standard.
*D&SM . . . Dressed (one or two sides), standard matched.
D2S&CM . . . Dressed two sides, center matched.
*D2S&M . . . Dressed two sides and (center or standard) matched.
D2S&Sm . . . Dressed two sides and standard matched.
Den. . . . . . Dense.
Dim. . . . . . Dimension.
D/Sdg. . . . Drop siding. Also D/S and D. S.
E. . . . . . . Edge. Also Ed. and Edg.
EB1S . . . . . Edge bead one side.
E&CB1S . . . Edge and center bead one side; i. e., surfaced one or two sides with a longitudinal edge and center bead on a surfaced face. Also B&CB1S.
E&CB2S . . . Edge and center bead two sides; i. e., all four sides surfaced and with a longitudinal edge and center bead on the two faces. Also B&CB2S.
E&CV1S . . . Edge and center V one side. Also V&CV1S.
E&CV2S . . . Edge and center V two sides. Also V&CV2S.
EG . . . . . . Edge Grain. Also VG (Vertical grain), rift-sawed; comb grain and quarter-sawed.
EM . . . . . . End Matched.
EV1S . . . . . Edge V one side.
exp. . . . . . Export (lumber or timber)
f. a. s.
  vessel . . . Free along side vessel.

Fac. . . . . . Factory (lumber). Also Fact. and Fcty.
F. G. . . . . . Flat grain. Also slash grain and plain sawed.
Flg. . . . . . Flooring.
f. o. b. . . . Free on board.
ft. . . . . . . Foot or feet.
ft. b. m. . . . Feet board measure.
G. R. . . . . . Grooved roofing.
hdwd. . . . . Hardwood.
Hrt. . . . . . Heart.
KD . . . . . . Kiln-dried. Also K/D.
lbr. . . . . . Lumber.
l. c. l. . . . . Less than carload.
lgth. . . . . . Length.
lin. ft. . . . . Lineal foot; i. e., 12 inches.
M . . . . . . Thousand.
M b. m. . . . Thousand (feet) board measure.
Merch. . . . . Merchantable.
Mldg. . . . . Molding.
Pat. . . . . . Pattern.
rdm. . . . . . Random.
Rfg. . . . . . Roofing.
r. l. . . . . . Random lengths. Also R/L.
S&E . . . . . Surfaced one side and edge.
S1E . . . . . Surfaced one edge.
S2E . . . . . Surfaced two edges.
S1S . . . . . Surfaced one side.
S2S . . . . . Surfaced two sides.
S1S1E . . . . Surfaced one side and one edge.
S2S1E . . . . Surfaced two sides and one edge.
S1S2E . . . . Surfaced one side and two edges.
S4S . . . . . Surfaced four sides.
S2S&CM . . . Surfaced two sides and center matched.
S2S&SM . . . Surfaced two sides and standard matched.
S2S&CG2E . . Surfaced two sides and center grooved two edges.
Sdg. . . . . . Siding. Also Sidg. and S/G.
Sel. . . . . . Select.
S. E. . . . . . Square-edge.
S/lap. . . . . Shiplap. Also Shlp.
SM . . . . . . Standard matched.
snd. . . . . . Sound.
sq. . . . . . . Square.
SE&S . . . . . Square edge and sound. Also Sq.E&S.
Std. . . . . . Standard.
stnd. . . . . . Stained.
Str. . . . . . Structural.
T&G . . . . . Tongued and grooved.
V. G. . . . . (See E. G.)
wt. . . . . . . Weight.

*—Abbreviation indefinite either as to surfaces dressed or to type of matching. Use other abbreviations which are more specific.

Courtesy, Southern Pine Association

LUMBER TERMS

BOARDS—Yard lumber less than 2 inches thick and 8 or more inches wide. Narrower material is usually referred to as "strips."

DIMENSION—All yard lumber except boards, strips, and timbers; that is, yard lumber 2 inches to but not including 5 inches thick, and of any width.

HARDWOOD—The botanical group of trees that are broad-leaved. The term has no reference to the actual hardness of the wood.

SAPWOOD—The outer layers of growth in a tree, exclusive of bark, which contains living elements, usually lighter in color than heartwood.

SOFTWOOD—The group of trees which have needle-like or scale-like leaves, often referred to as conifers. The term softwood has no reference to the softness of the wood.

STRUCTURAL LUMBER—Lumber that is 2 or more inches thick and 4 or more inches wide, intended for use where working stresses are required.

MENSURATION

Area of a square = length x breadth or height.
Area of a rectangle = length x breadth or height.
Area of a triangle = base x ½ altitude.
Area of parallelogram = base x altitude.
Area of trapezoid = altitude x ½ the sum of parallel sides.
Area of trapezium = divide into two triangles, total their areas.
Circumference of circle = diameter x 3.1416.
Circumference of circle = radius x 6.283185.
Diameter of circle = circumference x .3183.
Diameter of circle = square root of area x 1.12838.
Radius of a circle = circumference x .0159155.
Area of a circle = half diameter x half circumference.
Area of a circle = square of diameter x .7854.
Area of a circle = square of circumference x .07958.
Area of a sector of circle = length of arc x ½ radius.
Area of a segment of circle = area of sector of equal radius—area of triangle, when the segment is less, and plus area of triangle, when segment is greater than the semi-circle.
Area of circular ring = sum of the diameter of the two circles x difference of the diameter of the two circles and that product x .7854.
Side of square that shall equal area of circle = diameter x .8862.
Side of square that shall equal area of circle = circumference x .2821.
Diameter of circle that shall contain area of a given square = side of square x 1.1284.
Side of inscribed equilateral triangle = diameter x .86.
Side of inscribed square = diameter x .7071.
Side of inscribed square = circumference x .225.
Area of ellipse = product of the two diameters x .7854.
Area of a parabola = base x ⅔ of altitude.
Area of a regular polygon = sum of its sides x perpendicular from its center to one of its sides divided by 2.
Surface of cylinder or prism = area of both ends plus length x circumference.
Surface of sphere = diameter x circumference.
Solidity of sphere = surface x 1/6 diameter.
Solidity of sphere = cube of diameter x .5236.
Solidity of sphere = cube of radius x 4.1888.
Solidity of sphere = cube of circumference x .016887.
Diameter of sphere = cube root of solidity x 1.2407.
Diameter of sphere = square root of surface x .56419.
Circumference of sphere = square root of surface x 1.772454.
Circumference of sphere = cube root of solidity x 3.8978.
Contents of segment of sphere = (height squared plus three times the square of radius of base) x (height x .5236).
Contents of a sphere = diameter x .5236.
Side of inscribed cube of sphere = radius x 1.1547.
Side of inscribed cube of sphere = square root of diameter.
Surface of pyramid or cone = circumference of base x ½ of the slant height plus area of base.
Contents of pyramid or cone = area of base x ⅓ altitude.
Contents of frustum of pyramid or cone = sum of circumference at both ends x ½ slant height plus area of both ends.
Contents of frustum of pyramid or cone = multiply areas of two ends together and extract square root. Add to this root the two areas x ⅓ altitude.
Contents of a wedge = area of base ½ altitude.

—— Courtesy, A. C. Horn Co., Inc. ——

FREQUENTLY USED CONVERSIONS

1 Cubic Foot	1 94-Lb. Sack Cement
1 Cubic Foot	7.48 Gallons
1 Cubic Foot	1,728 Cubic Inches
1 Mile	1,760 Yards . . . . . 5,280 Feet
1 Acre	4,840 Sq. Yds. . . . . 43,560 Sq. Ft.
1 Kilowatt	1.34 Horsepower
1 Horsepower	0.746 Kilowatt
1 Gallon	231 Cubic Inches
1 Gallon Water	8.35 Lbs.
1 Cubic Foot Water	62.52 Lbs.
1 Bushel	1.24 Cu. Ft. . . . . 2,150 Cubic Inches

WEIGHTS AND MEASURES

APOTHECARIES WEIGHT

20 grains	1 scruple
3 scruples	1 dram
8 drams	1 ounce
12 ounces	1 pound

The ounce and pound in this are the same as in Troy Weight

AVOIRDUPOIS WEIGHT

27 11/32 grains	1 dram
16 drams	1 ounce
16 ounces	1 pound
25 pounds	1 quarter
4 quarters	1 cwt.
2,000 lbs.	1 short ton
2,240 lbs.	1 long ton

DRY MEASURE

2 pints	1 quart
8 quarts	1 peck
4 pecks	1 bushel
36 bushels	1 chaldron

LIQUID MEASURE

4 gills	1 pint
2 pints	1 quart
4 quarts	1 gallon
31½ gallons	1 barrel
2 barrels	1 hogshead

LONG MEASURE

12 inches	1 foot
3 feet	1 yard
5½ yards	1 rod
40 rods	1 furlong
8 furlongs	1 sta. mile
3 miles	1 league

SQUARE MEASURE

144 sq. inches	1 sq. ft.
9 sq. ft.	1 sq. yard
30¼ sq. yds.	1 sq. rod
40 sq. rods	1 rood
4 roods	1 acre
640 acres	1 sq. mile

SURVEYOR'S MEASURE

7.92 inches	1 link
25 links	1 rod
4 rods	1 chain
10 sq. chains or 160 sq. rods	1 acre
640 acres	1 square mile
36 sq. miles or 6 miles sq.	1 township

WEIGHTS

1 gram	0.03527 ounce
1 kilogram	2.204622 lbs.

1 metric ton	0.9842 English ton
1 ounce	28.35 grams
1 pound	0.4536 kilogram
1 English ton	1.0160 metric tons

SQUARE MEASURE

1 sq. centimeter	0.1550 sq. in.
1 sq. decimeter	0.1076 sq. feet
1 sq. meter	1.196 sq. yds.
1 acre	3.954 sq. rods.
1 hectare	2.47 acres
1 sq. kilometer	0.386 sq. mile
1 sq. inch	6.452 sq. centimeters
1 sq. foot	9.2903 sq. decimeters
1 sq. yard	0.8361 sq. meter
1 sq. rod	0.259 acre
1 acre	0.4047 hectare
1 sq. mile	2.59 sq. kilometers

CUBIC MEASURE

1,728 cubic inches	1 cubic foot
128 cubic feet	1 cord wood
27 cubic feet	1 cubic yard
40 cubic feet	1 ton shpg.
2,150.42 cu. in.	1 standard bushel
268.8 cu. in.	1 standard gallon dry
231 cu. in.	1 standard gallon liquid
1 cu. ft.	about 4/5 of a bushel
1 Perch	A mass 16½ ft. long, 1 ft. high and 1½ ft. wide, containing 24¾ cu. ft.

APPROXIMATE METRIC EQUIVALENTS

1 decimeter	4 inches
1 meter	1.1 yards
1 kilometer	⅝ of mile
1 hectare	2½ acres
1 stere, or cu. meter	¼ of a cord
1 liter	1.06 qt. liquid or 0.9 qt. dry
1 hektoliter	2.8 bushels
1 kilogram	2.2 pounds
1 metric ton	2,200 pounds

METRIC EQUIVALENTS— LINEAR MEASURE

1 centimeter	0.3937 in.
1 decimeter	3.937 in. or 0.328 ft.
1 meter	39.37 in. or 1.0936 yards
1 dekameter	1.9884 rods
1 kilometer	0.62137 mile
1 inch	2.54 centimeters
1 foot	3.048 decimeters
1 yard	0.9144 meter
1 rod	0.5028 dekameter
1 mile	1.6093 kilometers

ACREAGE AND AREAS SQUARE TRACTS OF LAND

Acres	One Side Square Tract	Area
1/10	66.0 lin. ft.	4,356 sq. ft.
⅛	73.8 "	5,445 "
⅙	85.2 "	7,260 "
¼	104.4 "	10,890 "
⅓	120.5 "	14,520 "
½	147.6 "	21,780 "
¾	180.8 "	32,670 "
1	208.7 "	43,560 "
1½	255.6 "	65,340 "
2	295.2 "	87,120 "
2½	330.0 "	108,900 "
3	361.5 "	130,680 "
5	466.7 "	217,800 "

Appraisals are also adjusted to compensate for items that add to the building's value, such as built-in kitchen equipment, hot water heat, extra fireplace, full insulation, and many others. In addition to such considerations, appraisals of older buildings must also allow for age or for neighborhood developments. FHA appraisers look for standard qualities.

Cubic foot method. Another method of securing a tentative estimate is to determine the building's cubic foot content and multiply this by an approximate cost per cubic foot. As with the square foot method, the approximation must be based upon known building costs of similar structures. NOTE: An average cost of $1.75 per cu. ft. can be used for *preliminary* estimation in lieu of an estimate based upon buildings of similar construction. This rough approximation is suitable only in learning how to estimate.

Estimating by Determining Exact Quantities

The most accurate way to estimate is to list every item needed. In addition, one must know how much the actual sizes will vary from the stated dimensions, the percentage of each material to be allowed for waste, shrinkage, or cutting. One must also know the unit cost of each item, the number of labor hours required for installation, and the labor costs per hour. One must determine the amount and cost of supervision and allowances for overhead expenses. After each item is calculated and recorded, the results must be totaled to determine their combined costs.

To select materials and determine their cost, use catalogues, manufacturers' specifications, and current price lists. For labor estimating, secure charts and tables that show labor requirements for individual jobs. It is necessary to know prevailing wage scales for all trades involved. Since they vary in different localities, accurate results demand they be secured for a specific locality. Tables showing labor requirements are available in books or magazines devoted to estimating. Individual manufacturers also describe methods of estimating materials and labor for their products. For your use, if you do not have the information described above, you may secure building material catalogues from large retail firms, especially those that call themselves discount houses. If these are not available in your locality, general merchandise firms frequently include building material listings in their catalogues.

Estimating procedure usually follows or approximates the construction sequence. That is, excavations are estimated first, then footings, foundation, floor framing, subfloor, and so on until all items are calculated.

There are two different ways of recording detailed estimates, with many variations of each. All labor and materials can be recorded in one listing; or material and labor can be compiled into separate lists. Sample estimating sheets done both ways are shown here to illustrate what information is frequently included and how it is compiled. The first excerpt from an estimate combines labor and materials, while the second one is for materials only. The titles at the top of each sheet help you identify them. The company name and address is usually placed in this location.

Quick pre-estimate of labor costs. Since the above method is so detailed and must rely upon labor tables, an abbreviated form for pre-estimating is handy. It consists of estimating all materials and then doubling the sum to compensate for labor. Of course, this is not as reliable as estimating actual labor requirements.

PREPARED BY

APPROVED BY

ESTIMATING
MATERIALS & LABOR

JOB

JOB NO.

DATE

NO.	QUAN.	NAME	DESCRIPTION	JOB HOURS		UNIT OR HR. WAGE		COST		COMBINED COSTS	
258	Lin Ft	Machine Excav for footing	Hours Req Per 100 Lin Ft	1/3	.85	12	00	10	20		
258	Lin Ft	Hd Labor Excav for footing	Hours Req Per 100 Lin Ft	5	12.90	2	50	32	20		
			Total Footing Excav							42	40
		Wood Forms for footing	No Purchase - Use Framing Lumber								
258	Lin Ft	Labor for Wood Forms	Hours Req Per 100 Lin Ft	2	5.16	2	50	12	90		
258	Lin Ft	Skilled Labor Wood Forms	Hours Req Per 100 Lin Ft	2	5.16	4	00	20	64		
			Total Form Labor							33	54
516	Lin Ft	Reinforcing Bars	#4 Deformed				11	56	76		
			Hours Req Per 100 Lin Ft	1/4	1.29	2	50	3	63		
			Total Rein Mat & Labor							60	39
206	Lin Ft	Conc Footing	8" x 16"	7 Yd		15	00	105	00		
206	Lin Ft	Labor	Hours Req Per 100 Lin Ft	4	8.24	2	50	20	60		
206	Lin Ft	Skilled Labor	Hours Req Per 100 Lin Ft	1/2	1.03	4	00	4	12		
			Total Conc Footing							129	72
138	Lin Ft	Field Tile									
138	Lin Ft	Labor	Hours Req Per 100 Lin Ft	1	1.38	2	50	3	45		
5	Cu Yd	Gravel Fill	Washed			2	00	10	00		
		15 lb Felt	Cover Joints					1	00		
		Labor	Hours Req Per Yard	1/4	1.25	2	50	3	13		
			Total Found Drain							31	38
		Wood Forms for Foundation	No Purchase Use Roof Sheath								
390	Sq Ft	Labor	Hours Req Per 100 Sq Ft	2	7.80	2	50	19	50		
390	Sq Ft	Skilled Labor	Hours Req Per 100 Sq Ft	2 3/4	10.72	4	00	42	98		
96	Sq Ft	Wood Forms	Heat Registers & Furn				25	24	00		
		Skilled Labor	Heat Registers and Planter		10.00	4	00	40	00		
										126	48

PREPARED BY

APPROVED BY

JOB

JOB NO.

DATE

NO.	QUAN.	NAME	SIZE	DESCRIPTION	UNIT COST		EXTENSION		COST
137	Ea	Studs	2" x 4" x 8'	Outside Walls	15	00	105	46	
411	Lin Ft	Plates	2" x 4" x __	Outside Walls	15	00	40	84	
144	Ea	Studs	2" x 4" x 8'	Inside Walls	15	00	115	20	
432	Lin Ft	Plates	2" x 4" x __	Inside Walls	15	00	22	00	
96	Lin Ft	Headers	2 x 10	Outside Walls	15	00	24	00	
96	Lin Ft	Headers	2 x 6		15	00	14	40	
66	Ea	Clg Joists	2" x 6" x 14'		15	00	128	60	
1	Ea	Porch Post	6" x 6" x 8'	Const. Grade	22	00	5	18	
2	Ea	Beam	2 x 10 x 12'	Built Up	16	20	6	48	
44	Lin Ft	Ridge Board	2 x 8		15	00	8	78	
66	Ea	Rafters	2" x 6" x 18'		16	20	192	46	
24	Ea	Studs	2" x 4" x 12'		15	00	38	80	
2,000	Sq Ft	Roof Sheathing	5/8" x 48" x 96"	Sheathing Grade Plywood		19	380	00	
1,096	Sq Ft	Wall Sheathing	25/32" x 48" x 96"	Treated Fiberboard	13	75	150	70	
1	Ea	Door Frame	3/0 x 6/8 - 1-3/4	O. S. - Wp.	18	00	18	00	
1	Ea	Door Frame	2/8 x 6/8 - 1-3/8	O. S. - Wp.	17	40	17	40	
160	Lin Ft	Fascia	1" x 8" W.P.	Rip to size	30	00	32	10	
90	Lin Ft	GI Starter Stp				10	9	00	
1	Ea	Window	#C-13 Single Alum Awning		35	94	35	94	
1	Ea	Window	#C-24 Triple Alum Awning		152	36	152	36	
3	Ea	Window	#C-24 Twin Alum Awning		100	10	300	30	
4,000	Sq Ft	Rock Lath	3/8 - 16 x 48		6	00	240	00	
65	Bags	Plaster		Lite Mix	1	82	118	30	
35	Bags	Finish Lime			1	05	36	75	
8	Bags	Gauging Plast			3	00	24	00	

RECEIVED BY

Questions to Reinforce Knowledge

1. What is construction estimating?

2. Why must one have much information to do it?

3. From your own reasoning can you define when estimating might be a full-time occupation, and when it might be only part-time?

4. Since this chapter does not cover the subject fully, explain how to get additional information.

5. Describe the square-foot approximate method of estimating.

6. How can one be reasonably accurate when using this method?

7. Is a garage or carport estimated at the same square foot price as the rest of the building? From your own reasoning, why or why not?

8. What is the approximate relationship of garage cost to house cost?

9. Explain how appraisal agents elaborate upon the square-foot estimating method.

10. What other items—in addition to the cost and number of square feet—do they consider?

11. Describe the cubic-foot approximate method of estimating.

12. Explain difference between approximate and detailed estimating.

13. When estimating materials, why must one specify a quantity larger than needed for the actual size of the area involved?

14. Where may one secure information concerning manufactured products?

15. Where may one secure data pertaining to labor requirements?

16. How may general merchandise catalogues be of value when doing estimating?

17. Describe a logical order for estimating.

The following questions are taken from the sample estimating sheets in the chapter.

18. How much time is required for machine excavating the footings of this house? How much time is required for excavating 100 lineal feet?

19. What is the hourly cost of the trencher and its operator? What is the total cost for machine excavation?

20. How many lineal feet of reinforcing bars are required for the foundation? What size are they? What is their price per foot?

21. How long must one allow for installing all foundation reinforcing bars?

22. What is the unit of measure for purchasing concrete? What is its cost per yard?

23. What are the dimensions of the porch post? What grade material is required? What is its cost per board foot? How does this compare in price with other dimension lumber?

24. What is the price of a bag of gauging plaster? How much will be needed?

Terms to Spell and Know

construction estimating
square foot method
cubic foot method
appraisal

53

Method of assembly. Small models may be glued together. Larger ones are usually fastened with glue and modelmakers' pins. Pins permanently secure parts and also simulate nailing.

Architectural Models

Architectural models are small scale structures that duplicate features of proposed buildings. There are three general types: small scale solid models, structural models, and presentation models. Each type shows different kinds and amounts of detail.

Models are usually constructed prior to the actual building so final form can be previewed and analyzed before construction begins. Models may also be used as sales tools for securing an architectural commission.

Small Scale Solid Models

Small scale solid models show how a proposed structure will fit into a total group. They may show sections of a city (as an area to be redeveloped), a college campus, a factory complex, or similar areas.

Amount of detail. Since solid models are small they usually include only general shapes and show little intricate detail. Models may be rectangular blocks, painted a solid color. Simplified outlines of doors, windows, and other features add to their appearance and create an illusion of reality.

Roof overhangs, balconies, terraces, and similar items help make appearance more lifelike. Landscape features give the model group a finished appearance.

Solid model scale. The size of a proposed building or complex determines model scale. Solid models are seldom larger than $\frac{1}{8}'' = 1'\text{-}0''$, and many are $\frac{1}{16}'' = 1'\text{-}0''$ or less.

Solid model base. All parts are mounted on a rigid base such as plywood or particle board. This holds individual pieces in position and makes the assembled unit easy to handle. Models are frequently attached directly to table tops, which can have folding legs to make them portable.

Structural models

Structural models show framing features, and frequently include all such building parts. All materials are cut to scale size and assembled in the same order as a full-size building. Like solid models, these are assembled upon a rigid base.

Structural model scale. The most frequently used scales are $\frac{1}{2}'' = 1'\text{-}0''$ and $1'' = 1'\text{-}0''$.

Presentation Models

Presentation models are the most realistic appearing of any type. Therefore all materials selected must be similar in appearance to their counterpart.

Presentation model scale. Presentation models are frequently built to a scale of $\frac{1}{2}'' = 1'\text{-}0''$ or smaller. The appropriate scale is determined by how large the model is to be and the amount of detail to be included.

Scope of the Discussion

This chapter discusses the planning and procedures necessary for constructing one featured model which is the presentation type with some structural features shown. The front, both sides, and landscaping are done as presentation. The back portions of the roof, and some interior finishing materials are omitted to show structural parts.

The model featured in this chapter is of the same building featured in the house plans of this book. It is a split three-level home. It is constructed to a scale of $\frac{1}{2}'' = 1'\text{-}0''$.

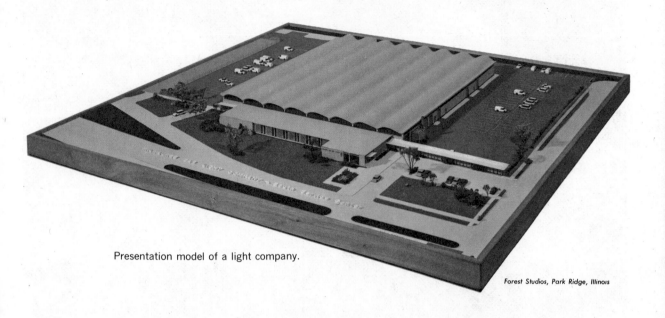

Presentation model of a light company.

Illinois School for the Deaf

Residence hall complex, Illinois State University, Normal, Illinois

Forest Studios, Park Ridge, Illinois

Determining Suitable Base Size

Careful study of the preliminary color rendering and the working drawings indicate a base size of 36″ x 56″ as suitable for the model and its landscape.

Location of Model on Base

With the long dimension of the base as the front, the model is centered in this space. However, the back wall is only 5″ from the rear edge of the base, to permit maximum landscaping in the front yard.

Building the Lower Level

The lower living level uses the plywood base as the house floor; therefore no foundations are required. Building outlines for this level are drawn on the plywood.

Floor finishes are exposed concrete in the workshop and tile in the laundry and recreation rooms. To prevent plywood grain pattern from showing through the floor finish, poster board that conformed to lower level outlines was contact-cemented to the base. All wall outlines were then drawn on the poster board.

The workshop floor was painted light grey to simulate concrete. Latex paint was applied with a stiff bristled brush for a textured appearance.

Tile on the laundry and recreation room floors was painted light beige. Floor tiles were drawn 9″ x 9″ with a 4H pencil and drafting instruments. All floors were then sealed with a clear fixative to protect the coating.

NOTE: Floor areas were covered temporarily to prevent damage during model construction.

The working plans specify concrete block for lower level walls, covered on the exterior with cut stone. The plans also show stepped footings and foundations with stone positioned on the steps; to simplify model construction the stone covering begins at floor level.

Wall heights and lengths were determined from the working plans and individual walls drawn on heavy illustration board. Openings for doors and windows were drawn in their proper location. Walls and all openings were then cut to size.

Lower level walls were glued to the plywood base but raised floors were also secured with wood screws.

This photographic enlargement shows the scribed and painted mortar joints of concrete block walls.

Illustration board may be cut with a knife, paper cutter, or small table saw. Since all lower level walls on this model are the same height, these were cut quickly on a table saw. Window and door openings were cut with a knife.

One may purchase paper or thin wood with concrete block pattern printed on it for a decorative wall finish. However, for a more realistic appearance, mortar joints on this model were cut into the illustration board. This produced a shadow line effect similar to actual concrete block walls.

Each wall was given a coat of sealer to prevent paint absorption. All lower level walls were painted with light green latex paint to blend with the overall color scheme. Before assembling the model, fine dark green lines were drawn in each mortar joint to further emphasize the shadow effect. Note the effect in the photograph of the block walls.

Using outlines previously drawn on the floor, all walls were glued to it and to each other. All wall intersections were secured with modelmakers' pins to hold them in position while the glue was drying.

After assembly, all exposed surfaces were given an additional coat of latex paint for a final finish.

Door and window frames for the lower level were constructed of basswood and glued in place. (More information concerning doors and windows will be given later). Doors were fitted for all required openings. These were cut from basswood, and then given a clear finish. Doors may be secured in place with cellophane tape or, if a more elaborate arrangement is desired, small hinges can be used.

Floor plans of laundry and workshop cabinets were drawn to a scale of $\frac{1}{2}'' = 1'\text{-}0''$ to serve as guides for construction. Cabinet bases were cut from birch lumber. All cabinets were made in sections so toe boards could be easily cut on each base.

Finishing procedures for lower level cabinet work and furnace room doors required much patience. After all items had been sanded, sealed, and sanded again, the toe boards were painted black.

Next, outlines for all doors and drawers were drawn in pencil on cabinet faces. Stiles, rails, and louvers were then drawn on furnace room doors. To make framework more clearly defined, all faces were masked so only frames were exposed. These were then sprayed with color tinted clear lacquer. Masking was removed and all exposed parts given a clear, three-coat finish.

Modelmakers' pins were used as door and drawer hardware to give the cabinets a realistic appearance.

Since the laundry sink required fitting into the counter top and cabinet, the cabinet interior was cut away to accommodate it.

Outlines of the laundry room counter top were drawn on patterned plastic laminate and cut to size. All exposed edges were filed and sanded to a smooth finish. The sink cutout was drawn on the counter top and a hole cut to receive the sink. Next, a coppertone laundry sink made of sheet metal and paper was glued into the counter top cutout.

A washer and dryer were also formed from sheet metal and painted coppertone to match the laundry sink. A backsplash for the counter top was cut to size and all edges filed and sanded. Cabinets and equipment were then glued into position.

The work bench and its wood top were completed in the same manner described above.

Close study of the accompanying photographs will show each detail described.

Middle Level Floors

This house was designed to be built upon a hill, so the second level is approximately 4' above the lower one. This is shown on the right half of the working plans.

Floor outlines for this level were drawn on $\frac{1}{2}''$ plywood and cut to size. "Lumber" strips representing the foundation walls were ripped to width to bring floors to the proper height. These were cut to proper lengths and fastened to the floor. The entire unit was then fastened to the original base.

Floor coverings for each room on this level were selected. Hard surfaced floors in the powder room, foyer, kitchen, and bathroom are composition tile. A small mosaic pattern was used in the kitchen and bathroom, and a pebbled pattern was used in the powder room. These finished

Floor framing is secured to lower level walls.

floors were cut to shape and cemented to the raised plywood base.

Slate floors for the foyer and fireplace hearth were cut from embossed vinyl asbestos tile. Individual stone shapes and mortar joints were cut into the surface and filled with light grey paint. For color variation, some stones were tinted slightly different tones. This color variation can be seen in the early model photographs.

Garage and Walk Level

The garage floor and outside front walk of the actual structure are 4″ lower than the kitchen floor. Bases for these were constructed and fastened to the original plywood base in the same manner as for the middle level floors.

Since part of the foundation wall is above grade level and all of the garage floor is visible, these were painted light grey to match those done earlier.

Upper Level Floors

A floor framing diagram of the upper level was drawn on paper to a scale of ½″ = 1′-0″ and taped to a plywood work surface. The framing diagram was covered with transparent plastic film to protect it while gluing framing members together.

Box sills. Box sills, consisting of bed plates and headers, were the first floor framing members needed, so small scale lumber was cut to length and the box sills were glued into shape. These parts were held together with tape while the glue was drying. After removing the tape, the box sills were temporarily pinned to the floor framing diagram so other structural parts could be positioned and secured to them. Interior wall plates were cut to length and pinned to the framing diagram. Next, all floor joists were cut to length and glued and pinned to the box sills and wall plates. Naturally, spacing conformed to the framing diagram. Next, floor bridging was cut to size, glued and pinned in place. The entire floor framing system was then removed from the diagram and glued and pinned to lower level walls. See the illustration above.

Cutouts in the plywood subfloor permit one to view floor framing construction.

Subfloor. The subfloor for this level is constructed of ¾"x48"x96" plywood panels. To simulate full-size panels, these were cut to scale from birch veneer. All panels were contact-cemented to the floor framing diagram. This made the entire subfloor a one-piece unit for easier handling. All panels terminate above joists, with no two adjoining ones ending on the same joist, as on a full-size building.

Outlines of upper level walls were drawn on the finished subfloor. Lines for the cutaway sections, to permit viewing the lower level were also drawn in. Subfloor cutouts were made on a jigsaw. Next, the entire subfloor was then sanded and sealed. This finished

unit was then glued and pinned to the floor framing.

Determining Wall System to Use

On this model all walls indicated on the plans as "frame" were constructed as the plans prescribed. However, this is not always necessary. Other wall materials, such as sheathing, and interior wall coverings may obscure the framework; so presentation models that do not show structural parts are most easily constructed with solid walls.

Wall Framing Diagrams

The model featured in this chapter required separate framing diagrams for each wall. Walls with gable ends above them were drawn as one single unit so studding could be aligned. However, walls and gables were constructed independently as an aid to construction. Each diagram indicated studding placement, splices in sole and top plates, plus all double framing at doors and windows.

Building Frame Walls

Each model wall was constructed individually as on an actual building and then set or "raised" into position and secured to the floor and other walls.

Framing diagrams were fastened to a plywood work surface and then covered with transparent plastic film. Walls were temporarily attached to these during assembly.

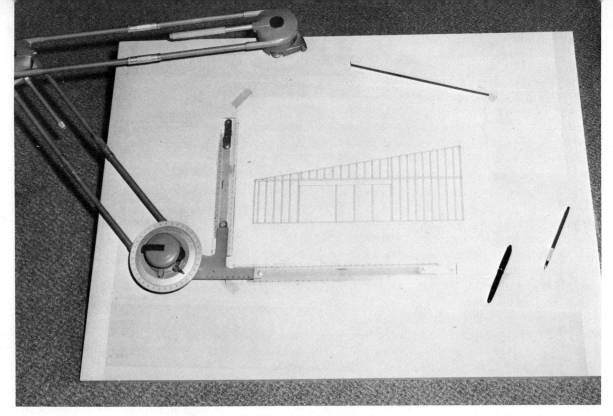

All floor and wall framing required framing diagrams.

This model wall is an exact duplicate of the framing diagram.

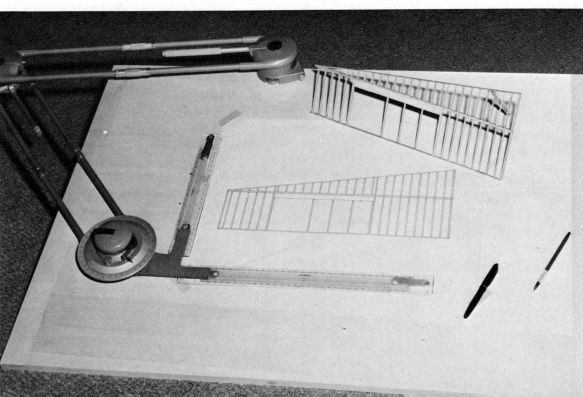

Straightedges about 3/16″ thick, ½″ wide, and slightly longer than the wall being framed were fastened above and below the diagram to hold plates and studding in alignment while gluing. The upper top plate was not fastened to the wall at this time so wall corners could be lapped to tie adjoining ones together.

Before construction began, all small scale framing lumber was cut to proper length, sealed, and sanded.

NOTE: Before constructing model walls, review information on wall framing, as corner studding, wall intersections, window openings, or door openings. Consult the Index for reference to appropriate pages.

Assembling frame walls. Sole plate and lower top plate members were positioned onto the framing diagram and pinned to the plywood work surface and straightedges described earlier. Built-up corner studs were preassembled and secured in their proper locations. Studs for wall intersections were then constructed and added where required. Headers were placed above all door, window, or other openings and glued to the top plate. Double studding was then positioned, glued, and pinned in place to complete rough openings.

Studding locations shown on the diagram that were not occupied by corner studs, wall intersections, or framed openings were filled in with single studs and secured in place. Crippled studs were added below window open-

ings to complete the frame wall. After the glue had dried, all pins were removed, excess glue trimmed away, and the completed wall frame put aside for future use. CAUTION: Do not remove the bottom plate at the door openings until the walls are set in place. This plate gives the wall rigidity while applying interior and exterior coverings.

Wall Sheathing

For display purposes, some model walls show exposed sheathing. The rear wall on this model does not require sheathing since only structural parts are to be shown. All other walls are covered on the outside with heavy black paper to simulate wall sheathing.

From the working plans, calculate the exact height and length of each wall that requires sheathing. Then check the measurements of the small scale walls just assembled and compare them with the working drawings. If discrepancies exist between the stated and actual sizes, make the necessary corrections. Using drafting instruments and proper techniques, draw the outlines of each sheathed wall onto the black paper and cut to size. NOTE: *Do not cut door or window outlines until after all sheathing is glued to the wall frame.* Sheathing will conform more closely to framed openings if cut with a knife after the sheathing is applied.

Before gluing the sheathing to the wall frame, pin the upper top plates temporarily in place so sheathing can be aligned with their upper edges. Apply glue

sparingly to the outside face of one wall frame and lay the sheathing in its proper location. Place the sheathed wall on a flat surface and put another flat surface over it. (Scrap plywood or a large book works well.) Apply sufficient weight to press all parts into contact and permit to remain in this position until the glue is dry. Continue applying sheathing to walls until all those requiring it have been completed. Then make all necessary cutouts for door, window, or other openings.

Interior Wall Coverings

After selecting interior wall coverings, they are cut and applied in the same manner as sheathing. Most walls on the middle and upper levels of the model were covered to simulate plaster; a lightweight cardboard was used. Three walls on the lower level required wood paneling; this was cut from walnut veneer. Veneers were measured, cut, and fitted to each wall. Then they were glued in place and weights applied to insure perfect contact at all points. After the glue had dried, door and window openings were cut out as described for sheathing openings.

Cased Openings

Door and window jambs were cut to size, finish applied, and then glued into their openings.

Wall Installation

Individual walls, complete with their coverings applied and all door and window trim installed, were then glued and pinned to the subfloor and to each other.

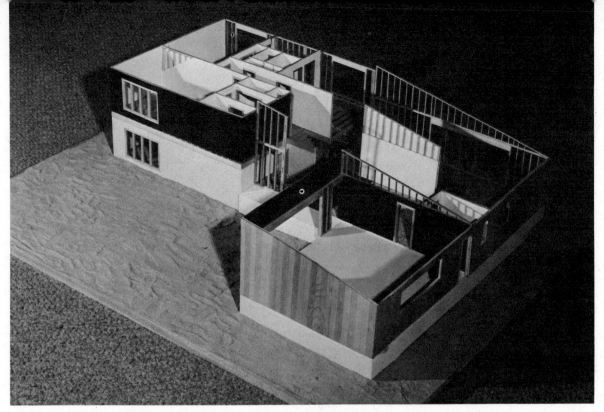

After wall frames were assembled they were covered with sheathing and exposed coverings.

A center bearing wall, with a "let-in" ribbon across the studs, supports ceiling joists and roof rafters.

Gable framing and roof trusses, a part of wall installation, bring the model one step closer to completion.

Walls were permitted to remain undisturbed until the glue was thoroughly cured. Wall intersections required additional finishing to achieve a smooth appearance; so all joints were filled and smoothed with white plastic putty. Closet shelves were fitted and glued in place. Walls were masked along all floors and around door and window trim to minimize painting effort. Each wall was given three coats of colored latex paint. Sliding doors were then glued in place and hinged doors were hung in their openings with transparent tape. Doors were left partially open and tape applied to the face of each door and to the door jambs.

Stairways

Since the stairway to the lower level simulates concrete while upper level stairs require carpet, both were formed of lightweight cardboard rather than wood. All risers and treads were made from one cardboard section. Lines were scored with a knife to aid in bending the steps to shape. Formed risers and treads were glued to a rigid backing to hold their shapes. Lower level ones were painted concrete color while upper level stairs were completed by contact-cementing carpet to all steps. Each stairway was then glued into its stairwell.

Bathroom Fixtures

Bathroom cabinets and counter tops were constructed in the same manner as those for the laundry room. After completion they were glued in place. Mirrors behind the lavatory cabinets were cut to size and contact-cemented to the walls. Soffits above the mirrors were fashioned from cardboard and pre-painted before installation. Joints at wall intersections were filled and smoothed with plastic putty. The soffits and puttied areas were then painted to match existing surfaces.

Water closets and the bathtub were shaped from potters' clay and finished with colored lacquer. They were glued in place.

Fireplace and Chimney

Fireplace and chimney parts were shaped from heavyweight illustration board and glued into a finished rectangular unit. The fireplace interior was painted black to simulate a used appearance.

All exposed surfaces were to simulate cut stone. Each surface was coated with contact cement and covered with ⅛″ of plastic putty. Stone outlines were cut into the surfaces while the putty was still pliable. Stone surfaces were then painted with a solid color latex paint to give a uniform background color. Mortar joints were painted a contrasting color. Tints of different colors were brushed onto individual stones to give variation in appearance of cut stone. The entire chimney was sprayed with fixative.

The chimney cap was shaped from potters' clay and glued onto the chimney. Cardboard flue liners were constructed, painted, and glued to the chimney cap. The completed chimney unit was then glued to the house floor and to an adjoining wall.

Kitchen Equipment

All kitchen cabinets were shaped from solid walnut to match wall paneling previously installed. Finishing procedures, counter top construction, and installation were done the same way as for laundry room cabinets. All soffits were pre-assembled and installed at the same time as other cabinet parts. The range hood was made entirely of cardboard. Rectangles representing the oven, surface unit, and refrigerator were also cut from lightweight cardboard. Each item was coated with colored lacquer. Outlines for doors, moldings, and surface unit burners were drawn with India ink. Each completed item was then glued into the finished cabinet work.

Ceiling Joists

Ceiling joist spacing was laid out on the top wall plates. All joists were then cut to size, glued, and pinned in their proper locations.

Exterior Stone Walls

Exterior wall surfaces requiring stone veneer were first covered with heavyweight illustration board to give a smooth joint free surface. They were then finished with contact cement, plastic putty, and fixative, as described for the chimney.

Windows, Doors, and Exterior Trim

Clear plexiglass was fitted and glued into window openings. The garage door and other exterior doors were fitted, painted, and glued in place. Remaining window and door trim and all sills were then fitted and glued in place.

Roof Construction

All garage roof trusses were pre-assembled, using the working plans as a guide. Each truss was constructed from the same diagram so that all parts would be identical.

The basic roof structure consists of two pieces of ¼″ fir plywood. These were cut to conform to the overall roof shape and serve as the finished lower face of the overhang. Most of the plywood over the house itself was cut away to reveal structural framing. (The roof cutouts are shown in photographs of the completed model.) The plywood was then covered on the top face with thin cardboard to serve as a smooth base for the roof covering. NOTE: Cutouts in the cardboard

are smaller than those on the plywood to permit gluing of roof framing.

To frame the left-hand or smaller roof, a ridge board was first fastened across the plywood cutout. Rafter spacing was laid out on the board, and this same spacing was duplicated along the lower roof edge. Rafters were cut and fitted to conform to the spacing, then glued and pinned in place. The entire unit was glued to the model walls. While drying, weights were applied to insure perfect contact of all parts.

A plywood and cardboard roof, as described earlier, complete with cutout spaces, was constructed and glued over the rest of the model. Girders and headers were constructed and installed as shown on the roof framing diagram. Individual rafters were cut and fitted to their proper locations.

Garage roof truss spacing was marked on the roof surface; then pre-assembled trusses were cut and fitted into the plywood opening. Each truss was glued and pinned in place.

Cardboard roof surfaces meeting at the ridge were filled and smoothed with plastic putty to obscure the joint. The entire roof surface was given two coats of colored latex paint.

The painted roof surface was coated with clear adhesive and small crushed-stone chips sprinkled onto it. After brushing the excess stone from the dry roof surface, all exposed framing members were covered with masking tape. The stone roof was then sprayed with colored lacquer.

This lacquer is tinted to match the base coat color. This final coat also serves as a sealer and affords additional durability.

Painting Fascia and Exterior Trim

To complete the model, two coats of latex paint were applied to the fascia, soffit, and all exterior wood trim.

The Base

A wood frame conforming to the land contour as described in the working plans was cut, fitted, and fastened around the plywood base. The frame was then sanded, sealed, and coated with clear finishing materials.

The Entourage

Early model photographs show the foundation walls protruding above the plywood base. The finished grade had to be raised to conform to the level shown on the working plans.

The rear terrace and all sidewalks were raised to their proper levels by building a wood framework for this use and covering it with plywood and cardboard as described for the garage and middle level floors.

Wood nailer strips conforming to the finished grade were fastened to the foundation walls and to the finishing boards around the plywood base. Two wood strips ¾" thick were shaped to the driveway contour but were cut ³⁄₁₆" less than the total finished height. A line was drawn down the center of the strip so the middle could be aligned with the driveway edge. This alignment also permitted the strips to serve as a solid edge for the lawn. Driveway width and length were drawn on ⅛" untempered hardboard and the piece cut to size. A cardboard

Views of the finished model with entourage. (Also see next page.)

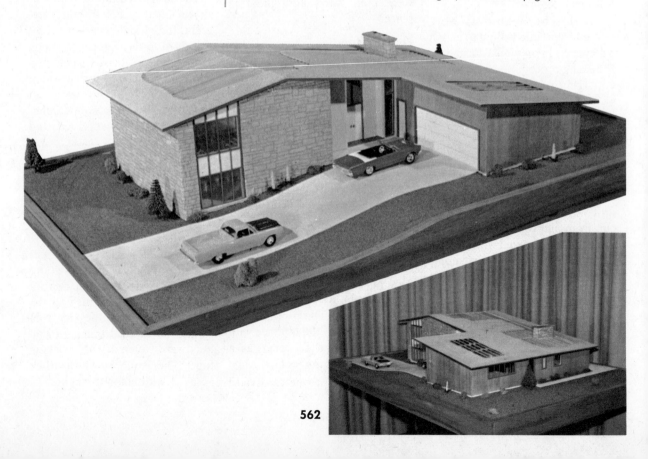

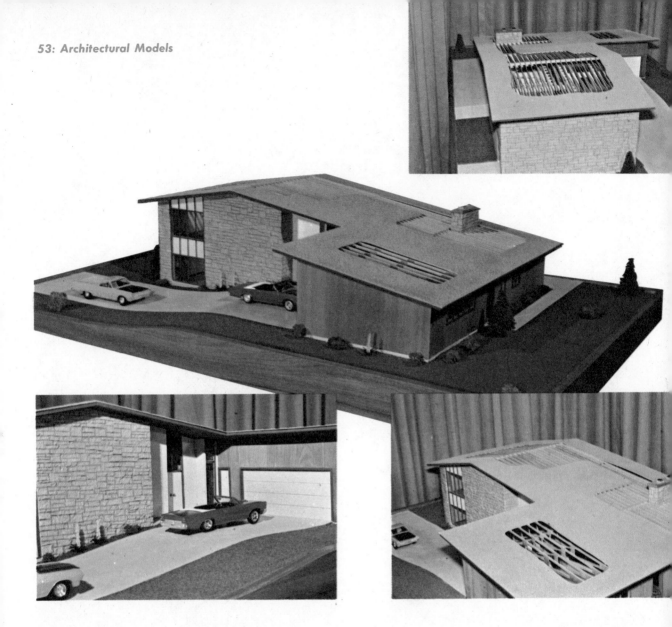

finishing surface was cut and contact-cemented to the hardboard base.

The driveway, terrace, and walks were painted light grey to match other concrete surfaces.

Screen wire was cut and stapled to the nailer strips to cover the entire lawn. The staples were driven about ¾″ apart to prevent buckling and to hold the screen in contact with the nailer strips. A thin coating of plaster was applied to the screen. When dry, a second thin coating was applied. NOTE: Papier mâché or other wet covering materials may also be used and still maintain the same finished appearance. Since plaster is porous, the entire lawn surface was coated with sealer. It was then painted green. When the paint was dry, the area was coated with clear adhesive and modelmakers' grass sprinkled on. For greater coverage and a more lifelike appearance, a second coat of adhesive and grass was applied.

Trees, shrubs, flowers, and automobiles were purchased from a hobby shop (in kit form), assembled, and fastened in their appropriate positions.

INDEX

Tables and Charts